THE CRAFT OF
PUBLIC ADMINISTRATION

George E. Berkley

Northeastern University

Allyn and Bacon, Inc. Boston London Sydney

for Patricia, tender comrade

© COPYRIGHT 1975 BY ALLYN AND BACON, INC., 470 ATLANTIC AVENUE, BOSTON, MASSACHUSETTS 02210

LIBRARY OF CONGRESS CATALOGING IN PUBLICATION DATA

Berkley, George E
    The craft of public administration.

    Includes bibliographical references and index.
    1. Public administration. I. Title.
JF1351.B47   350   74-26589

ISBN 0-205-04681-9

Contents

Contents

7 COMMUNICATION 217

Formal and Informal Means and Methods Up, Down and Across
Case Study: Action This Day The Question of Secrecy

8 BUDGETING 254

Traditional Budgeting The Coming of PPBS Case Study: What Price
Parking? The Pursuit of Productivity

9 CENTRALIZATION AND ITS CONCERNS 296

Case Study: Selective Service, Schools and Others MBO: The Search
for Answers Problems of Field Offices Case Study: The Federal Government Goes for Ten

10 THE CHALLENGES OF CHANGE 330

Agents of Change: Planning Agents of Change: Sensitivity Training
Agents of Change: Interdepartmental Committees Agents of Change:
Study Commissions and Task Forces Case Study: Seeking Shelter in the
Sixties Agents of Change: Consultants The Limits of Change

11 ADMINISTRATIVE LAW AND ADMINISTRATIVE CONTROL 369

The New Limits on Administrative Discretion Administrative Law at
Work Issues in Administrative Law Case Study: The "Trial" of J. Rob-
ert Oppenheimer Administrative Control Law and Control: How
Much Is Enough?

12 THE SEARCH FOR SUPPORT 409

Clientele Relations Public Relations Case Study: Two Police Forces in
Search of an Image Relations with Politicians Responsibility

13 THE ADMINISTRATIVE FUTURE 459

The Passing of the Pyramid Case Study: The New Administration at
Work "Democracy Is Inevitable"

Preface

Any writer of a textbook in a field already somewhat crowded with such works faces a crucial question. What does his book have to offer that the others lack?

He will not find this an easy question to answer since he is scarcely the best or most impartial judge of his own work. However, what can be said in this instance is that *The Craft of Public Administration* reflects an attempt to achieve two specific goals. One is to convey to the reader some measure of the genuine excitement which characterizes the world of public administration. The second is to provide some actual assistance to the reader if he plans to work, or is already working, in the public sector.

To meet these twin and, fortunately, essentially convergent goals, I have studded the book with examples. Not only have illustrations and illustrative anecdotes been scattered throughout the book, but each chapter has a case study designed to illuminate some of the points raised in the chapter. I have also sought to outline some of the techniques which successful administrators employ in coping with their manifold challenges. Thus, the book contains such suggestions as how to work with politicians, how to engage in collective bargaining with public employee unions, how to get rid of unwanted employees.

To meet the criteria of readability and utility, I have tried to include those recent developments in public administration which show signs of having some staying power. Consequently, the reader will find material covering such topics as planning, program budgeting, productivity measurement, management by objectives, systems analysis, the use of consultants and other emerging trends in the field. Furthermore, examples are drawn from such timely occurrences as the Vietnam war and the Watergate affair. At the same time, more traditional materials are by no means ignored. The works of such worthies as Frederick W. Taylor, Mary Parker Follett, Elton Mayo, Chester I. Barnard and others are at least briefly discussed.

In getting the book ready for publication I have piled up some debts which I should like to acknowledge. Thanks to my capable and considerate editor, Robert Patterson, I have had the benefit of valuable critiques of the manuscript by professors Thad F. Beyle of the University of North Carolina at Chapel Hill, Richard Chackerian of Florida State University at Tallahassee, Kent Chabotar of Michigan State University, Richard Hogarty of the University of Massachusetts at Boston and J. David Palmer of Georgia State College in Atlanta. I only regret that the pressures of an early deadline prevented me from making as full use of their suggestions as I might have wished. Two of my colleagues in the Department of Political Science at Northeastern have also given me valuable assistance. Professor David Barkley urged me to include many examples, while Professor David Schmitt suggested the title. I am grateful to them both.

I should also like to thank Louis Sheedy, Management Sciences Director for the U.S. Civil Service Commission in Boston for introducing me to the basic principles of PERT and supplying the two charts I have used to illustrate how it works; the American Society of Public Administration and, in particular, its Massachusetts chapter for helping me keep in touch with the "real world" of public administration during my academic career; and the staff of the Boston Finance Commission who have been consistently kind and helpful to me since I departed as their chairman in 1966. Most of all, I am indebted to my students, particularly the working practitioners in our MPA program at Northeastern. Bringing with them their experience and knowledge of the current state of the craft, they have furnished me with much information and many insights. Special thanks are due to Sheri Larsen, Edward Montminy and Ronald Lawson whose research papers were used as source material in certain sections of this work.

Finally, Miss Barbara Sladeck who performed the formidable task of translating rough-hewn material into neat typewritten copy deserves an extra measure of gratitude and praise for her efforts in behalf of the author and his book.

One Sunday in May 1962, he took André Malraux out to Glen Ora for luncheon, and, as Kennedy later described it, they fell into a discussion of the persistence of mythology in the contemporary World. "In the nineteenth century," Malraux said, "the ostensible issue within the European states was the monarchy versus the republic. But the real issue was capitalism versus the proletariat. In the twentieth century the ostensible issue is capitalism versus the proletariat. But the world has moved on. What is the real issue now?" The real issue today, Kennedy replied, was the management of industrial society—a problem, he said, not of ideology but of administration.

—Arthur M. Schlesinger, Jr., in *A Thousand Days*

1

The Administrative Craft

Not so very long ago, an author wrote a book dealing with the changes which organizations are undergoing in a technological society. He proudly entitled his work *The Administrative Revolution*. His publishers liked the book but hated the title. Why? The answer is simple. In their opinion, any book with the word *administration* in its title simply would not sell.[1]

Although they finally published the book under its original title, there is no gainsaying the fears and doubts which prompted their attempt to rechristen it. The work *administration* does conjure up connotations of colorlessness, and it does cause most readers to turn away or, to use a more current phrase, turn off. While administration, particularly public administration, is America's fastest growing industry, it arouses more apathy than ardor and inspires more distaste than devotion.

Without stopping to probe the roots of the anti-administration syndrome, let us take a look at the subject itself to see if such an attitude is justified. Is administration best depicted as a leafless tree growing sadly in a bleak landscape, or can it be thought of as a lush and luxuriant plant busily sprouting all kinds of interesting blossoms?

THE HEART OF THE MATTER

A classic textbook defines administration simply but graphically in this opening sentence. "When two men cooperate to roll a stone that nei-

---

1. The book in question is the author's own prior work, *The Administrative Revolution: Notes on the Passing of Organization Man* (Englewood Cliffs, N.J.: Prentice-Hall, 1971).

ther could have moved alone, the rudiments of administration have appeared."[2] Such a concrete if elementary illustration has much to tell us as to just what administration is and what it is not.

Administration, first of all, is *people*. A stone sitting by itself on the side of a hill is certainly not administration. Nor does a stone which, through some act of nature, rolls down a hill constitute administration. People have to be present before administration can take place.

Second, administration is *action*. Two men watching or admiring or leaning on a stone does not, it itself, constitute administration. They have to be doing something before administration can enter the picture. There is no such thing as inactive administration. (Although many who have to deal with administrative agencies sometimes believe otherwise.)

Third, administration is *interaction*. One man moving a stone or two men each independently moving stones in separate fields are not examples of administration in action. (And remember, there is no other kind). In order for their activity to become administration, their efforts must in some way be related. This does not mean that they have to be aware of each other's activity. But somewhere in the background there must be some coordination between what each of them is doing. Administration, by its very nature, involves *people relating to other people.*

People interacting with other people to accomplish tasks—this, indeed, is what administration is about. Yet that is not all that administration is about. A further ingredient is required, for not all work activity involving human interaction can bear the administrative label. The prisoner and his guard, for example, may have an intense relationship involving the moving of stones or, more likely in this case, the making of little stones out of big ones. Yet, we would not define this relationship as administrative in nature. Rather, the prisoner is the recipient of a network of administrative relationships involving the guard with his co-workers and his superiors. Strange as it may sound, the prisoner is a beneficiary, albeit in this instance usually an unwilling one, of administration. He is the client of an administrative service not a participant in the creation of such a service. Put in other words, he is closer to the administrative product than he is to the administrative process.

The line that separates administration from other types of human interaction often becomes blurred and fuzzy. Take the relationship between a professor and his students. In this case, the students are the clients, and, hopefully, somewhat more willing ones than the prisoner we just cited. They are the beneficiaries, although some of them might dispute the use of such a term, of an administrative process involving

---

2. Herbert A. Simon, Donald W. Smithbury and Victor A. Thompson, *Public Administration* (New York: Alfred A. Knopf, 1950), p. 3.

the professor, his colleagues, his dean, the department secretary and even the building custodian.

But now let us assume that the class is one in biology and the professor and students decide to undertake a joint project such as investigating the pollution of a nearby river in order to write a report for the state legislature. At this point, the relationship starts to change. Now, they are *mutually* involved in a joint endeavor. In their former relationship, they both might have had a convergent interest in that the students may have wanted to learn as much as possible about biology—you will note that this example is purely theoretical—and the instructor may have wanted to teach them as much as possible about biology. But the situation was nevertheless different. The students were there to obtain a product; the professor was there to dispense it. Consequently, the students were not more engaged in an administrative relationship with their teacher than are the customers of a department store administratively engaged with the store's sales clerks, buyers, etc.

This introduces a new element in our definition. Joint or cooperative activity is an essential part of all administration. This does not mean that such cooperative activity must always be spontaneous or voluntary. A young man may be drafted against his will into the army. He may be sent even more against his will to a foreign base. Yet, in performing whatever role may be assigned to him at that base, he will be participating in administration. Like it or not, unless he wishes to brook disciplinary action, he will be involved with others in a common effort, namely that of maintaining what at least his superiors will claim to be the nation's security.

To sum up, administration is a process involving human beings jointly engaged in working toward common goals. Administration thus covers much if not most of the more exciting things which go on in human society. Why, then, should anyone feel justified in wanting to color it grey?

ART, SCIENCE OR CRAFT?

The very title of this book indicates that it classifies administration as a craft. Why this classification instead of another? Why should we not consider administration an art or a science?

Science is characterized by precision and predictability. A scientific rule is one that works all the time. As a matter of fact, rules in science are considered to be so rigid and final that they are not called rules at all but laws. Two parts of hydrogen combined with one part of oxygen will *always* give us water—or steam, or ice, depending on the temperature—regardless of where and when the amalgamation of the two elements takes place. Of course, if the apparatus combining them is dusty or if someone switches it off at the wrong time or if any of countless thousands of other things happen, the formation of H_2O may not occur. But this does not invalidate the formula. With other factors kept out of the process, and in pure science it is often fairly easy to keep out intrusive factors, we can combine hydrogen and oxygen on a two-to-one basis with the certainty that we will derive some form of water.

Some sciences, or some aspects of science, do not, it is true, achieve such a 100 percent level of predictability. Quantum theory, for example, is predicated on the predicted behavior of only some, not necessarily all, of the particles involved. Many of the more scientific aspects of the social sciences similarly deal with expectations which govern only a portion of the elements being scrutinized, not all of them. For example, many social scientists feel that they have established pretty much as a scientific law the theory that political participation correlates with education and affluence. Put more explicitly, they feel that their research has proven that the more educated and/or the more affluent people are, the more they will tend to participate in democratic politics. To justify such an adamant stand, they point out that this theory has been tested under a variety of conditions in both this country and abroad and generally has been substantiated. Voting and other forms of political participation will almost invariably be greater in those communities or neighborhoods where education and/or affluence is greater. However, one cannot automatically assume that any person who has a Ph.D and a $50,000-a-year salary—the two do not always go together— will be a feverish participant in the political process. Indeed, one cannot even be sure that he will be a voter. In similar fashion, one cannot single out an individual at the bottom rung of the education-affluence ladder and automatically assume that he is estranged from, or antagonistic to politics. Obviously, *some* low income and less educated people participate quite intensively in politics while *some* of the well-educated rich have never even bothered registering to vote. Yet, with it all, the latter are much more likely to take a more active role in politics than are the former. Science here reigns, though somewhat imperfectly, by establishing degrees of probability.

What does all this tell us about administration? Actually, quite a bit, although it may not add up to a completely clear picture. (Few things involving administration ever do.) Administration makes or should make great use of scientific data, laws and theories. The use of mathematics and computer sciences in some aspects of budgeting is a fairly obvious example. The utilization in personnel work of somewhat less definitive but nevertheless statistically valid material developed by

4

psychologists is another. Thus, administration uses these types of scientific data, but is it a science itself?

In attempting to answer this question we should note that the utilization of science is not confined to the sciences themselves. Music, for one, bases itself on laws of harmony that are quite mathematical. Painting depends on laws dealing with the colors of the spectrum. Yet, both music and painting are arts, not sciences. In a sense, the same holds true for administration. Administrators make use of scientific laws, techniques and data. But they do so in ways that allow a great deal of free rein to the individual imagination and temperament. Usually a variety of successful ways exist for dealing with any particular problem and any administrator can devise yet another one. Furthermore, problems are rarely, if ever, identical and it would be difficult to evolve any equations that would cover all cases. In algebra we know that if $2x = 4$, then x will *always* equal 2. We are almost never that certain about any "law" in administration. The equations change depending not only on the circumstances but also on the personality of those dealing with them. And this should not be viewed as an erasable imperfection. It is, rather, an integral part of the administrative process. Like the painter and composer, the administrator uses science, but also, like them, he uses it in ways which tend to reflect his own mood and personality.

Does this make administration an art? Here, again, the picture is far from crystal clear. As we have noted, administrators, like artists, do tend to work in individual and often highly imaginative ways, employing a various mix of materials, including intuition, in their labors. One man's administrative product is never quite the same as another's, just as one composer's symphony differs from another's. Individual style tends to show through in both cases, though it is certainly more pronounced in the latter field.

But administration is not an art for there is a difference which, while often illusive, is nevertheless vital. Artists create works of aesthetics; administrators solve problems or at least attempt to do so. Therefore, their respective end products and the criteria used for evaluating them tend to differ. Although we can state with some certainty that Beethoven was a great composer, no one can state with the same certainty that he was greater than Bach. Nor can one say that Mozart was greater than Brahms or that Mendelssohn wrote better music than Liszt. Each was doing his own thing, so to speak, and our judgments of their accomplishments depend heavily on our tastes and inclinations.

To some extent, our personal tastes and inclinations enter into our judgment of administrators. But only to some extent. For in administration there are usually some objective standards that can be applied in evaluating the work that administrators do. Each administrator may

5

have his own way of proceeding and each administrator's problems may be unique, but in most cases there is an objectively desirable and determinable goal to be met. In his classic work *Administrative Behavior,* Herbert Simon ably addresses himself to this point. "The criterion which the administrator applies to the factual problems is one of efficiency. The resources, the input, at the disposal of the administrator are strictly limited. . . . It is his function to maximize the attainment of governmental objectives (assuming they have been agreed upon) by the efficient employment of the limited resources that are available to him. . . ."[3]

Admittedly, making judgments on administrative efficiency, particularly when it comes to weighing the efficiency of one administrator against that of another, it is not always an easy task. But to some degree, at least, it can be and is done. No such criterion would ever be utilized in evaluating a work of art. There is good music and bad music, good painting and bad painting. But who has ever heard an efficient symphony or viewed an efficient picture?

Consequently, if we turn to the last category, that of craft, we find a more suitable or at least a more comfortable classification. The man who paints a picture which hangs in a museum is an artist. The man who brings his easel and palette into the museum to copy this picture is a craftsman. The latter has an objective standard for the goal he is trying to meet and against which he can be judged. He may use a variety of techniques and materials in his effort to achieve this goal. But the goal remains the same. Another painter-craftsman with the same aim may mix his paints differently, shade his light differently, or do a host of other things which the former craftsman did not do. But he is striving for the same end and an outside observer can usually determine who was the most successful.

A more pertinent hypothetical problem will further point up the ability of viewing administration as neither a science nor an art but as a craft. Let us assume a city is divided for the purpose of garbage collection into two distinct and equal sections. One team of sanitation men under an assistant sanitation commissioner is assigned to each section with the objective of keeping the streets clean. One of the assistant commissioners may choose to have his men work straight eight-hour shifts five days a week; the other may choose to bunch the efforts of his men at key times in the week and work them for longer periods of time on fewer days. One may try to improve the conditions of work by conducting a promotional campaign designed to persuade the residents of his section to switch from garbage cans to cellulose bags. The other may

---

3. Herbert A. Simon, *Administrative Behavior* (New York: The Free Press, 1957), p. 186.

deem it more fruitful to ask the police to crack down on the street litter law. One may offer his men extra inducements if they do their job successfully while the other may hold out to his crew the prospect of more time off. The ways in which each team goes about its work may differ depending on the personalities of their administrative leaders, the personalities of the men and a variety of other factors. But an objective standard exists for comparing the relative efficiency of each, namely which produces cleaner streets.

Most administrative activity does not lend itself to such an easy evaluation as the example just given. When it comes to assessing the efficiency of a foreign policy operation, to take just one example, assessments and judgments can become very tricky. The administration of a policy often becomes hard to separate from the policy itself. (This is an important issue in public administration which we will explore in greater detail later on). Furthermore, there is not always agreement on the criteria or the objective against which success or failure is to be measured. And, in many cases, varying conditions will complicate our comparison. In the street cleaning case, for instance, one team may excel another team only because its streets are in a lower density section of the city which has less garbage. Or it may out-perform the other team because its district is closer to the incinerator, thereby cutting down the travel time needed to send its dump trucks back and forth.

Nevertheless, despite all these complicating factors, in most administrative situations, there is an objective standard lurking somewhere, shadowy and illusive and hard to apply though it may be. At the same time, there is almost never a precise formula that will invariably work best in all situations. The situations not only change but the ideas that may be applied to handling them are almost as infinite as the mind of man.

Another example, this one from history, will provide further support for our contention that administration may be more easily categorized as a craft than as an art or a science. As the New Deal reached its height, Harry Hopkins and Harold Ickes emerged as Franklin Roosevelt's most valued and trusted aides. Each man was given a substantial chunk of the federal public works and relief programs to administer. However, as they acquired power they became increasingly suspicious and jealous of each other. Word of their growing rivalry and animosity soon leaked out. This caused their respective partisans or opponents in the government, in the press and in the public at large to leap to the attack or to the defense as the case may have been. Washington was abuzz with rumors of the feud, and the fact that so many others were choosing sides was producing disruption throughout the governmental network.

The situation placed Roosevelt in a quandary. If he fired or encouraged the resignation of either of these men, he would not only lose a tried and tested aide but he would alienate and antagonize the man's admirers and supporters. On the other hand, if Roosevelt issued a statement denying the feud, he would only succeed in acknowledging and giving credence to the rumors. Here was an administrator with a problem.

Roosevelt decided to solve his problem by embarking on one of his famous conservation tours and taking Ickes and Hopkins with him. For nine days and nights the trio wound their way by train and automobile through the American countryside, inspecting dam sites, forestry projects and other New Deal undertakings. At every opportunity, Roosevelt lavished public praise on his two associates and played up their importance in his administration. And every night he sat down with both of them for a poker game.

By the time the presidential party had arrived back in Washington, the rumors of the feud had begun to dissolve. The steady stream of news and pictures of the men standing shoulder to shoulder had had their effect. And, in fact, it appeared that the two men ended the junket on much better terms. One administrator had solved a pressing problem.

Roosevelt used a great deal of artistry and imagination in dealing with this situation. Yet he was not creating a work of art but resolving a difficult problem. At the same time, however, Roosevelt was certainly not acting as a scientist for what he did does not lend itself to easy formularization. His solution, while it might provide some ideas for other administrators faced with similar dilemmas, certainly does not lend itself to an all-embracing equation. Such a solution, for instance, would not have proven of much use to George Washington when he confronted the somewhat similar challenge of dealing with the bitter fight between his two top aides, Alexander Hamilton and Thomas Jefferson. For one thing, there were no conservation projects to inspect, no trains to transport the visiting party and no photographers to take and send back pictures of their amicable visitations. Furthermore, Hamilton and Jefferson were probably not the type of men who would be amenable to such treatment and certainly it would be hard to imagine the somewhat austere "Father of our Country" sitting them down to nightly poker sessions.

In summary, administration uses artistry but is not an art. It uses science but is not a science. It is more properly thought of as a craft, seeking to achieve goals and to meet standards, and in so doing, often managing to utilize all the creativity and capacity that its harried practitioners can muster.

PUBLIC AND PRIVATE: IS THERE A DIFFERENCE?

Since we now hopefully have a better idea of what administration is, let us proceed to describe and designate the different forms it may take. In some respects these forms are as numerous as the various fields which apply it. There is health administration, welfare administration, factory administration, university administration. Within these fields each institution often has its own type of administration which can differ considerably from that of a counterpart institution. But in another sense, there are virtually no essential differences since administration deals with the working relationships of human beings, and this common denominator is often a stronger unifying bond than the disparateness of the numerators. It is sometimes said that administration is everywhere the same and to some degree this is true. Running a hospital or a factory, a small field unit or a large bureaucracy presents the essentially similar problems which tend to crop up when human beings seek to work cooperatively.

Be this as it may, it is helpful in furthering our understanding of administration to distinguish the two broad areas where it is utilized: the public and private sectors. Since this book will focus on the public sector, it might be useful to spell out those ways in which public administration differs from business administration.

The first distinguishing characteristic is public administration's much greater reliance on, and vulnerability to, the law. Legalism in general and laws in particular tend to circumscribe and influence the operation of a public institution much more than they do a private one. "This pervasive legal context is among the principal distinctions between public and private enterprise," note John F. Pfiffner and Robert Presthus. "In private management one is assured that he can do anything not specifically forbidden. In public administration, on the other hand, discretion is limited by a great number of laws, rules and regulations."[4] To put it more succinctly, in private administration the law generally tells the administrator only what he *cannot* do; in public administration, the law tells him what he *can* do.

The much greater preoccupation of public administration with the law is manifested in various ways. For example, a young campaign aide to a politician seeking high office in a New England state was horrified when he learned that the campaign committee had decided to make cash payments to reporters of a local newspaper in return for favorable publicity for the candidate. To the aide, this was rank corruption. However, there was nothing criminal in what was being done. The newspapermen were not working for a public institution but for a pri-

---

4. John M. Pfiffner and Robert Presthus, *Public Administration,* 5th ed. (New York: The Ronald Press, 1967), p. 427.

vate one. It was up to the newspaper itself to determine whether or not it would allow its employees to accept fees from political candidates for "public relations services." What the newspapermen were doing may not have been very ethical in terms of their profession but neither they nor those who were paying them were committing an illegal act. However, similar behavior by public employees would, in most jurisdictions, violate a conflict of interest law and disclosure could result in the employees not only being dismissed from their jobs but even prosecuted.[5]

Most newspapermen, of course, do not accept pay-offs but even so their conduct often varies greatly from what we expect from public employees. News concerning socially prominent people receives much greater space than the comings and goings of the less well off, and while this, to some extent, can be justified in terms of reader interest, the discrepancy often far exceeds justifiable limits. More significantly, the marriage of the daughter of the friend of an editor or the opening of a new store by an advertiser is likely to receive exaggerated attention. Even the newspaper's book review editor is likely to be heavily influenced by personal contacts and approaches in determining which few of the thirty thousand books published annually he will choose for review. Thus, even a newspaper that is vigorous and sincere in ferreting out and denouncing corruption in government can be committing numerous acts every day which, if done by a public agency, would bring the wrath of the community down on its head and land its officials and employees in jail.

This discussion of the discrepancy between the way newspapers behave and the way public agencies are expected to behave is not intended to show the veniality of the former but the vulnerability of the latter. A much more ethical and impartial pattern of behavior is expected and demanded from public organizations than from private ones. If the laws which govern the acts of public institutions were applied to private institutions, most of the management and staff of the latter would end up behind bars.

The legal limitations placed on public agencies contribute to, when they do not actually create, many of the other differences which demarcate them from private enterprise. Government organizations must usually operate in something of a goldfish bowl, subject to continual scrutiny from politicians, the public and the press. They must generally be ready to open their doors and their books to virtually any outsider, even though the outsider's interest in the agency may be prompted by no more than idle curiosity.

---

5. The reader will no doubt understand the writer's reluctance to give further details of this episode. However, he can personally vouch for its veracity.

There are, of course, exceptions to this rule. The Central Intelligence Agency (CIA) has not been known to maintain an open door policy to all and sundry who may wish to examine its records and find out just what it is up to around the world. The Defense Department rarely reveals the details on its deployment of troops and resources, particularly during the conduct of a war. On the local scene, a police department may not choose to open up its files on a current investigation and a welfare agency may refuse to make public the names and circumstances of particular clients. Nevertheless, while many exceptions and qualifications exist, public agencies are expected to be much more open to public inspection and public investigation than are private ones.

The legal context within which the public sector functions also helps explain why its employees usually enjoy greater rights as well as greater obligations. Public employees benefit in many ways from the legal restrictions and restraints which are customarily imposed upon government operations. Their jobs are more secure, their pensions and perquisites are more certain and their paths to promotion are more stabilized. Like most of the benefits in public administration, this one is a mixed blessing. If their risks are less, then so are their rewards. Public employees often experience fewer opportunities for rapid advancement, rotation and displays of individual initiative than do their counterparts in the private sector.

What is true for the employees is likely to be true for the organization. Public agencies frequently possess less flexibility than private ones. They find it much harder to shift direction, change procedures and revamp operations. Firmly enmeshed in a tight web of legality, the public organization typically must follow prescribed procedures and aim at traditional targets.

Underlying this state of affairs is the greater need of the public organization to hold itself accountable. Its obligations extend not just to a particular group of shareholders or sponsors but to the public at large. It is not supposed to do simply what it wants, how it wants. Rather it is supposed to do what the public wants in ways which the public, or its elected representatives have decreed. Responsiveness and responsibility—these are held forth and hailed as the hallmarks of public administration in a democratic society.

The private organization also suffers restrictions, of course, but these usually hinge on its need to make a profit. As long as it is advancing to this goal, it enjoys considerable latitude in the way it operates and in the specific targets it may set for itself. This profit motive accounts for another feature which many feel distinguishes the two types of administration, namely differences in their efficiency. There is a

11

widely held opinion that because private organizations work under the whiplash of profitability, and because they are freer to initiate and innovate, they are more efficient than public ones. The fact that an opinion is widely held does not in itself make it valid and this opinion has encountered heavy opposition. While comparisons between private and public operations are not always easy to make, given the divergent nature of their activities and ends, a case can be made for the potentially equal if not greater efficiency of the public sector.

This case was perhaps best expounded by Paul Appleby in his landmark work *Big Democracy.* Appleby put forth the claims of public administration in the area of efficiency by posing a series of questions. Which types of operations, public or private, he asked, are more subject to the pressures of pull and privilege? Which more readily puts the boss's relatives on its payrolls and which does more of its purchasing from favored friends rather than from the cheapest possible suppliers? Which has executives who are more apt to act on the basis of personal whim and caprice and who are more likely to hire, fire and assign employees for subjective reasons and in an irrational manner?

As for charges of wasteful duplication which are so often flung at the public sector, Appleby responded by asking about the duplication involved in retailers' selling the same goods, gas stations working all four corners of the same intersection and milk and oil deliverymen plying the same routes. Furthermore, in noting the existence of budget bureaus, legislative bodies, the press and other overseers of public spending, Appleby questioned which had the most oversight and control against waste. In a somewhat deeper vein, he posed these questions: which produces the most wasteful products and which engages in the most fundamental and most productive research?[6]

Moving from the theoretical to the practical, we can obtain some glimpse of the claims and counterclaims of the two contending sides by examining the efficiency of the public sector when it engages in private sector activities. There have been and are a host of public enterprises in this country and even more in other countries which produce goods in competition with private firms. What does the record show?

To a large extent, the answer depends on which part of the record one examines. In this country, United States government shipyards have often found few defenders when accused of inefficiency, and this is one reason why their activities have suffered drastic curtailments in recent years. On the local level, John Lindsay found on assuming the mayoralty of New York in 1966 that the city was making its own batteries and asphalt at costs far exceeding what these commodities could be

---

6. Paul H. Appleby, *Big Democracy* (New York: Alfred A. Knopf, 1949), Chapter 5.

purchased for on the private market. Overseas, the so-called Nora Commission appointed by the French parliament in the 1960's, discovered that the productivity of enterprises owned by the French government fell significantly below those in private hands. In Britain many idealistic socialists in the early sixties began expressing doubts and even despair over the questionable results chalked up by those industries that the Labour government had nationalized in the late 1940's.

There is, however, another side of the balance sheet. In this country, the Tennessee Valley Authority as well as many municipal power plants have operated with results ranging from merely satisfactory to superb. In Europe, many Swedish public enterprises have competed successfully with private companies. Similarly, government ownership of the controlling interest in Germany's Volkswagen plant and Holland's KLM Airline has not prevented these firms from registering impressive earnings records. And the entirely government owned and operated British Overseas Airlines Corporation has made a profit every year since 1964. This is an earnings record that many private airlines can only envy.

An article published, oddly enough, in a British bankers' magazine in 1970 provides new and interesting support to these public sector enthusiasts. It notes that while Britain's nationalized industries fared rather poorly between 1948 and 1958, during the ensuing ten years they performed markedly better. Productivity rose by almost two-thirds during this latter decade, far outstripping the productivity gains made in the country's private sector. Indeed, even after lumping in the previous ten-year rate of slower growth, the public sector came out ahead. Productivity increased in the nationalized industries at an annual rate of 3.4 percent from 1948 to 1968. This compares with an annual gain of 2.8 percent in manufacturing which was the greatest growth area in the private sector. After dealing fully and statistically with any doubts or qualifications which skeptics might voice, the writer of the article, economist R. W. S. Pryke concludes, "Certainly, the productivity comparisons and calculations which have been made in this article lend no support to the belief that the nationalized industries have during the last decade been lagging behind the private sector, which is normally supposed to be the repository of economic virtue."[7]

We may conclude by noting that public administration does differ in certain significant ways from private administration. These largely hinge on the greater legal accountability of the former as compared to

---

7. R. W. S. Pryke, "Are Nationalized Industries Becoming More Efficient?" in *Moorgate and Wall Street* (spring 1970). The magazine is published by the British investment banking firm of Hill, Samuel and Co., Ltd.

the greater flexibility of the latter. Determining which is the most efficient remains a complex question subject not only to variances in product and procedures but also to differences in conditions and criteria. Both public administration and private administration are and have been changing in ways which are stimulating to see and exciting to experience. And after completing our journey along the highways and byways of the administrative process, we will take another look at the fence separating the private and public domains. We may then determine if the fence these days is all that high, and we may wonder if, in the future, there will or should be any fence at all.

THE BUREAUCRACY AT BAY

While public administration's supporters do not lack materials for mounting a sturdy defense in its behalf, still, as America entered the last quarter of the twentieth century, it was becoming increasingly difficult for them to do so. Never popular at any time in its history, the public sector was being swamped by attacks on all sides. The Washington bureaucracy was being assailed as "Disneyland East," the "Marble Jungle," the "Citadel of Creative Non-Responsiveness," and the "Fuddle Factory." One Washington joke that was going the rounds had it that an unsuccessful weapon was about to be renamed "the civil servant" because "it won't work and you can't fire it." State and local bureaucracies were, if anything, being made the butt of even worse invectives. The volley of criticism crossed ideological lines, with liberals and conservatives joining radicals and reactionaries in voicing loud dissatisfaction and disdain for those institutions, along with their employees, which were charged with the delivery of public services. Moreover, this discontent and disenchantment was being steadily fed by what seemed to be a near deluge of documentation tending to show how poorly the public sector was performing.

For example, in the spring of 1972, a band of Oglala Sioux Indians aided by some white sympathizers, staged an uprising in western South Dakota. Many, perhaps even a majority, of the Sioux refused to support the insurgency but many others did, and it took the federal government several weeks to quell the disturbance. Yet, whatever the grievances of the angry Sioux insurgents may have been, they could not have complained that the federal government had failed to devote sufficient manpower to minister to their needs. In a book published shortly before the uprising, Washington columnist Jack Anderson and political scientist Carl Kalvelage pointed out that the federal government had at that time 1,400 full-time and 425 part-time employees at work on one of the Sioux

reservations. Adding the other federal employees working on reserva-
tion matters in district and regional offices would be enough, said these
authors, to "provide a live-in bureaucrat for every Oglala family."[8] Yet,
such an expenditure of effort had not prevented the most turbulent and
troublesome Indian rebellion since the closing of the frontier.

Anderson has since detailed other examples of what he calls bureaucratic bungling. To wit: The National Institutes of Health spending
many thousands of dollars for a research effort which only duplicated
what a British research team had investigated and published five years
before; the Post Office awarding a $168,000 contract to a private firm to
develop a safety belt for postal truck drivers only to turn around and
develop its own belt from existing hardware; the Department of Health,
Education and Welfare paying nearly a million dollars to find out
whether college students and other young people were capable of gathering information. Anderson quotes Oregon Representative Edith Green
as saying that she could have done this "study" for $1.50. According to
Mrs. Green the answer was basically simple. "Some can and some
can't."[9]

It was not necessary, however, to depend on Washington colum-
nists for examples of the federal bureaucracy's many shortcomings.
Regular news accounts were supplying a nearly continuous stream of
reports chronicling public sector problems. For example, on February
18, 1973, a few weeks after an article of Anderson's itemizing various
bureaucratic blunders had appeared in a national magazine, the *New
York Times* reported on Post Office studies showing that air mail was
taking about as long as surface mail. Moreover, a letter posted in New
York City to an address fifteen blocks away did not reach its destination
until eleven days later, while two letters to a Greenwich, Connecticut
man, one posted from New York City and the other from Eastern Asia,
both took the same number of days to arrive at his address. Less than
three weeks later, on March 8, newspapers throughout the country carried an Associated Press story disclosing details of a secret report prepared by a congressional subcommittee investigating hospitals of the
Veterans Administration. The investigators had found that care in these
hospitals was so bad that patients were sometimes in worse shape when
discharged than when admitted.[10]

If the federal bureaucracy's operations seem to leave a lot to be
desired, then those at the state and local level seem in many instances to
be suffering still worse problems. When state auditors began scrutiniz-

8. Jack Anderson and Carl Kalvelage, *American Government . . . Like It Is* (Morristown, N.J.: General Learning Press, 1972), p. 60.
9. Jack Anderson, "The Fuddle Factory," *Parade,* January 14, 1973.
10. *Boston Herald-Traveler-American,* March 8, 1973.

15

ing governmental operations in New York City in 1972, they found that the city's building inspectors were spending an average of one-half of their time loafing, the city's truck crews were averaging only about one-half a day's work per shift and the city's welfare workers were wasting two-thirds of their time performing such activities as napping, exercising, playing chess or cards and fixing each other's hair. If such studies may be thought to have been biased as a result of the tensions that existed between the state and city administrations at that time, there was an abundance of similar evidence from sources within the city government itself to support their basic thrust. The city sanitation department, for example, had found that while its permanent clerks would process 37 to 45 invoices a day, temporary employees would average 225 invoices a day. A retiring city greeter, meanwhile, claimed that the sanitation department's own work crews were going up into skyscrapers during parades and throwing down confetti so they would have more to sweep up afterwards, part of this work being done, presumably, at overtime rates.[11]

Although the problems which were afflicting governmental operations in New York City were not duplicated throughout the subnational system, nevertheless there were clear indications that they were by no means unique to the nation's largest city. An employee in a state-run welfare agency in another state wrote a report for his public administration class in 1972 specifying some of the things which went on in his district office.

> Case A: As stated previously, the Director and the Adult Supervisor have a one hand washes the other type relationship. The Adult Supervisor runs a laundry business on the side and does not do much as far as welfare is concerned. This, in no uncertain terms, has had a derogatory effect on his social workers. It should also be pointed out that the situation is not new and has been going on for roughly 10 years. With a supervisor that provided no guidance, no goals, and no interest in his staff, the workers held very little interest in their jobs and also had very little regard for them. One in particular, while on the Welfare Department payroll, held a side job as a bartender, working from 10-3 o'clock, 5 days a week, for five years. He just recently stopped this practice because he was getting old and was tiring of his bartender's job. Although everyone knew he was doing this, no one stopped him or, for that matter, seemed to care. There were, in spite of this, some social workers in the division who continued to try to do a good job, but they received no encouragement and no reward, either monetary or verbal, and lost just about all incentive to continue. This

---

11. *New York Times*, November 20, 1972.

same social worker does not, as previously stated, bartend anymore but does spend most of the 9 to 5 hours playing cards in the establishment that he previously worked in. This, in turn, has left many cases uncovered and has caused inconvenience and probably hardship for many many clients over the years. Net cost in this regard is hard to quantify but we can determine that he was paid roughly $10,000 per year for five years, for services he did not provide. Net loss—$50,000 plus.

Case B: The Director and the AFDC division have been at ideological odds for the past three years. Among the people in this division, though, are some of the best minds in the office . . . .This is what has resulted in our office. In one instance that I know of, a young female social worker, to protest the Director's "lack of feeling for the clients" doubled one particular client's grant from $350.00 per month to $700.00 per month. This went on for four months and is probably one of many cases of blatant waste. Net loss—$1400.00

Case C: Another of the AFDC social workers rebelled in her own way. She decided that she would advise clients not to pay their gas bills until their gas was shut off. She would then apply to the department's hardship fund for payment of these bills. There are at least five cases in which it is known that she did this and all the bills that were payed ranged from between 250 to 300 dollars. Net loss—$1400.00 plus.

Case D: Because the clerks in the office are severely understaffed, they are far behind in paying their bills. One clerk in the AFDC division has $500.00 worth of bills to pay, lying in stacks on her desk. They go back over a year. Besides being bad business, it has ruined clerical morale. The girls are given tasks that are humanly impossible to perform and they are working at half the staff they need and three-quarters of the staff they *legally* are entitled to yet all the Director says is, "Do the best you can." One of the problems that has arisen is that bills are being paid more than once, since the clerks do not have time to make an organized record of the bills they pay. The pressure is constantly on them, by the Director and vendors alike, to "get those bills paid." This they try to do but due to a chaotic situation, some bills are again paid more than once. The fault here lies not only with the Director, but the Regional Office as well. Net loss— thousands of dollars and growing.

Case E: Because the entire office is understaffed and because the workers are not motivated, many of the cases are not covered. Some cases, in fact, have not been visited for 2 years. I came across one case that hadn't been visited for 7 years. The result is that many people who deserve budget cuts do not receive them and, on the other hand, some people who deserve raises in their budgets do not receive them. Net loss—The difference between the amounts that legally should have been removed from certain budgets, and the amounts that legally should have been added.

The former always outnumber the latter, but the loss is incalculable because of the large amount of uncovered cases we have.

I could continue listing cases, but I believe that I have dedicated enough time to the negative aspect of this paper. . . .[12]

As the foregoing account indicates, such malfunctioning in the public sector imposes a heavy cost in terms of dollars alone. Other evidence supports such a claim. When Scottsdale, Arizona decided to contract out its fire services to a private company, it found it could obtain such service at about one-third the price it would cost to operate its own fire department. When New York City allowed a co-op of private plumbers to repair its water mains, the city saved a full four-fifths over what it had been paying to have the work done by city employees.[13]

More systematic studies were also pointing to widespread discrepancies between public and private sector productivity rates in the United States at this critical time. According to economist James W. Kuhn, output per man-hour in the private sector since World War II had generally advanced at a rate of 3 percent a year; output per man-hour in the public sector, he claimed, may have grown at only 0.3 percent per year or one-tenth as much. Again, the problem is believed to be worse at state and local government levels. From 1962 to 1970, a time during which the private sector was earnestly replacing manpower with equipment in an effort to increase productivity, the ratio of payroll expenses to overall expenses in state and local governments increased from 52 percent to 60 percent.

Kuhn accused the public sector of not just being inefficient but of actually spearheading the inflation which surged forward during the Vietnam war and even accelerated after the war came to an end. He noted that the salaries of government workers had pressed upward at a higher rate than did the pay of private sector employees, and this fact, accompanied by only a snail's pace advance in productivity, had contributed greatly to the rapid rises in the cost of living which had plagued the nation during the previous ten years.[14]

Many public administrators themselves were only too quick to acknowledge that something was amiss. In a 1973 report, the National Academy of Public Administration noted that "Americans face the confusing paradox of giving more attention, time, money and manpower to public problems than at any time in their history, but achieving indiffer-

---

12. For what should be obvious reasons, the writer cannot disclose the name of the author of the report or identify the office described.
13. *New York Times*, December 16, 1973.
14. James W. Kuhn, "The Riddle of Inflation—A New Answer," *The Public Interest*, no. 27, spring 1972.

ent or disappointing results. New policy and new programs have received thunderous legislative approval during the past decade only to produce miniscule results. Rightfully, people ask, why can't government—with all of its power and resources—deliver?"[15]

Despite this rising chorus of complaints which buffeted and battered the public sector, those who continue to champion its cause were not without resources for reply. They could point to the fact that most public sector activity is involved in the delivery of services not the production of goods, and it is much more difficult to score productivity advances in the former area than it is in the latter. Indeed, it is difficult even to evaluate the productivity of service delivery. "A fiddler does not increase his productivity by fiddling faster" was one phrase that was sometimes invoked. Furthermore, during the previous decade, governments at nearly all levels had greatly increased the number and extent of their programs, thus significantly and suddenly increasing the workloads of their bureaucracies. The Eighty-ninth Congress alone, which met in 1965 and 1966, enacted eighty-six new domestic programs, thus increasing the strain on public agencies at all levels of the governmental system.[16]

In spite of all these added and often aggravating burdens, many sectors of the bureaucracy still seemed to be performing well. Both the Social Security Administration and the Internal Revenue Service had been given a more than proportionate share of the federal government's increased workload, yet Social Security was still holding administrative costs to within one percent of its overall budget, while the IRS in 1970 spent only 45¢ to collect each $100 worth of taxes. (In 1914, the agency spent $1.52 to collect the same amount.)[17]

On a broader level, Labor Secretary James Hodgson announced in 1972 the results of a government task force which had conducted the first survey ever made of output per man-hour in the U. S. Civil Service. According to the survey, output rose at an annual rate of nearly 2 percent in the agencies studied, and while this still fell below the usual average increase in the private sector, it actually exceeded the private sector average productivity growth rate during the four years covered. (Largely due to problems generated by the Vietnam war, output per man-hour in private industry rose at only an average rate of 1.5 percent

---

15. Richard L. Chapman and Frederick N. Cleaveland, *Meeting the Needs of Tomorrow's Public Service: Guideline for Professional Education in Public Administration* (Washington D.C.: National Academy of Public Administration, January 1973).
16. *New York Times,* November 23, 1966 (column by James Reston).
17. "Diogenes," *The April Game* (Chicago: The Playboy Press, 1973), p. 65. The anonymous writer, an IRS agent, points out that tax payments have gone up considerably since then and it costs no more to process a large tax payment than a small one. Nevertheless, the IRS' track record over the years remains reasonably creditable in at least this respect.

during these four years.) True, the survey only encompassed some 55 percent of all the federal government's activities—the rest were considered unmeasurable by current techniques—and did not take into account state and local government which employ four-fifths of the nation's public work force. Still it did indicate that things were stirring in the "Marble Jungle."[18]

Things were also starting to stir at state and local levels as well. More states had enacted significant constitutional reforms during the previous decade than at any comparable period in our history. In 1973 alone, twenty-two states took some official action to modernize their constitutions. At the local level, a few cities had actually managed to make the leap to metropolitan government while many others were employing new techniques and new talents in seeking to tackle their problems. Even county governments were showing signs of adopting more serious and systematic approaches to their often underestimated responsibilities.

Yes, something was stirring. Some fresh breezes had begun to blow across the governmental landscape, and the administrative sector was starting to respond to their impact.

Public administration's need for such freshening currents, it should be noted, springs not just from its shortcomings but also from its significance. Most political scientists would no doubt concur in Carl Friedrich's assertion that the bureaucracy is the core of modern government, and most would go along with the contention of Marshall E. and Gladys O. Dimock that bureaucracy has become the chief policy-maker in government.[19] Bureaucracy, like a huge colossus, now bestrides nearly all of modern society. As former Federal Communications Commissioner Lee Loevinger puts it, bureaucracy is "the most pervasive institution of the modern age, the most characteristic social problem of the exponential growth of recent years . . ." Loevinger then goes on to describe bureaucracy as resembling "a passionate mob which can capture and conquer man unless he is wise enough to subdue it and shape it to his own purposes."[20]

It is with the hope of rendering some slight assistance in the task of subduing and shaping bureaucracy to the purposes of man that this book has been written.

---

18. *Time*, June 1972, p. 83. Also see *U.S. News and World Report*, June 19, 1972.
19. Marshall E. and Gladys O. Dimock, *Public Administration*, 4th ed. (New York: Holt, Rinehart and Winston, 1969), p. 3.
20. Quoted in Joseph C. Goulden, *The Superlawyers* (New York: Dell Publishing Co., 1973), p. 11.

2

The American Political System

As we saw in the foregoing chapter, public administration differs from private administration in many important ways. And while these differences appear to be narrowing, they are still significant enough to give the public sector a character all its own. It now remains for us to focus on those aspects which inhere to public administration in the United States. The American political culture and the governmental set-up which results from it are characterized by certain features that provide a unique environment for the delivery of public services. The public administrator must understand and appreciate these characteristics if he is to work efficiently to achieve his goals.

FRAGMENTATION

Probably no feature influences and shapes American public administration more pervasively and profoundly than the fragmentation of the political system of which it is a part. The American polity is easily the most decentralized of any country in the western world. Governmental power in this country is strewn in bits and pieces over a widely dispersed and variegated political landscape, and the impact this has on the conduct of public administration is immense.

We find this dispersion of political power operating at every level of our governmental system. At the national level, the United States has three separate and distinct branches of government: the presidency, Congress and the Supreme Court. The Constitution stipulates that Congress is to pass the laws, the president is to administer the laws and the Supreme Court is to see that all this and everything else that happens within the system takes place within the limits of its own continually changing interpretation of the Constitution. The actual balance of power among these entities is almost continually shifting, to be sure, but each branch retains essential prerogatives and woe to the administrator who fails to appreciate them.

Governmental fragmentation at the national level does not stop, however, with this simple tripartite division of power. Congress itself is divided into two houses, each of which jealously guards its rights and responsibilities. Furthermore, within these houses there are some fifty committees along with numerous subcommittees which function, in many cases, as separate islands of power. In some respects, these committees are almost immune to direction from the congressional chambers which have created them.

The presidency, at first glance, seems to provide a much more coherent and unified system of power, for the job of presiding over the executive branch falls on the shoulders of a single individual. As President Truman was fond of saying, "The buck stops here." But, as he was well aware, this does not mean that the president is almighty. Though the chief executive may be saddled with the ultimate responsibility, he by no means possesses any overriding authority. Truman once described his job, as "sitting behind this desk trying to *persuade* people to do what they ought to do." (Emphasis added.) And when he was getting ready to cede his office to Eisenhower, he said to a visitor, "He [Eisenhower] will sit here and say 'do this' and 'do that' and nothing will get done." The history of the Eisenhower administration indicates that Truman knew what he was saying.[1]

The inability of the American president to coordinate and control the far flung activities of his administrative sector has plagued even the strongest of our chief executives. When both the Army Engineers and the Bureau of Reclamation wanted to build the King's River Dam, President Franklin Roosevelt gave specific orders that the Bureau of Reclamation was to execute the project. Yet despite his firm directive, the Army Engineers built the dam. As political scientist Norton Long has remarked, "power [in the U.S.] is not concentrated by the structure of government or politics into the hands of a leadership with a capacity to budget it among a diverse set of administrative activities. A picture of the presidency as a reservoir of authority from which the lower echelons of administration draw life and vigor is an idealized distortion of reality."[2]

That the same problems of fragmentation exist in the 1970's can

---

1. In connection with this problem see William W. Boyer, *Bureaucracy on Trial* (Indianapolis: Bobbs-Merrill Co., 1964), p. 45.
2. Norton Long, "Power and Administration," *Public Administration Review*, 9, no. 4 (1949).

be seen readily. One of the crucial issues beginning to confront the country in 1972 was a shortage of energy. The *New York Times* in an editorial of May 20th in that year bewailed the fact that "there are now an estimated 61 governmental agencies that contribute in some way to the nation's energy policy—if it can be said to have one. No fewer than 18 committees and subcommittees of the 92nd Congress have so far in some way considered the subject." Thus, a unified procedure for tackling urgent domestic problems still remains to a great extent beyond the reach of the American political system.

At lower levels of the governmental structure, the problems of fragmentation are often still worse. In many American states, a governor has even less power to control his administrative branch than the president has over his. Some states have as many as two or three hundred separate agencies and it is impossible for the state's chief executive to keep tabs on what they are doing. Even if he were able to do so, he still would have a hard time bringing order out of chaos for in many states he lacks the power to appoint his own department heads and to have them serve at his discretion. Various top level administrative positions in most American states are filled either through elections or through fixed term appointment. The situation has started to change in recent years and, as we shall see later, state bureaucracies are becoming more unified and responsive to gubernatorial control. But the trend still has a long way to go.

A survey of political scientist Deil S. Wright, taken some years ago to be sure, vividly illustrated an important aspect of this situation.[3] Wright asked 900 top echelon administrators in 50 states to specify who exercised more influence over their activities, the legislature or the governor. Only 32 percent named the governor while 44 percent cited the legislature. A further 22 percent said both the legislature and governor wielded the same degree of control over them. In theory, the governor serves as chief administrator of the American state, but theory, as Wright's survey showed, does not always correspond to reality.

Compounding the problem is the fact that the legislatures of many states are themselves not unified. They are frequently loose amalgamations of shifting factions and therefore cannot impart much unity to the state's administrative processes even if they do tend to control them. It can be safely assumed that at least some of the top echelon administrators who gave the legislature as their number one control really did not mean the legislature as a body but rather one or two committees or even one or two key legislators.

---

3. Deil S. Wright, "Executive Leadership in State Administration," *Midwest Journal of Political Science,* February 1967.

Dropping down to local levels of government we find the same situation. Indeed, fragmentation at this level often becomes still more intense. There are counties, cities, towns, school districts and special districts to split up the power pie. Thus, in any particular locality, the county government may be providing some public services, special districts may be providing others, school districts may be serving the area's educational needs and the municipal governments may have charge of what is left. And even within the shrunken domain of the municipal governments, a good deal of fragmentation may be found.

"In Los Angeles, several departments of the city government control their own funds and are therefore largely independent of the mayor and council . . . . Minneapolis elects 49 officials. The Mayor can appoint no one except his own secretary without the approval of the council and he can remove only his own secretary, the superintendent of police, and the director of civil defense. The comptroller of New York City is elected and therefore not subject to the Mayor. Normally he is a political opponent of the Mayor's," note Edward C. Banfield and James Q. Wilson in their book *City Politics.* And they add, "in the smaller cities—those of them that do not have the council-manager form of government—the division of authority is even often greater."[4]

The special districts, such as transportation authorities or health districts, which proliferate at the sub-state level have, we should point out, their counterpart at the supra-state level. Each state usually has more in common with some states than with others and this fact has given rise to a plethora of regional commissions and boards. The Gulf States Fisherman's Commission, the Southern Interstate Nuclear Board, the New England Board of Higher Education, the Delaware River Basin Commission—the names show some of the flavor of these bodies and indicate some of the common concerns which have engendered their formation. However, the power of these regional agencies is often quite limited. To get anything accomplished, they usually must depend on the voluntary compliance of their constituent states.

One final observation is necessary to round out this picture of fragmentation. It should be evident that political power, and hence power over public administration, is widely distributed not only horizontally but also vertically. In other words, fragmentation occurs not simply at the various levels of government but between the various levels. Actors in the administrative process must not only share authority with many others on their own level of government but frequently with higher or lower echelons too. Many public services represent the com-

---

4. Edward C. Banfield and James Q. Wilson, *City Politics* (Cambridge: Harvard University and the MIT Press, 1963), p. 81.

bined output of federal, state and various local agencies, all of which must to some extent work together in order for the service to be delivered.

Such a wide dispersal of political power produces an even wider atomization of administrative authority. And this situation offers both advantages and disadvantages to the American administrator. Obviously, it provides many agencies with a greater degree of independence than they would enjoy under a more unified system. This in turn may permit a greater diversity of administrative styles and encourage experimentation. It also allows an agency to adapt more fully to its local environment and to achieve a greater rapport with its clientele. At the same time, it may prevent any one administrative agency from acquiring too much power since it must usually contend with other agencies which also have some jurisdiction in the same general area and whose consent it must obtain before taking action.

As James Madison wrote in his famous Federalist Paper #51,

> The great security against a gradual concentration of the several powers in the same department can assist in giving to those who administer each department the necessary constitutional means and personal motives to resist encroachments of the other. The provision for defense must in this, as in all other cases, be made commensurate to the danger of attack. Ambition must be made to counteract ambition. . . . In framing a government which is to be administered by men over men the great difficulty lies in this: You must first enable the government to control the governed; and in the next place oblige it to control itself.[5]

However, the system offers problems as well as possibilities and for many administrators the former are often the most significant. The first of these problems is simply the sheer difficulty of getting anything done. Such a fragmented system breeds the constant necessity for checking and rechecking, clearing and reclearing, creating numerous booby traps and pitfalls which may easily undermine the progress of nearly any program. Each agency tends to fight bitterly any encroachment on what it considers to be its own terrain and the American system allows many agencies to acquire considerable leverage in resisting such encroachments. Consequently, it becomes much easier to impede another agency's attempt to do something than it is to do something oneself. The net overall result is often a general feeling of weary frustration on the part of administrators as well as on the part of the public whom they serve.

---

5. Alexander Hamilton, John Jay and James Madison, *The Federalist* (New York: Modern Library, n.d.), p. 337.

Many administrative activities offer examples of this. Welfare, for instance, is a program that customarily involves inputs from federal, state and local governments. The federal government would seem to be in the driver's seat since it contributes nearly half the total funds and sets the guidelines for their dispensation. Any state or local government that fails to adhere to these guidelines faces a cutoff in funding. However, the process by no means works as smoothly and as simply as might appear to be the case. In her study of the relationships involved, Professor Martha Derthick found that "federal enforcement is a diplomatic process. It is as if the terms of a treaty, an agreement of mutual interest to government parties, were more or less continuously negotiated. . . . Negotiations over a single issue may go on steadily for several years and intermittently for a decade."[6]

Of course, many individual agencies do acquire considerable power over their own limited areas of competence. Some of the most notable of these at the federal level include the Army Engineers, the Forest Service and the FBI, all of which exercise an almost startling degree of independence from the cabinet departments in which they are placed. However, such independence often warrants grave concern for it can lead to irresponsibility and abuse of power in the carrying out of the agency's functions. Here, the Madisonian goal of power checking power is actually being subverted by the Madisonian principle of fragmentation.

The agency itself often suffers, albeit in subtle ways, from such independence, which all too often is more apparent than real. Or, to put it another way, the agency frequently pays a steep and onerous price for its presumed freedom from higher control. In many cases, these seemingly uncontrolled agencies are closely allied to key legislators in Congress, the state legislature or the city council as the case may be. And this alliance is one which frequently substitutes one kind of control for a less visible and less responsible kind of control.

One of the most independent of the cabinet departments is Agriculture. The president does appoint its top officials and they are supposed to carry out his policies. But while they undoubtedly make their presence felt, and while they do manage to execute some of the president's wishes, the department still retains a remarkable degree of immunity from White House influence in many matters. This does not mean that the department is without direction from other areas. An example provided by Nick Kotz in his book *Let Them Eat Promises: The Politics of Hunger in America* offers a telling illustration of some of the forces at work.

---

6. Martha Derthick, *The Influence of Federal Grants: Public Assistance in Massachusetts* (Cambridge: Harvard University Press, 1970), p. 209.

When the department completed its national nutrition survey in the mid-1960's, it found that Mississippi had landed on the list of states with a population suffering from widespread malnutrition. The head of the department's research service dutifully called Capitol Hill and informed Representative James L. Whitten of this fact. Whitten, a Mississippi congressman, was chairman of the House Appropriations Subcommittee on Agriculture, a post he had held for 18 years. Thanks to his longevity in this key position and the diligence with which he kept tabs on what the Agriculture Department was doing, Whitten had become known in Washington as "the permanent undersecretary of agriculture."

The 59-year-old congressman was understandably perturbed over any publication that would put his state in a bad light. He let his feelings be known and, as a result, no hunger list defaming the good name of Mississippi was ever issued by the Department of Agriculture. "Thus, in August 1967," says Kotz, "the Johnson Administration's first meaningful attempt to ascertain the facts about hunger in Mississippi was stopped cold by an executive department's fear of one congressman."[7]

The incident and the interplay of forces which it discloses is by no means unique in the annals of American public administration. It happens all too frequently, and at state and local levels as well as in Washington. (In some respects even more.) The fragmentation of power may allow an agency to escape, at least partially, from under the thumb of its administrative superiors only to end up in a forced and often demeaning alliance with certain key members of the government's legislative body.

Key legislators are not the only group from which the American administrator seeks support and to which he may become beholden. The public agency in the United States is also frequently driven into the arms of its clientele, and the embrace of this latter group, while it may be comforting, may also be crushing. As we stated earlier, fragmentation of political power may enable an agency to establish close rapport with its clientele. This, within limits, is an objective devoutly to be wished. The trouble is that the limits are often exceeded. In its quest for support, the agency may become responsive not only to its clientele's legitimate needs, but also to its whims and caprices. "A major and most time-consuming aspect of administration consists of the wide range of activities designed to secure enough 'customer acceptance' to survive. And, if fortunate, develop a consensus adequate to program formulation,"[8] Norton Long tells us.

---

7. Nick Kotz, "Jamie Whitten, Permanent Undersecretary of Agriculture," in *Inside the System,* Charles Peters and Timothy J. Adams, eds. (New York: Praeger Publishers, 1970). The article is an excerpt from Kotz's book, *Let Them Eat Promises: The Politics of Hunger in America* (Englewood Cliffs, N.J.: Prentice-Hall, 1969).
8. Long, *op. cit.*

We see examples of what Long means almost every day in American administration. Indeed, many cabinet departments such as Agriculture, Labor, Commerce, are at least to some extent captives of their constituencies. And certain sub-units along with independent agencies may be even more susceptible to clientele influence. Regulatory commissions in particular have long been ridiculed and attacked for allowing themselves to become spokesmen for, rather than supervisors of, the industries they are supposed to regulate. Fortunately this situation began changing, rather dramatically in some instances, during the 1960's and it is continuing to do so today. But the forces inherent in the system that lead to such a state of affairs still exist and still make themselves felt.

Thus, the fragmentation that so deeply characterizes the American political system constitutes very much a mixed blessing to the public administrator. It has its distinct advantages and we should not fail to keep these in mind. But at the same time it poses problems to those who wish to practice the administrative craft and it is important that all such practitioners fully understand what they are up against. (This is why, in this chapter, so much emphasis has been and will be placed on the drawbacks of the system.) Professor Long perhaps sums up these particular drawbacks as well as anyone when he writes:

> It is clear that the American system of politics does not generate enough power at any focal point of leadership to provide the conditions for an even partially successful divorce of politics from administration. Subordinates cannot depend on the formal chain of command to deliver political power to permit them to do their job. Accordingly, they must supplement the resources available through the hierarchy with those they can muster on their own, or accept the consequences in frustration—a course itself not without danger.[9]

In later chapters we will examine some techniques that administrators use to deal with the quest for support which our political system and the culture it reflects so rigorously require. At this juncture, we may heighten our understanding of the situation in the United States by taking a brief look at the way administration operates in another modern industrial society with a different political system. As any student of political science knows, Great Britain has a parliamentary government in which the legislature creates the executive out of its own ranks. The prime minister and his cabinet continue to hold their seats in Parliament and to vote on the programs which they themselves introduce. Parliament can oust its government at any time but it rarely does so for if it cannot agree on a new government then it must dissolve and hold

---

9. Long, *op. cit.*

new elections. This, plus the high degree of unity and discipline which the parties are able to maintain, means that the leaders of the majority party can run the government fairly free of interference from particular legislators. In Great Britain the Minister of Agriculture has no need to worry about any "permanent undersecretary of agriculture" within the parliamentary ranks.

Similarly, a government department or agency draws its support and its control from the majority party that is running the government. Clientele groups can and do make their desires and their problems known to their respective agencies. But while they may be able to gain a sympathetic hearing and even to secure some modifications in the agency's programs, these clientele groups cannot acquire the influence over their agencies that their counterparts so often manage to achieve in this country. The majority party in Britain has the final authority and bears the ultimate responsibility. Eventually it will have to answer to the voters. Consequently, it must weigh, for example, an increased subsidy to farmers against a rise in the cost of food. The majority party cannot easily escape the burden of being held accountable for everything which the government does since it knows British voters will vote for or against the party rather than for or against individuals when elections come around again.

Thus, the British system does not provide for a sharing of power at the national level in the way in which our system does. A generally unified majority party legislates and governs pretty much as it sees fit, subject, of course, to prying questions and caustic comments from the opposition in Parliament and also mindful of the wishes of the electorate who will eventually pass judgment.

Reinforcing this concentration of power in Great Britain is the weakness of the country's lower levels of government. Britain has no sovereign subunits such as the American states, and local government, though fairly vigorous, is overshadowed in almost all essential areas of activity by the cabinet and by the national bureaucracy. For example, Great Britain does have local police forces, but they number only 42 in all. Thus, a nation with over ¼ of our population has only 1/1000 as many police organizations. Furthermore, these constabulary forces are heavily subject to central supervision. The national government pays 50 percent of their costs and it lays down all their basic rules and regulations governing such matters as recruitment, pay, promotions, retirement. The Home Office in London must approve the appointment and can at any time require the dismissal of a local police chief. It can even abolish or merge local police units and has frequently done so since World War II.[10]

---

10. George E. Berkley, *The Democratic Policeman* (Boston: Beacon Press, 1969), pp. 24-25.

The same basic trend shows itself in other areas of government activity in Britain. Its Ministry of Education establishes educational policy to a degree that no federal commission of education in this country could even approach. And the situation in most other European countries, though variations do exist, is pretty much the same. The French, for example, have only one police force for the entire country and the educational system is so centralized that it is sometimes said that the Minister of Education can look at his watch and know just what every child in the French school system is studying at that moment. (This is an exaggeration, of course, but it is a revealing one nevertheless.) Certainly, no industrially developed land displays the elaborate degree of fragmentation that so pervasively shapes government activity in the United States.

None of this should be taken to mean that centralized systems are, ipso facto, better either for administrators or for the public they serve. Obviously, the United States is much too large and, more importantly perhaps, much too heterogenous to be administered on the unified basis that characterizes France and England. Furthermore, as we have noted, there are distinct merits in the diverse and dispersed system that we have. But there are drawbacks and deterrents too and they often make life difficult and occasionally impossible for an American administrator.

In his fascinating little book, *Science and Government*, C. P. Snow points out that the entire British government often appears to function like a small family firm. The British, he feels, have a knack for making their country of 53 million seem much smaller than it is while the United States seems to do just the reverse. In other words, our governmental system may exaggerate and compound our diversity and complexity. Snow speaks of "the smoothness, the lack of friction and the effortless speed" which the British government can exhibit once it firmly decides on a policy.[11] An American administrator soon learns that such a state of affairs seldom if ever holds true for the system in which he works. And if he wishes to be successful he adjusts himself accordingly.

A QUESTION OF BUREAUCRACY

Bureaucracy has many meanings, and to an American almost all of them are negative. Sometimes we use the term to describe any extensive complex of government, such as when we speak of the federal bureaucracy

---

11. C. P. Snow, *Science and Government* (New York: New American Library, 1962), p. 31.

or the state bureaucracy. More often, we apply the word to any organization whose methods of operation we dislike. There are few greater insults that one can hurl at an organization than to call it bureaucratic. In similar fashion when we label an official a bureaucrat we are rarely rendering him homage.

In administrative parlance, however, we usually use the word in a somewhat more specialized sense. Though an administrator will speak of the "federal bureaucracy" or the "state bureaucracy," nevertheless, when he refers to a particular organization as being "bureaucratic," he usually has something more specific in mind. Technically, the word *bureaucracy* stands for a particular *type* of administration, one which came into flower only in the modern industrial age.

Prior to the last century or so such public services as existed in most western countries were delivered by administrators who had obtained their position through either political favor or class position. These officials had little in the way of training and often possessed little in the way of competence. Administrative actions were frequently unsystematized and uncoordinated and were in many cases governed more by whim and whimsey than by reason and rationality. Supervisors could often hire, fire or promote subordinates at will while they, in turn, faced the same situation with their own superiors.

The advent of the industrial age initiated a process of change. Governmental leaders increasingly felt the need for expanding the number of public employees and for systematizing their methods of operation. They also had to respond to the growing pressures for democratization which were making themselves felt. All these forces began to prod them into establishing formal organizational structures which operated on a basis of systematized and impersonal rules and procedures. Thus the bureaucratic style of administration was born.

The burgeoning of bureaucracy—again we are using the term in its specialized sense—was a gradual process. However, like most social movements it gained impetus when it acquired a major theoretician. The theorist is this case was Max Weber, a prominent German sociologist who early in this century took a long and careful look at the way public administration was evolving and approved of what he saw. This led him to coin the term *bureaucracy* and to ascribe to it the following features:

1. A graded system of centralized authority based upon law with a fixed and official area of jurisdiction.

2. A professionalized system of work. (This does not mean that all its work is professional in the sense of employing highly skilled or highly educated people. Rather, it means that those who man the

31

bureaucracy work on a full-time basis and that this work normally constitutes their careers. Bureaucracy wars with amateurism in the conduct of government.)

3. Levels of authority arranged in a hierarchical scale with formal lines of communication between the various plateaus.

4. The reduction of all work to formal rules and procedures.

5. The execution of tasks without regard to personal feelings or favoritism. In other words, bureaucracy emphasizes office and function rather than personalities and informal arrangements.[12]

Bureaucracy, therefore, stands for a formalized and systematized method of administration which proceeds on the basis of what Weber called "calculable rules." It is depersonalized, objective and, supposedly, rational. It features a hierarchy but, and this is most important, this hierarchy is subject to distinct limitations on its authority. In a strict bureaucratic system, a superior may not interfere with those activities of his subordinate which have nothing to do with the subordinate's work. Similarly, subordinates are not obligated to superiors in the non-work connected aspects of their lives unless these aspects impinge in some way on their organizational performance. Bureaucracy is non-arbitrary, non-discriminatory and non-personal in dealing with its own employees as well as with its clients and the public at large.

"Bureaucracy," wrote Weber, "is like a modern judge who is a vending machine into which the pleadings are inserted along with the fee. The machine then disgorges the judgement based on reasons mechanically derived from the code."[13]

Weber felt that bureaucracy was the only rational way to organize and operate modern mass societies and most modern mass societies seem to have concurred. The bureaucratic ideals of formalization, systematization and depersonalization spread into wider and wider areas of administrative activity. However, the growth was by no means uniform. Generally speaking, the bureaucratic style of administration found much more favor in Europe than in the United States, and today administration here remains a good deal less bureaucratic than does administration there. To put it another way, American administration tends to be more personal, more informal and, in some respects, more flexible than the administration practiced in such countries as Great Britain, France and West Germany.

One way in which this difference reveals itself is in the vast num-

---

12. H. H. Gerth and C. Wright Mills, *From Max Weber: Essays in Sociology* (New York: Oxford University Press, 1946), pp. 196-239.
13. *Ibid.*

bers of administrative officials who arrive at their positions in the United States through political appointment or election. At local levels, we find many small towns as well as some larger cities electing various administrative officials such as assessors, controllers and even "fence viewers" (still an elective office in some New England communities). In cases where they are not elected such officials are appointed by others who have won office through the ballot. County governments in particular have chosen to go this route and many do not have a single employee who has achieved his post through a formalized personnel system.

The situation at the state level is often much the same. In a few states, formalized personnel systems exist only for those programs involving federal grants-in-aid. In these cases, the adoption of such a system is a federal requirement for receiving the financing. Many other state governments with more bureaucratic (i.e., impersonal and formalized) personnel systems still manage to employ vast numbers of political appointees at various echelons of their "bureaucracies." Furthermore, over four-fifths of the states have the long ballot which means that they elect other executive heads besides the governor. The number of such elected administrators varies from one or two in a very few states to thirteen in Oklahoma.

At the federal level, there are no elected executives other than the president and vice president, and bureaucratic norms are more accepted and obeyed. Yet, the president still makes 6,500 appointments pretty much unhampered by any bureaucratic machinery. Many newer federal operations such as anti-poverty programs make little use of formal personnel systems at all.

This situation presents a startling contrast with that of most other western countries. A party taking power in Great Britain will have just 64 governmental positions to fill, including those of the prime minister and his cabinet. Local and borough councils, who are the only elected officials below the national level, have almost no political appointments to make at all. Similarly in France, a cabinet minister generally has only three appointments at his disposal, all of them on his personal staff. And at the regional and local level in France virtually all administrative officials, with the exception of local mayors and one or two members of their office, are career employees who have had to make their way up through a complex bureaucratic system.

Another and more significant way in which the greater emphasis that European countries place on bureaucratic approaches reveals itself is through behavior. This difference is not so easy to document with facts and figures but perhaps a few incidents will tell the story. In 1966 a policeman in Cologne, Germany arrived at a courthouse to testify at a trial and had trouble finding a legal parking space. With time pressing on him, he parked his VW in a restricted zone and gave himself a parking ticket. Then, with a clear conscience, he hurried to give his testimony. However, when his superiors subsequently learned of his act they disciplined him. He should not have disobeyed the parking laws, they said, even though he was prepared to pay the penalty. Another case from the annals of the German police tells of a Hamburg patrolman who returned home after work to find his wife beating the carpets outdoors. Since this was in violation of the local ordinance, he dutifully gave her a summons. For a true bureaucrat, the rules always come first.[14]

Germans are perhaps more bureaucratically oriented than most other people and the situations just described may not have repeated themselves in quite the same way in other European countries. Yet, in most of them, a greater deference is shown to prescribed procedures than is usually the case here. One should, of course, be careful not to exaggerate this difference. Administration in the United States certainly offers many examples of truly bureaucratic behavior as anyone who has dealt with or worked in American administration well knows. Yet, on the whole, the establishment of elaborate systems of rules and regulations and a slavish dedication to them has been less characteristic of administration in this country.

Many benefits spring from the lessened emphasis on bureaucratic norms and values that mark our administrative system. American administration is often more flexible because its public servants are less bound by pre-set codes and formulas. Since those who deliver public services in the United States are somewhat less compelled to always "go by the book," they can be more responsive to special sectors of the population and their needs and problems. Also, American administration in some respects tends to be more representative and more heterogeneous and, as a result, less inbred and less remote from the people than that of many European countries. Moreover, the lack of a strongly bureaucratic culture enabled our administrative apparatus to more readily recruit minority members to man the poverty programs that came into existence during the 1960's. An overly elaborate and too deeply respected personnel system would have set up many formidable barriers to such a step. Finally, American administration often has less of that well-known and despised bureaucratic bugbear, red tape, than other systems. (Fragmentation, however, with its need for continual checks and counter checks, may add to red tape and this may more than offset the gains achieved by the use of less formalized practices and procedures.)

Europeans who visit our country have occasionally called atten-

---

14. Berkley (1969), *op. cit.,* p. 118.

tion to some of these more agreeable features of administration, American-style. In her book on the United States, *L'Amerique au jour le jour,* the French writer Simone de Beauvoir describes her visit to the Internal Revenue Service prior to leaving this country after a lecture tour:

> I have just been to declare the money I earned during the four months and to pay the necessary tax. In France, that operation would have demanded various steps and countersteps. Here the affair is a matter of dealing directly with one official and it is settled in a half hour. The functionary who sits in front of me to examine the accounts that I have drawn up asked only my word of honor for verification, nothing more. Then, he helped me set up deductions for transportation, secretarial services, receptions, hotels, laundry. . . .
>
> It is he who makes all the suggestions with a touching zeal. He is sad that the total of deductions does not add up to more and that I am left with some tax to pay. Two blows of his rubber stamp and that's all. I can leave America.[15]

Of course, American citizens do not by any means always find their visits to the tax man so pleasant. Yet, in most cases, they are at least able to settle their accounts directly with the official they deal with. They usually do not have to wait until the official's decision clears through various channels. This enables them to transact their business, unpleasant though it may sometimes be, on the spot without filling out additional forms or waiting long periods for various approvals. The French taxpayer, who has to deal with a much more heavily bureaucratized system, is not even this lucky.

But in administration, as in most every other aspect of life, every virtue has its vice and every bundle of blessings bears a price tag, sometimes an exhorbitant one. The fact that Weber's way of doing things never quite gained the same foothold on our organizational soil as it did on the European continent has fostered its share of fatuities and failures in our administrative system.

Let us look once again at our Cologne policeman. Though his actions and those of his superiors may seem excessive, they also are praiseworthy. In going by the book, they were obedient to the ideals of impartiality. And impartiality has a great deal to do with the ideals of democracy. The bureaucratic way may be ponderous, slow, and at times even ridiculous. It also tends to be non-discriminatory and non-arbitrary. If the rules must be slavishly applied, then this means they are applied to everyone without fear or favor. Some further incidents regarding European police activities will help point this up.

---

15. Simone de Beauvoir, *L' Amerique au jour le jour* (Paris: P. Morihien, 1948), p. 370.

In May of 1972, a Helsinki magazine reported that the country's Minister of Justice, while attending a conference of his political party in another city, had late one evening run into a noted strip teaser in the corridor of his hotel. He asked her if she would give a special performance for him and a group of his friends. The dancer replied that such performances were not allowed under the local law. The minister thereupon called the home of the local police chief, woke him up, and asked for a special dispensation that would enable the bosomy artiste to demonstrate her talents. The police chief told the cabinet minister to go to the devil and went back to bed. And that was the end of the incident until the press got wind of it. In Finland, it was not even possible for a Minister of Justice to obtain a minor relaxation of the rules.[16]

Great Britain also provides us with examples of how the bureaucratic way of doing things may lead to more fairness for everyone. Professor Michael Banton tells of two constables who stopped a woman motorist one night and, in examining her license, noted that it was unsigned. They also noticed that she was the wife of their chief inspector. They did not say anything to the woman except to ask her to show her license to her husband. A few days later the chief inspector reprimanded both constables for not having treated his wife in the same manner as they would have treated another motorist. In West Germany again, a policeman once gave a traffic ticket to the then Minister of Defense, Franz Joseph Strauss, when the official's chauffeur made a wrong turn. The cabinet minister protested loudly, saying he was on important business, but the policeman stuck to his guns (figuratively, more than literally) and the incident blossomed into a national controversy. The West German people lined up almost solidly behind the officious police officer and he prevailed in court.[17]

Needless to say the American police do not always act with such ruthless devotion to the established rules and procedures and consequently they do not always observe the democratic norms of fairness and impartiality. And as with the police so with many other sectors of our administrative establishment. Government in the United States, particularly at its more local levels, often shows much more partiality, favoritism, discrimination and arbitrariness than do the more bureaucratic operations of our sister democracies abroad. Harold Ickes once said that those who rail against "bureaucrats" are often attacking "conscientious public servants who won't make a quick decision in favor of a private as

---

16. The incident was reported in the Finnish magazine *Nyrkkiposti* of May 1972. It was subsequently related in the German magazine *Der Spiegel,* May 20, 1972.
17. Berkley (1969), *op. cit.,* pp. 117-118.

against the public interest."[18] It is interesting to note that Hitler hated bureaucracy and vilified civil servants as "pen pushers" and "sock knitters." He almost eliminated the seniority system in the public service and reduced the traditional entry requirements and probationary periods. As a result of Hitler's "reforms," nepotism, corruption and an assortment of other ills flourished in the administrative apparatus of the Nazi state.

Another aspect of bureaucracy which constitutes a two-edged sword is that of administrative competence. A full-fledged bureaucrat can indeed be a man or woman of limited vision who would allow a problem to continue and intensify rather than depart from the sacred rules. In the bureaucratic way of doing things, the means often takes precedence over the ends. But non-bureaucratic administrators can sometimes act in an even more counterproductive fashion. To the extent that they are elected or appointed without training or experience in their tasks, they may proceed not only arbitrarily but stupidly. An elected or politically appointed tax assessor or an elected sheriff and his politically appointed deputies may not only be less disposed to act fairly but may also lack the skill and capacity to do so even when they wish to.

Finally, there is the problem of rigidity. Bureaucratic organizations, as has already been noted, tend to be resistant to innovation and change. At the same time they tend to have a knack not only for perpetuating their routines but also for perpetuating themselves. Though all organizations, as we shall see in later chapters, tend to show a propensity to continue along their well-trod paths, bureaucratic ones often seem to show the most affinity for the tried and true. Furthermore, they exhibit a great deal of staying power in the face of the forces of change. "Nothing can equal the zeal of a functionary for his function," the French leader Clemenceau once said in despair over the often impermeable bureaucracy of his own country. He might have added that the same zeal is often as true for the organization as it is for the individual. Bureaucratic organizations seldom die and frequently do not even fade away. They just go on functioning, impervious to the turbulence and turmoil that may be rocking the society in which they operate.

But even this rather fearsome feature has its advantages. In some countries, the bureaucracy has provided needed continuity and stability during times when the whole social system seemed on the point of collapse and a worse social system appeared in the offing. The French

---

18. Harold I. Ickes, *The Autobiography of a Curmudgeon*. Originally published by Reynal and Hitchcock, New York, this interesting description of one honest man's odyssey through twentieth century American politics has been reprinted by Quadrangle Books, Inc., Chicago. The statement quoted appears on p. 274.

Third Republic which lasted from 1871 to 1940 was certainly not an ideal democracy but it was the most successful experiment in democracy that France had up to then. Its 70-year duration constituted something of a record in French history. One reason why it managed to do as well as it did, and to last as long as it lasted, was its bureaucracy. While politicians came and went, and while governments rose and fell during this period, the bureaucrats kept the country going and maintained a reasonably civilized society. In his detailed account chronicling the collapse of France's Third Republic, William L. Shirer points out how "these permanent officials stood like a rock of Gibraltar against the currents of what ever times." And he goes on to note:

> Honest to a degree unknown or unpracticed among the old nobility and aristocracy . . . and the later parliamentarians and cabinet ministers, industrious in a plodding sort of way and fairly efficient, possessed of a strong sense of public duty, of a remarkable *esprit de corps,* unprogressive and unresponsive to the demands of evolving society, they were a pillar of the state . . . the permanent bureaucracy served as a check upon parliament— there was no other—and saw to it that the business of government got done even at the most chaotic moments.[19]

Thus the balance sheet of bureaucracy—and do not forget we are using the term now in its technical sense as describing a particular type of administration—lists both assets and liabilities. American administration, in proving less receptive to bureaucratic norms and values, has both profited and lost. Again, the differences between the United States and other western countries in this respect should not be exaggerated. Bureaucratic methods are by no means foreign to administration in this country as we shall have ample chance to find out in the chapters that follow. However, there is no gainsaying the fact that administration in our country still remains less bureaucratized and, concomitantly, more personalized and politicized than that of most other industrially developed countries. And this is a fact which the would-be American administrator will ignore only at his peril.

LEGALISM

The American political system is a system designed by and, possibly, for lawyers. The prevalence and power of the legal profession in American public life has existed from our earliest days. Some 31 of the 55 men

---

19. William L. Shirer, *The Collapse of the Third Republic* (New York: Simon and Shuster, 1969), p. 83.

who wrote the American Constitution during that long hot summer of 1787 were attorneys, and members of the bar have played a determining role in our governmental operations ever since. Today about 300 of the 535 members of Congress are lawyers and so are a substantial number of our state legislators and local officials.

This heavy preponderance of lawyers in the ranks of our political leadership has helped to foster a heavy reliance upon legalistic methods and devices in our political system. Indeed, a substantial amount of our governmental operations take the form of legal activities. Not only are problems resolved but policies are established, modified, and even discarded through the use of legalistic means.

For example, race relations constitute one of our most significant and seering problems. Some would say it is the most serious domestic issue we face. Yet the problem over the years has probably been more influenced by litigation than it has by legislation. Since the Civil War and particularly since the early fifties, court decisions have perhaps played the single most determining role in shaping the manner and form of relationships between majority and minority in American life. It is safe to say that in no other country would such a sensitive and salient issue be left to such an extent in the hands of the legal system.

The way we handle the problem of monopoly provides another striking example of how the American political culture allows political decisions and administrative actions to be dealt with in the courtroom. The basically simple but somewhat vague standard of antitrust that exists on the books was laid down well over a half-century ago. Since then the economy has changed drastically and so have our antitrust activities. But nearly all our antitrust policy since that time has been made in the courtroom by men and women who are not necessarily trained in either economics or administration. Other nations would not normally dream of letting judges and lawyers make such decisions. As the British political economist Andrew Schonfield points out in discussing this matter, "In the British system there is no place for the use of the courts to further some evolving principle of public administration. In America there is."[20]

Crucial to this aspect of our system is the existence of our Supreme Court. Functioning somewhat as an *imperium in imperio* our highest court has no real counterpart in any other country. Great Britain, for example, has no court at all that can set limits for the political leadership or strike or modify any of its laws. France has a *conseil constitutionel* which, though modeled after the U. S. Supreme Court, in no way shares the latter's influence or lustre. West Germany's higher court has

---

20. Andrew Schonfield, *Modern Capitalism* (New York: Oxford University Press, 1965), p. 320.

somewhat more power as do the highest courts of a few other countries such as Canada. But none of them can compete with our Supreme Court in influencing governmental policy and shaping governmental operations.

But the legalistic orientation of the American political system does not reveal itself only through repeated resort to the courtroom. Lobbying frequently takes a legalistic form. Much of the lobbying that is done before federal agencies is carried out by large Washington law firms which often use fine points of the law to alter and deflect the course of administrative activity. In his book *The Superlawyers,* Joseph C. Goulden accuses these firms of blunting the thrust of the New Deal's revolutionary reforms, of reducing regulatory commissions to impotence or paralysis and even of drafting laws and administration regulation. As an example he cites the 1937 Civil Aeronautics Board Bill, which was drafted in the law firm of Covington and Burling.[21]

The deeply imbedded legalism of our political system is by no means confined to Washington. It permeates all levels and nearly all activities of American government. Take, for example, the problem of land use. In the United States it is common for state governments to grant zoning powers to their municipalities. This means the municipal government can draw up a zoning map which will specify what types of buildings can go up in the various sections of the community and what types cannot. Some streets may be designated for single-family homes, other streets may be earmarked for both single-family and multi-family dwellings, while still other streets may be allocated for light industry and so forth.

When the zoning map is ready, it is then enacted. In other words it has the force of law. However, an appeals board is usually set up which will grant exceptions, called variances, if the exception seems warranted. A person—say someone wishing to put up an apartment house on the street zoned for single-family dwellings—seeking such a variance will customarily hire a lawyer to plead his case before the appeals board. However, abutters, that is those who live next to or across from the site for which the variance is being sought, must be notified and given a right to be heard. Often times these abutters, if they strongly object to the sought-for variance, will hire a lawyer of their own.

At the stipulated time, the hearing takes place. Both sides make their presentations and the appeals board, after weighing the matter, will subsequently hand down its decision. If the decision goes against the abutters, as it does suprisingly often, then they may take their case

---

21. Goulden, *The Superlawyers,* Chapter 1.

to court and a new legal battle begins. And if the decision again goes against them, they usually can appeal to a higher court.

Such labyrinthine legalistic procedures in resolving land use disputes are foreign to most other countries. In Britain, for example, local planning authorities, which are under national supervision, make all decisions regarding land use. Anyone wishing to secure an exception applies to his local authority. However, the interested party will have no need for a lawyer. The planning officer who will decide the applicant's case is not a lawyer himself and once he has investigated the applicant's petition and made a decision, the matter usually ends.[22]

The American administrator must thus be able to work in a highly legalistic setting. This does not mean that he needs to be a lawyer. Indeed, in some respects he might be better off not being one since legal training does have its limitations. Edmund Burke once said that the practice of law continually sharpened a man's mind while it continually narrowed it, and an administrator in today's dynamic society can scarcely afford to have a narrow mind. Furthermore, legalistic training tends to focus more on methods than on results, and modern administration as we shall subsequently see, is becoming more and more oriented toward results. However, an administrator does need to have an awareness of the many legalistic aspects of American administration and he must be prepared to thread his way through a complex web of law and lawyers to achieve his ends. It is not always an easy task.

In concluding, it is interesting to note that, at least to some extent, the heavy recourse to legalistic approaches in solving administrative problems in the United States is aided and abetted by problems generated by our system's fragmentation and personalism. In other words, the law and its devices are often utilized, for good or for ill, as a way of getting around the deeply political character of our administration. As Professor M. S. Bernstein of the Duke University Law School has written, "the inability to come to terms with the political character of regulation has . . . sanctified the drive towards further judicialization of administrative regulation."[23]

ANTI-GOVERNMENTALISM

In many industrial countries government generally is viewed as a positive good which exists to protect and preserve its citizens. The powers

---

22. For an informative presentation of the contrasting ways in which the two countries handle land use problems, see Charles M. Haar, ed., *Law and Land: Anglo-American Planning Practice* (Cambridge: Harvard University Press, 1964).
23. Quoted in Schonfield, *op. cit.,* p. 321.

that it is given are not given reluctantly but expectantly. The citizen expects the government to act, and to act forcefully if need be, to resolve problems and to improve the conditions of life. Furthermore, those who work for the government are also viewed in a somewhat favorable light. Government service is not looked upon at all as being demeaning. On the contrary, it is sometimes considered to be a mark of prestige, even at its lower levels.

Unfortunately for the American administrator, such is not the case here. We Americans have decidedly mixed views about government activity and though we want to see public services delivered in an efficient manner and are increasingly outraged by its seemingly growing failure to do so, we are sometimes loath to invest our governmental structure with the scope and power to take the forceful action which the achievement of such a goal may require. "I own, I am not a friend to very energetic government," said Thomas Jefferson, and large sectors of the American populace have echoed his sentiments ever since. Deeply implanted in our political culture is the belief, or at least the feeling, that that government governs best which governs least.

The proliferation of regulatory commissions in the United States, somewhat ironically, provides evidence of this. The primary reason why we have so many regulatory commissions and European countries have so few is that the industries regulated in America are, in Europe, government owned. These include public utilities, telephone companies, railroads, airlines. Many European governments also own, in whole or in part, auto manufacturing firms, coal mines, steel mills, drug companies. As Andrew Schonfield points out, "Among the Americans there is a general commitment to the view, shared by both political parties, of the natural predominance of private enterprise in the economic sphere and the subordinate role of public initiative in any situation other than a manifest national emergency."[24]

Public service itself, except when it takes the form of a high level political appointment, rarely has been a mark of status in American society. Too many Americans for too long have regarded the civil servant as a dullard and a dolt who clings to his government job as if it were a security blanket. Even those who do not judge the government worker so harshly still tend to regard him as a cautious and colorless fellow, an exemplar of an industry whose presumed greyish tone was discussed at the beginning of the book.

This image of the public servant does seem to be changing. So is the public conception of what the government should be and should do. And, for that matter, change is coming to many of the other aspects

---

24. *Ibid.*, p. 328.

of American political culture which we have examined in this chapter. Merit systems are expanding and political appointments are gradually going out of style. Many governmental functions are passing to higher levels and are thereby becoming less fragmented. The federal government now intervenes in functions heretofore left to the states and the states are playing roles in operations that have hitherto been regarded as strictly local matters, such as education. Such trends are probably both a cause and a result of the public's growing impatience with what it feels is the public sector's ineffectiveness.

Yet, despite these trends, all the features we have noted still form an integral part of the American political system and are likely to continue to do so for a long time to come. To anyone embarking on an administrative career, they will continue to present both problems and possibilities. They will make his work day both more interesting and more frustrating. In any event, one thing is certain, American public administration for the foreseeable future will challenge and challenge fully all the administrative abilities which its practitioners may acquire or possess.

CASE STUDY

The Delaware Runs Dry[25]

The state of Delaware has little control over the river that bears its name. The 330-mile waterway originates in southern New York State, wends its way along the borders of Pennsylvania and New Jersey, and then passes through Delaware before emptying into the Atlantic. In its daily course, it manages to provide substantial amounts of water for all four states and some of their largest cities. Since the region which the Delaware serves holds almost one-tenth of the nation's population and employs almost one-seventh of its work force, the river has sometimes been considered the most important of America's waterways.

Until the spring of 1961, the Delaware had generally fulfilled the demands that its host states had placed upon it, and water experts confidently expected that it would continue to furnish sufficient water for the growing region until 2010. This, however, was the last time they expressed such a hope, for the following August a drought descended on the entire middle Atlantic region. The dry spell continued for four years and by the spring of 1965, New York City's water resources were down to about one-quarter of their capacity. Northern New Jersey's reservoirs were similarly afflicted, while the situation

---

25. Richard A. Hogarty, *The Delaware Drought Emergency,* Inter-University Case Program #107 (Indianapolis: Bobbs-Merrill Co., 1970). All material, including quotes, in this section are taken from this case.

in much of the rest of the region was as bad if not worse. The crisis precipitated a series of events which have been summarized and assessed by Richard A. Hogarty in an illuminating case study, *The Delaware River Drought Emergency.* The problems which the drought dramatized and the ways in which they were resolved shed valuable light on the political system within which the American administrator must ply his trade.

It should be noted that although the Delaware up to the time of the 1961 drought had managed to supply the water needs of all those who depended upon it, this had not prevented its beneficiaries from wrangling among themselves as to who was to get how much of its valuable resources. In 1928, New York City obtained state approval for a new reservoir system which would divert substantially increased waters from the Delaware. New Jersey and Pennsylvania became incensed at the proposed diversion and filed suit to halt it. Their case gradually climbed up the judicial ladder, reaching the Supreme Court in 1931. The Supreme Court ruled that the proposed diversion was subject to the doctrine of equitable apportionment, and that New Jersey and Pennsylvania had "real and substantial rights in the river that must be reconciled as best they may." The Court did grant New York City about two-thirds of the additional water it was seeking, but it indicated that this might not prove to be a permanent solution. In the prophetic words of Justice Oliver Wendell Holmes who wrote the majority decision, "the possible experiences of the future may make modifications of the plan as it now stands necessary in unforeseen circumstances."

In 1936, the four basin states formed the Interstate Commission on the Delaware River Basin (INCODEL), but they gave it little regulatory or operational power. The commission prepared a comprehensive plan for the physical development of the river in the early 1950's, but the plan fell by the wayside when it failed to secure the needed approval from one of the four states, Pennsylvania. With the failure of the plan, the commission ceased to play any significant role.

In 1952, New York City, once again eager to proceed with some reservoir construction, petitioned the Supreme Court to modify its 1931 decree and allow the metropolis to tap more water from the Delaware. The Court moderately increased the city's water allowance and agreed to a substantially greater allowance of water once its projected new reservoir system was completed. (The plans for the reservoir had still not been fully worked out by 1965. Consequently, New York was still operating under the modest increase permitted by the Supreme Court's earlier decree when the drought problem reached its climax.)

In 1953, the governors of New York, New Jersey and Pennsylvania decided to explore again the possibilities of developing a single governmental unit to handle the basin's water resources. The hurricanes of that year added impetus to their efforts, for they exposed and intensified the difficulties which the lack of a coordinated and cohesive mechanism had engendered. As Hogarty notes, "the region's water planning and policy machinery was balkanized, complex and cumbersome. Approximately 849 local governments, 42 counties, 4 states and an estimated 252 water supply enterprises had some sort of policy-making responsibility in water management. Superimposed upon this jurisdictional maze were about 18 federal agencies, 14 interstate agencies and countless private firms including giants like United States Steel."

By 1959 the governors had worked out a plan for a permanent basin agency to be established by an interstate-federal compact. By 1961 all the states and the federal government had approved it and the Delaware River Basin Compact (DRBC) came into existence. The compact was unique in many respects. For one thing, it was the first such arrangement to include the federal government as a voting member. Second, the interstate agency envisioned by the compact would have "strong regulatory powers and extensive authority over allocation, diversions and releases of water in the basin." It was given an office and a staff and was believed to be functioning well when the full impact of the drought began to be felt in the fateful spring of 1965.

It was on June 14 of 1965 that New York City suddenly shattered the uneasy peace which had for some years prevailed along the Delaware River basin. With no prior announcement, the city on that day began diverting substantially more water for its own use. Its action quickly triggered expressions of anger and alarm in the other three states which were already being deeply troubled by the developing drought. The city of Philadelphia was particularly worried, for with less and less fresh water coming in from the Delaware, the "salt line" in the city's existing water supply would rise to dangerous levels. However, the situation in most of the rest of the region was nearly as threatening.

Representatives of the four governors and the federal government hurriedly met on June 23 to discuss and, so they hoped, decide the issue. Their meeting, however, only produced a decision to call a public hearing in order to determine the full extent of a problem that was now as much political as it was physical. While such a hearing was required as a prerequisite to taking action under the Interstate Compact's emergency powers, it by no means guaranteed that such powers would be or could be invoked. All five signatories would have to consent to such action, and with New York State quite sensitive to the problems of its major city, such unanimity might prove hard to muster.

Following hard on the heels of the June 23 conclave, Governor Richard Hughes of New Jersey summoned a meeting of the governors, along with federal representatives, for July 1. Hughes acted in his capacity as chairman of the compact, but goading him on was the desperate turn of events in his own state. Some of New Jersey's cities were faced with the alternative of importing water in tank cars at enormous costs if the drought continued and if New York City's increased diversion was allowed.

The governors of New York and Pennsylvania, Nelson Rockefeller and William Scranton, declined Hughes' offer to attend the meeting though they did send representatives. Secretary of Interior Stewart Udall and Delaware Governor George Terry, however, did show up. New York City, though it had no official status at the conclave, sent a delegation of its own. The meeting failed to produce a mutually acceptable solution though one compromise plan did seem to have possibilities and was targeted for further study.

In the meantime, the public hearing authorized by the earlier meeting was held on July 7. It produced convincing evidence as to the severity of the crisis. It also produced much testimony blaming New York City not just for diverting more than its share of water from the Delaware, but for failing to undertake what others thought were necessary conservation measures. New York City spokesmen, as might be expected, vigorously denied such charges. After the hearing, the compact's commissioners and staff members, with New York City excluded since it was not a member of the commission, gathered in executive session for five hours. They managed to agree to some limitation on the amount of water which New York State could keep for itself and its communities. (New York State's representatives, ever mindful of the political importance of New York City, and not wishing to push it too far, gave only limited and grudging acceptance.) This was the first of several difficult and hard-fought agreements reached by the DRBC on its tedious and troublesome way to a solution. And though such bargaining and negotiation did produce progress, it took a new development to move the issue toward a real resolution.

The governors had been asking for federal aid almost since the crisis began. Particularly active in this regard was Governor Hughes, who had aggressively supported President Lyndon Johnson's election the previous year. The president himself, meanwhile, had been showing increasing interest in water problems, particularly in desalinization which he considered to be the most effective long-term method for "drought proofing" major metropolitan areas as well as farm regions. (He was also well aware of the importance of some of these areas to the future of the Democratic party, particularly in the congressional elections that would occur the following year.) On July 14 Johnson expressed concern over the drought and said he had asked federal officials to study the situation and suggest ways in which the federal government could help. On August 7, Interior Secretary Udall sent him a memorandum urging the initiation of coordinated intergovernmental planning and suggesting, as a first step, inviting the four governors, along with the mayors of the affected major cities, to a Washington meeting.

The meeting was held on August 11 after which Johnson moved swiftly. He launched a series of steps which, while they brought no short-range solution in themselves, produced prospects of long-term financial aid to the distressed states and localities. By using such prospective aid as an inducement, the federal government succeeded in prodding them to work out a "water bank" and take other immediate steps both to conserve water and to apportion it more equitably among themselves. The state governments came under particular pressure to exercise greater control in coordination of their own water resources and to show more leadership vis-a-vis their own communities lest they lose out on the federal government's generosity.

The case is, indeed, a complicated and a complex one, and this short summary does little justice to its many components and phases. However, even such an abridged version as this affords a glimpse of the American political system at work.

The most apparent feature is that of fragmentation. Not only were four quite sovereign states involved in the dispute but their largest cities played important and somewhat independent roles. New York City, Philadelphia, and other cities sent their own representatives to the various meetings that finally produced some solutions. Furthermore, the tensions which hampered the achievement of a resolution existed not just between the states themselves but, at least in some cases, between the state governments and their own communities. Governor Scranton's attempt to assert state government authority in Pennsylvania was opposed by the Greater Philadelphia Movement and other local organizations and leaders. As for Governor Rockefeller, he and his state water commissioner, in their dealings with New York City, "often found themselves," says Hogarty, "in the role of protectors rather than deciders." From the standpoint of the state water commissioner, "there was never any question about his backing up New York City. State officials could not concede that the city was violating the 1954 Supreme Court decree."

The case also illuminates the extensive role which legalistic techniques and devices tend to play in our political system. Although the courts were not dragged into the drought crisis, they had been utilized in two previous disputes concerning how much water New York City was to obtain. Actually, some of those involved in the drought decisions wanted to take New York City again to court, but others felt that such a step would take too long. They also pointed out that a functioning agency existed to handle such matters and the Supreme Court always required litigating parties to exhaust all administrative remedies before seeking its help.

Finally, the impact of personality presents itself throughout the case. Governor Scranton not only had trouble from local organizations in Philadelphia but had deep trouble from a leading member of his own party who opposed him at every step. The personality of the mayor of New York City played a major role in the proceedings. He had shrugged off all the initial warning signs of the crisis, and his rather lackadaisical attitude certainly precipitated some of the dramatic action which the city found itself constrained to take at a later date. And had the water commissioner of New York City been more amiable and also amenable to outside suggestions, the problems might have been resolved at a much earlier phase.

But perhaps the most startling and the most significant way in which the accident of personality intruded itself into the course of events occurred much earlier during the fight for the plan which the previous interstate commission (INCODEL) had devised during the 1950's. It will be recalled that this plan failed to be adopted because one state, Pennsylvania, had said no. However, Pennsylvania's rejection resulted from the fact that a subcommittee of its state senate failed to approve the plan by one vote. Thus, solely because one obscure state legislator in one of the affected states refused to give his approval, a physical development plan that might well have averted the entire crisis never saw the light of day.

3

The Anatomy of Organization

Stripped to its essentials, an organization consists of two or more people engaged in a cooperative effort, working toward a common goal. Thus, the two men engaged in stone-lifting that we depicted in a previous chapter constitute, whether they know it or not, an organization or at least the rudiments of one. All administration requires an organization of some shape, size or kind, and all organizations carry on some measure of administrative activity.

THE BASIS OF ORGANIZATION

The structure of most public organizations is a good deal more complex than that of the two imaginary stone-lifters that we have continually cited. In launching our foray into this rather formidable field, we may find it useful at the outset to examine what is called the basis of organization. We owe this concept to Luther Gulick, one of the trailblazers in American administrative theory.[1] Gulick classified organizations into four different types depending on their basis or fundamental orientation. Many dispute the utility of his classification scheme and nearly all will concede that his categories overlap. Yet, in examining them, we will, I believe, find much that can deepen our understanding of modern organizational life.

     The first category consists of organizations established on the basis of *purpose.* These organizations are oriented essentially toward

---

1. Luther Gulick and L. Urwick, *Papers on the Science of Administration* (New York: Institute of Public Administration, 1937), p. 15.

accomplishing some specific, though often broad, task. Examples of such organizations abound. A school system is structured to teach children. A fire department is arranged and operated to put out fires. An army is designed to fight wars. And so on. All of these organizations tend to include all the functions necessary to accomplish their essential purposes.

As the reader may quickly surmise, purpose has long been the most prevalent basis of public organization, at least in this country. Yet there are three other categories of organizational basis, and all of them seem to be growing in importance. One of these categories is that of *process.* A process organization is oriented not so much toward accomplishing a specific goal but toward performing certain types of functions. A good example of such an agency is a city law department. Typically, at least in a large city, this department will consist of a group of lawyers who service other departments. One lawyer may represent the city's urban renewal authority in the use of eminent domain. Another may defend the city's public works departments in lawsuits. A third may prosecute errant policemen in disciplinary hearings. All of them thus may be engaged in helping to accomplish a wide variety of specific purposes, but all of them are united through the means they utilize, namely the law.

A third basis of organization is that of *place.* Organizations put under this heading are structured primarily toward serving a particular locale. So far, only a few public agencies strictly meet the classification standards for this category. One example is the neighborhood city halls which Boston and a few other cities have established. These are centers designed to provide a variety of services to all the people who live in a particular neighborhood. In performing this task, they may utilize a variety of processes and strive to accomplish a variety of purposes. What underlies everything the neighborhood city hall does is the providing of services to those who live in a particular place.

If we wish to make our classification criteria less strict, we can lump a host of organizations in this category since nearly every field unit of every public agency is, in a sense, place oriented. The local firehouse, the local police station, the local elementary school are all designed to perform services for particular areas. Yet, they are all part of purpose organizations oriented toward putting out fires, preserving public order and teaching children. Consequently they cannot be properly labeled place organizations.

The fourth and last basis of organization which Gulick identified is that of *clientele.* Like place organizations to which they are often closely linked, clientele organizations have not been a common feature of our administrative landscape. These agencies are built around the need to serve a particular group of people. One notable example is the federal government's Bureau of Indian Affairs. This agency is designed to provide a variety of services to American Indians irrespective of where they may live. Though its efforts, judging from the discontent now being voiced on the reservations, may not have been all that successful, this at least has been its primary aim. Another example was the federal government's Children's Bureau which, from the time of its creation in 1912 to its dismemberment and virtual abolition in 1969, sought to furnish a variety of services to children. It proudly claimed that it serviced the *whole* child.[2]

As we have already noted, purpose organizations have traditionally dominated American public administration in theory as well as in practice. The Presidential Commission on Organization of the Executive Branch of the Government, better known as the Hoover Commission, warmly endorsed and embraced this organizational basis when it issued its report in 1950. Although most federal agencies already had adopted a purpose orientation, the commission felt that even more of them should do so. Recommendation #12 of its report addressed itself forcefully to this point. "The numerous agencies of the executive branch must be grouped into departments as nearly as possible by major purposes in order to give a coherent mission to each department." The commission's rationale was contained in a terse sentence that followed its recommendation. "By placing related functions cheek-by-jowl overlaps can be eliminated and, of even greater importance, coordinated policies can be developed."[3]

The commission, in throwing its weight so solidly behind the purpose concept, did not offer critiques of the other bases of organization. Others, however, have pointed out that place or clientele organizations offer too few opportunities for utilizing specialized services or even for establishing a satisfactory division of labor. Furthermore, both place and clientele organizations tend to become highly vulnerable to improper influences from the areas or the groups that they serve. Process organizations, on the other hand, while they provide the best opportunities for making use of specialization and for allowing specialists to practice and develop their skills, tend to lose sight of the main aim of public administration which, of course, is the delivery of basic services. In a process organization, professionally interesting activities tend to take precedence over vitally needed ones. Means tend to predominate over ends. Finally, these three other bases of organization tend to en-

---

2. For a more detailed critique of the various bases of organization see Schulyer C. Wallace, *Federal Decentralization* (New York: Columbia University Press), pp. 91–146.
3. *Hoover Commission Report* (New York: McGraw-Hill, 1948), p. 24.

courage a proliferation of departments and a disunity of action in solving public problems.

Despite long-term popularity of the purpose concept and despite the reservations which were long voiced regarding the other three bases of organization, signs began to appear during the 1960's that the pendulum was starting to swing in other directions. For instance, more and more administrative activity began focusing on clientele or place or a combination of the two. Some of these activities were brand new endeavors such as poverty programs which, in their overall concept, were and are designed to provide a package of services to a distinct group of people. Another example is agencies dealing with the elderly. From the Department of Health, Education and Welfare's Bureau of the Aging down to local Golden Age Centers, these organizations aim at aiding a particular group of citizens in a variety of ways.

The formation of the Department of Housing and Urban Development was something of a triumph for the clientele approach since HUD's essential reason for being is to service a particular clientele, primarily the nation's city-dwellers and to give them a voice in the cabinet. The same trend has manifested itself at the state level. Even the battle cry of the old Children's Bureau, to care for the *whole* child, began to re-emerge early in 1971 when the New York City Board of Education approved a $43 million appropriation to finance a new breakfast program in the city's schools. According to a report in the *New York Times,* the program was placed in the budget by the school system's Chancellor Harvey B. Scribner "probably as much to establish a philosophy as to meet a need." Said the *Times,* "Dr. Scribner appears to be insisting that unless the schools take care of the children's physical as well as intellectual welfare, those who need attention most are least likely to get it." The report, which was written by the newspaper's education editor, concluded with these words. "The question of how to deal with the whole child—including his family, if any, and including even such problems as disease and drug abuse—is real and must be faced."[4]

Clientele is not the only alternative basis of organization that is gaining in popularity. As we will see when we discuss staff services later in this chapter, process organizations are also growing in number. Place, too, as we will notice when we examine centralization later in this book is also acquiring increased acceptance as at least a partial basis for organizational structure. The point to keep in mind is that a single-minded emphasis on purpose, as typified in the Hoover Commission

---

4. "Role of the Schools: Should They Be Totally Involved in a Child's Life?" *New York Times,* January 24, 1971 (News in Review).

proposals, can no longer, if it ever did, meet the needs of modern administration. Delivering public services in today's technological society is a complex, delicate and ever changing task. As such, it is forcing administrators to review all the options they have available for organizational basis, and to modify their approach or even to adopt a totally new one as they strive to fulfill their goals in a rapidly changing society.

POINTS ABOUT PYRAMIDS

The pyramidal form tends to dominate the structure of most work organizations of any size. The reasons for this are fairly easy to discern. The organization must delegate its work to a vast number of individuals. In order to make sure that they do the work delegated to them, and to see to it that their efforts in doing it are coordinated, the organization typically establishes supervisors. These supervisors may themselves become so numerous that they require supervisors in turn. As a result one or more levels of hierarchy tend to emerge in any sizable work organization with each level dwindling in numerical size until the top is reached.

So pervasive is the pyramidal concept that it even characterizes the operations of organized crime. In his book *Theft of the Nation,* sociologist Donald Cressey points out that each of the twenty-four or more Mafia "families" in the United States is under the command of a boss or *capo*. The *capo* and his immediate aides oversee a group of *caporegime* or field managers who act as chiefs of the families' operating units. These field managers, all of whom are supposed to be of equal status, supervise a varied number of subordinates. Frequently these sub-units spawn further sub-units comprising five or so "button men" under a section head.[5] In many respects the Mafia family is organized along lines not dissimilar to those of, say, a municipal welfare department.

Perhaps the smoothest and most orderly pyramidal pattern found in the public sector is the infantry division of the army. The soldiers are grouped into squads under the control of sergeants. The squads are formed into platoons under the leadership of lieutenants. The platoons are collected into companies under the command of captains. The progression continues up to the apex of the divisional triangle which is headed by the division's commanding general.

However, and this is a point which bears continued emphasis, nearly every organization is part of a yet bigger organization, and so the infantry division and its general are answerable to still others above. The

5. Donald R. Cressey, *Theft of the Nation* (New York: Harper & Row, 1969), Chapter 6.

pyramidal process continues into the higher levels of the Pentagon where the Secretary of the Army joins the Secretaries of Navy and Air Force in being accountable to the Secretary of Defense. The latter, meanwhile, occupies one of twelve seats in the cabinet, a body which is presided over by the president of the United States.

Even much less authoritarian organizations than infantry divisions or Mafia families tend to assume, to a greater or lesser degree, this pyramidal form. A large university, for example, will often contain many diverse types of sub-units and many varying and shifting levels of authority. Yet we will generally find that the professors are under the leadership of their department chairman, the chairmen are responsible to their deans, the deans are answerable to their chancellors or whatever the heads of their respective colleges may be called, while the chancellors are accountable to the president of the entire university.

From the tendency of large and particularly bureaucratic organizations to shape themselves into a triangle, we draw certain important concepts. Among them are *unity of command, chain of command,* and *span of control.*

The meaning and import of unity of command is fairly obvious. It bases itself on the old proverb that no man can serve two masters. This maxim generally has been deemed true for a work organization, particularly one that is operating under the bureaucratic norms of delegation, specialization and accountability. Requiring an individual or a group to respond to the orders of two or more superiors will, it has been held, produce conflict, confusion and often chaos. If unity of command does not exist, such deficiencies, it is contended, will not only characterize those being commanded but those doing the commanding. In other words, multiple superiors will not only confuse their subordinates but also each other.

One of the most ardent admirers of the unity of command principle was Alexander Hamilton. "That unity is conducive to energy will not be disputed," he wrote in his famous Federalist Paper #70. "Decision, activity, secrecy and dispatch will generally characterize the proceedings of one man in a much more eminent degree than the proceedings of any greater number, and in proportion as the number is increased, these qualities will be diminished."[6] An old world contemporary of Hamilton, Napoleon Bonaparte, shared this view. The great French conqueror once said that when it came to fighting a war, he would rather have one bad general than two good generals.

The unity of command principle, it should be evident, frowns on the use of boards and commissions. Such multiple-headed bodies have

---

6.   Hamilton, Jay and Madison, *op. cit.,* p. 455.

been considered suitable only for organizations of a semi-judicial nature such as regulatory commissions or for certain policy-making or advisory functions. If an organization is administering a program, if it is *doing* things, then the reins of its authority should converge eventually into one pair of hands. Only in so doing will responsibility be pinpointed and conflicting orders, internecine warfare and a host of other organizational ills be avoided.

Unity of command usually requires a chain of command, for in any large organization the man at the top cannot oversee all that is going on below. He needs others to help do this for him. Frequently, these helpers themselves cannot supervise all those beneath them. As a result, several echelons of command may emerge through which authority is supposed to pour or seep downward in a neat, orderly flow. With unity of command, the captain of A company does not give orders to the soldiers of B company. With chain of command the battalion major does not give orders directly to soldiers from either company but works through their commanding officers. Even less structured organizations customarily observe, at least to some degree, the same principle. The college dean, if he has reason to be disturbed by the behavior of a particular professor, will usually first contact the professor's department chairman before taking any direct action against the troublesome faculty member.

A third concept which the pyramidal structure spawns is span of control. Unlike the first two, this does not in itself constitute a principle but rather serves as a frame of reference. In other words, span of control is not something which the organization *ought* to have but something which it *does* have. Span of control refers to the number of units, be they individuals or groups, which any supervising unit, be it an individual or a group, must oversee. The problem consists in making sure that the number of these sub-units is neither too many nor too few. Or, to put it differently, to make sure that the supervisor's span of control is neither too great nor too small.

How much is too great and how much is too small? Unfortunately, the slippery and shifty world of administration provides no hard and fast criteria for automatically determining such things. As with so many other questions concerning this capricious craft, the only intelligent answer is the highly unsatisfactory one of "it all depends." The proper span of control hinges on the type of work being done, the type of employees doing it, the degree of geographical dispersion of the employees, and a multitude of other factors. And these factors often can be deceptive.

To take a hypothetical example, it would appear that a foreman who is overseeing a group of laborers performing routine chores in a

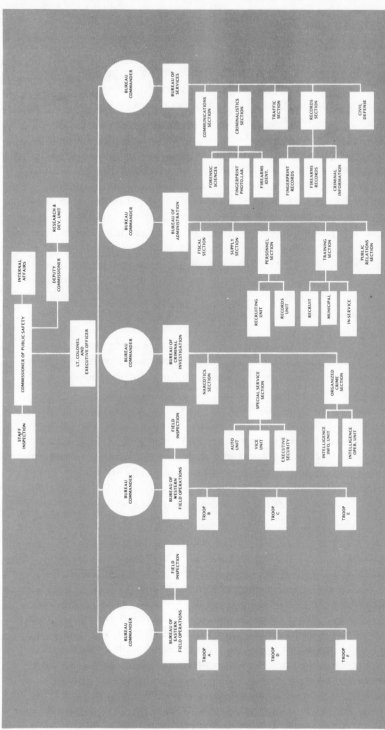

This is an organization chart of the Massachusetts State Police, a public agency which has 1,433 employees of whom approximately 868 are troopers. The five bureau commanders hold the rank of major while captains head up the six field troops as well as many of the other sub-units. Each of the six troops consists of 33 men including lieutenants and sergeants. Do the spans of control seem too broad or too narrow? Does the chain of command seem too short or too long? (Source: Massachusetts Department of Public Safety.)

compact work area would be able to supervise a greater number of people than can a senior scientist who is heading up a team of colleagues, each of whom is engaged separately in a unique and intricate task in various parts of a dispersed laboratory complex. Yet, the situation can be reversed. The scientists can work on their own and may insist on doing so. The assembly-line workers, on the other hand, may dislike their work and even each other. Thus the harried foreman's effective span of control may be less than that of the chief scientist.

The tendency in American government has been to make the span of control too broad, at least at the highest echelons. The president, most state governors and most mayors and city managers, it is widely felt, suffer from having too many different agencies and people reporting to them. It is not unusual to find state governors trying to oversee directly the workings of two to three hundred governmental units. The governor may, of course, have a staff including an administration commissioner to help him discharge this mission. But it still remains a formidable if not impossible task. Many state governments have undertaken reorganization plans in recent years and almost invariably one of their first orders of business is to consolidate agencies and set up intervening levels of authority so that the governor will not have to deal directly with so many components of his far-flung though loosely coordinated empire.

Such consolidations, however, often create problems as well as solve them. A good example of this is the reorganization which New York City has undertaken in recent years. Mayor John V. Lindsay during the last half of the 1960's sought to tame the city's many highly independent administrative agencies by consolidating them into ten super-agencies. This was designed to bring more coherence and unity to their operations and make it easier for the mayor to translate his policies into effective action. Lindsay achieved substantial success in getting his reorganization plans adopted but the results of their implementation were not an unalloyed joy.

Early in 1970, *New York Times* reporter Martin Tolchin, in discussing the recent and unexpected resignation by the city's commissioner of hospitals brought some of these misgivings to light. As a result of Lindsay's reorganization, the Hospitals Department, which previously was directly responsible to the mayor, was now situated in a consolidated Health Services Department headed by an overall health commissioner. According to Tolchin, the hospital commissioner had resigned because he felt he now suffered from "lack of access to the Mayor and lack of influence in critical decisions." Tolchin then went on to point out some of the questions which "democratic critics and experts on urban affairs" have raised in light of the hospital chief's departure. "Have these super-agencies, designed to encourage rational planning in city government, merely added to the red tape and imposed another bureaucratic layer between the city officials and the Mayor? Have they discouraged able men from taking commissionerships? Is Mayor Lindsay, in fact, less accessible to his commissioners than was Mayor Robert F. Wagner?"[7]

Some of the questions which the critics and experts were raising regarding New York City's reorganization accomplishment had already been suggested by Herbert Simon nearly twenty-five years before. In a widely heralded article published in 1946, Simon challenged much of the conventional wisdom regarding span of control. He noted that one of the "proverbs of administration" calls for limiting the number of subordinates and subordinate agencies which report directly to any one administrator. But, he pointed out, this contradicted another proverb of administration, namely that administrative efficiency will be increased "by keeping at a minimum the number of organizational levels through which a matter must pass before it is acted upon."[8]

The tighter the span of control, the more numerous are the intervening levels between top and bottom. This tends to increase both paperwork and procrastination. It also leads to decisions being made and policies being formulated too far from the scene of the action itself. And it leads, as the New York City example brings out, to difficulties in acquiring and retaining the services of topnotch people in vitally important but now no longer top-rated positions.

Simon's caveats and the New York City example may point up the difficulty of using span of control as a frame of reference but they do not render it useless. As with so much in public administration, it becomes a question of finding a proper balance for each particular situation. In finding this balance, we must assess all the specific circumstances involved and we must keep in mind that a gain achieved by moving in one direction will always be offset by *some* losses. These losses do not, however, have to cancel the gain out completely. If an executive has one hundred agencies under his tutelage, then some consolidation is nearly always called for, even at the expense of creating more administrative levels. However, every consolidation carries a price tag which we must be willing to pay if we wish to reap the benefits.

The span of control concept, it should be noted, is not the only point about pyramids which has come under attack. The unity of command and chain of command principles also present some problems. These we will be in a better position to evaluate after we examine the meaning and import of the terms *line* and *staff*.

---

7. *New York Times,* March 5, 1970.
8. Herbert A. Simon, "The Proverbs of Administration," *Public Administration Review,* winter 1946.

57

LINE AND STAFF

The paradigm pyramids that we erected above in discussing Mafia families, infantry divisions and large universities consist of what are called line personnel. Unfortunately, from the standpoint of neatness and orderliness in model-building, there is another group of people to be considered. These are the staff personnel. Again, as in the term *bureaucracy,* a confusion in the use and meaning of words may arise. In ordinary discourse, we are accustomed to using the term *staff* to describe all the working members of an organization. But in administration, *staff* has a more specialized meaning covering certain types of organizational personnel and not others.

Let us begin by first defining the line employees. They are the ones *directly* concerned with furthering the organization's goals. They catch the crooks, heal the sick, pave the roads, etc. The staff people are supposed to help them accomplish such ends. Staff personnel draw up the job classifications, program the computers, provide the legal services, coordinate and check (if they do not actually set up) the budgets. The personnel, finance, legal and other such units of an organization constitute its staff services and it is their employees who are most accurately referred to as the "staff."

Viewed as organizations themselves, the staff units are usually formed on the basis of process. For example, the organization's computer center typically comprises a group of people engaged in the same process while serving, within the context of the larger organization in which they operate, a variety of purposes, places and clientele. In a school system, the center may be simultaneously preparing figures on attendance records for the superintendent and principals, correlating statistics on retarded children for the director of special education and trying to pin-point certain cost trends for the budgeting department. This last-named chore points up the fact that staff agencies may not only serve line departments but also other staff units.

The bureaucratic pyramid, in its most pure and pristine form, makes no provision for staff units and their personnel. And traditionally, they have played only a small and shadowy role in the functioning of work organizations. What place they occupied was usually at the hands or feet of the organization's leader, providing him with advice and assistance of various kinds. The boss of a Mafia family, to cite one (traditional?) organization, usually has a *consiglieri* or counselor. The *consiglieri* is most often a partially retired older line official who now advises the boss but who gives no orders to anyone.

In modern times, staff services have increased tremendously and staff personnel have swollen in number. They are now occupying an ever greater place in the organization's structure, playing an ever greater role in its activities and consuming an ever greater chunk of its budget. In so doing, they are providing the organization with new strengths and also new problems.

The problems stem basically from what we noted at the outset, namely that the model pyramid makes no provision for staff units. It is hard, almost at times impossible, to establish their correct niche within the organization's hierarchy. Staff people tend to be specialists whose expertise does not lend itself to a scaled ranking except, possibly, within their own ranks. To phrase the problem in another way, the authority of a line unit is fairly definite. It knows what units are above it and which ones are below it. The authority of a staff unit is much more nebulous and elusive. Such authority will be determined by whatever need the line units have for the staff group at a particular time, the proficiency which it can exercise in meeting this need, the administrative and, if you will, political skill with which it handles its relationships with other units within the organization and a variety of other factors.

Underlying the uncertainties of this situation is the basic principle that specialization tends to destroy hierarchy. The more the members of an organization are differentiated from each other in terms of specific and separate skills, the harder it becomes to array them on a ladder-like scale. For, as Peter Drucker has pointed out, knowledge, in and of itself, knows no hierarchy. There are no higher or lower knowledges. Thus, the ever increasing presence of staff people is disturbing and disrupting bureaucracy and bureaucratic organizations. More specifically, they are undermining the cherished bureaucratic principles of unity of command, chain of command and span of control.

Once again, it was Herbert Simon who first called attention to this fact. In his article on "The Proverbs of Administration" cited earlier, he pointed out that to the extent that specialization comes in through the organizational door, unity of command goes out the window. Unity of command requires one channel of authority but specialization creates several channels of authority. The specialists, in one form or another, start giving orders. The fact that these orders are not labeled as such and stem not from rank but from expertise does not fundamentally alter the situation. If the organization intends to use their energies and abilities, it must respond to what the specialists say. And to the extent that their capabilities are utilized, the authority of line personnel, particularly those in a supervisory capacity is weakened and diminished.

Needless to add, this situation tends to generate a good deal of conflict. The staff are there to serve line personnel and sometimes their activities are accepted as such. Indeed, at times, line people will complain or get annoyed at the staff people for not sharing enough respon-

59

sibility. They will pressure the personnel department to handle some of their more ticklish employee relations problems such as getting rid of an undesirable employee. More often, however, the line personnel resent and repel the intrusions of the staff people. To the liners, the activities of the staffers frequently seem more subversive than supportive.

It is easy to see how this works. The head of a hospital's radiology department wants to buy some new equipment, and he has one particular make in mind which he deems the most suitable for his purposes. But the hospital's purchasing agent informs him that he must put his equipment order out to bid and accept the lowest quotation submitted. Then the radiology chief wants to hire a foreign-born radiologist whom he feels could be a valuable addition to his department. The hospital's personnel department tells him that the man does not meet certain residency requirements. While worrying about these problems, the radiology chief has to interrupt his work in order to supply certain data which the hospital's computer center has asked for. (One of the lesser complaints of line people is that the staff personnel take up too much of their time.) At this point, the chief radiologist wonders if things would be better if the hospital could do away with all these "outsiders" and let those whose task it is to heal the sick get on with the job of doing so.

Other less overt problems also color and cloud line-staff relations. Felix A. and Lloyd G. Nigro point out that staff employees are often younger and better educated than line officials.[9] Both differences provide a fertile terrain for the development of discord. When the line-men, who are often old-timers, see the new "whiz kids" moving into high paying jobs and starting to exercise authority over their activities, tensions rise. What aggravates the situation still more is that the line personnel fear, often with some justification, that the staff people will discover and point up deficiencies in their work and behavior.

The Nigros point out, however, that staff men also have their problems. The services they provide are indirect and often intangible. Their work is not only hard to evaluate but hard to credit. They erect no playgrounds, build no buildings, pave no roads. They do not even hand out driver's licenses or public assistance checks. In short, they produce no palpable products that the public can utilize let alone admire. This, in turn, often gives them another disadvantage vis-a-vis their confreres of the line. The latter can and frequently do build a base of political support among elected officials or among the organization's clientele. The staff man largely remains excluded from such sources of organizational strength.

---

9. Felix A. Nigro and Lloyd G. Nigro, *Modern Public Administration*, 3rd ed. (New York: Harper & Row, 1973), p. 122.

Line officials themselves often are skilled in the ways of politics and in some cases owe their positions to the use of such skills. They frequently possess, or at least aquire, more dexterity in the handling of people within the organization as well as without. In many cases, their ability at organizational gamesmanship more than compensates, in terms of power and position, for what they lose in lack of specialized expertise. They may also be tougher and more ruthless than their staff brothers. "You can always tell a staff man," sneers line business executive Robert Townsend, "by the number of people he has fired."[10]

To reduce the rivalry and rancor which may creep into line-staff relationships, organizations try to integrate the two as much as possible. They may make the staff people spend time familiarizing themselves with line functions and line personnel, sometimes to the point of requiring them to perform some line functions for specified periods of time. Or they may recruit their staff people from the ranks of the line personnel, giving them special training for their new positions. This is a practice which the Forest Service has used with some success. Unfortunately, however, this practice does not always provide the best trained or best qualified staff specialists. It also tends to make the organization too inbred, a problem we will examine in the next chapter.

As for handling the line personnel, organizations are supplying them with increasing doses of in-service training or encouraging them to take courses in outside educational institutions. One of the benefits of such educational programs is that the line people aquire more awareness and appreciation for the competences of the staffers and the complexities of their work. The liners frequently find that their teachers and many of their fellow students will be staff personnel and this helps build a base of understanding between the two groups.

The education of line personnel and the honing of their capacities illustrates a more fundamental trend leading to the gradual diminution of the gap between line and staff in modern administration. Both groups are actually becoming more alike. Staff employees are taking on quasi-line functions while line employees are aquiring specializations associated with the staff. In many a large metropolitan high school, for example, the social worker and the guidance counselor are participating, to some degree, in the instructional process. The teachers, meanwhile, through becoming more specialized, are developing some of the attitudes and ambivalences of the staff. The teacher of retarded children may technically be a line employee. But he or she may feel, act and relate to the organization in much the same way as a member of the staff.

---

10.   Robert Townsend, "Up the Organization," *Harpers,* March 1970.

Current organizational trends are, as Simon somewhat foresaw, making such concepts as unity of command, chain of command and span of control less and less useful. Modern organizations are paying diminishing deference to such bureaucratic and hierarchical rules all the time. But though less useful than they have been, they are by no means obsolete. While all organization members must become more attuned to responding to diverse and occasionally divergent lines of authority as the various specialists make their weight felt, the need for at least a coordinating nexus will remain. And while span of control and chain of command may become more frequently disrupted, these concepts still cannot be completely ignored. There remains the need for some orderly flow of communication and authority within an organization. The modern administrator confronts the challenge of retaining the basic benefits which these pyramidal points were designed to produce while adapting to the requirements which an age of increasing specialization and innovation imposes. It is no easy task. But, then, little that is worth doing in administration, or anything else for that matter, is.

CASE STUDY

Reorganizing Administration in Massachusetts.[11]

Governmental activities tend to grow and proliferate faster than the organizational structures designed to house them. As a result, we find at all levels of the political system numerous examples of bureaucracies that have burst their bounds, becoming too vast, complex and unwieldly for the organizational arrangements which encase them. At probably no level has this occurred with such marked and even malignant effect as at the level of state government. Although we hear much these days about the growing burdens of municipalities and about the swelling federal bureaucracy, it is actually at the state level where American government since World War II has grown the most. And most states have lagged and lagged badly in keeping their administrative structures abreast of their growing workloads.

During the 1960's, many states became increasingly aware of the problems involved in trying to operate at the high activity level of the modern age with an administrative apparatus set up in a more leisurely era. This growing awareness finally triggered a wave of state government reorganization movements. The Commonwealth of Massachusetts, a modern urban state laboring under the oldest constitution in the world (it actually predates the United States Constitution), was one such state. And in 1967, Massachusetts decided that it was time for a change.

Nearly half a century had elapsed since the state's executive branch had

---

11. The material for the case study is drawn primarily from "Reorganization of the Massachusetts State Government" by Sheri Larsen. Unpublished paper, Department of Political Science, Northeastern University, 1972.

undergone a major overhaul. Since that time, state programs had multiplied and state expenses had skyrocketed. Public dissatisfaction was exacerbated by the fact that the services which the state was seeking to deliver at such a high cost did not seem to have grown proportionately. It was generally felt that the state government's output in no way matched the state taxpayer's input, and the gap between the two seemed to be widening. To borrow an old Pentagon phrase, each additional new buck seemed to yield less and less additional bang. Adding urgency to the problem was the fact that the entire system faced increasing pressures and problems in the very near future.

Aside from these basic considerations, other factors were also favoring a re-examination and a reshuffle of the state's administrative sector. Thanks to some constitutional reforms put through by his predecessor, Governor John A. Volpe had become the strongest governor in Massachusetts history. These reforms which, among other things, gave the governor a four-year term and increased control over department heads had taken effect with the previous year's election. Thus, Volpe seemed to be in a better position than previous state executives to put a full-scale reorganization into effect.

Volpe was a Republican and though he had managed to win election the previous year, many other members of his party had not fared so well. Both branches of the state legislature had remained firmly in the hands of the Democrats. Thus, if Volpe was to achieve any major victories in the state legislature, they would have to come on non-partisan issues. Governmental reorganization seemed an ideal choice as an issue in which he could score a notable bi-partisan triumph and distinguish his gubernatorial career.

A further factor impelling the governor to take up the cudgels for administrative reform was the availability of federal funds to do the necessary ground work. There was approximately one-half million dollars to be obtained for carrying out the requisite research, and while Massachusetts would have to add another quarter-million to it, the state could pay for its share in the form of labor by employees already on the payrolls of its various agencies. The prospect of securing one-half million dollars to spend without any noticeable cost to itself usually exerts considerable attraction on any governmental entity.

Volpe secured a federal grant of $481,356 from the Department of Housing and Urban Development for a 12-month study of the state's governmental structure. The task of carrying out the project was given to the Office of Planning and Program Coordination, a unit that had recently been established in the governor's all-purpose staff agency, the Office for Administration and Finance. The reorganization study promptly became the OPPC's principal endeavor.

The following year, 1968, the OPPC reported its findings in a publication entitled *Modernization of the Government of the Commonwealth of Massachusetts.* It found that the state's administrative sector was mired in conflict and chaos, and was totally incapable of meeting the administrative challenges of the last third of the twentieth century. The OPPC researchers had little difficulty in documenting their discovery.

Essentially, they found that the state bureaucracy represented fragmentation run riot. There were 173 separate departments all reporting directly to the governor. Furthermore, there were an additional 132 agencies which, though nominally housed within the basic 173, were largely independent. For the most part, these 132 agencies also answered to the governor if they answered to any one at all. This meant that the Commonwealth's chief executive was expected to ride herd on 305 separate governmental units. It was clearly an impossible task. As the OPPC put it, "Neither the Governor nor the General Court [Legislature] can possibly provide consistent policy direction over this disorganized assemblage, nor can it be said that *anyone* can be held truly accountable for the total product of the work of this vast number of agencies." (Italics in the original.)

The OPPC was able to cite numerous examples of how this huge administrative potpourri was impairing the delivery of public services. There were, it noted, ten agencies that had something to with alcoholism. Twelve agencies were involved in mental retardation. Problems concerning youth came within the purview of twenty agencies. And the increasing concerns of the environment were shared among approximately thirty-two agencies. Such a dispersal of programs and policies made problem-solving difficult and often impossible. As the OPPC noted, "Divided responsibility sometimes means no responsibility" which is another expression for an old administrative adage that a job given to more than one agency is really given to none.

The costs of maintaining such a shapeless and sprawling administrative sector were deemed immense. The OPPC cited the simple question of telephone service as a minor but illustrative example of just how costly fragmentation can become. Thanks to the piecemeal character of the state's bureaucracy, the telephone company had to mail out 1,250 separate telephone bills to state agencies every month. It was estimated that the cost of merely processing such a vast array of bills was costing the Commonwealth several hundred thousand dollars a year.

If the situation was already bad, then, said the OPPC, it was destined to become worse, much worse. Massachusetts had already embarked on a program of regionalization, i.e., setting up regional offices and centers for many of its government programs. While the OPPC had no fault to find with this trend, such an effort made the need for reorganization all the more compelling. The imposition of regionalism, which is *territorial* fragmentation, onto such a pattern of existing *functional* fragmentation could lead to a breakdown of the whole system.

Having made their diagnosis, the researchers then offered their prescription. The basic remedy they advocated was the consolidation of the state's splintered administrative branch into eleven functional groupings. Eight of these were to be line departments that would bear the titles Human Services, Manpower, Communities and Development, Consumer Affairs, Transportation and Construction, Environmental Affairs, Education and Public Safety. The remaining three would be staff agencies devoted to Personnel, Finance and General Services. Each of the eleven new departments would be headed by a secretary and the eleven secretaries collectively would compromise a "cabinet." The members of this cabinet would be appointed by, and would be responsible to, the governor.

A fair amount of care had gone into the arrangement of the new departments and, for the most part, the arranging seemed to make sense. For example, the projected Department of Environmental Affairs would bring together all air and water pollution programs as well as all planning programs for water resources and land use. Waste disposal, recreation and tourism would also be included. The proposed Department of Public Safety would team up the state police with the Registry of Motor Vehicles along with the state's Fire Marshal's Office and the Civil Defense Agency. And nearly all the state's regulatory boards and commissions would end up in the contemplated Department of Consumer Affairs.

However, these recommended clusterings would produce, in some cases, giant public conglomerates. The Department of Human Services, for instance, would house such large existing departments as Health, Mental Health, Welfare (a purely state function in Massachusetts), Correction as well as a host of smaller agencies. Furthermore, there were grounds for disputing the cataloguing in a few cases. Tourism, for example, might belong in Environmental Affairs but it would also seem to fit into the Department of Communities and Development which was to include all other state functions aimed at maintaining and bolstering the state's economy. Vocational education, to take another example, was assigned to Education but it also might have been put in Manpower. Problems such as these invariably arise when it comes to grouping governmental functions.

It should be emphasized that the reorganization plan called only for the *grouping* of agencies and the establishment of secretaries over them. The OPPC planners shrank from offering specific proposals to merge existing agencies or to redistribute functions among them. Their reluctance to take such a step was certainly understandable. For one thing, such detailed recommendations would have required much more time and effort than was available. For another, and perhaps a more important reason, the researchers would have had to tread heavily on the toes of many of the existing agencies, and the heads of these agencies would probably have stirred up more than enough political backlash to kill the plan. Thus, instead of presenting such proposals themselves, they suggested that once the initial grouping of agencies was completed, each new cabinet secretary should then prepare further reorganization measures for those agencies under him and submit them by the spring of 1973.

As is obvious, the cabinet secretaries envisioned by the plan would not at the outset reign over streamlined and unified departments. Rather they would preside over clusters of still quite independent agencies. However, they were to be given certain powers to help them bring some degree of unity and coherence to their jurisdictions. Each would have the right to re-

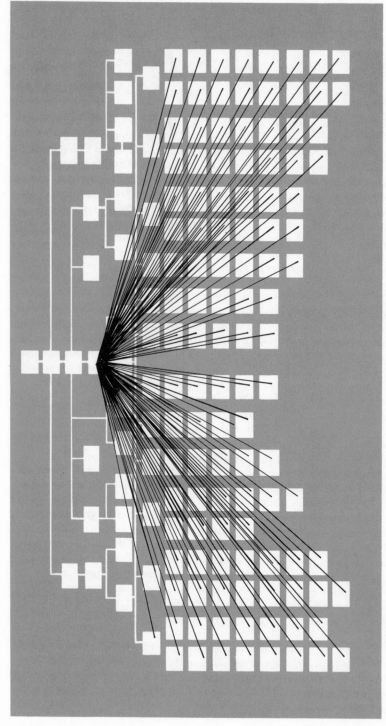

This chart shows the set-up of the Massachusetts state bureaucracy prior to reorganization. If the chart seems somewhat confusing, then this reflects very well the state's administrative organization at that time. (Source: Office of Planning and Program Coordination, Commonwealth of Massachusetts.)

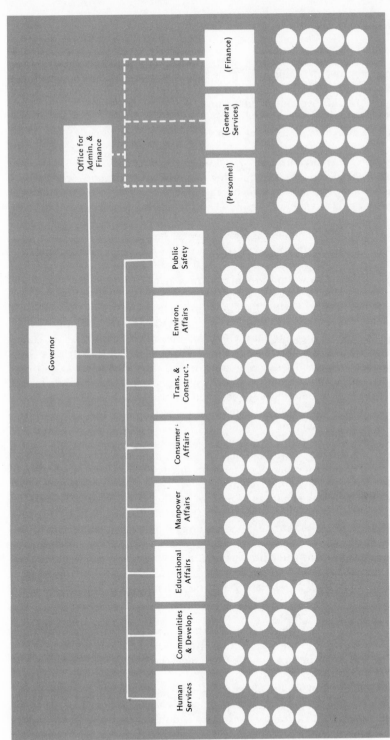

This chart depicts what the Massachusetts state bureaucracy was to look like after the reorganization was completed. Circles symbolize varying numbers of state agencies responsible to the secretary of each executive cabinet office. A secretariat for elderly affairs was subsequently added. (Source: Office of Planning and Program Coordination, Commonwealth of Massachusetts.)

view and approve the budgeting of all agencies in his secretariat. He would also have the right to examine all the records and documents of his constituent agencies and to conduct operational studies and comprehensive planning. Indeed, the latter was not just a right but a necessity since each cabinet secretary was mandated to develop the more thorough reorganization plans of the future.

Although the reorganization was designed to save money, hopefully as much as $100 million a year within a few years, its backers acknowledged that it would entail start-up costs. Each cabinet secretary was to have planning, legal, fiscal, public relations, personnel and system officers and each of these aides would have from one (for public relations) to four (for planning and systems) professional helpers as well as clerical staff. The total cost for maintaining the eleven proposed secretariats was thus set at $7.5 million annually although it was felt that through the use of existing personnel the figure could be reduced to around $4 million. The expense does not seem particularly exhorbitant for a state whose budget was already running in excess of $2 billion a year. Yet, as we shall see, the procurement of funds for the new secretaries has continued to plague the reorganization plan all along.

Governor Volpe presented the OPPC findings to legislative leaders, state employee associations and the news media in December 1968. He then announced that he would set up a broad-based advisory committee to go over the report, make any necessary changes and then draw up the requisite legislation. The following month Volpe resigned the governorship to become Secretary of Transportation in the cabinet of Richard Nixon. Thus, the task of developing and guiding the reorganization fell to his successor, former Lieutenant Governor and now Governor Francis Sargent.

Sargent completed the formation of the advisory committee which Volpe had begun. It contained members of both branches of the state legislature, representatives of state employee associations, businessmen, academics, the president of the Massachusetts League of Women Voters and a venerable former United States senator, Leverett Saltonstall. Sargent named his own chief administrative aide to head the group and he designated the OPPC to provide the committee with staff assistance. As a result not too many alterations in the proposals could be expected and, as it so happens, such was the case. The only major change made in the plan was the consolidation of the suggested three staff secretariats, Personnel, Finance and General Services, into one Office for Administration and Finance. This reduced the number of proposed secretariats from eleven to nine.

The committee drew up the necessary legislation by April 1969. Governor Sargent submitted it to the legislature with the warning that if the changes it called for were not put into effect, "state government will not work in the 1970's."

The legislature took up the bill and made no significant amendments in its basic design. However, the lawmakers did add a significant political revision. They stipulated that no cabinet secretary should be appointed until April

1971. The reason for requiring this delay was that Sargent would be up for re-election in 1970 and the Democratic majority in the legislature were hoping to unseat him and elect a member of their own party in his place. Indeed, the president of the state senate was himself planning to run for the governor-ship. Consequently, the legislators wanted to leave the way clear for a Democratic governor to make the cabinet appointments and put the plan into effect.

With this change, and a few other minor ones, the reorganization bill passed the legislature in August 1969. In signing it, Governor Sargent hailed its enactment as "one of the most significant events in the history of Massachusetts government."

Although pleased with what he regarded as a personal triumph as well as a blow for better government, Sargent could do little for the present but wait. It would be twenty months before he could begin to name the secretaries and move the plan into operation. However, in the interim the legislature came up with one substantive though scarcely shattering revision.

In the summer of 1970, the Speaker of the Massachusetts House suddenly filed a bill to set up a new cabinet secretariat for elderly affairs. Administration officials tried to block the measure, saying that such an agency would cut across the functional organization of the nine other secretariats. Instead, they offered to support the establishment of a deputy secretary for elderly affairs within the Department of Human Services. The Speaker expressed willingness to go along with the compromise but it was already too late. Massachusetts has a greater than average number of older citizens along with a large number of agencies to assist them. These organizations had already started to lobby for the new secretariat and, yielding to the pressure which these groups exercised, the legislature passed the original bill. Though the measure would create some difficulties, it would certainly not deal the reorganization plan a crushing blow and so the governor signed it into law. This brought the number of secretaries to ten.

In the fall of 1970, Sargent easily won election to a full four-year term in his own right but the Democrats retained firm control of both the House and Senate. This began to create some turbulance for the reorganization proposal. While the governor had little difficulty in naming the secretaries, he ran into considerable trouble in trying to secure the necessary funding to staff their offices. The legislators persistently made drastic cuts in the moneys he requested for such purposes. Thus, all the new secretaries had to make do with substantially smaller sums and smaller staffs than the reorganization plan had called for. The *Boston Globe* in an editorial on June 21, 1972 claimed that the legislators "seem to be using the secretariat funding as a patronage lever to pry jobs, appointments and favors from the executive branch."

The governor, however, experienced little difficulty in securing legislative approval for the one structural change which he requested during this period. He filed a bill in 1972 to set up an Office for Children's Affairs in the Department of Human Services. The measure, which he signed into law in

July of that year, would oversee and coordinate all the department's programs affecting children. It would also carry out some programs of its own in such areas as day-care services.

By the fall of 1972 the reorganization had already provoked its share of criticism. Its detractors claimed it was wasting rather than saving money and was simply piling a new layer of government on top of an already overly swollen administrative complex. Its defenders pointed out that it was too soon to pass judgment on the scheme and that in any case the new secretariats had lacked sufficient funds to prove themselves. OPPC director Robert Marden further maintained that despite these limitations of time and money, the new secretaries were prompting state agencies to take a broader view of their activities and to cooperate more fully with other agencies than they had ever done before. Further results would have to await additional funding plus submission and passage of detailed reorganization plans for each cabinet department.

The troubles and travails involved in reorganizing the state government of Massachusetts point up some of the issues which we have previously noted. First, though this aspect of administration was not stressed here, the case offers at least a glimpse of the deep and complex relationship that exists between administration and politics in the American political system. More importantly for our present purposes, it shows how such concepts as unity of command, chain of command and span of control enter into administrative theory and practice. The reorganization was designed to create a more developed chain of command and thereby a more manageable span of control for the governor. This, in turn, would, at least theoretically, provide more unity of command. Note that all three concepts are interwoven. Note also that they are scarcely an unmixed blessing. While Massachusetts' bureaucracy obviously needed restructuring—hardly anyone disputed this—the reorganization created problems of its own as well as additional expense. Time will tell just how effective it will be.

The case also sheds light on the increasing interest which is being directed toward the clientele approach. The initial reorganization itself somewhat reflects this in its proposal for a Department of Human Services that would bring together all or almost all of the services designed to aid people directly. The OPPC expressly stated that it hoped such an amalgamated department would encourage a more integrated approach to the various problems that beset individuals and families. The proposal to set up a separate department for the elderly scored an easy success and though the reorganizers opposed it, they certainly did not make its establishment a life-or-death issue. Indeed, the administration itself subsequently proposed the institution of the Office for Children's Affairs.

The case also indicates the growing prominence of staff functions and staff personnel. The entire plan was drafted by staff employees, and though they claimed to have interviewed each agency head and many sub-heads before framing their proposals, the recommendations that ensued indicate that the final decisions were mostly their own. (It can be presumed that few of the line chiefs expressed eagerness to have cabinet secretaries placed over them.) The initial plan called for three of the eleven secretariats to be concerned exclusively with staff functions, and while the three proposed officers were subsequently merged into one, there was little doubt that this combined secretariat would assume prominence if not dominance over the others. The secretaryship of Administration and Finance was referred to in the press as "the top cabinet post" and when Governor Sargent in 1972 shifted his secretary for Consumer Affairs to this position, the change was automatically regarded as a dramatic step upward for the individual involved.

But if the case spotlights the growing power of staff in relation to line, it also shows that this trend produces inevitable conflicts which the staff people do not always win, at least not right away. One goal of the reorganization plan which we have not yet touched on was better budgeting. The OPPC hoped to make the budgetary process more informative, more accountable, and, most importantly, more centered on achieving specific program goals.

To this end, the reorganizers developed what they called the Program-Based Management System Project subsequently known simply as PMS. This was a modified version of a new budgeting system called Planned Program Budgeting System (PPBS) which the federal government and some other state governments as well as a few municipalities had been developing.

While discussion of PPBS and other aspects of budgeting will be put off until chapter eight, it can be noted at this point that these new budgeting systems generally ask the administrator to define as specifically as he can the goals of his program or agency and then carefully weigh all the possible ways and means for achieving these goals. It calls for establishing measures of evaluation, and demands, in many cases, totally new attitudes on the part of the administrator.

Under the strategy evolved by the OPPC a "PMS specialist" would spend approximately two and a half months with each of the state's major programs teaching those who were running them how to think in terms of goals and achievement and how to budget accordingly. However, the program managers, who were, for the most part, line administrators, rebelled at this intervention and their resistance fueled the suspicions of the legislature. During 1971, the attempt at PMS gradually fell by the wayside, at least for the time being, though those few agencies that had accepted the new budgetary approach continued to make use of it.

The battle over PMS brings us to one further and much more significant point about administration and that is the primacy of behavior over structure. Although organizational anatomy is certainly important, and although it obviously affects organizational physiology, i.e., what goes on within the organization, it by no means plays an all-decisive role.

Organizational charts, like the best laid plans of mice and men, "gae oft aglay." At best, a structural analysis tells us only part of what an organization is. At worst, the information that it provides can prove misleading. The field of organization is a good deal more far-reaching and complex than the structural matters that have occupied much of our attention in this chapter would indicate. Unfortunately the problems of organization do not lend themselves to such approaches as that of comic strip administrator Charlie Brown when he says,

You know what our team lacked last year? It lacked organization! Well, this year its going to be different! I've written down the name of each player and what position he plays, and I've attached the paper to a clipboard . . . And if *that* isn't organization, I don't know what is.[12]

---

12. Quoted by Harlan Cleveland in "A Philosophy for the Public Executive," in *Perspectives on Public Management*, Robert T. Golembiewski, ed. (Itasca, Ill.: F. E. Peacock, 1968).

4

The Physiology of Organization

Early writers on organization were largely concerned with questions of structure. They tended to believe that any organization would function well if only it were well designed. One of the earliest and most influential of such thinkers was Frederick W. Taylor, a steel mill laborer who worked his way up to the rank of chief engineer. In his climb to the top, Taylor felt he had learned the basic secrets of good organization, and he incorporated his ideas into a book that he published in 1911. His short work, *The Principles of Scientific Management*, became extraordinarily influential.

Taylor claimed that there was "one best way" for doing every job and that it could be determined through scientific and systematic study. He believed ardently in task specialization and maintained that each job should be broken down to its smallest component before being assigned to one or more men. The assembly line may be viewed as a triumph of Taylorism. While he did not completely neglect the behavioral side of administration, he felt that high wages would generally suffice to elicit employee cooperation and compliance. And since any organization that structured itself along the lines he suggested would automatically be in a better position to pay such higher wages, scientific management, in Taylor's view, would eliminate nearly all causes of dispute and disagreement between employees and employers.

Taylor's ideas acquired their greatest popularity in the business world, but the same basic approach, that is, viewing administration as a matter of constructing scientifically thought-out organizational arrangements, permeated public administration theory as well. As early as 1887, a brilliant young professor of government named Woodrow Wilson wrote that public administration, like any field of business, could be organized strictly on a technical basis.[1] Such extraneous factors as politics need not intrude, for, said Wilson, public administration was a part of politics only as the methods of the counting house were a part of society or as machinery was part of the product it manufactured. By the early 1900's, Max Weber seemed to see such a development emerging in public administration. His bureaucratic model, with its emphasis on such things as hierarchy, systematized procedures and formalized rules, seemed to embody many of the basic approaches or at least attitudes of Taylor's scientific management.

In 1926 L. D. White published the first American textbook in public administration.[2] Basing himself on the premise that administration was destined to remain the central problem of modern government, White claimed that it was essentially a single process that was applicable everywhere. Its objective was efficiency and in striving to achieve this objective it could at least aspire to becoming a science. Although his book did not slight the role of theory and values in the administrative process, he felt that these would be obtained from political science. Social and emotional factors played little role in White's administrative world.

But while White, following in the path of Wilson and Weber, was attempting to construct a field of public administration along systematic and somewhat mechanical lines, a social worker and educator named Mary Parker Follett was marching to the beat of a different drummer. Follett had become impressed with the psychological factors that she had seen at work in her active life as an organizer of evening schools, recreation agencies and employment bureaus, and as a member of statutory wage boards. Already the author of two books on political science, *The New State* and *Creative Experience*, she embarked on a series of speculations in the 1920's that were to signal the advent of a new era in administrative theory.

In various papers and articles, Follett depicted administration as being essentially involved with reconciling individuals as well as social groups. An organization's principal problems, in her view, consisted not only in determining what it wanted its employees to do, but in guiding and controlling their conduct in such a way as to get them to do it. And this, she indicated, was a much more complex task than previous writers had suggested. Follett not only anticipated what was to become the human relations school of administration, but she also foreshadowed

1. Woodrow Wilson, "The Study of Administration," *Political Science Quarterly*, June 1887. Reprinted, in part, in *Basic Issues in Public Administration*, Donald C. Rowat, ed. (New York: Macmillan, 1961).
2. Leonard D. White, *Introduction to the Study of Public Administration* (New York: Macmillan, 1926).

the humanistic school that was to grow out of it. She urged organizations to stop trying to suppress the differences that may arise within their boundaries. Instead, they should seek to integrate these differences and thereby allow them to contribute to the organization's growth and development. She advocated replacing the "law of authority" with the "law of the situation" and she admonished organizations to exercise "power *with*" rather than "power *over*" their members.[3]

While Follett's writings did not go unnoticed, they failed to score the impact which similar ideas would later achieve. This was perhaps due partly to the fact that she was a woman writing in a society that was not yet attuned to taking women thinkers too seriously. A yet more severe and serious obstacle, however, may have been the fact that she was an iconoclast, challenging the sacred credos of her time. However, in 1932, one year after her death, the hallowed principles of scientific management received a more shaking jolt. A team of researchers headed by Harvard Business School Professor Elton Mayo completed five years of study at the Hawthorne plant of the Western Electric Company.[4] Their research showed that many problems of worker-management relations resulted not from insufficient task specialization or inadequate wages, but from social and psychological forces that were often quite complex. The Hawthorne experiments, as they were subsequently to be known, constituted the first systematic research to expose the "human factor" in work situations. The study marked a major turning point in the history of administrative theory and practice.

The role of the human factor in administrative thought gained further emphasis and importance when Chester Barnard published his landmark work *The Functions of the Executive* in 1938. Barnard was a former president of the New Jersey Bell Telephone Company who had also served as state director of the New Jersey Relief Administration. Basing himself on his rich background in the practical world, supplemented by some wide-ranging reading and some serious thinking, Barnard attempted to set forth an all-embracing theory of organization. He defined organizations as cooperative and essentially dynamic systems which are engaged in a process of continual readjustment to their physical, biological and social environments. The theoretical framework he set up was quite complex and not completely successful, but his work contained many new mind-opening insights, some of which we will be drawing upon later in this chapter.

---

3. Some of Follett's papers may be found in Henry C. Metcalfe and L. Urwick, eds., *Dynamic Administration* (New York: Harper & Row, 1940).
4. Elton Mayo, *The Human Problems of an Industrial Civilization* (New York: Macmillan, 1933). Also see F. J. Roethlisberger and William J. Dickson, *Management and the Worker* (Cambridge: Harvard University Press, 1946).

Follett, Mayo and Barnard were followed in the 1940's by numerous other thinkers and researchers including Dwight Waldo, William H. Whyte, and, perhaps most notable of all, Herbert A. Simon.[5] The latter's brilliant 1947 book *Administrative Behavior* rigorously challenged the sacred tenets of scientific management and opened additional vistas in this new area of human endeavor. From then on the writers and researchers become too numerous to mention, but some notice must be given to the humanistic school of administration which began to emerge in the 1950's and which has been receiving increased attention in recent years. Pioneered by such people as Chris Argyris, Douglas McGregor and Rensis Likert, humanistic theory accepted wholly the human relations component in administration but carried it still further, arguing for a more humanitarian approach to the whole administrative problem.[6] The humanistic school bases itself on the following assumptions:

1. Men are not naturally passive, lazy and dumb; on the contrary they are generally eager for opportunities to show initiative and to bear responsibility.
2. Work is a natural activity and people by nature want to perform it.
3. People work best in an environment that treats them with regard and respect and encourages them to develop and utilize their abilities.
4. There is no inherent and intrinsic conflict between the goals of the organization and the goals of the individual member. Meeting the goals of the individual will only make the organization itself more productive.

A still newer approach to administration appeared on the scene in the 1960's with the development of systems analysis. Systems analysis, with its elaborate diagrams, mathematical symbols and somewhat obscure and obtuse jargon, tends to frighten off some students. Yet, its essentials are fairly easy to grasp. In terms of administration, it views organizations as systems which absorb "inputs" and disgorge "outputs." The inputs largely take the form of demands and resources. To these are added "withinputs," which are new resources and/or demands generated inside the organization as it processes its initial inputs. Its outputs can also take many forms including some that were not intended. Fur-

---

5. Dwight Waldo, *The Administrative State* (New York: The Ronald Press, 1948); William H. Whyte, *Human Relations in the Restaurant Industry* (New York: McGraw-Hill, 1948); Herbert A. Simon, *Administrative Behavior* (New York: The Free Press, 1957); J. G. March and H. A. Simon, *Organizations* (New York: John Wiley, 1958).
6. The best known works of these authors are Argyris, *Personality and Organization* (New York: Harper & Row, 1957); McGregor, *The Theory of Human Enterprise* (New York: McGraw-Hill, 1960); and Likert, *New Patterns of Management* (New York: McGraw-Hill, 1961).

thermore, the outputs affect future inputs, thus providing a "feedback loop."

Within the organizational system, several subsystems or structures are at work. These include the production or technical system which carries out the organization's main mission, its maintenance and support systems which keep the organization itself functioning, the adaptive system which helps it adjust to new factors and forces. Every organization strives to achieve a balance among its subsystems as well as among all the other conflicting influences that continually threaten to disturb and disrupt its equilibrium. Its basic goal is to maintain itself in a steady state called homeostasis. Its survival hinges on its ability to achieve such an equilibrium as well as on its ability to ward off disorganization and disintegration (entropy). This it seeks to do by importing more resources than it expends.[7]

It is important to underscore the fact that the systems analysis school and the humanistic school are extensions rather than deviations from the human relations movement. Not only are they not in conflict with the human relations approach, but they are also not necessarily in conflict with one another. One of the most valuable books to emerge in administrative behavior in more recent years has been *The Social Psychology of Organizations* by Daniel Katz and Robert L. Kahn. A model of the human relations approach, their work utilizes systems analysis to present much research and data that support the humanistic viewpoint. (It will be referred to frequently throughout the pages which follow.)

A more important and much more obvious point to bear in mind is that the field of organizational behavior is extraordinarily rich and complex, and new developments are occurring in it all the time. In this chapter we will be concerned with only three aspects of the subject— motivation, the role of the informal organization and organizational pathologies, and even these will be treated in rather summary fashion. Subsequent chapters will also draw on materials in this field, but no introductory text can substitute for some well-rounded reading. This would include reading the authors previously mentioned as well as regular perusal of such magazines as *Public Administration Review*, published by the American Society of Public Administration, and *Personnel*, published by the American Management Association. The student may find the field of organizational physiology not only highly important but highly intriguing as well.

---

7. This brief summary of some of the elements of systems analysis as applied to organizational behavior is taken from Daniel Katz and Robert L. Kahn, *The Social Psychology of Organizations* (New York: John Wiley, 1966) and from David Eastman, *The Political System* (New York: Alfred A. Knopf, 1966).

MOTIVATING MEN

When, at the beginning of the book, we analyzed our two men lifting a stone, we failed to answer a very vital question: What induced them to lift the stone in the first place? This question brings us to the very core of the organizational problem. In order for an organization to function, indeed in order for it to exist, people must be willing and able to do the things it wants them to do. Thus, a primary task for any organization is to develop ways to motivate its members to fulfill the organization's purpose and pursuits.

It is no easy task. By the mid-1930's, Chester Barnard was able to note that "if all those who may be considered potential contributors to an organization are arranged in order of willingness to serve it, the scale gradually descends from possibly intense willingness through neutral or zero willingness to opposition or hatred." Barnard then went on to add, and the emphasis, please keep in mind, is his, "*The preponderance of persons in a modern society always lies on the negative side* with reference to any particular existing or potential organization. Thus of the possible contributors only a small minority actually have a positive willingness."[8]

Barnard further pointed out that while some would always feel more organizational loyalty than others, not only would they amount to less than a majority, but their positive feelings would also suffer lapses. Their loyalty would fluctuate depending on time, circumstance, etc. Consequently, any work organization confronts a basic dilemma. Its processes and pursuits usually require a stable and uniform degree of commitment, but those who are supposed to render this commitment often have quite different ideas.

Some writers have approached the question and its potential answers from the standpoint of what might be called needs fulfillment. In their view, formal organizations motivate their members through trying to meet certain of the member's needs. These needs are classified in varying ways but perhaps four basic categories can be distinguished: material needs, social and emotional needs, ego needs and a fourth category which one writer, Chris Argyris, calls "self-actualization" needs.

Before going on to discuss these various needs and the ways organizations seek to accommodate them, we should take note of a further aspect to this subject. The late psychologist Abraham M. Maslow maintained that man's needs formed an ascending scale with each need more basic than the next. In this manner, a person first wishes to gratify

---

8. Chester Barnard, *The Functions of the Executive* (Cambridge: Harvard University Press, 1968), p.84.

his physical needs, that is, he wants the physical means to survive. Once that need has been met, he wants to have his safety or security needs accommodated, and so on up the ladder. Thus, fulfilling certain primary needs only brings other needs to the fore. Or, looked at in another way, certain "higher" needs are not even perceived by an employee until his various "lower" needs have been met.[9]

Many writers on administration, most notably Douglas McGregor, became attracted to Maslow's "hierarchy of needs" theory and swallowed it whole. Others, however, have remained skeptical that man's needs could be grouped or scaled in such a fashion. There is research to support both sides. This book will try to sidestep the entire controversy. For our purposes, the examination of human needs and their meaning for organizational motivation will be put into the four basic areas already mentioned with no attempt made to claim that any one need is "higher" or "lower" than another, though the material itself may suggest such a hypothesis.

Material Needs

Meeting its members' material needs must perforce be for the average work organization its most basic means of motivating these members to work. Certainly, few employees are in a position to devote their full-time efforts to any work organization without receiving a paycheck in return. They will, however, give the organization that employs them a certain minimum of effort in order to obtain the wherewithal to support themselves and their families. In this sense, material needs can claim top priority in motivating people to help carry out organizational purposes.

There is little dispute over this rather elementary fact. The question that does arise is just how much will the employee give of himself for such material needs fulfillment alone? The answer supplied by those who have studied the subject is fairly unanimous: not very much.

Although he wrote in the midst of the Great Depression, that is, at a time when material needs satisfaction was in fairly short supply and hence could be a prime motivator, Barnard voiced the belief that pay or monetary rewards as such were among the weakest inducements an organization could offer to gain the support and allegiance of its members. Subsequent research was to bear him out. In the 1960's, a group of researchers at the University of Michigan took a survey of 1,533 working people, asking them, among other things, to rank various aspects of their work in order of importance. The respondents placed "good pay" in fifth position, after "interesting work," "enough help and equipment

---

9. Abraham M. Maslow, *Motivation and Personality*, 2nd ed. (New York: Harper & Row, 1970). See in particular pp. 35-38.

to get the job done," "enough information to do the job," and "enough authority to do the job."

Industrial sociologist Frederick Herzberg, who has devoted a good deal of attention to this problem, has attempted to put material needs and their satisfaction into perspective. In a book entitled *The Motivation to Work*, written in cooperation with two of his associates, Herzberg claims that money, fringe benefits and even working conditions only motivate people if they are *not* satisfied. In other words, the influence of such factors can only be negative, not positive. Or, to put it more explicitly, poor financial conditions can cause a person to give less than the minimum to his organization, but good financial conditions will not usually make him give any more than the minimum. As Herzberg puts it, "It would seem that as an affector of job attitudes, salary has more potency as a job dissatisfier than as a job satisfier."[10]

One question immediately arises. What about bonuses and pay promotions? Do not these tend to propel people toward increased productivity? Here, the subject becomes intertwined with ego need satisfaction, which we will be looking at shortly. However, when it is divorced from ego needs, then the answer remains the same. They do not motivate, at least not very much. When, for example, the organization gives its entire work force a pay increase, it usually does not receive back any appreciably greater output *unless* the salaries which they had been paying had been causing dissatisfaction. By removing or at least alleviating such dissatisfaction the organization may reduce turnover and curb malignancy as well as employee sabotage. It may also bring overall employee performance up to a basic minimum, but that usually is about all it can expect.

At this stage a further question arises. If material needs satisfaction is such a poor motivator of employee performance, then why all the constant fuss about it? Why do employees grumble so frequently over pay and benefits?

The answer is twofold. For one thing, pay and benefits which workers view as inadequate are, as we have noted, prime *dissatisfiers*, and this alone can cause grievances galore. More important, perhaps, is a further factor. Frequently an organization's members carp and complain about pay when they are really dissatisfied over lack of employer regard, boredom or something else. This can be seen in the frequency of employee strikes which, while they often cite increased pay boosts as their prime demand, will often end up costing the employees more than

---

10. Frederick Herzberg, Bernard Mausner and Barbara Block Snyderman, *The Motivation to Work* (New York: John Wiley, 1959), p. 83.

they can ever hope to exact from the organization they are striking against. Wages may appear to be the issue even to the strikers themselves, but the real causes may lie elsewhere.

Douglas McGregor pointed to a fatal flaw in the use of material needs satisfaction as an organizational motivator. Fulfilling such needs, he pointed out, gives the employee only the means to satisfy ends outside the work environment. The satisfaction is not found through the job itself, and therefore while necessary, this will never in itself move men to do much more than they have to do while on the job.

There are two further aspects to the limitation of material needs satisfaction as a motivator of men which should be taken into account. The first is that while meeting material needs does not motivate very much, refusing to meet material needs, that is, trying to motivate people by threatening to deprive them of their material needs, often renders even less satisfactory results. As Katz and Kahn point out, "The man who complies for fear of punishment plans and longs for the day when he can escape or overpower the person whom he obeys."[11] The same can be said of his attitude toward the organization which puts him into such a position. Here his deep-seated desires for getting back may take the form of employee sabotage, a persistent problem for many organizations.

A further limitation on the use of material needs satisfaction as a motivator is found in the current trends in modern society. As society becomes more affluent, and as this affluence trickles down to its workers in the form of increased possibilities for saving money, increased job opportunities, unemployment compensation, etc., material needs fulfillment, at least at a minimum level, becomes less and less of a problem. As McGregor noted, man tends to live for bread alone only when there is little bread.[12] The welfare state, even in its still imperfect form, tends to undermine the ability of an organization to use the manipulation of material needs as a motivator of employee performance.

Another trend of the technological society which is also shrinking the boundaries of this motivation technique is the growth of professionalism. Productivity for the professional means creativity, and creativity probably responds less to material inducements than any other form of employee output. Threats of material deprivation, on the other hand, can even prove counterproductive. A professor may be a poor teacher, and it is possible that a gentle prod such as a poor student evaluation may cause him to improve. But a threatening exhortation

---

11. Katz and Kahn, *op. cit.*, p. 303.
12. McGregor, *op. cit.*, p. 41.

from his dean to start teaching better within two weeks or face immediate dismissal would probably either so anger or alarm him that his teaching would fall to new lows.

As if all these limitations were not enough there is a final one which a public administrator must reckon with. Given the nature of most public employee personnel systems, the public administrator usually has a good deal less discretion in using monetary incentives than does an administrator in the private sector. Promotions often come only through examination or, in some instances, through political influence. Organizational discretion in terms of dismissal may be even more sharply curtailed. Therefore, the public organization in particular, while it certainly cannot discard the use of material motivators, must usually seek out and make use of additional ways and means of persuading its people to assist it in achieving its purposes and fulfilling its mission.

Social and Emotional Needs

It has long been known that work organizations usually provide their members with more than just a livelihood. Over a half-century ago, Max Weber pointed out that in seeking to control the actions and elicit the loyalty of their employees, organizations will often provide them with an identity and socialize them into a culture. People need a sense of social solidarity, a sense of belonging to a group. The "boys at the plant" or the "girls at the office" frequently develop ties not unlike those of members of a family or at least a clan. The pattern of relationships that evolves may not always be amicable, but it almost always becomes important in the lives of those involved.

If the work group becomes a sort of extended family, the work place may become a subcommunity. The organization members may come to think of themselves as its citizens or, if they are deeply disgruntled, its subjects. In any event, they often perceive the organization as playing a major role in their social and emotional lives.

Organizations frequently seek to capitalize on this situation to build organizational loyalty and thereby motivate members to serve organizational goals. Symbols, codes, rituals and other devices may be brought into play to enhance the employee's sense of oneness with the organization. Special dress such as uniforms also tends to foster such feelings. And if the employee can believe that he or she is part of the group that has a special and noble mission to perform, so much the better.

The organizations which most frequently come to mind when we think of such techniques are the armed services, particularly the marines, and the police, particularly, perhaps, the FBI. Members of such organizations tend to develop such a heightened sense of organizational identity that they start to develop the trappings of a distinct culture. Religious organizations may go even further in this respect. Take, for example, the Catholic priesthood with its codes of dress, codes of living and its special sense of pursuing a noble purpose. The rather awe-inspiring induction ceremony whereby the priest-to-be prostrates himself on the floor cannot help but instill in him the feeling that he is now becoming part of something which is much larger than himself, and which will henceforth govern and guide his life.

Probably the most important element in shaping organizational identification is shared experience. This is particularly true if such experience involves struggle and sacrifice. "After almost twenty years of working with and observing firefighters in every conceivable emergency," writes a battalion chief of the New York City Fire Department, "I've concluded that the glue which holds this great department together is a combination of brotherhood and love. The misery, suffering and pain which we firefighters share creates a bond which those outside the fire service cannot comprehend. Wives, mothers, sweethearts—none can intrude into this unique fraternity that comes from being truly brothers."[13]

Of course, most organizations cannot hope to elicit the obedience of the Roman Catholic priesthood or develop the bonds of brotherhood which may characterize a fire department. But nearly all of them benefit to some degree from the fact that most of their members manage to feel some sense of identity with their fellow workers, and thereby with the organization itself. At a minimum, this will help induce people to show up for work more often than might otherwise be the case. At a maximum, it can enable the organization to call upon its members for a degree of dedication and devotion far beyond the level that material inducements alone could ever achieve.

The meeting of social and emotional needs thus constitutes a valuable tool in the public administrator's kit, and wise administrators will know how to make use of it. They may not only allow but encourage employee groups such as bowling teams or credit unions. They may hold office Christmas parties and sponsor annual picnics. Through public relations and other devices they may try to build the image of the organization in the community, thereby giving their employees a sense of pride in being part of an agency that is playing a vital and positive role in community betterment.

However, in public administration as in most other things in life, everything has its cost and sometimes the cost of trying to meet social

---

13. Joseph E. Galvin, "Now Listen to a Firefighter's Plea," *New York Times*, January 20, 1972 (Op-Ed page).

and emotional needs becomes exorbitant. This does not simply include the financial outlays that may be involved but rather the side effects which such efforts, when successful, often engender. Strange as it may seem, an organization can inspire too much allegiance for its own good.

When an organization builds feelings of solidarity and a heightened sense of morale among its employees, it also tends to build walls around itself. The more self-sustaining and cohesive it becomes, the more self-contained and more self-involved it becomes. And self-involvement, of course, may make the organization increasingly isolated from its environment. This isolation can produce two negative effects.

The first of these effects has received little systematic study and remains somewhat speculative. However, there are indications that too much organizational isolation can actually backfire in terms of creating cooperative bonds between members and subunits within the organization. To gain an appreciation of this first problem in isolation let us turn back and examine the ancient city-states of Greece. In speaking of these city-states, political theorist George H. Sabine points out how "the very intimacy and pervasiveness of its life, which was responsible for much of the moral greatness of its ideals, led to defects which were the reverse of its virtues. In general, the city-states were likely to be prey to functional quarrels and party rivalries *whose bitterness was as intense as only rivalry between intimates can be.*"[14] (Emphasis added.)

What Sabine noted in Sparta and Athens, others have noticed in certain modern-day organizations, such as the police, the armed services and others. Those organizations known for their solidarity and cohesiveness tend to develop intense intra-group tensions, rivalries and hostilities. To an outsider, the police seem to display a remarkable degree of solidarity and mutual protectiveness. This to a great extent is true. Yet, when sociologist William Westley began studying American police forces in the 1950's, he was struck by the high degree of distrust that seemed to pervade relationships between policemen even when they belonged to the same unit.[15] Studies of the German Gestapo, an even more isolated organization, show that feuds flared up so frequently and so flagrantly within that grim organization that its policies met frequent defeat from within.[16] Studies of organized crime indicate a similar phenomenon. Sociologist Donald Cressey claims that members of crime syndicates engage in an intense amount of wrangling and rivalry.[17] Petty disputes easily become inflamed into major ones and attempts at adjudication frequently only add fuel to the fire.

---

14. George H. Sabine, *A History of Political Theory*, 3rd ed. (New York: Holt, Rinehart and Winston, 1961), pp. 15–16.
15. William A. Westley, "Secrecy and the Police," *Social Forces*, March 1956.
16. See, for example, Heinz Hohne, *The Order of the Death's Head: The Story of Hitler's S.S.* (New York: Coward-McCann, 1970).
17. Cressey, *Theft of the Nation*, pp. 209–210.

It may be argued that policemen and criminals are not typical and their behavior in response to organizational separation may not be reflective of other groups. Nevertheless, there are indications that this same response to isolation occurs elsewhere as well. Memoirs of those who have served in the armed forces, religious orders, underground movements and other organizations which tend to create a strong sense of organizational distinctiveness and demarcation from society reveal somewhat similar responses.

Poets and novelists have sometimes called attention to this pattern. In Dante's *Inferno*, the punishment for lovers is to be chained together so that they may never be separated. As a result they must endure the greatest of all punishments, that of seeing their love degenerate into hostility and hatred through perpetual propinquity. Charles Dickens in his novel *Hard Times* offers this trenchant observation: "All closely imprisoned forces rend and destroy. The air that could be healthful to the earth, the water that would enrich it, the heat that would ripen it, tear it when caged up."

The perceptive Mr. Dickens, in another of his novels, *Bleak House*, also called attention to a second and a more significant setback which organizational self-involvement can produce. In speaking of the Court of Chancery of his day, he said, "The evil of it is that it is a world wrapped up in too much jeweler's cotton and fine wool, and cannot hear the rushing of the larger world outside . . . it is a deadened world, and its growth is sometimes unhealthy for want of air."

Here Dickens put his finger on a phenomenon that has been noted by many modern and more systematic researchers. The more an organization and its members acquire a sense of separate identity, the less receptive they become to change and innovation. In his near classic study of the U.S. Forest Service, Herbert Kaufman emphasizes the strong sense of identification which the organization manages to develop in most of its rangers. This spirit of cohesiveness and unity enables the Service to gain many operational objectives. But, Kaufman also notes that "an individual imbued with the spirit of an organization, indoctrinated with its values, committed to its established goals and customary ways, and dedicated to its traditions, is not likely to experiment a great deal, nor even to see the possibilities suggested by unplanned developments."[18]

Kaufman's study *The Forest Ranger* was published in 1960. As the conservation movement gathered steam during the latter part of that decade, some of the problems he alluded to began to be seen. The Forest Service came under increasing attack from conservation groups

---

18. Herbert Kaufman, *The Forest Ranger* (Baltimore: Johns Hopkins Press, 1960), p. 235.

for going about its tasks in an overly methodical and unimaginative manner. To many outsiders, its operational manner and methods seemed to suggest an avoidance of, and even an aversion to, new scientific developments and new social concerns. For example, when some research indicated that fires were, in certain cases and under certain conditions, actually good for forests, the Service reacted with horror. The rangers had become too steeped in the tradition of firefighting ever to look on fire as anything but an enemy and a scourge.

The same problem has been noted by private industry. In 1972, Distiller's Corporation-Seagram Limited began deliberating on whether to move its headquarters from New York City to the city's suburbs. It finally decided to stay in Manhattan. Its decision was based on a study it had made which stated, among other things, that "if employees dealt almost exclusively with others from the company, there would be a tendency to reinforce existing patterns of behavior; there would be a danger of mental lethargy. In the long run this would have a deleterious effect on productivity."[19]

One interesting illustration which points up both the possibilities as well as the problems that organizational solidarity can produce occurred in the 1972 presidential election. The campaign organization put together by Senator George McGovern was infused with a remarkable esprit de corps. It inspired a sense of mission and it developed into a remarkably compact and cohesive unit for an organization of this type. This development played a great role in producing the string of primary victories which brought McGovern the Democratic party's presidential nomination. But afterward, this same development helped set the stage for his crushing defeat in November. His campaign organization had become too isolated and self-involved to cooperate operationally or compromise ideologically with other elements of the Democratic party such as precinct chairmen and labor leaders. The inability and even reluctance on the part of many McGovernites to build a broad coalition behind their candidate helped pave the way for the Nixon landslide in November.

Thus, we see that meeting social and emotional needs has its limits as far as achieving organizational purposes is concerned. The more the members are "at home" in the organization, the more they make it an integral part of their lives, the more they will tend to be cut off from their environment. Carried too far, this can prove counterproductive for all concerned.

Another factor also casts doubt on the desirability of seeking to elicit large amounts of organizational loyalty. For illustration of this fac-

---

19. *New York Times*, June 9, 1972.

tor, we once again look to a British novelist, this time the contemporary writer Graham Greene. Writing in late 1972, Greene recalls overhearing many years previous a farmer describing some laborers he was using. "They are admirable workers and they are so loyal," said the farmer. The workers he was describing were inmates of a neighboring insane asylum.[20]

Greene's recollection has some special significance for the modern administrator. Organizational loyalty does not correlate well with intelligence and discernment. Those who have the ability as well as the emotional stability to serve the organization well also are apt to be the most reluctant to render any exaggerated allegiance to it. For the modern organization, confronted with a growing complexity of tasks and a growing need for proficient people, this can prove a serious dilemma. High level professionals in particular tend to identify with their profession and not with their workplace. They can be quite critical of an organization which does not meet their professional goals. The modern administrator thus must deal with the ironical fact that the less fully a member identifies with his organization, the more likely such a member is to be valuable to the organization.

Current trends in our society tend to compound the problems which meeting social and emotional needs often produce. "The risks of concentrating attention and energies inward are directly proportional to the magnitude and rate of change in the world outside the organization," write Katz and Kahn.[21] The world, as we all know, is changing rapidly and those who have studied our contemporary technological society feel that this trend will continue and even accelerate. This makes it increasingly dysfunctional for organizations to try to meet their members' social and emotional needs too fully, for the more they do so, the more they enmesh the member within the organization and cut him off from outside influences. Organizations will find themselves less and less able to endure the risks of stagnation which separation from the outer society can produce.

All of this does not mean that meeting social and emotional needs no longer has any role to play in motivating organizational members. Even the most creative and critical professionals still have social and emotional needs which an organization can help to fulfill. And in so doing, the organization can evoke a modicum of loyalty which can prove helpful in achieving organizational goals. But the days when an organization can call upon its employees to take an oath of all-out allegiance are rapidly drawing to a close. The trend of the times makes

---

20. Graham Greene, "The Virtues of Disloyalty," *The Observer*, December 24, 1972.
21. Katz and Kahn, *op. cit.*, p. 42.

such occurrences increasingly less likely and increasingly less useful.

Ego Needs

One of the experiments which Elton Mayo and his colleagues undertook at Western Electric's Hawthorne plant was to place a group of women who were assembling telephone relays in a testroom and observe their responses to changing work conditions. For two years the researchers studied the response of the women as the lighting was increased and then decreased, as rest pauses were introduced and then abolished, and so forth. The one fact that stood out and which somewhat startled the researchers was this: No matter whether the changes they introduced were pleasant or unpleasant, the response of the women in terms of production moved in only one direction—up![22]

The conclusion eventually drawn from this important experiment was that attention and recognition *in and of itself* tends to generate a positive response. The women were thus seen as reacting to the fact that they had become objects of attention and, as a result, were responding positively no matter what particular form the attention took. Of course, had unpleasant changes been introduced as a real and permanent policy, the response would undoubtedly have been quite different. But, as a laboratory test, such changes only signalled continued interest in their behavior, and so their responses were uniformly favorable.

Another interesting bit of research which bears some relationship to the Hawthorne experiment involved the case of the weeping waitresses. In the late 1940's, William H. Whyte wanted to find out why waitresses so frequently broke into tears. He discovered that they often became caught in a cruel vise. The customers would clamor insistently for their orders, but the more urgently the waitresses relayed this to the counterhands, the more the latter would make them wait. To meet their own ego needs, the counterhands felt they had to show the waitresses and their customers that they were not to be bossed. Caught between these two obdurate forces, the waitresses often ended up weeping.[23]

Fortunately a device existed to eliminate the problem. This was the prong. When the waitresses put their orders on a prong, the counterhands no longer felt any threats to their egos and much of the tension evaporated.

The lessons, or at least one of the lessons, of both of these research studies is clear; employees want to be recognized. They have ego needs which require fulfillment and the organization by fulfilling these

---

22. Roethlisberger and Dickson, *op. cit.*
23. Whyte, *op. cit.*

needs can help achieve its own purposes. The recognition of such ego needs and their potential as motivators of men was not in itself a new and sensational discovery. Organizations and their leaders from earliest times have been aware of the existence of such needs and had often sought to utilize them. However, the Hawthorne experiment and Whyte's research showed how widely and deeply such needs extended and how varied were the ways which existed for responding to them.

Administrators seek to accommodate ego needs in a variety of ways. Promotions, bonuses, medals, a bit of praise or even a pat on the shoulder have all been pressed into play. Sometimes it is a matter of assigning a desk by the window or changing a title from assistant director to deputy director. (The latter was a device which found frequent usage during the 1960's as the term *assistant* fell into disfavor.) A new and more challenging assignment can also help fulfill ego needs. These are a few of the devices for dealing with the ego needs problem on an individual basis.

There are also ways of meeting such needs on an organizationwide basis. For example, an organization may set its recruitment standards high, or at least claim that it is doing so, in order to make its members feel that they are among "The Chosen." Similarly, the organization may boast of how small a percentage of its recruits make it through the training or probationary stage. The organization may seek to boost its own image in the community so that its members will take more pride in belonging to it. As Robert Presthus has noted, "The status of one's occupation can be augmented by the status of the organization in which one works."[24]

However, the assuaging of ego needs, like all the motivators we have been examining, poses problems as well as potentialities. Utilized on an individual basis, they can breed an excess of rivalry and competition. One man's reward is another man's deprivation. They can induce the individual to act in ways which can prove inimical to organizational purposes. "The man who competes for external rewards," say Katz and Kahn, "is likely to ponder how he can obtain the reward without the circuitous and strenuous business of compliance."[25] The pursuit of recognition can become an end in itself and its consequences may not always dovetail with the goals of the employing agency.

Trying to meet ego needs on an organization-wide basis is often difficult and sometimes almost impossible. A sanitation department may find it quite difficult to make the chests of its employees swell with pride through instilling them with the idea that they belong to an elite

---

24. Robert Presthus, *The Organizational Society* (New York: Random House, 1962), p. 291.
25. Katz and Kahn, *op. cit.*, p. 303.

organization engaged in a glamorous enterprise. Yet ego needs continue to count, and in a mass society where people frequently feel left out, the fulfillment of these needs acquires increased importance. The adept administrator will strive to meet such needs while avoiding some of the pitfalls which they present.

The "Highest" Needs

Earlier, when speaking of material needs, attention was called to McGregor's statement that such needs were satisfied only off the job. An organization trying to use material needs satisfaction to motivate its employees was utilizing a motivator that was not directly job-connected. And as we noted, this may account for the weakness of such satisfiers in inducing workers to do more than a bare minimum toward fulfilling organizational purposes.

In a more limited sense to be sure, something of the same problem may confront the organization when it tries to boost employee performance through meeting social-emotional and ego needs. While such satisfactions are more directly linked to the job, they are still somewhat extrinsic to the actual work process. They relate more directly to the workplace and the worker than to the work itself.

The humanistic school which arose during the 1950's sought to add a new and penultimate motivator to the list. This was the satisfaction that an employee obtains from simply working, regardless of ego, social, material or any other satisfactions.

One of the first writers to call attention to this new bundle of motivators was Argyris. In his 1957 book *Personality and Organization*, this psychologist claimed that the employee has a thrust toward "self-actualization" which the usual organizational setup continually tends to thwart. The traditional methods of running an organization, said Argyris, are really more suitable for handling children than adults. But, he argued, this does not have to be the case. It is possible to design and operate organizations that enhance rather than inhibit the individual's development and hence satisfy his basic need to realize himself in his work.[26]

Three years later Douglas McGregor published *The Human Side of Enterprise.* In this and in subsequent writings until his death a few years later, McGregor hammered away at the theme that work could be and should be a source of self-fulfillment in and of itself, and that organizations should reshape themselves so that this can occur. McGregor saw no inherent conflict between organizational goals and individ-

---

26. Chris Argyris, "The CEO's Behavior: Key to Organizational Behavior," *Harvard Business Review*, March-April, 1973.

ual goals. "People are not by nature passive or resistant to organization-al needs," he emphasized. They want to take on responsibility and express themselves through creative and productive work. The essential task of management, he insisted, "is to arrange organizational conditions and methods of operation so that people can achieve their own goals best by directing their own efforts toward organizational objectives."[27]

What are these conditions? McGregor and others who took up this theme call generally for less hierarchy and more humanity in organizational life. They stressed expanded scope and encouragement for individual initiative and enterprise through allowing employees to make many of their own decisions on the job and to participate in the making of others. Work should be designed not only to be challenging and changing, but it should also provide pervasive possibilities for the employees to experience what is called closure or the sense of completion that is obtained from finishing a measurable unit of work.

Subsequent research has, at least in part, validated much of McGregor's argument. Katz and Kahn report that "if there is one confirmed finding in all these studies of worker morale and satisfaction, it is the correlation between the variety and challenge of the job and the gratifications which accrue to workers." Although exceptions exist, still "by and large, people seek more skill-demanding jobs than they hold, and as they are able to attain these more demanding jobs, they become happier, better adjusted and suffer fewer health complaints."[28]

What about job performance and productivity?

Here the results of research are somewhat mixed. However, as reported by Katz and Kahn and others, there seems to be a "low but positive" correlation between job satisfaction and job performance, even though the relationship is not always as high as McGregor and his disciples might have wished.[29] Then there are some additional factors to be taken into account.

Job satisfaction tends to reduce turnover, tardiness and absenteeism. Many of the devises used to measure productivity fail to record this effect, but it obviously has a distinct impact on overall productivity. Also, job satisfaction tends to play a particularly important role in motivating and raising the productivity of professional workers, and the proportion of professionals in the public work force is steadily rising. Finally, there is a growing tendency for all workers to insist on work that is intrinsically rewarding or at least is not boring and dehumanizing.

---

27. Douglas McGregor, *Leadership and Motivation* (Cambridge: MIT Press, 1966), p. 15.
28. Katz and Kahn, *op. cit.*, p. 364.
29. For a fairly recent illustration of such research see Lawrence D. Prybil, "Job Satisfaction in Relation to Job Performance and Occupational Level," *Personnel*, February 1973.

91

Meeting self-actualization needs, like meeting any of the other needs we have been examining, is not without limits and liabilities. Increased participation in decision-making can mean delayed decision-making. Sometimes such participation may only serve to catalyze conflict. Furthermore, what makes an agency's employees happy are not always the things that make its clientele or the taxpaying public happy, though there is, fortunately, a more *inherent* convergence of interests in this relationship than one might suspect. Employees, for example, usually derive substantial satisfaction from increasing their output as long as they do not perceive such increased output as something being forced upon them. Research indicated that many workers, when allowed to set their own goals, will set larger goals than management was prepared to set for them.

All in all, the fulfillment of self-actualization needs does seem to be an area of growing importance in motivating modern man. Consequently, many organizations are earnestly seeking to develop more and more methods and means for meeting such "higher level" needs. The reader will find that the remainder of this text will reflect this growing trend.

THE "OTHER" ORGANIZATION

In our examination of ego needs we saw how a group of young female employees at Western Electric reacted positively to every change made in their working conditions while they were working in the "testroom." However, another experiment conducted along the same lines produced quite different results.

Mayo and his colleagues persuaded the management of the company to put a group of men engaged in making parts of telephone switches on a piece-rate system. Since this new system would allow the men to increase their earnings without undue physical strain, and since these were Depression times when most workers seemed desperate to earn more money, both the researchers and the company expected a great jump in productivity. Their expectations came to naught. The output of the men remained the same.

The research group then began to investigate why the workers responded, or rather failed to respond, in the way they did. Unlike the young female relay assemblers, most of whom had expected to get married and leave their jobs before too long, the male workers had developed a work culture of their own. They had become a cohesive and compact group with their own codes, rules and norms. Among these rules were prohibitions against doing too much or too little work. So solidly entrenched were these understandings among the male employees that they remained impervious to any blandishments from management. The men rationalized that the incentive plan was an attempt to eventually cut out some jobs or to reduce wage rates. The company assured them that such was not the case and pointed to its record which indicated no instance of its ever having acted in such a manner. But this failed to move the employees. They remained adamant and productivity went on at the same level as before.[30]

What Mayo and his associates had come up against was what is sometimes called the informal organization. This phenomenon has interested and intrigued organizational theorists ever since, and a good deal of research activity has been devoted to probing its ramifications. These ramifications have been found to be large indeed.

Organizational charts and manuals of procedure, it seems, rarely provide us with an accurate picture of an organization. There is a good deal more lying under the surface, and what is not official or even readily visible is often the most important. Even the most formal organizations that pride themselves on going strictly "by the book" rarely do so. For example, an informal system of authority may and often does arise which supersedes, at least to some extent, the formal one. In the army, the lieutenant clearly outranks the sergeant. But when the sergeant has had twenty years of army service while the lieutenant is fresh from a college ROTC program, it may well be the sergeant rather than the lieutenant who actually ends up running the platoon.

Communication is another thing that often flows through informal channels. The office grapevine is usually faster and more complete than the office memo. Aboard a ship, for example, the real communications center is often not the captain's office but the kitchen or galley, and navy cooks are usually better sources of news than commanding officers. This is how the term *scuttle butt* came to have its current meaning.

The informal organization may give rise to a network of relationships for which the organization chart and the manual of procedure provide few clues. All employees in the office may be of the same grade but Jones, the oldest, gets the seat nearest the window while Smith, the youngest, fetches the coffee for the 10:30 A.M. break. All the employees are to do the same work but since Black does better at processing form A while Brown performs better in processing form B, the A's end up on Black's desk and the B's on Brown's.

A case study frequently used in public administration courses offers a vivid example of how completely the informal organization can

---

30.   Roethlisberger and Dickson, *op. cit.*, p. 522.

diverge from the formal one. Entitled *The NLRB Examiner,* it deals with a series of events that occurred in the Los Angeles office of the National Labor Relations Board during the mid-1930's when the NLRB was in the early stages of its existence. The head of the office showed signs of being highly partial to employers and to the union organization which was closest to employers, namely the old AFL. The examiners themselves tended to favor the more militant CIO and became incensed over what they regarded as their boss' favoritism. So, they formed an organization of their own, hiding reports and information from the head of the office, leaking material and otherwise providing aid to the CIO unions and seeking to establish their own connections to headquarters in Washington. Anyone looking at the office's organizational chart and examining its promulgated rules and procedures would have obtained a wholly erroneous idea of just how the NLRB's Los Angeles office was operating in those hectic days.[31]

One of the most extreme examples of how the informal organization can overwhelm the formal organization is the American prison. Ostensibly, prisons are run by wardens and correction officers according to prescribed rules and regulations. In practice, this has rarely been the case. Sociologists and criminologists who have studied prisons have found out that traditionally most prisons have been run by the prisoners themselves. This does not mean that prisons are democratic institutions; they are indeed far from it. Rather, the supervisory personnel, faced with the enormous difficulties involved in everyday prison operation, eventually give up and surrender basic control to what are often the toughest inmates in the institution.[32]

There is much brutality and ugliness in the typical prison, but those who have studied prisons feel that more of it results from too little rather than too much application of official authority. There are some exceptions to this, particularly at smaller institutions, and it should be said that in recent years prison officials generally have been asserting more control over penal facilities. But traditionally prisons have evolved a whole subculture including beatings, homosexual gang rapes and other grim and gruesome rituals, while the prison officials avert their eyes and try to get through the day with a minimum of trouble.

Of course, in most cases the informal organization does not loom quite so large on the administrative scene, and its role should not be overstressed. It modifies and colors the formal organization but does not radically alter it. No matter how expert and experienced a sergeant

---

31. William H. Riker, *The NLRB Examiner,* ICP Case Series No. 15 (Indianapolis: Bobbs-Merrill Co., 1951).
32. Vincent O'Leary and David Duffy, "Managerial Behavior and Correctional Policy," *Public Administration Review,* November/December, 1971.

may be, and no matter how naive and nervous the lieutenant may be, it is the lieutenant and not the sergeant who bears the final responsibility for the platoon. Consequently, there is a limit as to how much authority the sergeant can acquire and how much the lieutenant may abdicate. Nevertheless, some informal elements influence the operation of nearly all organizations, and the administrator must keep himself alert as to what they are and what they do.

There are two aspects of informal organization that merit some special attention. One concerns the role of informal rules; the other concerns the role of small groups.

Whose Rules?

Nearly all organizations seek to prescribe a set of rules and have their members follow them. But what they seek they do not always find. If we take the entire country as an organization, we find that from 1919 to 1933 it prohibited the sale of liquor only to discover that during this period more liquor was sold than ever before. Today, the laws of many states regarding gambling, marijuana and prostitution are flouted with almost equal impunity.

Employees of organizations are like citizens of nations in that they tend to obey only those rules they believe in. As sociologist Alvin Gouldner has pointed out, workers will accept a rule only if it is legitimate in terms of their values. They will not accept it just because those who issued it had a legal right to do so.

Employees also become quite adept at evading rules or bending them to suit their needs and desires, and the more rules the organization tends to set down, the more dexterous its members may become in this respect. "Any complex maze of rules," write Katz and Kahn, "will be utilized by the guardhouse lawyers in the system to their own advantage."[33] In this fashion when the rules run into employee resistance, the employees may use them to defeat rather than serve the organization's purposes.

Sometimes employees do this by simply enforcing the organization's rules to the letter, thereby creating all kinds of pandemonium. Traffic policemen have driven their departments to despair by merely giving out a ticket to every motorist that deserved one. Such action floods the police department with a sharply increased workload and a sharply increased number of complaints from the community's more substantial citizens. In 1970, French customs inspectors, incensed over the failure of the government to meet their demands, staged a "strike" by simply inspecting thoroughly every piece of baggage that visitors

---

33. Katz and Kahn, *op. cit.,* p. 350.

95

brought into France. In doing what they were supposed to do, they virtually paralyzed operations at France's international airports and disrupted travel in Europe generally.

The informal organization not only achieves frequent and sometimes spectacular success in sabotaging the formal organization's rules, but it also manages to establish and enforce rules of its own. Many of these rules have to do with work output. Those who exceed the informal quota may be branded as "ratebusters" while those who fail to carry their fair share of the load may earn the title of "chiseler." Seniority is another rule that governs many procedures of many informal organizations. Those who have seniority on the job are to get the better assignments and the more congenial conditions. The most junior members may not only be given the short end of the stick but may also be subjected to various kinds of petty harassments such as being sent to fetch the "left-handed monkey wrench." Sometimes the harassment is not so petty. Hazing rituals of college fraternities at one time used to result in frequent injury and occasional death to initiates of those organizations.

Probably no informal rule is more widespread than the ban on "squealing." This prohibition is instilled in most Americans during their school years and tends to stay with them through the rest of their lives. The taboo against "tattling" is so widely and deeply ingrained that even those who would stand to benefit from it tend to dislike it. The "informer" or "spotter," no matter how useful he may be, rarely wins esteem in the eyes of management, and though he may increase his earnings, he seldom enhances his chances for promotion.

While the organization often encounters difficulty in enforcing its own rules, the informal organization usually succeeds quite well in securing support and adherence to its own codes of behavior. Sanctions against offenders can take many forms, not excluding violence. Prisoners who depart from the informal rules can meet injury and even death at the hands of their fellow inmates, and when a New York City policeman name Frank Serpico decided to inform on corruption within the police force, he received several death threats from some of his irate colleagues.[34] However, the sanction most frequently invoked is that of the "silent treatment." The erring member is cut off from all social intercourse and all unnecessary conversation. When West Point cadet James J. Pelosi refused to resign from the academy on being accused by his fellow cadets of cheating in 1971, he was forced to room alone and to eat alone at a ten-man table at the cadet mess hall. Protesting his innocence, Pelosi stuck out the "silence" until he graduated eighteen months later.[35] He was the only cadet in the academy's history ever to

---

34. Peter Maas, *Serpico* (New York: Viking Press, 1973).
35. *New York Times*, June 7, 1973.

survive such a protracted ordeal. (The next year the cadets abolished the practice.)

Many informal rules, it should be noted, are quite benign. Alvin Gouldner indicates that while the Golden Rule remains an unattainable goal, it has become a nearly universal norm and as such governs a good deal of organization behavior. If people do not naturally love their neighbors as themselves, they do tend to help others who have helped themselves or at least refrain from injuring them. Gouldner claims that this norm is as ubiquitous and as important as the incest taboo in modern society.[36] As such it counteracts the harshness which other rules, both formal and informal, may produce in organizational operations.

The Small Group

The basic unit for the formal organization may be the division, the department, the section or all three plus others as well. The primary basis for the informal organization is generally the small group. Although many informal norms and rules are organization-wide, many others are promulgated and enforced by small work groups. The small group consists of no set number of individuals. Rather, it designates any group whose members are in continual face-to-face contact with each other. Such groups often follow the structural lines of the formal organization. The small group in the army infantry is typically the squad. In the university it is usually the department. But whether or not it conforms to any formally recognized structure, forces from within itself customarily dictate a good deal of its behavior.

The importance of the small group springs chiefly from the importance of primary relationships over secondary relationships in human behavior. Those we work with every day on a person-to-person basis invariably become more important to us than those whom we see infrequently or with whom we conduct relations at a distance. Out of such primary relationships come norms, codes, procedures and the means for their enforcement. The famed "silent treatment" is most powerfully exercised on those with whom we are in daily contact.

An interesting example of how the small group develops and enforces its own rules is found in Peter Blau's *The Dynamics of Bureaucracy.* Blau reports on an office of a federal agency that had certain law enforcement powers over business. Many times businessmen caught violating the law by agents would make implicit if not explicit offers of a bribe. The agents uniformly rejected such offers for it was not only against organizational policy but against their own code to accept them. However, the agents also had learned to make use of these attempts to

---

36. Alvin W. Gouldner, *Patterns of Industrial Democracy* (Glencoe, Ill.: The Free Press, 1954).

suborn them. Such bribe offers became a valuable lever in prodding the businessmen into settling the case on their, the agents', own terms.

"Being offered a bribe constituted a special tactical advantage for an agent," writes Blau. "An employer who had violated one law was caught in the act of compounding his guilt by violating another one. Agents exploited this situation to strengthen their position in negotiations."[37]

In refusing to accept bribe offers the agents were abiding by the organization rules. However, these rules also called for agents to report such attempted bribes to their superiors. Here the agents departed from the formal rules, for to them reporting bribe offers constituted "squealing" and "squealing" constituted one of the most cardinal of sins. Blau could only find two cases in the recollection of all the agents present in the office where one of their number had ever reported the offer of a bribe. The agent in one of the cases had left the office. In the second, the agent concerned remained at work but was still undergoing the punishment of ostracism. This agent stoutly maintained his "innocence." claiming he had only turned in the businessman after the latter had pressed his bribe offer vigorously and in the presence of other parties. However, the agent's protestations were to no avail. None of his colleagues would have any dealings with him that were not absolutely necessary for the conduct of office affairs. Such are the workings of small groups and informal organizations.

The Informal Balance Sheet

The informal organization and the small groups which make it up can obviously do a great deal of damage. They may and often do subvert the very purposes of the organization since they show a persistent tendency to do what is most congenial to their members and reject organizational endeavors which may conflict with their own basic goals. The British sociologist Michael Banton was told, in studying an American police organization, that "first the front office decides and then the locker room decides."[38] He was left with the distinct impression that it was the locker room's decision that was truly decisive.

The informal organization cannot only make things difficult for the formal organization, but it can also make things hard for its own members. Not only are the "ratebusters" or the "chiselers" usually punished, but sanctions may also be invoked against the member who has a beard or who espouses radical views or who in any way speaks or acts in a manner that marks him as "different."

---

37. Peter M. Blau, *The Dynamics of Bureaucracy* (Chicago: University of Chicago Press, 1955), p. 152.
38. Michael Banton, *The Policeman in the Community* (London: Tavistock Publications, 1964), p. 117.

Sometimes, the informal organization acts in an entirely opposite way, but this can prove even more counterproductive to organizational goals. It may cover up for one or more of its members who fail to do what is expected of them. The alcoholic who arrives back from lunch in a stupefied state may be allowed to sleep it off in an unobtrusive place while the rest of the group tells the supervisor that he is gone on an official errand. Such practices not only harm the organization but also the individual since he is allowed to continue without confronting his problem or making attempts to resolve it.

Finally, the sense of team loyalty with which the informal organization imbues its members can generate a variety of evils. This could be widely seen during the U.S. Senate Watergate hearings in 1973. Queried as to why he did not speak up at meetings where "dirty tricks" were planned, Herbert Porter, the youthful scheduling director for the Committee to Re-elect the President replied, "I was not one to stand up in a meeting and say this should be stopped. I kind of drifted along." Pressed further by Senator Howard Baker as to why he remained silent, Porter added, "In all honesty, probably because of the fear of group pressure that would ensue, of not being a team player."[39]

Yet, the informal organization also has a positive role to play, and organizational theorists are coming more and more to accept and avow this fact. Note the following quotations:[40]

The incompleteness of the formal plan provides a vacuum which, like other vacuums, proves abhorrent to nature. (Simon, Smithburg and Thompson)

No organization chart and no book of policies and procedures can specify every act and prescribe for every contingency encountered in a complex organization. To attempt such specification merely produces an array of instructions so ponderous that they are ignored for the sake of transacting the business of the organization. Moreover, even if such specifications could be provided, they would soon be out of date. . . . (Katz and Kahn)

. . . It would not, in any sense, be an exaggeration to assert that any large organization would come to a grinding halt within a month if all its members began behaving strictly in accordance with the structure of responsibility and authority defined by the formal organization chart, the position description and formal controls. (McGregor)

---

39. *Time,* June 18, 1973, p. 19.
40. The quotations from Simon, Smithburg, and Thompson, and Katz and Kahn are from works previously cited. McGregor's statement is from his posthumously published book *The Professional Manager* (New York: McGraw-Hill, 1967). The quote from Crozier is from *La Societe Bloquee* (Paris: Editions due Seuil, 1970).

99

... Reduced to its formal power, to the theoretical pact which constitutes it, every organization, every human enterprise is incapable of adapting itself to its environment. (Michel Crozier)

What these writers are saying is obvious: The formal organization cannot exist without its informal counterpart. All organization design is inevitably incomplete and imperfect for there is simply too much complexity and variability in the interaction of human beings ever to be compressed into a formal system. As employees come and go, as new technologies develop and new problems arise, the formal plans and procedures, no matter how well designed originally, become increasingly outmoded. Periodic revamping can help but can never hope to keep pace with the rate and sweep of the changes taking place which affect organizational operations. Consequently, the all-important facts of organizational life frequently become the unofficial ones.

If Mr. Green tends to wield the authority that belongs to Mr. White, then more often than not, Green possesses some competence that White lacks. If the seasoned sergeant exercises more authority than does the neophyte lieutenant, then undoubtedly many a soldier's life has been saved because of it. As a matter of fact, young ROTC lieutenants used to be told, "Be good to your sergeant lest he carry out every order you give." And if small groups tend to call the shots as they see them, then oftentimes they see them much better than does top management.

This brings us to the question of how the informal organization affects organizational productivity. We have already noted several ways in which it can sabotage and subvert organizational goals. However it can also do the reverse. Elton Mayo and his colleagues found in their Western Electric studies that informal work group norms could affect productivity in a positive way. More recently, Katz and Kahn have stated that the correlation between the informal group norms and productivity is likely to go in the way the organization would like it to go. "Though the relationship of cohesion with productivity can go in either a positive or a negative direction," they write, "the relationship is more often positive than negative in the studies done to date."[41]

This brings us finally to the role of the small group. Research indicates that the larger the size of the work unit, the greater the rate of absenteeism and accidents is likely to be. Small groups meet social and emotional needs, and whether or not they are the "highest" needs, such needs remain important for organizational purposes. In another of his books, *Bureaucracy in Modern Society*, Peter Blau writes that "the effective enforcement of unofficial standards of conduct in cohesive work

---

41. Katz and Kahn, *op. cit.*, p. 379.

groups has important implications for official operations. Many studies," he adds, "have found that the existence of cohesive bonds between co-workers is a prerequisite for high morale and optimum performance of duty. . . ."[42]

This does not mean that the organization should remain oblivious to the harm which small groups can do, not only to the organization but also to their own members. By facilitating and even fostering rotation, organizations can alleviate many of these problems. Promoting organization-wide activities and stimulating employees to take training outside their subunit, even outside the organization itself, are other devices which may help prevent small groups from becoming too ingrown and hence too injurious to all concerned. But in general, administrators have shown an increasing disposition to accept the small group and to work with it. To quote Katz and Kahn again, "The effective supervisor . . . regards the value of the group to each individual as a potential asset rather than as a bureaucratic irrelevancy or a threat to authority. As a result, he devotes a good deal of effort to creating a cohesive work group, a group in which each member finds the fact of membership rewarding."[43]

The ultimate aim is to make the formal and the informal organization converge. Can this be achieved? According to Argyris, informal organization results from the desires of organization members to satisfy various needs which the formal organization neglects or even thwarts. He reports on studies he has done of two departments of a business corporation. One department did not attempt to meet such needs and consequently its members developed informal ways of satisfying them. The other department made ample provision to meet these needs through job security, personal recognition, variety and challenge in work assignment. As a result, says Argyris, morale was high, personal relationships were warm, and the need for informal organization was hardly felt.[44]

ORGANIZATIONAL PATHOLOGY

Organizations, like individuals, often act in strange, irrational, and even, at times, self-destructive ways. But, as with individuals, such organizational behavior usually has a logic of its own, albeit one that is frequently perverse and sometimes pathological. This aspect of administration is often classified as organizational pathology. The term is somewhat misleading for pathology implies an abnormal condition and

---

42. Peter M. Blau, *Bureaucracy in Modern Society* (New York: Random House, 1956), p. 56.
43. Katz and Kahn, *op. cit.*, p. 327.
44. Argyris, *op. cit.*

this is not the case with the pathologies of organization. They are wide-spread and deep rooted and few organizations manage to escape their pernicious influences completely. Consequently, the subject warrants a good deal of scrutiny and study.

The Pathology of Persistence

At one time tuberculosis was a widespread disease in the United States, as well as elsewhere, and many sanatoria were erected to treat its numerous sufferers. Then in the early 1950's, a new drug came on the market that could effect, at least in most cases, a prompt and complete cure. Soon the new medicine had reduced this hitherto scourge to minimal proportions. But it had no comparable impact on the institutions that TB had brought into existence. While the drug soon depopulated most TB sanatoria, it did not eliminate them. Many states—Maine is just one example—continued to operate TB sanatoria with as few as five or six patients until an increasingly exasperated U.S. Public Health Service finally forced some consolidations. However, as late as 1973, many states, probably the majority, were still operating some sanatoria that were being used only to about 25 percent of capacity. In TB, the physical pathology proved much easier to treat than the institutional one.

The first pathology of organization is, thus, persistence. Self-preservation is as much a law of organizational life as it is of biological life, and the institutional organism, unlike the biological one, usually achieves a much greater success rate. The ability of organizations to survive in the face of adversity has often amazed and even astounded administrative observers.

Persistence is probably the most widespread of all organizational pathologies. While the federal government did exert pressure on states in its partially successful attempt to close down or consolidate unneeded TB sanatoria, the federal establishment still retains a great many examples of the persistence pathology within its own house. To take one example, the National Screw Commission was set up during World War I to standardize parts for military equipment. It has not held a weekly meeting or issued a report in decades, but when last heard from it was still maintaining a suite of offices and a bureaucratic payroll. Another agency of dubious utility to the American weal is the National Tea-tasters Commission. Like the Screw Commission, it has not become known for the vigor of its efforts in carrying out any needed public purpose, and early in his first term, President Nixon issued an order abolishing it. But midway through his second term the order had still to be carried out.[45]

---

45. *Boston Herald-American*, May 4, 1973, see editorial "Do We Need All This Advice?"

Then there is the Subversive Activities Control Board which was set up under the Internal Security Act of 1950 to register communists as foreign agents. The Supreme Court soon stepped in and stripped the agency of its powers. But in so doing, the Court did not thereby end the board's existence. The SACB continued on largely unnoticed until President Johnson named the husband of one of his favorite secretaries to a $27,000-a-year position as a board member. President Nixon expressed his support for the outmoded agency and said that he would try to find something for it to do. But by the end of his first term, there were no indications that he had succeeded in giving the SACB anything of any usefulness to perform.

The problem is certainly not a new one. By 1937, the Commission on Administrative Management in the Government of the United States, the so-called Brownlow Commission, could say in tones of rather despairing humor, "there is among government agencies great need of a coroner to pronounce them dead, and for an undertaker to dispose of the remains."[46] The problem, it should be added, is not in any way peculiarly a part of American bureaucracy. A survey by the University of Rome's Department of Government Studies in 1972 showed that Italy had 58,000 government agencies.[47] They included

an office to grant loans to persons who had suffered damage in eruptions of Mt. Vesuvius. (The last eruption had occurred in 1906.)

an agency to take care of the orphans of World War II. (The youngest such an orphan could have been by that time was 28 years old.)

a bureau to license carrier pigeons.

an agency to administer pensions for veterans of a battle that was fought in 1896. (The agency would not tell the researchers just how many veterans of this encounter were still alive.)

The Pathology of Conservatism

Organizations not only show a remarkable ability to prolong their existence, but they also display a noticeable facility for prolonging their traditional ways of doing things. Their means and methods of operation frequently exhibit a persistent penchant for the tried and true. "Organizational logic is essentially conservative," writes Robert Presthus, "for it honors consistency, tradition, the minimization of individual ends in favor of collective ends, and the wisdom of history rather than the wisdom of men."[48] A British writer, R. G. S. Brown, in noting the same

---

46. *Administrative Management in the Government of the United States* (Washington, D.C.: Government Printing Office, 1937), p. 34.
47. *New York Times*, July 1, 1972.
48. Presthus, *op. cit.*, p. 291.

tendency, adds an additional perspective as to its causes. "A really creative idea is likely to disrupt the smooth flow of business and therefore leads to faction." Since organizations want to avoid disruption, they "will usually find it easier to turn down an unorthodox idea than approve it."[49]

Change, it should be kept in mind, always poses threats. It can alter career opportunities, favoring new skills and training and thus new leadership abilities. It implies new priorities along with a reallocation of resources. Even those who would seem to benefit from the change may find it fearful. For example, the decision to equip submarines with nuclear power meant a dramatic upgrading in the submarine's role in national defense. Yet, submarine commanders opposed the plan when it was first conceived in the 1950's. A nuclear submarine, among other things, would require two crews and two commanding officers who would alternate in operating it. This meant that no officer or crewman could claim the submarine as "my ship." Submarine commanders would not accept this and so they fought against its development.[50]

As organizations grow older, this problem of routinization becomes greater. Like individuals, organizations tend to become increasingly inflexible with age. Values and procedures become not only established but entrenched. And, again like an individual and even like a society, an organization develops a heritage and seeks to pass it on to its new generation.

William A. Wayson, Director of Urban Education at Ohio State University, sees these factors as explaining why school systems have often failed to respond to the pressures for change. In his analysis, which could also be applied to most other organizational settings, he notes that "ways of doing things gain validity with longevity. The length of their utilization is cited as proof of their effectiveness. . . . Newcomers enter as novices and are taught by tribal elders 'how it is done around here' . . . By the time they are eligible for promotion, they have incorporated these priorities and taboos into most of their thinking. . . When new and creative responses are demanded, the bureaucrat looks inept, feels paranoid and becomes defensive."[51]

Examples of rigid routinization abound. From 1937 to the fall of 1972, the Boston Fire Department did not reassign a single fire company. Yet during this 35-year period the city's population drastically changed and shifted. As a result, some sections now had more than double the

---

49. R. G. S. Brown, *The Administrative Process in Britain*, (London: Methuen and Co., Ltd., 1970), p. 248.
50. Harvey M. Sapolsky, *The Polaris System Development: Bureaucratic and Programatic Success in Government* (Cambridge: Harvard University Press, 1972), Chapter 2.
51. Quoted by Fred M. Hechinger in "Principals: Call for New Breed of School Leader," *New York Times*, March 21, 1971 (News in Review).

proportion of firefighters on a per capita basis than other sections, though frequently the former sections were the areas that were now having the least fires. Similar situations can be found in many other American cities. Indeed, some older cities still maintain a string of small and now decrepit firehouses dating back to the time when fire wagons were drawn by horses which had to be changed frequently while en route to the blaze.

The reader again should be wary of believing that such patterns of persistence are endemic only to local governments. The federal government is itself a frequent offender. In 1970, for instance, the Department of Agriculture was still subsidizing the production of pitch pine. However, pitch pine had become totally obsolete when the navy had decided to abandon sailing ships over a hundred years before.

When confronted with pressures to change, organizations can react quite rigorously if not ruthlessly. "If you must sin, then sin against God and not against the bureaucracy," Admiral Hyman Rickover once said, "for God may forgive you but the bureaucracy never will."[52]

Rickover's statement probably reflects the trials and tribulations he experienced in developing, against considerable internal resistance, the navy's nuclear submarine. However, bitter as his experiences may have been, at least one other navy innovator had an even tougher time. This was William Sims who, as a naval lieutenant at the turn of the century, sought to institute a new and vastly improved method of naval gun sighting. When stoutly rebuffed by the navy's top brass for his outlandish ideas, he appealed over their heads to President Theodore Roosevelt. The naval-minded president liked Sims' proposals and saw that they were implemented. Although the innovation is credited with transforming naval gunnery from a haphazard art to a rather precise science, and, in so doing, vastly increasing the navy's efficiency, the admirals were not appeased. Toward the end of Roosevelt's second term they started making plans to court-martial Sims once his benefactor had left the White House. Fortunately, Sims got wind of the scheme and communicated news of it to Roosevelt who managed to squelch the plot before he left office.

Another pioneer in the armed services did not fare so well. This was army General William "Billy" Mitchell who became impressed with the potential of air power during World War I and began to push for a strong air force after the hostilities ended. As part of his campaign, he offered to sink some captured German vessels to demonstrate just what

---

52. Quoted by a speaker from the floor during a panel session at the annual convention, American Society for Public Administration, Los Angeles, 1973. Though I was unable to find out the context in which Rickover made the statement, it sounds so typical of him that I have little doubt of its authenticity.

bomb-carrying planes could do. Congress and the press liked the idea and finally forced a reluctant military establishment into staging such an exercise. Despite numerous handicaps and restrictions designed to hamper his operations, Mitchell and a small group of pilots inflicted such heavy damage on the target vessels that some naval officers present actually broke into tears. They thought that they were witnessing the impending demise of everything they believed in and had devoted their lives to.

When the military authorities still refused to respond, Mitchell began taking his case more and more to the public, calling explicitly for a separate air force. He was demoted and transferred and eventually court-martialed. He died in 1936, only a few years before his outlandish ideas were all too grimly validated in World War II.[53]

The Pathology of Growth

Having devoted considerable attention to the seemingly innate and inherent tendency of organizations to conserve their existence as well as their existing ways of doing things, it is now time to consider one aspect of change which organizations actually welcome and often strive for. This concerns changes in size. Organizations do all they can to ward off threats to their stability except in the area of growth. Most of them tend to welcome and embrace opportunities to grow larger, so long as the growth involves only a change of magnitude or at least does not substantially disturb their established processes and procedures.

This growth syndrome was first spotted by that amusing and all-too-accurate British commentator, C. Northcote Parkinson. In his 1957 work, *Parkinson's Law and Other Studies of Administration*, Parkinson identified growth as the first and foremost law of administrative behavior. Although he furnished figures to back up his contention, Parkinson elicited more chuckles than concern. In 1970, he returned to the fray, and with even more complete figures. To cite just one of them, he noted that in 1935 Great Britain employed only 1,023 officials in London to administer a swollen empire upon which, so its proud boast went, the sun never set. In 1960 this once vast array of colonies that had included India, Ceylon, and a good deal of Southeastern Asia and Africa had dwindled away to a few outposts such as Bermuda and St. Kitts. However, the number of employees needed to run this now shrunken and quite miniature empire had grown to 2,827, an almost threefold increase.[54]

This deeply rooted drive on the part of organizations toward ex-

---

53. For an account of both Sims' and Mitchell's ordeals, see Clark R. Mollenhoff, *The Pentagon* (New York: Pinnacle Books, 1972), Chapters 3 and 5.
54. C. Northcote Parkinson, *The Law of Delay* (New York: Ballantine Books, 1970), pp. 4–5.

pansion can be seen almost everywhere in the public sector. The very fact that public employees now constitute nearly 20 percent of the nation's work force is at least partly attributable to this particular pathology. To take a more specific example, hospitals expanded their facilities tremendously during the 1960's as government aid to do so became available. By 1971, the American Hospital Association reported that on an average day over 186,000 hospital beds were empty.[55] In some areas such as greater Boston and Los Angeles, the number of surplus hospital beds had reached the one-quarter mark.[56] Yet, there were hospitals even in these cities that were eagerly and busily planning still further expansion.

This growth dynamic may appear to contradict the stagnation syndrome which was noted previously, but actually it more often reinforces it. One clue to this may be found in a statement by the noted eighteenth-century British conservative Edmund Burke. "A state without the means of some change," wrote Burke, "is a state without the means of its preservation."[57] As with a state, so with an organization. An organization often wishes to grow in order to continue in existence and to continue operating in its existing ways.

To see just how this works in terms of organizations, we refer once again to Katz and Kahn. Growth, note these two writers, creates new opportunities for promotion, transfer, prestige and power, and it can alleviate a good deal of internal conflict. "Because each subsystem will mobilize all its forces for self-preservation, it is easier for management to meet internal problems by adding rather than subtracting."[58] Almost all organizations are subject to some pressures for change from time to time, and adding new structures and functions is one way to avoid changing existing structures and functions. Thus, it is the forces that make for stability in the organization that help generate the forces for its expansion.

There are, of course, other forces at work. Parkinson cites two factors which foster the expansion urge. "An official wants to multiply subordinates not rivals," he claims, for subordinates increase his prestige and power while rivals obviously endanger it. Also, "officials make work for each other" since the more employees there are, the more memos they exchange, the more conferences they hold, etc.[59] Finally, there is the organization's own hunger for the prestige and potency which only size can confer.

---

55. *Christian Science Monitor*, August 1, 1971.
56. *Los Angeles Times*, April 2, 1973.
57. Michael Curtis, ed., *The Great Political Theories* (New York: Avon Books, 1962), p. 49.
58. Katz and Kahn, *op. cit.*, p. 24.
59. C. Northcote Parkinson, *Parkinson's Law and Other Studies of Administration* (New York: Ballantine Books, 1964), p. 17.

We will have more to say about some of these other growth forces shortly. At this point it would be useful to point out that some parts of the organization tend to grow much more rapidly than others. The two most favored growth areas seem to be the upper levels and the administrative and auxiliary spheres.

Let us return to Parkinson. From 1938 to 1967, he tell us, the number of vessels in the British navy declined from 308 to 114, a diminution of almost two-thirds. The reduction in tonnage was probably even more severe since it was the larger ships that were the most heavily phased out. Battle ships and aircraft carriers, for example, were eliminated completely. During this period, however, the number of admiralty officials and clerical staff increased from 11,270 to 33,574. Thus, a two-thirds cutback in the fleet was accompanied by a threefold expansion of headquarters personnel.[60]

Again we should not regard such phenomena as peculiar to any one country. At the end of World War II, the United States had twelve million men and women under arms. They were directed by 139 three- and four-star generals and admirals. In 1972, as Senator William Proxmire has pointed out, we had only 2.5 million men and women in our armed forces but the number of our three- and four-star generals and admirals had burgeoned to 190.[61] A reduction of over 75 percent in the military saw a 33 percent growth in the number of top-ranking officers. Such are the workings of organizational logic, if logic is the right term to use.

This phenomenon does not stop short with military organizations. The rule of what might be called "inflation at the top" can be found at work almost everywhere. From 1970 to 1973, the U.S. Postal Service determinedly embarked on a cost reduction program and in so doing eliminated over 63,000 employees. At the same time, the number of Assistant Postmasters General more than doubled, going from eight to seventeen. After three years of reducing costs, the Postal Service had twenty officials earning $42,000 or more a year.[62]

Both Americans and Englishmen can take some solace, however, from the fact that Italian taxpayers undoubtedly have it worse. A 1972 survey in Italy showed that the country's national government had nearly 60,000 individuals bearing the official title of "president," and all of them were collecting full-time salaries. The Italian army, meanwhile, had more generals than the United States army, although the Italian

---

60. Parkinson (1970), *op. cit.*, pp. 2–3.
61. William Proxmire, *Uncle Sam: The Last of the Bigtime Spenders* (New York: Simon and Schuster, 1972), pp. 66–67.
62. *Los Angeles Herald-Examiner*, April 2, 1973.

military force is less than one-third as large as ours. As for the Italian navy, it actually had more admirals than it had vessels.[63]

Inflation at the top meshes with the other characteristic of organizational growth, namely its tendency to take place in the administrative or non-line branches. Most of the additional generals, admirals, Assistant Postmasters General tend to be assigned to matters other than fighting battles or delivering mail. The student of public administration need look no farther for examples of this trend than his own institution. If he is seeking a good subject for a term paper in public administration, he should examine the proportion of administrators to faculty members in his own college or university and see how the ratio has changed over the years. Almost certainly he will find that the number of administrators has grown at a much faster rate than the number of employees directly engaged in the educational process. Although teaching is supposed to be the primary purpose of the university, the number of those actually performing this mission is rapidly being surpassed by the number of those handling the auxiliary functions.

Not all of this trend can be ascribed to organizational pathology. There are some perfectly valid reasons for organizational growth to occur disproportionately in the upper levels and in non-line functions. We noted in chapter three that staff units were growing faster than line units and why this was so. The increase in specialization and specialized services spurs on staff growth. And this increase in specialization, along with the increase in professionalization, accounts for much of the tendency for such growth to occur at the top. Professionals and specialists usually cannot be brought in at the lower levels.

However, there are other and less healthy forces at work in stimulating this type of growth. Much of the swelling that takes place in the higher levels may reflect the workings of the "Peter Principle." As developed by Lawrence J. Peter, the principle states that people are promoted to their level of incompetence. This means that a person who does a job well is advanced until he reaches a position that he no longer can handle. The organization tends to be cluttered with such people, claims Peter, and tends to deal with them in ways which aggravate the problems we have been examining. Two of the methods he cites are the "Percussive Sublimination" in which the incompetent is kicked further upstairs to an innocuous position, and the "Lateral Arabesque" in which the incompetent is sidelined to another innocuous position at the same level.[64]

---

63. "A Plethora of Presidents," *Time*, January 29, 1973.
64. Laurence J. Peter and Raymond Hull, *The Peter Principle* (New York: William Morrow, 1968).

Although Peter exaggerates his "principle," both in terms of amusement and analysis, it does contain a germ of truth. It has become quite difficult to get rid of people who can no longer, if they ever could, handle their jobs, and organizations have frequently attempted to solve this problem by creating new positions for them. There is, however, a still more basic reason for the organizational trend to top-heaviness. It relates very directly to the basic reason why organizations tend to grow in the first place.

Growth, as we saw earlier, allows an organization to smooth and settle conflicts through appeasing various forces and factions both within and without its boundaries. Growth at the upper levels only aids and abets this process of conflict resolution. By expanding promotional possibilities organizations give more people more prestige and power. They therefore meet their ego needs and keep them from becoming too dispirited. It is becoming quite common, for example, for a soldier, when his enlistment period is up, to bargain for a higher rating as a price for re-enlisting. One result is that the simple stripeless private, the supposed backbone of the landed military, now constitutes a minority in the army.

The Territorial Imperative

According to biologist Robert Ardy, all animals, human beings definitely included, are slaves to the territorial imperative.[65] They seek to carve out a space for themselves and to repel all those who would intrude upon it. Whether or not this is biologically true—the claim has been bitterly disputed by many biologists—it does seem to apply to organizations. Organizations are continuously accused of not only overzealously protecting their own boundaries, but also of constantly seeking to enlarge them. According to theorist Anthony Downs, "Every social agent is essentially a territorial imperialist. He seeks to expand the borders of his various zones and policy space or at least to increase his degree of influence within each zone." And, adds Downs, "even pure conservatives are imperialists in policy space."[66]

Administrative history is dotted with numerous examples of this bit of bureaucratic pathology. There were the aggressive attempts by the Department of the Interior to take over the Forest Service from the Department of Agriculture, the more successful attempt of the Federal Security Agency, now the Department of Health, Education and Welfare, to appropriate the Children's Bureau from the Department of Labor in the 1940's, and the serious struggle waged by the air force to keep the

---

65. Robert Archey, *African Genesis* (New York: Dell Publishing Co., 1963).
66. Anthony Downs, *Inside Bureaucracy* (Boston: Little, Brown and Co., 1966), p. 216.

navy from developing its own missile program. It can safely be said that most organizations have engaged in territorial disputes during some part of their existence, and some have been involved continuously in such battles.

Sometimes such altercations flare up on grounds that would baffle and bemuse outsiders. In the spring of 1973, a truly divisive dispute broke out in New York City between the Central Park Zoo and the Bronx Zoo over the custody of a ten-pound baby gorilla named Patty-Cake. The tiny simian had been born in the Central Park Zoo, but early in her infancy she had been sent to a hospital with a broken arm. After setting the arm, the hospital sent her to the Bronx Zoo for recuperation. However, once the arm was mended, the Bronx facility refused to give her back to the Central Park Zoo, saying that Patty-Cake was also suffering from malnourishment and other ills as a result of her previous poor treatment at Central Park.

Needless to say, the Central Park Zoo became incensed at such allegations and countercharged, claiming that Patty-Cake was being overcoddled at the Bronx Zoo where her attendant was feeding her with a bottle and dressing her in diapers and, occasionally, in tiny skirts. Central Park insisted that she be returned so that she could be raised by her natural mother who could best train her how to cope with the exigencies of gorilla life in captivity.

The battle between the zoos escalated to such a point that the city's Parks, Recreation and Cultural Affairs Commissioner had to hire an animal psychologist as a $100-a-day consultant to adjudicate the matter. (He eventually issued a 2,000-word report, recommending that Patty-Cake be returned to her natural mother at Central Park.)

The territorial imperative is an important bureaucratic pathology, but administration is replete with contradictions and here we confront one of them. Though agency aggrandizement is a common feature of administrative life, an opposite trend can also be discerned. While agencies may often show a pronounced penchant for empire building, they may almost as frequently display an annoying aversion to taking on new functions and activities as well as the desire to shed some of those they already have. Police departments generally dislike having to enforce traffic laws and have fought, successfully in most instances, attempts to have meter maids put under their control. School systems have exasperated more people by refusing to undertake additional activities than by aggressively seeking them. Many school departments had to be pushed into taking on many of the programs they operate today such as school lunches and vocational guidance. Herbert Kaufman and Wallace S. Sayre, in their study of New York City, found that both the Hospital and Correction Departments had tried to avoid taking on treatment programs for narcotics while the Department of Health was trying to have the inspection of buildings put entirely under the aegis of the Building Department.[67]

At the federal level, the Department of Agriculture resisted taking on many of Franklin D. Roosevelt's new farm programs, forcing him to set up independent agencies to operate them. When these new agencies developed their own clientele and expertise, they became more bothersome to Agriculture outside its organization than within it and so the department agreed to house them. In like manner, when Roosevelt set up new and special agencies during World War II, the established federal departments offered no resistence. As Chester Bowles pointed out, "It relieved them [the existing agencies] of new responsibilities in unchartered areas of government which could inevitably bring them into conflict with Congress and subject them to criticism from the press."[68] In 1953, the State Department actually took the initiative in having its information activities transferred into the hands of a new and independent United States Information Service.

To note two completely divergent pathological trends may seem somewhat illogical, but actually there may be some method in this madness. A possible guideline does exist for determining when agencies are most likely to practice the territorial imperative and when they are most likely not to do so.

From a lifetime of studying as well as working in bureaucratic organizations, David W. Barkley has observed that the fiercest and most frequent jurisdictional disputes seem to be *intra-agency* in character.[69] Barkley's observation may provide a clue to understanding why agencies can behave in such contradictory ways. It may well be that public organizations seek aggressively activities that fit or complement their existing functions. This may be particularly true when these activities might otherwise go to their rivals. On the other hand, they may, thanks to their innate conservatism, shun activities which would take them into new, unknown and possibly disturbed waters. Similarly, when they have no fear that an activity will be lodged in the hands of their competitors, they may even welcome an opportunity to get rid of some functions they already have.

An example of Barkley's rule could be the dispute raised within the military during the 1950's over who was to control missile development and funds.[70] The air force, as we have previously noted, sought to keep the navy from obtaining authorization to proceed with a missile

---

67. Wallace S. Sayre and Herbert Kaufman, *Governing New York City* (New York: Russell Sage Foundation, 1960), p. 262.
68. Chester Bowles, *Promises to Keep* (New York: Harper & Row, 1971), p. 155.
69. In observations made to the author.
70. Sapolsky, *op. cit.*, p. 78.

program of its own. This in itself can be seen as an intra-agency dispute since both services are branches of the Department of Defense. More significant is the fact that when the navy finally won out and secured such authorization, it then found itself with an even more vigorous dispute on its hands. Two of its own subunits, the Bureau of Aeronautics and the Bureau of Ordinance, began contesting so vigorously and even vehemently for jurisdiction over the program that the navy felt constrained to set up a new unit, the Special Projects Office, to handle the task. Such are the workings of the territorial imperative.

The Pathology of Status

That human beings in nearly all cultures tend toward status seeking is well known. That organizations also tend toward status seeking is becoming equally well known, at least by those who have observed them in operation. Organizations, as we have perhaps tiresomely noted, are simply collections of human beings, and so it is scarcely any cause for wonder that they reflect the foibles and failings of those who compose them.

The pathologies of growth and imperialism that we have already examined bear witness to such status strivings. But, status seeking may take many other forms as well. A subunit may seek to free itself from the organization of which it is a part in order to enjoy the greater status of being an independent agency. Next it may strive to secure recognition as a full-fledged cabinet department. Another subunit may seek to attach itself to the office of the chief executive, or, if it is already there, it may resist transfer to another agency since that might bring about a loss of prestige.

We see examples of this all the time. One reason the Children's Bureau resisted transfer from the Department of Labor to the Federal Security Agency in the late 1940's was that the FSA was not a cabinet department, and therefore the Children's Bureau, in becoming one of the FSA's subunits, would suffer a loss of status. Meanwhile, the upward-oriented FSA managed to evolve itself into a cabinet department in the 1950's, as did the Housing and Home Finance Agency in the 1960's. (The latter is now the Department of Housing and Urban Development.) For some years now pressure has been building up to do the same for HEW's Office of Education. Teachers' associations continuously call for the re-establishment of the office as a separate cabinet department, and personnel within the office scarcely seem desirous of halting such an effort.

Sometimes status struggles concern the use of physical space. An agency may seek a site that is closer to the seat of power or simply one that offers a prestige address. Or it may do battle for a bigger and/or more beautiful building at its existing site. Or, if it shares a building

113

with others, it may compete vigorously for more commodious floor space or for a top-floor location with a better view.

Other physical resources also easily become transformed into status symbols. The admirals of most navies eagerly sought the building of battleships long after it became apparent that airplanes could easily blast them out of the water. Today the American navy continues to press for the construction of mammoth and costly aircraft carriers despite the fact that many defense experts, including some ex-navy men, claim that such vessels are far too vulnerable to be worth the billion-dollar price tags they entail. Similarly, the advent of the missile age brought little diminution in the ardor of the air force for heavy bombers. As for civilian agencies, they can rarely boast of a more prudent approach. Hospitals, for instance, dearly love to acquire new and shiny apparatus even though such apparatus may not be needed to accommodate the health needs of the community. Pennsylvania's outspoken Insurance Commissioner Harold Denenberg claims that while New York City has seventeen hospitals that can perform open-heart surgery, only five such facilities are needed.

Open-heart surgery is not only a matter of equipment but also of activity, and this brings us to another and often crucial area where status struggles occur. Agencies and their subunits search for status through seeking to expand their role. If open-heart surgery provides one example of this, heart transplants offer an even better one. When such an operation was performed with some success in a South African hospital in the mid-1960's, other hospitals, particularly American ones, eagerly embarked on this new and prestigious pursuit. Considerable resources were consumed in the enterprise, resources which could have more profitably been used elsewhere.

The Pathology of Self-Service
Many of the bureaucratic pathologies that we have been examining are obviously interrelated. In like manner, many of them relate to a final pathology which serves as a partial basis for most of the others. This is the tendency of organizations to serve their own interests rather than the interests of their public or their clients.

One of the most complete examples of such a pathology has been found in mental hospitals. In his book *Asylums*, sociologist Erving Goffman points out that though such institutions are designed to treat and care for the mentally ill, they are also designed to provide a livelihood and an agreeable work place for their staffs. According to Goffman, the latter goal easily and customarily supersedes the former one. Institutions for the mentally ill are run primarily, he says, for the benefit of their employees, not their clients.

Goffman's judgment may have been too harsh. Certainly efforts have been made in recent years to open up these institutions, and the press, the public and political leaders have devoted increasing attention to their problems. Furthermore, we should note that mental institutions may have a particular ability to indulge in such goal displacement thanks to the fact that their clientele are not in a position to exercise any effective countervailing power. Therefore, we should not suppose all organizations can or do act in the same manner. Yet, a good many public bureaucracies do display the same tendency.

We have already seen instances of this in our examination of other types of organizational pathology. When hospitals insist on purchasing redundant equipment, performing expensive operations of dubious worth and increasing their already surplus number of beds, they are serving basic needs of their staff, particularly their physicians. The doctors like the new equipment and enjoy the opportunity to make a name for themselves by engaging in various medical experiments which often do not provide a proportionate payoff in *overall* patient care. And almost all the staff benefits from the opportunities which an enlarged capacity can provide.

Hospitals should not bear the brunt of this diagnosis. Libraries, for example, in deciding when they will stay open will usually choose daytime hours over evening hours and weekdays over weekends. The public would obviously benefit from a reversed set of priorities. A library that is open on Sunday and closed on Monday would most likely accommodate the citizens of the community in a much better way than one that is open on Monday but closed on Sunday. Yet anyone who has used libraries knows what the priority is most likely to be. Other institutions tend to behave in the same way. Few public agencies, as a matter of fact, hold any evening or weekend hours since the convenience of the staff must take precedence over the convenience of the public.

In our earlier discussion of informal organization, we noted how prisons have often been run more by their inmates than by their staffs. This too reflects, at least in part, the tendency toward institutional self-accommodation. Maintaining control in a prison is no easy job, and so it becomes more convenient to let the inmates, or rather a small group of inmates, take on the task. In recent years, with the continued growth of prison unrest, prison officials have resorted to another self-serving stratagem. According to former U.S. Attorney General Ramsey Clark, wardens have started "to release the most violent criminals before they cause trouble inside and are so relieved to see the dangerous ones go that they disregard the public safety—and the fact that most will be back before long."[71]

Perhaps no organization has developed self-accommodation into

---

71. Ramsey Clark, *Crime in America* (New York: Simon and Schuster, 1970), p. 214.

such a fine art as the art museum. A hypothetical example will best illustrate what is an everyday reality. Suppose a museum has twenty masterpieces which are viewed by one million people a year. Suddenly the museum obtains a bequest of $1 million which it can use either to acquire another masterpiece or to take steps, such as lowering its admission fees, which would bolster its number of visitors to 1.5 million a year. It if buys the masterpiece it will increase the total amount of art absorbed by the public by 5 percent. If it spends the money in the alternative manner it will increase the amount of art viewed by the public by some 50 percent. Thus, if the museum's goal is to maximize its aesthetic service to the community, it should adopt the second choice in spending its new bequest.

Unfortunately, the typical art museum would not dream of doing so. Rather, it will hungrily go after the additional masterpiece. After all, a new and valuable painting adds to the aesthetic enjoyment of the staff and gives them something to boast about in talking with workers from other museums. "The American art museum," writes art critic Robert Hughes, "still tends to be an institutional parody of the robber baron's castle, staking its prestige more on acquisitions than functions." And Hughes points out that though New York City's famed Metropolitan Museum speaks in lofty tones of "bringing art to the people," it reinstituted its admission fees during the same year it spent over $5.5 million to acquire one new painting.[72]

What is particularly pernicious in this bit of museum madness is that it has driven up the cost of masterpieces horrendously so that all museums now have fewer prized works than they would otherwise have been able to acquire. In recent decades, the prices of prized art works have soared to stratospheric levels, and Hughes claims that "the chief perpetrators" of this phenomenon are the museums who bid feverishly against each other in a massive and mounting ego race. The situation has enriched many art dealers and private collectors while it has resulted in fewer people seeing fewer works of art than would otherwise have been the case.

PATHOLOGY AND ITS PRICE

The portrait of museums forcing up the prices of paintings by desperately trying to outbid each other is only one of the more egregious examples of the costs of organizational pathology. Agencies that have no functions, hospitals with rows of empty beds, armies which maintain horse cavalry in the age of tank warfare (as ours did in the 1930's) are

---

72. Robert Hughes, "Who Needs Masterpieces at Those Prices?" *Time*, July 19, 1971, pp. 52-53.

obviously bestowing unnecessary burdens on the public's purse. These and other price tags of pathology are readily apparent. Organizational disease, however, poses further problems which are not so readily seen.

In our study of the reorganization of the Massachusetts state government we omitted discussion of what produced the more than 300 independent or semi-independent state agencies in the first place. As we have now seen, one reason for such a multiplicity of organizational units is the durability and the conservatism of organizations. Their refusal to die and their reluctance to innovate continually forces the political system to create new organizations to handle the constantly emerging demands for public service. This, in turn, tends to clutter up the bureaucratic landscape with more organizations than it needs or can possible handle.

One consequence of this is an ever increasing span of control and an ever decreasing accountability. Other states besides Massachusetts provide examples of how this works. When the Florida House Reorganization Committee set about reducing that state's 200-odd agencies to 25, it found it could not even locate 16 of these agencies! The proliferation of organizations at the federal level, meanwhile, has helped to encourage American presidents to try to centralize more control in the White House. In some instances this has amounted to setting up a whole new bureaucracy to run various key governmental functions such as foreign affairs and poverty programs.

Another and possibly more costly consequence of adding on agencies are the problems created in terms of coordination. Squeezing an ever increasing number of agencies into a relatively fixed amount of bureaucratic territory puts these agencies on a collision course with each other. This can cause not just confusion but calamity, for sometimes an agency will expend more energy and effort in curbing and even curtailing a competitor than in trying to achieve its own purported goals.

The pathology of growth presents similar problems. As an agency grows in size, not only does its output usually fail to grow proportionately but it may actually fall. In other words, an organization may increase its number of employees by 20 percent only to see its productivity *decrease* by, say, 10 percent. Here too the problem is one of coordination. As Peter Drucker has noted, "The more people have to work together, the more time will be spent on 'inter-acting' rather than on work and accomplishment."[73] Another management consultant, Martin R. Smith, claims that "contrary to popular belief, the overstaffed organization does not get out more work than the leaner organization. People devote their time to the wrong tasks in the fat department and

---

73. Peter Drucker, *The Effective Executive* (New York: Harper & Row, 1967), p. 31.

they are constantly tripping over each other."[74] Herbert Simon puts it in a more pithy manner. "It is not very easy to thread a needle if one person holds the thread and another the needle."[75]

As an organization becomes bloated, the costs of this interactional process climb. Former Deputy Secretary of Defense David Packard found this to be true in the Pentagon's defense procurement activity, his special area of attention during his term of service. Once noting that "we have a real mess on our hands." Packard went on to say, "We don't need more people in the act—we need fewer people. We overorganize, overman, overspend and underaccomplish."[76] Military history supplies substantial confirmation of Packard's observation regarding the dangers of overabundance. The Germans used only 150,000 men to defeat, in six weeks, a French army that was actually ten times as large. Genghis Kahn conquered half the world with an army that was only one-half the size of the present New York City bureaucracy. And the Israeli army, which is considered even by our own military establishment to be, man-for-man, a more effective fighting force, has one general for every 21,000 enlisted men. The American army has one general for every 1,600 enlisted men.

The price of pathology, we should remember, cannot be assessed in only monetary terms. There is also the cost in human suffering from services wrongly rendered or not rendered at all. George Teeling Smith who directs the Office of Health Economics in Great Britain has pointed out that a hospital will exert every effort to obtain funds for a new kidney machine. The same amount of money would alleviate much more human misery if it were spent on such simple but nonprestigious tasks as widening the front doors of the rooms and apartments of paraplegics who have to use wheelchairs.

A final point remains to be considered. To what extent are the organizational pathologies we have been examining limited to public and semi-public institutions? Does the private sector manage to avoid them?

There is certainly evidence to indicate that such has been the case. If the American army was still maintaining horse cavalry during the 1930's, the blacksmiths in the private sector were rapidly going out of business. Profit does provide a direct and decisive feedback to the private sector, and a business can and usually does go bankrupt if it is not providing in a reasonably efficient manner those goods and services which the public actually wants. While business can to some extent manipulate its markets through advertising, the annals of business are

---

74. Martin R. Smith, *I Hate to See a Manager Cry* (Reading, Mass.: Addison-Wesley, 1973), p. 9.
75. Simon, *op. cit.*, p. 238.
76. Packard quoted in Proxmire, *op. cit.*, p. 68.

strewn with products such as Edsel cars, Champale beer, chemise dresses and midi skirts, which the public rejected. Even supposedly monopolistic industries are limited in the extent they can ignore public needs and the needs of efficient production without suffering losses. The steel and auto industries have achieved much lower earnings growth than business as a whole during the past decade, while such giants as Dupont, Alcoa and even IBM have seen their share of the markets in their respective industries steadily fade. The winds of change cut through the private sector with a much greater force and greater impact than they do through the bastions of public bureaucracy.

On the other hand, however, profit seeking may generate its own pathologies such as an excessive and even counterproductive competitive atmosphere. Furthermore, business is becoming more bureaucratized all the time. Those who manage the typical large firm are no longer those who own it. Thus, many of the pathologies of the public sector are pushing their way into the private sector as well. Martin R. Smith tells of a firm which used to allow the manufacturer of its packaging machinery to provide all the engineering services needed to keep the machinery operating properly. This the machinery maker was willing to do at no additional cost. In time, however, the firm began to wonder if it could do a better job of servicing the equipment by itself.

It first hired a specialist for this purpose. The specialist soon decided he needed some specialized equipment for his work. Then, he persuaded the company to engage a technician to operate the testing equipment and a machinist to implement the machine design changes which the specialist was drawing up. By this time paper work was becoming a problem and so a secretary was added.

"Within two years after the company had hired an engineer to perform a very specific task," writes Smith, "it had established an Engineering Machinery Department with a payroll of six people and an expensive testing laboratory to maintain. This, mind you, supplanted the free services provided by the packaging machinery manufacturer!"[77]

CASE STUDY

Sorry State[78]

When Henry Kissinger became Secretary of State in late 1973, he took over a department that had reached a nadir in effectiveness and reputation. "Foggy

---

77. Smith, *op. cit.*, p. 7.
78. The primary source of factual material and quotations for the following case study was John Franklin Campbell, *The Foreign Affairs Fudge Factory* (New York: Basic Books, 1971). Other sources included Charles Frankel, *High on Foggy Bottom* (New York: Harper & Row, 1968); Arthur M. Schlesinger, Jr., *A Thousand Days* (New York: Fawcett World Library, 1967); and Stewart Alsop, *The Center* (New York: Harper & Row, 1968).

Bottom," as the department is known in Washington, never seemed more foggy or more at the bottom. Even its friends no longer showed it any affection or regard, and the midwestern isolationists and others who distrusted and often despised the "striped-pants set" at State had now found allies in such figures as George Kennan, the late and distinguished former Secretary Dean Acheson and a growing number of disenchanted ex-Foreign Service officers. According to former Ambassador to India John Kenneth Galbraith, "It's the kind of organization which, though it does big things badly, does small things badly, too."[79]

The diagnosis of advanced organizational pathology has actually been confirmed, at least in part, by the department itself. In 1970, Undersecretary William MaComber set up thirteen task forces to study what was wrong. The task force on creativity noted that for the past twenty years State had been "applying the principles of the late 1940's in an increasingly rigid way to international conditions that were constantly changing. . . . Its creative arteries hardening, the department as an institution was unable to meet adequately and in some cases even to recognize the innovative demands of the early 60's."

Arthur Schlesinger cites one example of this during his period as an aide to John F. Kennedy. State, says Schlesinger, continued to refer to the "Sino-Soviet bloc" for years after the bloc had all too noticeably split. Indeed, it was still using the term when Russia and China were actually engaged in some rather bitter border clashes. Schlesinger records how he spent three years in a "plaintive" effort to induce the department to drop the phrase. Though he spoke with the authority of the president, his efforts did not avail.

Presidents had become increasingly provoked by the State Department's intransigence as well as its insipidness. Faced with a fast-developing Berlin crisis early in his administration, John Kennedy asked the department to draft a response to the Russians. It took a month to get such a response to his urgent request, and when the response arrived, it turned out to be a compilation of old positions that was not even readable. From then on Kennedy began bypassing the department more and more, relying on his staff, his Attorney General brother and even outsiders to conduct foreign relations work. According to Schlesinger, "The President used to divert himself with a dream of establishing . . . a secret office of thirty people to run foreign policy while maintaining the State Department as a facade in which people might contentedly carry papers from bureau to bureau." The extensive use which President Nixon made of Henry Kissinger and his National Security Council staff during Nixon's first term leads one to suppose that the Kennedy dream may actually have come close to being fulfilled.

Like many pathological organizations, the State Department has experienced phenomenal growth. Its budget amounted to only $15 million in 1930 but was approaching the half-billion-dollar mark by the mid-1970's. Even after adjusting for inflation, this represented an increase of nearly 1,000 percent. While America's international responsibilities during this time grew

---

79. Quoted in Frankel, *op. cit.*, p. 11.

considerably, the growth in budget and staff does seem disproportionate. Former Foreign Service Officer John Franklin Campbell points out that the United States employs five to ten times more people in foreign affairs work than do Great Britain, France, West Germany or Japan. While no figures are available for the Soviet Union in this respect, Campbell notes that the American Embassy in any world capital is usually about twice as large as its Russian counterpart.

Campbell cites the experience of former colleague Ellis Briggs for an example of how such overstaffing takes place. When Briggs was Ambassador to Brazil, he received notice that a Ph.D. in physics had been assigned to his mission as a science attache. Briggs promptly sent back a cable saying, "The American Embassy in Rio de Janeiro needs a science attache the way a cigar store Indian needs a brassiere." Briggs received an icy reply from the department's Undersecretary for Administration: "Your telegram did not amuse the White House." A short time later the science attache arrived and began to make himself busy.

In his previous mission as Ambassador to Czechoslovakia, Briggs noticed how the department's zeal for overstaffing actually, though unwittingly, foiled an attempt by the Czechoslovakian Communist government to punish it. Angered over some incident and wishing to show its displeasure, the Czechs ordered the American Embassy to slash the size of its mission from 78 to 12. However, instead of hurting the Embassy it helped it, for the mission functioned much more efficiently with a much smaller payroll.

True to the logic, if that is the proper term, of organizational growth, the State Department's expansion has been disproportionately concentrated in the upper levels and in the administrative spheres. From 1938 to 1969, for example, the department's total number of American employees went from 963 to 6,874, an increase of about 700 percent. During the same period, the number of employees in its top-level secretariat jumped from 21 to 342, an increase of over 1,600 percent, or more than double the rate of growth for the department as a whole. Campbell cites an "elder statesman" who, in being recalled by President Kennedy to temporary duty, noted twice as many assistant secretaries and deputies as he remembered in his last term of service a decade before. Helpers of one kind or another had also mushroomed. "I have three people on my staff," he reportedly said, "who spend all their time attending meetings so they can come back and 'brief' me about what was said at the meetings. The funny thing is, I don't give a damn about what was said at any of those meetings."

When we examine the Foreign Service itself we find the same forces at work. The Foreign Service has eight grades starting with Grade 8 at the bottom and proceeding to Grade 1 at the top. By 1969, Grade 8 had only 26 members; Grade 1 had 324 or almost 12 times as many.

The growth in administrative staff also has proceeded apace. By fiscal year 1970, the department had 2,580 employed in purely administrative matters, while another 2,267 worked for the department's ten functional bureaus. As for the five main "action" or geographic bureaus, their personnel complement came to only 980, and even these "action" bureaus managed to assign a high percentage of their work forces to administrative concerns. "In the African bureau," writes Campbell, "some 44 of its 166 personnel or 27 percent were administrative staff dealing with such matters as budget, personnel assignments, selection of supplies for African posts, processing of official travel between Washington and Africa, and the like. But separate and much larger department-wide administrative offices already existed for all of these functions under the department undersecretary for administration. Thus much of the work was duplicated and 'coordinated' between two distinct offices."

The bulging service staffs here, as in most cases, encounter little difficulty in keeping themselves busy. Along with the time-consuming tasks of "coordinating," they insist on furnishing the department's missions with everything they could possibly need from paper clips on up. Supplying toilet paper for East European posts, for example, absorbs a good deal of their bureaucratic energies.

The costs involved in all this administrative activity are fairly immense. In 1970 it required $25,000 a year to maintain an average State Department employee in a foreign mission. Furthermore, other costs are incurred which, while they bear no precise price tag, may yet be more significant.

One of these costs is insularity. Since the State Department insists on supplying its overseas personnel with housing and other goods and services, instead of letting these people scrounge for themselves, it helps isolate them from the citizenry of the country to which they are assigned. In effect, the department maintains what Campbell calls a "PX culture." This refers to the PX's or canteens that American military bases set up to provide armed services personnel with various goods and services which are not easily or cheaply available outside the barracks. The State Department's administrative service units, like the military PX's, keep American personnel from developing and maintaining many useful contacts with, and acquiring increased knowledge of, the people of the country in which they are stationed. They also may lead directly to jealousy and bad feeling since the goods and services being supplied to the Americans may be unobtainable to the citizens of these countries.

Another cost involved is the growth of paper work that such inflated staffing produces. Schlesinger tells of how Averell Harriman, soon after rejoining the State Department, received a courtesy call from a foreign ambassador. When the ambassador was ushered in, a junior State Department officer mysteriously appeared and began taking notes. When Harriman asked what he was doing, the young man replied that he was preparing to write a memo on the conversation and circulate it to all interested bureaus and embassies. Harriman, "shuddering at the proliferation of paper and expenditure of energy involved," sent him away.

Paper proliferation in the Department of State often takes the form of expensive cables. Stewart Alsop reports that a spot check made on January 28, 1966 showed the department sending and receiving 1,283 telegraphic messages during a 24-hour period. The State Department's cable traffic surpasses that of the Associated Press and United Press International combined, and the 215,361 words contained on the cables on the day mentioned exceeded the total wordage in Tolstoy's monumental novel *War and Peace*. During the Arab-Israeli war a few months later, an order went out barring all telegrams except for genuine emergencies. Alsop quotes a State Department official as describing what happened. "People had nothing to do. There were no telegrams to initial or comment on. Everybody was going crazy, just sitting around reading the papers."

An excess of paper usually indicates an excess of control, and the State Department bears witness to this fact. Although the Soviet Union as a nation is far more centralized than the United States, its embassies operate in a more decentralized fashion than do our own. According to Alsop, a Russian ambassador can offer scholarships and even commit his nation to major projects such as dams. The American ambassador must clear even miniscule matters with Washington.

These heavy chains of control encumber those at headquarters as well as those in the field. "To send a cable to our embassy at Lisbon concerning the U.S. Naval bases in the Azores," writes Campbell, "the country director for Spain and Portugal must first 'clear' his draft message with several other offices—perhaps with the African and International Organization Bureaus because of colonial and U.N. ramifications, perhaps with the NATO office of the European Bureau since Portugal is a NATO member, perhaps with the Bureau of Politico-Military Affairs (and through it with the Department of Defense) since this is a military matter. After these 'lateral clearances' are obtained, the story is not over. The drafter may then try to consult his assistant secretary (going through one of several deputy assistant secretaries and a bureau staff). If the matter is of sufficient importance, the assistant secretary may pass the draft up through the executive secretariat to the undersecretaries or the Secretary of State on the seventh floor who may want the opinion of other assistant secretaries. The White House and other agencies such as the CIA and the Treasury may be consulted."

Top officials themselves are not spared such problems even when they are dealing with relatively minor matters. Nicholas Katzenbach on becoming number two man at State under President Johnson was startled to learn that clearing a routine cable on the subject of milk exports required twenty-nine separate signatures.

Arthur Schlesinger points out the relationship of the increasing control with the department's increase in employees and its concomitant decrease in effectiveness. "As it grew in size," he writes, "the Department diminished in usefulness. This was in part the consequence of bureaucratization. 'Layering'—the bureaucrat's term for the position of one level of administrative responsibility on top of another—created a system of 'concurrences,' which required every proposal to run a hopelessly intricate obstacle course before it could become policy. Obviously clearance was necessary to avoid anarchy, but it often became an excuse for doing as little as possible."

The layering described by Schlesinger is rigorously reflected in the department's physical set-up and appurtenances. Charles Frankel, on becoming Assistant Secretary for Cultural Affairs, found that his office was furnished with green wall-to-wall carpeting and a color picture of the president. Looking around he found all other assistant secretaries had the same furnishings. Office directors, however, who were one level below assistant secretaries, had to put up with gray nine-by-twelve carpets and black and white photos of the president. The offices of all other officials from the Secretary to the bottom ranks were strictly outfitted in ways to denote their position in the department's scheme of things.

Great emphasis, says Frankel, is placed on these variations in physical trappings. "A difference in power that wasn't evident in the color of a rug was not a difference." Even the altitude of the offices betokened the department's pecking order. Thus the Secretary and undersecretaries occupied the seventh floor, the assistant secretaries the sixth floor, the office directors the fifth floor, and so on.

But for most of the State Department's leaders, the symbols of power, potent and pervasive though they may be, only highlight their lack of ability to get things done. Like many pathological organizations, State remains a monolith almost impervious to efforts by an enterprising leader to change it. Indeed, the department has a knack for crushing those who would seek to ruffle its routines. Nicholas Katzenbach had achieved a reputation as a forceful and farsighted administrator as head of the Department of Justice under Lyndon Johnson. After becoming the number two man at State, his friends found him depressed, confused and uncertain. At a luncheon which foreign affairs writers tendered to him after he had spent six months at his new job, Katzenbach remarked, "I'm not sure I see much correlation between what I do here and how the State Department runs."[80]

The same feeling apparently pervades the lower echelons to an even greater extent. The Foreign Service resignation rate has climbed markedly in recent years, and, according to Campbell, would probably have risen even higher if more outside jobs were available for ex-FSO's. One officer who managed to find a position with another government agency said, "There is just not enough work for senior officers. The average officer is utilized to about 50 percent of his capacity. Many of them are sitting in offices with desks and secretaries, but with nothing to do." And while the resignation rate is rising, the recruitment rate is going down. The number of applicants for the Foreign Service plummeted nearly 50 percent during the late 1960's, says Campbell, and the raw scores of those passing the entrance tests declined noticeably all through the decade.

In all fairness it should be noted that State's weaknesses are not all of its own doing. Its problems, at least in part, result from problems imposed upon it. Although it has experienced a good deal of growth, the foreign affairs activities of other federal agencies have grown still more. It is estimated that

---

80. *New York Times Magazine*, November 12, 1967.

80 percent of all civilians officially representing the United States overseas work for other government organizations. State, overpopulated with personnel as it may be, is no longer a master in its own house.

This abundance of competition can produce all kinds of demoralizing effects. One former Foreign Service officer tells of serving as a political analyst in a European capital during the early 1960's. Alongside him were two other analysts, each of them assigned to monitor and report on one of that country's three major political parties. But working in the next office down the hall were three CIA men who were engaged in many of the same activities. "I remember once waiting to interview the leader of the political party I was assigned to when out of his office came one of the CIA men. He had probably just finished asking this man the same questions I was going to ask. Boy, did I feel foolish when my turn came."[81]

The cold war and its many manifestations did a good deal of damage to the department. State was one of Senator Joseph McCarthy's favorite targets, and his relentless attacks ended the service of many of the department's top people. The wounds that State sustained during those turbulent times have still not completely healed.

Then, the State Department, has suffered from poor leadership. John Foster Dulles, who headed the department during most of the Eisenhower years, was not only limited in his foreign policy perspectives but was even more limited in his administrative ability. A consummate lawyer—he had graduated at the top of his class at Yale Law School—Dulles was a soloist with little sense of how to delegate duties or how to operate an organization. He treated the department as a law office designed only to provide him with clerical assistance while he carried the department's business around in his briefcase, flying from country to country, in an attempt to settle all foreign affairs matters personally. Dean Rusk, who served during the Kennedy-Johnson years, traveled much less but allowed other agencies, particularly the Department of Defense, to dominate foreign policy. And William Rogers, President Nixon's first appointee to the secretaryship, was a genial lawyer with no foreign affairs experience.

Finally, though many presidents have bemoaned the department's lack of inspired initiative, they themselves have contributed to its sorry situation. Presidents customarily find foreign affairs much more interesting and important than domestic matters. They also usually have a much freer hand in the foreign arena than in the domestic one. These factors, aided and abetted by the advantages of improved communications, have induced presidents more and more to be their own Secretary of State and to ignore their Department of State. By continually slighting the department, they continually weaken it.

Defenders of State can also claim that the White House staff set up to provide something of an alternative State Department seems to be showing

---

81. The Foreign Service officer who is quoted on his experience in West Germany is an acquaintance of the author who prefers not to be identified.

some of the same characteristics. By 1972, the White House foreign affairs staff was employing about seventy people or about four times the number employed during the previous administration. Thus, it could be argued that the agency that was supposed to compensate for State's many shortcomings was itself becoming infected with the same disease. Such is the potency of pathology in organizational life.

5

People and Personnel

Since organizations are primarily clusters of people, it logically follows that personnel policies and practices play a primary role in organizational life. "Let me control personnel," George Kennan has said, "and I will ultimately control policy. For the part of the machine that recruits and hires and fires and promotes people can soon control the entire shape of the institution."[1]

Few administrative theorists or practitioners would dispute this statement, and in the course of history, few able administrators have thought or acted otherwise. However, their attitudes and approaches to the subject have often differed. Thomas Jefferson, for example, believed that civil servants should be provided with "drudgery and subsistence only" so that they would not want to stay too long in office.[2] This would enable the country to escape the establishment and growth of an administrative class, a development which Jefferson greatly feared. His fears were echoed by an American business journal in the 1920's which published an editorial stressing "the urgency of keeping this country's civil service ineffective lest it become dangerous."[3]

Most writers on, and practitioners of, administration have, however, taken a different tack, and through the years increasing effort has gone toward improving the capabilities and enhancing the stature of those who toil in the public sector. Today, the stress almost everywhere is placed upon strengthening the competency of civil servants, and it is with this goal in mind that the subject of personnel will be pursued here.

---

1. Quoted in Campbell, *The Foreign Affairs Fudge Factory*, pp. 139-140.
2. Quoted in Campbell, *op. cit.*, p. 47.
3. Berkley, *The Administrative Revolution* (1971), p. 141.

PROCEDURES AND POLICIES

Public organizations in this country essentially use óne of two different methods in establishing and operating personnel systems. One method stresses political appointment and election, the other emphasizes an objective determination of merit.

Political appointment and election has a long if not always proud history in the United States. Units of the Revolutionary Army frequently elected their own officers, and once the hostilities ended, states and their communities undertook to elect most of the administrators they would need. This practice has persisted in many places up to the present day, and no other major country in the world elects so many of its administrators as does the United States. Most state governments elect at least some officials whose tasks would be regarded as purely administrative in Europe or Canada. Many cities and towns, particularly older ones, follow the same practice. Some New England communities elect as many as fifty officials. Newer areas of the country such as the Far West disdain such practices, but even they maintain county organizations with a high number of elective posts.

Political scientists have tended to frown on this practice and with good reason. Although election is supposed to give the people a deciding voice in determining who will administer their government, it tends to lead to all sorts of abuses such as confusing and misleading promises and campaign funding from special interests. Underlying all such problems is the fact that most of the electorate finds it impossible to know all the candidates for whom they must vote. A study done some years ago in Michigan showed that 73 percent of those polled could not identify the state's secretary of state, 75 percent could not name the state highway commissioner, 77 percent had no idea who the superintendent of public instruction was, 80 percent did not know the state attorney general and a full 96 percent were at a loss to name the state treasurer. This survey was carried out shortly after a state election in which most of the respondents presumably had cast ballots for those whose names they now did not know.

Politically appointing administrators is a practice that also dates back to colonial times. Even John Adams, who considered himself something of a paragon of political propriety, felt constrained to provide his ne'er-do-well son-in-law with a government job. Such practices gained increased favor with the arrival of Andrew Jackson at the White House. Jackson strongly adhered to Jefferson's belief in rotating public servants in office. At the same time he did not believe that this would entail any loss of public confidence. As he put it, "The duties of all public servants are, or at least admit of being made, so plain and simple that men of intelligence may readily qualify themselves for their performance."[4] Of course, Old Hickory's espousal of this philosophy was fortified by the fact that he had a virtual army of job seekers at his back who were clamoring loudly for the plums of patronage.

From Jackson's time on American presidents found themselves frequently besieged by persons seeking positions on the public payroll. One aggressive appointment seeker jumped into Abraham Lincoln's carriage to press his case while the president was riding through Washington. Lincoln started to listen to him but then drove him away saying, more in despair than in anger, "No, I will not do business in the street."

When a disappointed job seeker assassinated President James Garfield in 1881, the nation's appetite for such administrative practices began to change. However, political appointment continued to play a prominent role in American administrative life. As we noted in chapter two, our presidents have nearly one hundred times as many appointments to fill as do British prime ministers. At the lower levels, political appointment still prevails in many American states. While the governor of Wisconsin has only twenty jobs to fill and the governor of Oregon has less than a dozen, New York State's chief executive has nearly 21,000 positions at his disposal and Pennsylvania's governor can name 50,000 to state posts.[5]

But the assassination of President Garfield did have its effect. It gave rise to an alternative method of recruitment, namely the merit system. Two years after the president's violent death, Congress passed the Pendleton Act, setting up a systematized procedure for hiring and employing vast categories of federal civil servants. The merit system principle has continued to grow ever since. Today it not only embraces over 90 percent of all positions in the federal government but includes increasing numbers of employees in state and local governments as well. About two-thirds of our states now have what are called comprehensive merit systems which cover the vast majority of their job holders. And even the remaining states make some provisions for merit system appointments. The federal government has helped prod states and municipalities to move in this direction, for federal grants-in-aid frequently require the recipient agency to operate a merit system of some sort. Thus, HEW will not hand out any funds to a local welfare department that uses political appointment to recruit its case workers.

Although the merit principle has consistently climbed in public favor, the more traditional method of political appointment continues to have its supporters. Its backers claim that such a system provides

---

4. Quoted in Paul Van Riper, *History of the United States Civil Service* (New York: Harper & Row, 1958), p. 36.
5. Martin and Susan Tolchin, *To the Victor. . .* (New York: Random House, 1971), p. 96.

government with more flexibility and responsiveness. Elected officials, or at least officials appointed directly by elected office holders, are in a better position to control administrative activities and translate programs into action. A merit system, its detractors claim, leads eventually to a triumph of mediocrity with initiative and enterprise sacrificed to the pressures for security and the forces of stagnation. Finally, even when a merit system actually encourages merit, it may only lead to a "meritocracy" which shuts out otherwise capable people who cannot pass its tests or meet its formal and often irrelevant requirements.

Some who articulate this view compare Chicago with New York City. The merit principle seems less firmly ensconced in the midwestern metropolis than in the eastern one, and in 1972 one could find politically loyal civil servants holding "temporary" appointments at $17,000 or more a year for over twenty years in defiance of the spirit if not the letter of the local merit system. The claim was often made at this time that "Chicago works" while New York City seemed to be faltering badly.

But though the merit system may have lost some of its luster through the years, it retains a good deal of support from both theorists and practitioners. If it leads to a "meritocracy" then, they say, this is still likely to be more egalitarian and more in conformity with democratic ideals than a system built on political contacts and allegiances. When operated properly it recruits the better people and encourages them to stay and develop their capabilities.

Its supporters also deny that merit system employees will automatically block the implementation of new policies by elected officials. They point to Great Britain where the top officials of the bureaucracy, despite the fact that they themselves were largely members of the upper classes, cheerfully implemented the rather sweeping socialist policies of the Labour government that took office in 1945. (A less appealing example of this same flexibility is the German civil service which displayed few qualms in carrying out Hitler's policies in the 1930's.)[6] If Chicago seems to "work" better than New York City, then a somewhat greater acceptance of the merit system in the latter city is probably not responsible. California cities seem to have less problems than New York City or even Chicago, but their bureaucracies are almost completely covered by well-enforced merit systems. An editorial in the *Los Angeles Times* of April 5, 1973 credited "the momentum of a strong and professional civil service" for the fact that America's third largest city did not suffer "some of the malignancies that infect other major American cities."

---

6. See Richard Greenberger, *The 12-Year Reich* (New York: Holt, Rinehart and Winston, 1971), Chapter 9 for an illuminating picture of Hitler's impact on the German civil service.

Recruitment

If the merit principle has become the most widely accepted basis for personnel operation in American administration, it nevertheless contin- ues to catalyze controversies and pose problems. In terms of recruit- ment there is first the task of making sure that the system is truly merit- rewarding. Most civil service systems make extensive use of comparative examinations to bring this about. While such exams may more impar- tially weigh the merits of the various candidates than would a system built on favoritism or capriciousness, they still offer difficulties of their own.

For one thing, the exams must be predictive. In other words, high scores on the examinations should correlate with high performance on the job and vice versa. Unfortunately, in the majority of cases little attempt has been made up to recently to ensure that such correlations exist. A joint survey by the Office of Economic Opportunity, the Depart- ment of Labor and the National Civil Service League in 1970 found that only 54 percent of all state and local governments conducted any test validation, and most of these governments limited such validation ef- forts to only a few agencies. Other recruitment standards were also found to have gone unvalidated, often with damaging results to all con- cerned. The survey team came upon one city which desperately needed 38 dogcatchers but could not hire a single one. The criteria for the job called for all recruits to have high school diplomas plus two years expe- rience in handling animals. None of the few people who could meet these qualifications wanted the job.[7]

The issue of the validity of tests and other recruitment criteria has come to the fore in recent years thanks to the stepped-up efforts to recruit members of minority groups into government service. Civil rights supporters claim that many of these criteria serve to exclude blacks, Puerto Ricans, Chicanos and others. In so doing, they thus fail to deter- mine the true capability of a job applicant. A study in Chicago found that a black police recruit would perform as well as a white recruit who scored 10 percent higher on the entrance exam.[8] In other words, the entrance test failed to measure the true ability of black applicants for police work in comparison with white applicants.

The federal government has been moving to require test valida- tion as a means of ensuring and expanding equal opportunity. In Janu- ary 1973 the Department of Justice filed suits against the fire depart- ments of Boston, Los Angeles and Montgomery, Alabama, charging that

7. Herschel Cribb, "Public Jobs and the Disadvantaged," *Opportunity,* October 1972.
8. Cited in Patrick V. Murphy, *The Criminal Justice System in Crisis* (Syracuse, N. Y.: Maxwell School of Citizenship and Affairs, 1972).

their recruitment tests, qualifications and selection standards generally "have not been shown to be required by the needs of the fire department or predictive of successful job performance."[9]

The move to include more members of minority groups in public administration is part of a larger movement aimed at making government agencies more representative of the public they serve. This brings us to another issue in administration. Government agencies have at times become "captured" by one or more particular sectors of society. The "captive" agency—the term is Professor Brian Chapman's—tends to recruit heavily from one particular ethnic, religious, social or geographical group. Many American police forces, for example, have long been dominated by men of Irish descent. The army at one time drew a disproportionate number of its members, particularly at the officer level, from white southerners. And the Foreign Service long leaned toward upper-class Anglo-Saxons with preparatory school and Ivy League backgrounds to fill its ranks.

Such tendencies, it should be noted, do not necessarily spring from any intentional policy on the part of the agency concerned. Often it may arise by chance and then continue as members of the particular group involved are drawn toward the agency where so many of their fellow members are employed. Some might even claim that certain groups possess characteristics that naturally lend themselves to certain types of work. If New York City's school department is over 50 percent Jewish, this may simply signify that Jewish Americans are more oriented to and equipped for educational work. In a similar vein, others might argue that Irish Americans have the physical courage and the social skills that make them better policemen, while upper-class Anglo-Saxons can lay claim to a background and culture that equips them, as well as inclines them, toward the practice of diplomacy.

Whatever the merits of these arguments, capture by a particular group does bestow some benefits on an agency. Having personnel from a similar background eases communication problems and creates more harmonious operations. However, there are also costs to be paid.

The spy scandals that blew up in Great Britain during the 1950's illustrate just what these costs can be. These spies, who were agents of the Soviet Union, were also, like most of their associates, members of the British upper classes and graduates of prestigious universities. As a result, their fellow members of the establishment could never believe that they could be traitors, though the behavior of some of them should have led their superiors and co-workers to wonder. Referring to two of

---

9. *Boston Sunday Globe,* January 28, 1973.

these Soviet agents, Guy Burgess and Donald Maclean, Robin Maugham writes "These two outrageous characters would never have lasted two months if they'd been working for some reputable business company. They would have been sacked. Why were they kept on by our intelligence service? Why? Because in those days our intelligence service was run by an 'Old Boy' network and backed up by an Establishment of crypto-queer ambassadors."[10]

Another example of the costs of "capture" was the domination of the German Foreign Office by members of the Junker class during World War I. According to historian Barbara Tuchman, the Junkers reinforced each other's provincial tendencies. Not only did they fail to win friends for Germany but they succeeded in losing many of the friends the country already had.[11]

An agency that draws its recruits from all sectors of the population will stand a better chance of escaping these problems. More importantly, such an agency will more likely become infused with new ideas and new energies. It is more apt to be responsive to other organizations as well as to the diverse publics it is supposed to serve. Katz and Kahn cite research showing that homogeneous groups "produced fewer high-quality solutions than did heterogeneous groups" and, so these authors claim, an organization which continues to recruit one type of employee comes to resemble itself more and more closely as time passes until it turns into a virtual caricature of itself.[12]

Public organizations should not only broaden their recruitment base but should make sure that they draw from this broader base the maximum number of A-1 applicants. Government agencies, at least in this country, have often been quite lax in this regard. Many have made little use of advertising and other publicity techniques. Furthermore, their competitive examinations, irrespective of their validity or lack of same, have often been cumbersome and costly to perspective employee and employer alike. Processing the tests, meanwhile, usually entails a waiting period during which time many of the better recruits receive and accept job offers elsewhere.

Here again, fortunately, change is slowly coming. Many agencies have begun to recruit more aggressively and some are abridging and even eliminating the examination process. The latter tendency has been particularly pronounced in certain professional fields. Thus, doctors, nurses and teachers who possess requisite certification are seldom subjected to examinations when they choose to work for a public hospital

---

10. Robin Maugham, *Escape from the Shadows* (New York: McGraw-Hill, 1973), p. 175.
11. Barbara W. Tuchman, *The Zimmerman Telegram* (New York: Bantam Books), p. 113.
12. Katz and Kahn, *The Social Psychology of Organization,* p. 404.

or school system. This trend seems likely to grow as professionalism increases in society and as the need for flexibility and responsiveness grows in public personnel policy.

Although it is desirable for public agencies to recruit aggressively, it is also important for them to do what is in effect the opposite. They should discourage the unsuitable as much as they encourage the suitable. A shy introvert or a violence-prone individual should not be induced to take a policeman's exam, while the person who cannot stand routine should not be encouraged to seek a file clerk position. The personnel administrator should try to dissuade the overqualified as much as the underqualified. A Ph.D. is likely to turn into as poor a sorter of mail as would the semi-literate who has difficulty reading simple addresses.

One government agency that takes great care to discourage the unsuitable from seeking to join its ranks is the Forest Service. Being a forest ranger means long hours of rigorous, responsible and often lonely work usually performed in rather isolated outposts. It also means constant rotation. In its recruitment efforts, the Service tries to make it very clear that those who would find such a life distasteful should seek their careers elsewhere.[13]

In 1968, the British army began trying a new device designed both to encourage those equipped for military life to join up and to discourage the unsuitable from doing so. Perspective enlistees were offered a chance to try out the army on approval. Any young man contemplating an army career could enlist for a four-day trial period. If he found it to his liking, he could then sign up for a full term. If, on the other hand, he found it was not his cup of tea, he could leave with no hard feelings and with $11.80 in his pocket, his pay for an abbreviated term of military service.[14]

The Post-Recruitment Phase

The personnel agency, once it has cleared a group of recruits, will then usually place their names on a list. Such a list is rarely alphabetical. Rather, it runs in order of eligibility with the top scorers on the exam placing first and continuing down the line. However, many other factors may also figure into the standings. One of these is veterans preference. The federal and most state and local civil service systems award some bonus points to those who have served in the armed forces. The federal government bestows five points for such service alone and five additional points if the applicant qualifies as a disabled veteran.

---

13. Herbert Kaufman, *The Forest Ranger* (Baltimore: Johns Hopkins Press, 1960), pp. 161–165.
14. *New York Times,* December 15, 1968.

Agencies customarily take their recruits from the top of the list, but here again there are some exceptions. In some cases, particularly for higher level positions, the rule of three may apply. This permits the appointing authority to skip the top scorer or even the second scorer on the list of qualified applicants. They can choose any of the top three. The advantages of permitting such discretion for certain positions are obvious. An applicant may score highest in a well-thought-out exam for public relations officer, but if he exudes unpleasant breath and body odors, changes his shirt every two weeks, and shows fondness for picking his nose in public, he is not likely to perform the agency's public relations duties in the most effective manner.

In addition to these perfectly proper ways of relaxing their requirement to take recruits from the top of the list, agencies sometimes resort to more surreptitious strategies. They may hold off taking any recruits at all until they can be sure that enough people at the top of the list will have found other jobs or moved away so that some favored person or persons further down the list can be reached. The lists themselves usually expire after one or two years, and an agency may wait until such a list expires in order to gain someone who will be on the new list. Or the appointing authority may let the list expire and discourage attempts to set up a new one, choosing instead to fill positions on a temporary basis.

There is nothing inherently suspect about temporary appointments and virtually all merit systems make some provisions for them. Usually such appointments can be made only for prescribed periods such as thirty working days. Abuses have come when such appointments are indefinitely extended. The federal government and some state and local jurisdictions have taken steps to counteract this by prohibiting any temporary appointee from serving successive terms in any particular position. However, many other jurisdictions are more lenient—hence, the ability of Chicago mayors to name precinct captains to temporary positions lasting several years and even decades.

Assuming the recruit has qualified for and received an appointment, he still has some hurdles to surmount before he can claim full-fledged membership in his organization. One of these is the probationary period. During this time he can be dismissed without the safeguards which protect those who have successfully passed such a phase. Probationary periods vary in length from six months to six years. The six-month term is common in some state and local governments, while the federal government and some other subnational jurisdictions require one year of service. However, it is common to vary the time somewhat depending upon the nature of the position. While a fledgling sanitation man may acquire permanent status in six months, his colleague on the police force may have to wait a full year. At the same time, the local schoolteacher may not be given tenure for three years. The largest waiting periods are usually found at colleges and universities where new faculty members may have to serve six years before becoming tenured. Some positions such as political appointments to high level posts confer no privileges or permanency at all.

Another aspect of the post-recruitment phase concerns training. Some agencies do nearly all their own recruit training. These include police departments, fire departments and the like. Other public bodies such as school systems and public health agencies expect the newcomer to have acquired the needed basic skills beforehand. Generally, the higher the professional level of the position, the more likely it is that the recruit for that position will have obtained his essential training prior to his appointment.

Training of all kinds is receiving increasing attention in public administration today. It has become an accepted fact that a fast-moving and fast-changing society exhibits a high need for, and must place increasing emphasis on, wide-ranging and high level skills. It was not so long ago that a typical policeman's training consisted of some on-the-job supervision. Now he is likely to receive many weeks and even several months schooling at a police academy. The same holds true for many other public positions. Street cleaners are now more apt to operate fairly complicated equipment rather than merely push brooms, and so they too must receive a minimum of instruction to cope with their once simple tasks.

The fastest growing area of attention in regard to training lies in what is called in-service training. The upsurge of interest in this subject arises from the growing realization that in a modern society such as ours, scarcely anyone is ever fully trained for the rest of his career. Not only must his skills be continually upgraded but new skills must frequently be acquired if the employee and his organization are to meet the shifting demands and the changing work patterns that are so characteristic of our present time. More and more administrators are accepting the notion that education is a lifelong process and that the organizations they manage must plan to provide training on a nearly nonstop basis throughout an employee's career.

This brings us to the question of whether an organization should seek to do its own in-service training or whether it should require or encourage the employee to obtain such training from an outside source. Distinct advantages accrue to the organization that does its own in-service training. It should know best just what skills it wishes to develop and what general abilities it wishes to foster. As a result, it can target its training accordingly. Also, the organization may achieve some financial savings in using its own training personnel and facilities. Finally, employees may accept such training more readily and absorb it more rigorously for they can see a direct connection between the training and their organizational life.

But calling in outsiders or sending employees to outside educational institutions may also afford advantages. First, it allows the organization to tap a much wider variety of training talent and training facilities than it is likely to have within its own boundaries. Then, while outside training can sometimes be more costly, it can also on occasion be cheaper. This is particularly true when doing its own training would require the organization to hire people and buy equipment which it cannot fully utilize. Most important of all, perhaps, is the fact that in-house training deprives the employee of the expanded range of educational experience and contacts which can come to him when he obtains his education at an outside institution. Attending classes where his instructor and most of his fellow students represent different intellectual and organizational backgrounds may enable him to absorb new ideas and perspectives which will invigorate his work performance and his entire approach to his work problems. The late philosopher Alfred North Whitehead once said that no mind that has been stretched by a new idea will ever shrink back to its original dimensions, and an organization interested in improving the intellectual capabilities of its employees will probably find that outside education often does this stretching process better than in-house training classes.

Some reasonably recent figures from the federal government illustrate a few of the training trends. In fiscal year 1971, the United States government spent over $200 million in training programs of more than eight hours duration for its employees. (Programs that ran less than eight hours were not reported.) The average length of these training programs was forty-eight hours. An although 74 percent of this training was administered by government agencies themselves for their own employees, these figures represent a modest decline from the 80 percent in-house figure for 1967.[15]

Promotion

Once an employee has cleared all the hurdles and achieved full status as a member of the organization, he then normally starts to think about the possibilities for promotion. Such advancement may come in the form of

---

15. "Employee Training in the Federal Service FY 1967," Report issued in 1968 by the U.S. Civil Service Commission, Washington, D.C.

a simple pay increase, an increase in grade at his present level, or a move up to a new level usually involving at least some new duties and responsibilities.

Merit systems customarily provide two basic criteria for promotion: seniority and merit. In the majority of instances, both factors enter into consideration. The question to be answered is which is the most conducive to effective administration?

The answer at first seems obvious. Merit is normally deemed the best and most beneficial method for determining who shall rise and who shall not. Seniority presents obvious drawbacks. It rewards the incompetent along with the competent. It offers little inducement for the employee to upgrade his skills or exert his best efforts. A seniority system may make it harder for an organization to attract the best and the brightest and may make it even more difficult for it to retain them once they find that moving upward merely is a matter of biding one's time. When those who occupy the upper positions are still enjoying good health, this wait can seem nearly endless.

For these reasons, seniority has often served as a whipping boy of civil service and the dominant role it has played in many merit systems has made them seem far from meritorious. Yet, seniority does have benefits of its own to bestow. First, it is the most truly impartial system possible for conferring promotion. No merit measures can ever achieve the complete objectivity of the seniority principle, for though a dispute may arise as to whether employee A is better than employee B, no dispute is ever likely to spring up over the question of which of them joined the organization first.

As a completely neutral system for promotion, seniority may also put a damper on disruption and discord. There is little incentive to backbite or backstab when such activities are doomed to go unrewarded. Strange as it may seem, the fact that employees have little motivation to seek shortcuts to the top *can*, at least in some instances, induce them to concentrate better on their existing work.

Seniority also can, and the emphasis again is on *can*, stimulate productivity in another way. An employee who knows that his promotion is assured through the gradual piling-up of seniority may have far fewer fears when it comes to speaking out as to what he thinks is wrong and what he thinks will make things better. Since his advancement does not depend on the benign approval of those above him, he may be more inclined to offer suggestions and criticisms when they seem warranted. This will be seen more fully when the problem of employee evaluation is examined.

A seniority system also tends to encourage employee identification with the organization and to reduce turnover. The employee's investment in his job grows every day, for each day's work brings him closer to promotion.

Seniority thus has its blessings and the wise administrator would do well to keep them in mind. It is particularly useful in deciding who gets first choice in such things as vacation time, desk location and the like. And it probably does not deserve the blame that it so often is made to bear for the poor efficiency of many public organizations. As we have seen, seniority has advantages of its own in terms of productivity, and some organizations, such as Japanese industrial firms and government agencies, have not found their rather rigid seniority systems any major deterrent to achieving an extraordinary high output.

However, the trend everywhere is for decreasing the emphasis on seniority in promotion. Civil service systems in this country are gradually whittling down the prominent position which they had previously accorded this method of promotion. The federal government today makes little use of it as such and many other jurisdictions are reducing its role. Most administrators favor genuine merit systems for at least major promotions and most writers on administration agree with them.

Promotion by merit requires some way of determining merit and this opens up another set of problems. Two basic means exist for making such determinations, examinations and performance. Competitive examinations are the most impartial, and as such may confer some of the benefits associated with the seniority system. They reduce the role of internal politics and ensure all employees something of an equal opportunity to move upward.

Be this as it may, using competitive examinations as a basis for determining promotion is going out of favor. Again the federal government now makes little use of such devices in deciding who is to be promoted and who is not, and many state and local civil service commissions are slowly starting to follow suit. There are many reasons for this trend. For one thing, exams are bothersome for administrators to give and for employees to take. Also, the exams cannot be given every day and once given they must be corrected and tabulated. This procedure usually entails a waiting period which can be exasperating to the employee and disruptive to the organization since it may need someone to fill the vacant post right away.

A much more important consideration is the fact that examinations do not, and in many cases probably cannot, determine just how well the applicant will fare in his new role. Supervisory positions, for example, require leadership qualities and these are difficult to determine by answers to written questions. Two examples illustrate some of the problems that may occur. The joint OEO, Labor Department and Civil Service League survey cited earlier found a case where a mechanic

139

had received seven provisional promotions to shop foreman. Each time, he performed outstandingly in his position, but each time he lost it when he flunked the written test. The other example concerns the case of a New York City patrolman who was found by the *New York Times* on February 20, 1973 to possess a Ph.D. in psychology. Why was he only a patrolman? It seems that Officer Harvey Schlossberg had been spending so much time doing his graduate work that he failed to study enough for the sergeant's exam and so had failed it. Consequently, despite all his education and his useful skills as a psychologist, Dr. Schlossberg was still pounding a beat.

But whether an organization relies on seniority or merit, and whether it measures merit through examination or performance, a further question arises: To what extent should an organization promote its own members at all?

This brings us to the issue of lateral entry. Organizations may fill upper level positions from within or without. When they accept outsiders for posts other than those at the bottom level, they are using what is called lateral entry. It is an almost universal practice in the private sector, but is far less common in the public one. Many public organizations such as most police departments, fire departments, sanitation departments make no provision at all for lateral entry except for occasional highly specialized positions. Other organizations such as school departments may allow lateral entry only at the uppermost level. Thus, the school superintendent may come in from outside the school department, but the assistant superintendents and the principals will all have come up from the ranks.

Lateral entry is distinctly a two-edged sword. Its flagrant use can easily undermine an organization, for it seals off promotional opportunities from those who are already serving it. Organizational employees who see the positions they prize go to those who, in their opinion, have not worked for them become disheartened and discouraged. The more able and aggressive employees will tend to leave the organization. At the same time, the caliber of those applying for its rank-and-file positions will tend to fall since these entry positions will hold out little chance for advancement. Carried to an extreme, lateral entry can lead to a caste system such as the one which characterized many European armies in bygone years when no soldier could ever hope to advance to officer level.

Lateral entry can also present other problems. The organization has obviously had far less chance to study the outsider than it has its own people, and so it runs a greater risk in giving him a position of responsibility. Furthermore, no matter how capable he may be, there is no telling how long it will take him to adjust to the way things work in the particular organization which is hiring him. In some instances, this adjustment may never take place.

Lateral entry thus seems like a dangerous device. Yet an administrator may find that lack of lateral entry can be even more dangerous. Only through a lateral entry system can an organization take advantage of the vast range of talent and techniques which society has to offer. This involves not just specialized positions, though they are becoming more numerous and important all the time, but also more generalist posts. In an age when increasing numbers of young people are starting their careers after having acquired one or more college degrees, an organization must be able to offer them posts commensurate with their abilities if it hopes to stave off stagnation. Finally, the outsider brings with him fresh ideas and different perspectives. He often sees things that are wrong which insiders do not see, and he may suggest and make changes which they would never have considered.

With such factors as these in mind, public organizations are beginning to look more favorably on lateral entry. State governments are starting to follow the federal government in instituting management intern programs. Police departments are beginning at last to give extra pay and credit toward promotion for education achieved beforehand. As O. Glenn Stahl, the author of the country's leading text on personnel administration, has written, "Policies which accept and encourage entry at all levels . . . are the order of the day."[16] It is not a question of abandoning entirely promotion from within. Such a step, for reasons that we have already seen would in many cases prove disastrous. Rather, it is a question of striking a balance. And striking balances is, of course, what administration in general is all about.

PROBLEMS AND PARADOXES

The foregoing constitutes something of a quick tour through the sprawling fields of personnel administration. As such, it suffices only to develop a nodding acquaintance with what some believe to be administration's most basic aspect. In this section we will center our attention on some particular personnel problems of the 1970's. They yield no easy answers, but, as has been persistently and perhaps tiresomely stressed throughout this text, little in modern day administration ever does.

Equal Opportunity
With the exception of trade unionism, which we will examine in a subsequent section, probably no issue of recent years has so engulfed per-

---

16. O. Glenn Stahl, *Public Personnel Administration*, 6th ed. (New York: Harper & Row, 1971), p. 20.

sonnel administration in controversy and confronted administrators with problems as the quest for equal opportunity. Public administration is obviously a very integral part of modern society, and as such it cannot remain oblivious to society's pressures and concerns. As the drive for minority group rights has gathered momentum, it has shaken and buffeted public personnel administration along with so many other aspects of American life. There is no question that personnel administration stood in need of a shake-up. Even the federal government cannot boast of a glorious history in this area.

Take the problem of women's rights. There is no disputing the fact that women consistently suffered from discriminatory practices in the federal government during most of its history. In 1864, Congress passed a law setting the maximum salary for women in the federal service at $600 a year. For performing the same work, men could receive up to $1,800. The passage of the Civil Service Act in 1883 did not appreciably change matters. The top scorer in the first civil service exam to be held following the law's enactment was a young Vassar graduate named Mary Frances Hoyt. But despite Miss Hoyt's proud performance, she, along with her contemporaries and successors, had to put up with deep-seated prejudice. As late as 1911, a civil service commissioner stated that the government should try not to hire women stenographers because blonds were "too frivolous" and brunets were "too chatty."[17]

Needless to say, blacks often fared even worse. Woodrow Wilson, according to historian John Morton Blum, "permitted several of his cabinet members to segregate, for the first time since the Civil War, whites and Negroes within existing executive departments. Throughout the South the discharge or demotion of Negro employees attended the New Freedom."[18] In response to liberal protest these policies were eventually checked, but discriminatory treatment still held sway over vast stretches of the federal bureaucracy. At the beginning of World War II, the army confined black soldiers largely to engineering and quartermaster corps, the navy only permitted blacks to serve as mess attendants and the marines simply refused to accept black recruits at all.

Yet, despite this record of intolerance and even ill will, the federal government during most of its history has been light years ahead of the private sector as well as many state and local governments in offering opportunities to minority groups and women. Blacks frequently

---

17. For an informative article covering these and other developments in the federal government's policies and attitudes toward women employees, see "The Best Is Yet to Come," by Jayne B. Spain in the *Civil Service Journal*, January-March 1973. Ms. Spain is vice chairman of the U.S. Civil Service Commission.
18. John Morton Blum, *Woodrow Wilson and the Politics of Morality* (Boston: Little, Brown, 1956), pp. 115–116.

found federal employment something of a haven in the whirling tide of prejudice that encompassed so much of American life in previous eras. Women, from 1923 on, benefitted from the Classification Act which stipulated that "the principle of equal compensation for equal work irrespective of sex shall be followed."

The outbreak of World War II saw a good many discriminatory barriers burst asunder. All the armed services began establishing black units in branches hitherto reserved for whites, and all of them eventually opened up their officer ranks to black candidates. They also set up women's auxiliary corps. Furthermore, President Roosevelt issued an executive order outlawing discrimination in defense industries as well as in government. The policies adopted and the results obtained appear rather slight by today's standards, but by the standards of those times they seemed momentous.

The wheels of progress continued to spin forward in the postwar era. President Truman integrated the armed services, thereby making the military the most racially advanced institution in American society. He also created a Fair Employment Board within the Civil Service Commission. In 1955, President Eisenhower replaced the board with the President's Committee on Government Employment Policy. This marked a shift from a passive to a positive stance. The new body was charged with not just hearing complaints but with taking active steps to see that equal opportunity was afforded to all in federal employment.

Under John F. Kennedy the pace accelerated and the scope broadened. Kennedy set up the President's Committee on Equal Employment Opportunity and named Vice President Johnson as its chairman and the heads of eleven federal departments and agencies as members. The young president began tackling the problem of sex discrimination as well. The first year of his administration saw the creation of the Presidential Commission on the Status of Women designed to investigate problems and initiate solutions in this area of concern. President Johnson continued the effort. In 1967 the word "sex" was added for the first time to an executive order stressing the need to combat discrimination in federal employment.

The arrival of a more conservative tenant at the White House in 1969 failed to arrest this growing trend. On August 8 of that year, President Nixon emphasized in the strongest language ever used the need to rule out discrimination in any form from federal employment. The passage of the Equal Employment Opportunity Act in 1972 instructed the Civil Service Commission to institute "affirmative action" programs to make equal opportunity a living reality in all government agencies under its jurisdiction, and it gave the commission the power to take action against agencies and individuals who were found failing to take vigor-

143

ous measures in this direction. Such powers as the commission had held in this area in the past had come from executive orders of the president. Now congressional action had sanctified and strengthened its role.[19]

What have been the results of all these efforts? As of November 1972, minorities constituted 20 percent of all federal workers, a substantially higher percentage than their proportion of the general population. And while their representation in the federal government's higher levels, the so-called supergrades, was far less, it was growing. From 1971 to 1972, the number of minority employees in the top grades of the federal service increased by 1,845, while the number of whites holding such jobs actually declined by 419.[20] (There was an overall drop in federal employment during this period.) Women also saw their horizons in the federal government expand. Not only did their numbers in the upper-middle and upper echelons sharply increase, but 1972 saw women for the first time receiving appointments as FBI agents, forest rangers, narcotic agents, sky marshals and air traffic controllers.[21]

What about state and local government where, after all, nearly four-fifths of all government workers are employed? A study by the U.S. Commission on Civil Rights published in 1969 showed blacks holding nearly one-quarter of all full-time government jobs in the subnational governmental system. It also found that while black employees were clustered disproportionately in the lower range of jobs, they were still better represented in supervisory and white collar positions than they were in private employment in their respective communities.[22]

Equal Opportunity—Continuing Controversies

The progress achieved by 1973 had generated considerable controversy on both sides of the issue. Many civil rights enthusiasts insisted that all the policies promulgated and actions taken had only yielded moderate if not token results. They could point to some impressive figures to back up their claims. If minority employment in the supergrades seemed to shoot up from 1971 to the end of 1973, it still left minorities holding only about 5.5 percent of all jobs in the top third of the federal government's classification scheme. The same can be said for women who made up only 4 percent of those working at such jobs. Furthermore, even rank-and-file positions in some of government's most sensitive activities, such as education and law enforcement, continued to show an underrepresentation of minority members.

---

19. These historical efforts are recounted in "Equal Opportunity," by Tommie Sue Leaky in the *Civil Service Journal,* January-March 1973.
20. American Society for Public Administration, *News and Views,* March 1973.
21. Spain, *op. cit.*
22. *For All the People. . .By All the People, A Report on Equal Opportunity in State and Local Government Employment* (Washington, D.C.: Government Printing Office, 1969).

Underlying these sad statistics, so the complainants claimed, were a host of policies and procedures which served to hinder and hamper minority group members from moving into and up the ranks of public employment. These barriers are not always explicit or even intentional, they say, but they are nonetheless real. For example, the need to pay $3.00, take a test and then wait six months to become a janitor can prove an effective deterrent. The perceptions which government employers have of poor people and the perceptions which the poor have of themselves may constitute a woefully effective "hidden dissuader" to minority group employment. Or the fact that minorities are not plugged in to the type of networks which disseminate information on government jobs also deprives them of equal opportunity. Many openings become known through word of mouth, and a person isolated from the mainstream of society may never get the word.

It is with such facts as these in mind that William A. Brown III, the black chairman of the Equal Opportunity Commission, called for more sweeping reforms to open up the ranks of public employment. Educational requirements, he claims, are often needlessly high. Some 88 percent of all state and local agencies require recruits to pass a written test. In addition, about 22 percent demand a high school diploma for unskilled jobs and 94 percent do so for entry-level office jobs. Such requirements, maintains Brown, could and should be substantially modified.

Brown has also flayed such government employment features as job classifications, which we will shortly examine, and the already discussed rule of three. Rigid job classification schemes may freeze groups of employees into certain categories, he said, while the rule of three, or the rule of five as it is applied in some jurisdictions, prevents the employer from choosing any qualified applicant. "Merit principles," said Brown in a 1972 article, "were not implemented to assure the rigid following of procedures which no longer serve their purpose. They were not implemented to require the utilization of 'phoney credentials,' nor were they implemented to protect the jobs of those who design, administer and interpret written tests."[23]

Women's rights enthusiasts also had complaints to lodge and recommendations to make. Provisions for part-time employment, long-term leave and day-care facilities were frequent steps which they were demanding to increase the possibilities for more women to enter and to stay in government employment.

However, every issue has its other side, and while some were

---

23. William H. Brown III, "Moving Against Job Bias in State and Local Governments," *Good Government* (winter 1972).

accusing government employers of not having done enough, others were claiming they were going too far. One cannot, said the opponents, hold the employer responsible for poor schooling, deprived environments and other conditions which were holding back minority groups from advancing faster and further than they have. Furthermore, low percentage figures do not ipso facto denote discrimination. For example, while the percentage of blacks in most city police forces is disproportionately low, the relative percentage of some other groups such as Jews and Orientals is usually even lower. If the Chinese community of New York City was fully represented in the City's Police Department, then New York would have between two and three hundred Chinese policemen. The department has had only one Chinese police officer in its recent history and no one has cited or claimed discrimination. Blacks, many claim, are often dissuaded from joining the police by community pressures and attitudes. Consequently, they argue that judging discrimination simply on the percentages of representation which a group may have within it is neither reasonable nor just.

The controversy became more intense when the Civil Service Commission in 1971 directed agencies to set "goals" for employment of minority group members and to establish timetables for the achievement of such goals. Soon, the air was rife with rumors that a quota system was now operating that was discriminating against non-minority group members. Although the commission subsequently felt compelled to clarify its policy and to affirm that it was not mandating quotas, the charges of "discrimination in reverse" continued to be made.

A certain amount of evidence had accumulated to fuel these fears. In 1973 Civil Service Commissioner L. J. Andolsek cited two complaints of discrimination which had recently been brought before the commission. One was made by a black, the other by a white. Each claimed that a member of the opposite race had received a promotion for which the complainant was better qualified. Each complaint was found to be justified. In the case involving the white complainant, the superior finally admitted that he had promoted the black because of his race.[24] In another case, Samuel Solomon, a special assistant in HEW's Office of Civil Rights, investigated twelve cases of "reverse discrimination" in colleges and universities, some of them public ones, and found all these cases justified. Said Solomon, "I'm getting the impression that most institutions are engaged in some form of discrimination against white males."[25]

A dispute that flared up in Massachusetts regarding state civil

---

24. L. J. Andolsek, "No Matter What Boat," *Civil Service Journal,* January-March 1973.
25. *Parade,* June 3, 1973, p. 18.

service exams for policemen illustrates how involved the problem can be and how inflamed it can become. In 1971 Boston Federal Judge Charles Wyzanski Jr. declared a newly given batch of police tests invalid on the grounds that the questions they posed placed minority applicants at a disadvantage and resulted in a substantial percentage of such applicants failing to obtain qualifying marks. The state's Civil Service Commission prepared a new examination and gave it the following year. This time, more blacks and Spanish-speaking applicants passed but many still failed, and some of those who did brought the case once again before Judge Wyzanski. Again the judge castigated the commission, contending that, among other things, the test was unnecessarily rigorous. He demanded that all fifty-three minority group members who had failed the second exam be passed and that all of them be given jobs before any white applicant was hired. He also claimed that the state Civil Service Commission was setting unnecessarily high standards for education in requiring a high school diploma.[26]

This understandably horrified some state and local officials. They pointed out that one applicant who would thus be certified under Wyzanski's ruling had scored an absolute zero on the test while a few others had not done much better. The president of the Massachusetts Police Association, Captain Joseph V. Cavanaugh, branded the judge's move "discrimination in reverse" claiming that Wyzanski was setting back the long worked-for goal of upgrading the police. "It took us twenty years to establish the fact that a high school diploma was needed to become a police officer, and in a single sweep of the pen all this is wiped out," lamented Cavanaugh.[27]

Eventually a compromise was worked out whereby only those minority group members who passed the second test were deemed eligible but would receive jobs at a faster rate than the others.[28] The issues that the controversy raised, however, remained unresolved.

Thus, while personnel administration has acknowledged and accepted the goal of "equal opportunity," it has split in many different ways as to what the goal is and how it is to be obtained. One thing, however, seems reasonably evident. While the struggle to achieve such an end may have produced exaggerations and excesses, it has on the whole yielded benefits for personnel administration in general as well as for minority group members in particular. It has spurred public employers to broaden and intensify their recruiting efforts, examine the validity of their exams and question the necessity for many of their recruitment and promotion criteria. It has opened up government organizations and

---

26. *Boston Herald-American,* March 28, 1973.
27. *Boston Herald-American,* April 5, 1973.
28. *The Boston Globe,* April 16, 1973.

stimulated innovation. The debates and disputes it has sparked constitute in themselves a badly needed invigorating force in American administration.

Performance Ratings

If an organization is going to use merit rather than sheer seniority as a basis for promotion (or demotion), and if job performance rather than test performance is to provide the basis for determining merit, then just how does one determine job performance? The most common device used is a performance rating system. Such a system essentially calls for superiors to rate their subordinates. The system seems simple, but in practice it generates all kinds of complications and controversies.

The nub of the performance rating problem lies in the lack of objective data and procedures for making it work effectively. Even when a supervisor desperately wants to be fair and impartial, he still often has little in the way of neutral criteria which he can apply and which can protect him from his own whims and caprices. And when a superior does not feel such impartiality to be imperative, he can be very whimsical and capricious indeed.

The most common result of a performance rating system is ratings that are too high. "In any bureaucracy," writes management consultant Chester Burger, "the general attitude is to give the underdog the benefit of the doubt. Because after all, I have nothing to lose by it, if he gets promoted, it isn't interfering with me in any way, it's not costing me anything."[29] So superiors, wanting to be popular with their personnel, tend to give most of them and sometimes all of them ratings of at least satisfactory whether they deserve it or not. If an employee demonstrates weaknesses, the superior may find excuses. In this manner, mediocrity manages to score another of its many triumphs in organizational life.

Less widespread but much more injurious, perhaps, is the reverse reaction. Supervisors may and sometimes do use performance ratings to arbitrarily damage and even destroy a person's career. This can sometimes take the form of a seemingly innocuous statement such as "The individual is well placed at his present level of management." Or it can take a more virulent tone and produce much more vicious effect.

Vietnam produced many such efficiency-rating casualties. In his book *The Best and the Brightest*, David Halberstam cites one high-ranking State Department official and several military officers whose realistically pessimistic reports from the conflict area when American involve-

---

29. Chester Burger, *Executive Under Fire* (New York: Macmillian, 1966), p. 223.

ment was getting under way incensed their superiors and earned them disastrous performance ratings. In one case that was reminiscent of the story of Admiral Sims (see preceding chapter) the army actually gave serious thought to court-martialing a lieutenant-colonel named John Vann, ostensibly for talking to newsmen, but actually, according to Halberstam, for his annoying appraisals and pessimistic predictions on the course of events.[30]

Another Vietnam case involving an army officer's efficiency rating became much more prominent. This concerned Lieutenant-Colonel Anthony Herbert who had the temerity to file charges against his superior, accusing him of ignoring his (Herbert's) previous reports of war crimes and atrocities allegedly being committed by both American and South Vietnamese troops. Although Colonel Herbert had won a Silver Star and other decorations during his service in South Vietnam, he was promptly yanked from his command and made the subject of an adverse efficiency report which accused him of having "no ambition, integrity, loyalty or will for self-improvement." Two army review boards refused to overturn the adverse report, and only after his case had become the object of nationwide comment and congressional furor did the Secretary of the Army expunge the poor performance rating from the colonel's personnel record.[31]

Since adverse performance ratings, even if not widely used, constitute a potential threat to any employee, the whole performance rating system may engender behavior that is far from consistent with organization goals. Fear of a poor rating frequently will cause subordinates to become too subordinate, i.e., to conform too much to their superior's whims and wishes. Such fear stifles innovation, constructive criticism and even communication. In a study of a federal law enforcement agency, Peter Blau found that agents "were reluctant to reveal to their superiors their inability to solve a problem for fear that their ratings would be adversely affected."[32]

Some organizations such as the Foreign Service and the navy operate under a "selection-out" rule whereby a person who has a consistently poor rating or who has not earned a promotion in a stipulated period of time is subject to dismissal. This personnel procedure makes performance ratings even more important, for now they not only determine advancement but employment itself. As such, selection-out only intensifies the problems which performance ratings present. Arthur

30. David Halberstam, *The Best and the Brightest* (New York: Random House 1969), pp. 202-205 and pp. 248-249.
31. *New York Times*, February 26, 1973.
32. Peter Blau, *Bureaucracy and Modern Society* (New York: Random House, 1956), p. 50.

149

Schlesinger describes the Foreign Service system as "in effect a conspiracy of the conventional against the unconventional,"[33] and apparently many Foreign Service officers view it even more harshly. According to former FSO William Bell, members of the Service speak of their promotional system as resembling a "high-rise outhouse, constructed so that each person—except for those at the very bottom—is subject to deposits from those above but can deposit in kind upon those below." Adds Bell, "Whether it is accurate or not, *belief* in its validity creates a formidable operating reality."[34]

One of the most caustic critics of performance ratings was Douglas McGregor who filed a lengthy bill of particulars against such devices. According to McGregor, performance ratings are as bothersome and unsettling to superiors as they are to subordinates. They consume too much time in preparation, review and frequent argumentation. What is more, they can rarely claim much validity for usually it is impossible for the superior to make with precision the fine distinctions they often demand. Subordinates often say they want such ratings, claiming that they like "to know where they stand," but McGregor disputed this. Usually the employee just wants reassurance, he said, and if the rating is a bad one, it only makes him more anxious, more defensive and more unrealistic in his behavior.[35] The more the subordinate is likely to merit criticism, the less likely he is to respond effectively to it. (It might be interesting to compare the problems of performance ratings with those posed by the grading systems used in American higher education.)

McGregor suggested as an alternative that an employee be allowed to rate himself, with the rating being based on progress toward certain goals which he will have previously determined in cooperation with his superior. This proposal seemed outlandishly naive when McGregor first articulated it in the late 1950's. Today, however, a few private firms such as the Gillette Company and Stone and Webster Engineering, Inc. have adopted such a plan. It calls for the employee to fill in his own rating sheet and his superior to add to it his own comments if he in any way disagrees.

Few public agencies have gone as far, but many are at least allowing the employee to see his performance rating and to append his own comments to it if he feels it is in any way unfair or inaccurate. In the wake of the controversy over Colonel Herbert, the army on April 30, 1972, instituted a new system which allows an officer to see his ratings

---

33. Arthur M. Schlesinger, Jr., *A Thousand Days* (Boston: Houghton Mifflin, 1965), p. 386.
34. William A. Bell, "The Cost of Cowardice: Silence in the Foreign Service," in Peters and Adams, *Inside the System*, p. 223.
35. McGregor, *The Theory of Human Enterprise* (1960), p. 85.

and to determine how he ranks by mean grade average among all other officers of his rank. The system still requires a rater, an endorser who rates the rater and a reviewer who double checks both of the others. It also makes no provision for the rated officer to add his own remarks. But its proponents hope that it may reduce some of the army's personnel problems which the Vietnam war brought so glaringly to the fore.[36]

Job Classifications

Nearly all public personnel organizations have some system of job classification. The federal government, for example, divides its positions into eighteen basic grade levels ranging from Grade 1 to Grade 18. Each level pays more and, ostensibly, requires more in terms of ability and output than the level below it. Within each grade level there are twelve steps, each paying more than the preceding one. The upper steps of any grade actually pay more than the lower steps of the grade just above it. Consequently, an employee who is working at the eleventh step of Grade 12 will be earning more than an employee who is at the first step of Grade 13. Of course, the latter will eventually outdistance the former since he is working in a higher level classification. Advancement from one step to another takes place chiefly on the basis of time served. Advancement from one grade level to another is based more on merit, though in practice seniority often plays a large role.

The premise underlying classification schemes is that different jobs require varying degrees of ability and impose varying amounts of responsibility. The adoption of a classification plan has long been considered essential for the effective operation of a merit system, for it is designed to place the emphasis on *what* a person knows rather than *who* he knows. It provides a basis for, though it does not guarantee, a neutral and workable personnel operation which without fear or favor, can reward good performance and penalize its opposite. Furthermore, it can do this in open and objective ways.

One crucial question among the many which job classification poses is how many classifications should there be? Should the various jobs be strung out into a large number of separate grades and levels or should they be compressed into a comparatively few broad categories? If the Federal government's personnel system features eighteen grades with twelve steps each, is this too many or too few or just about right?

The problem is obviously a relative one to which there can be no precise answer since there are no precise criteria defining narrow and broad classifications. To some the federal government's eighteen grade

---

36. *New York Times,* January 3, 1972.

levels may seem too many; to others they may seem too few. However, we do know that moving in either direction will yield various advantages and disadvantages.

A personnel system employing many and hence relatively narrow classifications will be able to tailor its jobs more precisely to a particular level. If there are two classifications for typists rather than one, then better typists can be placed in the upper class and less capable typists can be put in the lower one. Thus, if typist A does better work than typist B, then A can be given a higher rating than B. It is further assumed that A will not only be given more money and more status but will also be given more difficult and more responsible assignments. In this sense, using many relatively narrow categories can be fairer to all concerned.

Narrow categories also permit more extensive use of promotion as an incentive. More levels mean more possibilities for moving up. At the same time, such promotional opportunities can be used as a sanction against those who fail to perform adequately. If typist B makes many errors in her copy or is unduly slow in getting out her assignments, she may find herself forgoing the better pay and prestige which advancement to a higher level would bring.

Many public organizations have relatively few classification levels, particularly in the lower range of jobs. Postmen, policemen, firemen and others can usually move up only to a position of command. Since there are relatively few such positions in most organizations, opportunities for promotion remain limited. Some 60 percent of all Post Office employees retire at the same job level they had when they started work. The majority of policemen face the same fate despite the additional possibility they have of moving up to detective as well as to the command position of sergeant. This contrasts with, say, the German system whereby a policeman can advance several notches in rank before assuming any substantial supervisory responsibility. The Germans find their system enables them more easily to reward a policeman for good work. Conversely, they can more easily discipline him for poor performance by simply delaying his upward advancement.[37]

Despite these merits, however, narrow and therefore numerous job classifications present distinct difficulties. The more classifications there are, the more personnel work the organization must do. Each classification must be carefully described and demarcated, and then each job must be carefully plugged into the right classification. This results in a system that is not only costly but also cumbersome and complicated.

Although utilization of numerous and narrow classifications can alleviate discord, since those performing somewhat more demanding

---

37. Berkley, *The Democratic Policeman.*

tasks can then more easily receive recognition for doing so, it can for the same reasons create tensions of its own. "Why should he or she be classified higher than I am when my job requires as much or more responsibility as his or hers?" is a constant complaint. Arguments frequently flare up over whether a position should be put in one class or another. For example, in a regional office of one federal agency, a personnel officer balked at classifying a job at Grade 14 level despite pleas and exhortations from the agency's other top officials that he do so. It seems the personnel officer himself held only a Grade 13 position, and it was felt that he could not bring himself to categorize the new post at a higher level than his own. Problems such as these run rampant when classifications are numerous.

Generally, the more classification levels there are, the more different kinds of personnel games may be played. One of these is called "job evolution." An employee finds himself stuck at his present level and unable to move up due to the lack of openings above him, so he strives earnestly to get his existing job reclassified upward. A sympathetic supervisor may assist by adding to his job some new duties, thereby strengthening his case. If the employee is finally successful, then others seek to follow suit and so the game begins all over again. This is the basis of some of the "inflation at the top" which we noted in a previous chapter. Jobs have a tendency to keep evolving upward.

Probably the most important impediment which a highly scaled classification scheme imposes on effective administration is inflexibility. The more numerous and narrow the classifications, the harder it is to rotate people from one job to another. In similar fashion, it becomes more difficult to change the nature of the work assigned to any individual for the new assignments may mandate a change in his grade level. An employee may protest vigorously that the task he is being given is below his level or above it.

To gain a better awareness of how this operates, let us take a somewhat extreme hypothetical case. Imagine two identical agencies doing the same work and having the same number and types of personnel. The first arranges its employees into five categories; the second groups its people into twenty-five categories. In the first agency, anyone holding a job equivalent, say, to Grade 3 in the second can be easily moved to what would be a Grade 1 or Grade 5 job in the second agency. Or his work can be altered in the same manner. Thus, the first agency is in a much better positon to innovate and change.

McGregor was a constant critic of tight and constricting classification schemes. He pointed out that no two people will ever perform in the same position in the same way and even one person does not do the same work in the same position over a period of time. Conditions

153

change as do skills, abilities and perceptions of priorities. Consequently, the position is actually changing continually. Hard and fast position descriptions, he contended, not only promote inflexibility but signify a lack of realism.[38]

One final aspect of the issue is also worthy of note. The broader the classification scheme it uses, the more egalitarian the organization is likely to be. Numerous, narrow classifications result in a complex pecking order which creates many social as well as economic distinctions between employees. To take what might be called the limiting case, assume that an organization had only one job classification. It would then be completely egalitarian as far as its personnel system went. The more an organization approaches this situation, the more "democratic" it is likely to become.

What are the trends for the future? Contemporary society is generating considerable pressures on public organizations to hold down administrative costs, to encourage innovation and flexibility and to increase democratization. For these reasons it seems likely that the direction of personnel administration will be toward broader rather than narrower classification schemes. We will see examples of this in chapter thirteen. At this point it is useful to keep in mind that such a trend may increase administrative effectiveness in many ways. Research indicates that the fewer the differences in prestige and status within a group, the more stable the group tends to become and the more likely are its members to accept internal leadership. In addition, communication most probably will improve. It is possible that some organizations will need to retain relatively narrow classifications, and some might benefit from even more classifications than they now have. But the overall tendency seems to lie in the opposite direction.

Centralization of the Personnel Function

The growth of civil service merit systems brought the development of centralized personnel agencies. Such centralization was deemed necessary to provide the resources for drawing up and administering a comprehensive merit system. In performing such a task, most personnel agencies also take on a significant control function vis-a-vis the various line agencies. To the extent that such centralized personnel agencies recruit and train personnel, set up classification and pay schemes, establish the standards for promotion, demotion and dismissal, they exercise a good deal of influence over line administrators.

There are many advantages in having centralized personnel agencies, usually called civil service commissions or boards, undertake such

---

38. McGregor, *op. cit.* (1960), Chapter 7.

functions. It impedes, when it does not block, the pressures of patronage and the forces of favoritism. It also produces more professionalism in personnel practices since a central personnel agency can obviously assemble more data, expertise and knowledge in this field than can an individual line agency.

Centralization of the personnel function also provides distinct advantages in recruiting and rotation. The prospective government employee who is willing to work for more than one particular agency does not need to file separate applications. Instead, he can file with the centralized personnel agency. Sometimes, he can take one test to qualify for several different jobs. For example, the New York City Civil Service Commission gives the same examination to applicants for the Housing Police, the Transit Authority Police and the City Correction Department, and the successful examinee can move into any one of these agencies on the basis of available openings and his own preferences. There are obvious savings here in expenditure of time by all concerned. In like fashion, if an employee wishes to rotate to another agency, he may find the way smoothed by a centralized personnel unit that not only knows which agencies need which people at which time, but that also, through its recruiting and staffing function, can more easily arrange the transfer.

But, a strong centralized personnel agency also has its negative aspects. The line agency often feels it knows better just what kind of people it needs and resents having to let the personnel people have the last word. Furthermore, it is time consuming to have to wait for the central personnel agency to draw up and administer examinations or to approve promotions, or new job classifications or changes in existing ones. A centralized personnel agency may also drain administrative energies and consume administrators' time in yet other ways since negotiations, sometimes protracted ones, are frequently required before the line department can move in many areas. Finally, such a system robs a line agency of authority and discretion and in so doing it can make the achievement of its goals more difficult.

When civil service merit systems were starting to become established, the trend was definitely toward centralizing personnel functions. Today, however, the currents of change may be blowing in the opposite direction. The mounting need for flexibility and expediency is prompting a tendency in some areas to strengthen the authority of the line agency and its administrators in regard to personnel matters. The fact that a technological society makes technical competence more important and political contacts less useful in administrative performance reinforces this trend, for it reduces the need to have a central personnel agency to prevent abuses. Central personnel agencies will still be needed, for they offer the advantages cited earlier, but their role may change to one of providing advice and assistance rather than constraint and control.

Residency Requirements and Moonlighting

Questions involving residency requirements and moonlighting are often slighted by writers on administration, yet they are sources of a good deal of conflict in many state and local governments. Years ago, when government jobs were regarded as prized plums, it was customary to restrict them to residents of the constituency being served. Outsiders, it was felt, have no right to enjoy the fruits of other people's taxes. The emergence of the welfare state and the (generally) full employment society has somewhat changed this attitude. Public positions are no longer quite so prized. Yet, residency requirements continue to exist in many jurisdictions. The U.S. Civil Rights Commission found in its 1970 survey that 28 percent of local governments still use residency requirements for some jobs. And in many cases where they are not formally written into the law, tacit rules or informal pressures exist to force certain public employees to live in the jurisdictions in which they work.

A case can be made on behalf of such restrictions. The resident employee is closer to the scene of work and can therefore be called to duty more expeditiously. This can prove advantageous to the local government particularly when it comes to such employees as policemen and firemen whose services may be required in emergencies. Residency requirements also are believed to give the employee more knowledge of, and more of a stake in, the constituency he serves. Finally, many still consider it only fair that he make his purchases and pay his taxes in the locality that supplies him with the wherewithal to do so.

But residency requirements are, first of all, hard to enforce. They are frequently honored more in the breach than in the observance. Then their constricting effect adds to employee dissatisfaction and may make recruitment more difficult. The question of proximity to the work place in case of emergency may be moot since bordering communities may lie closer to the employee's scene of work than some sections of the municipality which employs him. A fireman who is employed in, say, the Queens borough of New York City will be able to respond to an emergency call much faster if he lives in Long Island City than if he resides in any of the other four boroughs of New York City. Finally, requiring municipal employees to live within the city limits may make them too formidable a force in city politics. In many cities and towns, municipal employees have become the most influential pressure group in local politics.

The equal opportunity problem weighs in on both sides of this issue. Civil Rights Commission Chairman Brown has called for the abolition of such requirements since they may be used to deter minorities from obtaining and maintaining government jobs. However, the issue could cut the other way. As Spanish-speaking and black citizens come into control of more municipal governments, they may find that residency requirements can be used either to make sure the work force of such cities provides increased opportunities for minority group members, or, conversely, to keep members of the white majority from fleeing the city altogether. Newark, for example, turned down a white out-of-state applicant for a high financial post when the prospective job taker refused to agree that he would live in the city proper.

Moonlighting is another issue often neglected in discussions of personnel administration. Yet it too has become a matter of abiding concern to many administrators. Like residency requirements, moonlighting or the practice of holding one or more additional jobs outside one's regular public employment is a phenomenon that chiefly plagues local governments. However, many state governments and even some federal agencies have not gone unaffected. Prison and jailhouse guards, policemen, sanitation men, building inspectors and others are frequent moonlighters. Firemen are possibly the biggest moonlighters of all since their professional employment not only provides them with the opportunity but even with the accommodations to sleep during their normal working hours.

Moonlighting poses problems, some obvious and some not so obvious. In the first category is the dissipation of the employee's energies away from what should be his main focus of attention. A former commander of the Chicago police once noted that moonlighting reached such a level within his department that for many of his men police work had actually become their second job.[39] The situation in many other government agencies in Chicago and elsewhere is almost the same. In a time when public organizations are being pressed to produce more and better results, many find their efforts to do so being sapped by widspread employee moonlighting.

In the not-so-obvious category are the problems involving conflict of interest. Public employees will naturally tend to look for and accept off-duty work in areas in which they have some expertise. This will often bring them into conflict with their governmental responsibilities. The policeman who serves off-duty as a bouncer in a cabaret or the building inspector who does off-duty maintenance work for a real estate firm may find themselves placed in a position where they cannot always serve the public interest and at the same time the interest of their employers.

---

39. In a statement to the author. The former official wishes to remain anonymous.

Despite these concerns, many state and local governments have found that barring moonlighting, as many of them do, proves ineffective. The moonlighting still goes on, only now it is practiced in a secretive and *sub rosa* manner. Furthermore, employees grow resentful since they feel that what they do on their own time is and should be their own concern. It should also be noted that employee moonlighting can in some instances prove useful to a public organization. It may alleviate organizational in-groupism and may provide the employee with useful experience and contacts with the larger society. Sometimes, the off-duty job supplements rather than conflicts with the public one. For example, when New York City policemen were officially allowed to moonlight, many took outside jobs as taxi drivers. Soon, a wave of arrests occurred as would-be robbers of taxi drivers found themselves confronted by seasoned and armed police officers.

The best solution may lie in allowing but controlling moonlighting. Employees can be required to report the name or names of their outside employers, the nature of the employment itself and the hours involved. Certain restrictions may also be imposed. British fire departments, for example, allow their men to moonlight even though firefighters in Britain are required to be on the job 54 hours a week in comparison to the 40- or 48-hour week worked by their American counterparts. However, no British fireman is permitted to work in outside employment for eight hours prior to a tour of duty.[40] Public employers should also move to make their employees' regular jobs more challenging and rewarding. In the long run, this is probably the best if not the only true solution to the moonlighting dilemma.

The Public Employee and Politics

The Civil Service Act of 1883, often referred to as the Pendleton Act after the name of its congressional sponsor, stipulated that no civil service employee could be punished or threatened with punishment for refusing to make a political contribution. In 1907, President Theodore Roosevelt expanded these safeguards through an executive order which prohibits any classified employee from taking an active part in a partisan political campaign. In 1939 Congress formalized and strengthened these provisions through enactment of the Hatch Act. A year later it passed what was known as the second Hatch Act which extended these restrictions to numerous state and local employees whose work was financed to any extent by federal funds. States, meanwhile, began enacting legislation to place similar constraints on their own employees. Today about

---

40. This information was obtained by the author through interviews conducted in London, December 1972.

four-fifths of the states have laws curtailing the political involvement of state and even local government workers, although in many cases these state laws lack the rigor and inclusiveness of the federal legislation.

The Hatch Act does permit federal employees considerable freedom in non-partisan politics. They can not only participate but can run in campaigns for school committee and city council when these elections are non-partisan. They can also sign a nomination paper, vote in a primary and contribute up to $5,000 in a partisan contest. Acitve campaigning in such elections, however, is taboo.

Although the effort to depoliticize public employment was originally designed to protect employees, it has in recent years started to produce the reverse. In 1972, the National Association of Letter Carriers along with six individual employees and six local Democratic and Republican committee chairmen filed a suit claiming the Hatch Act was unconstitutional. The postal union won an initial victory in the Federal District Court of Washington, D.C. The judges held the act unconstitutional on grounds of an "overbreadth in the sensitive area of free expression" and also on grounds that it was too vague. The court stressed the latter point particularly. In its words, the act "talks in riddles, prohibiting in one breath what it may be argued to have allowed in another, leaving the citizen unguided but at hazard for his job."[41]

On June 25, 1973, however, the Supreme Court, in a 6-3 decision, overturned the lower court's finding and upheld the Hatch Act's constitutionality. The restrictions which the law imposes, said the Court, are necessary "if the government is to operate effectively and fairly." The similar state laws also received the Supreme Court's blessing.[42] Hence the legal aspect of the issue has been, at least for the time being, resolved. But other aspects of the issue continue to pester and plague present-day administrators. The Hatch Act may be accepted as lawful but that does not mean it is universally accepted as just.

Critics of the act claim that it makes public employees into second-class citizens. They further note that with the growth in public employment, the act is depriving nearly 20 percent of the nation's work force from full participation in the democratic process. What is more, it is disfranchising a group that is on the whole more knowledgeable about government than is the public generally. As a result, valuable inputs into government decision-making are being lost.

Sentiment for at least liberalizing the Hatch Act seems to be on the increase. President Johnson's Commission on Political Activity of Government Personnel recommended some loosening of the Hatch

---

41. *New York Times,* August 1, 1972.
42. *New York Times,* June 26, 1973.

Act's restrictions in its 1968 report. It called for permitting a federal employee to hold any local office, not just a non-partisan one, as long as the post was not full-time and did not provide more than a nominal compensation.

The commission split down the middle on whether federal employees should be allowed to become party, ward or precinct committeemen and women. The same split is apparently reflected among public employees themselves, for a poll by the commission showed that one-half of the federal government's work force favored some easing of the Hatch Act's constraints but a sizable minority did not. Unions in particular have been spearheading a drive to broaden the perimeters of public employee political activity and doubtless the issue will continue to count among the concerns of both public employees and their employers for some time to come.

PUBLIC UNIONISM

At the beginning of the 1960's, not a single written contract existed between a teachers union and an American school system. By 1972, hundreds of such contracts were in existence covering over one million teachers. And the number of operational contracts and the number of teachers they covered was increasing every year.

This rapid change of events reflects the most sweeping and significant development in public employment since World War II: the emergence of public employee unionism. The upsurge began in 1962 when John F. Kennedy signed his soon-to-be-famous Executive Order 10988. This order granted all federal employees the right to join employee organizations of their choice and to bargain collectively with federal agencies. With the signing of this order, public unionism started its Topsy-like growth. President Johnson gave the movement his blessing, and even President Nixon, despite his generally more conservative posture, did not attempt to arrest it. In a memorandum to all department and agency heads on September 6, 1972, Nixon stated "I support collective bargaining for Federal workers. . . . Good labor-management relations has high priority in my administration."

By the start of 1973, an estimated 64 percent of all federal workers were members of trade unions. No complete figures were available for state and local government employees but their number of union members had also mounted. Subnational America had in most instances quickly followed Washington's lead in sanctioning, if not actually supporting, public employee unionism. By mid-1973, the American Federation of State, County and Municipal Employees was growing at the rate of one thousand members a week. And it was experiencing such growth despite the fact that its membership was one-third female and one-third black, two groups which have traditionally been difficult for unions to organize.

Although public unionism is now an established fact, its right to exist, let alone flourish, remains hotly disputed. Examining the arguments made for and against public employee unionism may provide a perspective on just what it implies for public administration.

Unions as Problems

On a philosophical basis opponents of public employee unionism claim that such unionism is unjustified and unwarranted. The public employee does not labor to provide a profit to his employers. Thus, no basic divergence of interest exists between management and labor since the former do not benefit by depriving the latter. All are public servants, charged with executing the people's wishes as expressed through their elected representatives, votes on referenda and other means. Trade unionism in general and collective bargaining in particular, say the opponents, erode the whole concept of government work as a public service.

Unions are also accused of perpetuating and even expanding some of the worst features of public personnel systems. These include promotion by seniority and rigid tenure rules which make it difficult to fire or demote a delinquent or deficient employee. They also make public managers ever more careful about having employees work out of grade. Public employee unions, say those who oppose them, encourage public organizations to meet challenges and solve problems by simply adding more people. Writes a former New York City budget director, "If you have five men on the back of a fire engine, the union wants seven, and if you've got seven, they want nine."[43] All these practices increase costs, reduce flexibility and impede innovation.

The impairment to innovation can take a variety of forms. In January 1968, New York City announced the consolidation of eight of the city's seventy-two police precincts. This was the first step toward implementing a long existing and carefully drawn out plan. However, the Patrolmen's Benevolent Association, the policemen's union, organized mass meetings of one thousand or more citizens in every affected area, and after two precinct houses were closed, the consolidation efforts came to an abrupt halt. The city's police department also launched an experiment involving the use of one-man patrol cars in a residential

---

43. *Creative Budgeting in New York City: An Interview with Former Budget Director Frederick O'R. Hayes* (Washington, D.C.: The Urban Institute, 1971), p. 27.

middle-class section. The demonstration project resulted in a 35 percent reduction in response time, a lower accident and injury rate and good visibility of, and citizen support for, the police. But the PBA has managed to keep the experiment confined to the small district in which it originated.[44]

Unions can undermine management in still other ways. They diffuse responsibility and make accountability more difficult to pin-point. The problem becomes still worse when public managers themselves form unions, or associations that take on a unionist coloration. In order to bargain collectively they sometimes even resist efforts to classify them as managerial employees. In February 1973, New York City school principals, contesting a Board of Education ruling that they held managerial positions, appealed to the State's Public Relations Board to reclassify them in a non-managerial category.[45]

Unions also increase the political involvement of public employees. In 1963, postal unions financed a testimonial dinner for Representative Thaddeus J. Dulski of Buffalo, the chairman of the House Post Office and Civil Service Committee. At the statehouse and city hall level, the efforts of public employee unions to exercise leverage in behalf of favorite candidates frequently determines the outcome of many elections. New York City, where nearly 20 percent of the vote in municipal elections is cast by muncipal employees, is a city that many considered to have been captured by its own workers. From 1965 to 1972, wages of New York municipal employees more than doubled, reaching a level that substantially surpassed private sector salaries for equivalent work. Other cities have experienced nearly equal problems.

Finally, and perhaps most seriously, public sector unions stand accused of fostering and embittering labor disputes. Critics have noted that the rise of public employee unionism has paralleled a rising wave of public sector strikes. Such behavior has drawn the disapproval of even those who are generally pro-labor. Franklin Delano Roosevelt, who was rightly considered a supporter and ally of America's then weak labor movement, once castigated strikes by public servants as "unthinkable and unsupportable."[46] More recently, government officials have pointed out that a private firm when faced with a strike can shut down, but government enjoys no such option. Strikes of public employees are strikes against the public, and as such they may not only impair the public's welfare but endanger its safety.

What makes the strike issue so sensitive is that efforts to curb or outlaw such action seemed to have scored only limited success. Although the federal government and most states have passed legislation

---

44. *Ibid.,* pp. 26–27.
45. *New York Times,* February 27, 1973. See editorial "Schools Without Leaders."
46. *New York Times,* March 22, 1972, Section 6.

prohibiting strikes to all or at least some of their employees, strikes still occur and efforts to suppress them often fail. This is in large part due to the growing political strength of public employee unions. Even judges, particularly elected ones, are often loath to crack down. When non-teaching employees of Cleveland's public schools defied an express court order and went on strike on January 31, 1973, the judge who issued the court order said he would wait to see the extent of the strike before "deciding the ramifications."[47] Some ten years after President Kennedy signed his historic executive order, George Bennet of New York City's Office of Collective Bargaining was able to note that "even though public sector strikes are illegal and penalties often can be and are invoked, the fact is that the overall strike rate in the public sector is proportionally about that of the private sector."[48]

Unions as Possibilities
The lengthy list of accusations that can be and has been made against public employee unionism does not shake the faith and determination of the movement's supporters. They continue to stand firm, not only in discounting the negative but in affirming the positive. And a rationale does exist for viewing the growth of unionism as a beneficial factor in the development of public administration.

Let us start with the issue of strikes. David Ziskind, a onetime official of the U.S. Department of Labor, wrote a book entitled *One Thousand Strikes of Government Employees*. The book was published by the Columbia University Press in 1940, a time when there were few public employee unions of any significance. The incident is illustrative of a point which trade union proponents zealously propound: Unions in themselves do not cause strikes. On the contrary, they more often prevent strikes from occurring and shorten those that do occur.

In many if not most public employee strikes of recent years, the union's membership has spoken and acted more militantly than its leadership. Often, the union officials have called strike actions only in response to intense membership pressure. And, when they have not responded promptly enough, the union leaders have often found themselves with a wildcat walkout on their hands. A famous sixteen-hour Montreal police strike that broke out in October 1969 was a wildcat operation which union officials actually helped bring to a speedy end. A New York City police strike the following winter saw some enraged strikers actually storm their own union offices because they felt the union leadership had not been sufficiently aggressive in fighting for their rights. The big Post Office strike of 1970 began with disgusted

47. *New York Times*, February 1, 1973.
48. George Bennet, "Tools to Resolve Labor Disputes in the Public Sector," *Personnel*, 50, no. 2 (March-April 1973).

postal employees calling in sick. Said *Newsweek* magazine, "Union officials have been warning Congressional Postal Committee members, the administration and the Post Office that they were rapidly losing control of an increasingly unruly membership."[49] When it came to getting the strikers back to work, AFL-CIO President George Meany helped postal union leaders in urging the men to accept the government's proffered terms.

Economist Thomas C. Schelling has pointed out how "in war one may hope that the enemy government remains intact, thus assuring that there is an authority to negotiate with and to discipline the enemy troops themselves."[50] In a sense, the same holds true for warfare between labor and management. The existence of an organized union with a reasonably strong leadership provides an authority to negotiate with and to "discipline the enemy troops."

But if unions can help to end strikes, they can help even more in preventing them. At the outset it should be noted that union leaders tend to fear strikes for such actions drain union treasuries and, if unsuccessful, can turn the membership against the union. Thus, union leaders much more prefer to resolve disputes through negotiation. In so doing they offer management many opportunities for alleviating and avoiding disruption and discord in its labor relations. The union can bring problems to management's attention in time for management to act on them before they explode. It will provide employee representatives that management can talk to and, if they see some validity in management's case, they can transmit it to the employees with more credibility than management can ever hope to achieve.

Unions will, it is true, usually insist on making an input into administrative policy, but such an input need not, though admittedly it often does, constitute a roadblock to administrative improvement. Unions naturally tend to favor at least some generally approved administrative practices. For example, they will usually fight against favoritism, for favoritism, by its very nature, benefits a few over the many, and the many always have more potential votes at union meetings. Unions may, therefore, resist any policies which permit discriminatory or arbitrary treatment. Then, in order to improve the prestige of their membership, union leaders will often seek to raise recruiting requirements and promote professionalism. Some unions even run career development programs. Union publications usually carry some material concerning new developments in the vocational fields of their membership.

---

49. *Newsweek,* March 30, 1970.
50. Thomas C. Schelling, "Economic Analysis of Organized Crime," Appendix D, *Task Force Report: Organized Crime,* U.S. President's Commission on Law Enforcement and Administration of Justice (Washington, D.C.: Government Printing Office, 1967), p. 122.

When it comes to innovation and change, unions can also play a constructive role. This is the conclusion of Anthony F. Ingrassia, the Director of Labor-Management Relations for the U.S. Civil Service Commission. According to Ingrassia, employee resistance to change is usually a defensive reaction which arises when the employees feel that something is being imposed upon them. If they or their representatives are included in the planning process, then they may not only go along with the plans but can even contribute to their formulation. He recommends the establishment of "meaningful cooperative committees" which will solicit and listen to employee ideas and reactions.[51]

To cite just one example of what Ingrassia may have had in mind, the Federal Bureau of Prisons in 1971 decided to set up a pilot project for training federal correctional personnel. Union leaders were included from the very beginning of the project and the president of the Council of Prison Locals was made a member of the "Board of Visitors." The result was a successful program which has improved the operation of the federal prison system. (The bitter prison unrest which swept over the United States in the early 1970's, it should be noted, was almost exclusively confined to state and local institutions.)[52]

One final feature which can be credited to public employee unions is the ability to bring public sector problems before the public. Teachers unions have often done this and the unionized teachers of Los Angeles even passed up a 5 percent pay raise in 1969 in order to secure improvements in the city's educational system. The union representing New York City's correction officers repeatedly called attention to the severe overcrowding in the city's jails. Unfortunately, their pleas, in this instance, went unheeded until rioting broke out in 1972.

That public employee unions can improve as well as impair public administration has not gone unrecognized by administrators themselves. Picot B. Floyd, the City Manager of Savannah, Georgia, claims unions offer municipal administrators such advantages as "clarification of the role of management in the urban setting; a decrease in labor problems; better employee performance; an increased *esprit de corps*; and a source of support for changes that may be needed in personnel administration." Floyd urges his colleagues to "take advantage of the opportunities that are presented to city governments by organized labor groups."[53]

---

51. Ingrassia's remarks were made during a panel session at the annual convention of the American Society for Public Administration in Los Angeles, 1973.
52. See "Designing and Selling a Staff-Training Program: A Case Study," by Norman A. Carlson, *Public Administration Review*, November/December 1971.
53. Picot B. Floyd, "Some Aspects of Staffing for the Urban Crisis," *Public Administration Review*, January-February 1971.

The Bargaining Process

An administrator who is entering into negotiations with a recently established union will often feel like an early Christian entering a lion-filled arena. He should remember that a union usually arises as the culmination of a long and mounting series of disputes and disgruntlements. Consequently, the union's first aim is often revenge, and its first negotiations are often the most militant. Added to these problems is the fact that the union representatives are inexperienced and untested. They know that their members are waiting to see what they can do, and so they feel they must at all costs prove themselves.

As a result of these conditions, the initial phases of union-management relations are likely to prove much more trying than later ones. If an administrator fails to keep this in mind, he may let himself in for more turmoil and trouble than necessary. Later, when collective bargaining becomes an established and even routine procedure in organizational life, he may find the atmosphere starting to ease. However, rarely will such negotiations become a simple cut-and-dried operation. Each round of talks presents its own problems. Administrators who have weathered many such bargaining sessions usually have developed a series of strategies and strategems to deal with them. While each may have his own special techniques, there are a few general rules that many have found helpful.

First of all, to bargain effectively with unions an adminstrator must believe in such bargaining. This is essential for two reasons: (1) a disbelief in such a process will most likely communicate itself to the labor representatives and only make them more hostile and recalcitrant, and (2) no administrator can ever learn how to make full use of collective bargaining, of how to turn it to his and his agency's advantage, unless he believes that such a possibility exists.

Turning to another rule, it is important for administrators who are involved or who are about to get involved in contract negotiations to encourage the involvement and elicit the support of middle management and even first line management such as foremen. This is not always easy to do since many low-ranking managers identify with the rank and file. Indeed the union may indirectly bargain for these people as well as for its own members, for a pay increase for the rank and file will usually bring a pay increase for middle management as well. In some agencies, the pay of first level supervisors is fixed at a certain percentage over that of the people they supervise.

Nevertheless, despite these difficulties, it is worthwhile to seek their support, since middle and first line managers can often contribute much to the bargaining process. They usually know best what the rank and file really want and what will satisfy them. Also they will be the ones who will have to implement the new contract. This means that the contract is likely to prove more workable if their comments are obtained before it is worked out. Finally, excluding middle managers or paying little heed to what they have to say may only alienate them all the more from the administrative side and intensify their identification with those they supervise.

The public manager should also take care to come to the bargaining table with proposals of his own. In other words, he should not simply react to labor's demands but make some demands himself. Furthermore, he will be well advised not to negotiate all of the union's demands first. Instead, he should press forward with settling some of management's claims before all the union's requests have been dealt with, lest management lose all its leverage before its own concerns are thrashed out.

Administrators should be careful, however, to see that the union's negotiators do not leave the bargaining table empty-handed. They must be given some victories. Managers who seek to undermine the union representatives will only succeed in making these representatives or their replacements more intractable. The management negotiator should remember that his union counterpart may have to contend not only with competition from within but also from without, for other unions may be eager to supplant the existing one. Finally, the union representatives will almost always be needed to enforce whatever settlement is arrived at. Weakening their position is not going to help management in accomplishing this enforcement task.

For some of the same reasons, administrators would do well not to let the negotiations drag on too long, for this too may make the membership more militant and hence more difficult for their representatives to control. Another factor which may create similar problems for management is negotiating during an election. And once issues have been negotiated, the settlements should be put in writing so that the union spokesmen cannot easily repudiate them if they later find the situation more propitious for making even stronger demands.

One final fact should be kept constantly in mind. In the public sector as in the private sector, trade unions are not primarily economic organizations, and their fundamental role is not merely to secure economic benefits. They are essentially a means whereby employees seek to avoid manipulation. Employees form unions to protest against their dependent position and to assert their rights to self-determination. The economic issues that so often dominate the dialogue, while by no means unimportant, are still more often than not secondary. The more fundamental issues are those that involve human dignity and human rights.

When Collective Bargaining Fails

When the two sides become stalemated and the bargaining process breaks down, alternatives are available for avoiding a strike. The first of these is what is called *fact-finding*. Under this process, an individual or, as happens more frequently, a panel is set up to review the disputed issues and make recommendations. These recommendations are not binding, but if the fact-finding machinery has been properly constituted, and if its analysis of the facts is accurate, then both sides will be under a good deal of pressure to accept its suggestions.

In the late 1960's, New York City set up its Office of Collective Bargaining as a way of escaping the constant stream of labor disputes that were playing havoc with the city's government. The office is headed by two representatives of the city government, two representatives from city employee unions and three public members selected by the four management and union representatives. One of the public members serves as the full-time director of the office and as chairman of what is called the Board of Collective Bargaining.

The office maintains a roster of available "impasse panelists" and when negotiations reach an impasse in any sector of the city government, the disputing parties select names from the list in order of preference until a panel is set up. This panel then holds hearings and issues a report along with recommendations. Failure by either side to react to the panel's recommendations within two days constitutes acceptance. Nearly all panel recommendations have been accepted, although in some instances this has required further hearings and subsequent modifications. In 1972, these panels were strengthened by being given the right to make final decisions after holding additional hearings.[54]

To be effective, the fact-finders must be acceptable to both sides. During the Philadelphia school strike of 1972-73, the teachers union asked for either fact-finding or arbitration. The Pennsylvania Labor Relations Board finally appointed a fact-finder but it was one that the union found unacceptable. As a result, the fact-finder's subsequent recommendations were rejected and the strike became the second longest school strike in American history.[55]

Another device that is sometimes used when labor-management negotiations founder is *mediation*. The mediator or, in some cases, mediators actually help carry on negotiations between the disputing parties. They may group both sides around a table and try to find ways to open up previously entrenched positions or to point out possibilities for conciliation. On occasion, when a dispute has gotten out of hand and

---

54. Bennet, *op. cit.*
55. Albert Shanker, "The Philadelphia Story, 1973," *New York Times,* February 25, 1973 (paid advertisement).

tempers have reached a boiling point, the mediator may put the two sides in separate rooms and run from room to room in a continuing effort to break the deadlock. Some jurisdictions authorize fact-finders to mediate when their recommendations have failed to dissolve the differences separating the parties involved.

Needless to point out, mediation is quite an art. According to one experienced practitioner, a good mediator should:

have a good sense of timing, knowing when to advise each side on when to make each move;

avoid relieving the parties themselves of responsibility to solve the dispute;

be able to distinguish the power contest between the parties from internal power considerations (such as union leaders fearful of losing face with their own members);

avoid passing on the merits of the respective positions.[56]

Neither mediation nor fact-finding assures a peaceful settlement to a labor dispute. For that type of guarantee we must turn to a third alternative, *arbitration.* This device differs from the other two in just one crucial respect; it produces a definite decision, and usually one that is binding on both sides. When binding arbitration has been agreed upon, the arbitrator's word is final and there is no further appeal.

Of course, if arbitration is not accepted by either party at the outset, then it does not guarantee a peaceful resolution. But it is rarely utilized without such prior concurrence. One typical way of going about the process is for each side to choose a representative, and for the two representatives to choose a third member of what then becomes an arbitration panel.

Administrators tend to view third-party proceedings such as fact-finding, mediation and arbitration with mixed feelings. While they recognize that such devices help considerably to avoid strikes, they often feel that they result in decisions which, from a management perspective, are more often injurious than not. Third parties have nothing at stake except their own future business in getting cases to mediate or arbitrate. Thus, they show a tendency, it is felt, to split the issue down the middle with perhaps some leaning toward the labor side. Some administrators question not only the leaning toward labor but whether most disputes should automatically be split down the middle in any case. Many issues, they feel, simply do not lend themselves to that type of decision. In any case, management loses control in such proceedings

---

56. Bennet, *op. cit.*

and decisions are made by those who cannot be fully aware of all their implications, and who in any case do not have to live with them.

Unionists have tended to look more favorably on third-party intervention. They have particularly favored arbitration. As one fireman union official once expressed it, without compulsory arbitration in the background, collective bargaining for employees becomes collective begging.[57] Beyond that, public employee unions continue to strive for the right to strike. They may not wish to make use of it very often for reasons stated previously, but possession of such a right gives them the most valuable weapon a union can usually possess when it starts to bargain collectively. "One cannot deprive 20 percent of the work force of the essentials of democracy without harming the basic freedom of all Americans," Jerry Wurf, the president of the American Federation of State, County and Municipal Employees, has stated, while AFL-CIO President George Meany has noted that "a free collective bargaining system contemplates that at the end of the road there can be a strike. . . . If you don't like that then take out the word 'free.' "[58]

In behalf of this position, it is useful to point out that employees of privately owned hospitals, electric companies, water works, gas plants and shipyards enjoy the right to strike. Why, it is sometimes asked, should employees of comparable government-owned institutions not possess comparable privileges? Drivers on certain bus lines in Manhattan and the Bronx operated under a private contract in 1962 and thus had the right to strike. A few years later, when the lines had been taken over by the metropolitan transit agency, this right was lost. Yet the men were doing the exact same work they were doing before.

A perhaps more telling argument in favor of granting the right to strike is that in jurisdictions where such a right has been granted, it does not seem to have led to any noticeable increase in strike actions. On the contrary, it may even have served to prevent them. Hawaii and Pennsylvania now allow all public employees except policemen and firemen to strike, and except for the bitter and protracted Philadelphia school walkout referred to earlier, these two states, if anything, seem to have suffered fewer strike actions than many other states that prohibit such activity. The same can be said for many European countries which grant much more freedom to their public employees in this respect. Sweden, for example, even permits policemen to strike. Yet, the Scandinavian country seems to have experienced substantially less public employee strike action than has the United States.

The American Assembly, a non-partisan institute affiliated with

---

57. *Boston Herald-American,* March 28, 1973
58. These and similar statements will be found in "Collective Bargaining in the Public Sector: A Symposium," in *Public Administration Review,* March/April 1968, p. 131.

Columbia University, reached the conclusion at its fortieth gathering in the fall of 1971 that it was time to move in this direction. A panel of seventy top-level government, legal, academic, business and labor leaders recommended that public employees be allowed a limited right to strike after "obligatory procedures" have been exhausted. In making this recommendation, they cited not only some of the considerations already noted, but pointed out that management itself may be better off, for such strikes "often result in lost wages [for public employees] and no real discomfort for public employers whose revenues continue unimpaired."[59] The issue of the right to strike will continue to provoke discussion and debate as the public employee union movement continues to grow.

CASE STUDY

Turbulence at the Tower[60]

On March 25, 1971, as the Easter weekend was getting underway, some one thousand air controllers failed to report for work. Their action disrupted air traffic throughout the nation, hitting with particular force the key cities of the Northeast. By late the following day almost sixty jet airliners were grounded at John F. Kennedy Airport in New York City, unable to take off. Overhead, more than fifty other jets circled for as long as two hours waiting to land. Conditions in many other airports were almost as bad. The air controllers' strike of 1971 was underway.

This was not the first time that the disgruntled controllers had staged such a job action. There had been a six-week slowdown in 1968, a three-day "sick-out" in 1969 and a three-week "sick-out" in 1970, the latter involving about 15 percent of the controllers. The issues were primarily equipment and working conditions although pay was also a factor. As a result of these actions, the Federal Aeronautics Administration had raised salaries and speeded up its modernization program. But the underlying discontent continued to simmer while the wounds that had been opened by these events refused to heal.

The issue which had precipitated the current dispute was the FAA's reassignment of three controllers from Baton Rouge, Louisiana to other cities. The three had rejected the new assignments, only to be told that they would be suspended on March 30 if they were not then at their new posts. The three controllers were active members of the Professional Air Traffic Controllers

---

59. *New York Times,* November 1, 1971.
60. This case study was constructed out of news stories appearing in the *New York Times.* The stories appeared one day after each of the events they describe. The long quotations from E. L. Jack Embrey which conclude this secton are from his address "Recovering a Working Relationship in FAA Following a Strike," which was presented at the annual convention of the American Society for Public Administration in Los Angeles, 1973.

Union, PATCO, and PATCO officials had interpreted the move as an attempt to break or at least weaken the union. It had requested that the matter be turned over to the Federal Mediation and Conciliation Service, but the FAA refused.

However, as with most strikes, the precipitating factor was more of a symptom than a cause. Other issues included the union's desire to have certain rights restored which it had forfeited as a result of the previous strikes. These included recognition as a bargaining agent for the controllers with a dues check-off. The union wanted the FAA to once again deduct union membership dues from controllers' pay envelopes and turn them over to PATCO.

Still more basic were the repeated requests by the controllers for better equipment and less overtime work. The public, they claimed, had a distinct stake in this request, for fatigued controllers and obsolete equipment, so they maintained, were endangering the nation's air safety. The FAA, said the union, had not moved vigorously enough to modernize and expand the nation's air traffic control system and this had placed too much work and too much responsibility on the shoulders of its members.

The union had given advance warning of its contemplated action. It had sent a letter to Secretary of Defense Melvin E. Laird stating that numerous controllers would call in sick on grounds of fatigue on the stipulated day. However, in so doing they would not, said union spokesmen, be violating the federal government's strict no-strike edict. Rather, they would simply be taking advantage of their sick leave.

As might be expected, the FAA did not accept such an explanation. Shortly after the wave of "sickness" broke out, the agency dispatched the following hand-delivered telegram to every "sick" controller:

If your absence continues more than 24 hours after the receipt of this telegram, and if you fail within that time to furnish medical proof of your ailment or illness, prompt action will be taken against you under the statutes and regulations of the courts, the agency and the Civil Service Commission.

FAA Administrator John H. Shaffer claimed the strike was a product of union manipulation of its membership. "I think these people have been ill-advised and misled by a handful of men whose actions have been characterized consistently by a thirst for power and utter disregard for the law," he stated a day after the strike began. He also dismissed the union's contention that the FAA's policies were endangering the public safety. "We never sacrifice safety in an effort to cut delays," said the administrator.

However, on the same day that Shaffer was issuing his statement, the union obtained some unexpected support for at least one of its basic positions. In what appears to have been a sheer coincidence, the National Transportation Safety Board released a report criticizing some of the FAA's safety practices. It called on the agency to alter, among other things, its system of rotating controllers periodically from the night to the day shift. The board said that a plane crash the previous December may have been caused by a fatigued controller who had had only five hours of sleep after switching shifts.

On April 3, the *New York Times* published an analysis of the strike. It found that the dispute was mainly a power struggle between PATCO and its executive director, F. Lee Bailey, and Administrator Shaffer. Both sides were judged guilty of having misbehaved. The union had acted in an unruly fashion but Shaffer had also conducted himself in an antagonistic manner. The *Times* said it had polled leaders in the industry before arriving at this conclusion. It also quoted a report issued on January 1, 1970 by what was called the Panel on Controller Careers.

The committee found that employee-management relations with the FAA are in a state of extensive disarray due to ineffective internal communication, to failure on the part of the FAA to understand and accept the role of employee organizations, and to ill-considered and intemperate attacks on FAA management by certain unions.

Meanwhile, the FAA had secured a temporary restraining order requiring PATCO to withdraw any support from the strike. As the strike continued, the government took the union to court. Since the air controllers were a small and spread-out group with little political clout, and since federal judges are appointed and not elected, the courts were willing to act. On Friday, April 2, a federal judge got the union and the FAA to agree on a four-point program under which the union was to urge its members to return to work while the government was to cancel its contempt proceedings against PATCO's officers. A separate contempt of court proceeding against the union itself, however, was allowed to stand.

When numerous air controllers continued to call in sick, the court began to act more vigorously. Faced with threats of suspension, lost pay and even dismissal, the air controllers drifted back to work and by April 15, the strike was just about over.

FAA Administrator Shaffer refused to claim victory. He conceded that the agency "had not worked hard enough on labor-management relations in the past" and had used the federal government's ban on strikes as a sort of "security blanket" to protect the FAA against the repercussions of its own failings in this regard. At the same time, however, he held the union leadership primarily responsible for the strike action, and he announced that disciplinary action would be taken. Subsequently, the FAA fired about 80 controllers for their role in the strike and gave suspensions ranging from six to twenty days to 2,200 others for their participation. Union efforts to have the courts nullify these disciplinary measures proved unavailing.

The FAA's labor problems then faded from public view. However, two years later, E. L. Jack Embrey, the FAA's new union-management relations chief, gave an accounting of lessons that had been learned and actions that had been taken in the wake of the Easter sick-out.

We think it fair to say that all parties learned a good bit from the strike. The individual controller learned he could not disregard Federal laws and regulations, even though he believes his cause is just. The union learned that we would not allow it to dictate to management and foster an illegal job action. As for FAA? We learned more than anyone! First of all, we learned that a strike by Federal workers is a tragic affair in which no one wins. We learned that we simply must do a better job of really listening and really communicating with our work force to insure that such an event will not happen again. And finally, we learned that tactics used by our employees may be inappropriate—even illegal—but that their demands may well be legitimate and justified.

Embrey then went on to discuss some of the actions which the FAA took as a result of this learning experience in labor relations.

First, both the Secretary of Transportation and the Administrator of FAA issued statements to all managers in the air traffic service urging them to exercise reason, carry out the disciplinary actions with good judgment and understanding, and to be a positive force toward reconciling the differences among employees when the strikers did return to work.

We gave immediate attention to training every first line supervisor in managerial skills. We established a management training center at Lawton, Oklahoma and within 2½ years after the strike every supervisor, and newly designated supervisor (approximately 7,000 total) have had three weeks of intensive training to help them to recognize their potential as managers of human resources, teach them how to deal with unions and their functions as team members in FAA's job of accomplishing its mission.

Communication has had much attention. There is an established system for upward communications as well as down and across. As one example, the agency produces a video-tape at least once each month on topics of interest to everyone in the agency and all employees are urged to set aside approximately 30 minutes during their work time to view each presentation. Some of the video-tapes have featured employees asking top agency officials unrehearsed questions about various things of interest to them.

We have revitalized our organization for dealing with unions which represent our employees. A separate office of labor relations, with ready access to the Administrator of FAA, has been established. We have fostered a concept of nationwide bargaining units for those unions which represent discrete occupational groups and which win nationwide recognition elections. We now have two nationwide units of recognition with meaningful labor contracts already negotiated.

We have accelerated our recruitment and training efforts to the point that we no longer have the critical staffing shortages which was one of the major reasons for the strike.

The modernized equipment which was on-order but not delivered at the time of the strike is now on line at every major facility. Further, we are encouraged by the passage of the Airport/Airways Improvement Act of

1970 which will make some 15 billion dollars available for modernization of our airports during this decade.

A comprehensive second career and early retirement law was recently gained from the Congress. This has enabled us to acquire needed improvements to the air traffic controller career field.

Almost all of the approximately 80 controllers who were fired for their leadership roles in the strike were rehired after many of them had been off the payroll for some two to two and one-half years. Further, we have proved, through management actions, that even though some 2,000 were suspended without pay from 6 to 20 days each for strike participation, we have not been vindictive nor taken actions prejudicial to their long-range careers. Our fair treatment of the strikers has effectively removed a major obstacle to the improvement of FAA's relationship with the offending union.

The remedial action taken in the aftermath of the strike has not been confined to the FAA's management. PATCO's leadership has also learned a lesson or two. Says Embrey, "They too have taken action to gain a more reasoned and responsible approach toward making their grievances known in ways which are not counterproductive to the interests of those who use the nation's airways." As a result, "Unions are considered a part of the fabric of our day-to-day dealings with our employees."

Thus, the turbulence that engulfed the air towers of the nation in the spring of 1971 seems to have provided the basis for smoother and safer air travel for the foreseeable future.

6

Leadership

During the late 1930's, J. Robert Oppenheimer seemed to have found happiness teaching theoretical physics at the University of California at Berkeley. A shy and nervous man, he was pleased with the fact that he seldom had to venture into the laboratory, let alone the work-a-day world outside the campus. Instead, he could spend much of his time working out equations on his blackboard and indulging in his favorite hobby which was reading mystical Hindu poetry in the original Sanskrit. True, he contributed money to political causes that seemed to meet his ideals, and he did enjoy a reasonable amount of social life. But he was largely occupied with theoretical physics and esoteric poetry when World War II broke out.

The war wrought great changes in Oppenheimer's peaceful and sheltered existence. In a few years, he found himself assembling and directing a task force of over one thousand scientists and technicians in developing the atomic bomb. This involved, among other things, running an entire community since the scientists, along with their wives and children, were forced to live in sealed-off seclusion in an isolated area in New Mexico. As everyone now knows, the Los Alamos community stayed together, the scientists accomplished their work and the bomb was built. Afterwards, many of the physicists involved agreed that no one but Oppenheimer could have done it.[1]

The rapid transformation of the shy and nervous professor into the forceful and effective administrator is but an extreme example of one of the most fascinating phenomena in administration, namely the mystery of leadership. For leadership and the qualities it demands have puzzled and perplexed many an administrative theorist over the course

---

1. The material on Oppenheimer in this chapter is drawn mainly from Nuel Pharr Davis, *Lawrence and Oppenheimer* (New York: Simon and Shuster, 1968).

of time. Peter Drucker, a noted business writer and management consultant, reports that "among the effective executives I have known and worked with, there are extroverts and aloof, retiring men, some even morbidly shy. Some are eccentrics, others are painfully correct conformists. Some are fat and some are thin. Some are worriers and some are relaxed. Some drink quite heavily and others are total abstainers. Some are men of great charm and warmth, some have no more personality than a frozen mackerel."[2]

Thus, anyone who hopes to spell out the qualities of a leader is embarked on a perilous and problematic mission. One helpful and by now rather obvious observation, however, can be made at the outset. Leadership is to a great extent determined by the needs of the situation. "It is more fruitful to consider leadership as a relationship between the leader and the situation than as a universal pattern of characteristics possessed by certain people,"[3] McGregor once noted. In a similar vein, William J. Reddin, after surveying the research on management style, concluded that "no single style is naturally more effective than others. Effectiveness depends on a style's appropriateness to the situation in which it is used."[4] There is, in short, no ideal leadership style and most probably no ideal leader who can ably handle all situations.

Adolph Hitler offers an interesting illustration of this. His great though gruesome career as leader of Germany is certainly well known. Less well known is his career in the Austrian army during World War I. Although he served over four years in combat, and although he was decorated twice for bravery, Hitler ended his military career at the age of 29 holding the rank of corporal. Since promotion comes quickly in wartime to those who survive, anyone assessing Hitler's record in 1918 would have rated him a poor prospect to become even a shop foreman in civilian life.

The fact is that Hitler's peculiar leadership abilities needed a particular situation in which to flourish. This meant not only the conditions which existed in Germany during the postwar period, but also the requirement that Hitler be the number one person in any movement or government that he should become connected with. In a subordinate post, no matter how high it might have been, *Der Fuehrer* would most likely have been a washout. Some leaders simply cannot lead unless they occupy the pinnacle position. As Paul Appleby once noted, "there are men who would be poor as ordinary section heads in a bureau but who would be able and effective as Secretary of the Department."[5]

---

2. Drucker, *The Effective Executive* (1967), p. 22.
3. McGregor, *Leadership and Motivation* (1966), p. 73.
4. William J. Reddin, *Managerial Effectiveness* (New York: McGraw-Hill, 1970), p. 35.
5. Appleby, *Big Democracy*, p. 41.

If some leaders can only lead when no one is above them, others can only lead successfully when the reverse is true. There are men who would do well in the second highest position of a very large organization but who would flounder if placed in overall command of even a quite small one. In other words, they are natural seconds-in-command. Arthur Schlesinger puts Dean Rusk, who served as Secretary of State during the Kennedy and Johnson administrations, into this category. "He was a superb technician: this was his power and his problem," writes Schlesinger of Rusk. "He had trained himself all his life to be the ideal chief of staff, the perfect number-two man. The inscrutability which made him a good aide and a gifted negotiator made him also a baffling leader. When Assistant Secretaries brought him problems, he listened courteously, thanked them and let them go; they would depart little wiser than they came. Since his subordinates did not know what he thought, they could not do what he wanted. In consequence, he failed to imbue the Department with positive direction and purpose. He had authority but not command."[6]

Situational differences requiring different leadership styles do not just concern matters of hierarchical level. Different types of organizations may also demand different types of leaders. Many a successful business executive has failed miserably when he thought he could transfer his administrative prowess to the public sector. Few public sector executives have had the opportunity to test their leadership skill in commanding a business firm, but probably they would produce a comparable failure rate. Furthermore, any particular organization may need different leaders at different stages of its existence. Revolutions, for example, often bring to the fore vastly different kinds of leaders depending on the stage they are in. Thus, a fiery Trotsky may give way to a crafty Stalin, and a charismatic and flamboyant Marat may be replaced by a stolid and ruthless Robespierre.

The relationship of leadership ability to the particular situation requiring it makes the task of defining and detailing a list of general leadership qualities difficult and possibly even deceptive. Yet, certain qualities do seem to characterize at least many if not all leaders in many though not all situations. And although the list does not constitute a formula—one could possess all the qualities on the list and still be unable to lead—it does provide something of a basis for the student to gain a perspective on one of the most intriguing and enigmatic aspects of the administrative craft.

---

6. Schlesinger, *A Thousand Days*, p. 403.

QUALITIES OF LEADERSHIP

Probably no quality is more pertinent and pervasive among successful leaders than the quality of optimism. To lead successfully, one must believe that his leadership will make a difference. No matter how dark and dismal the journey, he must be able to see a light at the end of the tunnel.

Harlan Cleveland who has served successfully in many leadership roles—he is currently president of the University of Hawaii—lays particular stress on this quality of leadership. "Prophecies of doom," he reminds us, "do not in fact move people to action."[7] Indeed, they are more likely to have the reverse effect. In order to be happy, a man must believe in the possibility of happiness, the great Russian writer Tolstoy once pointed out. The same holds true for leadership. In order to exercise leadership, one must believe in its possibilities.

That energy and enterprise must accompany such optimism should be fairly obvious. This does not mean that every luminary in the ranks of leadership must put himself forth as a whirlwind of activity. Yet, even if his leadership position has been thrust upon him, he cannot hope to meet its obligations without some deliberate and diligent application of his talents. Leaders often do not seem to be working hard at their jobs, but such appearances can be deceptive. A leader may be relaxed and easy going, but if he is lazy and indolent, he will usually fail.

What about intelligence? Certainly, it is rare to find a leader who is both dumb and successful, and some have been extraordinarily brilliant. Take Napoleon and William Pitt, those young titans who confronted each other across the English Channel at the beginning of the nineteenth century. Each was at home in a variety of disciplines including mathematics, languages and the law. In this country, meanwhile, a president had come to power who was accomplished in architecture, science, agriculture, law, political theory and nearly every field of study of his time. Nevertheless, when it comes to correlating mental ability with leadership, some qualities seem much more crucial than others.

One vital intellectual skill is verbal ability. Skill in the use of communication generally accompanies leadership ability no matter what the particular situation may be. A ditch digger who becomes the foreman of his work gang will most probably be able to communicate better than all or at least most of the other members of the gang.

An interesting study on this point was done many decades ago. Researchers tested people from various occupations as to their vocabu-

---

7. Cleveland, "A Philosophy for the Public Executive."

laries. It was a multiple choice test which presented the testee with numerous words ranging from the commonplace to the obscure. Each word was followed by four others, one of which was a synonym. The object was to pick the synonym. The group that placed highest on the test were business executives who outscored all the professional groups including college professors. The test was given at a time when relatively few businessmen had a college education. Yet, as a group, they demonstrated the greatest facility at word recognition.

An ability to communicate, at least when he wanted to, apparently played a key role in Dean Rusk's rise to administrative prominence. Though sharing Arthur Schlesinger's view that Rusk was more suited for a number-two than a number-one position, journalist David Halberstam points up this valuable Rusk quality in his book *The Best and the Brightest.* "A brilliant expositor, he had a genius for putting down brief, cogent and forceful prose on paper—a rare and much needed quality in government," reports Halberstam.[8] It was this ability, reflected in the cables that he sent back while serving with the army in India during World War II, that led to Rusk being "discovered" by his superiors and being slotted for the wider opportunities that came his way when the war ended.

A much more complex question when it comes to relating leadership with intellectual skills concerns the qualities of creativity and judgment. The problem is that these two qualities are not always compatible. The good idea man, as Katz and Kahn point out, tends to be enthusiastic and somewhat impulsive and may fail to subject his ideas to searching criticism. He frequently has a hard time translating his ideas into action and when he does succeed in doing so, he may fail to follow through because he soon sprouts another idea that he wants to work on.

Katz and Kahn maintain that leadership puts more of a priority on reasoned judgment than creativity, and if a leader can have only one of these qualities, he is better off with the former. He can always make up for his lack of creativity by surrounding himself with people who possess such a trait.[9] This to a great extent was true of Oppenheimer. Though a brilliant physicist, he was not considered a particularly creative one. His talents lay in being able to analyze the work of others and, in so doing, to spur them on to greater efforts.

The question of judgment leads us to another quality which is still more difficult to define. Perhaps an illustration will serve as the best introduction to its discussion.

---

8. Halberstam, *The Best and the Brightest,* pp. 318–319.
9. Katz and Kahn, *The Social Psychology of Organizations,* pp. 293–294.

The story is told of the president of a major steel company who was inspecting one of his plants. He suddenly noticed two men puffing on cigarettes in an area where smoking was forbidden. He went over to the two men, handed each of them an expensive cigar and said good-naturedly, "Smoke these outside, boys."

This simple incident conveys some of the flavor of successful leadership. Good leaders rarely lose their heads or give in to their emotions. Instead, they deal with situations and the people involved in a disinterested manner best designed to achieve the results they have in mind. This observation is confirmed by research. Burleigh Gardner cites one study of several hundred executives which showed that they maintained a detached, objective view of their subordinates. Other studies, says Gardner, tend to corroborate this finding.[10]

This does not mean that a good leader should be a cool and clammy individual lacking all the human qualities of warmth and empathy. It rather indicates that he is able to keep his personal feelings in check and to appraise objectively the needs of the situation.

To the late Dean Acheson, who served as Secretary of State during the late 1940's and early 1950's, Henry A. Wallace and General George C. Marshall provided contrasting examples of the presence and absence of this quality. In his book *Present at the Creation,* Acheson recalls listening in 1945 to Wallace, who was then Secretary of Commerce, testifying on a bill. Acheson says Wallace gave, in a few minutes, a complete demonstration of how his weak points completely destroy his strong ones. He was well informed and gave excellent testimony. However, on two or three occasions hostile questions made him quite lose his temper, whereupon he made some ill-considered remarks and the whole hearing turned into a brawl."[11]

Two years later, while working in the State Department under its then Secretary George C. Marshall, Acheson came upon a man of quite different capacities in this regard. Marshall demanded "complete and even brutal candor" from all his staff and when he got it, he rarely seemed to show displeasure. "He had no feelings, he said, 'except those which I reserve for Mrs. Marshall.'"[12]

Of course, the annals of history are filled with petulant and peevish people who have seemed at times to display a flair for leadership. And it is true that some situations seem to require the qualities of detachment and objectivity less than others. But many of those who appear to have flouted this rule have not really done so. Adolph Hitler is

---

10. Burleigh Gardner, "Successful and Unsuccessful Executives," *Advanced Management,* September 1948.
11. Dean Acheson, *Present at the Creation* (New York: W. W. Norton, 1969), p. 151.
12. *Ibid.,* p. 286.

one example. Although undoubtedly a neurotic if not pathological individual, he was also, at least in the earlier stages of his career, a man who could make good use of this principle. Hitler's chief architect and subsequent minister for war production Albert Speer tells in his memoirs of the first time he saw Hitler. The Nazi leader had come to address the students at Berlin University prior to his assumption of power.

> His appearance . . . surprised me. On posters and in caricatures I had seen him in military tunic, with shoulder straps, swastika armband and hair flapping over his forehead. But here he was wearing a well-fitted blue suit and looking remarkably respectable. Everything about him bore out the note of reasonable modesty. Later I learned that he had a great gift for adjusting—consciously or intuitively—to his surroundings.[13]

His speech itself, notes Speer, also showed that Hitler knew his audience. Instead of an intellectually vapid harangue, the Nazi leader delivered to the students a rather carefully worded lecture on history that was mixed with a good deal of humor.

The Swiss psychologist Jean Piaget, well known for his pioneering work with children, offers an observation which may aid in summing up this rather illusive leadership quality. Piaget points out that when a child stands in front of another person, he will tend to identify the other person's left arm as his right and vice versa. This is because the arm of the person he is facing is on the same side as his own. The child is unable to put himself in the other person's shoes.

As people grow older, they usually manage to make this change, at least to the point of distinguishing between the right and left sides of a person they are facing. But everyone still retains some degree of difficulty in seeing situations from the other person's position, particularly when more than physical position is concerned. The good leader will be able to do this better than most. By being able to coolly assess situations from the various points of view of those concerned and to act accordingly, he exercises the influence that leadership betokens.

Qualities in Question

The above list of leadership qualities is admittedly a short one and may seem more notable for what it omits than for what it includes. Left out are at least three characteristics which are usually associated with leadership: technical proficiency, decisiveness and charisma. Let us examine them in turn.

Government in the United States has traditionally placed a great

---

13. Albert Speer, *Inside the Third Reich* (New York: 1970), pp. 18-19.

emphasis on technical competency in selecting leaders for its various administrative agencies. Americans generally insist that school superintendents be educators, public health commissioners be doctors and public works commissioners be engineers or at least men with some engineering background. Appointing technically trained people to administrative positions is often equated with progressive government and is considered a repudiation of administration by political hacks. A city manager-run city will more likely appoint a professional law enforcement specialist as its police commissioner than will a city dominated by political bosses, though the latter also seem to be bending to this trend. As for the federal service, a 1966 report by the Committee on Economic Development stated that nearly half of the top executives in the federal government were trained in mathematics, science, engineering or medicine.[14]

Many European countries, however, view the matter quite differently. They stress administrative skills and background rather than demonstrated technical expertise. When France consolidated its two major police forces in 1968, the government appointed as its new police head a man who had previously been the chief of staff in the Ministry of Education. He was neither an educator nor a policeman but simply a professional administrator.

Which is the right approach? There are no hard and fast answers to this question. Certainly technical expertise has much to commend it. A person who understands the actual work of his subordinates will possess very definite assets when it comes to directing them. Katz and Kahn cite studies done on railroads, power plants and heavy industry which showed that those foremen who were the most technically competent were generally the foremen whose work teams were the most productive.[15] At a minimum, a supervisor who is technically expert can gain the respect of his subordinates in a way that a non-technician would be unable to do.

Yet, administrative theorists even in this country have long looked askance at the "specialist syndrome." The leader of an organization or an organizational unit must be able to relate the unit to its external environment. This, so the claim goes, is best done by a professional administrator. He is much more likely to possess the expanded frame of reference which the leader needs to manage his organization in a productive manner. Failure to assess the external environment can be and has often been disastrous to many organizations.

Furthermore, the technically trained and experienced leader has

14. John J. Corson and R. Shale Paul, *Men Near the Top*, Supplementary Paper No. 20 issued by the Committee for Economic Development (Baltimore : Johns Hopkins Press, 1966).
15. Katz and Kahn, *op. cit.*, p. 328.

usually built up a network of prior associations and preferences. His very background makes him more prone to favor some activities than others and to listen to some people more than others. He may lack the overall and objective perspective that the generalist administrator can provide.

These considerations acquire heightened importance the more one moves up the organizational ladder. As many writers have pointed out, the higher the administrative level, the more time the administrator spends on "external" in contrast to "internal" matters. Furthermore, as Katz and Kahn note, the larger and more complex an organization becomes "the greater will be the commonality of their management substructures."[16] This indicates that since organizations are becoming larger and more complex all the time, their administrative positions are becoming more and more alike and thus demanding less and less specialist skills.

Other factors also lend support to the oft-heard administrative adage that "the technician should be on tap and not on top." As David E. Lilienthal has said, the technician's work usually has a terminal point. There is the bridge to be built, the vaccine to be discovered, the patient to be cured and discharged. The administrator has to think in different terms. His task is never done since in administration there is never any real completion.[17]

We see some of these problems at work in the Vietnam war. According to former Undersecretary of the Air Force Townsend Hoopes, the military leaders could only think in terms of winning the war. They avoided the question of whether some means of achieving victory might produce more problems than they solved or whether it would even be in America's interest to win the war in the first place. Theirs was a "can do" policy which, while productive and useful in some situations, can prove disastrous in others.[18] Indeed, as specialists, the military in Vietnam even went further and failed to question the efficacy of the means they were using to achieve their own limited goals. Thus, instead of questioning the usefulness of airpower to begin with, they devoted their efforts to trying to make it more efficient.

One thing is certain and that is that the abilities that make a person a proficient specialist in his field do not automatically equip him for administrative leadership in that field. The first-rate teacher all too often turns into the third-rate principal. In writing about scientists and administration, C. P. Snow observes that "to be any good, in his youth at

---

16. *Ibid.,* p. 115.
17. David E. Lilienthal, *Management: A Humanist Art* (New York: Columbia University Press, 1967), p. 17.
18. Townsend Hoopes, *The Limits of Intervention* (New York: David McKay, 1969), pp. 79-80.

least, a scientist has to think of one thing, deeply and obsessively, for a long time. An administrator has to think of a great many things widely, in their interconnections, for a short time."[19] Of course there are exceptions such as Oppenheimer, or, for that matter, Snow himself. But more often than not, the qualities that make for excellence in a speciality do not coincide and frequently conflict with the qualities that make for excellence in administering organizations devoted to that speciality.

In summary, then, we may say that technical competence in the field is an advantage to an administrator presuming that everything else is equal. The problem is that everything else is usually not equal. Thus, while such competence may have its uses, particularly at the first level of supervision, it tends to pose increasing disadvantages as one moves to the higher reaches of organizational life. Thus, it is omitted here as a necessary quality for administrative success.

Another quality that is often imputed to successful administrators is the ability to make quick decisions. To be sure, decision-making is what administration is basically all about. George C. Marshall maintained that the capacity to make decisions was the rarest gift that the gods could give a man.

However, when one scrutinizes the record of many notable government executives, one frequently finds not a chronicle of speedy decision-making but almost its opposite. Historians have constantly commented on Franklin Roosevelt's persistent penchant for procrastination. Some claim it was his most characteristic trait. Winston Churchill was also not keen on making decisions that did not demand immediate action. Unless it was imperative to make a major decision at once, Churchill would approach it by calling a meeting, asking for various views. Then he would ask for memoranda on the subject and then hold another meeting. It is also interesting to note that while John F. Kennedy sought to present himself as a firm and decisive leader, his favorite book was a biography of a British prime minister named Melbourne. And Lord Melbourne was a leader who ardently espoused and acted on the belief that "when in doubt what should be done, do nothing."[20]

Business leaders sometimes show the same trait. Alfred P. Sloan, Jr., the man who is credited with building General Motors into the giant it is today, never made a decision involving personnel the first time it came up. He might make a tentative judgment and even doing that

---

19. Snow, *Science and Government*, p. 73.
20. Anyone who believes that dynamic dictators are immune from such a tendency may find the following quotation from Adolph Hitler of interest. "Unless I have the incorruptible conviction: *This is the solution,* I do nothing—not even if the whole party tried to drive me to action. I will not act. I will wait, no matter what happens." Quoted in *The Mind of Adolph Hitler* by Walter C. Langer, M.D., N.Y., Basic Books, 1972, p. 81.

might take him several hours. Then, he would put the matter aside and tackle it again in a few days time. Only when the same name came up two or three times in a row would he proceed. It was this practice, says Peter Drucker, that helped give Sloan his wide reputation for picking winners.[21]

The Sloan example provides an insight into the reasons why successful leaders often seem loath to exercise the foremost prerogative of their position, decision-making. They realize the complexities and implications that may arise from any significant decision they may make. This is particularly true in government where there are so many different interests to contend with. A decision by a governmental administrator may cause reverberations throughout his staff, other governmental agencies, the legislative branches, clientele groups, the press and the public. And all of them must be taken into account. Furthermore, a good decision-maker must be like a good billiard player: Everytime he goes to hit the ball, he must figure out just what will happen when that ball hits another ball which in turn will hit another. Any decision of consequence is likely to set off a chain of events whose ultimate impact may prove difficult to discern.

For reasons such as these, speedy decision-making does not always make for good decision-making and good decision-makers have usually taken cognizance of this fact. While there is little disputing the fact that any administrator has to be able to make decisions before time runs out on him, many of the best executives have persistently preferred to stretch the time limit to the near maximum. As society and the apparatus that governs it becomes increasingly complicated, we may find that quick decision-making, although it occasionally will be necessary, will become less and less characteristic of successful administration.

The final item on what might be called the "left-out list" of leadership qualities is charisma. The capacity to be colorful and heroic, to stir the emotions of men and capture their hearts and minds, has long been regarded as a powerful leadership tool. Many of those we regard as outstanding leaders have possessed this trait. They include not just political leaders such as Roosevelt and Churchill but also some more purely administrative leaders such as Robert Moses, New York City's famous builder of bridges, highways and parks and Harry Hopkins, FDR's dynamic aide.

But charismatic leadership can not only be disadvantageous but even dangerous. Charisma, say Katz and Kahn, "is a means by which people abdicate responsibility for any consistent, tough-minded evaluation of the outcome of specific policies. They put their trust in their

---

21. Drucker (1967), *op. cit.*, p. 32.

leader who will somehow manage to take care of things." In so doing, charisma reduces democracy and equality in an organization for "charisma requires some psychological distance between leader and follower."[22]

The dangers of such a state of affairs are readily apparent. A charismatic leader will usually fail to develop fully the capacities of his subordinates. Instead, they will become overly dependent upon him. When he is absent, the organization will tend to flounder and when he departs for good, it may fall to pieces.

Charismatic leaders usually inhibit communication. Subordinates become too deferential to supply the leader with unpleasant information or to check him in policies that may be unwise. Often, they lose the ability to discriminate between wise and unwise policies for they have surrendered much of their capacity for independent judgment. This can be crucial since a charismatic leader may not only be forceful but also foolish.

History provides us with numerous examples of charismatic leaders who vigorously led their nations down the road to ruin. Hitler and Mussolini are two examples that come frequently to mind. But we do not have to reach so high to find instances of how charismatic leadership can malfunction. Robert Moses may have built more bridges, tunnels and highways than any man in recent history, but many New Yorkers today are questioning the wisdom of all his activity. His final masterpiece, the New York City World's Fair of 1965, turned out to be a startling disaster.

Another instance of how charisma can lead to catastrophe is the case of Ernest Lawrence. A University of California physicist like Oppenheimer, Lawrence seemed to possess certain charismatic qualities. As a result, he soon headed up an important laboratory at the university and persuaded many young scientists to work with him. They ended up going along with his plans to build a super calutron and later, a materials testing accelerator. Both were giant and highly expensive contraptions which turned out to be unworkable. Physicists elsewhere had branded both as silly and impractical from the start, but the charismatic Lawrence was able to wrangle sufficient support while his star-struck subordinates offered no resistance.[23]

It is perhaps fortunate, then, that charisma seems to be dying out as a leadership quality. As columnist James Reston of the *New York Times* has remarked, we are becoming a nation of the bland leading the bland. Some have bemoaned this fact since the charismatic leader often

---

22. Katz and Kahn, *op. cit.,* p. 318.
23. Davis, *op. cit.*

lends color and excitement to administrative activity. However, he also imbues it with other and less desirable elements as well. Furthermore, there are much more genuine ways of making administration exciting and some of these may become apparent as we proceed to examine other aspects of the leadership question.

TECHNIQUES OF LEADERSHIP

Can leadership be learned? Many writers on administration believe it can be, at least to some extent. Certainly, there are tools and techniques that administrators make use of in accomplishing their tasks. To cover them all would be impossible for not only space but knowledge is lacking. Every successful administrator manages to create one or two new ways of operating which are useful to him though they may not be utilizable by others. However, observers have noticed that some basic techniques seem to prove helpful to most administrators in seeking to accomplish their trying tasks.

Budgeting One's Time
A good manager must know how to manage his time. More specifically, he must know how to keep events from crowding in on him and consuming too much of his working life. He must know how to reserve time for himself and not be continually at the beck and call of the worried subordinate or the anxious client.

To Peter Drucker, this is a cardinal element in successful leadership. None of those he has ever known, he says, has managed to accomplish very much unless he could carve out of his working day fairly large slices of time for himself. He needs to do this in order to apply his energies to the broader and more long-range implications of the problems and decisions which constantly come before him. And unless he carefully budgets his time, he will expend his energies putting out brush fires and never treating the underlying causes. "The effective decision maker . . . always assumes that the event that clamors for his attention is in reality a symptom," writes Drucker. "He looks for the true problem. He is not content with doctoring the symptom alone."[24]

The annals of administration offer several examples of what Drucker means. Winston Churchill, says his wartime secretary Lord Normanbrook, would pick two or three matters of greatest urgency and give them his full attention. "He was thus able to control the use of his own

---

24. Drucker (1967), *op. cit.*, Chapter 6.

time, and to prevent its being eaten into by the demands of colleagues wishing to have his help in solving their own problems."[25]

Many administrators, however, often neglect this admonition. C. Brooklyn Derr found, in a study of a major metropolitan school department, that the top administrators were spending about 80 percent of their time on matters that required their immediate attention. As a result they were "managing by crisis."[26] Chester Bowles who served for a time as first Undersecretary of State under Dean Rusk found that Rusk's "energies and efforts were invariably directed at the problems that were presently on his desk with little evidence of concern about how and why they arose in the first place."[27] And Albert Speer speaks perceptively of how Hitler, in his later years, "flouted the old rule that the higher his position, the more free time a man should have available."[28]

Naturally, the process of reserving time for oneself can be overdone. Churchill was often accused of neglecting matters of lesser importance. President Nixon in particular may have overused this technique. According to one article that was published before the Watergate hearings, Nixon wanted "chunks of time that are not planned, partly to give himself an opportunity to react, partly to initiate on his own terms rather than on someone else's."[29] While a laudable goal, it eventually led him into conferring too much authority and responsibility on his chief aides, notably H. R. Haldeman, with rather unfortunate consequences for the president and the country. But Nixon's case, while perhaps not unique, is exceptional. Most administrators err too much in the opposite direction and this tendency produces unfortunate consequences of its own.

Putting First Things First

This principle reads like a truism. Of course, an administrator must put first things first. Still it is often disregarded, largely because of the problems raised above. To establish proper priorities requires the chunks of time which administrators too frequently fail to allocate to themselves. Time in itself, of course, will not necessarily give the administrator all he needs to order his priorities. Some guidelines are also necessary. Peter Drucker offers the following:

Pick the future as against the past;

25. Sir John Wheeler-Bennett, ed., *Action This Day: Working with Churchill, Memoirs of Lord Normanbrook and others* (New York: St. Martin's Press, 1969), p. 21.
26. C. Brooklyn Derr, "Conflict Resolution in Organizations: Views From the Field of Educational Administration," *Public Administration Review*, September-October 1972, p. 498.
27. Bowles, *Promises to Keep*, p. 429.
28. Speer, *op. cit.*, p. 351.
29. R. W. Apple, Jr., "Haldeman the Fierce, Haldeman the Faithful, Haldeman the Fallen," *New York Times Magazine*, April 6, 1973.

Focus on opportunity rather than on problems;

Choose your own direction rather than climb on the bandwagon;

Aim high, aim for something that will make a difference, rather than for something that is "safe" and easy to do.[30]

Franklin D. Roosevelt in many ways seems to have followed such a course. He was almost entirely future-oriented and his focus was definitely set on what could be done rather than what could not. In the words of Frances Perkins, his first Secretary of Labor, Roosevelt "did not like to make a recommendation *not* to do something. He liked to recommend things to be done."[31] Though he kept himself open to advice and counsel, he certainly chose his own direction and, in war and peace, he kept his aims high, sometimes, perhaps, too much so.

The Maintenance of Options

Anyone who manages to travel down the corridors of power will likely receive more than once the admonition to "keep your options open." This is a tactic used by leaders throughout government whether their seat of power is in a legislative body or an administrative agency. It is one reason, and probably the most important one, why so many shrewd leaders are so slow in making decisions. Every decision that a leader makes tends to commit him in some way; it therefore tends to narrow his options.

The advantages of keeping one's options open are fairly obvious. It increases flexibility and maintains wider ground in which to maneuver. It provides more leeway for shifting and changing if the situation itself calls for it. Essentially, the more options a leader has, the more power he has. Consequently, a leader will often be as reluctant to surrender his options as he will be to sacrifice his formal power.

Option maintenance, however, can be and often is carried too far. Through postponing definitive action in order to maintain his options, a leader can acquire a reputation for temporizing and vacillating. Also, he may end up losing all his options, for events will have overtaken him.

President Lyndon Johnson may have been guilty of both types of errors in his conduct of the Vietnam war. At the beginning of 1964, says David Halberstam, Johnson decided to hold off making a decision on what to do until after the fall elections. During this year, "opportunities were lost for possible political negotiation, of re-evaluation of American

---

30. Drucker (1967), *op. cit.,* p. 111.
31. Frances Perkins, *The Roosevelt I Knew* (New York: Harper & Row, 1964).

attitudes, of perhaps convincing the American public that it wasn't worth it, that the Vietnamese themselves did not care that much about the war. Instead," says Halberstam, "they . . . decided not to deal with Vietnam, but to keep their options."[32] During this period the situation deteriorated while the United States became increasingly entrapped. Disengagement was still possible but was, at least politically, much more difficult. And so Johnson moved toward escalation.

Later in the war, Johnson and his administration foreclosed his options by making too many commitments. As Townsend Hoopes points out, by sponsoring supposedly "free" elections in the South, the administration committed itself to the government that these elections produced. This in turn restrained the United States from carrying on serious negotiations which might call for a coalition government. Indeed, we had gone so far in pledging support to the shaky Thieu regime that we could not risk anything that might topple it. Our own prestige was at stake. As Hoopes has put it, "in short, President Johnson and his close advisors had so defined our national purposes and so conducted the war that a compromise political settlement would be tantamount to a resounding defeat for United State policy and prestige. Accordingly, it could not be faced."[33]

Sunk Costs

President Johnson and his associates who brought us into Vietnam can also be judged guilty of committing another commonplace blunder in leadership: falling prey to sunk costs. We have already encountered this problem in our discussion of organizational pathology in chapter four. It is one that haunts all administrations and all administrators. Indeed, it influences many different types of people in many different areas of life.

To gain a better appreciation of how pervasive this particular problem is, let us turn for a moment to the stock market. If a small investor with little knowledge of the market buys a stock and sees it go down in price, he will most likely hold on to it. To sell it would mean taking a loss and this he is usually reluctant to do. Instead he will hold on, hoping that it will eventually recover and enable him to "get out even." The seasoned speculator, so books on the stock market tell us, adopts a completely different approach. When a stock goes down, he usually disposes of it fairly promptly. In this manner, he cuts his losses.

One of the reasons why so few people ever become successful in the stock market is their inability to cut losses. It is also a reason why

32. Halberstam, *op. cit.,* p. 303.
33. Hoopes, *op. cit.,* p. 125. Also see p. 68.

there are so many unsuccessful administrators. For the same principle holds true for government and most any enterprise. Only the proficient practitioners know when to bail out of a losing proposition.

Peter Drucker calls this the practice of "sloughing off yesterday" and he enshrines it as a near sacred precept for the effective executive. Such an executive, he says, periodically reviews his organization's programs, the good as well as the bad, and then poses the question: Would we go into this now if we weren't already doing it? "And unless the answer is an unconditional 'yes,' they drop the activity or curtail it sharply."[34]

The American government obviously failed to do this in Vietnam. Halberstam quotes John McNaughton, an assistant secretary of defense, as saying early in the war, "I think it gets harder every day, each day we lose a little control, each decision that we make wrong, or don't make at all, makes the next decision a little harder because if we haven't stopped it today, then the reasons for not stopping it will still exist tomorrow, and we'll be in even deeper."[35]

The problem with sunk costs, as McNaughton's statement implies, is they tend to pile up. The more an administrator puts into an effort, the more he becomes wedded to it. He has committed not only such resources as time and money but also prestige. Each day spent upon the losing project increases his investment in the undertaking, and thus makes its abandonment still harder. The books written by Halberstam and Hoopes on Vietnam vividly illustrate how difficult "sloughing off yesterday" can become.

Vietnam was not the first war that was perpetuated and expanded because of an inability to cope with the problem of sunk costs. According to historian Barbara Tuchman, the contending powers in World War I had reached a virtual stalemate by 1916. Neither side could advance. Yet, neither side responded to President Wilson's constant pleas for peace. Their obduracy was dictated in part, says Tuchman, by the fact that they did not know how to explain to their respective citizens why so much bloodshed had been incurred with so little to show for it. So the war continued and intensified.[36]

Sometimes the issue of sunk costs is deliberately put forth to prolong a project. During the Vietnam war, the argument was frequently made that withdrawal from this seemingly senseless conflict would mean that all the American lives that it had taken would have been expended in vain. Consequently, according to the rather strange but

---

34. Drucker (1967), *op. cit.,* pp. 104–108.
35. Halberstam, *op. cit.,* p. 368.
36. Tuchman, *The Zimmerman Telegram,* p. 123.

effective logic that was sometimes used, we had to stay in the war and sacrifice more lives. Similarly, in 1971 when Congress was debating whether to end subsidies to the proposed supersonic transport plane, the plane's backers pointed to the near billion dollars which had already been spent as a reason for continuing the dubious project. Fortunately, Congress refused to buy the argument and the program ended.[37]

The average administrative leader does not deal in such grandiose projects as wars and supersonic aircraft. Nevertheless, he too is likely to find himself spending too much of his agency's resources prolonging a policy or a program that has been tried and found wanting. While he will take care not to jettison every project as soon as it shows a few flaws, he will also make sure that he does not let his investment trap him into a deepening quagmire. He will know how to slough off yesterday.

Mobilizing Resources

A newly appointed school principal in taking stock of the resources at his command may itemize such things as his staff, his equipment and his school building, together with the budget that he has been alloted to keep the school operating. However, if he is a good administrator, he will know how to muster many more resources than these alone.

He will first of all familiarize himself with all the staff services that may be available at the school department's headquarters and try to make maximum use of them. Then, he will check other governmental institutions such as libraries and recreation centers to see what possibilities they may hold for assisting him in his mission of educating children. Then, he will look to the community for additional aid. He may ask mechanics, carpenters and the like to drop into the classrooms and demonstrate and explain their skills to the youngsters. He may ask businessmen to donate certain commodities which the school can use. He may call upon the parents for all kinds of help. For example, if the father of one child works on the local newspaper, he may ask for some help in publicizing a school project or event.

As with the principal, so with most other administrators, the wise ones will know how to mobilize resources. This technique of leadership is much more important for a public administrator than for a private one for he is usually in a better position to ask for and obtain help without having to pay for it. True, he may not be in as good a position as a school principal since schools enjoy a rather special place in the hearts and minds of the community. But nearly every public manager

---

37. See the *New York Times,* March 7, 1971, Section E, p. 4, for an account of how this factor was finally overcome.

can develop some outside sources of support. A police chief, to take another example, can ask the local bar association to help in drawing up a legal manual for his police officers or he can ask the schools to publicize a new traffic safety program or he may request a local university for research assistance in compiling and evaluating data. The possibilities are almost endless.

Friends and Enemies

One resource which a good administrator is always trying to increase are his friends. This does not mean that successful leadership requires a charming, ingratiating personality. Friendships in government are usually constructed in other ways. The adept administrator will seek to build and expand a network of friendships based for the most part on what he does rather than on what he is.

He will rarely hesitate to do a favor as long as it does not involve a sacrifice of integrity or a disproportionate loss of another resource such as time or influence. He knows that doing favors is like putting money in the bank, i.e., he is building up an account that he may need to draw upon sometime in the future. He also realizes that he cannot know in advance just whose support he may sometime need, so he does not confine his amicable responses merely to those who currently possess substantial degrees of influence. The politician who is out of office may someday be in office, the obstreperous and seemingly uninfluential client may turn to writing letters to the newspaper.

This may seem somewhat cynical and manipulative but it need not be. Indeed, an administrator who naturally likes to provide help and assistance will probably perform this role not only more naturally but also more effectively.

One thing that the wise leader pays particular attention to is the keeping of promises. He realizes that nothing can lose him more support and respect than commitments made but not kept. Consequently, he does not make commitments rashly. As Robert Townsend says, "The world is divided into two classes of people: the few people who make good on their promises (even if they don't promise as much), and the many who don't. Get in Column A and stay there. You'll be very valuable wherever you are."[38]

While building up a base of friendship and support, a public administrator will simultaneously go out of his way to avoid making unnecessary enemies. Professor Charles Frankel, after a stint as an assis-

---

38. Robert Townsend, "Up the Organization," *Harper's*, March 1970.

tant secretary of state, noted that "a man—or his wife—isn't seriously committed to the business of government if he is prepared to disagree with people just for the pleasure of speaking his mind. The art of politics consists in not making enemies unintentionally."[39] A nineteenth century English writer, Henry Taylor put it this way: "A statesman should be by nature and temper the most unquarrelsome of men, and when he finds it necessary to quarrel, should do it, though with a stout heart, with a cool head."[40]

Taylor's comment also provides some clues as to how a leader should conduct himself during those times, and such times are inevitable in every administrative career, when he must confront enemies and not friends. Good administrators do not usually seek out fights but they realize that they cannot always avoid them, and one of the cardinal rules in waging them successfully is to maintain a cool head. As one big city mayor once remarked, never get angry unless it's intentional.

The cool-headed administrator will also observe some other rules when he is engaged in a bureaucratic battle. He will try to determine as much as possible the conditions of the fight such as the time, the place, the issue. He will also seek to avoid fighting more than one battle or fighting on more than one front at the same time. As a New England town manager once noted, "I make sure that if I'm fighting with one of my selectmen, I'm on excellent terms with the other two."[41]

The battling bureaucrat eschews personalism as much as possible. He does not make personal attacks and he seeks to side-step personal issues. He also appreciates the fact that symbolic issues are often more incendiary than real issues and so he often will attempt to defuse and de-emotionalize the controversy by continuing to pay homage to the appropriate symbols. Thus, a welfare administrator who is seeking to liberalize his benefits program may still find it useful to reaffirm his belief that people who can work, should work.

Like a good chess player, the good leader is prepared to lose some pawns and even an occasional knight or bishop in order to win the game. In other words, he is prepared to sacrifice the less important for the more important. Furthermore, he knows that total victories are rarely possible in a democratic government and may not even be desirable. He at all times leaves his opponents with a face-saving retreat route and will usually stand ready to make some conciliatory gesture. If it is a question of phasing out a program that his opponents want continued, he may offer a short reprieve and some further study. If it is a

---

39. Frankel, *High on Foggy Bottom*, p. 98.
40. Henry Taylor, *The Statesman* (New York: New American Library, 1958), p. 77. This fascinating little book was originally published in 1836.
41. In a statement to the author. Anonymity was requested.

question of blocking a program that he believes is wrong, he may offer to go along with a demonstration project to test it out.

John F. Kennedy observed these rules during the Cuban missile crisis and thereby helped prevent this critical turn of events from igniting a war that no one really wanted. When he clamped a naval blockade around Cuba, he also gave Russia's Premier Khrushchev a promise not to invade the island nation. This promise enabled Khrushchev to back down without too great a loss of prestige.

When a leader manages to score a complete victory, he will, if he is truly wise, be magnanimous rather than vindictive to his vanquished opponents. Churchill spent most of the 1930's bitterly assailing the appeasement policies of his own party's prime ministers, Stanley Baldwin and Neville Chamberlain. But after being vindicated and installed in office himself, Churchill took great care to keep Chamberlain, then dying of cancer, personally informed of events. And when Churchill heard that angry Britons had stoned Baldwin's car, he invited his discredited opponent to a well-publicized two-hour lunch.

Of course, not even the best of leaders always win their battles, but when they lose, they know how to accept it with good grace. They do not nurse personal grudges for they are well aware that such feelings will in the end hurt them more than those at whom they are directed. Dwight Eisenhower once said that when anyone had played him false, he would simply write the man's name down on a sheet of paper, throw it into the wastepaper basket and forget it. Good administrators will learn how to take their defeats without embitterment and, realizing that government still goes on, will prepare themselves to do better next time.

Ruffling the Waters

If the smart administrator shows more discretion than valor in picking fights, then this does not mean that he always tries to suppress conflict. To some extent he may even encourage it—within his own organization. It may seem strange but actually a certain amount of tension has its place in any effective organization. Conflict, provided it does not get out of hand, may uncover the weak spots in the organization that need remedial action. It may also improve the flow of communication and increase the number of policy options.

Many observers have called attention to this fact. Herbert Simon pointed out how "jurisdictional disputes are an important means of bringing to the top administrator significant issues of policy, and of preventing these from being decided at lower levels without his knowledge. Similarly . . . they are a means of informing him about the characteristics and viewpoint of his subordinates."[42]

42. Simon, *Administrative Behavior,* p. 145.

Other writers go even further in stressing the value of discord. For Peter Drucker, the right decision requires a certain amount of disagreement, for only such disagreement will bring out all the issues involved and thereby enable the decision-maker (or makers) to arrive at a full understanding of just what is involved. Such disputes prevent the administrator from becoming a prisoner of his subordinates, stimulates his and their imagination and provides more alternative areas of action than would otherwise be the case. An effective decision, says Drucker, is not a consensus based on the facts but a judgment based on disagreeing opinions.[43]

Harlan Cleveland claims that organizations are actually too peaceful. Co-operation, he says, comes too easily and "people are, if anything, too conformist." He admonishes public managers to pay heed to the "fruitfulness of friction" and create within their organization an adequate "web of tension." The tension should be de-emotionalized and de-personalized. No one should argue out of personal animosity for another or out of fear for his own personal security. But people should argue. "The muscles of an organization are like the muscles of a drunk: if they are too relaxed, he doesn't achieve much real coordination."[44]

THE MANAGEMENT OF MEN

The public manager primarily is concerned with managing people. It is on how he performs in this area that his effectiveness will largely be judged. Never an easy task, managing subordinates has become increasingly difficult during the past decade or so. But there are ways of making this job more agreeable and effective.

To begin with, the good administrator exerts every effort to obtain the best possible subordinates. He puts aside any fears that they might outclass him or show him up. He knows that the better they perform, the more his organization will achieve. And the more the organization achieves, the more successful he, as its leader, will be. Furthermore, top-notch people will stimulate him and spur him on to performing more effectively.

Many administrators, to be sure, do not take this approach. In this way they signal their own shortcomings. Princeton mathematician Andre Weil has promulgated what he calls "Weil's rule." According to "Weil's rule," a first-rate man will surround himself with his equals or his betters; a second-rate man will surround himself with third-rate

---

43. Drucker (1967), *op. cit.,* p. 148.
44. Cleveland, *op. cit.*

men; and a third-rate man will only be able to tolerate fifth-rate subordinates and co-workers. C. Northcote Parkinson has said much the same thing. In his own inimitable style, he notes that "if the head of an organization is second-rate, he will see to it that his subordinates are all third-rate; and they will, in turn, see to it that their subordinates are fourth-rate. There will soon be an actual competition in stupidity. . . ."[45]

Top-notch subordinates do present problems. Aside from their propensity to outshine their chief and to insist on speaking up for what they believe, both of which are assets to an administrator, they will very likely not stay with him very long. They will tend to seek out other opportunities when they feel they have pretty much exhausted the possibilities of their present position. And since they are high caliber people, they will usually experience little difficulty in finding something better or at least something different. But this is a situation which a wise administrator is prepared to live with. He will even boast of the many subordinates he had who have gone on to make their mark.

In short, the capable administrator will appreciate the lines which steel magnate Andrew Carnegie chose for his tombstone: "Here lies a man who knew how to bring into his service men better than he was himself."

Delegation

When Moses assembled his people for the Exodus, he picked the ablest among them and put them in charge of groups of varying numbers. Those selected were given the authority to settle all lesser matters and make all lesser decisions themselves, passing up to the prophet only the most important issues. Delegation has played a crucial role in administration ever since. No administrator can hope to do everything himself. He must delegate. And if he picks the best possible people for his subordinates, he must delegate even more for they will insist on substantial chunks of authority in order to exercise and hone their capabilities.

Administrative history abounds with examples of the success that can come when an administrator knows how to delegate authority to others. It was one of the reasons responsible for the success of George C. Marshall. As Secretary of State, Marshall always divested himself of his authority when he had to leave on a mission. As Acheson puts it, "General Marshall was meticulous that when the door to his aircraft closed, the command passed. He even on occasion asked for instructions when a wholly novel and unexpected point arose."[46]

Another military man who showed an unusual capacity for delegation in handling a civilian position was General Ismay, Churchill's

---

45. C. Northcote Parkinson, *Parkinson's Law* (New York: Ballantine Books, 1964), p. 103.
46. Acheson, *op. cit.*, p. 193.

chief civilian aide during World War II. Ismay had two assistants but he allowed them almost as much authority as himself. Contrary to traditional military practice, for example, he did not require all matters to pass through his hands before going to Churchill. As a result, whenever any of the three men were absent, the other two had no trouble filling in. The fact that his assistants could deal directly with anyone prevented bottlenecks from arising.

The value of delegation has also been substantiated by more systematic research. According to Katz and Kahn, "the extent of delegation has proved to be one of the predictors of productivity of many kinds."[47]

But delegation also has perils and pitfalls that, to be avoided, require adherence to a few guidelines. First of all, the leader should not just delegate trivia. He should, rather, delegate substantive assignments along with the authority to carry them out. Sending a subordinate on a mere errand is delegation of a sort but it is not the sort which makes for wise administration. He should remember that when it comes to delegating an important assignment, the subordinate, though he may have less knowledge and experience than the delegator, will, at the same time, be able to devote more time, effort and, most likely, zeal to the task than will his superior.

Beware of delegating to too few people. The administrator who relies on just one or two subordinates to handle his major assignments may end up as their captive. Moreover, as Seymour Berlin and his associates point out, "They can become screens and filters rather than eyes and ears, and they can get between you and the rest of your agency. To accomplish your mission, you need numerous ties into your agency."[48] President Eisenhower, who relied heavily on Sherman Adams, and President Nixon, who depended greatly on his aides John Ehrlichman and H. R. Haldeman, were both brought to grief partly as a result.

Finally, the administrator should bear in mind that some things cannot be delegated. These include responsibility for

creating the climate of the organization;

representing the organization;

establishing the basic policy of the organization;

the overall performance of the organization.

Participation
In a sense, participation in decision-making is merely delegation writ large. In another sense, delegation of authority is participation writ

---

47. Katz and Kahn, *op. cit.*, p. 332.
48. Seymour S. Berlin et al., "A Guide for Political Appointees: Entering the System," *Good Government*, winter 1972.

large. In any sense, both are integrally interwoven strands of the same mosaic.

Participation, however, can take in many more people and many more aspects than can be accounted for by the term delegation, at least as it is commonly understood. Essentially, it means allowing as many people as possible to make as many decisions as possible and to share to the maximum extent possible in making other decisions. It means giving subordinates a "piece of the action."

How big a piece? The answer usually given to this question is "as big a piece as they can handle." However, this is an answer that tells everything and nothing since how much they can handle is all too often wrapped up with the superior's estimate of their abilities in this respect.

Many modern day theorists believe that the average subordinate can participate much more than he is now allowed to do with positive results for all concerned. The real problem, they claim, is that managers are too reluctant to permit or too unable to stimulate such increased participation. A bureau or office head may call in his subordinates, tell them of a decision he has reached and then ask for their comments. This, he may feel, is participatory management. And so it is, after a fashion. Others, however, would say that the better approach would be to call in his people before he makes any decision. He would then explain the problem and get their suggestions first. In the former instance, they may be too cowed to give him their frank reactions once they know what he has in mind. And even if this were not the case, their framework for thinking would be somewhat curtailed by the presence of a tentative decision already lying on the table.

Participation can take many forms. Employees can be allowed to determine many of their work conditions such as hours. They can be asked to contribute their ideas to overall organization policy. They can even play a role in selecting their own superiors.

Its advantages are also many. It generally leads to more informed and better decisions since more minds and more varieties of experience have gone into making them. It also leads to better executed decisions, for those who are to carry them out have had some say in their formulation. And it stimulates employee development. "One of the most important conditions of the subordinate's growth and development," wrote McGregor, "centers around his opportunities to express his ideas and to contribute his suggestions before his superiors take action in matters that involve him."[49]

Participatory decision-making does have drawbacks. For one thing, it delays, sometimes extensively, the taking of action. It does not

---

49. McGregor (1966), *op. cit.,* p. 60-61.

always lead to a better decision and occasionally may produce a worse one. It can be terribly time-consuming to all involved and can at times lead to increased bickering. Furthermore, as we noted in discussing delegation, the responsibility still remains in the hands of the person in charge and he must bear the brunt of the burden when the decision turns out to have been wrong.

Sometimes participatory decision-making is hampered by the reluctance or the inability of the employees themselves to make use of it. Many may react with fear and distrust at being offered such a new role. Others may rush in before they realize the responsibilities it entails. Public managers wishing to embark on the participation route are usually well advised to begin by taking small steps, letting their employees first share in the making of minor decisions and then gradually proceeding to more major ones.

Participatory management has chalked up its score of failures but it has also achieved many notable successes. The California State Insurance Compensation Fund adopted wide-scale participation in a reorganization it undertook in 1967. It produced a dramatic reversal in the fund's hitherto declining fortunes. The United States Forest Service has allowed a certain amount of participation through taking surveys of how rangers feel about certain issues and then using the results of these surveys as a basis for action. Abroad, extensive use of participation has contributed to the dazzling growth rates recorded by Yugoslavia and Japan. The Israeli army allows its soldiers to help select candidates for officer training while the Israeli communal settlements or kibbutzes decide almost every issue through member deliberation and vote. Certainly, both these Israeli institutions have given a good accounting of themselves in the development of that tiny but formidable nation.

Education and Rotation

If participation can improve the employee's knowledge and skills, then it is only one of many devices for doing so. The perceptive public manager will make use of a variety of techniques for encouraging employee growth. These may include formal education and training, discussed in chapter four, and rotation.

Through rotation, an employee enlarges his work experience and increases his abilities and knowledge. He also acquires a broader and deeper understanding of the organization and how its various parts interrelate. Even if his main job is comparatively limited, he will be able to perform it better if he sees how it fits in the overall scheme. Rotation also helps to keep people from becoming bored or growing stale. And it prepares the better ones for more responsible roles.

The Forest Service has made extensive use of rotation and one reason why it does so is to develop the ranger's capabilities. As Herbert Kaufman writes, "The Service does not wait until vacancies occur; it shifts men to replace each other in what looks like a vast game of musical chairs but for the serious purpose of giving them a wide range of experience in preparation for advancement to positions that require a broader understanding of national forest administration than can possibly be gained in long assignments at a single duty station."[50]

Too much rotation, however, can produce adverse effects for both the organization and the employee. If the latter feels that he is a mere pawn being shuttled arbitrarily about at will, he can become quite dispirited. Even if he perceives the value and need for such rotation, he may, if it occurs too rapidly, fail to immerse himself deeply in any one assignment, preferring merely to keep things running smoothly until he goes on to something else.

The State Department, among all its other ills, suffers, so it is thought, from too much rotation. According to John Franklin Campbell, it was unusual during the 1960's for an assistant secretary of state to serve much longer than two years and, says Franklin, it usually takes that long to learn how to maneuver "through the intricate structure of bureaucratic Washington." Foreign Service officers are regularly rotated from post to post as part of department policy. In his book *Anatomy of the State Department*, Sloan Simpson says this encourages them to spend too much time thinking about their future opportunities and to spend too little time confronting their existing challenges.[51]

But while it does have its limits and while it can be abused, rotation is still a valuable tool for increasing employee and organization performance. It can and should be applied on an inter-organizational basis as well. Employees should be allowed and encouraged to move from one organization to another. Here, suitable retirement policies will help. Transferable pensions, for one thing, will facilitate inter-organizational mobility and keep employees from "drying out" in an organization. Possibilities for early retirement are also advantageous. They make organizational change easier and create promotional opportunities. Good circulation can be almost as vital to a healthy human organization as it is to a healthy human organism.

Speaking Out for Subordinates

McGregor once told of a mechanical superintendent of a small manufacturing company who swore at, drove and severely disciplined his

---

50. Kaufman, *The Forest Ranger,* p. 176.
51. Sloan Simpson, *Anatomy of the State Department* (Boston: Houghton Mifflin 1967), pp. 36–37 and pp. 39–40.

202

men. Yet, somehow he managed to maintain a remarkable high morale and productivity in his shop. His behavior did not bother his employees as much as it did a staff group who were seeking to carry out a human relations program in his shop. They could not understand how he managed to break all the "rules" of good management and still do as well as he did.

When they examined the situation further, they found other factors at work. First, the barking superintendent was considered a "square shooter" who, if he behaved rather roughly, also behaved with scrupulous fairness. Then, he took a genuine interest in his subordinates and was always ready to advance them a few dollars until payday or to render some other form of aid without adopting a patronizing attitude.

However, the most important means through which he elicited his men's loyalty was in his constant readiness to go down the line for them with his own superiors. During a ten-year period he had twice stormed into the "big boss' office," as his men fondly recalled, to protest a decision that he felt was unfair to "his boys." When in one of these instances the boss rejected his protest, the superintendent promptly resigned, clamped his hat on his head and strode out of the yard. The "big boss" actually ran after him, caught him as he was going out the gate, and capitulated on the spot.

According to McGregor, the story illustrated a valuable principle of leadership: The leader must be willing, and he must be able, to represent his subordinates to his own superiors. He must have influence higher up and he must use it to protect the rights of those beneath him.[52]

McGregor's observation and the anecdote he provides are supported by more systematic research. Katz and Kahn cite a study done at the Detroit Edison Company which found that supervisors who were following what are considered good human relations practices were not developing any greater morale or productivity in their units than those engaging in less desirable supervisory practices. Further study indicated that the "good guy" supervisors were not effectively relating either themselves or their subordinates to those higher up.

"The conclusion urged on us," says Katz and Kahn, "is that the most effective leader in a pivotal organizational role is not the perfect bureaucrat (rational, role-actuated, heedless of primary bonds) but rather the successful integrator of primary and secondary relationships in the organizational situation."[53]

---

52. McGregor, *The Theory of Human Enterprise* (1960).
53. Katz and Kahn, *op. cit.,* p. 321.

Praise, Censure and Sanctions

As we saw in chapter four, people have ego needs and any organization would do well to acknowledge them. The same holds true for the organization's leaders. They should make adequate provision to recognize the ego needs of their subordinates.

The easiest and cheapest way of doing this is through praise. A few laudatory words cost the giver little while they may mean much to the recipient. Praise is a device that belongs in every administrator's tool kit.

But praise is not quite so cheap as many imagine. Like money, the more of it there is, the less it is worth. An abundance of praise depreciates its value. Consequently, an administrator will do well not to lavish it about. Only when used sparingly, though not necessarily stingily, does it achieve its greatest effect. If an employee needs continual praise, then something is usually wrong either with the employee or with the organization. The latter may have created conditions which require the employee to look for continual reassurance.

George C. Marshall was a leader who was far from prodigious in giving praise. This made his employees appreciate it all the more. Dean Rusk, who served under Marshall in the State Department after World War II, says he only once evoked a favorable comment from his chief. As Rusk was wearily getting ready to leave after having worked a 14-hour day, Marshall remarked, "You've earned your pay today, Mr. Rusk." Commented Rusk later, "So I took that lesson from the greatest man I've ever known. If you have very good people it isn't necessary to compliment them. They know how good they are."[54]

Not all public managers will want to be as parsimonious with praise as was George Marshall. However, they will find it useful not to overspend in this direction. They may also find some other guidelines helpful:

Praise at the appropriate time. A compliment loses its value the longer it is delayed.

Praise the deed not the person. It is not who the person is but what he does that is important. Praising the person can lead to all sorts of problems, including, oddly enough, an increase in the individual's insecurity. He may become too fearful of falling from favor.

Praise in descriptive terms, not qualitative terms. Do not say simply "That was a good report." Say, rather, "That report covered all the matters I needed to know about."

---

54. Halberstam, *op. cit.,* p. 321.

What holds true for praise also, to a great extent, holds true for censure. All employees will need criticism at one time or another but here too it should be rendered at an appropriate time and on a somewhat impersonal basis. Martin R. Smith offers some helpful pointers in this regard:

Stress the positive aspect, encouraging the employee to build up his skills and proficiency in the area or areas where he has shown himself weak.

Concentrate on performance and those aspects of his personal behavior that are distinctly job-related.

When possible, be indirect, though at the same time make sure that the employee gets the message. One device is for the manager to talk about mistakes which he himself has made in the past.

Pick the right time. One good occasion for giving criticism is when the manager is also conferring praise. Calling attention to weaknesses while singling out strengths makes the former action more acceptable.[55]

Smith stresses that criticism to be effective must be directed toward a *correctable* fault that is substantially detracting from a person's *performance*. It does little good to criticize someone for something that does not bear on his job and it may do harm to criticize him for something he cannot change. Peter Drucker goes a step further. He urges executives to focus on what a person can do rather than what he cannot do. Everyone has weaknesses, notes Drucker, but the effective executive, instead of becoming overly concerned with them, concentrates on his subordinate's strengths. These he seeks to build and utilize while, at the same time, he looks for ways to minimize the impact of the employee's liabilities. Drucker claims this is what makes Japanese organizations function with such remarkable efficiency despite the fact that they almost never fire anyone. They accept a person for what he or she basically is and concentrate their attention on developing whatever assets the person may have.[56]

These are wise admonitions for an administrator to follow. Yet even the best of administrators will come across employees who seem unable or unwilling to make any positive contribution at all to organizational goals. Invoking sanctions such as suspension or transfer may help in some cases but not all. The manager will then be faced with the question of dismissal.

---

55. Smith, *I Hate to See a Manager Cry*, p. 108.
56. Drucker (1967), *op. cit.*, Chapter 3.

Firing an employee is often the hardest job an administrator has to do. It is always unpleasant not only to the subordinate and the superior but also to others in the organization. For the public manager, it poses particular problems since he often has to deal with civil service regulations which make dismissal difficult. Usually he can only take such action when the superior is prepared to go before an appeals board and offer solid grounds for his action, backed up by reasonably hard evidence.

Yet discharging the hopeless employee can confer benefits on all concerned. Not only does it make the manager's subsequent task easier but also, in most cases, it lightens the load of his other employees as well. As Parkinson says, "All experience goes to prove that the effective leader must be pitiless toward the disloyal, the careless and the idle. If he is not, the work falls too heavily on the willing men. The sense of belonging to a picked team is soon lost in an organization where the useless are still included."[57] The head of a large chemical laboratory had similar sentiments in mind when he said he would like to automatically fire his lowest producing employee every year. When asked "Why?" he replied, "Simply to keep up the morale of all the others."[58]

There are two additional people who are likely to benefit whenever the dismissal process is appropriately invoked. One is the person who could and wants to do the job that the malfunctioning employee is holding. The other is the dismissed employee himself. "Any person holding down a job that he is unable to do is tense, angry and frustrated," says Smith. "This situation is almost certain to affect his health and his family life."[59] Often a malfunctioning employee could do well at some other post. Retaining him at his present position only keeps him from realizing his own potentials. And if his problems are too severe for him to hold any job, and if he refuses to take any action on these problems while employed, then dismissal may help him finally to confront them.

Dismissal does not need to be unnecessarily difficult. In many cases, the manager may wish to call in the employee for a talk about his performance and in the midst of the conversation raise the suggestion that the employee might be happier working somewhere else. He may offer to ease up on the man's duties to let him shop around for a more congenial position.

Some leaders have resorted to other stratagems. When Franklin Roosevelt wanted to get rid of an official, he would gradually reduce the

---

57. Parkinson, *op. cit.*
58. William English, retired director of chemical research at Polaroid Corp. in an interview with the writer.
59. Smith, *op. cit.*, p. 186.

man's authority and responsibility while also consulting him less and less. Gradually, the official would get the hint and tender his resignation for "personal reasons." Roosevelt would accept the resignation "reluctantly," voicing great public praise for the departing official's "untiring efforts."

John F. Kennedy would proceed somewhat more harshly. He would plant newspaper reports that the official was planning to resign. After reading a sufficient number of these reports, the official would grasp what was happening and turn in his resignation.

Lower-level administrators have made use of both tactics. They will take away a man's assignments and fail to invite him to meetings, or they will circulate a rumor through the office that the individual in question is planning to leave. The first tactic is used more widely than the second and is certainly less offensive. Sometimes a variation of this method is used whereby the man is simply assigned to something he does not want to do. This can also hasten his departure.

But no matter what strategies he may wish to use, any manager must be prepared to fire people on occasion. One of the most important traits a leader can possess, it has been said, is the willingness to give pain. This may be harsh but it is also humane. Almost anyone who has worked in or studied public organization in present-day America would agree that a more aggressive policy in dismissing people would diminish rather than increase overall employee frustration, to say nothing of the frustration experienced by clients and taxpayers. Thus, the good public manager must be prepared to fire people. He owes it to all concerned.

Managing the Manager

Many of the precepts which the manager should use in handling his subordinates he should also apply to himself. In particular, he should be as concerned with his own development as with the development of his employees. Otherwise, he may find that his administrative skills, instead of improving, may actually decline with accumulating experience.

One administrator who zealously followed this rule was Napoleon. "The art of government is not to let me go stale," he once said. He showed in the course of his life that he meant what he said. Napoleon read widely and deeply and made a point of picking the brains of the best men of his time. When he sailed on his ill-fated expedition to Egypt, he took along a group of France's greatest scientists and scholars for his own entertainment and enrichment. While exiled to Elba, he developed an enthusiasm for agriculture and soon invigorated the tiny island's agrarian economy. The fact that Napoleon not only conquered most of Europe but left France with legal and governmental institutions

207

which exist up to the present day is in part a tribute to his almost constant self-development.

Administrators who toil in lesser vineyards can still take a page from Napoleon's book. And the fact that they work within a democratic setting only adds urgency to the task. They must continually reach out for new knowledge and experience both from within and without their organizations.

This can mean more than just reading books or attending executive seminars and conferences, though all these things are important. It can mean joining and participating in other organizations. The Forest Service, for example, has found that its better executives usually participate, and often quite actively, in civic, fraternal and religious organizations. They do so on their own time, but the outside expenditure of energies apparently does not detract from but enhances their work as foresters. Many other organizations have had the same experience, and some private organizations, though unfortunately very few public ones, encourage such activities.

In recent years some executives have found more dramatic ways of broadening their experience pattern. Trans-World Airlines, for example, actually requires its top officials to spend one day a month at a lower level job such as writing out tickets or handling baggage. Few executives may wish to go so far but it may be a good practice for the head of the clinic to see a few patients and for the head of the welfare office to continue to carry a small caseload of clients. An administrator who never does anything but administer the activities of others may eventually lose perspective on just what those activities entail. At a minimum, he should on occasion get "out in the field" and talk with those whom he does not normally talk to in the course of his daily activities.

One administrator who really went far afield to widen his range of experience was Dr. John R. Coleman, president of Haverford College. Coleman decided that his life had become too wound up with "words and politics and parties" and that he was forgetting certain elementary things about people. So, in 1972, he took an unusual sabbatical. Keeping his true identity secret, he wandered throughout the eastern seaboard working at whatever jobs he could find. Before the 51-year-old college head returned to the campus, he had been employed as a garbage man, ditch digger, farm hand and kitchen helper. Not all of his experiences were pleasant but they were all useful.[60]

But even such dramatic gestures as Coleman's may not suffice to keep an administrator on his toes and sooner or later he should start

---

60. *New York Times*, June 10, 1973.

thinking of moving on. "Nobody should be chief executive of anything for more than five or six years," says Robert Townsend. "By then he's stale, bored and utterly dependent on his own cliches—though they may have been revolutionary when he first brought them to the office."[61] Five or six years may be too early, particularly if he takes advantage of some of the other devices we have discussed to keep himself fresh and invigorated, but, nevertheless, the time will usually come when he has ceased to grow in his job. When that time comes, the good manager will pass over the reins to someone else and move along. For that is the way good managers go on to become still better ones.

CASE STUDY

The Supreme Allied Commander[62]

When the *New York Times* polled a group of historians in 1961 as to how they ranked America's presidents, Dwight D. Eisenhower scored a rating of 22. This placed him in the low average category, even below that of Herbert Hoover. Eisenhower's place in history fortunately does not rest on his presidential record alone. Ten years prior to entering the White House, he assumed command of what has been called "the most extensive and cooperative military alliance in history." His conduct of this command provides an excellent example of administistative leadership and assures Eisenhower a notable niche in the history of democratic leadership.

When World War II first broke out, Eisenhower was only fifty years old and held only the rank of lieutenant colonel. Yet, he had already given signs of the promise that was soon to be fulfilled. As a cadet in West Point, he had always remained in the upper third of his class and would undoubtedly have finished near the top if he had not been something of a minor hell-raiser. (He rated in the bottom third of his class in conduct.) Later, he attended the Army War College at Fort Leavenworth and graduated from its one-year course as valedictorian of his class.

His military career itself had also supplied indications that he was no ordinary soldier. He early saw the value of the tanks, and while George Patton was writing articles boosting the tank in the *Cavalry Journal*, Eisenhower was doing the same in the *Infantry Journal*. Both men, of course, saw their pleas go largely disregarded. (In France at this time, an elongated colonel named Charles de Gaulle was making the rounds of Parisian publishers with a book urging a greater role for tanks. His superiors had already turned down his outlandish suggestions.) Eisenhower showed equal prescience and even

---

61. Townsend, *op. cit.*
62. The principal source of material for this case study is E. K. G. Sixsmith, *Eisenhower as Military Commander* (New York: Stein and Day, 1973). Another source is Ladislas Farago, *Patton: Ordeal and Triumph* (New York: Dell Publishing Co., 1970).

more enterprise when it came to airplanes. Seeing in them another major weapon of the future, he took flying lessons at the age of 46 and earned a pilot's license. He was not a man to let himself go stale.

Eisenhower had also showed that he understood something about the behavioral side of management. "Morale," he once wrote, "is at one and the same time the strongest and the most delicate of growths. It withstands shocks, even disasters, on the battlefield, but can be destroyed utterly by favoritism, neglect or injustice." He also had committed himself to the goals of maintaining a mature objectivity in his working life. Among the principles he had written down for himself were "Remember that belligerence is the hallmark of insecurity" and "Forget yourself and personal fortunes."

Finally, Eisenhower had also demonstrated a fairly good capacity at verbal communication. This will come as a surprise to those who are old enough to recall the stumbling syntax which so often characterized his press conferences as president. Yet, as an aide to General MacArthur in the 1930's, Eisenhower drafted most of the eloquent general's speeches. During his mission as commander of the allied forces in World War II, he drafted delicate orders that were considered models of tact and understanding, wrote over 100 letters to his own commander, George C. Marshall, and managed to carry on a fairly lively personal correspondence as well. In one letter to a former West Point classmate, he wrote, "I think sometimes that I am a cross between a onetime soldier, a pseudo statesman, a jack-legged politician and a crooked diplomat. I walk a soapy tightrope in a rainstorm with a blazing furnace on one side and a pack of ravenous tigers on the other. . . . In spite of this, I must admit that the whole thing is interesting and intriguing."

The above description not only indicates an ability to put ideas into words but also provides a fairly accurate description of just what his job entailed. For heading up the allied forces turned out to be one of the most challenging administrative tasks in history.

Eisenhower was picked for this difficult assignment by George C. Marshall, who had spotted his abilities and had started grooming him for higher responsibilities once he, Marshall, had become chief of staff. When Marshall found that he could not take on the commander's role himself, since Roosevelt wanted him to stay in Washington, he sent Eisenhower in his place. It proved to be a fortunate choice.

The difficulties confronting Eisenhower stemmed not so much from the military as from the political situation. There were all kinds of people, parties and pressures that had to be skillfully managed. They included the various British armed forces and their various leaders, British public opinion, British political leaders, many different and often conflicting French interests, other allied forces and their governments including the exile governments in London, and then, of course, his own troops, their commanders, his military and political superiors in Washington and the American press and public opinion. All these, plus the persistent pressure to bring the European war to as speedy an end as possible with a minimum of allied bloodshed, required masterly managerial skills.

Eisenhower approached this trying task with modesty and geniality. He would share his thoughts with his subalterns as if they were his co-equals and he framed his commands as if they were advice. In the view of one of his biographers, the British brigadier general Sixsmith, he was a superb delegator of authority, and yet he was able "to keep his finger on all that was going on. His subordinates were able to see that they were expected to act, they were told what was in Eisenhower's mind, and they knew he would not shrink from his responsibility."

Regarding this latter point, Eisenhower issued a directive early in the campaign that newspaper stories criticizing him should not under any circumstances be censored. When it came time for the cross-channel invasion of France, he prepared a statement for use in the event that the invasion misfired. In this statement he accepted full blame for its failure. And during the actual campaign across Europe, he shrugged off persistent attempts in the British press to give all the credit for allied successes to the British generals, Montgomery and Alexander.

One good illustration of Eisenhower's managerial skill was his handling of General George C. Patton. Eisenhower recognized that Patton was in many ways an excellent combat commander, particularly when it came to tank warfare. He further realized that the Germans had a very high estimation of Patton and feared him as they feared no other allied combat general. But Eisenhower also was painfully aware of Patton's many weaknesses, such as his egoism, his officiousness and his reactionary cast of mind.

When Patton on two occasions slapped American soldiers who had been hospitalized with bad nerves or battle fatigue, thus setting off an uproar in the United States, Eisenhower refused to take the easy course and relieve him of command. Instead, he ordered Patton to make personal apologies to the slapped men, the medical personnel and all others concerned. Patton, who was desperate to continue in command, complied. Two years later when the savage Nazi counterattack almost upset the allies in the historic Battle of the Bulge, Patton's adept rescue of the besieged American forces vindicated Eisenhower's action.

He tolerated Patton as long as he could, but after the war ended and Patton persisted in employing ex-Nazis in his zone of occupation, Eisenhower moved to replace him. However, even at this point he tried to ease the aging general's humiliation. He asked Patton whom he would like as a replacement, and when Patton named someone who was acceptable to Eisenhower, the American commander appointed him.

His tact and concern were not only in evidence in handling his commanders. He also regularly toured the ranks, talking with the soldiers and looking after their well-being. He sharply reproved any base commander who utilized his best facilities for administrative quarters instead of giving them up for the rest and relaxation of the men who were doing the fighting.

Behind his modest geniality lay a great singleness of purpose. He realized that the alliance would falter and flounder unless there was a single overall commander and he made sure that this was accepted and acknowledged. He also took steps to see that throughout the allied forces all issues would be discussed and decided on considerations other than national pride. His creation of an integrated command, integrated not only in combining the forces of several nations but in also combining both the army and navy of these nations, is considered his greatest accomplishment.

He also knew how to put first things first. Thus, in North Africa he deferred his integration scheme, important though it was, in order to capture Tunis before the bad weather set in. And when Roosevelt urged him to lead the troops into Rome, thus glorifying his own and America's role in the city's liberation, he refused in order to get to England more quickly and thus have more time to work on the coming invasion of France.

Regarding the French invasion, Eisenhower had originally wanted to have an invasion of southern France accompany the cross-channel attack. Due to a shortage of landing craft and other factors, he continually had to scale down his plan but he did not scuttle the idea until the very end. In Sixsmith's view, this decision "was typical of the man" for "he liked to keep his options open."

As a military strategist, Eisenhower did make his share of mistakes. He allowed the German military divisions in Sicily to escape, he balked at sending his airborne division to capture Rome, and he opened up a hole in his front that permitted Hitler to launch the perilous and costly Battle of the Bulge. It took the allied forces, despite their complete domination of the air and their vast superiority on the ground, nearly a year after the time they crossed the channel to bring Germany to defeat.

But, according to Sixsmith, he was by no means a poor strategist either. And he was constantly beset by conflicting pressures. In the north, Montgomery was insisting that the full allied thrust be put into his own hands. He was supported by a feverish public opinion in England, not simply because he was their general but also because they feared the German rockets that were being launched from the area that Montgomery was trying to capture. Farther south, there was Patton, champing at the bit, demanding more gasoline and other scarce supplies as well as men. Since American public opinion needed a hero of its own, Patton could not be completely restricted. Meanwhile, the French were clamoring for the liberation of Paris, a move that would not only detract from the route of advance but could hinder further advances since supplies and the trucks to carry them would have to be siphoned off to maintain the city afterwards.

On balance, Eisenhower handled his strategist role adequately and his administrative and political role superbly. This is Sixsmith's view and it seems to reflect the consensus of others who were in a position to know. When Germany finally surrendered, General Marshall, who was not, as we have seen, overly given to effusive praise, sent him a long and truly effusive letter of congratulations: "You have commanded with outstanding success . . . you have met and successfully disposed of every conceivable difficulty . . . you have triumphed over inconceivable logistical problems and military obstacles

. . . you have made history, great history for the good of mankind. . . ."

Churchill shared much the same view. Shortly before Roosevelt died, the British prime minister wrote him expressing "admiration of the great and shining qualities of character and personality which he [Eisenhower] has proved himself to possess. . . ." But most important of all was the judgment of British Field Marshal Montgomery, the petulant prima donna who chafed and complained at the way Eisenhower had restricted him all during the war. Said Montgomery afterwards, in words reminiscent of those used by the Los Alamos physicists to describe Oppenheimer, "No one but Ike could have done it."

But if Eisenhower performed so well in the highly sensitive and highly political role of Supreme Allied Commander, why was he such an undistinguished president?

There are many possible answers to this question and all of them may contain some element of truth. For one thing, he may not have been such a poor president as historians have believed. Eisenhower himself thought that his greatest contribution was to keep the United States out of war, and in view of the actions of his successors, that accomplishment may not have received its due. Eisenhower, like Kennedy and Johnson, also came under pressure to invade Vietnam, but when such a course was urged on him by his Secretary of State and his military chief of staff in 1954, he asked that Congress and other nations be sounded out first. When reaction from both quarters was negative, he scuttled the idea.

Another answer may be found in his age. He was ten years older when he entered the White House than when he took over the Supreme Allied Command, and while 62 is not an unusually advanced age for high political office—Churchill was in his late 60's during World War II and Clemenceau was in his late 70's when he headed France during World War I—the years take their toll on some people more than others. The fact that for over three years during the war he worked day and night, smoking four full packs of cigarettes a day and getting no exercise, certainly did not contribute toward his later vigor.

But most of all, the answer lies in the point raised at the start of this chapter and that is the situational nature of leadership. Leaders create their situations, to be sure, but situations also create their leaders. Such was the case with Dwight D. Eisenhower.

LEADERSHIP AND ITS LIMITS

A new textile mill manager once decided, on assuming his new responsibilities, that things would go best if he indicated to one and all that things were going to be run his way. On his first day in the job, he strode into the weave room, walked up to the union business agent, and, after making sure the latter was the person he was seeking, announced, "I am the new manager here. When I manage a mill, I run it. Do you understand?"

The business agent nodded and then waved his hand. The workers who had been closely watching the encounter promptly shut down every loom in the room. The union official then turned to the manager and said, "All right, go ahead and run it."

This story illustrates one very real yet often overlooked or at least underestimated aspect of leadership: it is very much a two-way street.

"In a bureaucracy that contains people with brains and consciences," writes Charles Frankel following his tour of duty in Washington, "an unspoken bargain binds the man at the top to his subordinates. If they are to be the instruments of his will, he must, to some extent, be an instrument of theirs."[63] Most writers on administration would agree. "A manager is often described as someone who gets things done through other people," notes the British organizational theorist Rosemary Stewart. "We tend to forget that this means he is dependent upon them."[64]

In a complex bureaucracy the problem intensifies. Tsar Nicholas II was one of the few truly autocratic rulers of his time. Yet, he experienced consistent frustration in getting his smallest orders carried out. "I do not rule Russia," the weary monarch once sighed. "Ten thousand clerks do."[65]

American presidents have consistently discovered their office to provide far less power than they had thought. Franklin Roosevelt depicted Lincoln as "a sad man because he couldn't get it all at once, and nobody can." Roosevelt's own battles with his bureaucracy are almost legendary. He once wearily described his efforts to handle government agencies as akin to boxing a featherbed.

Roosevelt's successors suffered from the same problems. Truman's and Eisenhower's difficulties in doing what they wanted to do were pointed out in chapter two. John F. Kennedy took office with the idea of changing all this. But he found that when he wanted a simple sign taken down, it did not come down even after he had given the order for its removal three times.

President Nixon, at the time that the Watergate scandals were breaking, was widely said to have amassed a frightening amount of power. Yet, Watergate, in many respects proved the opposite. He tried

63. Frankel, *op. cit.,* p. 56.
64. Rosemary Stewart, *The Reality of Organizations* (New York: Anchor Books, 1972), p. 48.
65. For an interesting and informative view of some of the Tsar's leadership problems, see the earlier chapters of Rober K. Massie, *Nicholas and Alexandra* (New York: Atheneum, 1969).

to get the Internal Revenue Service to crack down on his enemies, but all he could manage to achieve was a few simple audits, something that almost any citizen could engineer with a well-worded letter to his regional IRS representative.

Nixon, or at least his administration, was also thwarted in attempts to halt anti-trust prosecution of ITT, to obtain funds from the CIA for the incarcerated Watergate burglars, to prevent disclosure of the break-in by his "plumbers" of the office of Dr. Ellsberg's psychiatrist, to limit certain investigations by the Securities and Exchange Commission, etc. etc. The fact that the Nixon administration approved plans for breaking and entering and other felonies is certainly frightening. Yet the fact that it felt constrained to do so may indicate a lack rather than a plenitude of power. And in any event, Nixon's master plan for such incidents was stymied by a bureau chief, J. Edgar Hoover, who was supposedly serving at the president's pleasure.

The limitations of lesser executives are even greater. To many students, the president of their university may seem like an omnipotent figure, at least as far as their immediate needs are concerned. Yet, college presidents usually find themselves walking a very narrow tightrope, having to balance carefully the needs and wishes of trustees, faculty and administrative staff, students and community officials. As for deans, their plight is still worse. The relationship of a dean to his faculty and students, so one dean has said, is that of a fire hydrant to a dog.

Even when he seems to possess sufficient power to command obedience, the leader still may find the going rough. Stewart relates how "one unpopular manager worked himself almost into the grave as his subordinates always did what he asked them to do and never did anything else." And she adds, "The more a manager needs the cooperation of his staff—and the more skilled and interrelated the work, the more he will need it—the less he can rely on formal authority to obtain it."[66]

It would seem from all this that the leader's lot is scarcely a happy one. Many who view it with awe and wonder from the outside would find it sheer torture to experience from the inside. Yet it does have its challenges and its charms.

David Lilienthal, who held such posts as the chairmanships of the Tennessee Valley Authority and the Atomic Energy Commission, once defined leadership as a humanistic art. It requires, he said, "a humanistic outlook on life rather than mere mastery of technique. It is based on the capacity for understanding of individuals and their motivations, their fears, their hopes, what they love and what they hate, the ugly and the

---

66. Stewart, *op. cit.*, p. 82.

good side of human nature. It is an ability to move these individuals, to help them define their wants, to help them discover, step by step, how to achieve them."[67]

The challenge of leadership is thus the challenge of humanism itself. Its successful exercise lies less and less in giving orders and more and more in developing the innate capacities of human beings. But to this must be joined something else, a sense of mission bolstered and buttressed by some degree of vision. The story is sometimes told of three stonecutters who were asked what they were doing. The first replied, "I am making a living." The second, busily at work, answered, "I am doing the best job of stonecutting in the whole country." The third looking up with a gleam in his eye said "I am building a cathedral."[68]

The conclusion is obvious. Only the third can become an effective manager.

---

67. Lilienthal, *op. cit.*, pp. 16-17.
68. Peter Drucker, *The Practice of Management* (New York: Harper & Row, 1954), p. 122.

7

Communication

Through the years, administrators and administrative theorists have placed increasing emphasis on communication. In the 1930's, Chester Barnard called attention to the fact that "a common purpose must be commonly known, and to be known must in some way be communicated. With some exceptions, verbal communication between men is the method by which this is accomplished."[1] Writing in the 1950's, Herbert Simon put even greater stress on the role of communication. "It is obvious," he noted, "that without communication there can be no organization, for there is no possibility then of the group influencing the behavior of the individual. Not only is communication absolutely essential to organization, but the availability of particular techniques of communication will in large part determine the way in which decision-making functions can and should be distributed through the organization . . . ." Simon went on to conclude that "only in the case where the man who is to carry out a decision is also the best man fitted to make the decision is there no problem of communication—and in this exceptional case there is of course no reason for organization."[2]

More recent writers have assigned communication an equal if not more important role. They consider such organizational ingredients as solidarity and support, along with command and control, to be closely tied in with organizational communication. Some even view organizations as essentially systems of communication and regard all or nearly all organizational problems as communication problems. Such an approach may well go too far but it can sometimes prove helpful. For example, Charles Redfield tells of one successful consultant who, when he embarks on an organizational study, stations himself in the mail

---

1. Barnard, *The Functions of the Executive*, p. 89.
2. Simon, *Administrative Behavior*, p. 154.

room and "by plotting the lines of actual communication, he can some-times build a more accurate organizational chart than the one that hangs on the wall in the president's office."[3]

Communication presents as many problems as any other aspect of administration, if not more. There are, first of all, the technical prob-lems. When the Germans invaded France in 1940, they utilized tele-types, advanced field telephones and other devices to maintain a rapid flow of communication among all the parts of their fast moving military organization. The French, however, relied heavily on the old dispatch system whereby orders issued from Paris would be carried by dispatch runners on motorcycles. This not only seriously slowed down communi-cation but often eliminated it altogether, for the runners sometimes never reached their destinations. They would either become the victims of accidents or of strafings and bombings from the ubiquitous German aircraft.

The French had other communication problems besides merely technical ones. Prior to the German onslaught, they had received from Vatican sources the proposed route through Belgium which the Ger-mans were planning to use. Yet, Paris refused to believe the report since the proposed route did not seem to them militarily sound.[4] This illus-trates a further communication problem: sometimes the information is properly sent and received but then is simply disregarded.

Many countries have experienced this problem. During the same war, the Germans paid handsomely for some British battle plans that had been carefully photographed by a valet of the British ambassador in Turkey.[5] However, once they obtained possession of the documents, the Nazis failed to act on them. Similarly, the Soviet Union was repeat-edly warned of an impending German attack in 1941. One source was the famous double agent Richard Sorge who supplied them with the exact dates of the scheduled invasion. Yet, Stalin shrugged them off. In the postwar period, the United States received numerous reports from our embassy in China forecasting the impending collapse of the Chiang Kai-shek regime and the communist assumption of power. But when the predicted event occurred, it caught everybody in Washington by surprise.

Experience alone does not necessarily solve such problems. When World War I broke out, the French general staff fell into posses-sion of authentic German documents clearly indicating that the Ger-mans would march through Belgium. This would normally call for the

---

3. Charles Redfield, *Communication in Management* (Chicago: University of Chicago Press, 1953), p. 7.
4. Shirer, *The Collapse of the Third Republic*, Chapters 27, 28 and 29.
5. Ludwig C. Moyzisch, *Operation Cicero* (New York: Coward-McCann, 1950).

French to shore up their left flank to counter and turn back the thrust. But the French had based their strategy on a strong center and clung to this position despite their new information. Thus, their later experience in 1940 was a duplicate of their 1914 errors.

A more common problem is simply failing to request information from the right parties. Khrushchev in his memoirs blamed Russia's abortive invasion of Finland in World War II on such a failure. The Soviet intelligence services had known about the powerful Finnish defense system all along but no one in the high Soviet command bothered to ask them about it. The disaster cost the Russians nearly a million lives.[6]

Not all manifestations of this problem are so sweeping and dramatic. But they occur all the time. A detective investigating a case may fail to consult the policeman who first handled the case and did the initial investigation. This failure, which happens in police forces all the time, scarcely contributes to efficiency in fighting crime. The detective may spend days and weeks tracking down a suspect when the policeman who first dealt with the matter knows all along where the suspect is living.[7]

However, it is not only a failure to consult that makes the work of detectives more difficult than it needs to be. Often, the patrolman will not tell the detective what he knows even when the detective asks him, for he may be angry at not being allowed to pursue the matter on his own or he may have a grudge toward that particular detective. Thus, information can be impeded as much, if not more, by intention as by error.

Parties involved in a communications network of any kind may not only withhold information but may also intentionally distort it. But the distortions that come about through maliciousness are far and away exceeded by those which occur through mischance.

To obtain an idea of how widespread a problem this is we have only to examine the most simple and most intimate organization in current society, the married couple. In their highly respected book, *The Mirages of Marriage,* William J. Lederer, M.D., and Don D. Jackson estimate that husbands and wives miscommunicate about 20 percent of the time. To offer an example, they cite a case where the wife has a habit of rubbing her nose when she is angry. An occasion arises, however, when, in talking to her husband, she rubs her nose simply because it is itching. The husband, who is well aware of what this usually means, assumes she is angry. Since he cannot imagine any reason why she should be, he starts to get irritated at her for allegedly becoming so. His defensive tone

---

6. Edward Crankshaw, ed., *Khrushchev Remembers* (Boston: Little, Brown, 1970).
7. Joseph M. Jordan, *Theory Y: An Urgent Need,* Unpublished Paper, Department of Political Science, Northeastern University, 1972.

then starts to make her annoyed which in turns confirms him in his initial reaction. And so their marriage has to ride over another bump on the road to bliss.[8]

Communications problems arise not just from information that is too slow, too incomplete or too distorted but from information that is simply too abundant. This is the problem of communication overload. Harold Nicholson claimed that this was one of the greatest problems at the Paris Conference that followed World War I.[9] The conference's forty-eight committees generated so much information that it was impossible for anyone, including the conference's major decision-makers, to know what was going on. James MacGregor Burns blames too much communication for the failure of the United States to take advantage of concessions from the Japanese in 1941, concessions which might have averted the Pacific war. "The problem was too much information, not too little—and too much that was irrelevant, confusing and badly analyzed."[10]

Occasionally, this communication problem also arises through intent. School superintendents, for example, sometimes purposely flood their school board members with reports and other documents which, though completely accurate, are so voluminous as to make it impossible for the board members to know what is happening. As the board members struggle in vain to keep abreast of the swelling tide of information, the superintendent calmly proceeds to do pretty much what he wants to do.

Most overload problems, however, arise from sheer force of circumstances. And the circumstances which make for too much communication are increasing all the time. The growth of complexity, specialization, interdependence and some of the other features of today's organizational world is constantly leading to the generation of more and more information. This process is being aided and abetted by the growth of communications technology. Consequently, an organization may take great care and achieve great success in developing excellent lines and flows of communication only to sink under the profusion of information which may develop as a result.

To sum up, in tackling the problem of communication, the administrator would do well to keep in mind a statement attributed to the nineteenth-century British novelist Samuel Butler. "Communication of all kinds is like painting—a compromise with impossibilities."

---

8. William J. Lederer and Don D. Jackson, M.D., *The Mirages of Marriage* (New York: W. W. Norton, 1968), Chapter 42.
9. Harold Nicolson, *Peacemaking 1919* (New York: Harcourt, Brace and Company, 1939).
10. James MacGregor Burns, *Roosevelt: Soldier of Freedom* (New York: Harcourt Brace Janovich, 1970).

FORMAL AND INFORMAL

Communication falls into two basic categories: formal and informal. They are easily defined. Formal communication is written communication; informal is oral. Of course, not all communication is verbal. Attitudes and even ideas can be transmitted through inflection, gesture and "body language." But though non-verbal communication definitely has a place in organizational life, its role is usually not very great and in any case is hard to analyze and define. Consequently, our attention will be directed to verbal communication.

What factors govern the use of one form of verbal communication over the other? Under what conditions does formal communication take precedence over informal and vice versa?

Generally, two factors foster the use of formal communication. One of these is size. As organizations grow, they tend to make increasing use of formal communication and, correspondingly, diminishing use of its opposite. The other factor is public character. Public organizations tend to rely more heavily on formal communication than do private ones. A brief examination of the merits of formal communication will show why this is true.

Formal Communication: The Advantages

Formal communication fosters accountability. This factor alone makes it indispensable for governmental affairs, particularly in a democracy. Unless the public and those who serve its information needs, such as the press and legislators, can find out what orders were given and who gave them, it cannot make the judgments needed to insure truly democratic government.

By facilitating accountability, formal communication puts a restraining hand on arbitrariness, capriciousness, favoritism and discrimination of all kinds. Through proceeding on formal instructions and keeping records of their transactions, public officials find it much more difficult, though certainly not always impossible, to depart from acceptable standards of impartiality and fairness. Of course, the rules and standards themselves may be unfair, but if so, then this is at least a matter of public record and can be easily determined.

Many of the scandals and other sensational events of recent years that have shed valuable light on governmental operations point up this advantage of formal communication. Take, for example, the case of the Pentagon papers. These disclosed a great deal of valuable information on the country's conduct of the Vietnam war. Had Defense Secretary Robert McNamara not directed that such reports be written, much of this information would have escaped public view.

221

The Watergate affair also provides a good illustration of the relationship that formal communication has with pin-pointing responsibility in government. Had there not been a certain amount of documentation regarding these events, then exposure and prosecution of the misdeeds it involved would have been greatly impeded and possibly nullified. Had there been still more extensive use of formal communication, then many more elements of this nefarious affair might have been more deeply and successfully explored. Without formal communication, the work of the journalist, to say nothing of the work of the historian, would frequently become implausible and even impossible.

Watergate and the Pentagon papers are only two of the more dramatic incidents which spotlight the utility of formal communication, at least when it comes to serving the interest of the public. Other illustrations occur on an everyday basis. Early in 1973, a special commission set up by New York State to investigate New York City's property tax situation found there were no written procedures or manuals to guide the city's assessors in their work. The absence of such formal materials resulted in the "frivolous application of discretionary standards" which in turn had opened the door to favoritism and other forms of political abuse.[11]

To pursue the matter further, let us suppose that all of the city's assessors were deeply committed to performing their tasks accurately and fairly, and let us further suppose that the city administration was determined to let them do so. Could New York City's property tax payers then be assured that they were being treated rationally and impartially?

The answer is no. Without a uniform and written set of standards and criteria, the chances are that assessments would still be unevenly imposed and administered. What one assessor is likely to emphasize in making his assessment, another assessor is likely to slight. To one assessor, high ceilings in a building give it added charm and space and hence add to its value. To another assessor, high ceilings may mean additional heating and cleaning costs and hence detract from a building's value.

Formal communication thus tends to curb the disparities and discrepancies which can occur even without express design. With all the best will in the world, distortions can and usually will creep in when formal communication is totally absent. Written communication allows everyone concerned to receive the same message and to check back on it if he is at any time uncertain as to what it says.

This brings us to still another asset of formal communication. It

---

11. *New York Times,* February 20, 1973.

saves time. In any large organization, it would be difficult indeed to issue all instruction orally. Not only would distortions occur as the message was relayed from person to person or group to group but time would be needlessly consumed. Written communication allows an almost infinite number of people to receive the same message at the same time and if they forget any portions of it, they do not have to check back to the sender of the message for they now have it in front of them.

Written communication can also save time when it travels in the other direction. It would be virtually impossible for any large and complex organization to receive orally all the information which it may need to obtain from its far-flung operations. Its phones would be constantly tied up and its offices would be continually filled with people relaying what they think headquarters needs and wants to know. In the same way, putting things in writing can save a superior's time in handling information from his subordinates. He can usually read memoranda from several different people in the time it takes to talk to just one of them. This also allows him to schedule his time better for he can allocate certain periods of the day or week for going over such messages.

For reasons such as these, busy executives have often encouraged their aides to put things in writing even though such aides may work in close physical proximity to them. Robert McNamara was especially emphatic on this point. He always discouraged oral briefings from anyone because, as he put it, "I can read faster than they can talk."[12]

Written communication also allows information to be more fully developed with all of its ramifications discussed. Issues of any importance usually require such treatment. The document that results can then be circulated to others for still further analysis until all possible points of view have been solicited and all aspects have been explored.

Finally, written communication not only helps inform the recipient but may also do the same for the sender. Francis Bacon once said that an index is chiefly useful for the person who makes it and the same can be said for many of the memoranda, reports, etc. which flow through the corridors of bureaucracy. By putting down his data and ideas in writing, the administrator or his aide frequently sees things which he did not see before. Expressing ideas in written form usually assists the person doing it to seek details he previously disregarded and to see relationships and implications which he previously missed. Many a bureaucrat will testify that frequently in his career he did not fully understand an issue until he wrote a memo about it.

---

12. Halberstam, *The Best and the Brightest,* p. 215.

There are thus good reasons why the written word looms so large in the operations of government. We should bear them in mind when we discuss some of the less attractive aspects of this phenomenon.

Formal Communication: The Disadvantages

Shortly after he was appointed Secretary of Housing and Urban Development in 1969, George Romney held a press conference and displayed a stack of paper that stood 2.5 feet high and weighed 56 pounds. This, he said, represented all the paper generated by an application for a single urban renewal project.[13]

Although the problem, as Romney explained it, was caused more by faulty organization than by a sheer obsession with formal documents, it does illustrate that one of the ways in which organizational pathologies work is through a profusion of paper. The very use of the written word tends to encourage its further use and many a governmental organization, and not a few private ones, have found themselves swamped in a sea of documentation.

Romney's display is only one of many incidents which have from time to time cast a chilling light on this problem. During World War II, for example, there was a celebrated Office of Price Administration price order on fruitcake which consumed six pages of fine print. It was one of the most famous orders which the red-faced OPA ever turned out.

But though the paper problem is as old as bureaucracy itself, it seems to show great resistance to correction. A congressional report in 1966 estimated that there were 360,000 forms in use by the federal government. By 1972, the number of such forms was thought to have grown to more than 800,000. Harold Koenig, the head of a National Archives team that was trying to reduce the paper explosion, estimated that at least 30 billion copies of these forms were circulating every year. He estimated the annual cost of such communication at $10 billion. A Senate subcommittee, however, put the total cost of printing, shuffling and storing the forms at closer to $18 billion.[14]

Few organizations have managed to escape the ravages of the paper revolution. Former FBI Director J. Edgar Hoover consistently boasted that the FBI was not a bureaucratic agency and when one considered the highly personalized manner in which he ran the agency, he was to some extent right. Yet, the FBI did not manage to avoid the maze and craze of documentation. Its agent's manual encompassed 32,000 rules and regulations and its files would have filled an area equal in space to twelve football fields. When an agent in Philadelphia was

---

13. Frederick V. Malek, "Executive in Washington," *Harvard Business Review*, September-October 1972.
14. *Boston Record-American*, November 19, 1972.

scheduled to speak at a dinner, his office sent out a report on the event to headquarters and 37 other field bureaus and then filed the report under eleven different categories in its own files.[15]

The problem is certainly a universal one. Although Italy is a much smaller country than ours, its bureaucracy consumes twenty tons of printed forms each day. By 1973, its archives were bulging with ten million *bundles* of records and papers.

Dictatorship also can suffer from this problem. Albert Speer says he struggled continuously against the ever threatening paper tide when he headed Nazi war production during World War II. To damp down the flood of correspondence, he had unimportant mail stamped with the message "Return to sender. Not critical for the war effort." At times, he even welcomed the allied bombing raids for they destroyed some of the government's ever growing files. After the destruction of part of his own ministry by allied bombers in late 1943, he issued a statement saying, "Although we have been fortunate in that large parts of our current files have burned and so relieved us for a time of useless ballast, we cannot really expect that such events will continually introduce the necessary fresh air into our work."[16]

Today, communist countries seem to be particularly afflicted with this spreading scourge. In May of 1974, Romanian President Nicolae Ceausescu, aghast at the two million directives being sent within and among the various ministries of his government every year, decided to act. He decreed a 50 percent cut in paper supplies for all government offices effective almost immediately.

The growing crush of paper is in many respects a symptom of other organizational problems rather than a problem itself. One frequent cause is an insufficiency of delegation. A superior who insists on making all decisions himself and who needs to know everything that is going on down to the smallest detail will find his desk piled high with memoranda, reports, requests. In like manner, an agency that has split duties among several subunits when they could be handled by one will also add to its paper problems. This, according to Romney, was the problem at HUD. An urban renewal application had to travel through the hands of too many assistant secretaries.

Some of the very advantages of written communication lead to its abuse. If it promotes accountability, then it also fosters self-protection. A person may put something in writing so that he cannot be accused of having done something improper, or so that he can point to the record later on and show where he was right. "A civil servant's job is

15. *Newsweek*, May 10, 1971, p. 30.
16. Speer, *Inside the Third Reich*, p. 255.

precarious," a French police official once remarked in the American television program *McCloud.* "We stand on a mountain of paper. The higher the mountain, the more secure the civil servant." Though the speaker was fictional, the tendency he called attention to was very real. Harold Macmillan, who served as a British aide to General Eisenhower in World War II, and as such was the recipient of a constant stream of written communication, once claimed that "directives are more useful in protecting the writer than in instructing the recipient."[17]

Sometimes people write more than they need to simply to show how industrious they are. And often superiors are quite impressed with such industry. Joseph Califano was a prodigious writer of memoranda when he served on Lyndon Johnson's staff. Although in Califano's case the motivation was probably a genuine desire to reach the president on many issues, his diligence did not go unnoticed. Once when Johnson heard another aide speak somewhat disparagingly of Califano, the president retorted, "Don't criticize Califano. There's never been a man around me who wrote so many memos."[18]

Whatever the causes of paper profusion, its costs can be immense. We have already seen some estimates of the cost involved in printing, storing and circulating forms. Other costs may also be included. A memo may save the superior's time but may consume inordinate amounts of the subordinate's time and his time also bears a price tag. It is not uncommon for a public employee to spend a day or more drafting a memorandum on an issue that could have been settled with a ten-minute conversation with his superior. When this occurs, the time factor involved in formal communication is usually working against the organization instead of for it.

Each piece of paper, we should also remember, tends to spawn offspring of its own. One person's contribution evokes a similar or even greater contribution from others. If A sends a memo to B, then B must often send a memo back. B may at the same time send a memo to C asking him for his comments. C may not have even waited for B to act. If he has heard about B's memo, then he may feel inclined to do some memo-writing on his own initiative. In order to make his memo better, he may send a memo to D seeking some additional information which produces in return a memo from D. And so it goes.

Meanwhile, the ever bulging files start to produce problems other than just the costs of storage. J. C. Masterman, in describing Great Britain's remarkably successful effort to convert German agents to double agents during World War II, says the files on some of these double

---

17. Harold Macmillan, *The Blast of War 1939-1945* (New York: Harper & Row, 1968).
18. Halberstam, *op. cit.,* p. 432.

agents grew to over 35 volumes. This, he said, made it "difficult and wearying and time consuming to master the essentials of each case in a resonable space of time and with some degree of certainty that no essential feature has been overlooked."[19] Thus, completeness of information, carried too far, can lead to less information, or at least less information that can be easily used.

Needless to say, all these problems have an impact on the organization's employees. Formal communication by virtue of being formal is less humane. It may have a dispiriting and even deadening effect on human relations. Indeed, people actually start to turn off when too many formal communications pour in on them, and the messages themselves end up in wastepaper baskets unread.

Finally, we should note that while formal communication usually is clearer and less liable to be misunderstood than its opposite, this is not always the case. The story is told of how J. Edgar Hoover became irked at the sender of a memo because the sender had not left wide enough margins for the FBI chief to scribble his comments. Since wide margins were a bureau policy, he wrote on it "watch the borders" and sent it back. For the next week FBI agents fanned out on the Mexican and Canadian borders in the bewildering belief that their boss wanted them to keep a vigil.

Informal Communication

Oral communication offers a solution to many of these problems. It does not flood the person or clog the files. It can evoke immediate feedback which in turn can lead to a resolution of any issues and clarification of any points that may be involved. In so doing, the one who is doing the communicating can be assured that his information has been received. It permits the use of shading and emphasis and gesture. And it certainly is more human and often more humane. People are now dealing together directly.

Informal communications is heavily used in Japanese industry and government. The Japanese prefer face-to-face contact and rarely send inter-office memoranda. Superiors spend considerable time "walking the floor" and talking with their employees. Conferences are common at all levels and are often conducted in an informal and relaxed atmosphere. Judging from Japan's growth rates and productivity levels, it does not seem to have hurt their administrative processes.

Efforts are also underway in this country to substitute oral for written communication. President Johnson's task force on cutting red tape, for example, urged federal officials to make more extensive use of

---

19. J. C. Masterman, *The Double Cross Game* (New York: Avon Books, 1972), p. 55.

227

the telephone and less use of "time-consuming written communications."[20] It is quite possible that the use of oral communication will grow apace in governmental agencies though it will most likely never replace formal communication altogether. For reasons that we noted earlier, the written word and the printed document will probably continue to serve as the mainstay of the communications process in any developed democracy.

A Note on Grapevines

Any agency that has an informal organization will also have an informal communications system that is often referred to as the "grapevine." And since informal organizations are found in almost all organizations, grapevines tend to be ever present.

Grapevines can also be terribly efficient. "With the rapidity of a burning powder train," says Keith Davis, a professor of management who has studied grapevines for over twenty years, "information flows out of the woodwork, past the manager's door and the janitor's mop closet, through steel walls or construction-glass partitions."[21] What is more, Davis claims that well over three-quarters of all this information is accurate.

Even when it is not accurate, says Davis, it may convey a psychological truth for many rumors that run rampant through an organization are "symbolic expressions of feelings." If the rumor has it that a certain employee is planning to quit, it may reflect the wish on the part of his fellow employees that he would quit. Or it may simply reflect the employee's own desire to leave.

Davis advises managers to pay careful attention to the grapevine's information for it may tell them more than they know about what is going on within their organization. He also urges them to disseminate whatever information they have in order to counter whatever errors the grapevine may be spreading. Beyond that there is little that the administrator can do because the grapevine, he says, "cannot be abolished, rubbed out, hidden under a basket, chopped down, tied up or stopped." Managers might just as well accept it for it "is as hard to kill as the mythical glass snake which, when struck, broke into fragments and grew a new snake out of each piece."

MEANS AND METHODS

Modern-day administration can avail itself of an ever growing number of devices as it seeks to cope with its communication needs. Some

---

20. *Detroit Free Press,* September 28, 1967.
21. *Time,* June 18, 1973, p. 67.

might argue that the current plethora of communication tools and techniques is aggravating rather than alleviating communication problems since the more such means are available, the more they may be used. Others would argue the contrary, claiming that organizations are not making enough use of the vast variety of current techniques. It is possible that in this case both sides are correct.

In this section we will examine a few of the basic components of organizational communications systems, leaving some others for the following section when communication flow will be discussed.

Memoranda

The memo has come to symbolize the communications process of present-day bureaucracy and well it might. It is easily the most used and probably over-used communications device in many public organizations. Administrative personnel not only send memos to each other but even to themselves.

Self-directed memos are actually some of the most useful. They not only help an administrator organize his thoughts but provide him with a record of important events which have transpired in his administrative life. This can be particularly valuable when it comes to matters which are crucial or controversial. For example, when a client or a politician has tried to exert unwarranted and unacceptable pressure on him, he may dictate a memo for his file covering all the details of what happened. This he may need to refer to if the disgruntled favor seeker tries to take action against him.

Memos will also be needed for other matters, but the good administrator will utilize them with care. He will, first of all, make his memos brief and encourage others to do the same. Some executives have laid down a rule requiring all memos sent to them to be only one page in length. As an unvarying rule, this is probably a bad one. Many matters simply require more explication than can be handled in one page and an arbitrary cut-off may lead to arbitrary action on the matter being covered. If the memo is to be the basis for decision-making, then the recipient should want to know all the possible decisions that can be taken along with their respective pros and cons.

The difficulties and potential embarrassment that may result from trying to promulgate and enforce a "one-page rule" are illustrated by what happened to one city manager when he issued a memo to his department heads instructing them on the art of writing brief, one-page memos. His own memo attracted nationwide attention for it took him several pages to get his one-page idea across to his subordinates.[22]

But if it is unwise for public managers to decree one-page

---

22. *Boston Herald-American,* May 9, 1972.

memos, they should encourage them or at least encourage brevity and not only in memoranda but in all forms of communication. Good students usually learn in writing their academic papers that they cannot and should not use all the material they may have compiled, no matter how fond and proud of this material they may have become. Good bureaucrats should learn the same lesson.

Communications Professor Marvin H. Swift provides a pungent example of the long and the short of memo writing.[23] Sam Edwards, a mythical manager, finds that everybody in the company is taking advantage of the company copying machines for their personal use. It is costing the company a pretty penny. So he fires off the following memo:

To: All Employees

From: Samuel Edwards, General Manager

Subject: Abuse of Copiers

It has recently been brought to my attention that many of the people who are employed by this company have taken advantage of their positions by availing themselves of the copiers. More specifically, these machines are being used for other than company business.

Obviously, such practice is contrary to company policy and must cease and desist immediately. I wish therefore to inform all concerned—those who have abused policy or will be abusing it—that their behavior cannot and will not be tolerated. Accordingly, anyone in the future who is unable to control himself will have his employment terminated.

If there are any questions about company policy, please feel free to contact this office.

Such a memo, says Swift, is not only discourteous to the employees but is also unnecessarily verbose. The message could be better conveyed in the following way:

To: All Employees

From: Samuel Edwards, General Manager

Subject: Use of Copiers

Copiers are not to be used for personal matters. If there are any questions, please contact this office.

A comparison of the two memos will further show that not only is the second one shorter but it is also clearer. Brevity and clarity often

---

23. Marvin H. Swift, "Clear Writing Means Clear Thinking Means . . . ," *Harvard Business Review,* January-February 1973.

go hand in hand and the latter is as important as the former in effecting good communication. The wise administrator will encourage simple, straightforward sentences that get directly to the point. Sometimes, of course, sensitive matters will require more indirect treatment but even in those instances there is little need for the prolix prose which characterizes so much organizational writing.

A memo once sent by the State Department to its division chiefs offers some helpful hints along this line. It read in part:

> . . . It has become increasingly apparent that the sophisticated, legalistic and prolix prose sometimes employed in intragovernmental communications is predictably inappropriate in replying to relatively simple questions from the general public, which has little experience with or tolerance for such language.
>
> A useful check on the readability of prose is [the] Fog Index. It is based on the length of words and sentences. The Fog Index of the first paragraph, above, is 23, well above the graduate student level, 17. The Fog Index of this paragraph is 9, slightly over than that of *Time* magazine. Our goal will be to replace the former with the latter.[24]

Humor, as the above suggests, is a valuable ingredient in many memoranda. As we noted earlier, one of the big problems in formal communication is that recipients tend to throw it away unread. Attempts to overcome this by requiring them to initial it do not really solve the problem for almost anyone who has worked in a large public organization will have initialed many a memo to which he has given only the most cursory attention. Humor, along with brevity, clarity and a minimization of memoranda generally, can help any administrator in getting his memos read. But here, too, pitfalls may await him. Witness the case of New York City school principal Maurice Shapiro.

In 1968, the New York City Board of Education temporarily suspended Shapiro, giving as one of its reasons a memorandum in the form of a letter which the 60-year-old educator had sent to each of his teachers on January 4, 1966. The communication read as follows:

> I wish to welcome back all of you and I am sure we will have a wonderful year for 1966.
>
> I would like to call the following to your attention:
>
> 1. Be attractive at all times. Shave face and chin before coming to school. This applies to men also. We are inviting talent scouts and Hollywood producers to P.S. 96, Manhattan, so we wish you to be at your best at all times.

---

24. *The Atlantic,* December 1967, p. 40.

2.   You wear high heels at your own risk. They are especially dangerous if you are doing Folk Dancing.

3.   Dress attractively, not as if you were pushed out of bed by an exuberant lover. If you wear a low cut dress, we do not approve of falsies.

4.   Unless you are bald, please have your hair combed suitably.

5.   If you wear a dress above the knees, be careful how you sit, unless you are in the teacher's lunchroom, or in my office.[25]

Forms

Few communication devices cause as much aggravation and annoyance as forms. And our preceding discussion showed how extensive and expensive their use can become. Yet, they are, if properly used, savers of time, energy and money. Policemen, for example, often find report writing the hardest part of their jobs. Few, however, would argue the need for providing some written information covering their activities. Court cases alone make such information necessary. However, some police forces have begun developing forms to cover accidents and many of the other matters which demand police involvement. If such a form is clear and complete, it can be a boon to all concerned.

Clarity and completeness in forms are not qualities that can be taken for granted. Although some forms are too long, many are too short. This leads to faulty action or to further efforts to provide the necessary information. Clarity is another important ingredient which is often lacking. Robert Townsend urges any executive to fill out every form himself before permitting it to be used by his organization. This will give him an idea as to how effective—and how necessary—it is.[26]

Reports

A somewhat less symbolic but perhaps still more controversial communications tool is the report. That ebullient Englishman C. Northcote Parkinson flays this device with all the verbal vigor—and it is considerable—at his command. One of his famous laws contends that reports will be written regardless of whether the writer has anything to say.[27] Many who have worked in bureaucracies that stress them will share Parkinson's belief. It is truly amazing how sometimes the most unproductive person can turn out impressive reports filled with information attesting to his productivity.

Writing and reading reports also consumes the valuable time of more productive people. As such, reports can be quite costly. When John P. Fishwick took over the presidency of the Norfolk and Western

---

25. *New York Times,* February 6, 1968.
26. Townsend, "Up the Organization."
27. C. Northcote Parkinson, *The Law and the Profits* (New York: Ballantine Books, 1971), p. 181.

Railroad in 1970, he cut the number of reports which his executives had to write by almost one-third. The railroad's accountants estimated that this simple step saved the company over one-half million dollars a year, enough to purchase two new locomotives.[28]

Nevertheless, reports do have their place in administration. Martin T. Smith offers two guidelines for their intelligent use. First, they should be limited to one page; second, they should be written and filed only when the project discussed is completed. "Periodic progress reports," he claims, "inevitably waste time. Besides the author who sweats out filling empty space with empty words, there are the frustrated readers who are impatiently attempting to glean the information they need from ten pages of rubbish."[29] Unless limited to concise summaries of completed action, people will end up spending their time writing about progress rather than accomplishing it.

Copies of Correspondence

One truly excellent way of disseminating information is through circulating carbon or Xeroxed copies of correspondence. Such documents can often be substituted for memoranda with much better effect. The material that a memo would cover is often available in a letter which the would-be memo writer has either received or sent. Through simply having copies of this correspondence sent to all those who might have an interest in, or a need for, the information, he not only saves himself the time of doing some additional writing but also insures himself more likelihood that the information he is seeking to convey will be absorbed. People will read such messages with much more alacrity than they will read memos. In some cases, they will be pleased and flattered to have received it. This is particularly true when the superior is circulating his own correspondence to his subordinates.

Manuals

Most organizations of any size prepare handbooks for their employees to guide them in their work as well as in their organizational life generally. The Forest Service at one time used to issue a manual which ran to seven volumes of about 3,000 pages each. It was designed to cover almost any possible aspect or potential problem of a forest ranger's job. The physical format consisted of looseleaf binders so that new material could continually be added to or substituted for existing material in the appropriate categories.

This manual, which served as the agency's Bible or Baedecker,

---

28. *Time,* February 7, 1972, p. 57.
29. Smith, *I Hate to See a Manager Cry,* p. 26.

was slated for three additional volumes when complaints over its unwieldiness began to mount. The agency then cancelled the scheduled new volumes and began to scale down the existing opus. This illustrates anew one of the problems with such communication devices. They are not only expensive to prepare and revise but are also time-consuming and tedious to read. Furthermore, if an employee always has to check the manual for every decision, he will fail to develop much decision-making capacity of his own. And since no manual, no matter how complete, can hope to cover every conceivable contingency, the pre-formed decisions which it prescribes will in many instances be less satisfactory than the ones which can be made by those at the scene.

Nevertheless, such manuals can have their uses. One personnel specialist, Don E. Jones, recommends that such handbooks provide the employee with the general policies and philosophy of the organization, including a statement as to what the organization is trying to accomplish. At the same time, they should cease and desist from trying to spell out details for handling every potential problem that may arise. Policies that are clearly stated will allow employees to make more decisions on their own—and usually better ones than the organization can make for them.[30]

Staff Meetings

Prior to the battle of Mechanicsville early in the Civil War, General Robert E. Lee summoned all of his general officers to a joint meeting. The gathering, unprecedented in the annals of American military history, aroused some alarms. Many feared the risks it would present in terms of secrecy and security. Yet it went off smoothly and secretly as some forty men with star-spangled epaulets on their gray uniforms sat around their new commander on the lawn of a country home in Virginia exchanging information. Lee skillfully solicited their ideas and discussed his own, taking care, however, not to divulge anything which could prove harmful if leaks did in fact develop.

The meeting yielded many benefits. It helped the generals to know and understand each other and gave them an overall grasp of the situation which confronted the Confederacy at what seemed a rather dark hour. As for Lee himself, it not only provided him with much useful information on the condition of his troops but also on the temperaments and talents of those who commanded them. And it established his authority as their commander. It thus set the stage for the rather spectacular series of victories that were to ensue.[31]

---

30. Don E. Jones, "The Employee Handbook," *Personnel*, February 1973.
31. Burke Davis, *Gray Fox* (New York: Rinehart and Company, 1956), pp. 80-81.

The staff meeting, so rare in Lee's day, has become a fixture of modern-day organizational life. Its development has, in certain respects, paralleled the development of democracy itself for the staff meeting is, at least to some extent, a manifestation of the democratic impulse. However, its successful utilization can be furthered by the observance of a few simple guidelines.

The good staff meeting should have some structure. A brief agenda should be prepared and, if possible, circulated beforehand. And an effort should be made to finish the agenda before the meeting breaks up. This means that the chairman of the meeting must exercise some care to stick to the agenda while the meeting is in progress.

But this rule is often breached and sometimes rightly so. A meeting that sticks too closely to a printed document will not generate the ideas and information which make such meetings most successful. Furthermore, an approach that is too businesslike may annoy and alienate its participants, particularly if they are people who possess humanistic orientations, such as many social workers, or artistic temperaments, such as many architects. A former executive vice president of one of the country's largest breweries once related that when anyone said something that was not absolutely relevant to the issue being discussed at his company's board of directors' meeting, there would be a slight and chilling pause, after which the meeting would proceed as if the person had not spoken. Such techniques will usually not work in the public sector.

The adroit meeting chairman must thus engage in a careful balancing act, trying to keep the meeting from wandering too far afield while at the same time taking care not to keep it under too tight a rein. Setting a reasonable but fairly firm time limit and announcing this at the outset can help.

Through his conduct of the meeting, the chairman should try to encourage the interchange of all information and ideas that can be useful for those attending to know. He should at the same time discourage detailed discussion of matters that concern only a few of the participants. They should be encouraged to get together by themselves later on. It is imperative to provide an atmosphere where anyone who thinks he has something to contribute will feel free to do so. It is equally imperative to make sure that no one feels obligated to speak when he has nothing to say.

Seating arrangements can also play a role in making these meetings successful. Grouping the members down the sides of an elongated table with the chairman at the head may help in getting through the agenda quickly but may also inhibit communication, particularly between the members themselves. Attention naturally focuses on the person sitting at the head. Consequently, many administrators find that a circle arrangement works much better. A creative brain-storming session may require an even more open and relaxed atmosphere.

At the end of every meeting, the chairman should sum up the ground that has been covered and the decisions, if any, that have been made. He should also point out what further activity will have to be taken persuant to the matters raised in the meeting. He may find it useful to back up his oral wrap-up with a subsequent written summation which could be circulated to those who may not have attended the meeting as well as to those who did.

How often should staff meetings be held? There is no hard and fast answer to this question. Some mutual funds have staff meetings twice a day, once in the morning before the securities exchanges open up, and again in the afternoon when they close. A team of detectives working on a tough case may also meet at the start and at the end of each working day. In most cases, however, fewer meetings are desirable. Lenin once warned his comrades on the dangers of "meeting sickness" and Peter Drucker has noted that "meetings are by definition a concession to deficient organization. For one either meets or one works. One cannot do both at the same time."[32] This may be something of an overstatement but there is little dispute that too frequent meetings can not only consume time but can also lead to a preoccupation with details that only exaggerate their significance.

Generally, the larger the organizational unit involved, the fewer the meetings. Thus, a field office staff may meet once a week while the head of the field office may attend regional meetings once a month.

Another problem which frequently arises in connection with meetings is that of who should be invited. A general staff meeting should, of course, include almost everybody. Even file clerks and typists can benefit from at least learning what the organization's problems are and what efforts are under discussion to resolve them. They also may have something to contribute to decision-making. Furthermore, their sense of affinity to the organization is likely to increase if they are invited to its conferences.

But many meetings do not even require all members of the professional staff and inviting everyone to attend not only lengthens the meeting but keeps other work from going forward. The problem is that failure to invite some employees to the meeting can badly hurt their feelings as well as damage their position in the organization.

Sometimes this is consciously done. It was noted in the previous chapter that one technique some administrators use to get rid of an

---

32. Drucker, *The Effective Executive* (1967), p. 44.

unwanted employee is to drop his name from the meeting list. This technique can also be used simply to indicate that the subordinate is in disfavor. When Hubert Humphrey as vice president voiced objections to bombing North Vietnam in 1965, he soon found himself omitted from all White House conferences. The vice president soon became an object of pity or scorn in official Washington as he sent his small staff scurrying around the city desperately trying to find out what was going on. Humphrey found that many journalists knew more about what was happening in the executive branch than he did. Within a year, he had changed his mind and climbed aboard the bombing bandwagon.[33]

Usually, however, omitting people from meetings is not intended to show disfavor or disdain and this confronts the administrator with the need to see to it that the omission scars no egos and injures no feelings. Drucker suggests an approach such as the following: The executive issues a notice saying he has invited certain members of the organization to meet with him at a certain time to discuss a particular matter. Any staff member who felt he had something to contribute or who wanted the information could then be told to "feel free to drop in."[34]

This discussion of the problems of staff meetings should not obscure their potentialities. Essentially, they remain an excellent device for exchanging information, building morale and making better and better-executed decisions. As such, they are, when properly used, an important part of every public manager's means for accomplishing his mission.

UP, DOWN AND ACROSS

Information moves in three basic directions, upward from subordinate to superior, downward from superior to subordinate and horizontally from one organizational unit to another. No matter which way it flows, however, it runs into problems.

Perhaps the most difficult route is upward. As information wends its way up the organizational ladder it becomes increasingly stale. Just how severe the problem becomes is a question of the particular situation involved. It may take a fireman inside a blazing building only a few minutes to convey information to his immediate superior but in that few minutes his information may have become tragically outdated. Most matters, fortunately, are not quite so urgent but even so the information needed to act on them may come too late. The situation may

---

33. Halberstam, *op. cit.,* p. 534.
34. Drucker (1967), *op. cit.,* p. 39.

have already changed or at least developed nuances which make the information less satisfactory as a basis for action.

This problem affects all communication flow no matter what its direction. Communicating consumes time and nearly all delays involve some disadvantage. (Of course, delays often turn out to be helpful to an organization in that they permit a reappraisal of the situation or the introduction of new elements into the decision. However, in this case, the information itself has changed. If it is a question of communicating a specific piece of valid information, then usually the quicker it reaches its destination, the more effective it is.)

A much greater problem with upward-moving information is that it tends to change as it advances. This, too, is a problem of all communication flows. If A relates a message to B and B, in turn, relates it to C, then the information which C has received is likely to be a little bit different than the message which B received. However, when B is A's superior and when C is B's superior, some special factors often magnify the problem.

Consciously or unconsciously, subordinates frequently distort information as they pass it to those above them. They may do this for a variety of reasons. First and probably foremost is their simple reluctance to serve as bearers of ill tidings. All too often in human history the bearer of ill tidings has become identified as the producer of such tidings, and as such has incurred the wrath of those to whom he bears them. Even when the bearer has no such fears for his fate, he may still try to soften and shade unwelcome news out of a simple desire to protect his harrassed superior from unpleasantness. As former New York City Mayor John Lindsay once wrote, "I think nothing is more dangerous to an executive than isolation from the people and reliance on advisors who, however competent, may tend to tell the executive what they think he wants to hear. It's not very likely that an aide will say 'Mr. Mayor, they think you're a nigger lover in my neighborhood and they hate you for it.' But it is likely that in some neighborhoods that is precisely what I will hear."[35]

Sometimes subordinates are merely trying to spare their superiors from simple fatigue. George E. Reedy, who served for a while as Lyndon Johnson's press secretary, tells of being called in by one of the president's most trusted assistants and finding him furious over the fact that two separate staff members had submitted memos offering contrary advice on a particular matter. Said the presidential aide indignantly, "That man is exhausted enough and has enough problems on his mind without assistants coming at him from every direction. I think I should send

---

35. John Lindsay, *The City* (New York: W. W. Norton, 1969), p. 89.

both memos back and tell them to get together before I allow anything to go in."[36]

Subordinates sometimes have more selfish reasons for withholding or manipulating information. They may fear that the action such information would produce would prove disadvantageous to their interests. Or, if others stand a chance of being adversely affected, they may be fearful of being cast in the role of the informer.

This particular problem in upward communication, it should be noted, reflects problems inherent in hierarchy itself. As the French writer Albert Camus once noted, "There is nothing in common, in effect, between a master and a slave. One cannot speak or communicate with a subjugated human being. In place of that natural and free dialogue by which we acknowledge our resemblance and consecrate our destiny, servitude causes to reign the most terrible of silences."[37] Of course, bureaucratic relationships are rarely those of a master and slave but wherever hierarchy is introduced, it will tend to act in this fashion. Chester Barnard once noted that information received from a low status person will often receive scant attention while information received from a high status person may set off a reaction well beyond what was ever intended.[38] Katz and Kahn point out that a superior is supposed to give orders and a subordinate is supposed to receive them. This means that upward communication goes against the organizational grain for the subordinate is not used to telling things to his superior and his superior is not used to listening to things from his subordinate.[39]

History is replete with examples of how these various factors can influence and infect the communications process. During World War I, Kaiser Wilhelm of Germany received his ministers no more than necessary and then did most of the talking in order to avoid hearing, in the words of Barbara Tuchman, "their reports of inconvenient facts that did not fit in with his schemes."[40] His opposite number in the United States, Woodrow Wilson, had somewhat similar difficulties. Wilson not only disliked unpleasant information but tended to shy away from first-hand reports of any nature, preferring to get his news from his chief aide, Colonel House.

The Vietnam war provides the administrative analyst with a virtual treasure trove of illustrations as to how the upward flow of communication can become distorted out of all proportion. Vietnamese peas-

---

36. George E. Reedy, "What the White House Does to Presidents," *Boston Sunday Globe Magazine,* April 4, 1970.
37. Albert Camus, *L'Homme révolté* (Paris: Editions Gallimard, 1951), p. 340.
38. Chester I. Barnard, *Organization and Management* (Cambridge: Harvard University Press, 1948), Chapter 9, especially footnote on p. 231.
39. Katz and Kahn, *The Social Psychology of Organizations,* p. 245-246.
40. Tuchman, *The Zimmerman Telegram,* p. 24.

ants, being interviewed by American officials in the field would give the answers which they thought the Americans wanted to hear. The translators would usually touch up the answers still more before rendering them in English. When the information reached Saigon, its negative aspects would be pruned still more. This process would continue right into the White House where aides would cull those items which they thought Walt Rostow, who was Johnson's chief conduit, would most want to receive. Rostow in turn would package it into as agreeable a form as possible and pass it on to the president.[41] Rostow performed a similar tailoring operation on information coming in from other sources as well. As a result, Lyndon Johnson, in some respects, knew less of what was going on in Vietnam than did the average American newspaper reader and television viewer.

Within the military itself, there were numerous instances where the upward flow of communication took an erratic and erroneous course. According to one writer, Morris J. Blackman, the ineffectiveness of the bombing of the North was consistently distorted because those who were carrying out the missions did not want to tell those who ordered them the truth. As Blackman puts it, "It would have taken a certain amount of courage for a colonel to tell a general that the air strike the general had ordered—and for whose success the colonel felt he would be held responsible—was a failure."[42]

Then there were the famous or rather infamous massacres at My Lai and Song My. On March 27, 1970, the *New York Times* published a story under the headline "Panel Finds Songmy Data Diluted at Each Echelon." The news story recounted how the field investigators of the massacre estimated the number of innocent Vietnamese killed at 175 to 200. This, in itself, represented a scaling down of other estimates that had put the reported number of dead at closer to 400. However, as the lower figures were forwarded "from echelon to echelon up the military chain of command, the reported number of Vietnamese killed became smaller and smaller," said the *Times*. "By the time these reports reached the headquarters of the American Division, where they stopped, the number of Vietnamese killed had been reduced to an estimate of 20 to 28."

Unplugging the Upward Flow

Perhaps, the most important step which an administrator can take in resolving or at least reducing these impediments to the upward passage of information lies in his own conduct. If he genuinely believes and acts on the belief that all information should move swiftly and surely up-

41. Hoopes, *The Limits of Intervention*, p. 218.
42. Morris J. Blackman, "The Stupidity of Intelligence," in Peters and Adams, *Inside the System*.

ward, then the information is much more likely to do so. If he shows his subordinates that he wants to be told the bad news along with the good, and in as fresh and pure a form as possible, then they will not only be more inclined to do so but will also be more likely to deal with their own subordinates in the same way.

However, in an organization of any size and complexity, this will not be enough. Fortunately, there are other ways and means of seeing to it that those above are kept adequately informed by those below.

One such device is the trade union. As we saw in chapter five, informing those on top of what is happening beneath them is one of the major contributions which unions can make to the administrative process. Many an executive who has been shielded by his middle management from much of what is going on at the rank-and-file level finds the unions a valuable supplier of needed information. And he can usually be assured that the union's representatives will not spare him any unpleasant news.

Another means for improving the upward information flow is through formal devices for hearing complaints. These may include grievance committees, appeals boards and various clientele service units. For example, a mayor who sets up little city halls throughout his city in order to receive and process complaints may find that these complaints will give him some excellent clues as to where problems may exist in his administration.

Investigatory units can also prove helpful in this regard. Many large police departments have a special unit to investigate policemen. The head of the "shoefly squad" as it is usually called can often provide the police commissioner with information that he might not hear from his other subordinates.

Sometimes executives make their own field inspections, talking directly with rank-and-file personnel. This does not always have to take the form of a formal inspection. When Jerome Kretchmer was Environmental Protection Commissioner of New York City, he made it his practice to leave home once a week at 6:00 A.M. in order to stop off at a car barn and talk to the sanitation men as they were assembling for work. He would listen to their complaints and suggestions, usually, of course, receiving more of the former than the latter.[43]

An executive can also disregard the chain of command on occasion and call someone several levels below him to his office for some direct conversation. Or he may stipulate a period each week or month when his office door will be open to anyone within the organization who has a matter he would like to discuss.

Suggestion boxes can also play a helpful role in getting informa-

---

43. Fred Powledge, "Can Kretchmer Make a Clean Sweep?" *New York Times,* March 22, 1971.

tion from the bottom to the top. Not only will the suggestions sometimes be useful in themselves but they may well illuminate problems
which the manager may not know about. Surveys and polls of the organization's members and of its clients may also provide valuable information as well as indications as to how the upward communications
process is working.

There are, in short, many means available to insure a relatively
swift and smooth flow of upward communication. Any public manager
who truly wants an undistorted picture of what is going on in his organization should experience no great trouble in obtaining it.

Communicating Downward

While information may run downward a bit more smoothly than upward, it also encounters numerous obstacles and impediments. When it
is oral, downward communication is subject to almost all the alterations
that can creep in when it moves the other way. The captain tells the
lieutenant to have the men ready at 0800. The lieutenant, to protect
himself, tells the sergeant to have the men ready at 0700. And the sergeant, in a further manifestation of the same fear, makes sure the men
are ready at 0600. Thus, the captain then finds the men sleepy and disgruntled when he orders them into action.

When communication moves down in written form, it can also
develop difficulties. It may be misinterpreted either because it is not
complete or because the recipient is simply not willing to accept its
message. The biggest problem, however, is probably the inability or the
refusal of the recipient to absorb all the information which seems to be
cascading onto him. As we have already seen, memoranda senders encounter persistent problems in this respect.

Organizations have tried to get around this in many ways. In
some organizations, important messages are sent to the recipient's
home, occasionally by special messenger, as an insurance that he will
read it. And at least one school system makes a practice of following up
the written messages which it distributes to its teachers in the school by
broadcasting the same message through a loud-speaker.

There are other and usually better ways of surmounting this difficulty. People will often read material on bulletin boards that they might
ignore if placed in their agency mail slots. This is particularly true if the
bulletin board also carries other information besides that which ema-
nates from the "front office." Consequently, a notice placed on a bulletin board can score a greater impact than if it is sent individually to each
organization member.

Another useful device is the organization publication or house
organ. Such publications usually depend for their appeal on the report-

ing of a wide range of personal items within the organization. However, the adroit administrator will seek to sandwich in useful information regarding company policy, etc. Some private organizations have begun using in-house TV. They broadcast interviews with employees, both managerial and non-managerial, along with news of what the company is doing. Some of them also televise the company's annual stockholders meeting.

Whatever the means used, the wise public manager will develop some techniques for checking up to see that the information he has sent has truly gotten through to those for whom it is intended. And he will check for feedback as to how they have responded. Not infrequently, the way in which a decision has been communicated will have a greater effect on agency operations than the substance of the decision itself.

Cross-Communication

A generation or so ago, lateral communication received relatively little attention from administrative thinkers. Now, it is becoming as important, and in some cases more important, than communication up and down. The growth of specialization and interdependency is making it increasingly vital for information to flow *through* the organization as well as to move up and down its ranks.

Staff meetings can be particularly helpful in stimulating cross-communication. This assumes, of course, that they are genuine interchanges of ideas and data and not just monologues by the person who presides. Within a broader context, interdepartmental committees may also aid the lateral communications process. And house organs, bulletin boards and many of the other devices already cited can and usually do aid in spreading information from one section of the organization to another.

Physical arrangements can also play an important role in either helping or hampering cross-communication. Organizational units put in one building will tend to communicate more than when they are housed separately. Spreading them along the same corridor will usually encourage more communication than placing them on separate floors. And removing partitions that divide offices and work places from one another may greatly assist the cross-communication flow.

Organizational practices designed to resolve other problems may foster cross-communication as well. In-service training, for example, may bring people from various parts of the organization together and result in a good deal of cross-communication taking place. Organization-wide activities such as bowling teams or hobby clubs and an organizationally run cafeteria or dining room will also bring employees together and thus may lead to an interchange of information. Many of

243

the tough problems which arise on Israeli kibbutzes are solved over the dining room table in the evening.

Rotation of employees is also useful in improving cross-communication. The rotated employee can give his new co-workers a better understanding of how things operate "over there." More importantly, his former relationships can be used to maintain some communication flow with his former work unit. In any case, he is likely to meet his ex-colleagues from time to time and fill them in on what is happening at his new assignment.

As the technological society advances, and as organizations become more complex, cross-communication will become increasingly important. It is a subject that administrators will have to devote much more attention to in the future than they have in the past.

CASE STUDY

Action This Day[44]

Words always came easily to Winston Churchill. As a young man, he engaged in many daring exploits while serving as a lieutenant with the British forces in India and later in South Africa. But it was not so much the exploits themselves but his skill in writing about them that gained him the prominence that was to win him a seat in Parliament and launch his political career.

His bitter denunciations of Britain's appeasement policies during the 1930's acquired sharpness and thrust through the pungent language he so often employed. "These are the years when the locust has eaten" was one of the phrases he used to describe that sorry period. And when he served as prime minister during the war that ensued, he managed to warm the hearts and rally the spirits of his countrymen with the stirring speeches he delivered in what he called "England's darkest hour."

Churchill's abilities as a communicator also characterized his administration and they offer an interesting illustration of how a particular administrator sought to handle his many communication problems at a crucial time.

From the outset of his administration, Churchill placed a heavy emphasis on the written word. "Let it be very clearly understood," he informed his war cabinet, "that all directions emanating from me are made in writing, or should be immediately afterwards confirmed in writing, and that I do not accept any responsibility for matters relating to national defense on which I am alleged to have given decisions unless they are recorded in writing."

The message itself indicates one of the main reasons he adopted such a policy. War administration is crisis administration and as such can lead to

---

44. Material for this case study was largely drawn from *Action This Day: Working with Churchill, Memoirs of Lord Normanbrook and others,* Sir John Wheeler-Bennett, ed. The quotation of Robin Maugham is from his *Escape from the Shadows,* pp. 108-109.

considerable confusion. Orders given in a hurry and quickly passed down can easily be misunderstood with dire results. Other orders that are vital may go unheeded or become lost in the far-flung and fast moving governmental machinery. Churchill wanted none of that and since he had no problem in handling the written word, he used this facility to keep intermediaries at a minimum and to stay in direct touch with a vast number of people.

Through the time-saving device of formal communication Churchill was thus able to direct personally much of Britain's governmental activity. He retained for himself the cabinet post of Minister of Defense and there is no indication that wearing two hats in the cabinet impeded Britain's war effort in any way. Indeed, most accounts of Britain's history during this time indicate that the country was better off with the prime minister playing such a dual role.

His extended use of personal memoranda, all of which carried the imprint of his personal style and bore his signature or initials, also had an invigorating impact on the whole government. An official several ranks below him might find on his desk a message from the prime minister himself directing him to do such and such. In the words of cabinet secretary Lord Normanbrook, such messages often had a "startling effect."

There was yet another reason for Churchill's heavy reliance on written communication. This was the discipline it imposed on him. He was less likely to get carried away by some whim of the moment if he made it a point never to give orders that were not confirmed in writing afterwards.

Although the profuse stream of memoranda which issued from his office bore his distinct personal style, usually opening with the phrase "Pray tell me . . .," they were by no means literary extravaganzas. He could be remarkably concise as when he once ordered the mass production of a controversial new weapon. His memo read, "Sticky bombs—make one million—WSC." As he once noted, "It is sheer laziness not compressing information in a reasonable space."

Churchill also insisted that subordinates follow the same policy in dealing with him. He spent little time in interviewing people; instead they were to address him in writing. All such correspondence was put into a box and he would work on it at the beginning or the end of the day or at odd moments through the day. When any crisis erupted, he never had to cancel a lot of personal appointments.

He demanded that those who addressed him adhere to the rules of brevity as closely as he did himself. In 1941 he sent the following memo to the First Lord of the Admiralty: "Pray state this day, *on one side of a sheet of paper,* how the Royal Navy is being adapted to meet the conditions of modern warfare." (Emphasis added.) He was particularly hard on the needless use of banalities and truisms. He once replied to an official's memo by pointing out to the hapless fellow that his memo had employed every cliche in the English language except the British men's room admonition "Please adjust your dress before leaving."

None of this is meant to imply that Churchill disdained the use of the

245

spoken word, rather that he reserved it for those times and occasions when it could be used most effectively. When Eisenhower was in London, Churchill made it a part of his regular schedule to lunch with him every Tuesday. As he said later, nothing but shop was ever discussed on these occasions. He encouraged spirited discussion in meetings, at least at the beginning of his administration, and urged anyone having a dissenting viewpoint to "Fight your corner." When one attendee once remarked "I have tried to present my case fairly," Churchill growled at him "That's a very dangerous thing to do."

Churchill made sure that he did not spend all his time talking to higher-ups. He kept his lines of communication continually open to those down below. As Robin Maugham writes, "Throughout the war, Churchill was always more interested in talking to junior officers than to the top brass—partly from pure kindness, partly from his knowledge that it was from the men in the field that he could discover what was really going on." Maugham, who served as a lieutenant in the tank corps during the war, mentions how Churchill asked him after the fall of France if he and his fellows were ready to repel a German invasion. When Maugham replied that many of their tanks could not move for want of a spring in their trackpins, Churchill exploded in fury and immediately set the whole British government into action. By nightfall, the springs had been delivered and were in place.

Despite the personal manner in which he conducted his administration, Churchill did not neglect the use of that traditional British device, the committee. As we saw in the preceding chapter, he would frequently set up one group to give him information on a subject and then establish another group to supply him with advice on what to do with the information. On a more informal level, he would often set up dinner parties or after-dinner gatherings with some of the best minds both within and without the government for stimulating, if sometimes rambling, conversation. This institution, which became known as the "Midnight Follies" due to Churchill's predilection for staying up into the wee hours of the morning, was the source of many of the ideas which enlivened his administration.

However, his communications style did present drawbacks. He would frequently try to handle too much and consequently many matters would go neglected. Things that did not interest him would tend to pile up, and the stack of paper in his box would remorselessly rise until his secretaries could cajole him into spending more time trying to whittle it down. His personality was such that it too easily dominated any meeting at which he presided and toward the end of the war, when fatigue and possibly age was setting in, he showed himself less and less receptive to ideas from others within the coalition cabinet. The Labour party ministers began protesting that his cabinet meetings were becoming monologues.

Although he continued to remain more open to advice on the scientific and technical level, even here he became somewhat more remote as war weariness set in and, perhaps, as he became too infatuated with his own way of doing things. He listened too exclusively to his own science adviser F. A.

Lindeman (later Lord Cherwell) and failed to consult other scientists. As a result, he ordered, on the basis of Lindeman's faulty statistics, the rather fruitless and possibly even counterproductive saturation bombing raids on Germany.

Churchill's communication policy reflected his leadership policy and both reflected the man himself. As such, the question becomes one of judging whether his communications style suited the role he had to play at the time and in the circumstances in which he had to play it. On balance, the judgment of history seems to be that it did.

THE QUESTION OF SECRECY

The practice of government always requires some degree of secrecy. Negotiations with another government would often prove difficult and even dangerous if conducted in the open glare of publicity. There is little doubt that the sensitive talks which finally brought the Vietnam war to a close would have soon collapsed had newsmen been invited to sit in on the negotiating sessions. Indeed, so important is secrecy to the conduct of foreign affairs that Alexis de Tocqueville claimed that no democracy would ever succeed in carrying out a foreign policy since democracy, he reasoned, by its very nature must continually lay itself open to public view. While democracies have learned to conduct foreign relations, they have managed to do so only because they have learned to keep some things secret.

Sometimes it is necessary for a government not only to hide the truth from other governments but even from its own people. When Franklin Roosevelt sought to cover up the extent of the damage which the Japanese had inflicted in their raid on Pearl Harbor, he did so not just to mislead the Japanese but also the American citizenry. If the country had realized how badly the Japanese had crippled our Pacific fleet, public morale would have fallen to a dangerous ebb.

Secrecy is also essential in many less spectacular functions of government. Few people would want to have their income tax records available for anyone to inspect. Few welfare clients would want to have their status easily ascertainable by any neighbor who might choose to check on them. Adoption agencies require a great deal of personal data from a couple seeking to adopt; making this data available to all would doubtless deter many couples from making such a move. And a police department that allowed complete access to its files would not only imperil many of its investigations but would also jeopardize the rights and damage the reputations of many innocent people.

247

The need for secrecy also makes itself felt in the university. A committee on academic standing would probably need to have a student's psychiatric history and other personal data before it could make an intelligent and humane judgment on whether to put him on probation or suspend him. If, for example, he had a bad record but was currently undergoing psychotherapy, then this would undoubtedly temper their action. However, to allow such information to become general knowledge on the campus would obviously be unjust to the student. In a possibly parallel problem, New Jersey teachers fought for two years to prevent the state from releasing the results of state-wide reading tests. The teachers, along with other opponents, argued that making such data public would put counterproductive pressures on teachers and damage the self-image and possibly the future achievements of pupils in the poorer performing schools. Many also claimed the tests were culturally biased. However, others contended that the public is entitled to know how well the schools are performing and that the reading tests provide a measure of accountability.[45]

Thus, no government and few organizations, no matter how democratic they may be, can hope to dispense completely with secrecy. Some covert elements find their way into most administration and most administrations. Few administrators may wish to go so far as Frederick the Great when he said that if his coat knew of his plans he would burn it. But most administrators at one time or another have felt compelled not to reveal all that they know.

Yet, secrecy imposes a heavy price and presents an obvious peril to the practice of administration. "Everything secret degenerates," observed Lord Acton, and he added "Nothing is safe that does not show it can bear discrimination and publicity."[46] His contemporary countryman C. P. Snow puts it even more forcibly. "The results of closed politics can run precisely contrary to the results of open politics," he has said.[47]

What are some of the dangers and difficulties which secrecy presents? To quote C. P. Snow again, "The most obvious fact which hits you in the eye is that personalities and personal relations carry a weight of responsibility which is out of proportion greater than any they carry in open politics. Despite appearances, we are much nearer in ordinary government to personal power and personal choice.[48] Secret government therefore tends to become government by whim and caprice. Accountability withers away and objectivity also shrinks. Favoritism, discrimination and arbitrariness flourish in an environment of secrecy.

---

45. *New York Times,* April 7, 1974.
46. Quoted in Berkley, *The Democratic Policeman* (1969), p. 159.
47. Snow, *Science and Government,* p. 37.
48. *Ibid.,* p. 53.

Secrecy creates inequalities which did not previously exist and exacerbates those which did. Those who are "'in the know" tend to develop an arrogance and contempt for those who are not. Even when they manage to avoid such feelings, they still become sealed off from those who are excluded from the charmed circle of insiders. Secrecy obviously reduces communication and leaves decision-makers, even when they possess the best will in the world, with diminished capacity to make the best decisions.

Richard Neustadt has pointed out how the secrecy which World War II imposed on much of Franklin Roosevelt's activity severely curbed his effectiveness. He could no longer assign the same projects to more than one person or group of people and thereby obtain more than one point of view before making a decision. He could no longer dispatch trouble-shooters, observers and assistants wherever and whenever he wanted. And he could not utilize the knowledge and the opinions of outsiders in quite the way he liked to, for now such outsiders simply would not know enough to be of maximum helpfulness.[49]

In limiting decision-making to a relatively few insiders, secrecy tends to limit discussion and debate. Frequently, the decision is made by those who are too personally involved and have too much at stake. Morton H. Halperin of the Brookings Institute and Jeremy J. Stone of the American Federation of Scientists found this to be true in a study they undertook of the Central Intelligence Agency. The supersecret atmosphere tends to limit participation in covert decisions to those who support them and earn their living from them, they said. "The lack of vigorous dissent, so common in other proposals of a controversial nature, tends to lead to routine approval."[50]

The effect of secret knowledge can also prove injurious to those who possess it, even to the point of disturbing their mental balance. "It takes a very strong head to keep secrets for years and not go slightly mad," says Snow. And he adds, "it isn't wise to be advised by anyone who is slightly mad."[51]

Finally, trying to keep a matter hidden may only result in it becoming better known. Secrecy sows suspicion; the more secret an agency is, the more it arouses fear and distrust. The more secret any activity is, the more interest the press and the public will show in trying to find out about it. It then becomes too easy and too tempting for a disgruntled participant or employee not to covertly reveal what the covert operation is all about. Some do not have to be disgruntled to leak

49. Richard E. Neustadt, "Approaches to Staffing the Presidency: Notes on FDR and JFK," *American Political Science Review,* 57 (December 1963).
50. *New York Times,* May 20, 1971.
51. Snow, *op. cit.,* p. 65.

out the knowledge. They may just want to enjoy the sense of power which revealing important information can provide.

History affords no shortage of examples to illustrate all the many problems and pitfalls which secrecy engenders. The Watergate affair, in all of its many ramifications, provides a graphic illustration of most of them. However, the same difficulties posed by secrecy can also be seen in previous presidential administrations, although usually in considerably diminished form. The abortive invasion of Cuba during the early months of President Kennedy's administration owes its failure, at least in part, to the veil of secrecy in which the venture was enshrouded. The *New York Times* and *The New Republic* both learned of the event beforehand but both publications decided out of a misguided sense of patriotism not to disclose their information. Afterwards, President Kennedy told them that they would have done both him and the country a tremendous service if they had.

Secrecy and American Administration

American administrators can take comfort in the fact that secrecy imposes fewer restraints on administration here than it does on administration abroad. With the possible exception of the Scandinavian countries, American administration is the most open in the world.

Great Britain, for example, operates under what is called the Official Secrets Act. This legislation authorizes a remarkably stringent set of controls. Early in 1973 a British postal clerk was accused of violating the act when he wrote a letter to his local newspaper saying that the delay in processing mail at the local post office was caused by a shortage of help. When the *Sunday Times* of London published a report by consultants to the British Railway Board which raised the prospect of a drastic cut in rail service, it also ran afoul of the act. Detectives from Scotland Yard visited the newspaper's editor and informed him that he might have committed a crime.[52]

On the continent, similar if not stricter rules governing secrecy exist. In the fall of 1962, German police, acting on the express orders of their country's Ministry of Justice, descended on the offices of a magazine called *Der Spiegel*. They stopped publication, arrested the editor and inquired into the whereabouts of the publisher. When they learned that the latter was vacationing in Spain, they notified Spanish authorities who seized the publisher in his hotel room at 3:00 A.M. The magazine's "crime" consisted of having published a report showing that in recent NATO maneuvers, the German army had earned NATO's lowest rating on its performance.[53]

---

52. Anthony Lewis, "Official Secrets," *New York Times*, February 19, 1973.
53. Donald P. Kommers, "The Spiegel Affair," in *Political Trials*, Thomas L. Becker, ed. (Indianapolis: Bobbs-Merrill Co., 1971).

But if Americans can feel themselves fortunate in enjoying a much freer flow of information than their European counterparts, this should not blind them to the fact that secrecy still poses problems here as elsewhere. These became painfully apparent in the early 1970's when the controversy over the Pentagon papers and other information concerning the Vietnam war cast the whole problem of secrecy into bold relief.

Among the many incidents indicating abuse of administrative secrecy that came to light in this period were the following:

The General Services Administration had refused to allow public disclosure of the rent it was paying to lease office space in a privately owned building;

The Justice Department had withheld a report on expense-paid trips to shooting matches by border-patrol inspectors;

The State Department refused to allow newsmen to see gifts which foreign governments had given certain federal officials on grounds that the gifts were stored in a "classified building."

The Forest Service refused to release the names of persons who had been granted permits to graze cattle in a national forest;

The Civil Service Commission declined to divulge the results of an investigation it had conducted into alleged irregularities of an examination for rural mail carriers;

The Department of Health, Education and Welfare had clamped a tight lid of secrecy on a report that listed studies of human reproduction problems.[54]

It was the Defense Department, however, that became the greatest target for those attacking alleged abuses of administrative secrecy. The air force was accused of having put the stamp of secrecy on pictures of the interiors of transport planes because it did not want the public to see the plush lounges which had been installed for the comfort of traveling military officials. The navy still had a secrecy stamp on a report of attacks made by sharks on seamen in New York Harbor in 1916. The navy also had classified as secret a series of published newspaper articles until a red-faced official issued an order saying that newspaper clippings should no longer be considered secret. When one of the joint chiefs wrote a note to the others suggesting less use of the secrecy stamp, his note was stamped top secret. According to William G. Florence, who retired in 1971 as a security classification expert, only one-half of one percent of the Pentagon's 20 million classified documents truly merited being shielded from public inspection.

---

54. *Time*, July 5, 1971, p. 14.

In many cases, the use of secrecy was found to be not only excessive but inconsistent. Thus, while the Washington Zoo in 1960 was proudly exhibiting a monkey that had a sign on its cage saying that the animal had flown in space, the State Department was withholding all news that a monkey had ever been sent up in a space capsule.[55] In 1965 Dean Rusk gave a talk before a group of high school students outlining his views of the Vietnam conflict. The next day, he sent a memo on the same subject to the president. Although he labeled his memo "eyes only," meaning that it was strictly to be read by the president himself and no one else, the message, according to reporter David Halberstam, contained "word-for-word" the exact presentation he had made the previous day to the high school students.

Faced with a rising clamor of concern over secrecy excesses in the federal bureaucracy, President Nixon moved in 1972 to ease access to public documents. In an executive order that went into effect on June 1 of that year, the president stipulated that papers labeled "confidential" must be opened to the public after six years; papers bearing the imprint "secret" must be released after eight years and documents carrying the "top secret" stamp could not be kept secret more than ten years.[56]

His order provided for some exemptions but permitted anyone to challenge them. The burden of proof for keeping any document secret would then fall on the government. This marked a reversal of previous policy which had left to the applicant the task of showing why it should be made public. Furthermore, the number of federal officials allowed to wield secrecy stamps was reduced by more than two-thirds, from 55,000 to 18,000, with only a little over 1,000 having the power to assign the "top secret" rating.

The president's directive does seem to have produced some results. In the first five months after it was promulgated, federal agencies received 177 requests for information that had previously been classified. Of these requests, 83 were granted in full and 4 in part. Another 38 were still pending while only 53, less than one-third, had been denied in full.[57]

However, antagonists to administrative secrecy were not appeased. They pointed out that the government was still requiring someone seeking such information to know precisely what he wanted and this was often impossible until the requester had a chance to go through the files. In addition, the person requesting declassification must agree in advance to pay the cost of locating, identifying and re-

---

55. *New York Times,* April 9, 1973 (speech by Edmund C. Muskie).
56. Richard Halloran, "The Word Now Is: 'Easier on the Stamp,' " in the *New York Times,* March 12, 1972 (News in Review). Also see editorial "Crack in the Secrecy Wall" in the same edition.
57. *New York Times,* April 25, 1973.

viewing the material even though it may not turn out to provide the information he is seeking. Then, there is also no provision for holding to account and punishing federal officials who abuse the classification system. And, most important perhaps, there are no precise definitions and criteria for determining what material should be classified and, if classified, in what category it should be placed.[58]

A bipartisan congressional committee set up to review the government's secrecy procedures called attention to many of these concerns.[59] The Watergate affair has only focused more attention on the whole problem of secrecy and the dilemmas it presents to a democratic society. Consequently, administrators can expect to confront increasing pressures for more and more openness and less and less secrecy in the future.

---

58. *New York Times,* November 22, 1972.
59. *Boston Evening Globe,* May 24, 1973.

8

Budgeting

Students of public administration frequently shudder when the course turns to the subject of budgeting. They tend to regard the budget as merely a ponderous tome of dreary figures and to view the process of budgeting as simply a tedious and humdrum chore which lacks all the human interaction that makes things like personnel and leadership so much more palatable. In responding in such a way, they could not be more wrong.

Most, though certainly not all, of the issues and conflicts which spring from the administrative process take the form of contests over monetary allocations. If politics is sometimes defined as the process of deciding who gets what, administrative politics often becomes the process of deciding who gets what amount of money. Consequently, whether or not one department or individual is to be favored over another or whether or not one program or policy is to be supported over another usually becomes translated into a budgetary decision. In this way, budgets are not just political documents in addition to being other things as well; budgets are political documents before they are other things as well.

This does not mean that deciphering budgets in terms of what they have to tell us about administrative politics is an easy task. If budgets are essentially political documents, the politics is often veiled. To the untrained eye, a budget often conceals much more than it reveals. Expertise in clouding over or cloaking some of the political aspects in a budget has advanced more than one administrator's career, while skill in figuring out what was being done has helped more than one politician enhance his power. The late Senator Richard Russell of Georgia became one of the most influential men in the United States Senate—he was the senator whom Lyndon Johnson most listened to and deferred to when Johnson was Senate Majority Leader—in part because of his ability to read a budget. As one Johnson aide once said, Russell "could glance at a Defense Department budget request that is sixty pages long and in 30 seconds could pick up the tricks."[1]

It is not enough, however, to call attention to the political aspects of budgeting in order to define just what budgeting is. Budgets are also instruments of coordination, control and planning. They thus govern nearly all aspects of administration and confer a great deal of power on those who prepare them. In New York City, to take just one example, the post of budget director is considered the most influential non-elective position in the city government. In Washington, to take another example, President Nixon transformed the Bureau of the Budget into the Office of Management and Budget, thus giving the budget agency extensive formal power over the entire federal bureaucracy.[2] And in Great Britain and Canada, to take still other examples, the Treasury Department, which makes up the budgets in these countries, has traditionally exercised many managerial functions as well. Indeed, the prime minister of Great Britain was long known as the First Lord of the Treasury.

As for the fledgling administrator, he will frequently find that a term of service in his organization's budgetary branch will furnish him with knowledge and insights that he can obtain from few of the organization's other subunits. And if he does start out in a line department or on another staff unit, he will usually discover that budget preparation constitutes one of the unit's most important survival activities, sometimes overriding in care and concern the unit's main focus of operation. As long as resources continue to be relatively scarce in terms of what any organizational unit wishes to do, the budgetary process will continue to cast a long shadow over administrative activity.

TRADITIONAL BUDGETING

As might be expected, traditional budgeting is a lengthy process. It usually begins with comparatively small subunits figuring out what they need or feel they need for the coming year and submitting these figures as requests to higher levels. At each stage, the figures are customarily reviewed and frequently reduced. Eventually, all the requests will converge in the organization's budgetary office or in the office of its chief executive or both.

From the organization, the figures travel to the government's overall budgetary department which in the federal bureaucracy is the

---

1. Halberstam, *The Best and the Brightest*, p. 146.
2. Presidential message in the *New York Times,* March 13, 1970.

Office of Management and Budget. There they are once again reviewed and often reshaped. The tendency here, as at previous review stages, is to cut down rather than to expand the requested amounts. Oftentimes, the agency heads and the budgeting office officials find themselves in adversary positions. The former stoutly maintain that they need all the money they are requesting and even more, while the latter keep insisting that they are overstating their organization's needs and inflating its role.

After fashioning an overall spending blueprint, the budgetary office and the chief executive submit it to the legislative body. Here it will almost always be initially assigned to one or more committees before being adopted by the body as a whole. And here, as previously, the tendency will be to pare down the proposed sums. If the legislative body consists of two chambers as does the Congress of the United States and all but one of the country's state legislatures, the process may have to be repeated a second time before a final budget becomes enacted.

With some exceptions, budgets in this country cover only one year, which makes the budgeting process an annual one. However, preparation for the budget may begin, as it does in the federal government, well over two years prior to the period which it is designed to cover. Thus, a president inaugurated in January will find that the spending policies of his administration are already committed for the most part for the forthcoming 18 months. (The federal government's budget, it should be pointed out, does not coincide with the calendar year; rather, it runs from July 1 to July 1 which forms the fiscal year. Many states and municipalities use the same system.)

Capital Budgets

Most of America's 80-odd thousand governments divide their budgets into two sections, one for capital projects, the other for expenses. Often they are considered as two separate budgets.

The rationale for segregating capital expenditures in a separate budget is easily explained. Such projects usually entail a considerable expenditure that may incur only once in a generation or even once in several generations. Trying to cover the expenditure involved in one year would be troublesome and often impossible. A small community faced with building a new high school could bankrupt many of its citizens if it sought to pay for the cost through one year's collection of taxes. Capital budgeting enables the community to break out of the one-year budget cycle and spread the cost over many years. Since such projects are usually financed from the sale of bonds which are to be paid over 20, 30 or even 40 years, placing such expenditures outside the annual expense budget makes a good deal of sense.

Another aspect of capital improvements also warrants spreading out their costs. Capital projects confer benefits for extended periods of time. Modern-day Rome, for example, is still using some of the sewers built in the time of the Caesars. Consequently, it is only equitable that those who will subsequently benefit from the expenditures should shoulder part of the burden. A capital budget permits them to do so.

Because capital projects do not involve immediate expenditures—usually they do not get launched until a year or two after they are authorized—there is a tendency to utilize them in political ways. Some state legislatures have been known to pass bloated capital budgets as a way of appeasing their constituencies without imposing any new immediate tax burdens. The legislator can return to his district boasting about how he has wrangled a new road, dredging project, etc. for his constituents while at the same time escaping the onus of having voted for new taxes. Of course, eventually new funds will be required to pay off the debts incurred for the approved capital expenditure. But for the present at least, the lawmaker is "home free."

A more common abuse of the capital budget process is the simple one of putting into the budget items that really belong in the expense budget. Here again, the reason is to avoid increasing the constituent's present tax burden. In mid-1973, for example, the Citizens Budget Commission of New York City, a non-official watchdog agency, claimed that a full 25 percent of the city's current capital budget was being used for operating expenditures. And it estimated that about one-third of the city's projected 1973–74 capital budget was made up of such items.[3] This means that the city was selling bonds to pay for increasing amounts of its day-to-day expenses. Since such bonds must eventually be repaid with interest, the practice only worsens the city's financial plight in the long run. As the commission put it, "Unless this vicious cycle is stopped, the end result will be ever-increasing borrowing and debt service and ever-increasing real estate taxes."

For its part, the city administration had consistently claimed it was justified in that its expenditures were rising at about 15 percent per year while its revenues were going up by only about 5 percent. However, borrowing to pay current expenses is bound to be a losing proposition. It may be justified for a short period of time when unusual conditions dictate unusually high expenditures and/or unusually low revenues. As a consistent policy it obviously will lead to dire conse-

---

3. *New York Times,* July 8, 1973.

quences. Its political appeal is that the consequences in terms of subsequent increased taxes can be shifted to a later administration, and usually are.

But if capital budgeting can lead to political abuses, its absence may produce even worse consequences. The federal government does not make use of capital budgets, and in some respects there seems to be no compelling reason why it should. Unlike states, municipalities and other governments, federal agencies are rarely faced with one-shot expenditures that would completely disrupt their budget cycles. They are so large that capital projects of one kind or another are a continual activity. Furthermore, the federal government is not compelled to float bonds to finance its projects since it controls the money supply.

Nevertheless, the failure of the federal bureaucracy to use capital budgeting has drawn the fire of many critics in recent years. They claim that the lack of a capital budget has promulgated or aggravated an assortment of ills.

For one thing, the absence of a capital budget at the federal level means an absence of systematic review procedures to establish the economic desirability of capital projects. To put it more simply, capital projects are made too haphazardly. Accounting practices flourish which do not properly consider the total and unit costs. Useful and accurate estimates of the cost savings which a capital expenditure may produce are difficult to come by.

Furthermore, despite the fact that the federal government is constantly making capital expenditures, the refusal to segregate them in a separate account may and often does make any particular agency head, division chief or branch manager more reluctant to initiate such expenditures. Such outlays will simply bulk too large in his current all-in-one budget and thus make him look like a heavy spender. If those who review his budget approve a substantial capital project, they may cut him back in other areas as partial compensation. Furthermore, in terms of his own career, he may not be around to take credit for the economies that such capital expenditures may eventually yield. As a result, an administrator will often feel inclined to let his successor set up the new computer system or purchase the new maintenance equipment.

According to Senator William Proxmire, the lack of a capital budget at the federal level has induced government agencies to resort to various stratagems. These include hidden subsidies to sponsor various programs, many of which are, in themselves, quite deserving of public support. He cites as an example several of the federal government's housing programs. Backers of such programs, says Proxmire, devised an array of tax, credit and other subsidies to escape the fiscal and political impact of putting such items in a one-year budget. "As a consequence, the ultimate costs of the program skyrocketed in order to preserve a small annual cost. In this way costs rose while control over the program was lost."[4]

To sum up, capital budgeting, as a device to be used within the framework of traditional budgeting, makes a good deal of sense for most state and local governments. It might also prove useful for the federal government as well. It does, however, lend itself to certain manipulations and machinations which have proven costly to some states and municipalities. But then the expense budget is even more prone to the playing of political games, as we shall see.

Expense Budgeting

The basic document in traditional budgeting is the expense budget. This details the operational expenditures for the coming year. Like the capital budget, it is an array of things to be purchased and the prices to be paid. The "things" include manpower as well as heat, electricity and less tangible items. Nearly all the basic objects of expenditure are customarily covered and set down clearly in page after page of neat rows.

Usually, some attempt is made at categorizing the various objects of expenditure. Thus, there may be one account for permanent personnel, another for temporary personnel, a third for consultants and so forth. And within each of these categories there will most likely be subcategories. Thus, there may be one or more rows in the permanent personnel account listing the number of employees needed for each job classification and the total amount of expenditure they represent.

The traditional line-item budget is often highly detailed. It frequently provides the viewer with precise data on where every dollar is being spent. Yet, at the same time, such budgets tend to reflect and reinforce the organizational pathologies which we noted in chapter four.

The basic problem of traditional line-item budgets is that they fail to show what the money is being used for in terms of *programs*. The Public Works Department budget may specify the amount of machinery on hand and what will be needed to keep it in repair, as well as any new machines which may be purchased. It may tell us how many employees will be used to operate the machinery and how much they will be paid. And it may indicate how many temporary employees may be hired and how much private equipment may be rented to cover specialized tasks or emergencies. But it will not tell us, for instance, just how many miles of streets all this expenditure is designed to tar or pave and whether tarring a street is cheaper than paving it and if so, how much cheaper.

---

4. William Proxmire, *Uncle Sam: The Last of the Bigtime Spenders* (New York: Simon and Shuster, 1972), p. 35.

Because of this lack of program information, the line-item budget lends itself to stagnation. Possessing little information as to the costs and effectiveness of its various activities, the organization tends to base its budget requests on simply what it has used in the past. Last year's appropriation becomes the basis for this year's requests. Outmoded programs are not phased out and new programs are not eagerly embraced. By failing to provide program information, line-item budgeting tends to perpetuate the status quo.

The Defense Department budget during the 1950's offers a vivid illustration of how the stagnation factor enters into traditional budgeting. During the eight years of the Eisenhower administration, the proportion of defense funds going to the three military services remained almost constant. The air force received around 47 percent of the department's appropriation, the navy received about 29 percent and the army approximately 22 percent. Slight changes occurred from year to year, but essentially the proportions at the end of the decade did not appreciably differ from those at the beginning. Yet, during this time, great changes took place in defense technology, changes which, so it would seem, should have forced some substantial reallocations of the department's budget.

The status quo reinforcing effect of traditional line-item budgeting—often referred to as incremental budgeting since it concerns itself with increments of change rather than program change—can influence whole governments. Ira Sharkansky attributes to incremental budgeting the fact that the relative spending positions of the American states has remained basically the same since the turn of the century. Despite the fact that many states have experienced startling growth and change while others have suffered relative decline, those that were the big spenders in 1903 are still at the top of the spending list today. Incremental budgeting, claims Sharkansky, tends to lead to static governmental expenditure policies.[5]

The term *incremental,* however, does imply some change. What it indicates is that the change will occur in terms of spending more or less rather than in terms of spending money differently or for different purposes and programs. This is, indeed, what happens. However, incremental changes, it should be noted, tend to go in just one direction. They almost invariably take the form of more rather than less.

There are many reasons for this, some of them perfectly legitimate as far as administration is concerned. Population tends to grow, hence requiring more expenditures to serve more people. Furthermore, price levels have also shown a pronounced predilection for going up,

---

5. Ira Sharkansky, *Spending in the American State* (Chicago: Rand McNally, 1968).

particularly in the inflation which has characterized most societies since World War II. Then, people seem to expect more and more from government. And increasing prosperity itself takes its toll. The more cars we have, the more highways, parking lots, traffic policemen, etc. we will need.

However, there are other factors inherent in the incremental budgeting process which tend to push expenditures to ever higher plateaus. For one thing, there is little inducement to the administrator to save money. On the contrary, traditional line-item budgeting tends to punish the parsimonious public manager. If he cuts his costs and hence finds himself with a surplus at the end of the fiscal year, then his overseers, such as his hierarchical superiors and particularly members of the legislative committee which approves his budget, will decide that he did not need all that money in the first place. Instead of receiving a medal, he will most likely be given a cut in appropriations the following year.

Dr. Matthew Dumont, a psychiatrist who once served in the Department of Health, Education and Welfare, provides a pertinent and rather pointed analogy to describe how stupid it would be for an agency head to return unspent money which Congress has appropriated for his agency. "It would be like a bum asking for a handout for a cup of coffee. A passerby offers a quarter and the bum returns 15 cents, saying 'coffee is only a dime, shmuck.' "[6]

This feature of incremental budgeting has given rise to what in Washington is called the "Spring Spending Spree." As the fiscal year starts to run out in April and May, agencies and subagencies with unexpended balances in their accounts begin casting about frantically for ways to spend the excess money. They do so simply because they fear the consequences from Congress if they are caught with a surplus once the fiscal year ends. The Nixon administration tried to put a halt to this by making agencies report their unexpended balances every three months. However, the practice apparently still goes on. In February 1972, for example, Admiral Elmo R. Zumwalt sent a telegram to the heads of the various Naval commands urging them to make haste in meeting their "outlay targets" for the current fiscal year in order to "avoid resultant adverse effects" on next year's appropriations.[7] As another federal official once noted, "The political process abhors a surplus."

Incremental budgeting not only provides an administrator with few inducements to cut costs, it actually adds to the pressures on him to

---

6. Mathew Dumont, "Down the Bureaucracy!" *Transaction,* October 1970.
7. *New York Times,* March 29, 1972. For Admiral Zumwalt's reply see his letter to the editor on April 28 and for Senator William Proxmire's counter reply see his letter to the editor on May 8.

increase his costs, i.e., to ask for money. Thomas J. Anton points out that an administrator must try to appease three separate "audiences."[8] One of these is his own employees who look to him to preserve and, if possible, enhance their working conditions and their status. Such considerations can be met through increasing the organization's appropriation. Then, there is the agency's clientele group. They also desire increased funds for the agency since they are usually the most direct beneficiaries of the agency's expenditures. These two pressures for budget increases would probably exist under any form of budgeting. However, there is a third audience to be appeased. These are the review officials including hierarchical superiors, budget bureau officials and legislators. All of these, but particularly the latter, have an interest in being able to cut his budget. In making cuts they achieve a sense of fulfillment and importance.

All of these factors translate into a simple process that characterizes budgeting all through the American political system. Agency heads greatly inflate their appropriations requests; review officials continually pare them down. However, the agency is more often than not allowed some additional funding.

Many administrators have become quite adroit in procuring increased allocations. They will usually ask for money for one of their more popular activities regardless of whether or not all or even part of the new funds will actually be targeted for that purpose. They may latch on to a popular cause or concept and say they need the money to do something more or something new in response to it. Or they may ask to undertake a new activity and seek only limited funds to get started. This is known as the "foot in the door" approach. However, once launched, the new enterprise tends to cost more and more.

The Department of Defense has made frequent use of the "foot in the door" approach. It will set down a low initial cost to get a program started and Congress will often grant the money without fully realizing what the final bill will be. Another related device employed by the Defense Department has been the creation of shortages. The department will overextend its commitments and then urgently plead for more money. Thus, the army will set up a goal of so many divisions and then bemoan the fact that it lacks the funds to maintain them. "The worst thing you can do to a service," one observer once noted, "is to take away its shortages."[9]

Similar stratagems are employed by other organizations as well.

---

8. Thomas J. Anton, "Roles and Symbols in the Determination of State Expenditures," *Midwest Journal of Political Science,* November 1967.
9. Alain C. Enthoven and K. Wayne Smith, *How Much Is Enough?* (New York: Harper & Row, 1971), pp. 17–18.

Universities are by no means exempt. As Katz and Kahn have pointed out, an academic department may ask to teach new courses claiming it can do so with existing personnel. It may be perfectly sincere, but as its work volume expands, it finds itself asking for additional funds.[10]

All of these pressures and policies converge to force the level of spending to ever higher levels. In his study of budgeting in the state government of Illinois, Anton compares the budget document "to a huge mountain which is constantly being pushed higher and higher by geologic convulsions." He describes the governor as a blindfolded man "seeking to reduce the height of the mountain by dislodging pebbles with a teaspoon."[11]

Of course, elective officials are not completely powerless in this situation. Except for "earmarked" funds that have to be allocated and spent because of constitutional restrictions, prior commitments, etc., they can wield the scalpel as deeply as they wish. However, in addition to various outside political pressures, such as the agency's clientele group, many other considerations may stay their hand, for budget cutting can be a hazardous game.

The problem once again is related to the lack of program direction and content in the traditional line-item budget. As a result, a budget cut can be translated into various forms. And sometimes it can end up actually increasing costs.

A line-item budget will generally include categories for personnel, equipment and maintenance, among others. An administrator confronted with a general slash in funds will often cut maintenance costs first and personnel costs last. The reasons are fairly obvious. Reductions in maintenance disrupt his agency's operations the least, in the short run. Reductions in personnel are apt to disrupt operations the most, particularly when the morale of those remaining on the job is taken into account. Unfortunately, equipment and buildings that are not properly maintained eventually increase an agency's costs over what would otherwise be the case.

To be sure, administrators will sometimes respond to a budget cut by actually phasing out whole programs or dismissing personnel. But all too often this is done for the express purpose of generating pressure for their restoration. For example, when a new administration in one major American city attempted, as part of a needed austerity program, to cut the budget of its main library, the library's director announced that he would be forced to close the library building two evenings a week and on Saturdays. As it so happens, Saturdays and

---

10. Katz and Kahn, *The Social Psychology of Organizations,* p. 103.
11. Anton, *op. cit.,* p. 146.

DEPARTMENT	FUND	ACCOUNT NO.
Public Works	General Revenue	1 03-11

BUDGET COMMENTS

The Public Works Department was created in 1911 under the provision of Chapter 486, Acts of 1909, through the consolidation of the existing street, water and engineering departments. The department is in the charge of a Commissioner who is required by ordinance to be a Civil Engineer. The department now operates through its Central Office - Engineering and four major divisions. These divisions carry out the major programs of the department; namely, the maintenance and construction of highways, street lighting, snow removal, sewerage construction and maintenance, water construction and maintenance, street cleaning, and removal of garbage and rubbish.

EXPLANATION OF DECREASE

1972 Collective Bargaining	235,576
1973 Collective Bargaining	140,146
Step Rates	49,477
Decrease in Rubbish Contracts	(554,144)
Increase in Supplies and Materials	71,128
Decrease in Equipment	(87,765)
Total Decrease:	(145,582)

COST SUMMARY BY PROGRAM ELEMENT

PROGRAM ELEMENT	1971 EXPENDITURE	1972 APPROPRIATION	1973 BUDGET REQUESTED BY DEPARTMENT	1973 BUDGET RECOMMENDED BY MAYOR	INCREASE OR (DECREASE)
Adm. Support and Direction	1,371,783	1,742,639	1,985,476	1,726,032	(16,607)
Transportation	7,722,760	9,066,738	10,979,774	9,351,574	284,836
Sanitary - Solid Waste Control	8,442,970	9,697,936	10,541,669	9,431,328	(266,608)
DEPARTMENT TOTAL					

COST SUMMARY BY CLASS

DESCRIPTION	1970 EXPENDITURE	1971 EXPENDITURE	1972 APPROPRIATION	1973 BUDGET REQUESTED BY DEPARTMENT	1973 BUDGET RECOMMENDED BY MAYOR	INCREASE OR (DECREASE)
Personal Services	6,722,370	6,860,852	7,506,206	9,879,543	8,069,593	563,387
Contractual Services	7,770,632	9,579,328	10,904,702	11,108,393	10,355,358	(549,344)
Supplies and Materials	634,880	692,021	876,405	947,533	947,533	71,128
Current Charges and Obligations	11,790	36,585	30,000	49,215	39,215	9,215
Equipment	80,032	51,297	500,000	412,235	412,235	(87,765)
Structures and Improvements	451,026	317,430	690,000	1,110,000	685,000	(5,000)
Land and Non-Structural Improvements						
Special Appropriation						
DEPARTMENT TOTAL	15,670,730	17,537,513	20,507,313	23,506,919	20,508,934	1,621

This is the summary page of the city of Boston's Public Works Department budget for 1973. It is primarily a line-item budget and subsequent pages itemize the various expenditures in each of the main categories listed at the bottom of the page. Note, however, that some attempt has been made to group expenditures by program element as well. (Source: Boston Finance Commission.)

evening hours were the most popular periods of library use. (During the morning hours, the library actually had more staff than readers on its premises.) The public outcry that ensued from the library director's announcement forced the mayor to temper his proposed cutback in funds.[12]

In addition to promoting static though swelling administration, incremental budgeting has also been criticized for many other ills. Though its numerous details on expenditures would seem to make it a good vehicle for public scrutiny, the reverse may be the case. Indeed, the more detailed the data on objects of expenditure are, the more they may obscure. Large bulky documents filled with page after page containing row after row of expenditure items may reveal very little of what an agency is doing and how well it is doing it. Appropriations for any one activity may be scattered throughout the budget and almost impossible to piece together. Foreign military assistance was thought to be costing the United States about one-half billion dollars a year at the beginning of the current decade. It took an exhaustive study by Senator Proxmire's Subcommittee on Economy and Government to bring out the fact that such assistance was actually amounting to three or four billion dollars a year.[13]

The stratagems which administrators often have to employ in working with incremental budgets do little to enhance their own integrity or that of the budget process itself. Incremental budgeting has been accused with some justification of "making liars out of honest men." Requesting more money than one needs or expects simply to satisfy the rules of the game would scarcely seem a way to promote rationality and honesty in administration.

Such considerations as these have spurred efforts to find newer and better ways of dealing with the budgetary process in modern administration. It is to some of these efforts that we will now turn.

THE COMING OF PPBS

As government grew in size and complexity, dissatisfaction with traditional budgeting grew apace. The failure of line-item budgets to reveal the impact of expenditures on programs, to show future costs and effects, to analyze the relationships between capital and operating costs and to propose alternatives—all these and other problems came to ran-

---

12. The incident is based on the author's experience as an aide to Mayor John F. Collins of Boston in 1960.
13. Proxmire, *op. cit.,* pp. 94–103.

kle more and more of those who were dedicated to improving administrative performance. Surely, they reasoned, there must be a better way of budgeting than simply drawing up a list of expenditures every year, a list which, based as it is on last year's list, tends to change in only being larger. A better way of budgeting, one more conducive to change and evaluation, was felt to be needed.

By the early 1950's, the Hoover Commission was proposing a new type of federal budget. It would be a budget "based upon functions, activities and projects." Such a budget would be a "performance budget" and it would include, along with the mass of itemized objects of expenditure, some additional information as to what all this expenditure was to provide in the way of public services. If the public works department was to spend so much for personnel, equipment, etc., then how many miles of streets would be paved as a result? Early performance budgeters attempted to provide this information by adding an additional column in the traditional budget and setting down within it the actual work to be performed.

Some, however, were still not satisfied. They felt that simply tacking an additional column onto the existing line-item budget did not go far enough. What was needed was a whole new budget geared to actual programs, that is, to what the agency is really doing. C. Northcote Parkinson had once noted that the budget for the British army was broken down into a series of accounts. Account number one covered pay, account number seven comprised supplies, and so forth. The navy's budget was similarly classified. "But," bemoaned Parkinson, "neither the Navy nor the Army is organized like that. The Navy is organized into units afloat and ashore. The Army is organized into battalions, batteries, depots and schools for which individually no cost is shown."[14]

The problem which Parkinson noted was as prevalent in America as it was in Britain. And, in some quarters at least, it was causing even more concern. Finally, with the inauguration of John F. Kennedy in 1961, steps began to be taken to respond to Parkinson's complaint.

Kennedy's Secretary of Defense, Robert MacNamara, found his department's budget organized into the following broad categories:

Military Personnel

Operations and Maintenance

Construction

Research and Development

Although he had probably never read Parkinson, this method of budgeting bothered MacNamara. By the time he left the Defense Department

---

14. C. Northcote Parkinson, *The Law and the Profits* (New York: Ballantine Books, 1971), p. 11.

seven years later, the department's basic budget categories read as follows:

Strategic Forces
  Offensive forces
  Defensive forces
  Civil defense
General Purpose Forces
Specialized Activities (Intelligence)
Airlift and Sealift

Note well the difference between the two sets of categories. The first simply lists expenditures grouped according to the *type of expenditure*. The second groups expenditures according to the *purpose these expenditures are to achieve*. The first grouping would not tell us just how much the country is spending for, say, offensive forces as compared to other defense activities. The second grouping bases itself on providing just such information.

However, grouping expenditures on the basis of program rather than on merely type of expenditure was only part of MacNamara's new system. The rationale for putting expenditures into program categories was to find out whether the Defense Department was spending its money wisely. To make such a determination, a further tool was needed. This was cost-benefit analysis.

The use of cost-benefit analysis actually pre-dated MacNamara's arrival in the federal government. Many years before, economists had been weighing the costs versus the benefits of certain water resource projects in an attempt to find out just what projects would be most effective in terms of dollars spent. Otto Eckstein in his book *Public Finance* gives an example of using such an approach to determine the most effective way of dealing with a flood control problem.

Plan	Cost of Project	Average Damage	Benefit (reduction of damage)
No Protection	0	$38,000	0
Levees	$ 3,000	$32,000	$ 6,000
Small Reservoir	$10,000	$22,000	$16,000
Medium Reservoir	$18,000	$13,000	$25,000
Large Reservoir	$30,000	$ 6,000	$32,000

Source: Adapted from Otto Eckstein, *Public Finance* (Englewood Cliffs, N.J.: Prentice-Hall, 1945), reprinted in Virginia Held, "PPBS Comes to Washington," *The Public Interest*, summer 1966.

Which of the above projects is the most desirable method of dealing with the flood damage in question? On a percentage basis, the best project appears to be levees since their construction would return double the amount of benefit in relation to outlay. On an absolute basis, the best approach might be found in constructing a large reservoir, for it provides the greatest dollar amount of benefits. However, Eckstein says the estimates show that the medium reservoir is the productive project because it provides the *greatest amount of dollar benefit in relation to cost.* The net savings which a medium reservoir would produce amount to $7,000 a year as compared to $3,000 a year from levees and only $2,000 a year from a large reservoir.

Note that the savings and cost are figured on an annual basis. However, most of the money involved in such projects is spent at the outset in constructing the levees or the reservoir. Maintenance and operation costs during the time the facility is in use are usually minimal. However, in order to arrive at an annual cost figure, the amount of the initial outlay is spread over the life of the project.

This would mean that a project costing $10 million to build and lasting ten years would be figured as costing $1 million a year in addition to any operational, maintenance and other costs that may be involved in operating the project. But cost-benefit analysis does not stop with simply dividing up the initial outlay over the project's projected life. It also uses what is called the discount rate or interest rate to arrive at a more accurate picture of both costs and benefits.

To understand the use of a discount rate, imagine that you have the chance to receive one thousand dollars right away or one thousand dollars a year hence. Which would you accept? Obviously, the one thousand dollars right away. Even if you do not wish to spend it, you can put it in the bank and earn, say, 5 percent interest on it during the coming year. This means that one thousand dollars now is worth at least one thousand and fifty dollars next year.

Or take the reverse situation. Suppose you have the alternative of paying a one-thousand-dollar bill this year or next. Obviously, even if you have the money, you will prefer to pay it next year, for in the meantime you can use the money for another purpose or, at a minimum, let it accumulate interest in a bank. Thus, a bill for one thousand dollars actually will cost you less next year than if paid right away.

These two simple illustrations indicate that the value of money must be calculated in relationship to the time it is spent or received. Cost-benefit analysis incorporates this concept through what it calls the discount rate. If a project involves an initial cost of $10 million and will provide benefits of $11 or $12 million at the end of ten years, then the project will be considered a losing proposition. Why? Because even if one figured that money was worth only 2 percent a year, this would still make $10 million worth more than $12 million at the end of ten years. (We are, of course, compounding the interest.) Similarly, if a project provides an initial savings of $10 million but a cost of $12 million after ten years, then it would more than pay for itself.

The discount rate used by the federal government is 5.75 percent which many feel is too low. The lower the discount rate, the easier it usually becomes to justify an expenditure. A little thinking on this subject will show why.

MacNamara joined cost-benefit analysis to his new budget classifications. Not only would expenditures be grouped according to programs but cost-benefit analysis would be used to decide whether such programs were actually effective, or, if they were effective, whether they were the most effective approaches available in terms of the expenditure involved. This amalgamation of budget classification according to program with cost-benefit analysis for deciding program effectiveness produced a new method of budgeting called the planned program budgeting system, better known as PPBS.

PPBS is obviously not always an easy system to use. For one thing, it requires a whole new way of thinking, not just about public expenditures but about public policy in general. To use it effectively administrators must think not just about what they are doing but about what they are trying to achieve. PPBS stresses goals and achievements over processes and procedure, and many administrators prefer to emphasize the latter.

Furthermore, even with the best will in the world, the administrator may have trouble putting down his goals in the form of tangible objectives. This is particularly true for those working in the "soft" areas of human services. What is the goal of a welfare agency? Is it to extend assistance to as many needy people as possible and thereby increase the welfare rolls? Or is it to get as many people as possible off welfare? Or is it both?

Then, how does one measure the effectiveness of one program over another? Is it better to spend a given amount of money rehabilitating alcoholics or improving the schooling of retarded children? If we stick to evaluating just one program, how do we identify all the units of costs and benefits? Even in terms of the "hard" areas such as defense forces and water resource projects, there are many complex costs and benefits to be taken into account, and some of them are quite difficult to measure. For example, purchasing a new weapon might produce sufficient added defense capability to permit a sizable reduction in defense manpower. However, let us assume that the new weapon is expensive, more expensive than the actual payroll savings to be obtained from reducing the number of men and women in military service. Does this rule out its purchase? Not necessarily, for there may be benefits for the country in allowing more men and women to work in the civilian sector. But how does one calculate the less tangible social benefits that accrue from having a smaller military establishment?

Such problems failed to daunt early PPBS enthusiasts who plunged forward into developing their new craft. The system made great strides in the Pentagon, despite continual criticism and complaints from many military chiefs. It also began to spread to other areas of the federal bureaucracy. In 1966, President Johnson, impressed with MacNamara's efforts in the Defense Department, instructed other government agencies to adopt the same budgeting method. Some states and municipalities also began using program classification and cost-benefit analysis in their budgeting process.

Yet the path of progress was by no means easy and the system attracted a growing number of critics. Some of these foes were administrators and politicians who were hostile to change generally, particularly change which they either could not fully understand or which might threaten their own power and their pet projects. Other criticism, however, took a more thoughtful and disinterested approach. A review of the criticism made by its opponents, along with the claims put forth by its defenders, may shed considerable light on both the potentialities and limitations of PPBS.

PPBS and Its Critics
One of the most trenchant attacks on PPBS has come in the form of an article written by Aaron Wildavsky in the spring 1966 issue of *Public Administration Review.* Entitled "The Political Economy of Efficiency: Cost-Benefit Analysis, Systems Analysis and Program Budgeting," the lengthly article scores the new budgeting method on several points.

In 1970 Montgomery County, Maryland adopted a program budget. This figure shows the program groupings for Category I, Protection of Person, Rights and Property of the Individual. (Other categories were Promotion of the Individual's Physical and Mental Well-Being, Intellectual Development, etc.) On the right-hand side are the governmental units that will be involved in each program of category I. Some of these units appear more than once which means that portions of their budgets will be allocated or charged off against various programs. (Source: The Six-Year Public Services Program, Montgomery County, Maryland, p. 31.)

CATEGORY I. PROTECTION OF PERSON, RIGHTS AND PROPERTY OF THE INDIVIDUAL

A. Crime Prevention and Control
   1. Crime Prevention — Patrol Div, Dept of Police (PS); Canine Div, Dept of Police (PS)
   2. Crime Investigation — County Medical Examiner (PS); Invest Div, Dept of Police (PS); Juvenile Court Committee
   3. Supporting Services — Headquarters, Dept of Police (PS); Services Division, Dept of Police (PS)

B. Adjudication of Criminal Offenses
   1. Adjudication of Adult Offenses — Circuit Court (GG); People's Court (GG); Off of State's Attorney (GG); Off of Public Defender (GG)
   2. Adjudication of Juvenile Offenses — People's Court for Juvenile Causes (GG)
   3. Supporting Services — Circuit Court (GG); Judicial and Adm Sec, People's Court (GG); People's Court for Juvenile Causes (GG); Off of Co Sheriff (PS)

C. Rehabilitation of Criminals
   1. Rehabilitation While Not Confined — People's Court (GG)
   2. Rehabilitation While Confined — Detention Div, Dept of Gen Serv (PS); Correction Advisory Committee

D. Adjudication of Civil Cases
   1. Investigation of Civil Suit — Circuit Court (GG)
   2. Judgment of Civil Suit — People's Court (GG)
   3. Protection of Minors — People's Court for Juvenile Causes (GG)
   4. Domestic Relations — Circuit Court (GG)

E. Safe and Efficient Movement of Traffic
   1. Traffic Movement and Control — Bur of Traf Eng, Dept of Pub Wks (PW); Div of Traf Ops, Dept of Pub Wks (PW); Maryland State Roads Commission
   2. Enforcement of Traffic Regulations — People Court (GG); Traffic Division, Dept of Police (PS); Parking Meter Enf Sec, Dept of Pub Wks (PW)
   3. Traffic Accident Prevention — Sign Review Board (PS)
   4. Supporting Services — Div of Traf Plan & Surv, Dept of Pub Wks (PW)

F. Fire Prevention and Control
   1. Fire Prevention — Div of Fire Prev, Dept of Gen Serv (PS); Div of Bldg Elec & Plbg Insp, Dept of Insp & Lic (PS)
   2. Fire Fighting — St Dept of Forest & Parks
   3. Supporting Services — Div of Comm, Dept of Gen Serv (GG); County Fire Board

G. Protection From Animals — Animal Shelter, Dept of Insp & Lic (PS); County Resident Veterinarian

H. Protection From Natural and Made-Made Disasters
   1. Civil Defense and Protection from Disasters — Div of Civil Defense, Dept of Gen Serv (PS); Civil Defense Advisory Board
   2. Emergency Rescue Squads — Vol Fire Departments Rescue Squads

I. Prevention of Food and Drug Hazards, Non-traffic Accidents and Occupational Hazards — Div of Bldg Elec & Plbg Insp (PS); Div of Envir Hlth Serv, Dept of Health (PH); Range Approval Committee

J. Research and Planning — Services Division, Dept of Police (PS); Law Enforcement and Crim Justice Committee

K. Supporting Services — Services Division, Dept of Police (PS); Police and Fire Training Review Committee

Wildavsky first of all questions whether one man's benefits can be intelligently and fairly weighed against another man's losses. Cost-benefit analysis, he says, purports to do this in many instances but it faces an impossible task. A river project may aid an upstream user while it disadvantages a downstream user. Who can really pronounce judgment on the overall desirability of the project?

Then, can PPBS really develop all the data needed to arrive at a full assessment of the costs and benefits? Wildavsky doubts that it can. There are simply too many aspects, too many spillover and external costs and benefits to take into account. Most public activity of any scope or dimension produces all manner of side effects which elude computation. And even assuming that all this information can be obtained, the outcome of any project based upon it will still remain uncertain.

One feature which Wildavsky singles out for special attention is the discount rate. It is, he says, simply too arbitrary a device for rational decision-making. Lowering the rate a point or two will frequently make a project seem effective while raising it a point or two will make it look ludicrous. Another capricious element in PPBS evaluation is the time factor. If a projected facility is costed out over a twenty-year period, for example, it may not seem worthwhile. If the time span is increased to twenty-five years, then it may take on a different hue. Yet, who can say for sure whether it will last 20 to 25 years or, for that matter, 15 or 30 years?

PPBS also fails to assess political costs and benefits. A program may be ineffective but popular and launching it may yield benefits which cannot be tabulated with an adding machine or a slide rule. Wildavsky cites federalism itself as possibly having a poor cost-benefit ratio, as being, in a word, inefficient. Yet, it may represent a political value that is well worth retaining and promoting.

Wildavsky even sees PPBS as weakening the political process itself. It redistributes power, taking it from political leaders and the people they represent and putting it into the hands of experts. And it is doubtful if the experts will come up with a more rational approach for, he contends, the whole basis of PPBS is erroneous. It seeks to replace the *partial* view of the public interest, which characterizes incremental budgeting, with a *total* view of the public interest. The former may be a piecemeal approach, but it is more consistent with human capabilities and needs. Wildavsky doubts that anyone or any group can arrive at a sure view of a whole problem with all its ramifications and implications.

Even the admitted virtues of PPBS are seen by some critics as containing inherent evils. A PPBS budget based on categorization by program and supported by cost-benefit analysis may reveal a great deal more than a conventional budget, but is this an unmitigated good? Does specifying goals lead to more or less conflict? Some argue that it can widen or inflame conflict. As Virginia Held puts it, "How honest can an agency be in declaring its intentions without getting into difficulties, how open can it be about its criteria of evaluation? If the Department of Agriculture, for instance, is trying to shift a lot of people out of farming, would it be useful to advertise this objective?"[15]

Furthermore, PPBS is complicated. It requires a lot of manpower, and rather skilled manpower at that, to amass all the data and make all the evaluations. This alone can represent a considerable cost in time as well as money. And even with all the care in the world, erroneous decisions can result.

One PPBS fiasco which critics like to cite is an HEW study on ways to reduce motorcycle injuries. After what they thought was a careful assembly of data and a painstaking evaluation of alternatives, analysts at HEW proposed spending $1.7 million over five years in an advertising and public relations campaign to encourage motorcyclists to wear helmets. Such a program, they reasoned, would have a cost-benefit ratio of 55 to 1.

Just how they arrived at this proposal and the benefits it would produce illustrates some of the quagmires and quandaries which PPBS users can fall into. They started with a study of a foreign country which had significantly lowered the number and severity of its motorcycle accidents after implementing such a promotional program. This, in itself, provided a dubious starting point, for the experience of other countries is not always transferable to the United States. Then, they decided somewhat arbitrarily that introducing such a program in this country would be 20 percent effective the first year and 55 percent effective by the fifth year. In other words, they assumed that after five years of promotional effort, over half the country's motorcyclists would be regularly wearing helmets. Then, basing their calculations on the growth of motorcycle registrations, they decided that the program would save 4,006 lives during this five-year span, which worked out to a cost of $180 per each death averted. Questionable as these projections already seem, the HEW analysts did not stop there. Basing themselves on the life earnings of those whose lives would be saved by the program, they arrived at their cost-benefit ratio of 55 to 1.[16]

This particular example of cost-benefit analysis evoked a good deal of well-deserved critical scorn. The analysts were saved from further embarrassment only when Congress enacted a law cutting off high-

---

15. Virginia Held, "PPBS Comes to Washington," *The Public Interest,* summer 1966.
16. Outlined by Graeme Taylor of the Brookings Institute in a seminar on PPBS for Boston City officials in May, 1970.

way funds to any state that did not pass legislation requiring motorcyclists to wear helmets. This, of course, rendered any promotional program along this line unnecessary.

Even MacNamara's use of PPBS at the Pentagon has drawn caustic comment. Though initially he won much praise for his attempt to introduce what was regarded as a much-needed element of rationality into overly open-handed defense spending policies, later observers have viewed his efforts in a much more critical light. They note that defense spending rose consistently during MacNamara's reign and that he and his new whiz kids did not prevent us from getting into and fighting a war that was not only morally and politically dubious but was also waged with questionable effectiveness.

Opponents of PPBS also see vindication in the fact that the popularity of the new budgeting system in government circles seems to be waning. A study done in 1968, three years after President Johnson had directed all federal agencies to start making use of the new budgetary technique, showed that of 16 federal agencies, 11 were no longer making any effective use of the system.[17] And on June 21, 1971, the Office of Management and Budget sent out a memorandum stating, in effect, that federal agencies were no longer required to submit their budget requests in PPBS form. PPBS frequently has found the going rough in state and municipal government as well. As we saw in chapter three, those who sought to reorganize the Massachusetts state government failed to secure the implementation of what was a modified version of the PPBS approach.

Thus, by the mid-1970's, the PPBS movement seems on the defensive and appears, in some instances at least, to be losing ground. Yet, the system retains its defenders and it is their viewpoint that we will now examine.

PPBS and Its Backers

Backers of the budgetary system often respond to attacks upon it with considerable contrition. They frequently admit that the state of the PPBS art remains woefully imperfect. As one PPBS advocate concedes, the system is a lot like Richard Wagner's music in that "it sounds better than it is."

Another federal official, however, warns against confusing "the product with the process. The numbers are lousy and always will be in

---

17. Edwin J. Harper et al., "Implementation and Use of PPBS in Sixteen Federal Agencies," *Public Administration Review*, November/December 1969.

the civilian area. But the need to produce them pushes people in the right direction."[18]

It is on this last element that most PPBS supporters focus their support. Allen Shick, for example, sets down three potential benefits from PPBS. First, it usually will rule out the worst programs even if it does not always designate the very best ones; second, it will usually provide some improvement in existing programs; and third, and perhaps most important, it encourages politicians, administrators and even the public at large to start thinking along different and more constructive lines.[19]

PPBS stimulates those involved in the process of government to start specifying their goals. This, in itself, say its supporters, can produce many valuable benefits. Furthermore, it spurs them into thinking analytically and objectively about ways and means of achieving those goals. As former New York City Budget Director Frederick O'R Hayes has said, "The habit of examining the facts instead of taking second-hand representations, the habit of analysis as a substitute for tradition and custom can scarcely help but yield dividends. Moreover, the complexity of our problems suggest that we can go only a limited distance with intuitive decisions, that, increasingly, solving problems requires explicit analysis."[20] In laying such stress on explicit analysis, PPBS, its supporters say, brings a vital new element to the spending of public money and the formulation of public policy.

Merely thinking in terms of cost-benefit analysis has already produced at least a few dramatic successes. In the field of corrections, for example, reformers for years argued for the expanded use of parole, probation and outside work programs. Now, their endeavors are bearing fruit largely because the cost-benefit equation works in their favor. Analysis shows that recidivism does not increase but may even go down when jail sentences are reduced or abolished or when prison inmates are put on work-release programs. And since such programs save money, their desirability becomes apparent even to those who have taken a much less liberal approach to the subject.[21]

More systematic uses of cost-benefit analysis illustrate its ability to single out the *least* productive methods of accomplishing objectives. One HEW study examined eight alternative methods of reducing inju-

---

18. "Putting a Dollar Sign on Everything," *Business Week,* July 16, 1966. Reprinted in James W. Davis, Jr., ed., *Politics, Programs and Budgets* (Englewood Cliffs, N.J.: Prentice-Hall, 1969).
19. In remarks made to a seminar on PPBS for Boston City officials in May 1971.
20. Hayes, *Creative Budgeting in New York City . . .,* p. 34.
21. John Conrad, "Law, Order and Correction," *Public Administration Review,* November/December 1971.

ries from automobile accidents. The cheapest way was found to be a seat-belt program which, calculations showed, would cost only $87 for each death averted. The most expensive would be a nationwide driver-training program which would cost $88,000 for each life saved.[22] Thus, the most expensive safety program would cost over one thousand times more than the least expensive. Such a wide gap leaves a lot of room for faulty data and fuzzy figuring before the basic fact that seat belts are cheaper than driver-training programs comes into doubt.

The following HEW study illuminates another aspect of PPBS. The department made an assessment of programs for detecting and treating cancer at four different sites on the human body: uterine-cervix, breast, head and neck and colon-rectum. It found that a uterine-cervix detection and treatment program would cost only $3,500 per death averted compared to a cost of $43,000 for each life saved through a colon-rectum program. This means that the same amount of money needed to save one life under one program would save twelve lives if spent on another program. However, HEW did not recommend an abandonment of all efforts to cope with colon-rectum cancer. Rather, it called for new techniques and technology for detecting and treating this form of malignancy.[23]

This points up a further aspect of cost-benefit analysis which its supporters firmly and often feverishly stress. It does not dictate decision-making but merely provides a more intelligent basis for decision-making. Confronted with figures such as those provided from the cancer program analysis and assuming they are *essentially* true, i.e., a uterine-cervix program costs a lot less than a colon-rectum program, officials and the public they represent are still left with choices to make. In HEW's case, the department continued to support the more expensive program while stimulating efforts to bring down its cost.

True, setting down goals and then developing all the information possible on how to achieve them can touch off a good deal of controversy. But, PPBS advocates claim, controversy is often productive in itself. Furthermore, even traditional budget methods can breed discontent. As a budget official during the Eisenhower years once expressed it, the budget is "a unified system for distributing dissatisfactions." Admittedly, incrementalism can mute these dissatisfactions to some extent since it can allow nearly every party of interest at least some attention. The basic line-item budget, for example, could more easily make provision for some sort of nationwide driver-training program as well as a seat-belt program. However, since the same amount of money would

22. Elizabeth B. Drew, "HEW Grapples with PPBS," *The Public Interest,* summer 1967. Reprinted in Davis, *op. cit.*
23. *Ibid.*

produce fewer reductions in automobile injuries, public dissatisfaction with overall government performance might only increase.

The case of sugar beet subsidies offers a good illustration of this problem. In the mid-1960's, Kermit Gordon, who was then director of the Bureau of the Budget, pointed out that the domestic sugar industry was receiving various types of assistance, including government price supports and import quotas, and that analysis had shown that the total cost to the citizenry in higher prices and taxes came to nearly one-half billion dollars a year. The net income to domestic sugar producers from all this expenditure was only $140 million a year.[24] Discontinuing these various subsidies would produce a good deal of discontent among sugar producers, but an argument could be made that it would be more than offset by less public discontent with high food prices. In any case, the analysis only develops the data. It is still up to political leaders to make the decisions and in this case the subsidies continued.

The fact that decision-making still lies in other hands comes to the fore once again when we consider MacNamara's operation of the defense establishment. While defense costs rose even before the Vietnam war, this reflected a change in American policy. The Eisenhower administration, in an effort to hold down defense costs, had concentrated on developing the country's nuclear deterrent as its primary defense mechanism. President Kennedy and many of the liberals who supported him feared this policy for it left the country with few options in an emergency other than a resort to nuclear weaponry. During the early MacNamara years a fairly sweeping attempt was made to build up conventional forces in order to reduce the threat of nuclear warfare. This produced some increases in defense spending.

As for the Vietnam war, it can in no way be blamed on MacNamara's budgeting techniques. As a matter of fact, the systems analysis office which he set up recommended against the bombing of North Vietnam, a step which, when taken, dramatically escalated the conflict. It is also interesting to note that the military chieftains by and large fought the new budgeting techniques every inch of the way. So did many administrators in the civilian bureaucracies and this, more than any inherent failure of the system itself, was largely responsible for the fact that it did not catch on as well as had been hoped in many government agencies.[25]

---

24. Held, *op. cit.*
25. The difficulty which PPBS encountered in securing congressional acceptance may likewise have been due more to political factors than considerations of its effectiveness. Harry McPherson, an aide to President Johnson, refers to the new budgetary system as "a rational concept, but difficult in practice. Congress, for example, did not take to the idea that there should be only one program for subsidizing sewage treatment plants and not four or five under the patronage of as many committees."

In any case, PPBS is by no means dead in the federal bureaucracy. Gordon T. Yamada of the Office of Management and Budget reports that "even though it is no longer required, many agencies are continuing to apply either PPBS or some of its desirable features, such as systems analysis."[26] Indeed, the OMB's current Management Improvement Program incorporates most of PPBS' salient features such as the identification of program objectives and the execution of cost-effectiveness analyses. Furthermore, the Office of Management and Budget in 1973 was pilot testing a performance management system which, according to Shick, combines features of PPBS with those of the older scheme of performance budgeting.[27]

Congress has also been showing increased interest in having a PPBS-oriented budget document to work with. The Legislative Reorganization Act of 1970 calls for restructuring of budget classifications along with five-year cost estimates for new programs. It also, as Shick puts it, directs the Comptroller General "to review and analyze the results of government programs and activities carried on under existing law, including the making of cost-benefit studies." As Shick notes, "These requirements now written into law strive for the very objectives which executive PPBS failed to accomplish." And he concludes, with apparently some justification, that "it is probable that under a different label and with somewhat different approaches and techniques there eventually will be a return to the aims of PPBS."[28]

At lower government levels, the push for PPBS is also continuing. Wisconsin seems to have scored some signal successes with such techniques. California, too, is moving forward with an adaptation of PPBS which it calls its resources management system. First introduced in 1968, it saw its first full year of implementation in 1972. Despite hostility from some quarters including the local John Birch Society, which castigates it as a "thought control system," all of California's state departments are gradually making use of it. The California legislature, like the Wisconsin legislature, has backed the new budgetary system.

Finally, although PPBS is an American product, it has already caught on overseas. Again, the labels often differ. In Britain, where it is called output budgeting, it is being used to plan highways, health centers and other projects.

In summary, PPBS, while it does pose problems and suffer serious

---

26. Gordon T. Yamada, "Improving Management Effectiveness in the Federal Government," *Public Administration Review,* November/December 1972.
27. Allen Shick, "A Death in the Bureaucracy: The Demise of Federal PPB," *Public Administration Review,* March/April 1973.
28. *Ibid.*

limitations, still seems to have something to offer modern-day administration. And we may expect to see its influence increasingly felt as new administrators replace older ones and as pressures for more governmental effectiveness continue to mount.

CASE STUDY

What Price Parking?[29]

Like most American cities, Boston after World War II became engulfed in a swirling and swelling tide of automobile traffic. And like so many American cities, Boston set out to meet this increasing influx through a policy of accommodation. By 1964 it had built seven municipal garages to house some of the cars that were thronging into the city every day. The garages were leased to private operators on a highest bid basis. Each lease ran only for three years at which time it was again put up for bid.

The city was pleased with the program. The revenues it was obtaining from the leases were more than enough to pay off the bonds which had been floated to acquire the land and build the garages. Thus, in addition to housing cars, the program was also, so the city felt, making money.

The city's Finance Commission, however, did not share the administration's satisfaction. It was growing increasingly dubious as to the effectiveness and the cost of the municipal garage program. With some assistance from Professor Otto Eckstein of Harvard University, it decided in 1964 to undertake a reasonably rigorous cost-benefit analysis of the program to date.

On the plus side of the cost-benefit equation, the commission found that the total revenue which the garages had brought in through 1963 came to $6,830,000, a rather formidable sum, particularly in those days. To this must be added the revenue which could be expected over the remaining life of the garages. The commission adopted twenty years as the time period for each garage's existence and projected its current annual income over the years remaining in its assumed twenty-year life span. To put it differently, it subtracted the years each garage had been in existence from twenty and then theoretically multiplied the number left by its current annual rental fee.

The word theoretically is used for this process, for it fails to take account of the time value of money. It was necessary to add interest to these figures. The discount rate the commission chose was a low one of 3.5 percent for it decided to base itself on just what it cost the city to borrow money during these years. Thus, if a garage had been in existence for ten years and was being leased for, say, $100,000, the Finance Commission did not simply calculate its future income at $1,000,000 for the ten years remaining. Rather, it took

---

29. The material for this case study was taken from the author's "Municipal Garages in Boston: A Cost-Benefit Analysis," in *Public Policy 1965* (Cambridge: Harvard University Press, 1965).

the present year's income and compounded it over ten years at 3.5 percent, then it took the following year's income and compounded it over nine years at 3.5 percent and so on. The total projected income for all the garages computed in this fashion came to $11,828,000.

However, although a twenty-year period was used to estimate the total income from the garage, there was no question that at the end of this period each garage would have a considerable residual value. This was even more true of the land on which it was built. To arrive at a figure for this residual value, the commission took the cost of the land and half the cost of the building, figuring that the structure would only be half depreciated or worn out in this time. Adding up the residual value of all the garages provided a figure of $3,345,000.

The reader with some background in finance or real estate may already have noticed that despite the use of an interest rate, the above figures probably understate the true income from the garage program. This is because land values usually rise and the value of the land may be worth more after twenty years. However, we will allow these figures to stand for the time being.

What other possible benefits may be attributed to the garage program? There were the presumed advantages of fewer cars on the street. This, however, was by no means certain and could even be argued the other way, i.e., that the garages attracted cars to the city and hence aggravated rather than alleviated congestion. Another possible advantage was an increase in property values for buildings located in the vicinity of the garages. Since this would be impossible to calculate, the commission's analysis merely noted it on the benefit side of the analysis. As for the overall impact of the garage program on the city's economy, this was put off until all the direct costs and benefits were computed.

However, while the benefits of the garage program may have been greater than would at first appear, then this proved to be doubly true for its costs. First there were the sums expended to acquire the sites and construct the buildings. The commission took the cost for each garage and computed it at 3.5 percent over twenty years. Since bonds at that interest rate had been issued to carry out the program, the use of a discount rate in this instance was directly in accord with the governing reality.[30] The total figure arrived at came to $17,512,532.

Some additional and rather appreciable costs also had to be taken into account. One of these was the tax loss. In acquiring property for municipal

---

30. The use of a discount rate would certainly not have been a mere theoretical device in any case for even if the city had financed the garages out of cash on hand, it would still be foregoing the interest which the money could be earning at a bank. The reader should also be careful not to become confused into thinking that "discount rate" always means reducing a sum of money. An immediate benefit projected over a time period is actually discounted "up," as we saw when we examined the garages' income figures.

garages, the city was taking real estate off its tax rolls. Municipally owned land and buildings pay no taxes; privately owned properties do. Consequently, the garages were costing the city money in terms of lost tax revenue. The commission, in figuring this loss, took the assessed value of each parcel of taxable property that was taken for these garages and tabulated the amount of tax income it would have brought in at the prevailing tax rate over a twenty-year period, again compounding at an interest rate of 3.5 percent.

Another major cost was somewhat more indirect but quite palpable. Boston at the time was served by a fairly extensive and expensive public transportation system called the Metropolitan Transit Authority or MTA. To the extent that the garages induced people to drive their cars into the city instead of taking public transportation, they were adding to the MTA's deficit. Through a survey of garage users, the commission was able to determine that approximately 21 percent of these garage customers would utilize the MTA if the municipal garages did not exist. Taking into account prevailing MTA fares and the number of likely days per year that the average such garage customer would use the transit system, the commission determined that the total cost in lost MTA fares to the city over the life span of all the garages amounted to $2,634,125.

Here it could be argued that this is not a total loss to the city since the lost passengers might also have caused some additional expense. Hence, the loss figure should be reduced by the amount saved in not having to accommodate these garage users as transit authority passengers. However, since the commission felt it had been quite conservative in estimating the amount of lost fares, and, more importantly, since the transit system was then greatly underutilized, it assumed that the 1,470 additional passangers which the garages had taken away could have been served with no additional cost.

There were, in addition, an assortment of other costs which could only be noted since no figures could be ascertained. These included the legal costs in acquiring the property, the processing costs of floating the bonds, the costs of arranging and overseeing the construction involved, and the cost of putting the garage leases out for periodic bidding and auditing the accounts. To be added to these was the cost of any structural maintenance problems that might occur.

Less tangible and more contestable were the costs involved in congestion and property depreciation. If the garages were taking cars off the street, they were reducing congestion. But if their net effect, as seemed indicated, was to encourage more people to drive into the city, then this aggravated the city's congestion problems. Property depreciation was also a two-edged sword. While parking garages, as we noted on the plus side of the ledger, may enhance the value of certain properties, they may detract from the value of others. A garage is a dead spot on a street and diminishes its attractiveness. Furthermore, to the extent that they were drawing people away from the transit system, they could have a negative effect on properties located near transit stations.

Leaving aside the more controversial and less computable costs and benefits, while at the same time taking note that the former would seem to exceed the latter, the commission arrived at the following balance sheet on the city's municipal garage program:

Costs	Benefits
	6,830,000 (income received)
17,512,000 (site acquisition and construction)	11,163,000 (projected income)
15,415,000 (tax loss)	
2,634,000 (MTA loss)	7,345,000 (residual value)
35,561,000	25,338,000
Total net loss: $10,223,000 or $510,000 a year.	

Thus, the commission's analysis arrived at a quite different picture than the one that had been so often portrayed in the past. The garages were costing Boston in excess of a half-million dollars a year.

Of course, the figures are only projections and are subject to many qualifications. On the benefit side, they would seem to be distinctly understated. In projecting the return from the leases, the commission's estimates are based on the current rental figures. But succeeding lease arrangements might well bring in higher rentals if for no other reason than because of increases in the general price level. More significant, perhaps, was the commission's assumption that the land at the end of twenty years would be worth only what it was worth at the time it was taken for the garage. It would seem likely that the land would increase in value, possibly substantially, over a twenty-year period.

The commission took notice of these factors. However, it felt that they were more than compensated for by greater underestimates on the cost side of the balance sheet. If, for example, the market value of the property were to go up, then so would its assessed value and this means that it would have been bringing in substantially greater sums in tax revenue. Thus, the tax loss figure would be understated. Another factor which further depressed the tax loss figure below what ordinarily might be expected was the possibility of a change in the tax rate. Any increase in the tax rate would only increase the amount of money lost through removing the property from the tax rolls. Since the tax rate was showing a tendency to move upward—it actually doubled in the ensuing decade—this further understated the loss in foregone taxes.

The MTA loss figures were also projected on the basis of the current fare schedule. But, here again, any increase in fares would increase the cost to the city in lost riders. And, as it so happens, within a few years after completion of the study, the transit system's fares were substantially raised.

The commission thus felt that while it could not provide completely accurate figures on the cost and benefits of the garage program, it did present a valid case for deeming it a net cost to the city government instead of considering it a financial bonanza as city administrations had previously done.

The commission's work, however, was not over. It now had to try to calculate whether the garages, despite their net cost to the city administration, were generating enough revenues to downtown business to warrant their construction and operation.

This proved to be a much more difficult task, but with the assistance of Professor Eckstein, the commission plunged forward. First, it went back to its survey of garage users. This indicated that 68 percent of the garage program's customers were all-day parkers. Presumably, they would come in anyway. The number of shopper and visitor vehicles using the garages came to only 1,330. Estimating that each vehicle brought in an average of 1.5 people, the commission projected a total count of 1,995.

The question now presented itself of how many of these people would have come into the city even if the municipal garages had not been built. The survey indicated that 54.6 percent would have stayed home. (The rest would have come in by MTA or would have parked in a privately owned, tax-paying garage at a higher parking cost.) Multiplying the overall figure of 1,995 by 54.6 percent produced a figure of 1,089 shoppers and visitors whose presence in the city was directly attributable to the garage program.

But how much benefit were downtown businesses deriving from these people? The commission felt that all it could do was to take a safe *maximum* figure and see how it worked out. An official of the city's retail trade board agreed that the average shopper, theater-goer or other such visitor spent no more than $50.00 during his visit. (Keep in mind that this was in 1964 when $50.00 was a lot more than it is today). Figuring that the shopper-visitor schedule as amounting to 250 days a year to take care of Sundays, holidays, snowstorm days and the summer months when the number of people coming into town drops dramatically, this provided a total annual revenue of $13,612,500 generated exclusively by the garage program. Since the average profit in retailing at that time was 2.4 percent of sales (it has since gone down), this meant that the garages, which cost the city some $510,000 a year, were producing profits to businessmen of only $326,000 a year. Consequently, the commission said, the city could simply pay the merchants all the money the garages were making for them and still save nearly $200,000 a year.

The figures, of course, are by no means accurate. Nevertheless, the commission felt that it had proved its case and that more precise figures would only widen the discrepancy between what the garages were costing the city and what benefits they were producing. The heart of the problem, said the commission, lay in the fact that over two-thirds of all garage customers were commuting workers who could—and should—take public transportation or park in private garages. The commission called for including in the leases, as they come up for bid, a rate structure designed to encourage short-term parkers and discourage the all-day variety.

What happened to the commission's study is also interesting for students of the budget process. The study was reprinted in two publications and was put on the selected bibliography on traffic issued by the federal government's Bureau of the Budget. It also became the basis for a widely used PPBS exercise. However, within Boston itself it aroused considerable hostility from the merchants and from one of the city's newspapers. Consequently, it has gone almost completely ignored.

THE PURSUIT OF PRODUCTIVITY

As we saw in chapter one, public administration entered the decade of the 1970's under heavy attack, particularly in regard to its presumed lack of productivity. Faced with a growing climate of distrust and confronted with a rising clamor for greater results, public administrators began to direct increasing attention to the productivity problem. Their efforts were spurred on by various PPBS-oriented studies which indicated that the problem was a real one that was not being successfully met. But in order to deal with it, one must first have some way of measuring its dimensions. For many reasons, this is a troublesome task.

Measuring Public Productivity: The Pitfalls

The public sector usually deals in services, and services almost always present problems in productivity measurement. Services are intangible and often widely variable. How does one compare the productivity of heart surgeon A versus heart surgeon B. Surgeon A may perform more operations per week and his patients may show a greater recovery rate, but how do we know that they are suffering from roughly the same heart problems as surgeon B's cases? And what if surgeon A's patients are richer and can afford more follow-up care or are more educated and thus are perhaps more likely to adhere to recommended diets and other advice than are the patients of surgeon B?

Even if one analyzes what might seem to be a fairly routine operation in health care, namely the administration of chest X-rays, one can encounter measurement difficulties. X-ray unit A may consistently outperform X-ray unit B in number of chests examined each week. But perhaps unit B operates in poorer areas or in areas with large numbers of non-English speaking people. Or perhaps B's unit handles more children than A's, and children, so it turns out, are harder to X-ray. Measuring productivity of services is a troublesome and touchy task.

284

Many government experts concede that some public sector operations are simply not measurable, at least with the tools currently at hand. Posing particular difficulties, among others, are numerous staff operations, such as personnel work, as well as much case work. As for the latter, one has only to think of the complexities involved in trying to measure the productivity of a case worker in a public welfare office. Should he be rated on how many cases he clears from the welfare rolls or on how many people he adds to the welfare rolls? Using either standard can produce all kinds of distortions.

Related to these problems is the central one of distinguishing between efficiency and effectiveness. Efficiency is sometimes defined as doing things better, while effectiveness means doing the *right* things better. As one commentator once noted, a man might be efficient in driving nails into a table. Effectiveness enters the picture when we question whether he should be driving nails into a table at all.

Numerous examples exist to illustrate some of these hazards in productivity measurement. On April 20, 1971, for instance, the New York Police Department announced changes in the operations of its narcotics squad. Before, the squad had worked under a quota system with each officer being put under pressure to make at least four arrests a month. The result had been that detectives were bringing in too many street corner peddlers and were ignoring the complicated and time-consuming cases involving major dealers. The department decided to abandon the quota system in order to concentrate on fewer arrests of more substantial drug dealers.[31]

Measurement of productivity of poverty programs is also susceptible to distortions. In order to show impressive rehabilitation rates, for example, many programs have practiced what is called "creaming." This means that they take only the most easily rehabilitated cases and leave the harder cases untouched. In some instances, they may take a case which they know will fail in the long run but will show good results in the short run. Thus, in one such case, a man on welfare who had a good work motivation and some basic skills was trained as an auto mechanic and put to work in a garage. The agency then credited itself with a success. However, the man was unemployed to begin with because of a bad back, and soon this same problem forced him to give up his new trade and go back on welfare.

This brings us to a further dimension of the problem of productivity measurement. It may produce behavior which is actually antithetical to good results. Correction officials may release inmates before they are rehabilitated and then send them out of the state to hold down their recidivism rates. Hospitals, if placed under carelessly drawn productivity

---

31. *New York Times,* April 20, 1971.

measures, could end up turning away the hopelessly ill since they would not show up well on the balance sheets. Deceptive practices may also find favor. Some drug "communities" established to house and hopefully cure addicts have reported "cure" rates of 50 percent or higher. However, in some cases they were counting only those who had stayed in the program until completion. Since about 75 percent of those who were entering such programs in the early 1970's were dropping out before completion, the "cure" rate represented only 50 percent of the one-quarter who finished the program.

Productivity measures can produce counterproductive behavior in employees even when the organization itself is attempting to use such measures for perfectly legitimate ends. Peter Blau has described a public employment agency where interviewers were evaluated on the number of applicants they interviewed each month. This led the interviewers to dismiss clients who would require too much of their time. The agency then changed its system to judge interviewers on the number of jobs they actually filled. This caused the interviewers to try to outdo each other in getting hold of the slips which reported job openings, even to the point of hiding the slips from each other.[32]

Sometimes, an agency may know what measurement device to use but may not know how to scale it. The Division of Social Security one summer placed college students in offices of the Internal Revenue Service to check tax returns for what are called Schedule C forms. It is a very simple exercise that can be executed at a speedy pace. Social Security officials set a work norm of 4,500 a day per student. However, it was found that in an office where no norm had been set, the students were checking 9,000 to 12,000 per day!

Accounting problems also add to the administrator's travail in setting productivity measures. Shall man-hours or cost-per-output be used? Cost-per-output is sometimes almost impossible to measure while man-hour tabulations may not reflect the cost of new equipment. Another item which is often hard to figure is overhead costs. Then there is the problem of a changing and usually rising price level. Shall the costs be figured in current dollars which do not adjust for price level changes or shall they be calculated in terms of constant dollars which do? Both approaches create difficulties. And there is the problem of side costs which the private sector can often ignore but which the public sector cannot. A new street cleaning program may show measurable improvements in productivity but may also require more police costs. Or it may require residents to bring their barrels to the curb. In this latter case, whose productivity has been increased, the sanitation crew's or the residents'?

---

32. Peter Blau, *Bureaucracy in Modern Society* (New York: Random House, 1956), pp. 58-59.

The legal problems entailed in establishing productivity measures can also impede and impair the use of productivity measures. Civil service rules and regulations are examples of these. New York City's former Deputy Mayor Edward K. Hamilton has claimed that "parts of state civil service laws sometimes appear to have been written precisely to frustrate a productivity effort."[33] Even laws not specially related to public employment can bog down a productivity drive. One New York State law requires all medical admissions into hospitals to be in handwriting. With admission to some hospital emergency wards having risen 400 percent and more during the past decade, one can see why hospitals are having problems and why those who are attempting to ease these problems are sometimes experiencing difficulties.

Needless to add, labor unions may often resist productivity measurements. Many work contracts are written in such a way as to nullify the use of nearly all such criteria. Fortunately, unions, if properly handled, can help as well as hinder the implementation of productivity measures.

Finally, there are the political problems involved. Like PPBS to which they are obviously related, productivity measures can collide with the interests of many elements in the politico-administrative process. These include administrative office holders who find such measures threatening to their own pet ways of doing things, legislators who react negatively to measures which may show their favorite programs misfiring, and public interest groups whose preferred projects may fail to measure up under the new criteria.

Productivity measures can even prove upsetting to whole sectors of the public who otherwise may be clamoring for increased public sector productivity. For example, conservatives are often in the forefront in demanding more efficient government. But productivity measures may show that incarceration of criminal offenders is much less productive in terms of crime control than parole and probation. Other measures may show that much of the nation's extensive military hardware such as aircraft carriers produce little in the way of added security. Since incarceration and defense are programs that conservatives tend to favor, they may react with outrage.

Liberals, too, are not immune from the dangers which productivity measures can pose to programs which they ideologically support. Liberals have responded angrily when the use of productivity measures showed that many initial programs designed to help the poor, such as Head Start or Job Corps camps, yielded little or nothing in the way of measurable benefits.

33. Edward K. Hamilton, "Productivity: The New York Approach," *Public Administration Review*, November/December 1972.

All of these factors make the introduction and implementation of productivity measures an exacting and often excruciating undertaking. Yet, there are numerous indications to suggest that the problems are far from insurmountable, that the task is far from hopeless.

Productivity: Progress Report

Despite all the difficulties and dilemmas which they engender, productivity measures have started to assume increasing importance in public administration. Progress has been neither smooth nor swift but it has occurred. In some instances remarkable successes have been achieved.

One of the first federal agencies to use efficiency measurements was the Division of Social Security. In the mid-1950's, it began its work sampling program. Under this program, an employee of every office periodically measures the amount of work being done by various employees. These samples are not taken in an attempt to judge the employees' efficiency but only to determine just how long it takes to handle the various operations which the office is performing. This information from all Social Security offices is then compiled into averages and each office is subsequently rated as to how it performs in respect to the overall averages for its region and for the nation as a whole.

The averages provide a useful yardstick to measure just how any one office is operating. Of course, numerous factors may make any particular office rate above or below its regional or national average. An office may be so small, for example, that maintenance functions, as opposed to line operations, consume too large a proportion of its man-hours. However, the averages, once all such factors have been taken into account, do provide a tool which indicates which regions, which offices and even which individuals are performing well and which are not.

By 1962, the Bureau of the Budget had become interested in applying productivity measures more generally and it selected five agencies for an experiment. The results released in 1964 confirmed that productivity indices could be developed for many other activities of the federal government. This endeavor undoubtedly contributed to the early enthusiasm for PPBS which, among other things, concerns itself with productivity problems and ways to resolve them. And in June 1970, after the Nixon administration had decided that PPBS techniques would no longer be required in federal agencies, a National Commission on Productivity was set up to improve productivity in both private and public activities.

The following year, the General Accounting Office joined with the Office of Management and Budget and the Civil Service Commission—a rather unusual alliance since the General Accounting Office is a branch of Congress—to study productivity trends in federal agencies.

The joint effort produced productivity measures covering some 56 percent of the federal government's civilian work force. On May 24, 1972, OMB instructed each federal agency with 200 or more employees to report annually on what progress it was making in improving productivity.

The movement has gradually spread to lower echelons of the governmental system. New York City embarked on a drive to develop and utilize productivity measures in 1971. In March of 1973, the city sponsored a two-day conference on productivity measurement which attracted city officials from throughout the East. Overseas, productivity has also started to generate increasing interest and concern. Great Britain's Civil Service Department has published quite a few papers on such things as clerical work measurement.

It is generally felt that productivity measures lend themselves most easily to certain types of operations and these are often operations that may be common to many agencies. In other words, particular functions rather than whole programs may provide the productivity measurer with the most fruitful terrain in which to launch his labors. Gordon T. Yamada, chief of management systems information for OMB, offers an example of how productivity measures could be employed in processing applications whether the applications are for urban renewal projects, grazing permits, university admissions, or what have you. Here is how four different criteria could be used to determine productivity in such an operation:

Applications Processing		
	FY 1	FY 2
Productivity Applications processed per man-year	7,600	8,300
Service Total processing time per application in minutes	12	10
Quality Percentage of applications requiring reprocessing	7.5	7.2
Cost Unit cost per application in dollars	$1.00	$.98
(FY = Fiscal Year)		

Source: Adapted from Gordon T. Yamada, "Improving Management Effectiveness in the Federal Government," *Public Administration Review*, November/December 1972.

289

It is also possible, at least in many cases, to determine the productivity of a particular facility. Harry P. Hatry and Diana R. Dunn, in their study *Measuring the Effectiveness of Local Government Services: Recreation* published by the Urban Institute, offer some ways of measuring the effectiveness of a recreation facility.

First, one can measure the number of people within so many miles or so many minutes of the facility in order to determine its *accessibility*. If it is a specialized facility such as a tot lot, then the measure could be limited to the number of children in the appropriate age group. Census maps, police listings, and other data can be used to discover whether the facility is conveniently located. The proximity to public transportation can also be taken into account.

From there we can go on to measure *usage*, taking into account how many persons actually use the facility, how often they use it and for how long. This can be estimated by visiting the facility at representative times and taking random samples of the participants, asking them how often they come, what services they use, how long they stay, etc. Some estimate of crowdedness can also be made through examining sign-up sheets or through observation of waiting times. The evaluator can also ask users if they feel crowded.

Safety is another factor that should enter into the evaluation. What is the rate of drownings and injuries? What about crime? This data can be supplemented by asking users if they felt the facility was dangerous. The accidents and the crime that may occur in the facility must be balanced, however, with the accidents and crime which it may have averted elsewhere. Unsupervised swimming and playing on public streets also leads to accidents while lack of recreational outlets can also stimulate increased crime. Has the facility had any impact on crime and accidents in the neighborhoods it serves?

Attractiveness is another, though perhaps lesser, criterion which can be utilized in weighing the productivity of a recreational facility. Does it contribute to the neighborhood's physical design? Does it upgrade the neighborhood? Here, in addition to the opinion of residents, one can check the effect, if any, on property valuations and possibly on the amount of business done by nearby commercial establishments.

Then, there is the final and determining factor of *overall satisfaction*. People in the area served by the facility can be asked such questions as "Would you say that the recreational opportunities in this community are excellent, good, fair or poor?" Doing this on a yearly basis will provide some idea of trends.

It will be noted that much of the evaluation will be achieved through polling. This, however, need not be extensive or expensive, for only a reasonably representative sample is required. The results can be matched against other data. If, for example, the community served by the facility had a population of 100,000 and attendance at the facility came to 50,000, and if a random sample of 100 users showed that they used the facility 2.5 times a year, then it can be estimated that about 20,000 people, or one fifth of the community, are being served.

Hatry and Dunn claim that evaluations of recreational programs can be done at a cost of no more than 1 or 2 percent of the recreation budget. It would seem to be an expenditure that might well be worth making.

It is also possible to develop productivity measures for entire programs. The Institute of Traffic Management at Northwestern University, for example, has worked out what it calls a law enforcement index for evaluating the effectiveness of a police department in enforcing traffic laws. It is based on a simple equation in long division, namely the number of citations divided by the number of fatal and personal injury accidents. To wit:

$$\text{Enforcement Index} = \frac{\text{citations with penalty}}{\text{number of fatal and personal injury accidents}}$$

The institute says that the EI or Enforcement Index should equal 20. In other words, a police department should give out penalty citations equal to twenty times the number of fatalities and personal injury accidents caused by motorists.

It should be noted that the approach differs considerably from the more simplistic quota system used by many police departments. Under the latter system, traffic officers are instructed to hand out a fixed number of citations every day or week. The Enforcement Index established a *relationship* between enforcement and accidents and, since evidence indicates that accident rates do respond positively to traffic enforcement, the number of citations is allowed to fall as the number of accidents declines. Thus, if a department could reduce its number of such accidents to one a year, it would need to give out only twenty citations in order to meet the standard set by the index.

Crime control, however, remains much more illusive when it comes to establishing productivity measures. It is possible, for example, that improved police work can bring about an *increase* in the *reported* crime rate. Why is this? Simply because most crimes do not get reported. If a police department starts improving its operations, including the strengthening of its relationships with the community, this could cause more crimes to be reported. For this, as well as other reasons, crime rates by themselves do not provide a basic reliable measure of police effectiveness.

Yet, crime rates often do tell us something and when used in conjunction with other measures may offer valuable clues in assessing the quality of law enforcement. What are some of these other measures? They include such things as attitude surveys (i.e., do people feel they are better protected), pedestrian flows, particularly at night, merchants keeping open after dark, the number of arrests and the number of cases won in court (the latter element is often omitted in reports of cases cleared by the police), the number of complaints against the police, the number of policemen and civilians killed or injured in police-civilian encounters. The task of evaluating police effectiveness in fighting crime is by no means easy but, at the same time, it is by no means impossible.

One city which appears to have achieved some notable initial successes in the use of productivity measures is New York. A brief look at some of the areas in which they have been applied along with the results obtained will indicate the potential of this new trend.

Rat control, an important problem in the nation's largest city, had traditionally been handled on the basis of complaints. In January 1971, the city introduced a more systematic procedure based on the selection of target areas. Within a year this new systematic approach increased the number of premises inspected per man-day from 6.1 to 20.1. At the same time, the cost per inspection fell from $9.10 to $2.74.[34]

The introduction of productivity measures in the Fire Department also produced some welcome changes. The Fire Department began responding with fewer men and less equipment to many calls and began using chemically treated water which, through increasing water flow by 70 percent, permitted the use of lighter hose.[35]

However, it was in the Sanitation Department where the most startling results were achieved. The number of tons of refuse collected per truck per shift went up 21 percent in one year while the number of missed collections fell from 10 percent to .1 percent. Applying productivity measures in the department's repair shops reduced the number of trucks sidelined for repairs at any one time from 36 percent to 8.5 percent.[36]

Introducing and implementing the productivity measures which made such accomplishments possible proved no easy task. Union officials and their members both resisted the attempt. However, by a combination of devices, including the prospect of increased pay as a result of increased output along with subtle appeals to professional pride, the crews of the Sanitation Department were induced to go along. Some

---

34. Hamilton, *op. cit.*
35. Richard A. Armstrong, "The Re-education of John Lindsay," *New York Times Sunday Magazine*, October 8, 1972.
36. Frederick O'R Hayes, "Things Are Picking Up in the Sanitation Department," *New York Times*, July 9, 1973.

city officials thought they could at least see an end to the spiral of ever increasing expenditure coupled with what had seemed to be ever declining quality of service.

Productivity and Its Pay-Offs

Assuming that productivity measures can be developed and implemented, then the benefits to public administration and the public in general would seem to be immense. First and foremost, of course, is an increase in output both in terms of efficiency and effectiveness. Katz and Kahn claim that "knowledge of results in itself motivates people toward improving their performance. Level of aspiration studies," they say, "indicate that individuals tend to raise their sights when they see the outcome of their efforts. If there is continuous feedback on the basis of some objective criterion of behavior, people will be motivated to improve their scores."[37]

It must not be assumed that this reaction leads to exhausted and eventually exasperated employees. On the contrary, such goal-raising is likely to increase employee satisfaction. Marshall Edward and Gladys Ogden Dimock cite research indicating that employee work satisfaction goes up when standards are raised.[38] Productivity measures therefore, despite the fears and frustrations which they may initially arouse, should lead to increased employee morale and increased work satisfaction.

Evidence of this has already been seen in New York City. Deputy Mayor Hamilton describes how under a productivity improvement program, the city Parks and Recreation Department abolished their policy of assigning one or more men on a permanent basis to take care of a particular park. Instead, the men were grouped into three-man crews and sent from park to park as a team. According to Hamilton, not only did the output of the crews double that achieved by men working alone with permanent assignments, but "the morale of the work force increased noticeably because, as they said, they could see the results of their work and they took the new system as evidence that someone was taking an interest in their jobs."[39]

Productivity measures tend to work for, rather than against, the public employee in other ways as well. In the absence of productivity measures and ratings, the bad often tends to show up more than the good. Attention is more easily aroused when things go wrong than when things go right. Productivity measures make it easier to bring to light superior as well as substandard performance.

37. Katz and Kahn, *op. cit.*, p. 421.
38. Marshall E. and Gladys O. Dimock, *Public Administration*, p. 377.
39. Hamilton, *op. cit.*

In doing this, productivity measurement offers a better method for determining promotions of one kind or another. Use of such measures may obviate the need for traditional efficiency ratings and all the problems which they present. They also may permit a reduced emphasis on seniority. A good set of productivity measures can provide administrators with an impartial method of determining and rewarding merit.

Measuring productivity may also provide a basis for de-emphasizing rules, regulations and even supervision itself. Working with a good set of productivity measures, the employee can often become his own boss, at least to a substantial extent. Objective criteria rather than his supervisor guide his labors and determine his achievements.

All of these factors can foster innovation, for once specific goals have been set they should tend to become more important than the procedures for achieving them. The increased flexibility which results, along with the spur to use it, can widen and enrich the employee's scope of work. To cite one example, Wisconsin Correction Department officials, responding to a productivity effort, abolished the rule limiting female probation officers to counseling only women offenders. By doing away with this rule, the department was able to equalize work loads and reduce the overall number of probationary employees needed. At the same time, it broadened the work experience of one group of probation officers.[40]

Productivity measures may also strengthen the good features of the small group while modifying its less advantageous aspects. The genial alcoholic whose failings were previously covered up by his associates may now find himself forced to confront his problem as his comrades balk at his failure to contribute his share to their measurable output. A misanthropic member of the group, on the other hand, who may have been ostracized for reading poetry rather than joining in the lunch-time card game, may win a greater measure of acceptance if he makes a worthwhile contribution to the group's performance.

Management, too, may start to alter its attitude in beneficent and beneficial ways. A 1972 study, commissioned by the U.S. National Commission on Productivity, of British experiences in productivity bargaining found that it "induced management to abandon its defensive posture toward work rules and practices and to take the initiative in improving both the health of the enterprise and the welfare of the workers."[41]

In summary, then, productivity measures, despite the problems

40. Patrick J. Lucey, *Wisconsin's Productivity Policy,* November/December 1972.
41. U.S. Civil Service Commission, General Accounting Office and Office of Management and Budget, *Measuring and Enhancing Productivity in the Federal Sector* (Washington, D.C.: Mimeograph edition, June 1972).

they present and the limitations under which they must work, may have much to offer present-day public administration. At a session of the New York City conference on productivity, Ford Foundation President McGeorge Bundy called such initiatives "the beginning of the kind of human endeavor in which nearly everybody wins."[42]

42. *New York Times,* March 20, 1973.

9

Centralization and Its Concerns

The issue of centralization has haunted and hounded public administrators for centuries and even millenia. Ancient Chinese and Egyptian writings indicate that the emperors and pharaohs of those early days devoted much care and consideration to the ways and means of controlling field officers. And while these rulers eventually passed from the scene, problems involving centralization persisted. Ancient Rome, the medieval society and finally democratic governments all had to come to grips with this issue and most of them found satisfactory solutions to be in short supply.

America's response to the centralization controversy has been remarkably clear-cut, albeit one-sided. As was indicated in chapter two, our political culture has almost from its inception tended to favor the forces of fragmentation. In the minds of many of our founding fathers, centralization was associated with tyranny while decentralization was considered a necessary component of democracy. Predictably, American administration reflected this sentiment. Thus, Alexis de Tocqueville could write in 1830 that "in general the prominent feature of the administration in the United States is its excessive decentralization."[1]

This same high regard for decentralization has continued to characterize American thinking, if not American administration, up to the present day. As a matter of fact, decentralization has enjoyed a fresh burst of popularity in recent years. While the United States already benefits, or suffers, from more decentralization than any other nation in the industrialized world, critics on both the right and left insist that the answer to many of our social ills lies in creating more of the same. As

---

1. Alexis de Toqueville, *Democracy in America* (New York: Random House, 1945), Vol. 1, p. 86.

Irving Kristol has observed, decentralization in the United States in recent years has moved from an idea to an ideology.[2]

The decentralization issue, like so many other public administration issues, provides an abundance of argument for those on either side. One method for approaching the subject is to set up a balance sheet in order to examine the assets and liabilities of decentralization. This should enable us to obtain a better understanding of the problems involved and put us in a better position to seek solutions.

Decentralization and Its Delights

Decentralization tends to encourage flexibility. The closer decisions are made to the scene, the more likely it is that such decisions will be characterized by speed and suppleness. The decision-makers can take into account those factors affecting their particular situation and act accordingly. Decentralization makes provision for the fact that conditions, problems and people are not everywhere the same.

In stimulating quicker and more flexible decision-making, decentralization may improve the decision-making process. "We have learned," wrote Douglas McGregor, "that if we push decision-making in an organization as far down as we possibly can, we tend to get better decisions." However, McGregor, an enthusiastic advocate of decentralization, did not stop there. He also claimed that decentralization not only improved the quality of the decisions but also the quality of the decision-makers. "People tend to grow and develop more rapidly and they are motivated more effectively" when decision-making becomes decentralized, he maintained.[3]

There is undoubtedly some truth in McGregor's assertion. Conferring more authority on those who are down the line or out in the field makes their jobs more challenging and interesting. In this manner, the decentralized organization may not only find it easier to hone the capacities of its personnel, but it may also find it easier to recruit and retain high caliber personnel. Top-notch people do not like to work for organizations that curtail the scope of their initiative and enterprise. Consequently, they are not likely to be attracted to organizations which are close-fisted when it comes to allowing discretion.

While the benefits of decentralization seem to fall most heavily on subunits and subordinates, those at the center do not necessarily find themselves disadvantaged, for decentralization can improve their work experience as well. It eases the burden of decision-making and control at headquarters and gives headquarters personnel more time to

---

2. Irving Kristol, "Decentralization for What?" *The Public Interest,* spring 1968.
3. McGregor, *Leadership and Motivation* (1966), p. 121.

concentrate on formulating policy and shaping programs. We have already seen the importance of free time in fullfilling the functions of leadership. Decentralization can confer increased amounts of this valuable commodity on those who need it most.

Many of the advocates of decentralization go further and point out the ways in which it can alleviate the work load throughout the organization. If a decision has to be referred from field office to headquarters, then this demands more work all the way along the line. Field office must communicate to headquarters and headquarters must communicate back to the field. The work of both has thus been increased. If the field office can make the decision on its own, then it stops right there. There is less paperwork for both units and the problem of communication overload is alleviated.

An interesting example of how this principle works is supplied by Sir Ian Hamilton in his memoirs of British army life in India at the turn of the century. His experience involves only two people but it illustrates the same principle that so often affects relations between headquarters and subunit operations.

In 1896 I was Deputy Quartermaster-General at Simla; then, perhaps still, one of the hardest worked billets in Asia. After a long office day I used to get back home to dinner pursued by a pile of files three to four feet high. The Quartermaster-General, my boss, was a clever, delightful work-glutton. So we sweated and ran together for a while a neck and neck race with our piles of files, but I was the younger and he was the first to be ordered off by the doctors to Europe. Then I, at the age of forty-three, stepped into the shoes and became officiating Quartermaster-General in India. Unluckily, the Government at that moment was in a very stingy mood. They refused to provide pay to fill the post I was vacating and Sir George White, the Commander-in-Chief, asked me to duplicate myself and do the double work. My heart sank, but there was nothing for it but to have a try. The day came; the Quartermaster-General went home and with him went the whole of his share of the work. As for my own share, the hard twelve hours' task melted by some magic into the Socialist's dream of a six hours' day. How was that? Because, when a question came up from one of the Departments I had formerly been forced to compose a long minute [memorandum] upon it, explaining the case, putting my own views, and endeavoring to persuade the Quartermaster-General to accept them. He was a highly conscientious man and if he differed from me he liked to put on record his reasons—several pages of reasons. Or, if he agreed with me, still he liked to agree in his own words and to "put them on record." Now, when I became Quartermaster-General and Deputy-Quartermaster General rolled into one I studied the case as formerly, but there my work ended: I had not to persuade my own subordinates: I had no superior except the Commander-in-Chief, who was delighted to be left alone: I just gave an order—quite a simple matter unless a man's afraid: "Yes," I said, or "No!"[4]

Finally, decentralization is often said to facilitate and foster more rapport with the organization's clientele. Subunits such as field offices are obviously in a better position, at least most of the time, to know what the special needs of their own clientele may be. With more authority in their hands, they can respond to these needs more effectively. The clientele, on its part, will frequently find it easier to communicate their desires and demands to a branch office in their own area than to a central office far away.

Decentralization and Its Disappointments

While the case for decentralization seems quite compelling, there are some less appealing aspects to be considered. Decentralization, for one thing, curbs specialization. The large unit can afford to develop and retain a much greater variety and depth of expertise than can the subunit. A simple and hypothetical, though essentially realistic, example may serve to illustrate this problem.

A city may have a choice between maintaining a central health center with ten doctors or operating ten smaller neighborhood health centers with one doctor each. If the latter option is chosen, then obviously each doctor must to a great extent be a general practitioner, able to deal with a variety of health problems. If the centralized center is chosen, then it becomes possible to employ a pediatrician, a gerontologist, etc. The centralized health unit can offer a variety of services which the neighborhood units cannot hope to approach without substantial increases in the overall health services budget.

This brings us to another aspect of the question. Operating the ten neighborhood centers is likely to be more expensive. It may require ten different custodians to take care of the physical plant of these centers while one large facility, though it might need more than one such custodian, would probably require less than ten. The combined heating bills for these neighborhood centers will likewise be much greater than the heating cost of one larger unit. And, perhaps more importantly, there is the expense of sophisticated medical equipment which may be required, but which would not be in constant use, at a local health center. Thus, for these and many other reasons, it should be possible to

---

4. Sir Ian Hamilton, *The Soul and Body of an Army* (London: E. Arnold and Co., 1921), pp. 235–236, quoted in Simon, *Administrative Behaviors*, p. 237. This example also illustrates the costs involved in over-staffing and over-organization discussed in chapter four.

provide greatly increased health services for the same amount of money if the service remains centralized:

The potential economies from centralization should not be exaggerated. Centralization itself has its costs and these tend to become greater the more extensive it becomes. Any function can only be centralized just so far and then any economies which may have been produced start to diminish and finally turn negative. Still, centralization does permit a grouping of activities, bulk purchases of supplies, the use of heavy equipment such as large computers, and other practices which can lower overall costs.

Centralization can also open up as well as seal off opportunities for the organization's personnel. As we have already seen, it allows more chances for a person to develop specialized skills and to work with others in his specialty. It may also simplify and expedite transfers from one subunit to another. A case worker employed in a municipal welfare system may find it hard and almost impossible to move if he discovers, for example, that he has few opportunities for promotion at his present job or that he cannot get along with his boss. In a statewide system, he can more easily move on to another office in another locality.

The American correctional system offers an illustrative example of some of the drawbacks which decentralization may entail. In writing about prisons, former Attorney General Ramsey Clark notes that "some 125,000 employees are scattered through an impossible maze of jurisdictions throughout the country. Jails across the street from each other—one run by the county, the other by the city—are still commonplace. The time spent moving prisoners from one facility to another and the risk involved each time are reasons enough to abolish one. . . ." Clark then goes on to say "Local prisons do not, and in the nature of things cannot, have the staff, the range of skills or the number of prisoners necessary to provide the services required. They are less able to provide the special services needed by female and juvenile offenders."[5] It is for reasons such as these that Clark advocates statewide prison systems.

Lacking centralization, an organization may experience a lot of expensive and injurious duplication. A study of a Michigan high school which allowed its teachers considerable leeway in picking their books found that the seniors had read George Orwell's *Animal Farm* three times, once in an English course, once in a government course and once in a social relations course. Some of the seniors had also read Hawthorne's *The Scarlet Letter* three times. John Lindsay, on becoming mayor of New York City, found that three city departments maintained

---

5. Clark, *Crime in America*, p. 234.

street paving programs and eight departments ran youth programs. Not one of them knew what the others were doing.[6]

Those who distrust decentralization even find its presumed virtues a cause for concern. A subunit in a decentralized organizational setting may achieve more closeness to its clientele but, they ask, is this always a good thing? The clientele may have ideas of its own that run contrary to the interest of the broader public which the organization is supposed to serve.

The Forest Service has long been sensitive to this issue and it is an additional reason why the Service rotates its rangers as a regular policy. The Forest Service is afraid that they will become captured, as it were, by their immediate constituencies, thus doing damage to its proclaimed ideal of providing the greatest good to the greatest number. Herbert Kaufman, in his study of the rangers, found that this fear was no idle concern.[7]

Kaufman reports that one ranger who was an active member of the local chamber of commerce in his district mentioned how he "looked the other way" when he had reason to believe that the businessmen's group was operating a resort area without the rather expensive liability insurance required under the terms of its special-use permit. Another ranger sought to dispose of timber through many small sales. This allowed many local people to bid for the wood but it involved more paper work for the Service and brought lower prices to the government. At least one ranger allowed grazing permits for small herds to help local farmers, another permitted a dump to continue, and so forth. If the Forest Service, with its high degree of cohesion, is still vulnerable to constituency capture, one can imagine what can happen to other organizations whose members have not been so heavily imbued with an organization's ideals and codes and who are not subject to regular rotation.

What makes the problem of constituency capture still more serious is that in many cases it is not the entire constituency that does the capturing. Usually, a subunit becomes most susceptible to influence from only the more organized and articulate elements among its clientele. And these elements may have interests that not only diverge from the general public, which is paying the bills, but which also diverge from and even contradict the interests of the majority of the other clients. For example, an organization of nursing home operators will usually be able to exert much more pressure on a local administrator than

---

6. Nat Hentoff, *A Political Life: The Education of John V. Lindsay* (New York: Alfred A. Knopf, 1969), p. 91.
7. Kaufman, *The Forest Ranger,* pp. 76–80.

will their unfortunate patients. And the interests of the operators are by no means always consistent with the interests of those entrusted to their care.

Of course, clientele groups can and sometimes do exercise undue pressure at headquarters as well as on the field office but it is usually much more difficult for them to do so. This is true for a variety of reasons. For one thing, people removed from the scene are likely to be more neutral and impartial. Familiarity may confer knowledge; it also engenders entanglements. In one of Voltaire's short stories entitled, "La Vision de Babouc," there is the following dialogue between the protagonist and an angel who wishes to send him to Persia:

But, seigneur, said Babouc humbly, I have never been in Persia; I don't know anyone there.

So much the better, said the angel, you will not be partial.

It is for reasons such as this one that the Italian police when they recruit a young man from, say, Naples will send him after his training to serve in Genoa. A Genoan, on the other hand, may find himself policing Naples. The lack of intimate knowledge and associations with the area he polices enables the Italian policeman to enforce the law, so it is felt, without fear or favor.

Another factor which contributes to the vulnerability of subunits to clientele capture is that such subunits are often less visible and less easily held to account by the public, politicians and the press. Let us go back to our hypothetical health centers. If the city decides to maintain one central health facility, then it becomes much easier for everyone concerned to determine just what the city's health department is doing and how well it is doing it. If it decentralizes into ten centers, then the local newspaper, the city councilor and the interested citizen must try to keep tabs on ten times as many operations. Furthermore, since none of these neighborhood centers would be anywhere near as important as one central health center, none will arouse much outside interest generally.

This lack of visibility permits and even encourages abuses. With the press, the public and others giving less attention to the individual, decentralized facility, other interest groups will usually find it easier to exercise influence. And since the local administrator will lack the support as well as the control which a higher visibility operation tends to evoke, he may find himself more and more disposed to yield to neighborhood pressures. If the entire neighborhood becomes concerned with the center, this is one thing. However, it is unlikely that it will. Indeed, the neighborhood residents will probably not know too much about it since each center, as we have seen, will not be receiving much attention from the news media, city councilors and others due to its being only a neighborhood institution. As a result, those with the most direct interest in the center, such as those who are seeking certain forms of patronage, may become the center's "public."

If all of this seems somewhat farfetched and involved, then all too many examples exist to show that this is precisely what often happens. However, before passing on to some concrete instances of the difficulties which decentralization may produce, we should take note of the fact that centralization and decentralization are by no means absolutes. Every organization is to some extent centralized and, similarly, every organization is also somewhat decentralized. Decentralization and its opposite are basically matters of degree. Consequently, the foregoing should be viewed as describing the costs and benefits entailed in moving in one direction or the other. Progress in either direction will provide payoffs along with some price tags as well.

CASE STUDY

Selective Service, Schools and Others

Although the Roosevelt era is generally regarded as a time when American government became vastly more centralized, it was also a time when some interesting experiments in decentralization got underway. One of these occurred in military conscription. Faced in 1940 with the task of implementing a controversial draft law—the conscription bill had passed the House of Representatives by only one vote—the Roosevelt administration decided to have it carried out through local boards consisting of three citizens each. These local citizens would decide who was to be drafted and who was not, under the provisions of the act.

The system survived World War II, the Korean war and the Vietnam war and continues up to the present day, although actual conscription, at the time of this writing, is now suspended. As a result, the history of military conscription in this country, with the exception of the rather abortive attempt at a draft during the Civil War, has, to a great extent, been a highly decentralized affair. Any young man subject to the draft can be assured that three citizens from his own locality will determine whether or not he is required to serve in his country's military forces.

However, as to whether such a young man would actually find this reassuring or not might depend on who he is and whom he or his family knows. Researchers who have studied the operations of these boards have uncovered a persistent tendency on their part to make judgments based on less than the most objective types of criteria. One researcher, Gary L. Warmsley, found that board members generally shared "middle class values" and more often than not a "legionnaire mentality." (Veterans outnumber non-veterans on the boards by about seven to one.) They also lacked information and comprehensive criteria for decision-making. As a result, mannerisms, bearing, dress and attitude took on exaggerated importance when it came to deciding who would go and who would stay.[8]

It is quite possible that many other considerations might also enter into the selection process. A board member who owed a favor to the family of one potential conscriptee might argue persuasively for the young man's exemption. If, on the other hand, he carried a grudge against the fellow or his relatives, he might argue the other way. Economic interests under such a system could also find their way into board deliberations. Somehow, those who held economic or other forms of power in the community seemed to have more success in getting their sons, nephews or valuable employees exempted from the draft.

The fact that selective service boards were local bodies did not make them necessarily more visible or more acceptable to their constituencies. Two other researchers, James W. David, Jr. and Kenneth M. Dolbeare, found in a 1966 survey of adults in Wisconsin that only a bare majority were even aware that conscription was handled by local boards. (The local boards had by then been in operation for more than a quarter of a century.) What is more, of those who did not know about them, over one-half disapproved of the idea of allowing local agencies to make such decisions.[9]

In 1969, Daniel Moynihan, then serving as an advisor to President Nixon, released some figures which offer some possible indications as to how the local boards had performed. According to Moynihan, only 24 percent of all elementary school graduates had been found medically disqualified for military service while 38 percent of all college graduates had received such exemptions.[10] Although Moynihan did not attempt to relate this disparity to arbitrary behavior on the part of local draft boards, others might well draw such an inference. College graduates, it would seem, should, if anything, enjoy better health than those from poorer environments. However, they should also enjoy, at least on the whole, somewhat better contacts with their local draft board members. In the light of what other researchers have noted about the behavior of such boards, this latter factor may have been partly responsible for their higher number of medical deferments.

Another experiment with decentralized administration that flourished during the New Deal, and to some extent has continued since then, occurred in agriculture. Vigorous moves were made to stimulate community participation in the government's agricultural programs and these resulted in a network of about 30,000 elected farmers' committees. Professor Lewis Mainzer, in reviewing this decentralization effort, cites a 1939 study of the agricultural ex-

---

8. Gary L. Warmsley, *Selective Service in a Changing America* (Columbus, Ohio: Charles E. Merrill, 1969), p. 154.

9. James W. Davis, Jr. and Kenneth M. Dolbeare, *Little Groups of Neighbors: The Selective Service System* (Chicago: Markham, 1968), Chapter 7.

10. Daniel P. Moynihan, "The Schism in Black America," *The Public Interest*, no. 27 (spring 1972).

tension agency. The study, according to Mainzer, found that "the necessity of pleasing the dominant economic and political leaders because of dependence on county appropriations as well as a natural tendency to conform to social and economic patterns has resulted in service by the county agent primarily for more prosperous farmers." Stockmen, in being invited to serve on "advisory boards," only "buttressed the old system of local control of the range by rural elites." Concludes Mainzer, "Local control in agricultural administration serves the well established, not the poor farmers."[11]

These same tendencies presented themselves in even more magnified form when the Johnson administration undertook its heralded but scarcely well thought out "War on Poverty" program in the 1960's. An attempt was made to involve the poor in planning and executing the program, and to this end elections were held in slum neighborhoods of various cities to choose representatives for the local Community Action Program. Despite much fanfare and publicity, the turnout of potential voters usually amounted to less than 5 percent and in one city, Los Angeles, failed to reach 1 percent.[12] Those elected thus often represented only themselves and their friends. And all too often they behaved as if such a circumscribed circle defined the limits of their responsibilities. Funds were spent largely on salaries and sometimes disappeared completely. Indictments of anti-poverty workers stemming from alleged forgeries, kickbacks, embezzlements and other abuses occurred in New York, Connecticut, Arizona, New Jersey, Pennsylvania, Arkansas, Rhode Island, Utah and other states.[13]

The decentralization of the anti-poverty war also raises some larger and deeper issues. Even if the numerous abuses had not taken place, was it still the right way to proceed? Would it not only reinforce parochial attitudes and dysfunctional behavior? In his book *The End of Liberalism,* Theodore Lowi writes that "the War on Poverty will never integrate the city, racially or culturally. Narrowed perspectives are created by and reinforced by the neighborhood concept. The call for decentralization is a sound of great joy to liberals. But decentralization is an absurdity at the beginning of a program whose major goal is (or ought to be) reeducation toward new social values. Decentralization in this case is abdication; worse, it provides additional powers of resistance."[14]

Community Control Comes to the Schools
Our peculiar American penchant for reducing governmental authority and operation to its smallest components sharply characterizes our system of education. With the exception of law enforcement, education has quite possibly been the most decentralized function in our political and governmental

---

11. Lewis C. Mainzer, *Political Bureaucracy* (Glenview, Ill.: Scott, Foresman, 1973), p. 137.
12. Theodore J. Lowi, *The End of Liberalism* (New York: W. W. Norton, 1969), p. 246.
13. *Boston Herald-American,* May 1, 1973. See editorial "Poverty War: Won or Lost?"
14. Lowi, *ibid.*

system. Originally, there was a school board for nearly each ward in the country and up to a few years ago, there were still thousands of school districts whose "districts" consisted of a single school.[15]

The system produced more than its share of critics. The incapacity and often unwillingness of these local school boards to educate children in an optimum manner aroused not only irritation but alarm. Many Ohio districts, for instance, at one time taught all their subjects in German. It was scarcely a way to help their charges participate fully in the life of their country or utilize to the fullest their abilities in an English-speaking society.

Progressive educators fought long and hard against such splinterization of the educational function, and after World War II, they began to make substantial headway. The number of school districts dropped markedly as small school systems consolidated to form larger ones. However, during the 1960's a reaction set in. The renewed interest in decentralization, now often expressed in the phrase "community control," gave rise to a new impetus to break up the school systems of the larger cities and "return" their schools to the neighborhoods they served. It was widely believed that such a move would greatly benefit minority groups whose many problems, it was felt, were compounded by the fact that the school systems which served them were in outside hands.

In Detroit, community-control-oriented blacks joined with anti-integrationist whites to introduce a school decentralization bill into the state legislature. The measure was designed to set up eight school districts drawn almost wholly along racial lines. With wide support from both black and white legislators, the school decentralization bill was enacted into law in 1970. The first school elections under the new scheme failed to produce any increased influence for blacks. Although black pupils were in the majority in six out of the eight districts, black representatives won a voting majority on only two of the boards. As for the city's central board, only three of its thirteen seats were won by blacks. Of the remaining ten whites who were elected, six were staunch anti-integrationist conservatives. As William R. Grant, the education editor of the *Detroit Free Press,* subsequently commented, "The song may be 'community control' but the tune was 'Dixie.'"[16] Turmoil within the schools following the adoption of the new system seemed, if anything, to increase and the city's highly respected superintendent resigned.

In New York City, meanwhile, another and much more significant attempt at school decentralization was underway. Mounting dissatisfaction with, and distrust of, the city's school system prompted Mayor Lindsay to name a study commission in the mid-1960's to see what could be done. In late 1967 the commission issued its report calling for the establishment of between thirty and sixty school districts within the city, each having its own elected school board. The central city board was to retain only minimum control over the elementary schools though it was to continue operating the high schools.

---

15. Robert Bendiner, *The Politics of Schools* (New York: Harper & Row, 1969), Chapter 12.
16. William R. Grant, "Community Control vs. Integration—The Case of Detroit," *The Public Interest,* no. 24 (summer 1971).

The plan was enthusiastically received by many black and white political and educational leaders as well as by reform groups generally. As a full-page advertisement inserted by the Urban Coalition in the *New York Times* put it, "If it works in Scarsdale, it can work for Ocean Hill," Ocean Hill being a slum section of the city. The *New York Times* itself eagerly backed the plan as did the New York City *Post.*[17]

Without waiting for the state legislature to act on the overall proposal, the Ford Foundation sponsored an experimental district in the Ocean Hill-Brownsville section of the Bronx. From the start, the district was embroiled in controversy. Much of its opposition came from the city's teachers' union which was suspicious of decentralization in general and hostile to the leadership of this particular district. When the local board attempted to transfer out of the district some teachers it did not want without going through what the union claimed were the proper procedures, the teachers' union went on strike throughout the city.

While the teachers were accused of obstructing progress, the experimental board and its superintendent, Rhoddy McCoy, were charged with flagrant misuse of patronage and with failing to accomplish their educational mission. Despite massive funding from various sources which permitted reduced teacher-pupil ratios and many new modern materials, reading scores in the experimental district fell. Pupils who were reading a little more than two years below grade level in 1967 had slipped to a full three years below grade level by 1971.[18]

In the meantime, a bill to decentralize the city's entire school system had been introduced into the state legislature and was enacted in 1969. It broke the system into thirty-one districts each of which was to be governed by a nine-member elected school board. Each board was to appoint the district superintendent, as well as the principals, and was to exercise general operating authority over the elementary and intermediate schools within its district. The central board, meanwhile, exercised some overall control in terms of budgeting and other matters, but even here the districts enjoyed some degree of discretion.[19]

The first elections for the new district school boards were held in 1970. Although they received intense newspaper, radio and television coverage, and although a goodly number of candidates vied for election in each district, the voters failed to respond. The turnout amounted to only 15 percent. Since more than two slates of candidates were running in most districts, many a new school board member secured his or her seat with little more than 5 percent of a district's potential vote. It was hoped that as the boards swung into operation, voter interest would increase. However, this proved not to be the case. In the next election three years later, only 10 percent of those eligible turned out at the polls.[20]

17. See, for example, the editorial page of the *New York Times,* November 9, 1967.
18. Diane Rovitch, "Community Control Revisited," *Commentary,* February 1972.
19. A good summary of the decentralization law appeared in the *New York Times,* April 20, 1973.
20. *New York Times,* May 2, May 3, May 5, 1973. Also see editorial on May 12, 1973.

The results have been particularly disappointing in terms of minority representation. Despite the fact that white pupils comprised only 38 percent of the city's public school population in 1970, white candidates won 72 percent of all board seats.[21] To be sure, the proportion of white eligible voters is somewhat higher than the number of white public school children would suggest since whites tend to have fewer children and to place a much higher proportion of the children they do have in non-public schools. Still, the proportion of black candidates elected proved disappointing to many.

Parent groups were organized to maintain liaison and keep tabs on the local school boards, but their effectiveness in truly representing their communities was often called into question. Although each such group was to consist of 1,500 to 2,000 parents, frequently as few as 15 people showed up to elect the group's leaders. When parents did make their voices heard, it was not always gratifying to those who had backed the decentralization scheme. For example, in the fall of 1972 the city began bussing a few black students into the Canarsie district of Brooklyn. The white residents of Canarsie, fearful that this would lead to a black majority in their already delicately balanced district, organized a mass boycott which culminated in name-calling and even some violence. The parents based their protest on the rights they supposedly had achieved through school decentralization.

School decentralization has undoubtedly proven expensive, although just how expensive cannot be precisely determined. The New York City school budget has gone up considerably to the point where the city was spending over $2,200 per pupil in 1973. While much of this was a result of other pressures, some of the increase was undoubtedly due to decentralization. It was now necessary to pay thirty-one district superintendents a salary of around $35,000 a year plus the costs of maintaining their staffs. Each school district had a separate office to handle Title I grants while previously one office had processed them for the entire city. Money expended to maintain the elaborate administrative network which a decentralized system may require is, of course, money that is not available for educational purposes.

More disquieting to many were the increasing indications that the money was not being spent properly. On June 10, 1974, three district board members pleaded guilty to charges stemming from the illegal use of school funds. Earlier, a Board of Education hearing examiner had found that a local board had acted improperly in handling many contracts and leases. He also found "substantial questions" regarding the district's use of patronage in filling jobs.[22] Another board, meanwhile, had hired as an advisor a man who was already under indictment for murdering a moderate civil rights leader. (He was subsequently convicted of the charge.) Still another board hired a superintendent who had made anti-Semitic as well as anti-black statements and who was subsequently found to have collected two full-time salaries from

---

21. *New York Times,* April 29, 1973.
22. *Ibid.*

two different boards.²³ Other school boards had employed school security guards with criminal records, and some of them were subsequently involved in later crimes.²⁴

Adding to these administrative abuses was a good deal of administrative inefficiency. The first year of operation saw the school system running up a multi-million-dollar deficit. This led to the institution of stronger controls by the central board. Two years later, a state audit found that new teachers and other employees were frequently forced to wait months for their first pay-checks. At the same time, paychecks were still being sent to former employees who had long ago left the system.²⁵

The most important issue concerning decentralization, however, was how it would affect the way the schools were performing their primary mission, that of educating the children. Here again problems arose. Each district developed its own system of instruction and pupils who moved from one district to another found the continuity of their education disrupted. It also became difficult to gauge a pupil's progress. In a Brooklyn district where one hundred children were tested in a reading project, only thirty-two were present to be tested a year later. The other sixty-eight had changed schools. Complained one school official, "We were testing two different sets of pupils. How can you measure progress that way?"²⁶

When it came to testing the school system's overall achievement in instruction, the initial results proved disheartening. City-wide reading tests administered in April 1972 showed a rather dramatic drop in reading scores for nearly all grades since 1969. This came about despite the fact that teacher-pupil ratios had improved and many more dollars as well as much more effort had been devoted specifically to the reading problem. On a city-wide basis, 66.3 percent of all elementary pupils and 71.3 percent of all junior high and intermediate pupils were now reading one or more years below grade level.²⁷ While demographic and other factors may help to explain the drop, the results proved discouraging to the decentralizers.

Prior to the announcement of the 1972 reading tests, the ranks of the decentralizers suffered a major defection. Dr. Kenneth Clark, a black psychologist who had played a leading role in instituting the decentralization scheme, announced that he had done a "180-degree turn" on the issue. The new system, said Dr. Clark, had led to "selfish" and "racial" politics and had generated "intimidational pressures." He was now "vehemently opposed" to decentralization which, he said, had been a "disastrous experience."²⁸ The *New York Times* and others who had so fervently supported decentralization were

23. *New York Times,* June 17, 1973.
24. *New York Times,* February 27, 1973 and May 24, 1973.
25. Leonard Buder, "Run Like a 'Candy Store,'" in the *New York Sunday Times* (News in Review), April 29, 1973.
26. *New York Times,* May 27, 1973.
27. *New York Times,* March 18, 1973.
28. "Turmoil over Local Control," *New York Times,* December 3, 1973 (News in Review). Also see "Just Teach Them to Read," *New York Times Magazine,* March 18, 1973.

also beginning to express some misgivings although none was as outspoken as Clark.[29]

A more cheering note came in the fall of 1973 when the results of more recent reading tests were announced. It was found that the reading scores of the city's children had started to rise. The school system's newly appointed chancellor, Irving Anker, attributed the turnaround to the increased resources being expended for this purpose such as special diagnostic reading programs, para-professional aides, the lower teacher-pupil ratios, as well as a deeper commitment on the part of all concerned to do something about the problem. Whether or not decentralization had facilitated or hindered this development remained a matter for conjecture.[30]

MBO: THE SEARCH FOR ANSWERS

The dilemmas which decentralization poses, along with the very real benefits it can confer, have puzzled and perplexed administrators since the inception of their craft. How can one take advantage of the flexibility, immediacy and responsiveness which decentralization affords while still maintaining standards of accountability and without piling up costs?

One possible answer has come from the private sector. In 1954, Peter Drucker published a book entitled *The Practice of Management* which offered a potential method for reconciling the two contrasting approaches. Drucker called his method "management by objectives."

The new system was essentially simple and, in many respects, perhaps not all that new. Drucker advised executives to set measurable objectives for their subordinates and their subunits and then let them have a fairly free hand in how they would seek to attain them. As he has since expressed it, "All one can measure is performance and all one should measure is performance."[31] Everything else is secondary, if not actually superfluous. Thus, an organization, once it has devised an agreed set of objectives for its subunits can allow them to make their own decisions on just how they will meet these objectives.

Management by objectives (MBO) soon won wide acceptance throughout the business world. It led firms to establish "profit centers" in which the manager of a subunit enjoys nearly the same scope and freedom as the owner of a small business. All he has to do is see to it

---

29. As an example, see the editorial page of the *New York Times*, May 12, 1973.
30. Leonard Buder, "They Go Up, But Nobody Is Sure Why," *New York Times*, December 23, 1973 (News in Review).
31. Drucker, *The Effective Executive* (1967), p. 86.

that his "profit center" returns a suitable profit to the company. (Not that this is always an easy task!) Headquarters, aside from occasionally checking as to how his unit is doing in meeting its goals, provides very little day-to-day or even month-to-month supervision. Rather, it stands ready to aid and assist him in meeting and, if possible, exceeding his target.

This technique of centralizing objectives but decentralizing the decision-making necessary to meet these objectives obviously permits, and even encourages, a good deal of latitude at the lower levels and/or out in the field. Subunits are expected to adapt and adjust their operations to respond to local conditions and to cope with their own particular problems. All that top level management cares about, basically, are the results. Headquarters may still offer specialized equipment and services in order to take advantage of the economies of scale. However, if the subunit can find a cheaper way of doing things, such as contracting out locally for such services, it is often permitted to do so.

Management by objectives or, as it is sometimes called, management by results has won a respected position in the business school curriculum and has also become a fundamental operating feature of many business firms. One such firm is the Jim Walker Corporation which saw its sales quadruple from 1968 to 1973 after it initiated such an approach. In the process, it became the nation's largest producer of building materials.

This corporation allows the planning and sales office managers of many of its divisions to actually set their own goals. (Based, partly, to be sure, on research provided by headquarters.) These goals are then reviewed by headquarters. In the process of doing this review, the central office may modify a local manager's set of objectives but only after the manager has agreed that he can meet the revised goals. Headquarters maintains an audit staff to monitor his progress and he may receive a call if his monthly reports indicate that he is falling behind. But the call is likely to be an offer of assistance more than a rebuke. After all, the company has as much interest in his success as he does.[32]

By the late 1960's, MBO had begun to interest an increasing number of public organizations and their managers. To many, it seemed to offer a way of decentralizing while avoiding the problems which previous attempts at decentralization almost consistently encountered. If it worked in the private sector, they reasoned, then why couldn't it work for us?

However, developing and implementing an MBO system in the

---

32. Peter Vanderwicken, "'Collegial Management' Works at Jim Walters Corporation," *Fortune,* March 1973.

delivery of public services is no easy task. Probably the most trouble-some of the obstacles it presents is the difficulty of defining and quanti-fying objectives. Business has a comparatively easy measuring stick, namely profit. But how can one calculate the profitability of a welfare office, a police station, a school? As we saw in our discussion of PPBS and productivity measures, it is often difficult to gauge not only what a service is accomplishing but even, in some instances, how much the service is actually costing. And even when we can do this, problems remain. As one commentator has noted, "One can calculate the dollar cost of teaching a disadvantaged child to read, for example, but how does one measure the 'profitability' of this service to society?"

Then there are the political problems which beset the public sec-tor when it seeks to adopt such an approach. It is frequently hard and sometimes impossible to secure agreement on objectives once they can be identified with some precision. A private firm essentially must satisfy its stockholders; a public firm has to satisfy a variety of publics who may have different and even contradictory demands. And, of course, there are the constraints of legislation, legislative oversight, annual budgeting, civil service requirements, etc.

We are, however, learning how to cope with the accountability problem in public organizations. The path of progress, to be sure, has not been smooth and the record is scarcely one of unflawed success. Yet, with the aid of such techniques as PPBS and productivity measures, public managers in many instances have managed to put MBO to work.

MBO at Work in the Public Sector

As was noted at the outset, MBO is in some respects not all that new. Good leaders have always recognized the priority of performance over procedures. When Napoleon was once asked how he picked his gener-als, he replied, "I pick lucky generals." In other words, Napoleon liked generals who could win battles. Anything else was secondary. Lincoln had the same considerations in mind in choosing Grant to head the Union forces and in continuing to back him despite numerous attempts by others to undermine the new military chief. When informed that Grant liked to drink too much, Lincoln is said to have replied that he wished his other generals would drink the same kind of liquor. "He makes things git," said Lincoln of his controversial commander.[33]

The Dutch school system provides a more current and compre-hensive example of the MBO approach. In Holland any group of quali-fied educators who can guarantee some minimum enrollment can start up a school with the assurance of a full government subsidy based on

---

33. Smith, *I Hate To See a Manager Cry,* p. 179.

the number of pupils they teach. They are free to use whatever methods of instruction they may wish. However, the government requires that all pupils take certain standardized tests at frequent intervals and any school with a high failure rate will start losing pupils and, as a result, government funding. Schools that show up well on the tests will usually attract more pupils as parents shift their children from poorer performing schools. As a result, the successful schools will be able to expand.[34]

A more modest but nevertheless major MBO effort was scheduled to be introduced into America's largest school system in the fall of 1974. New York City was planning to institute accountability measures into nearly 100 of its schools. If successful, the criteria would be extended to all 950 schools in the city's decentralized system.

Schools would be evaluated by their results which would be determined by such data as the percentage of pupils who were failing to register minimum achievement, student development indexes showing how much progress each school was making with its children each year and a profile of each school. A planning and operations committee consisting of the principal, teacher representatives, parent representatives and others would be established in each school to help make the system work. The teachers' union greeted the new plan with considerable enthusiasm, claiming that it would help teachers determine those factors which make for effective learning.[35]

An American state which has successfully utilized an MBO approach in one facet of its educational process is Michigan. In the early 1970's, Michigan launched a $25 million-a-year compensatory education program. The program, as it has evolved, bases itself on what is called a "performance pact" between the state and the local school district. The state sets a basic objective for each child in the program, namely a month's gain in achievement for each month's instruction in the fundamental areas of reading and mathematics. The local school district can go about meeting this objective in any way it wishes but if it fails to achieve at least 75 percent of the objective it loses its program funding for the following year. "If they can teach a kid to read by taking him to the zoo three times a week, fine," says the program's acting director Alex Canja. "If not, they'd better stop taking him to the zoo." Data released in 1973 indicated that almost 60 percent of the pupils enrolled in the program were achieving a month's gain for a month's instruction and many of these children were scoring even greater achievements.[36]

Management by objectives is also spreading to higher education. The president of the University of Pennsylvania, Martin Meyerson, has

---

34. *The New Republic,* August 15, 1970, p. 11.
35. *New York Times,* April 9, 1974.
36. *New York Times,* December 11, 1973.

adopted some key elements of MBO to administer the university's network of 22 schools and institutes. Each of these units has been designated a "responsibility center," and as such bears the main responsibility for supporting itself. At the same time, it also enjoys the freedom to make its own decisions on just how its earned income, which is mainly from tuitions, is to be used. Instead of simply applying to the university for financing, each school now has its own revenue but must learn to live within these means.

The new system permits a good deal of decentralized and diversified decision-making. A school can decide on its own whether to increase or decrease its faculty-to-student ratio, student aid, number of courses, etc. Each responsibility center is given its share of the university's general income, but it is also assessed for whatever use it makes of centralized university facilities such as libraries. The university even maintains a sort of bank from which a responsibility center can "borrow" to meet, say, the start-up costs for a new program. However, all such "loans" must be repaid with interest out of its subsequent income.

Meyerson claims the system is producing results. Professor John Hobstetter who chairs the university's budget committee agrees. They say the method of operation is inducing deans and faculty to relate the academically desirable with the financially possible, and to show more concern for the general problems of the university.[37]

Perhaps the most extensive and systematic use made of MBO so far has occurred at HEW. According to Rodney H. Brady, a former assistant secretary for administration and management at HEW, this came about because "there was no adequate provision for stating program objectives that were based on specific measurable results. Consequently, program success was often assessed on wrong criteria such as the number of grants awarded rather than on the number of people helped or problems solved."[38] Information for policy development and guidance for program managers were both in short supply since no formal mechanism existed for generating a continuing dialogue throughout the operating cycle.

To overcome such problems, writes Brady, HEW set up a six-stage procedure for setting objectives.[39]

1. The Secretary determines the goals of the various HEW agencies in consultation with the heads of these agencies and encourages them to sharpen and refine their objectives in the light of such goals.

37. Associated Press dispatch in the financial section of the *Boston Sunday Globe,* April 14, 1974.
38. Rodney H. Brady, "MBO Goes to Work in the Public Sector," *Harvard Business Review,* March-April 1973.
39. *Ibid.,* pp. 68–69.

314

2. The Secretary's staff then draws up the budget and sends it to the president and, through him, to Congress. (Actually, of course, it really goes through the Office of Management and Budget.)

3. The Secretary, having determined priorities during the budgetary process, now formalizes them in a paper to provide planning guidance to agency heads and regional managers.

4. These executives now make sure that their own objectives conform to the priorities and overall department goals as reflected in the budget document. Typically, they select eight or ten objectives "that represent the most important results expected of their respective programs."

5. The agency heads and regional managers then submit their lists of objectives "along with milestones that must be reached and resources that must be expended" to accomplish them to the Secretary's office where his staff gives them a thorough perusal.

6. The Secretary then selects certain objectives that he will personally keep tabs on. He may add or detract from the list as the year unfolds, depending on new ideas of his own, the passage of new legislation or other developments. In the 1972 fiscal year, Secretary Elliot Richardson personally monitored about 70 such objectives. The agency heads and regional managers had a total list of 300 objectives, which included, of course, the 70 that the Secretary was watching. The various agency bureaus, meanwhile tracked a total of 1,500 more specific objectives derived from the 300 established by their superiors.

A typical procedure for tracking objectives is to set up a chart designating various milestones along the way to their fulfillment together with the approximate times when these milestones are expected to be reached. The Secretary confers bimonthly with the agency heads and regional directors to discuss their problems and to see how they are doing. They are encouraged to keep in contact and to seek advice and assistance from the Secretary's office whenever they feel they need it.

Some ten days prior to his bimonthly meeting with the Secretary, the agency head or regional head submits a report showing the status of all the objectives for which he is responsible. Three gradations are used to describe progress in meeting an objective: satisfactory, minor problem and major problem. The designation of "major problem" signifies that the objective may not be reached without some substantial corrective action. Each of the executives also submits a year-end evaluation of his unit's progress.

The conference itself is designed to be a reasonably relaxed and free-flowing affair, providing a dialogue between the Secretary and the manager and giving them both an opportunity to identify and resolve problems. The agenda of matters to be discussed is planned jointly ahead of time and may be altered during the interchange at the suggestion of either and with the approval of both.

How is the system working? There have been problems. Writes Brady, "Some managers have viewed their roles as principally involving policy making, development of legislation and defense of their budget requests. They have tended to slight their responsibility in formalized management planning and control." Also, many have become overwhelmed by crisis—HEW has had more than its share of these—and consequently "have dealt with management issues on an ad hoc, rather than on an anticipatory, results-oriented basis."[40] (The reader will recall what was said in chapter six on the need for leaders to budget their time and resolve fundamental problems rather than treat symptoms.)

HEW has also found, according to Brady, that giving the executives access to the Secretary has actually, in some cases, impeded the operation of the system. Many of the managers are still too deeply imbued with the traditional notion that discussing problems with their superior means that somehow one has failed. This has led some managers to propose "only those areas for control under MBO which would not prove a source of embarrassment in face-to-face dialogues at management conferences."[41]

A final difficulty has been the tendency on the part of some of the executives to establish objectives that are too easy. In 1972, for example, one HEW agency set a goal of reducing by 2 percent the number of people in certain areas that would need a certain type of rehabilitation assistance. It exceeded the goal by 1,000 percent!

But not withstanding all these difficulties, the system, even in its initial phase, has, says Brady, already yielded substantial pay-offs. In Fiscal Year 1971 (FY 71), the first full year of MBO's operation, the Social and Rehabilitation Service determined that it would train 35,000 welfare recipients and place them in "meaningful" jobs. Despite the fact that this is not an easy task, and despite the fact that the Service would have to secure the cooperation of state agencies (which is also no easy task), it managed to shift some 40,000 people from welfare rolls to payrolls. It followed up this success by doing the same with 50,000 welfare recipients the following year. And it set a target of 69,000 for FY 73.

The Food and Drug Administration, to cite another example, decided it would try to increase the number of imported products it inspected by 50 percent in FY 72. It achieved this goal despite a severe dock strike on the eastern seaboard which disrupted shipping.

---

40. *Ibid.*, p. 71.
41. *Ibid.*, p. 72.

All told, one-quarter of HEW's objectives fell short of achievement in FY 72 and half of these fell very far below the targets that had been set. However, Brady does not regard this as a bad average, for "if an organization is consistently accomplishing 100 percent of its objectives, there is probably reason for concern rather than celebration." In order for objectives to play an effective role, he says, "an organization must 'stretch' to reach them."[42]

The Uses and Abuses of MBO

Management by objectives, as applied to the public sector, may be viewed as providing *administrative decentralization* within a framework of *political centralization.* Policy-making remains at the center, though the subunits can and should contribute to it. However, once the policies are formulated, the subunits can then be given considerable discretion in *how* they wish to implement them. With a system to monitor the results, headquarters should feel little need and, hopefully, little desire to keep track of day-to-day decision-making.

But just how much actual decentralization would such *administrative* decentralization involve? Theoretically, at least, a good deal. Let us return to the New York City school system. Under a fully developed and fully utilized system of MBO, a principal could, for example, hire unlicensed teachers if he felt that they would produce measurable results that would better meet his objectives. It is possible that in certain situations some carefully selected ex-convicts might prove more successful than trained teachers in bringing the benefits of education to the children. On the other hand, however, the principal and the district superintendent could lose their jobs if they consistently failed to meet their target goals. In this sense, there would be somewhat less decentralization than now exists.

An MBO approach might well satisfy the demands of Dr. Kenneth Clark who sponsored the present decentralization scheme and who now looks upon it as a failure. Clark suggests "that instead of talking about prerogatives and power and what not, we all concentrate on one absolute responsibility—the development and implementation of a reading and arithmetic program, monitoring it, evaluating it, maintaining a system of accountability to see that it works and modifying it if it isn't working."[43] Management by objectives would seem to fit this approach.

MBO, like PPBS and productivity measures to which it is closely related, may also interject other beneficial developments in organiza-

---

42. *Ibid.,* p. 74.
43. "Just Teach Them to Read," *New York Times Sunday Magazine,* March 18, 1973.

tional life. It reduces the role of personalism in administration. A superior will find it more difficult to advance a poor employee or hold back a good one since there is now an objective system for evaluating their work. The employee has to concern himself more with meeting his objectives than with pleasing his boss. A fully developed and practical MBO program can render traditional efficiency ratings nearly useless.

MBO should also ease the burden on managers. When a subordinate has performed poorly, the manager may no longer have to call it to his attention. The employee can now see it for himself. Managers can delegate more and certainly need not supervise as much. Thus, they can enjoy more of the free time which, as we saw in chapter six, a leader needs in order to manage effectively. At the same time, the public manager will feel an increasing compulsion to review his unit's *overall* operations and goals and to think about what he and his subordinates are really trying to accomplish and why.

A good MBO system should stimulate initiative and innovation. Since meeting objectives becomes the paramount purpose of the organization, it will feel itself pushed and prodded into trying new techniques for reaching and, if possible, exceeding these targets. It is much more likely to review its organizational structure, examine closely its methods of operation and consult with all those who may have some information or ideas that could be utilized. As a paper issued by the Civil Service Department of Great Britain entitled *Management by Objectives in the Civil Service* puts it, "A most useful feature of a Management-by-Objectives programme is that it obliges superior and subordinate not only to concentrate on the content of a job but to think about ways in which it can be done better."[44] The authors of the paper then go on to sum up some other benefits of MBO.

> The benefits of Management by Objectives go beyond providing a system of managerial control based on personal accountability. There are benefits of conducting a regular review of the purpose of the organization in the light of its changing environment; of examining the purpose and contribution to the total task of every part of the organization, and every managerial job; of establishing priorities for action and of allocating individual responsibility for seeing that action is taken; of introducing participative management in organizations that have traditionally been strongly mechanistic and hierarchical in character.[45]

However, despite the plethora of praise that it has evoked from some quarters, MBO is not without failings and faults. Objectives can

---

44. John Ganett and S. D. Walker, *Management by Objectives in the Civil Service,* CAS Occasional Paper/Number 10 (London: Her Majesty's Stationery Office, 1969), p. 5.
45. *Ibid.*

be artificially contrived to make the organization or its subunits look good. Or, if not actually contrived, then manipulated to cover up rather than expose existing deficiencies. Furthermore, many activities will not easily lend themselves to the establishment of quantifiable objectives. Pure research and many staff functions fall into this category. Attempts to apply MBO in many areas could lead to erroneous goals that could, in turn, lead to behavior that hurts rather than helps the organization's overall performance.

In short, MBO is no magic elixir that removes all the difficulties inherent in decentralization. It does not by any means automatically guarantee an organization a "best of both worlds" situation. Yet, it can provide the basis for moving in this direction. MBO thus constitutes a tool of some promise to the modern public manager as he wrestles with the dilemmas of decentralization.

PROBLEMS OF FIELD OFFICES

Essentially, there are two ways through which authority and responsibility are divided in an organization. One is on the basis of function; the other is on the basis of area. Most organizations of any size make some provision for both. They maintain some offices in the field and, at the same time, they operate some functional bureaus at headquarters.

One of the big questions which the organization must answer at this point is how much authority it will confer on one type of subunit versus the other, for the two different kinds of subunits tend to be competitive with each other. Strong functional bureaus usually imply weak field offices and vice versa. Consequently, the issue of *functional* versus *areal* responsibility can and often does generate a considerable degree of tension.

To see just how pervasive this issue is, let us step outside the area of public administration and take a look at the world of journalism. A large metropolitan newspaper may maintain bureaus, perhaps consisting of only one or two reporters each, in certain municipalities throughout its coverage area. Let us assume that a statewide organization of educators decides to hold its annual convention in one of these communities. The local correspondent wants and expects to cover the convention. However, the newspaper's education editor feels he should be the one to report on the convention's proceedings. Each can claim certain qualifications for the assignment. Whom should the managing editor choose?

In *The Kingdom and the Power,* a book on the *New York Times* which contains many interesting insights into administrative activity,

319

Gay Talese chronicles the persistent problems which that newspaper has had in keeping its Washington, D.C. field office under control. When the newspaper's labor editor, A. H. Raskin, was covering a labor proceeding in New York which happened to move to Washington, Raskin attempted to continue covering it from its new site. However, when he arrived at his newspaper's Washington office to seek a desk and a typewriter, he was informed that since it was now a Washington story, the local office would handle it. Raskin protested to the home office editors but to no avail.[46] In this case, areal power won out over functional authority.

When we examine public administration in terms of this issue of functional versus areal authority, we come across one of the ironies which so often characterizes public administration in this country. Although American administration does function in a highly decentralized political setting, and thus can be considered highly decentralized, the emphasis within most individual governments and their agencies has long been placed upon retaining a great degree of authority at headquarters and lodging it in functional bureaus. As a result, field offices have often played a strictly secondary role in our administrative life.

In his 1964 book *Area and Power,* James W. Fesler called attention to this fact in noting that "the basic distribution of administrative authority within each of our governments is functional." Only the State Department, the Tennessee Valley Authority and, to a lesser degree, the Department of Interior have "unique area responsibilities," he said in discussing the federal bureaucracy.[47] His observation has been backed up by many others. Professor Doris Kearns, after winding up a tour as a White House fellow in 1969, commented that "the [functional] bureau chiefs really run the government."[48]

What these and other observers have noticed are not things which they have approved. *Functional fragmentation* in the federal bureaucracy is not a suitable substitute for *areal decentralization.* And although some of both may be required, many have felt that an imbalance exists within the federal bureaucracy which needs to be redressed. The government would work better if those in the field could do more and those in Washington would do less.

The problem, it should be kept in mind, is not unique to the United States. In France, for example, considerable tension has arisen over the years between the prefects, who are the regional representatives of the central government, and the various ministries who operate

---

46. Gay Talese, *The Kingdom and the Power* (New York: World Publishing, 1969), pp. 21–22.
47. James W. Fesler, *Area and Power* (University, Ala.: University of Alabama Press, 1964), p. 49.
48. In a statement to the author in 1970.

bureaus within each prefect's district. French President De Gaulle made an earnest attempt in 1964 to strengthen the powers of the prefects and to reduce somewhat the authority of the ministries in Paris in overseeing their own field operations. It should be kept in mind, however, that what was involved was an attempt to achieve *administrative* decentralization not *political* decentralization since the prefects themselves are officials of the central government.

Similar attempts, from time to time, have occurred in this country. When Chester Bowles became director of the Office of Price Administration during World War II, he immediately set about transferring authority and resources to the field. Within 90 days he had worked out a plan for transferring two-thirds of the OPA's 12,000 Washington employees to the regional offices. The regional offices, in turn, were instructed to place most of these employees in their own district offices. However, here he ran into difficulty. There is a tenacious tendency for any headquarters to increase its own staff and authority at the expense of its field units and the OPA's regional offices proved no exception. As Bowles tells it, "We soon found that the regional offices suffered from the same zeal for building up their own staffs as had the Washington office, and a second effort was required to persuade the regional offices that we were serious in our intentions."[49]

Bowles eventually succeeded but his success failed to encourage other federal agencies to follow suit. However during the 1960's, as the federal government became more and more involved with hitherto strictly local problems, the need for creating more areal authority became increasingly apparent. And during the first term of the Nixon administration things finally started to happen.

How to Site a Field Office

The first problem that one confronts in attempting to set up a system of effective field offices is the not-so-simple one of location. For field offices to function effectively they must be put in the proper places. Determining what are the proper places is not easy, and before going on to examine how the Nixon administration dealt with it, let us first consider some of the basic issues involved.

In his book which was cited above, Fesler lists some six "considerations" which have to be weighed in establishing a network of field offices.[50] The first of these is the obvious one of span of control. If there are too many field offices, then their individual workloads may be too small to permit efficient operations. Also, they will be harder and more

---

49. Bowles, *Promises to Keep,* p. 82.
50. Fesler, *op. cit.,* pp. 50–60.

expensive to supervise. If, on the other hand, there are too few, then their individual workloads may be too great to be efficient and the areas they serve may be too large for them to respond flexibly and sensitively to local problems. The actual number will therefore depend on variables such as the amount of work, the complexity of the work, the degree of diversity in the areas served. An agency such as Social Security which has clients throughout the country may need more field offices than the Department of Agriculture which serves only rural areas. (It may be of interest to note in connection with Social Security that this agency has found that offices of between twenty and thirty-five employees seem to be the most efficient. Larger or smaller offices generally perform less well.)

A second consideration cited by Fesler is the location of the activities with which the agency is concerned. An agency dealing with rivers might want to established its offices around river systems. An agency that was involved with fishing would probably have little need for an office in the Texas panhandle.

The third of Fesler's considerations concerns workload. It should be relatively uniform among offices in the same category. In other words, there should be no great disparities between the workload of one office and that of another.

A fourth consideration concerns the other units which the field office has to do business with. If the agency, for example, dispenses grants-in-aid to states, then it may want to have an office in every state. If its activities primarily bring it into contact with the governments of large cities, then it may wish to use these cities as its field office locations, and this may mean more than one office in some states and no office in others.

Number five on Fesler's list of considerations is what he terms "administrative convenience." This includes travel time and costs in visiting offices, availability and cost of rental space, the work force available to man the office, etc.

The sixth and, as we shall soon see, perhaps the most important consideration is politics. A field office serving a congressman's district may prompt him to give the agency more support. Similarly, an office in each state may engender increased support in the Senate. However, this may also work to the agency's disadvantage, for "claims to patronage are always most insistent from political organizations and leaders whose constituencies embrace the total area within which a prospective appointee will have administrative jurisdiction." Fesler cites the controversies which arose during World War II over the selection of state directors of the OPA. A more contemporary illustration would be the inability of the Customs Bureau to close down operations in areas

322

where they are not needed. For example, there is little need to maintain a customs office in Rhode Island since so little international traffic comes through that state. Yet, political pressures, presumably emanating from the state's congressional delegation, have prevented the Customs Bureau from phasing out its Rhode Island operations.

CASE STUDY

The Federal Government Goes for Ten

The Departments of HEW, HUD and Labor, along with the Small Business Administration and the Office of Economic Opportunity, maintain substantial field office operations. Since the 1940's, there has been talk of realigning them. This sentiment grew more pronounced in the 1960's as the number of federal programs proliferated and the work of these agencies mounted.

Various reasons supported this sentiment. The first was the need for what was called "one-stop shopping." State and local officials had been voicing increasing complaints over the fact that they would often have to go to different cities to transact their business with the federal government because each department located its field office in different places. Bringing the field offices of the various federal agencies together in one place would cut down considerably the time and expense these officials sustained in dealing with these agencies. Then, the agencies themselves would benefit, it was felt, by having their regional offices in the same city, preferably under the same roof. Such an arrangement would encourage more cooperation or at least more communication between them. Finally, it would lay the basis for increased decentralization of authority since it would make it easier to provide overall areal leadership.

In 1967, the Bureau of the Budget prepared a draft report recommending that the regional offices of all these agencies be situated in the same cities and that their regions be made congruent with each other. This report led to a presidential order on March 27, 1969 promulgating such a realignment of regional headquarters and districts.

John E. Rouse, Jr. has studied the reorganization plan and how it fared when the Nixon administration attempted to implement it.[51] His study, plus a report by journalist John Fisher,[52] offers some interesting insights into the politics and administration of field office locations.

According to Rouse, the improvement in coordination between agencies with closely related activities which the realignment envisaged ran into two

---

51. John E. Rouse, Jr., "The Politics of Realignment of the Field Offices of the Social Agencies of the Federal Government," Paper presented at the annual convention, American Society of Public Administration, Los Angeles, 1973.

52. John Fischer, "Can the Nixon Administration Be Doing Something Right?" (The Easy Chair) *Harper's*, November 1970.

323

initial difficulties. One was the varying workloads that would occur from agency to agency if they were all to serve the same geographic region. The second was the start-up costs and other problems entailed in the transfer of personnel, staff recruitment and moving expenses.

The 1967 draft report had taken into account the fact that drawing up the new congruent regions would not be easy. The report had set forth the following factors to be considered in designating the new multi-purpose regions:

1. location and geographic dispersion of clientele;
2. distance or travel time between locations;
3. availability of work force;
4. distribution of workload;
5. mobilization requirements;
6. availability of space and real property;
7. political and economic impact;
8. relationship to other organizations;
9. existing political, economic and natural geographic boundaries.

These factors, it will be noted, not only parallel those mentioned by Fesler but also would apply, at least in part, to any state or local government seeking to accomplish the same purpose. A city, for example, would have to deal with many of the same considerations in establishing school districts, police precincts, etc.

Initial discussion within the federal bureaucracy on the proposed realignment centered on whether to divide up the nation into seven or eight regions. It would be seven if New England could be combined with New York State into one northeastern region. However, the New England congressional delegation insisted on a separate region for their six states. Consequently, it was decided to plan for eight regions and this was the number that was subsequently announced.

Now, however, some further political pressures appeared. The eight cities designated as regional headquarters under the plan were Boston, New York City, Atlanta, Chicago, San Francisco, Philadelphia, Denver and Fort Worth. The selection of the first five cities aroused no resistance. Boston had been selected to ward off an adverse reaction from the New England senators and congressmen; the other four cities were already serving as regional headquarters for the three cabinet departments. However, the choice of Philadelphia, Denver and Forth Worth ignited considerable controversy.

In the case of Philadelphia, there were three competitors for its designation as a regional headquarters. These were Washington, D.C., Chambersburg, Pennsylvania and Charlottesville, Virginia. Each of these three cities was already serving as a regional headquarters for at least one of the agencies involved. The Bureau of the Budget had given the nod to Philadelphia, however, for that city already housed the regional headquarters of two of the agencies with a combined work force of 700. Philadelphia also offered more administrative convenience in terms of transportation and accessibility than the other three cities with the exception of Washington itself and in Washington office space was scarce and expensive.

However, Charlottesville was not prepared to give up without a fight. The Virginia city's chamber of commerce pointed out that travel costs for the HEW headquarters already located in Charlottesville would be increased 35 percent if this office was moved to Philadelphia. And the costs of the actual move would in itself amount to a one-shot expenditure of $2.5 million. The Charlottesville advocates also maintained that their city could provide the needed new office space more easily and more cheaply than could the Pennsylvania metropolis.

The influential Virginia congressional delegation predictably sprang to Charlottesville's support. And the congressmen succeeded in gaining allies, particularly among the congressional delegations from North Carolina and Kentucky. These two states had been put into the region that was to be served by the Philadelphia headquarters. Their states would naturally prefer a headquarters situated in a state that was not only geographically but also culturally closer to their own.

On this issue, the administration was not so willing to yield. President Nixon and his crew rejuggled the scheme, transferring North Carolina and Kentucky to the southern region whose headquarters was to be in Atlanta. This caused the congressmen and senators from those two states to drop out of the fight and removed Charlottesville's main argument, i.e. its location. Without Kentucky and North Carolina in the region, the Virginia city found itself no longer in the region's center but in its southern half. Finally the city was given a military installation which did a great deal to ease the pain of loss.

A more severe problem emerged farther west. The Bureau of the Budget had decided to make Denver rather than Kansas City the headquarters of a region serving both cities despite the fact that Kansas City already had three regional headquarters while Denver had only two. In making its decision the bureau pointed out that Kansas City was situated in a corner of the designated region, more than 1,500 air miles from some of the region's major cities. Furthermore, air travel and auto routes generally made Kansas City less convenient than Denver.

However, the largely Democratic Missouri delegation teamed up with the largely Republican and hence, in terms of the Nixon administration, more influential Kansas delegation to oppose the BOB's plan. They not only presented an impressive political front but were also able to muster some impressive arguments to support their case. At a May hearing, they showed that:

more residents of the region lived within 400 miles of Kansas City than lived within a similar distance of Denver;

about 75 percent of all federal expenditures by OEO, Labor and HEW went to communities closer to Kansas City than to communities closer to Denver;

325

approximately two-thirds of all school children in the proposed eleven-state region lived nearer Kansas City than Denver;

approximately 65 percent of all the new region's Social Security offices were situated nearer Kansas City than Denver and these offices served more than twice as many beneficiaries.

Basing themselves on facts such as these, and wielding in addition considerable political clout, the two delegations demanded that Kansas City be made the headquarters for a new six-state region. They pointed out that such a region would still contain some 10 percent more people than New England which the bureau had previously accorded the status of a separate region. The BOB had little choice but to say yes.

The state of Washington was also eager to have a regional headquarters, and the state's two senators joined forces with the Kansas and Missouri delegations to press for the establishment of two new regions, one with its headquarters in Kansas City, the other with its headquarters in Seattle. The Seattle advocates lacked the strong factual case which underpinned the Kansas City argument, but in some respects they possessed almost greater political power. Senator Warren Magnuson was considered one of the Senate's most influential figures while Senator Henry Jackson was needed by Nixon to spearhead the administration's controversial Anti-Ballistic Missile program through the Senate.

The upshot was that on May 21, 1969, less than two months after he had announced his eight-region plan, President Nixon disclosed what was in effect a reorganization of his reorganization. It was now a ten-region plan with Kansas City and Denver serving as headquarters for two new regions and with Atlanta now serving as headquarters for an expanded southern region which included Kentucky and North Carolina. (The decision to make New England a separate region had been made prior to the first announcement.)

But although the original scheme had been modified, it had not been greatly damaged. "In summary," writes Rouse, "the ten-region realignment offers considerable potential for eventual decentralization within the American political scene, despite the difference in regional workload. The immediate result of realignment may mean a significant cost to the government. However, in the long run, the realignment should allow more efficient operation and delivery of government services."

The Follow-Up

A consolidated system of field offices is in itself no guarantee of adequate decentralization. The regional headquarters could serve as mere receptacles of various local inputs, passing them on to Washington for processing. Or they might process most of the work themselves but under guidelines so strict and tight that they would have comparatively little discretion. On the other hand, of course, the field offices might become too independent, operating at their own will and whim and neglecting and even subverting the goals of their agencies.

Since it was generally felt that the problem with the federal bureaucracy was that field offices had too little rather than too much authority, and since the basic goal of the reorganization was to allow them to do more, thereby easing the burden of work not only on Washington but also on themselves and their constituents (it will be recalled that too much centralization can increase everybody's work requiring much more processing and review up and down the line), the field office reorganization was followed up by further decentralization measures. Health services offer one example of how this was done.

On July 1, 1970, prior to taking formal steps in decentralizing health service administration, HEW announced the development of several "coordinating mechanisms." These included:

1. a new review-processing schedule for all decentralized grant-in-aid applications;
2. a new Regional Office Operations Manual to promulgate guidelines and provide information to the regional health directors;
3. provision for an in-house ad hoc study group, to be known as the Joint Staff Conference. Each regional health director would establish such a group to review all grant applications and make recommendations;
4. provision for the establishment of Health Services and Mental Health Administration (HSMHA) Regional Resources Teams to monitor the activities of those receiving grants and provide them with technical assistance where needed.[53]

As a result of HEW's decentralization drive and the "coordinating mechanisms" which it established to help make it work, the department was able to delegate to its regional health directors authority to administer twenty-four different types of grants-in-aid. The regional health administrators would still have to notify Washington of every grant they gave, but they would no longer have to secure Washington's prior approval, at least for those grants which fell within the twenty-four designated categories. The types of grants selected for such decentralized discretion numbered only 24 percent of all grants which the Health Services and Mental Health Administration distributed, but they accounted for three-quarters of all of HSMHA's grant dollars.

HEW Secretary Richardson stressed the role of evaluation in making the new decentralization work. He said it was now more urgent than ever before "to apply objective measures to the performances of our programs." (The reader will note the connection of decentralization with management by objectives discussed in the previous section.) Richardson also exhorted the department's Washington personnel to support the decentralization. In a briefing of main headquarters employees on December 17, 1971, he noted "If we are to be of maximum use to the front-line forces engaged in health and

---

53. Edward Montminy, "Decentralization at HEW," Unpublished paper, Department of Political Science, Northeastern University, 1972.

education and welfare services, we must make our support of those forces as accessible as possible, as flexible as possible and as adaptable as possible to the needs of their communities *as they perceive them.* It follows that our support functions must be moved up as close to the front as we can. This, in turn, requires that we place increasing reliance on our regional offices—that we give them the staffing, the authority and the resources necessary to enable them effectively to exploit their accessibility."[54] (Emphasis added.)

By 1973, the decentralization effort in Health Administration seemed to be yielding results. Grant requests that had taken up to 150 days were now, on the average, consuming no more than 50 days. Response in rendering technical assistance had also noticeably quickened. The amount of paper work was down by some 20 percent and the cost of grant administration overall had been reduced by an estimated 33 percent. Furthermore, morale and general efficiency in the field offices seem to have increased.

This is not to say that the new decentralization has been implemented without problems. Consistency was often lacking and some regional health directors were reluctant to make full use of their newly granted authority. But on balance, the decentralization seemed to be providing more benefits than costs to all concerned.

Turning to the Department of Housing and Urban Development, we find a similar story of at least partial success. For example, HUD formulated a set of eight criteria for evaluating applications for low-interest loans to construct low-rent housing. The criteria included such questions as the relationship of the projected housing to its physical environment, the record and reputation of the developers, the housing need in the area which it would serve. Armed with these criteria, regional offices could process many of these applications themselves. And they, in turn, were to pass on these criteria to their subunits to help them in making the initial determinations on such requests. Each regional administrator was given the final authority on all such applications.[55]

Adoption of the new system not only cut the time of processing applications by about one-half but also helped to screen out political influences and pressures. Political leaders now had to make sure that their pet projects could pass muster on the new criteria before they could expect a favorable reply.

Thanks to this expansion of the regional office's authority, conflicts and confusion are being handled more expediently and more successfully. The regional officials can use their new power to force mayors and other local officials to coordinate projects within their own jurisdictions and to settle their own disputes. For example, one regional official pointed out that the heads of the housing authority and the urban renewal authority of one city in his region came to see him about a problem. The housing authority head wanted a parcel of land for a housing project in one of the city's urban renewal areas but the urban renewal chief refused to give it to him. The

---

54. Quoted in Montminy, *ibid.*
55. Information obtained in an interview with a regional official of the Department of Housing and Urban Development who asked to remain anonymous.

regional officer told the two officials to straighten out their problem themselves or they would both lose their federal assistance. Within ten days, they had reached a satisfactory solution. "The irony is," said the regional official, "I had an almost identical problem involving these same two men a few years back and that time it dragged on for over a year and was never really resolved."[56]

As with HEW, the new decentralization at HUD has encountered difficulties. According to the regional official just cited, the agency still needs new forms, further internal reorganization and a better management information system that would provide officials with up-to-date data on the status of each application, project, etc. Also, many HUD employees need additional training in order to handle the widened, generalist responsibilities which the new decentralization calls for. But all in all, the decentralization must be judged a success. "Things are working better than they have in the past," he said, "and I am hopeful that they will work still better in the future."

---

56. *Ibid.*

10

The Challenges of Change

To many, the most distinctive feature of the modern age, the one which demarcates it most heavily from previous times, is its rapid pace of change. Ours is an age where alteration and amendment, mutation and permutation, have become the natural order of events. Innovation seems to follow innovation at an accelerating rate and the individual who fails to adjust to successive shifts in the pattern of his existence may soon find himself outmoded.

What holds true for the individual holds equally true for the organization. It, too, finds itself caught up in the currents of change and it can hope to shield itself from its onslaughts only at the risk of atrophy and decay. Today's organization must do a good degree of running simply to stand in the same place; to move forward requires still greater exertions.

Unfortunately, as we noted in chapter four, such flexibility rarely comes easily to an organization. Katz and Kahn have pointed out that an organization naturally tends to proceed on the principle that it is easier for the world to adjust to it than for it to adjust to the world. When change in the external environment causes the organization to malfunction, it tends to assign the blame to the external forces rather than undertake internal alterations to correct the problem.

This natural reluctance to change becomes especially noticeable in the administrative sphere. Although technical changes may be welcome since they are more easily demonstrable and provable and may not involve emotional and personal values, administrative changes strike much deeper and may affect those things which the organization holds most dear. As Katz and Kahn note, this tendency parallels the response of an individual.[1] A person may easily discard his icebox for a refrigerator and give up his car for a better one. However, he will not so lightly yield his political and religious beliefs. The same holds true for organizations. They also possess ideologies, attitudes and patterns of behavior which they do not lightly surrender.

This aversion to administrative change is particularly marked in public organizations. With private companies, change is often a *sine qua non* of survival. For example, in an age of automobiles, a buggy whip manufacturer who insists on turning out the same product will find it hard to meet his payroll. A public organization is not usually confronted with the same bracing pressures. On the contrary, public organizations may actually come under pressures to retain the status quo. These pressures are not just internal, such as resistance by their employees to alter their patterns of performance, but external as well. An organization's clientele or its political overseers or both may want things to stay the way they are.

Consequently, public organizations have often found the task of transforming themselves to accommodate the winds of change to be difficult indeed. Many have avoided the task almost completely. However, an increasing number of public agencies are becoming cognizant of the fact that they do so at their peril. In the face of the growing hostility to public organizations, and in the face of their increasingly apparent inability to meet the challenges which confront them, they are starting to stir themselves out of the ruts and routines into which they so easily become enmeshed. They are increasingly feeling the need to make innovation a part of their way of life.

PPBS, productivity measures, management by objectives and many of the other emerging developments in public administration help to stimulate and support the forces of change. In this chapter, we will examine other mechanisms that are more specifically oriented toward this end. These devices are diverse and disparate and their examination will take us into varying aspects of administrative activity. Yet, they all have some capability for responding to the freshening currents now coursing through the corridors of contemporary organizational life.

AGENTS OF CHANGE: PLANNING

The last quarter-century has witnessed a great growth in government planning. Such nations as France, Sweden and Japan have developed highly articulated techniques for anticipating future economic and so-

---

1. Katz and Kahn, *The Social Psychology of Organizations,* p. 92.

cial problems and for preparing to meet them. These nations have generally been rewarded with high rates of economic growth and increasing prosperity. Many business firms have also learned how to plan, and the ones that have planned the best have often fared the best. IBM is only one of the more notable examples.

Planning also has much to offer public administration. Here, as elsewhere, planning permits the organization not only to anticipate and prepare for change but also, at least to some extent, to select and shape such change as will come. Planning offers a way of institutionalizing vision and stabilizing innovation. It permits the future to shape the past rather than the opposite. An organization that plans is an organization that, at least theoretically, has accepted the value and necessity of change.

The role of planning, it should be stressed, is not just to encourage change but to encourage proper change. When new equipment for learning languages came on the market, many schools rushed to buy it. They often set up "language labs" with a full-fledged array of audio-visual apparatus without weighing carefully the merits of the various devices and, more importantly, without defining, or redefining, their long-term goals in language instruction. As a result, these expensive language labs failed to yield results commensurate with their costs. Proper planning could have prevented this, for it cannot only facilitate change but can forestall change that is too rapid or too little considered.

Planning can also be a way of sparing the organization the abrupt changes which may occur through any number of events, such as a change in leadership. It can smooth out a transitional process and allow it to take place in a way that will not shatter or shake the organization in a traumatic manner.

In helping to deal with the problems of change, planning can also help the organization in other ways. It can and should stimulate the minds of its members, jogging their brains and leading them to discover new ways of doing things. Planning, like all change, can create tensions, to be sure. But in many instances these will be tensions that were festering long before the change was contemplated. Planning may only bring them to the surface where they can be dealt with. At the same time, planning can also reduce various strains and stresses within the organization for it may modify annoying conditions and alleviate monotony. "The quest for a change of pace by people caught in routinized jobs, the introduction of elements of risk or uncertainty in situations providing only a boring regularity," writes Wilbert E. Moore, "offer testimony to the need for change as a way of alleviating strain as well as a source of further tension."[2]

---

2. Wilbert E. Moore, *The Conduct of the Corporation* (New York: Random House, 1962), p. 191.

Planning, properly conceived and executed, also provides two further benefits for the employees of the organization. One of these is increased participation, the role of which we will be examining shortly. The second is predictability. The employees now have a better idea of what to expect and can make their personal plans accordingly. As Herbert Simon has noted, "A major purpose of the planning and organizing that precedes any administrative activity is not merely to put each participant in the job he can best fill, but to permit each to form accurate expectations as to what others are going to do."[3] Simon was speaking only of the casual planning required in all administrative operations. More developed planning enables an employee to decide more intelligently just what role he may want to play in the organization in the future or whether he wants to play any role at all.

Planning also affords management an additional tool for evaluating the employee. Innovation, so it seems, is one way of helping to sift the wheat from the chaff for, generally speaking, it will be the better employees who will be the ones to respond most positively to the challenges of change. In a federal agency studied by Peter Blau, most of the less competent half of the employees resisted changes in the agency's rules and regulations. The more competent employees welcomed such changes. Ironically, then, those agents who were the most adept at working with the existing procedures were the ones who were the most willing to see these procedures altered or eliminated. Change appeals to the more capable, and an organization that accepts the need for change by making planning an integral part of its operations is one that is more likely to recruit and retain capable employees.

The Planning Process
Planning in the public sector encounters many obstacles. In addition to the problems of administrative conservatism noted earlier, there is the problem of administrative personality. "Administrators," C. P. Snow has written, "are by temperament active men. Their tendency, which is strengthened by the nature of their job, is to live in the short term, to become masters of the short-term solution."[4] Ron A. Webber, in his book *Time and Management,* echoes the same belief and develops it more fully. Managers, he says, believe in keeping busy and actually acquire guilt feelings when they are not bustling with activity. Planning, on the other hand, requires thought and contemplation. It also requires an expenditure of resources for results which will not be immediately realizable. Furthermore, the future is always uncertain and ambiguous,

---

3. Simon, *Administrative Behavior,* pp. 71–72.
4. Snow, *Science and Government,* p. 73.

and formulating plans for it can be not only difficult but even threatening.

Why threatening? According to Webber,

> The threat is two-fold: first, because managers tend to fear the kind of time necessary for such thought; it must be unstructured, open and seemingly ill-directed—all attributes which run counter to time-haunted, efficiency-minded men. Wide open time like space can be frightening. Second, incorporating concern about the future into the present necessitates clarifying what we really want, and this means defining fundamental values of management, organizations and society.[5]

These problems may loom particularly large in American administration. "Our difficulty," writes Townsend Hoopes, "is that, as a nation of short-term pragmatists accustomed to dealing with the future only when it has become the present, we find it hard to regard future trends as serious realities. We have not achieved the capacity to experience as real and urgent—as demanding action today—problems which appear in critical dimension only at some future date."[6] Hoopes believes that our lack of planning greatly helped to entrap us into the Vietnam quagmire.

The American administrator who hopes to plan faces still other problems beyond those of his own and others' temperaments. The American political system with its deep fragmentation of authority makes administrative planning difficult and even dangerous. No matter how large the agency and no matter how sweeping its mandate of authority, it rarely can carry out meaningful planning without concurrences and clearances from numerous other sources. Annual budgets further tend to crimp administrative planning, for an agency can seldom be sure of what its financial resources will be from one year to the next. Political appointments complicate the planning process still more, for they can lead to abrupt changes in agency leadership and agency policy. Finally, planning, if not handled with political astuteness, can put an agency on a collision course with its legislative overseers. A legislator, concerned with his power and prerogatives, may regard the planning function as a threat to his right to exercise continual supervision and influence over agency actions.

Nevertheless, despite all these and other constraints, administrative planning, even in a system such as ours, can take place. The first planning task is the most obvious but often the most difficult one,

---

5. Ron A. Webber, *Time and Management* (New York: Van Nostrand Reinhold, 1972), pp. 160-161.
6. Hoopes, *The Limits of Intervention*, p. 1.

namely deciding what the goals of the organization really are and what they should be. What are the purposes of our organization? What should it be doing? What does the public really want us to do? These are only some of the questions which must be answered before planning can begin.

Successful planning next requires information, a great deal of information. To begin with, the planners have to find out all they can about their own organization, its purposes and policies, its culture and characteristics, its strengths and weaknesses. Then they must find out what other organizations like their own are doing and what successes or setbacks these organizations are experiencing and why. At the same time they must also keep tabs on the doings and designs of organizations which are not like their own but which can affect their organization's activities in many ways. And finally, the planners have to know the total environment in which their organization functions. They must acquire an awareness of what is going on in society and an appreciation of how the changes occurring in society may influence their organization's future. Thus, before anything else, planning is an information-gathering function.

To meet this information need, planning requires large-scale participation. All the organization's members, from those at the very bottom to those at the very top, will usually have something to contribute to the planning process. At the operating levels, the front lines, so to speak, people see the specific problems much more clearly. Even if it is assumed that they lack the education and development to make proper evaluations, an assumption that is often incorrect, they still will have a kind of knowledge that those higher up will almost never be able to attain. The lowly porter who pushes a mop through the corridors will have perspectives and insights into the organization's physical plant that even the supervisor of maintenance will lack.

In its quest for information, the planning process must reach up as well as down, for top management also has a role to play in this initial phase. People at the top often have a better view of the "broader picture." They can more easily grasp the interconnections between components of the organization. They can, or at least they should, be able to see much more fully the relationship of the organization to its environment. Successful planning thus requires that all elements of the organization be brought into the process.

There is yet another reason why successful planning requires large-scale participation. Good plans are nothing in themselves; to acquire significance, they must be implemented. This, in turn, requires a measure of acceptance from all levels of the organization. Employees who have had a chance to share in the formulation of plans will gener-

335

ally be more willing to implement them, even when the ideas that are finally adopted go contrary to their wishes, for at least their own ideas will have been heard and in most cases some accommodation will have been made to their concerns. Here, too, the participation of those at the upper levels as well as those at the bottom is important, for if those at the top have not been actively involved in the planning process, they may evince little enthusiasm for the results of that process. "Real and lasting change requires the sustained involvement of top management," writes Argyris, and he notes that an executive who has helped design the new system is more likely to make an "internal commitment" to its realization.[7]

The requirement of wide-scale participation in order to meet these information and implementation needs obviously becomes a determining factor in setting up the organizational arrangements and apparatus for planning. An organization may create an office staffed with full-time employees expressly for the purpose of planning. Or it may set up one or more committees of employees whose full-time assignments lie elsewhere in the organizational nexus. Or it may use any combination or variation of these two approaches. But in any case, those who do the planning must seek to involve as large a proportion of the organization's membership as fully as possible in the planning process.

One device developed by Floyd Mann and his colleagues at the University of Michigan's Survey Research Center calls for setting up what are called organizational "families." Each such family consists of a supervisor and those reporting to him. This means that each supervisor actually belongs to two families, the one consisting of himself and his subordinates and another consisting of his colleagues and his own superior. Such a system establishes linkages up, down, and, to some extent, across the organization and provides feedback to guide the planning process. Each organizational "family" enjoys discretion to consider and work out the implications of matters at its own level though the designation of the basic problem areas may come from above. This device has been used successfully in many instances.[8]

The "family" system satisfies another requisite for good planning besides the participation necessary to meet its information and implementation needs. This is the opportunity it creates for those who do the planning to execute it. This relates to the implementation problem but carries it one step forward. Just as it is important for those who are to execute the plans to have some say in their formulation, so is it important for those who formulate the plans to participate in their execution.

---

7. Chris Argyris, "The CEO's Behavior: Key to Organizational Development," *Harvard Business Review,* March–April 1973.
8. Katz and Kahn, *op. cit.,* p. 418.

A planning staff or a planning committee should not go out of existence once the plans have been made. They should continue on, assisting in the implementation of the plans and continually checking on their status. As Henry Taylor noted over a century ago, "There are few things more important in the business of the state than that the results of inquiry and research should be realized by those who have had the conduct of it."[9] In other words, the planning function cannot be strictly demarcated from the operating function. Those who execute must plan and those who plan must execute. A planning group not actively involved *as a planning group* in the fulfillment of its plans will soon fail to function properly.

The reasons for this stipulation are many. In being allowed and even required to play a role in the implementation of their plans, the planners acquire a more realistic awareness of the problems involved. This should in itself result in better formulated plans. Furthermore, it will spare the planners the agony of seeing their efforts dissipated through the errors of those who lack the knowledge of, or the commitment to, these efforts. If the policies adopted strike a sudden snag, then those who were most instrumental in drafting the policies should be best prepared to modify or adapt them to the needs of the situation. Successful planning is not an isolated exercise.

Although actively involving the planners in the implementation of their plans should place some realistic constraints on their planning activities, in general the planners should enjoy a great deal of discretion. The best planning takes place under conditions of maximum freedom. Planning groups should work within the confines of prescribed goals and guidelines but these should be kept as broad as possible. Restricting the lines of inquiry will tend to restrict the results.

In utilizing their discretion, planners should take into account two important but often neglected aspects of the planning process. The first is the need for alternative plans in the event that one or more basic elements of the initial plan become outmoded or in some other way do not prove successful. Given the uncertain environment within which the planning process takes place, and given the variety of variables which may influence its outcome, plans should be kept fluid and flexible, subject, almost like an airline schedule, to change without notice.

A good example of this failure to have contingency plans occurred when Congress in 1971 killed the long worked-on plans for the supersonic transport plane. Following the SST's congressional defeat, it soon became appallingly apparent that the plane's backers both within and without the government had devised no arrangements to deal with

---

9. Taylor, *The Statesman*, p. 123.

such a setback. They were completely unprepared for such tasks as finding jobs for the 14,000 workers who had been employed on the project, disposing of $850 million worth of hardware, patents and blueprints, and liquidating the numerous obligations and contracts which the project had created. "At every level of government," wrote the *New York Times,* "the new questions were being discussed in a mood of general confusion and incredulity that the long SST fight was over. One federal official commented, 'I can't comprehend that there was never a Plan B, but it's obvious now that nobody ever considered the chance of an SST defeat.'"[10] A good planning group will always have a plan B ready, and possibly a plan C as well.

Another aspect of planning that is often neglected is the decision of what *not* to do. This involves not simply rejecting ideas for future action but also eliminating things which the organization is already doing. According to Robert Townsend, "It's about eleven times as easy to start something as it is to stop something," and he urges all organizations to "make it a practice to wipe out their worst product, service or activity every so often."[11] We have, in earlier chapters, called attention to such bureaucratic pathologies as the tendency to resist elimination or even modification of any function and to such leadership failures as the reluctance to "slough off yesterday." Good planning is designed to reduce these and other perversities in organizational life.

The Tools and Techniques of Planning

If planning, to paraphrase Thomas Hobbes, is characterized by a perpetual and restless desire for information, a quest that ceases only with the death of the planning group or its parent organization, then how is this information to be obtained?

The starting place in most instances is the organization's own records. What are its expenditures for various activities and how are these related to results? This is an obvious key question. It shows the relationship which fruitful planning has to proper budgeting whether it is programed budgeting or some other system. Well-developed and well-utilized accounting practices are also mandatory. In short, the planners must have a good grasp of what the organization is currently doing and how it is doing it if they are to map a path for the future.

However, many other sources of information exist besides those which are linked to the organization's budgetary and accounting process. Complaints, for example, form a valuable planning resource. So do requests for service. A police department planning unit will want to

---

10. *New York Times,* March 26, 1971.
11. Townsend, "Up the Organization."

keep a careful check on the quantity and variety of police calls and it will also go over the various reports submitted by patrolmen, detectives, etc. An urban renewal agency will want to study the number and kinds of applications it receives, along with their eventual disposition. And both agencies will want to carefully tabulate and evaluate the complaints they receive.

In making such studies, the planners will usually want more than just a picture of what is happening at one moment in time. In cataloguing and classifying police calls, for example, they will want to compare one year with the previous year and possibly with other still more previous years. In this way, they may be able to detect possible trends. For example, if the number of calls involving family disputes is rising every year, this could indicate a need for providing patrolmen with special training to cope with such problems. (Of course, straight-line projections of current trends can be hazardous and should always be subject to close evaluation of all the factors involved.)

Surveys of one kind or another can also help meet the information needs of planning and help satisfy its participation requirements as well. Organizational planners will want to obtain inputs from as many members of the organization as they can and often a survey is the only means for doing so. In making such surveys, employees may be interviewed individually or may simply be asked to fill out a form. At some stage of the planning process, however, it is usually advisable to have all those who will be affected by the plans participate in a dialogue regarding them. This is more apt to bring out information hitherto undisclosed and to ease the task of subsequent implementation.

Such surveys should not be confined to people within the organization. It is important and often imperative to involve the agency's clientele in the information process as well, for they obviously have aspects and angles that will be worth considering. Furthermore, their cooperation may be as crucial to making the plans work as the cooperation of the organization's own employees.

This restless and relentless quest for information will not stop at the organization's boundaries. As was noted earlier, the planners will normally reach out into the organization's total environment. They should examine what other organizations are doing through writing letters, paying on-site visits, going over the reports of these organizations and reading about their activities in journals that cover their affairs. They will also want to know what plans these organizations are making for their own future. Finally, the planners will show some interest and concern in finding out what is happening and what is likely to happen in society which could in some way influence their future course.

Once they have amassed all this information, they then face the

339

formidable task of digesting it. Here, they will find it necessary to establish some sort of system for classifying all these inputs. This should assist them in arriving at certain quantitative assumptions regarding what it has to reveal. And this, in turn, will enable the planners to utilize it more effectively. Some information can even be fed into a computer which can be programed to calculate a wide range of consequences and consider a wide range of alternatives. The final decisions, however, will always have to be made by the individuals concerned.

However, even if all the safeguards regarding information gathering and assessment along with participation are zealously and minutely followed, planning will still remain a risky business. Future events can seldom be foretold with complete accuracy and the effects of planned developments can often be quite different from what was anticipated. This state of affairs frequently leads a planning group to undertake one or more experiments before finalizing their planning efforts.

One great advocate of the need for experimentation was Franklin Roosevelt. "It is common sense," he once said, "to take a method and try it; if it fails, admit it frankly and try another. But above all, try something."[12] Experimentation, at least on occasion, is indispensable to productive planning.

Experimentation often takes the form of a demonstration project. The organization will try out an idea in one of its subunits or on one sector of its clientele to see how it works. Then, it assesses the results and determines whether or not the new concept is essentially workable, and, if it is, what further modifications or amplifications may be necessary to put it into practice. Demonstrations may also serve a further purpose, one that may be more important than that of providing the organization with information as to a new idea's workability. This is the persuasive function. The demonstration may help to convince the organization's employees, clientele or political overseers that the new way of doing things is sound and helpful. In this way, the demonstration may help break down resistance to, and generate support for, the planned change. (It goes without saying that the demonstration project can also serve a contrary purpose. It may be used to demonstrate to one or more employee, clientele or political groups that an idea which they are urging upon the organization is unsound and unworkable.)

Demonstration projects are not, however, without problems of their own. It is difficult, for one thing, to find a "pure" situation. The scientist in his laboratory can carry out an experiment free of any external conditions which could influence the experiment's outcome. The social scientist rarely enjoys such a happy state of affairs. For example, a

---

12. Perkins, *The Roosevelt I Knew.*

new idea may be tried out in field office A and may be found to have worked successfully. But field office A may be different in one or more respects from field office B. Its employees may be more eager for change, its clientele may be less organized to resist change, its geographic location may lend itself to the proposed change. Consequently, the fact that the demonstration goes well in field office A does not necessarily signal its success as an organization-wide policy.

This problem is further compounded by what has come to be known as the "Hawthorne effect." The reader will recall from chapter four how the group of working girls who were put in the testroom during the experiments conducted at Western Electric's Hawthorne plant responded positively to nearly every change that was made in their working conditions. Similarly, field office A, if asked to try out a planned change, may make the change work more effectively than it otherwise would simply because the office knows it is being watched. The fact that it is engaged in an experiment makes the field office function differently than it would if it were simply adjusting to a change which was being implemented throughout the organization.

These difficulties, it should be kept in mind, encumber experimentation in other fields besides administrative planning. In medicine they have prompted experimenters to create what is sometimes called the "double-blind" study. Under the double-blind approach, one group of test subjects receives the medicine while the other receives placebos and neither the test subjects nor those conducting the test know which are which. Such a method was used at the Universities of Toronto and Strathclyde in 1972 to test the efficacy of vitamin C in preventing colds. Only after they had made up their lists of those student volunteers who had gotten colds and those who had not and had tabulated how long and how severe the colds were did the researchers as well as the students learn which students had received the vitamin C.

Demonstration projects in administrative planning usually require safeguards such as these if they are to yield valid results. In the case of the California State Insurance Compensation Fund referred to briefly in a previous chapter, proposed changes were first tried out at a field office. However, two other field offices were established as "controls." One of these field offices was told that it was serving as a basis of comparison; the other was not. In this way, the experimenters were able to eliminate, or at least allow for, the influences of the Hawthorne effect.[13]

Even when such steps are taken, however, result evaluation in

---

13. Berkley, *The Administrative Revolution* (1971), p. 29.

administrative demonstration projects can be troublesome. One basic difficulty consists in finding definitive ways of measuring the results. We have already covered these snags and snarls in our discussions of PPBS, productivity measures and MBO. It goes almost without saying that demonstration projects, and indeed, virtually all administrative planning requires some systematic and sound method for evaluating results, and an organization will have a hard time planning successfully unless it confronts and conquers this particular problem. But assuming that an organization has done so, it still has to deal with another difficulty. It takes time to run a demonstration project and to calculate costs and benefits. Sometimes, by the time the final report is ready, the situation has changed to the point where the contemplated plan would no longer be applicable. And so the planners have to start all over again, hoping that this time they will not be overtaken by events.

One final problem remains for the evaluators. This is the need to distinguish between short-term and long-term results. Sometimes they can be quite different. For example, an organization might try out a system of tighter supervision which in the short term might produce substantial benefits in terms of reduced waste and increased output. Yet, the long-term effects could prove disastrous as the better workers, chafing under such constraints, leave the organization while others turn hostile and begin sabotaging it. It is sometimes necessary to show short-term results in order to convince the organization, its clients or its political overseers that something is being accomplished. But it is also necessary to exercise caution and care lest such considerations weaken or even wipe out long-term achievement.

Putting the Plan to Work

As was noted earlier, planning does not stop when the proposed change or changes are finally drawn up, packaged and handed on for implementation. The planning process must include the implementing process as well. And not only should the planners help execute their plans, they should even draw up plans for such execution.

One tool which has evolved to assist in this task is PERT, an acronym which stands for program evaluation and review technique. PERT was developed by the navy's Special Projects Office to implement the service's newly authorized ballistics missile program. According to Professor Harvey Sapolsky, it is characterized by four main features. The first is "a network that geographically describes the inter-relationship of steps (called events) involved in developing a specific end item." The second consists of "three time estimates for reaching each event in the network." These estimates are categorized as the most optimistic, the most likely and the most pessimistic. Then, a formula is arrived at "for

NETWORK DIAGRAM

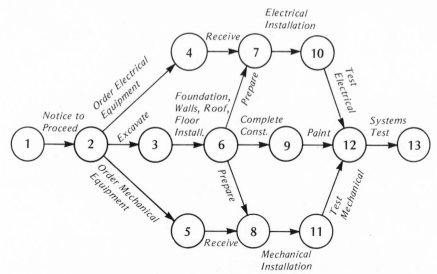

This is a sample PERT chart which could have been drawn up to construct a building. The numbers stand for events while the arrows signify the activities necessary for reaching the events. Note that after event 2, three arrows branch out simultaneously to events 3, 4 and 5. This means that these activities can be undertaken at the same time. (In PERT parlance, this is called a "burst point.") The "merge point" occurs at 12. The "critical path" is the longest path through the network yet it represents the shortest time possible for completing the program. Can you think of why? (See diagram on next page for answer.) (Source: U.S. Civil Service Commission.)

calculating the probability distribution of the 'expected' time for completing the expected activity." Finally, the implementers identify "the longest expected time sequence through the network, which is labeled 'the critical path.'" It is understood that the total project will not be realized until this critical path has been completed.[14]

This new technique seemed to have worked well for the navy during the 1950's and gradually became adopted by other agencies. NASA has made use of it in the development and construction of its space vehicles as well as in its moon shot program. Even private industry has perked up its ears and borrowed at least some of its techniques. For example, the DuPont Chemical Company now sets up a critical path for various projects and then calculates the variances along the "path" to

---

14. Sapolsky, *The Polaris System Development* . . . , Chapter 4.

CRITICAL PATH DETERMINATION

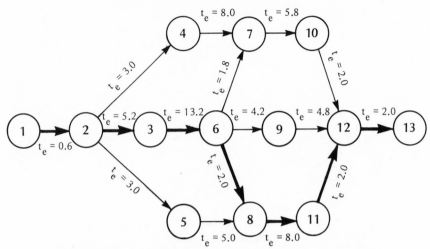

The symbol t_e simply represents the estimated time necessary to reach an event while the figures stand for units of time which can be days, weeks, months or even years. The critical path consists of 1, 2, 3, 6, 8, 11, 12 and 13. If any other route is used, it would not provide enough time for all the events to be realized. (If we proceed from 6 to 9 to 12, we would reach event 13, or completion, more rapidly but we would not leave enough time to complete events 8 through 11 though we would be able to achieve events 7 and 10.) The chart shows us, among other things, that it would be unwise to pay overtime to complete events 7 and 10 earlier since they are not on the critical path. Can PERT be used in other activities, such as planning a dinner party? (Source: U.S. Civil Service Commission.)

determine the probability of finishing on schedule. However, the company uses only one time estimate per task along the way, not the three that are utilized by the navy.

Sapolsky, who has written a scholarly study on the navy's use of PERT, claims it was largely a public relations stunt and "had little to do with the effectiveness of the effort to develop the polaris" submarine. He presents strong evidence to support his claim and, in fact, the loud hosannas which were originally sung to the new system have begun to die down. However, it does tend to encourage more systematic thinking, and its basic approach can lead to improved results.

As an example of how the PERT approach can work, New York City found in 1966 that its capital construction program was floundering. It was taking the city government ten years or more to build a school, hospital or other major capital facility. The site-selection and planning phase alone frequently consumed more than five years. A study of the problem showed that such construction would often involve twelve or more different agencies, most of them operating under strict state regulations. As a result, the process of building a new school required some 4,000 separate steps. By the time the process was completed, population changes, technological innovations or political realignments may have made the completed facility somewhat outmoded.

The following year the city set up its Capital Construction Information System to provide monthly reports on progress and completion projections for 2,300 projects. Milestones for each project were established and monthly progress reviews were prepared for the officials bearing responsibility for them. The mayor also named a single director of construction for projects under control of City Hall. Planning and construction time for capital projects was cut almost in half as a result.[15]

The New York City system lacks, of course, some of the main features of PERT and may seem in some respects more closely related to MBO which was discussed in the previous chapter. Actually, it is related to both and, as such, serves to show how deeply interrelated so many elements in the administrative process are. A clear understanding and an ability to cope with these manifold interrelationships can help administration and administrators meet the challenges of change.

AGENTS OF CHANGE: SENSITIVITY TRAINING

Organizational change imposes a certain amount of change on the organization's members. And just as the organization cannot cope intelligently with change unless it knows itself fairly thoroughly, neither can the individual member. To promote this self-knowledge which is desirable not just for smoothing the processes of change but for dealing with the stresses and strains of everyday organizational existence, many organizations have made use of a new human relations tool called sensitivity training.

Sensitivity training was developed by the National Training Laboratories for Group Development, a division of the National Education Association. The training itself is performed by means of a training group often referred to as the T-Group. This unit consists of approximately ten to sixteen people including one, and occasionally two, trainers. The group may meet intensively for a whole weekend or for one

---

15. Hamilton, "Productivity: The New York City Approach."

and a half to two hours each day over a period of two weeks, or in any variation of these two approaches. The purpose is to teach the participants human relations communications and leadership skills.[16]

How do they seek to accomplish this? Essentially by trying to help each member of the group gain a better grasp of the thoughts and feelings of others and of himself. It attempts to do this by establishing what Warren G. Bennis calls a "counter-culture." More specifically, it encourages the participants to interact freely and openly with others, letting the others know what he really thinks and feels about them and in the process learning what the others think and feel about him.

The T-Group operates without an agenda, rules of procedure or structure of any kind. Instead, the trainer, who is usually a qualified psychologist or even psychiatrist, will begin by calling the participants' attention to the fact that they are assembled to learn from each other and that they will proceed in any way which they, the members of the group, feel will be helpful. Confronted with such an ambiguous situation, the members respond as they see fit.

The primary aim of the training session is to foster what might be called authenticity. The members are encouraged to set aside the defenses and facades of everyday life and open themselves up to the group learning experience. As NTL Research Director Charles Seashore has put it, "Each participant is responsible for his own learning. What a person learns depends upon his own style, readiness and the relationship he develops with other members of the group." Seashore singles out the experiential role of T-Groups in promoting the self-learning process. "Most learning is a combination of experience and conceptualization," he says. "A major T-Group aim is to provide a setting in which individuals are encouraged to examine their experiences together in enough detail so that valid generalizations can be drawn."[17]

The role of authenticity in allowing this to happen is cardinal. "A person is most free to learn when he establishes authentic relationships with other people and thereby increases his sense of self-esteem and decreases his defensiveness," says Seashore. "In authentic relationships persons can be open, honest, and direct with one another so that they are communicating what they are actually feeling rather than masking their feelings."[18]

Obviously the achievement of such ends does require some guidance and assistance and here is where the trainer comes in. Although he will refrain from clamping any preconceived structure or

---

16. "Commonly Asked Questions About Sensitivity Training," *Management Forum,* XIX, no. 4 (December 1969).
17. Charles Seashore, "What Is Sensitivity Training?" *Management Forum,* no. 2 (June 1968).
18. *Ibid.*

method of operation on the group, and although he will scrupulously avoid trying to manipulate it, he will help the participants, in Seashore's words, "to focus on the way the group is working, the style of an individual's participation, or the issues that are facing the group." To accomplish this, he may at times encourage nonverbal communication such as body movement, dramatic improvisation and the use of art materials. He may also suggest exercises which are like games but which have serious learning goals.

The T-Group movement started during the late 1940's, began to take hold during the fifties and enjoyed a burst of popularity during the sixties. By the seventies, however, interest in this approach had begun to dim. Responsible for this waning affection were the disappointments and occasional disasters which the movement seemed to have caused.

The disasters came about when the T-Groups were used as a substitute for psychotherapy and were conducted by trainers who were not adequately trained. Participants with severe psychological problems were thus sometimes harmed by the emotional unmasking which goes on in such sessions. (Although even in these cases, advocates of sensitivity training could argue that the participant who emerged from the sessions emotionally overwrought was learning at least some of the dimensions of his own problems. He was therefore more likely to seek psychotherapeutic or other assistance as a result of his T-Group experience.)

The disappointments came about largely, perhaps, because sensitivity training was oversold and sometimes improperly done. As for the latter, Dr. Stanley G. Klein, a Boston psychologist, points out that the qualifications needed for a trainer cannot be easily acquired. Not only should the trainer be a trained psychologist but he should also have a fair degree of experience in T-Group work. Another important requirement that is often overlooked, says Klein, is that sensitivity training will not work unless the participants are participating of their own free will. No one should take part in a T-Group unless he or she really wants to. If the participant is taking part because of pressures, no matter how subtle, from his colleagues or superiors to do so, the experience will usually have negligible or even negative effects.[19]

However, even when all these requirements are met, sensitivity training has often failed to yield the results expected of it. Katz and Kahn claim that such problems are often due to the fact that it works on the individual and not the organization. If the individual emerges with a heightened sense of self-awareness and with potentially better skills for coping with human relationships, the organization may only suc-

---

19.   Berkley (1971), *op. cit.,* p. 77.

ceed in snuffing them out. When the individuals return to their old structures, they step back into the same definitions of their roles, say these authors. What is more basic, these roles are intimately related with a number of other organizational roles; the converted returnee may want to re-define his way of functioning, but the expectations of superiors, subordinates and colleagues have not changed, nor has there been a change in organizational sanctions or rewards. As a result, the T-Group participant finds himself slipping back into his old patterns of behavior.[20]

One way of remedying this situation is to involve top management in the sensitivity training process. Only through helping them attain the insights which T-Groups are designed to impart will enough change be introduced into the organization itself to allow the change which the other members have experienced to become realized. Thus, to be successful, a sensitivity training program must involve those at the top as well as those below.

But here, too, problems may yet arise. Argyris tells of doing a follow-up study of a group of company presidents who had attended one or more T-Group sessions. One of them had actually participated in seven. Argyris says he found in analyzing tape recordings of the sessions that while the chief executives did pretty well in "owning up" themselves, they did poorly in getting others to "own up." "In other words, no chief executive's behavior in the sample was of the type to encourage human and organizational development. They did not invite others to share responsibilities, did not develop cooperative relationships, and did not present opportunities for others to take the initiative and assume new responsibilities." Nevertheless, Argyris notes that in a few cases "the chief executive was able to change significantly, and his new leadership style helped some of the vice presidents to 'unfreeze.' His insights started chain reactions that continued throughout the organization."[21]

Argyris claims that this would happen much more frequently if T-Groups were better arranged and conducted. The most important factor in inhibiting change, he says, is that most sensitivity laboratories last only one week and this is too short a time for most people to learn new behavior and "internalize patterns that will not vanish under stress." Attending several different T-Group sessions does not help matters, he says, because one does not build on the other. It takes a T-Group with continuity to score a significant impact on organizational behavior.

Given all these requirements, sensitivity training can help to

---

20. Katz and Kahn, *op cit.*
21. Argyris, *op. cit.*

change individuals and the organizations they serve. The effect will in most cases not be as great as early enthusiasts of the movement believed, but it can be useful and further development of the device may make it more so. As Katz and Kahn express it, "The organizational T-Group, in short, is a promising development, but its properties and potentialities require continuing exploration and research evaluation."[22]

AGENTS OF CHANGE: INTERDEPARTMENTAL COMMITTEES

Let us assume that a city manager suddenly finds that a particular neighborhood in his city is suffering from an outbreak of teenage crime and general juvenile misbehavior. He definitely wants to do something about it. What should he do?

Several suggestions come to mind: consult the neighborhood institutions, the parents and even the teenagers themselves. But in order for their ideas to be sifted, refined and, most important of all, implemented, the city government must come into play. Which agency of the government should this be? Although the police would seem to be the most directly concerned, they have neither the resources nor the capacity to deal with the problem in a deep and comprehensive manner. What now?

One solution would be to set up an interdepartmental committee. Such a committee could include representatives from the police, the school department, the parks and/or recreation department, the health department, the welfare department and any other agency that might have some input to make in diagnosing the problem and some contribution to make in alleviating it. Working with neighborhood groups and citizens, they could jointly undertake a program of what might be termed "meaningful change."

In ways such as this, an interdepartmental committee can serve as an agent of change. It is a device that frequently serves other functions, of course, primarily those of coordination and adjudication. It is particularly useful in dealing with disputes involving jurisdiction, i.e., determining which agency has authority in which area. It can also serve, as we shall shortly see, as a means of preventing or forestalling change. But despite such other and sometimes contradictory functions, interdepartmental committees have been and are used for adapting organizations to new problems and new processes.

In a sense, the interdepartmental committee has a long history in American administration, for its origins go back to the beginnings of the

---

22. Katz and Kahn, *op. cit.,* p. 406.

republic. The president's cabinet is, at least to some extent, such a committee, and George Washington, who took his cabinet fairly seriously, used it for this purpose. However, the really great growth of interdepartmental committees occurred during World War II when American officials had to work closely with various agencies of the British government. They found that the British were making extensive use of this device, seemingly to good effect.

One particularly outstanding British example of such a committee was the famed "Twenty Committee" which met weekly from January 1941 to May 1945. This committee was set up to decide what information to give the string of German agents which the British had managed to convert to double-agent status. In order to build up their credibility with their Nazi superiors, the agents had to be supplied with bona fide information and even had to be allowed to carry out some successful sabotage. Handling the double agents in this way required intensive cooperation from many government agencies and the "Twenty" managed to obtain it.[23]

While few if any Americans learned much about the "Twenty Committee" at the time, they did acquire a knowledge and appreciation of how skillfully the British seemed to be able to use such an administrative tool in less secret situations to improve communication, encourage cooperation and respond to vicissitudes of war. By the end of the war, the interdepartmental committee had become firmly entrenched in our own federal bureaucracy.

After the war, many interdepartmental committees disappeared but many continued while still others came into existence. The most notable of the latter—it is today the most important such committee in the nation—is the National Security Council which was formed in 1947. It consists of the president and essentially whomever the president wants to have on it. The other members usually include the vice president, the Secretaries of State, Defense and the Treasury, the directors of the Office of Management and Budget and the Central Intelligence Agency, the chairman of the Joint Chiefs, and others. Some, such as the Secretary of State and the chairman of the Joint Chiefs, participate in nearly all committee deliberations. Others may only attend on occasion. The council has a small staff but no operational responsibilities.[24]

The National Security Council became fairly active under Eisenhower, but according to James W. Davis, Jr., it seemed to decline in importance under Presidents Kennedy and Johnson.[25] Both presidents also made little use of cabinet meetings, preferring to handle matters

---

23. Masterman, *The Double Cross Game*, pp. 36–37.
24. James W. Davis, Jr., *The National Executive Branch* (New York: The Free Press, 1970), pp. 25–26.
25. *Ibid.*, p. 26.

pertaining to security with ad hoc groups whose membership might even include persons holding no official government position. The council seemed to experience a revived role under President Nixon. When Nixon issued a low-keyed alert to the armed forces during the 1973 Arab-Israeli war, it was suggested by some that he was doing so only to divert attention from the exploding Watergate scandal. Secretary of State Henry Kissinger sought to squelch such speculation by pointing out that the president's action was taken only in response to a unanimous National Security Council decision.

Many other less lustrous interdepartmental committees have also thrived within the federal bureaucracy. One little known but quite successful one was the Federal Committee on Pest Control which was set up in 1964 to combat a rather serious agricultural problem. Its membership consisted of representatives from the Departments of Defense, Interior and HEW as well as Agriculture. The departments cooperated well, bringing about productive and reasonably prompt results.[26]

The interdepartmental committee has also secured a measure of acceptance and usage at the state and local government level. Many mayors during the 1960's, such as John Lindsay of New York and Kevin White of Boston, began holding weekly meetings of their department heads to encourage greater interdepartmental cooperation and a more unified and comprehensive approach to problem-solving. Lindsay also set up an interdepartmental committee on industrial development comprising representatives from the city's Department of Housing and Redevelopment, the City Planning Commission, the Department of Marine and Aviation, the Department of Real Estate and the Mayor's Office. It was considered something of a revolutionary concept in the history of New York City's fragmented administration.[27]

The interdepartmental committee, however, cannot be given a clean bill of health. Although such committees are designed to smooth out and speed up interagency action, they sometimes do the reverse. They add still more units to the administrative network and thus increase its complexity and possibly its confusion as well. This is particularly true when such committees start creating a staff of their own. They then become more and more like operational agencies and in so doing they can make for less rather than more unified action.

Depriving the committee of any separate staff, facilities, etc. may ease this problem but, at the same time, may only aggravate another one. If committee decisions are to be effective, they must be implemented, and without a staff to at least check up and follow through,

---

26. *The Federal Committee on Pest Control. What It Is, What It Does* (Washington, D.C.: Government Printing Office, February 1967).
27. Hentoff, *A Political Life . . .* , p. 119.

such implementation may not take place. What further hampers implementation is the fact that top officials tend to be overburdened with demands made on their time and start assigning lesser officials to serve on the committees. The lesser officials may have the time to serve on the committee or committees and may do so faithfully and intelligently. However, when it comes to putting the committee's decisions into practice within their own agency, they frequently find that they lack the power to do so. An agency will normally feel less obliged to abide by an inter-agency decision when the decision is brought back by someone of lesser stature. Of course, if the agency representative can persuade his superiors to push forward with the decision, this may substantially solve the problem. However, higher officials will feel much less committed to implementing a decision when they did not participate directly in making it.

The problems of getting participant agencies to abide by the decisions which these committees make is a constant one but is often superseded by another problem, namely arriving at a decision in the first place. While interdepartmental committees can serve as agents for change, they can, as was noted above, also serve as a bulwark for the status quo. Agency representatives may attend the meetings not so much to create change as to protect their own agency's powers, prerogatives and position. In an effort to appease its various members, the committee either ends up as a talking shop or arrives at decisions that are so watered down as to be virtually meaningless. As Dean Acheson once noted, "One can always get an agreed paper by increasing the vagueness and generality of its statements. The staff of any inter-departmental committee has a fatal weakness for this kind of agreement by exhaustion."[28]

Finally, such committees become prone to many of the bureaucratic pathologies that were cited in chapter four. These include in particular the one of persistence. Even when formed to deal with only a single, transient problem, the committee may linger on and on, particularly if it has established a staff. The Hoover Commission, while finding that such committees could prove worthwhile, expressed concern over their tendency to survive long after they had outlived their usefulness. It recommended a reappraisal of all such committees every year with the termination of those whose work was no longer necessary. This recommendation failed to take hold and as new committees arose, the number of such groups increased to approximately 850 by 1970. The State Department alone chaired 62 such committees and sat on many others.

Dean Don K. Price of the John F. Kennedy Institute of Politics at Harvard University has sought to come to grips with both the problems

---

28. Acheson, *Present at the Creation*, p. 242.

and potentialities of interdepartmental committees, drawing upon a lifetime of service in and out of government. According to Price, such committees can be useful if not too much is expected of them. The most important issue, says Price, is "whether the departmental representatives are sent to the meeting to come to an agreement or with instruction to prevent anything from happening." Another criterion he puts forth concerns their formal status. "If . . . such a committee acquires legal status, *esprit de corps* and jurisdictional interests of its own, and is looked to by Congress and the public as the source of policy, the only outcome can be a muddle."[29] Thus, he argues that interdepartmental committees should not be given any formal authority but rather should be used as auxiliaries in a responsible system of executive organization.

In the meantime, an approach has evolved to ease some of the problems of translating committee decisions into departmental policy. This allows the head of an agency to send a representative to committees involving his agency rather than attending himself. However, all the representatives attending are permitted to make decisions which will be binding on their respective agencies if no agency head objects to the decision within a stated period of time. For example, the governors of New England meet four times a year as the New England Regional Commission. However, their representatives, called alternates, meet every six weeks. The alternates hammer out decisions on various matters and if no governor casts a veto within ten days following their meeting, the decisions become final.

These and other ways of improving the operations of interdepartmental committees will hopefully become more widespread as time goes on. Certainly, such committees will continue to be needed, for in a society in which problems are becoming increasingly multi-dimensional, the need for interdepartmental decision-making will doubtlessly grow apace.

AGENTS OF CHANGE: STUDY COMMISSIONS AND TASK FORCES

During his second term, President George Washington confronted a crisis which threatened not only the authority of the president but that of the federal government itself. A band of irate Pennsylvania distillers, angry over a federal tax on their products, had refused to pay it. The governor of Pennsylvania was no help since he was fearful of losing his own popularity in the state and, in any case, had a Jeffersonian outlook

---

29. Don K. Price, *The Secretary of State,* Eighteenth American Assembly (Englewood Cliffs, N.J.: Prentice-Hall, 1960).

which made him reluctant to take harsh governmental action. It was up to Washington and his administration to meet this initial test of federal sovereignty.

Washington eventually summoned a force of 15,000 militiamen from four states and stamped out the Whiskey Rebellion, as it was called. But before taking this step, he appointed a commission to study the problem. The commission authorized his hitherto unprecedented action. The authority of the federal government had weathered its first major test.

Since that time, presidents, along with lesser chief executives and administrators, have set up commissions and task forces to help them resolve pressing problems. As was the case with Washington's commission, these bodies are by no means exclusively agents of change. They serve a variety of purposes, including, on occasion, the prevention of change. Yet, they are usually intended to bring about some form of change and hence warrant our consideration.

The use of commissions at the presidential level has become particularly pronounced in the last forty years. Franklin Roosevelt made fairly extensive use of this device and so did his successor, Harry Truman. Both presidents, for example, established commissions to study the executive branch of the federal government and to suggest ways of improving its operations. President Eisenhower appointed a commission to seek ways of shifting some of the federal government's activities back to the states. And John F. Kennedy had appointed a variety of task forces to help him map policy before he even took office.

The presidential commission, however, reached its finest flowering under Lyndon Johnson. This hyperactivist president had a variety of study commissions at work during his tenure in the White House. Many of these became well known, such as those concerned with law enforcement, riots and violence. Others remained more obscure, such as the Commission on Crime in the District of Columbia. The popularity of the device diminished during President Nixon's first term but did not die out completely. Nixon named commissions to study such matters as nutrition, heart disease and federal statistics.

As has been noted, a commission, be it presidential or otherwise, may serve a multitude of purposes, only some of which may be conducive to fostering change. Elizabeth Drew, who is perhaps the country's outstanding journalist when it comes to reporting on administrative matters, has listed in somewhat cynical if nevertheless perceptive fashion eight such purposes.[30]

---

30. Elizabeth B. Drew, "On Giving Oneself a Hotfoot: Government by Commission," *The Atlantic Monthly,* May 1968.

The first, according to Mrs. Drew, is "To obtain the blessing of distinguished men for something you want to do anyway." This is probably the oldest rationale for establishing a commission and was most likely the main motivation behind George Washington's appointment of commissioners to study the Whiskey Rebellion. It certainly played a role in the appointment by Presidents Roosevelt and Truman of commissions to study the executive branch. Both men, Roosevelt in particular, wanted to strengthen the hand of the president in running the bureaucracy. To have suggested this themselves would have brought a storm of controversy on their heads. But an impartial commission of distinguished men—Truman's commission was headed by former Republican President Herbert Hoover—could make such a move seem quite legitimate.

Governors, mayors, city managers and even department heads and bureau chiefs can and sometimes do use the commission device for the same purpose. This does not mean that they always "stack" the commission with people who will do their bidding or that they try to manipulate it for this covert purpose. Rather, it may often indicate that what they want to do is what any group of intelligent people who have studied the situation would recommend, and so they appoint a commission knowing full well that it will come up with suggestions along the lines of what they already have in mind.

In serving such a function, the study commission is still serving as an agent of change. However, according to Mrs. Drew, another frequent purpose of such a commission is to postpone action while giving the impression that work on the problem is proceeding apace. Tied to this purpose as well as to the first purpose is a third motivation, namely "to act as a lightning rod, drawing political heat away from the White House."

Some would see an example of this latter motive at work in the first concrete step suggested by President Nixon in response to the Watergate affair. In the spring of 1973, as the scandal was starting to unfold, the president called on Congress to set up a seventeen-member bipartisan commission to study the electoral process. The reaction from Congress and the press was decidedly negative. The *New York Times* pointed out that the study commission was a "traditional temporizing device."

Howard E. Schuman, who served as executive director of the Commission on the Problems of the American City, agrees that study commissions can often be used in this way. "A presidential commission," he has written, "is generally established to buy time on an immediate and politically tender issue—or, as someone else has said, to treat the politics of a situation rather than the situation itself. Commission members are expected to go into seclusion and not rock the boat. They usually report many months later—after public clamor has died down—and their work gets filed with the great unread literature of the World."[31] However, Schuman does say that commissions can aid and abet the process of change. The work of his own commission, he claims, did have some impact in the shaping of policy, although probably much less than the commission and staff members had hoped and expected.

Mrs. Drew also admits that commissions can prove a positive force in policy-making. In addition to helping secure public acceptance for doing something that needs to be done, they educate their own members in the problems they are confronting. They may also lay to rest rumors and "convince the public of the validity of one particular set of facts." She cites the Warren Commission which probed and reported on the assassination of President Kennedy as an example of the latter type. (Although the rumors of a widespread conspiracy being responsible for the president's death still continue to circulate.) Finally, she concedes that a commission can uncover facts which the administrator has not uncovered and can suggest programs and policies which he and his staff have not devised. With all their shortcomings and their susceptibility to political manipulation, study commissions can serve as agents of change.

The Study Commission at Work

Setting up a study commission is a delicate task. Obviously, it must contain people with some acknowledged expertise in the problem or problems to be investigated. A committee on nutrition that has no physicians or nutritionists among its members would scarcely command any public support. At the same time, however, the commission must be representative of all the groups who are most directly concerned. Thus, while a commission on urban problems should contain some recognized urbanologists, it should also include representatives of those sectors of the population, such as minority groups, who may have the most at stake in the resolution of urban problems. Finally, the commission must number among its members some distinguished representatives of the general public. A commission composed solely of experts and clientele representatives will often lack the perspective as well as the political clout for drawing up proposals which are both essentially sound and administratively feasible.

Particular care should be taken in the selection of the chairman. He should almost always be a public member or at least someone with

---

31. Howard E. Schuman, "Behind the Scenes and Under the Rug: One Man's Presidential Commission," in Peters and Adams, *Inside the System*.

no direct and personal interest in the commission's outcome. He should, at the same time, be someone who can command the respect of the public and, hopefully, the support of the political figures whose cooperation will be needed to implement the findings. Harry Truman's selection of Herbert Hoover to head his commission on reorganization of the federal bureaucracy was probably a masterstroke in this respect. Hoover, as an ex-president, could be considered well qualified for the task. At the same time, he had long since retired from politics and consequently had no personal involvement in what the commission was studying. Finally, Hoover was a Republican and any Republican congressman who might choose to contest the commission's recommendations would thereby have to repudiate the former leader of his own party.

If the commission is authorized and funded to have a staff, then appointment of this staff constitutes one of its first and probably its most important task. What makes the staff so important is that if the commission is representative, and if it consists of distinguished people, then it will be composed of people who lack both the expertise and the time to delve fully into the designated problem areas. Thus, the role of the staff looms large. Frequently, the commission will become a captive of its staff, ratifying with only minor changes the proposals which the staff members devise.

Given the prominence of the staff in shaping the commission's output, great care should be exercised in selecting it. Unfortunately, this cannot always be done. The commission is usually under instructions to get going as soon as possible. More importantly, it can only offer temporary employment. Since many able people are not immediately available for what is essentially a one-shot opportunity staffing commissions presents problems. On the positive side, however, is the fact that the prominence and often dominance of the staff in deciding what the commission shall eventually recommend makes service on such commissions appealing to many who would otherwise not be interested.

The commission may have to confront other issues as it winds its way toward its final report. Should it issue interim reports along the way or should it wait until it has its final report ready? There are advantages in both procedures. Interim reports may come at a time closer to the events which prompted the commission's formation and therefore may score a greater impact. They may also allow speedier action to be taken by presenting proposals for action sooner than would be the case if the commission waited until it had completed all its work. And the interim report may whet the public interest for the commission's subsequent findings. On the other hand, interim reports may be premature and lack completeness even if they are confined to certain aspects of the problem area. They may lead to fragmented action and may hinder the public from obtaining a broad view of the entire situation. They may also weaken the impact of the final report.

The commission will usually face a more vexing problem in getting agreement within itself on just what is to be said in its report or reports. There will often be a clash of viewpoints. The danger then arises that, far from swallowing the staff's reports whole, the commission waters them down to the point where they become almost meaningless. This is the same danger which, it will be recalled, Dean Acheson warned about concerning interdepartmental committees. Many members as well as the staff personnel of Lyndon Johnson's Commission on Law Enforcement and the Administration of Justice wanted to discuss in detail the problem of police corruption. However, the law enforcement members on the commission managed to block any in-depth treatment of this subject.

However, if the conflicting viewpoints on the commission result in a report that is less specific and hard-hitting than many might wish, they will at the same time help produce a report that will stand a better chance of acceptance. As Harold Wolman has pointed out, "The benefits derived from a 'representative' outside task force are several. Most important, if the task force report is unanimous, a supporting coalition representing most of the major elements in American society will already have been built. Issues dividing builders, labor, financiers, cities, civil rights groups and others will have been bargained out and settled prior to the Congressional battle."[32] Wolman was speaking in particular reference to commissions on housing, but the same factors apply to commissions on other matters as well. It might be just as well to deal with the political problems involved before the report as after it.

How effective are outside study commissions? Few, if any of them, have seen all their recommendations translated into firm operational policy. Perhaps the most successful in this respect were the two Hoover commissions. Their proposals brought about the unification of the armed services into a single Department of Defense, a modernization of the federal government's budgetary procedures and several other changes. Others have not fared so well, but most have seen at least some of their suggestions acted upon. Furthermore, their proposals, along with the data upon which they are based, become published and often constitute a valuable source of information for those who are interested in the problems they have tackled. Used in college courses, for example, such material may influence the next generation of leadership.

---

32. Harold Wolman, *Politics of Federal Housing* (New York: Dodd, Mead & Co.), p. 90.

Finally, there is the role they play in educating some influential people, namely their own members, in some of the crucial issues of the day. As a member of Johnson's staff noted in pointing out how appointing conservative members to a commission on housing can create change,

> We . . . in effect, co-opt them. We rub their noses in the problem and bring them along with the solutions. Hell, some of them have never seen slums and ghettos before. We bring them into the slums and they are amazed that such things can exist. Its surprising how radical some of them become.[33]

CASE STUDY

Seeking Shelter in the Sixties

During the 1930's and the 1940's, the federal government sought intermittently to come to grips with the nation's housing problems. It launched a public housing program during the New Deal and a limited and quite controversial urban renewal program during the postwar era. Then came the relatively quiescent Eisenhower period when federal action on many domestic fronts slowed down considerably. The return of the Democrats to the White House in the 1960's, however, saw a revival of interest in housing and related problems. How this revived interest manifested itself has been well documented and described in Harold Wolman's *Politics of Federal Housing*. His account provides an interesting insight into the role of study commissions and interdepartmental committees as agents of change.[34]

John F. Kennedy set up a task force on housing prior to his inauguration. However, it formulated few of the proposals which he subsequently sent to the Congress. Instead, an interdepartmental committee consisting of representatives of the Bureau of the Budget and the Housing and Home Finance Agency and chaired by HHFA head Robert Weaver drafted most of the new president's housing legislation.

What was wrong with the pre-inaugural task force? Its members did not lack political and administrative experience. Indeed, its chairman was Joseph McMurray, a highly respected former chairman of New York State's Commission on Housing. However, according to Wolman, its members, despite their expertise and background, "had no institutional attachments to the policy process." They were essentially outsiders. Wolman suggests that if Kennedy had named McMurray head of the HHFA or, conversely, if he had appointed Weaver to head the pre-inaugural group, then the task force's efforts might have fared much better. However, the fact that it was not plugged into the

---

33. *Ibid.,* p. 88.
34. *Ibid.,* Chapter 4.

relevant institutions, plus the fact that the HHFA was now under new leadership and was bristling with ideas of its own, prevented the first study group from playing any significant role in mapping housing policy.

During the rest of his administration, Kennedy relied mostly on the HHFA and its Office of Program Policy to initiate housing legislation and to work for its enactment in Congress. There were no further outside task forces in this area.

The arrival of Lyndon Johnson to the presidential helm, however, saw a renewed interest in, and use of, the task force approach. According to Wolman, Johnson was more disposed to call in outsiders for housing ideas because the bureaucracy was heavily loaded with Kennedy appointees, and while he may not have wanted to get rid of them, at least not right away, he wanted suggestion sources of his own. Thus, in 1964 the new president set up a task force consisting largely of academics and specialists under the chairmanship of Political Science Professor Robert Wood of the Massachusetts Institute of Technology.

This group had, if anything, even less ties to the Washington establishment than did Kennedy's pre-inaugural assemblage. However, its proposals fared much better. For example, it originated the rent supplement law which Congress enacted in 1965. Wolman attributes its success to the fact that despite its lack of connection with the federal bureaucracy, it did enjoy a high degree of support from the president. This presidential preference contributed to its effectiveness. (This does not mean that Kennedy did not trust his own initial task force; only that Kennedy also had his own people in the bureaucracy and tended to give their efforts more sanction.)

The first Johnson task force on housing was followed by a second one in 1965. Like the previous one, this task force was extra-governmental. However, it differed from its predecessor in one very crucial respect; its membership was not confined to academics and specialists but, in Wolman's words, "reflected major centers of power in American society." While Wood again served as chairman, only one other academic served along with him. The rest of the membership consisted of the heads of two large business corporations, the president of the United Auto Workers union, the executive vice president of a non-profit housing development corporation in Philadelphia, the executive director of the Urban League, the director of the Bureau of the Budget, and a member of Congress, Senator Abraham Ribicoff of Connecticut. In this manner, business, labor, the cities, blacks, the executive branch and Congress were all represented.

Its broad representation in the relevant sectors of society created difficulties but in the end it made the commission more effective. Some wanted to concentrate on building small structures while others wanted to create large ones. Walter Reuther, the UAW head, for example, felt that a real housing industry was needed and this could only be achieved through focusing on large housing developments. While majority rule generally governed its decisions, exceptions occurred. Most of the membership, for instance, wanted to

360

shift the Community Action Program from the Executive Office of the President to their proposed new Department of Housing and Urban Development. But when Urban League Director Whitney Young argued that blacks distrusted HUD and would interpret the move as an attempt to kill off the program, the other members gave in.

The government members helped considerably in making sure that the task force's efforts resulted in proposals that were feasible. Budget Director Kermit Gordon continually reminded the group of budgetary considerations and constraints. Senator Ribicoff kept pointing out the political problems involved, often suggesting ways they could be overcome. Thus, when the task force decided on a limited model cities program, Ribicoff urged that the number of such projects be increased so that they could be distributed to more states. This would make the program more acceptable to Congress. The Model Cities program and the new Department of Housing and Urban Development were two of the major proposals of the task force that were subsequently enacted into law.

In 1966 Johnson set up still another task force. This one reverted to the 1964 model in being top heavy with academic members. As a result, it produced a report which some described as "too radical" and which others termed more philosophic than legislative. It focused more on the problems of racism than housing, although the two were obviously interrelated. However, Wolman says that Johnson may not have particularly wanted another sheaf of feasible legislative proposals. Congress had already swallowed quite a good deal of housing legislation by this time and needed a respite to digest its fare. Wolman suggests that Johnson, conscious of this, had constituted his new task force of academics in order to develop some long-range and deeper perspectives on the housing problem, not to draft pragmatic and specific laws. The recommendations of the 1966 task force, says Wolman, had very little, if any, immediate impact on public policy.

The year 1967 actually saw three different governmental groups studying housing and related problems. The first of these was the National Commission on Urban Problems which was set up by Congress under the chairmanship of former Senator Paul Douglas. This body delved into such matters as zoning ordinances, building codes, tax rates and a host of other matters. It held hearings around the country and drafted a mammoth report. (The commission had to furnish reporters shopping bags to cart it away.) However, the commission had no base in the presidency and even less of a rapport with HUD which it had criticized. Consequently, its effect on policy was minimal.

The second group was another presidential commission, this time chaired by Edgar Kaiser, the president of Kaiser Industries. Its eighteen-man membership also included a past president of the National Association of Home Builders, an official of the Association of General Contractors, four union heads including AFL-CIO President George Meany, the executive director of the Urban League, the mayor of Pittsburgh and only one professor. Johnson set up the commission with a good deal of fanfare and the commission's staff maintained close liaison with the White House all through its existence. As a result, its recommendations received a good deal of presidential support. Johnson incorporated its suggestion for a National Housing Partnership, to consist of a private corporation to provide equity capital for low and moderate-income housing, into his 1968 housing program. The president also accepted and espoused its goal of 26 million new dwellings over the next decade, although HUD had submitted a more modest figure.

The Kaiser commission comprised a good many influential and representative people. However, this made it a large task force of busy men. Consequently, the staff virtually ran the commission, setting up agendas, developing and writing the position papers. This marked a departure from the earlier task forces chaired by Professor Wood who wrote many of the papers himself and used the staff mostly for technical back-up.

The third group at work on the problem was an interdepartmental committee which consisted of representatives of seven government agencies, including the White House staff. This body exhibited many of the less appealing features characteristic of such committees. Wolman quotes one HUD official as describing the meetings he attended as "fluff, speeches, the exchange of paper, but most of all lies. The various agencies strive to protect their own jurisdictions. They are imperialistic and it is difficult to get any kind of results from them. They will work only if Califano (Johnson's aide) rides them and makes it known he wants results."[35]

In the end, however, the committee did produce results, setting national housing goals and recommending a new home ownership program and a new method of rent supplementation. Wolman attributes its success largely to HUD's dominant position on the committee. Weaver, HUD's Secretary, chaired the committee and he and his special assistants wrote most of its papers. Another factor contributing to its ultimate effectiveness was the fact that Johnson was now more interested in improving existing programs than in embarking on new ones. This is perhaps a task that an interdepartmental committee can often perform better than a broad-based commission whose membership lies largely outside the government. Certainly, a group of government officials are less likely to concern themselves with brand new ideas and are more likely to focus their energies on existing programs. In any case, the interdepartmental committee, according to Wolman, probably had the greatest impact on Johnson's 1968 housing proposals.

AGENTS OF CHANGE: CONSULTANTS

In an attempt to keep abreast of the currents of change and their impact on their own operations, organizations have begun to make increasing use of consultants. The practice of calling in such outside experts for aid

---

35. *Ibid.*

and assistance is already far advanced in the private sector and is gradually becoming more common in the public sector as well. By the early 1970's it was estimated that non-profit institutions of one kind or another were generating $100 million worth of business for managerial consultants every year.

This growing trend has not failed to incite a drumfire of criticism. A consultant, in Robert Townsend's definition, is a person who borrows your watch to tell you what time it is and then walks off with it. Ida Hoos is somewhat less sarcastic but more specific in her reservations. "When outside information experts descend on in-house staff, with the blessing of oversold executives, they make demands for 'cooperation'— the gathering of data, records, etc. that often interrupts necessary tasks and interferes with normal activity. Free from the cost/benefit sword of Damocles that hangs over the in-house planners and programs, they generate and perpetuate systems that are cumbersome, often unworkable and even an impediment to the achievement of goals."[36]

If consultants, in addition to being expensive, tend to interfere with the normal operations of an organization and to make recommendations which, because of their necessarily limited knowledge of the organization, tend to be dysfunctional, why are they so often used? In the views of their detractors, consultants are used to serve three purposes.

First of all, consultants can be a way of getting around civil service laws. An agency can hire the people it wants when it wants and for how long it wants without having to put up with civil service restrictions if it can classify and fund them as consultants. This practice can easily lead to a second abuse, namely the use of consultantships as a means of patronage. Contracts for professional services are rarely put out to bid for the members of the profession usually have strict rules regarding such competitive practices. Thus, the contract can be awarded on grounds other than that of the lowest price. Ostensibly, the grounds should be those of quality of performance but since this cannot be predetermined with any exactitude, the awarders of the contract have a fair degree of discretion in deciding who is going to get it. As a result, consultants who contribute to the campaigns of winning mayoral candidates, for example, frequently find themselves favored when city hall needs some consulting services.

Perhaps the greatest and most widespread criticism leveled against the use of consultants, however, is that often they are engaged to tell those who are engaging them what they want to hear. In other

---

36. Ida R. Hoos, "Systems Techniques for Managing Society: A Critique," *Public Administration Review*, March/April 1973.

words, they are hired not so much to present the contractee with new ideas but to legitimize the ideas he already has.

In an interesting paper which he presented to the American Political Science Association in 1972, Lewis A. Dexter sketched some of the dimensions of this aspect of consulting.[37] The first consultant he ever met, said Dexter, told him that he always wrote two reports after he had completed an assignment with an organization. The first report presented the situation as the head of the organization wanted to see it; the second report presented the situation as it really was. Apparently, this consultant and any others who follow the same or similar practices are wise in doing so, for Dexter goes on to quote a highly placed government official as expressing little regard for a consultant which his department frequently engaged. Why, then, did he contract for the consultant's services so often? "We have to use him," said the official. "He always tells us what we want to hear."

Of course, many times an organization or even its leadership is not unified as to what it wants to hear. There may be splits over various policy matters. These can pose quite a problem for many consultants. He may find himself, says Dexter, allied with one group and opposed to another. "Consultants," says Dexter, "are not neutral. People who advise on anything one can think of may be inclined to one interest or another in a way of which they are unaware until they get to work." Consequently, even if a consultant is determined to "tell it like it is," his work may yield little in terms of positive results. The fundamental rule, according to Dexter, is that "advice and advisors are likely to be accepted, esteemed, hired and rejected in terms of the internal politics of the commissioning organization, as viewed by the members of the organization."[38]

But while consultants can be expensive, meddlesome, irresponsible—after all, they do not have to live with their recommendations—and encumbered with all manner of political considerations and constraints, they nevertheless have their uses.

Marvin Bower, a director of the international consulting firm of McKinsey and Company and a former president of the Institute of Management Consultants, has stressed two advantages which the outside consultant can bring to an organization.[39] One is the diversity of his background. He has worked with a variety of organizations including many with similar functions or similar problems to the one which has engaged him. He thus draws from a broader range of knowledge. He

---

37. Lewis A. Dexter, "The Internal Politics of Organizations and the Role of the Consultant," Paper presented to the American Political Science Association annual meeting, 1972.
38. *Ibid.*
39. In a letter published in the business section of the *New York Times*, March 4, 1973.

most likely has seen other organizations wrestle with the same or similar dilemmas, and how they succeeded or failed in resolving them gives him some valuable knowledge which he can offer to the organization which has commissioned him.

The second advantage which the consultant possesses is his independence. This may sound strange in view of what was noted earlier about the consultant's need for proclivity to play politics with the organization if he is to gain its favor. However, if an organization is really determined to utilize what the consultant has to offer, it may find that the most valuable thing he has to offer is his detached perspective.

The consultant is not wedded to the everyday operation and is not enmeshed in the habits, customs and culture of the organization. He can thus see things which the organization's own members do not see. Furthermore, given the right conditions, he may speak up and out more candidly than an insider since he has not the same fears for his future or the same ties of everyday association which may constrain the organization's own members. Along the same lines, many of the organization's members may speak more candidly to him than they would to their own colleagues and superiors. Similarly, his recommendations may secure greater acceptance from them since his relationship is relatively uncolored by the experiences and emotions, the attachments and animosities, which can influence reaction to suggestions made by superiors, subordinates or colleagues. Thus, a good consultant will almost invariably come up with information about the organization that the organization's top management would find hard to obtain and/or accept.

The fact that he is not an integral part of the organization and has no day-in, day-out duties benefits the consultant and the organization which commissions him in still other ways. It was pointed out previously how important it is to treat problems not symptoms. The consultant does not have to treat symptoms since he has no connection with the daily business and routine of the organization. He can concentrate his efforts fully on the more substantial areas of concern.

One final advantage involved in consultant usage is worthy of note for it is of particular applicability in the public sector. Consultants, unlike most public employees, are easily disposed of. Although the public manager cannot fire or phase out an unwanted or unnecessary employee without undergoing a great deal of trouble and turmoil, he usually has no such problem in handling consultants. The utilization of outside experts brings a note of flexibility into what are often overly rigid personnel structures. It can thus be argued that the employment of consultants to circumvent civil service laws is not an abuse as long as the consultants only consult and do not administer.

Consultants, in short, can aid and abet the processes of change. "If there is a feature of the medieval court which the modern office needs to reproduce," writes C. Northcote Parkinson, "it is the ancient office of fool or jester. It was the fool's privilege and duty to put forward another point of view, neither that of the establishment nor that of the group currently out of favor. If the traditions of the office mean anything, the official jester would seem to have been at least as clever as any other official. There was no need to take his advice seriously, but neither was there much excuse for taking offense at anything he said. After all, to talk out of turn was what he was paid to do. There is reason to think that he served a useful purpose and there is even some reason to suspect that he might be useful now."[40] The properly utilized modern-day consultant may be or could be what Parkinson has in mind.

Dos and Don'ts in the Use of Consultants

Consultants rarely come cheap and consequently those who hire them should take care to see that they obtain their money's worth. A few pointers gleaned from those who employ them as well as from consultants themselves may prove helpful in this regard.

At the outset, the commissioning organization should make sure that it knows just why it is hiring a consultant and just what it wants him to do. "The clearer the notion we had on what we wanted, the better the results we got out of consultants," says former New York City Budget Director Frederick Hayes.[41] No public agency should sign on a consultant in order for the consultant to tell the agency what it wants the consultant to do. If the agency wants the best return on its expenditure, it should take care to sort out its wishes and wants and define them in a way in which they will be clear to whatever consultant it may hire. Of course, the agency may err by going too far in this direction and thereby constrict the consultant's scope of work. A consultant needs a certain amount of freedom in order to come up with the best range of ideas. Yet, when forced to choose between giving the consultant freedom or focus, it is usually better to stress the latter than the former. Consultants do have to know what is expected of them if they are to help the organization in a significant way.

Then, those hiring the consultant should make sure they hire the consultant or consultants with the right expertise. A psychiatrist is not an industrial sociologist, and a certified public accountant is not necessarily imbued with a good grasp of government budgeting. It is particularly important to acquire consultants who have skills, background and even viewpoints that are *not* too similar to those found within the or-

---

40. C. Northcote Parkinson, *The Law of Delay* (New York: Ballantine Books, 1970), pp. 48–49.
41. Hayes, "Things Are Picking Up in the Sanitation Department," p. 13.

ganization. There is no point in paying outsiders to tell you what people whom you are already paying can tell you anyway. (We are assuming, of course, that those who are hiring the consultant are not looking for ways of justifying what they already know or feel, an abuse of the practice that was noted above.)

It goes without saying that once the consultant starts work he should be given the aid and assistance he needs to do what he was hired to do. He should have access to those who will ratify and implement his recommendations. This usually includes top management and thus constitutes another burden on their time. However, if a consultant is worth hiring then he is worth keeping in touch with as he pursues his mission. Confining his contacts to those who will not have the final say on his product will result in a weaker product.

But if successful consulting requires input from the implementers, then successful implementation demands input from the consultants. Too often, the consultant is hired for a certain study, does it and then is sent on his way. The agency should, instead, make sure that he plays a role in putting the proposals into effect. As a matter of fact, many consultants as well as those who hire them stress the undesirability of using consultants on a one-shot basis. It is better to engage a consultant intermittently over a longer period of time than on a continuous basis for one long and terminal stretch. The consultant's assignment should not end with his final report.

Last and most important, organizations and those who manage them should not overuse consultants. Most organizations have more capability in-house than they realize and they should seek to utilize it to the utmost. In so doing, not only will they save consultant fees but they will also boost the spirits and develop the capacities of their own members. Consultants themselves will often admit that many organizations resort to their services to handle matters which they, the organizations, could deal with internally. Consultants do have a role to play as agents of change and have often played it well. (Much of the dramatic turnaround in productivity which New York City finally began to achieve in the early 1970's was stimulated and guided by experts from the famous Rand Corporation.) Yet, any government or government agency that relies too much on their services may fail to develop its own capacities for coping with the challenges of change.

THE LIMITS OF CHANGE

As we stressed at the outset, change comes hard for public organizations, and this condition itself must change if they are to keep in step with the societies they serve. Much of the current disfavor which public bureaucracies are now experiencing can be laid at the door of their static and stagnant patterns of behavior. Change itself must become a built-in feature of the public agency if it hopes to meet its increasing and evolving responsibilities.

Yet, no administrative admonition can be set down without at the same time issuing some caveats and cavils. Like nearly every other principle, precept and prescription we have examined, change is fine *up to a point.* When that point is reached, it becomes costly and counter-productive. While the process of change can be an exciting and ener-gizing experience, it can also be an exhausting and enervating ordeal.

Seymour Berlin and his associates point out some of the disbene-fits and dysfunctions of change. "The organization can't work while it knows it's going to be changed, it can't work while it's being changed, and it takes a long time for it to start working following a change."[42] Those who so sharply condemn the old and so eagerly grasp the new would do well to remember the price that will have to be paid. The Environmental Protection Administration went through a series of reor-ganizations early in its existence and their cumulative effect nearly crip-pled the agency.

Viewing the problem from a broader perspective, we should bear in mind that sometimes the completed change represents a step back-ward rather than forward. There is scarcely any public organization that is doing such a bad job that it could not be altered in such a way as to make it do a still worse one. In other words, not all change is change for the better. Hitler, Mussolini and many of the other tyrants of history, so Frank Marini reminds us, were agents of change.[43] Transformation is not an end in itself, and the impetuous and impatient would do well to keep this in mind as they and their organizations struggle to respond to the challenges of change.

42. Berlin et al., "A Guide for Political Appointees . . . "
43. Unwritten remarks made during a panel session at the annual convention, American Society of Public Administration, 1974.

11

Administrative Law and Administrative Control

During the first hundred years of American history, several factors conspired to keep the administrative sector of our many governments comparatively small and weak. These factors relate to the characteristics of our political system which we examined in chapter two. Fragmentation and personalism, for example, deterred the growth of large and formalized bureaucracies like those starting to emerge in Europe. The antigovernmental attitudes of the American people probably acted as an even greater deterrent. But our legalistic approach to governmental problems may have served as the greatest deterrent of all.

Just how American legalism imposed limits on, and even substituted for, administrative power was noticed by Lord James Bryce, that perceptive British observer who began visiting our shores late in the nineteenth century. In his 1888 book *The American Commonwealth,* Bryce wrote "It is a great merit of American government that it relies very little on officials [administrators] and arms them with little power of arbitrary interference. . . . [The government] has taken the direction of acting through the law rather than through the officials. That is to say, when it prescribes to the citizen a particular course of action it has relied upon the ordinary legal sanctions, instead of investing the administrative officers with inquisitional duties or powers that might prove oppressive."[1]

As the quotation suggests, Bryce wholly approved this approach.

---

1. James Bryce, *The American Commonwealth* (1888), quoted in Lowi, *The End of Liberalism,* pp. 128–129.

Had he been more legalistically trained or oriented himself, he might have pointed to a particular legalistic feature of our system which served as the main roadblock to a greater assumption of power and responsibility by American administrators. This feature was our consti-tutionally enshrined principle of separation of powers.

As nearly everyone knows, the Constitution stipulates that the legislative branch shall enact the laws and the executive branch shall execute and enforce them. Through the first century of our existence, the courts took a particularly rigorous and righteous attitude toward this demarcation of authority. They ruled that Congress could not give away its power even if it wanted to. Consequently, all efforts to bestow sub-stantial discretion on any administrator or administrative agency drew the Supreme Court's prompt disapproval. Congress, said the Court, could not delegate its powers. Rules and regulations that would have the force of law would have to be passed by the body charged with passing laws.

However, as Bryce was writing his book, the Court was getting ready to alter the whole course of American administrative history. Con-gress, confronted with the pressing need to regulate the country's grow-ing and sprawling railroad industry, and appreciative of the fact that it could not possibly devote the continuous time and effort which such a task demanded, passed the Interstate Commerce Act of 1887. This act set up a new agency, the Interstate Commerce Commission, to carry out this function. In a landmark decision that signaled a major change in policy, the Supreme Court ruled the act, along with the agency it estab-lished, to be constitutional.

It should be pointed out that the newly created ICC was scarcely given carte blanche discretion. Congress set down specific standards regarding its jurisdiction and prescribed rather detailed criteria for use of its discretionary power in policing the railroads. Congress even spelled out the various forms of misbehavior which the ICC was to police such as rebating, rate-discrimination, pooling. The new regula-tory commission was, in the words of Theodore Lowi, "relatively well shackled by clear standards of public policy, as stated in the statute and as understood in common law."[2]

From this time on, Congress, along with most state legislatures, began delegating more and more legislative power to administrative agencies, and the Supreme Court became increasingly cooperative in permitting them to do so. Thus, when Congress added to and amplified the ICC's powers by passing the Transportation Act of 1920, the Court let the act stand even though the increased powers were accompanied by

---

2. Lowi, *op. cit.,* p. 131.

far fewer hard and specific criteria to guide and control their application.

But though the Court had backtracked considerably over its once hard-line stand on delegation, it was still not ready to capitulate completely. The Court, for example, played havoc with the Federal Trade Commission during the first twenty years of its life, invalidating order after order of the agency on the ground that the congressionally imposed standard of "unfair method of competition" which the agency was charged with enforcing was too vague. Such vagueness, said the Court, gave the agency too much discretionary power.[3]

The New Deal brought the issue to its head, as President Roosevelt, trying to wield broad executive power to pull the country out of the Depression, found himself on a collision course with the nation's highest tribunal. While Roosevelt managed to obtain from Congress wide-scale discretionary authority for his New Deal agencies, the conservative Court frequently balked at approving such sweeping delegations of power. This led to a series of hostile Court decisions, culminating in the famous Schecter case of 1935.[4] In this case, a majority of the justices struck down the National Recovery Act and with it the elaborate planning machinery and the wide blanket of administrative power which the act had promulgated.

The Schechter case, however, marked the end of a long era. Although Roosevelt's subsequent effort to change the composition of the Court through adding more justices failed, some of the older and more conservative justices retired, and FDR replaced them with jurists more to his liking. The Supreme Court's attitude toward delegation has never been the same since. It has allowed Congress steadily increasing leeway in delegating power to administrative agencies, insisting only on some sort of standard to govern the application of such authority. And since 1935, it has failed to find any standard so vague as to warrant an act being outlawed on grounds of improper delegation of power.

A good example of the Court's new thinking was its upholding of the Economic Stabilization Act of 1970. This act authorized the president "to issue such orders and regulations as he may deem appropriate to stabilize prices, wages and salaries at levels not less than those prevailing on May 25, 1970" together with such adjustment as might be necessary "to prevent gross inequities." As the language of the act clearly indicates, it constitutes what in former times would have seemed an awesome grant of power, particularly when one remembers that the act left it up to the president to decide when and where he would

---

3. *Ibid.*, p. 132.
4. *A.L.A. Schechter Poultry Corporation* v. *United States,* 295 U.S. 495 (1935).

choose to exercise such power. Yet, when the Amalgamated Meat Cutters union contested the constitutionality of the act in 1971, the courts rejected the suit, claiming that the criterion of a legislatively prescribed standard had been met. In reviewing the Court's decision, the *Duke* (University) *Law Journal* noted that "the case leaves the impression that Congress would be hard put to contrive a delegation that would *not* be judicially sustained."[5] (Emphasis added.)

Spurred on by what might be called the permissive attitude which the Court has taken toward the delegation issue during the past forty years, the administrative sector has surged forward. Administrative agencies have acquired increasing functions along with increasing powers to carry them out. They may prescribe rules and issue orders which have the force of law and they may impose penalties on those who disobey. Some agencies have even acquired the subpoena power and/ or the contempt power. What were once the closely guarded prerogatives of elected officials have been increasingly placed into the hands of non-elected functionaries. American government has entered the era of the administrative state.

The actions which administrative agencies may take under their new and increasing grants of authority often have distinct policy implications. For example, when the Post Office decided in 1968 to require all shipments of firearms through the mail to be clearly labeled as such, and when it announced that it was planning to report all deliveries of such shipments to local law enforcement authorities, it was clearly playing a role in the policy-making arena. Similarly, when the Internal Revenue Service announced on April 10, 1973 that it would henceforth allow abortions, vasectomies and birth control pills to be deductible items, it was making policy as well as executing it. Sometimes administrative power has been used to get at problems which lie beyond the immediate scope of the agency involved. Mayor John Lindsay, for example, used New York City's rent control agency to prod landlords to observe the building and sanitation codes. Exasperated over the failure of the courts to crack down on delinquent real estate owners, Lindsay ordered the board to lower the rents of those buildings that were persistently found to be in violation of the codes.

The penalties which administrative agencies can impose are sometimes more severe than those usually levied by courts. Thus, an alien can be deported, a stock brokerage firm can be put out of business and a motorist can lose his license, all through administrative action. As for the last-cited action, some states empower their automobile registration agency to lift a driver's license only *after* he has failed to pay his

---

5. "Administrative Law Developments—1971," *Duke Law Journal,* Vol. 1972, no. 1.

parking tickets. In this instance, the administrative agency actually functions as a higher court and imposes the final penalty.

Many have viewed the increasing discretion being vested in administrative agencies with anger and alarm. Others have claimed it is inevitable since no legislative body can hope to prescribe all the detailed rules and regulations which government needs to cope with the problems of a complex and rapidly changing society. Congress or a state legislature, for example, may pass an air pollution control act but can such a legislative body really specify all the various steps that should and should not be taken to resolve all the situations which may arise within the air pollution control agency's jurisdiction? The flexibility and expertise required to handle such problems, it is contended, demand loose grants of authority.

In any case, whether or not Congress and the courts have gone too far in bestowing increasing influence on the administrative sector, they have accompanied such bestowals with certain restrictions and restraints. The growth of administrative authority has ushered in a parallel growth in administrative law.

THE NEW LIMITS ON ADMINISTRATIVE DISCRETION

Although administrators today find themselves blessed with powers their predecessors little dreamed of possessing, they also find themselves subjected to new restraints as well. The other two branches of government have not been content to stand aside and let administrators run the country subject only to broad policy prescriptions and rather vague standards regarding the public interest. And one way the other two branches have acted to limit administrative discretion is by imposing increasingly strict standards on *how* administrators may use their new prerogatives.

Congress first took action in 1946 through passage of the Administrative Procedures Act. This detailed piece of legislation set down fairly specific rules as to the ways in which administrative agencies were to proceed. The courts have since taken up the task, and basing themselves on broadened interpretations of the "due process" clauses in the Fifth and Fourteenth Amendments to the Constitution as well as on the Administrative Procedures Act itself, they have subjected administrative actions to stricter and stricter review.

It is important to note that judicial review since the Schecter case has focused not so much on matters of substance as on matters of procedure. In other words, the courts have concerned themselves less and less with *what* the administrative sector is doing and more and

373

more on *how* it is doing it. The judges have, in effect, admitted that they do not have the expertise to determine whether or not a drug is safe, a welfare payment is adequate, or a highway route is well designed. As long as the administrative agency can show that its decisions in such matters are not arbitrary but are based on some legitimate rationale, the judges will not be inclined to interfere. However, they have become increasingly disposed to speak out when they find that the agency has gone about doing what it is doing in a manner that is contrary to what has become known as administrative due process.

What is administrative due process? Practically speaking, writes Lewis Mainzer, "Administrative due process is that procedure which will normally be accepted by the courts as reasonable under the circumstances, whether or not the judge thinks the substantive decision was correct."[6] Kenneth Culp Davis puts it this way: "The dominant tendency in both state courts and federal courts is toward the middle position known as the substantial-evidence rule . . . the court decides questions of law but limits itself to the test of reasonableness in reviewing findings of fact."[7]

Due process, however, is not fully encapsulated by the criterion of "reasonableness" alone. It also implies what the Supreme Court has referred to as the criterion of "fundamental fairness." In attempting to set up standards for administrative due process, the courts, basing themselves on the federal government Administrative Procedures Acts and the similar acts which most states have enacted, as well as on their new interpretations of the Constitution, have worked out a fairly strict set of rules which administrators must follow if the requirements of due process are to be met.

Adequate Notice

Before an administrator or his agency can take any action that would directly affect one or more persons or institutions, they must generally give such affected parties adequate notice. How much notice is adequate? This depends on the circumstances and often becomes a matter for litigation before the courts. Rarely is a period of less than thirty days deemed to be adequate and frequently a much longer interval is required.

In some situations, however, administrative agencies are empowered to act with scarcely any notice at all. Thus, if a building inspector finds a structure so unsafe as to be in danger of collapse at any moment, or a health inspector finds a restaurant serving contaminated food, they

---

6. Lewis Mainzer, *Political Bureaucracy*, p. 62.
7. Kenneth Culp Davis, *Administrative Law and Government* (St. Paul, Minn.: West Publishing Co., 1960), p. 463. Quoted in Mainzer, p. 50.

can usually order the situation remedied immediately. However, unless it can be shown that the public safety demands precipitate action, the rule of adequate notice must govern.

Disclosure of Reasons

In addition to giving adequate notice, administrative agencies are usually required to state their reasons for taking the action they intend to take. In most instances the affected party may demand that the agency put these reasons in writing. This, in itself, tends to deter agencies from acting in an arbitrary and capricious manner. And when it does not have this effect, it at least gives the affected party written evidence to use in seeking subsequent redress in the courts. (See, in this connection, chapter seven on the advantages of formal communication.)

The Right to a Hearing

Beginning in the late 1960's, the courts began to broaden dramatically the right of aggrieved parties to have a hearing. Motorists deprived of their licenses, welfare clients deprived of their benefits, public housing tenants faced with eviction and prisoners sentenced to solitary confinement all sued for the right to be heard and were sustained by the courts.[8] Even the private sector found itself coming under this dictum as students faced with expulsion were also granted such a right.

The expansion that has taken place in requiring hearings has also affected rule-making. Today, agencies which seek to promulgate new rules must usually schedule hearings and allow those who think differently to state their case. Even those who may not be directly affected by the new rule can have their voices heard.

At one time, the courts were not prone to require a hearing when what was at stake was a benefit. However, starting in 1970, the Supreme Court began insisting that such benefits as welfare payments, passports, unemployment insurance, driving licenses and public housing accommodations could not be denied or removed without an evidentiary hearing, even though these were customarily termed privileges and not rights. Essentially, the Court held that when the government has issued a benefit to an individual, it cannot take it away from him on mere administrative and fiscal considerations without a prior hearing.[9]

Hearings, of course, are not court trials but they are increasingly coming to resemble them. An aggrieved party now can often demand not only the right to appear in his own behalf but to be represented by

---

8. For an interesting though scarcely disinterested account of a leading decision regarding prisoners' rights see "Due Process for Prisoners," by Tom Wicker in the *New York Times*, June 18, 1970 (editorial page).
9. "Administrative Law Developments—1971," *op. cit.*, Section III.

counsel. In many instances, he or his counsel can cross-examine witnesses who may be testifying in behalf of the agency. The affected party can further ask that the hearing be made public. Here, however, the courts may allow the agency some discretion in denying such a request. In two cases involving students protesting their expulsion, the courts allowed their respective universities to hold closed hearings. The grounds, in one case, were that a public hearing might endanger the public safety; in the other, that the reputations of innocent students might be injured.[10]

The Right to Further Appeal

If after a hearing, the protesting party is still not satisfied, he may appeal to a higher echelon within the agency and, as a last step, to the courts. Such figures as are available suggest that increasing numbers of citizens are taking this final step. One estimate made during the 1960's indicated that 20 percent of all Supreme Court decisions dealt with administrative matters.[11] And according to the *Statistical Abstract* of 1970, approximately 28 percent of all the civil cases begun in federal district courts in 1969 involved the federal government as either plaintiff or defendant.

The aggrieved party may seek judicial redress on grounds that he was not given adequate notice, that the agency's procedures are not clear, that the agency is not abiding by administrative due process or even its own procedures, that it has behaved in an arbitrary or discriminatory manner, that the agency lacks jurisdiction in doing what it did or plans to do. As Mainzer points out, "Despite the Administrative Procedures Act and mountains of court opinion, the standards of administrative due process are extraordinarily indefinite."[12] Thus, numerous possibilities exist for carrying administrative issues into the courtroom.

However, there are at the same time numerous limitations on utilizing the courts to reverse or mitigate administrative actions. First, the courts will not entertain the case until the petitioner has exhausted all the remedies available to him within the administrative agency itself. Furthermore, the courts will not intervene in cases where there is no remedy. Finally, as was previously noted, the courts nowadays balk at deciding questions of fact or weighing the validity of one expert opinion against another. They prefer to confine themselves to questions of law and procedure.

To see how this works, let us assume that a citizen wishes to

---

10. *Ibid.* For a more readable but less profound account of the expansion of this right see "Toward Greater Fairness for All." *Time,* February 26, 1973, p. 95.
11. Martin Shapiro, *The Supreme Court and Administrative Agencies* (New York: The Free Press, 1968), p. 13.
12. Mainzer, *op. cit.,* p. 37.

contest a decision on a new highway route that will require the taking of his house. He protests the decision to the highway commission, is turned down, and so takes his case to court. He may argue in court that an alternate route would have been a better one and may offer evidence and expert witnesses to support his view. But, if the highway commission can show any evidence and bring forth any expert testimony of its own to indicate that it had a valid reason for choosing the route that it did, the court will generally turn a deaf ear to the citizen's plea. However, if the irate homeowner can show that the highway commission's selection flies in the face of nearly all logic and expert opinion, and if he can further show that the commission may have a reason for being prejudiced against him and consequently would have a motive in picking a route that would take his home, then he will stand a chance of getting the commission's action struck down.

This, of course, is a hypothetical case. Let us now turn to some actual cases which will shed further light on the nuances and ramifications of present-day administrative law.

ADMINISTRATIVE LAW AT WORK

In February 1968, the Federal Aviation Administration fired a 36-year-old traffic controller on grounds that he had engaged in "sexual relations with a woman other than his wife." To make matters worse, the other woman was a former employee of the agency. The FAA further alleged that the dismissed controller had been involved in a car accident while under the influence of alcohol.

The controller, a father of five, was understandably upset. He pointed out that he was separated from his wife during a large portion of the alleged affair and that he had actually reconciled with his wife prior to his discharge. More importantly, he contended that his sex life had nothing to do with his efficiency as an air traffic controller. He took his case to the FAA's Board of Appeals and lost. He then asked for a review by the Civil Service Commission and lost again. Thereupon, he went to court.

In February 1970, the U.S. Federal District Court in Washington, D.C. found that the government had failed to show any correlation between the air controller's love life and his efficiency as an air traffic controller. Since a hearing examiner who had studied the controller's work record had rated it "satisfactory in all respects," the court ordered the FAA to reinstate the man in his former position.[13]

Three years after this case, a discharged local government em-

---

13. *Parade,* March 15, 1970, p. 4. I have omitted the name of the individual concerned to spare needless embarrassment to him and his family. The same policy will be used in certain other cases which will be mentioned subsequently.

ployee won a somewhat similar vindication from a U.S. district court. In January 1973, the Federal District Court in Portland, Oregon ruled that a local school board had no right to fire a school teacher on grounds of "immorality" simply because she was a lesbian. The school board was ordered to give the woman one-and-a-half years back pay and expunge from her records all references to "immorality" since lesbianism by itself did not constitute proper grounds for such a charge.[14]

Then, there is the case of John F. Shaw, an FBI agent who in 1971 wrote a letter that was critical, in part, of the FBI and of its then director, J. Edgar Hoover. Shaw's letter was designed to be read only by the person for whom it was intended. This was a professor who had made some derogatory remarks about the agency in a college course which Shaw was taking while he was stationed in the FBI's New York City office. Shaw's letter to the professor was actually a defense of the FBI, but in certain passages he did make reference to some of the agency's failings. When the letter was discovered by his superiors, Shaw was given a transfer to Butte, Montana, the FBI's "Siberia" office. Aware that the transfer meant a limited future in the FBI and unwilling to leave the East in any case, Shaw resigned. Hoover accepted his resignation "with prejudice."

Shaw then filed a suit in federal court claiming that he had been the victim of a "capricious and vindictive act of personal retribution" by the FBI's director. The FBI, sensing, perhaps, the new spirit now animating court decisions on administrative discretion, settled with Shaw out of court. The agency agreed to remove the phrase "with prejudice" from his resignation record and, in addition, to pay him $13,000, partly as the salary he would have received during the previous nine months.[15]

These incidents illustrate the new approach which the courts are taking toward the problem of administrative discretion and they show how this approach is starting to affect even such autocratic agencies as the FBI. This is not to imply that all the questions which may arise over employee dismissals have been settled. Many issues still remain. For example, can an agency dismiss an employee when he invokes his Fifth Amendment privilege and refuses to answer questions which his superiors put to him? Generally, the courts have held that a public agency may discharge an employee who refuses to answer questions that are directly related to his job. At the same time, the Supreme Court has emphasized that the invocation of a constitutional privilege cannot, in and of itself, constitute grounds for the imposition of a penalty. Thus, no

---

14. *Boston Sunday Globe,* February 4, 1973.
15. *New York Times,* June 18, 1971.

simple rule governing all "Fifth Amendment dismissals" has been or can be set down.[16]

The new protectiveness which the courts have begun to evince toward people affected by administrative actions is by no means limited to administrative employees. Members of the public who find themselves similarly affected have also been scoring victories before the bench.

During the Vietnam war, many college students burned their draft cards or returned them to the Selective Service System as a way of protesting America's involvement in the conflict. Many of them also sought to interfere with the work of the Selective Service System or with that of military recruiters. Insofar as their activities violated the law the students became subject to criminal prosecution. However, when the Selective Service System itself began to penalize them for such behavior, the courts intervened.

One landmark case was that of *Oestereich v. Selective Service System Local Board No. 11, Cheyenne, Wyoming, et al.* which was argued before the Supreme Court on October 24, 1968 and decided the following month. Oestereich was a theological student and consequently had been classified as IV-D and exempted from the draft. However, the preceding year he had returned his draft registration certificate "for the sole purpose of expressing dissent from the participation of the United States in the war in Vietnam." His board then declared him delinquent for failing to have his registration certificate in his possession and for failing to notify the board of his change in classification and his new status. After turning down his appeal, the Selective Service ordered him to report for induction.

Oestereich then brought his case to the Supreme Court. In its decision, the Court struck down the board's action on the grounds that it had exceeded its powers. The Selective Service System had no authorization, said the Court, to devise regulations governing delinquency and then use them to deprive registrants of their statutory exemptions. "There is no suggestion in the legislative history that, when Congress has granted an exemption and a registrant meets its terms and conditions, a Board can nonetheless withhold it from him for activities or conduct *not material to the grant or withdrawal of the exemption.* So to hold would make the Boards free-wheeling agencies meeting out their brand of justice in a vindictive manner."[17] (Emphasis added.)

Increasingly, those injured by the acts of government agencies

---

16. *Garrity* v. *New Jersey,* 385 U.S. 493 87 S.Ct. 616 17 L.Ed. 2nd 562 (1967).

17. For an account of the Supreme Court's disposition of some other cases involving Hersey's attempt to use the authority of his office to punish draft protesters, see the *New York Times,* January 27, 1970.

are finding it easier not only to win judicial vindication but also financial compensation. The Federal Tort Claims Act of 1946 allowed the federal government to be sued "in the same manner and to the same extent as a private individual," subject to a limited number of exceptions. In subsequent decisions, the Supreme Court has expanded and strengthened this right. For example, it has held that federal law enforcement agents can be sued for engaging in an illegal search of a person's home. Furthermore, those state governments which have shown less disposition to surrender their sovereign immunity in this regard are gradually being stripped of it by the courts. In a landmark decision in 1973, the New Jersey Supreme Court denied the state's defense of sovereign immunity in a suit brought by the parents of a three-year-old girl whose arm was ripped off by a bear in a state park. Said the court, "It is plainly unjust to refuse relief to a person injured by the wrongful conduct of the state."[18]

In some situations, administrators have personally become liable for damages in suits brought by clients of their agencies. Early in 1973, a federal judge in Richmond, Virginia ordered the head of Virginia's penal system to pay $21,265 in damages to three former inmates of the system. According to District Court Judge Robert R. Merhige, the three men had received cruel and unusual punishment at the state penitentiary and that the director of the state's Division of Corrections, W. K. Cunningham, had sometimes encouraged through "affirmative action" such unconstitutional mistreatment.[19]

As was noted earlier in this chapter, the courts, in their dealings with administrative agencies, have generally confined themselves to questions of procedure and law and have tended to avoid questions of fact and substance. However, the boundaries between the two obviously overlap and many decisions seem to go beyond the limits which the courts have generally set for themselves since the Schecter case. One example of this was the Overton Park controversy.[20]

Overton Park lies in the center of Memphis, Tennessee. Its 170 acres include a zoo, golf course and other recreational facilities. In the late 1960's the Department of Transportation gave final approval to a plan that would have run a six-lane expressway through the park. The proposed road would have severed the zoo from the remainder of the park, removing 26 acres of park land in the process.

Many Memphis citizens were understandably upset over the decision, and, joined by various conservation groups, they took the case to court. The plaintiffs pointed out that the Department of Transportation

18. Leon Friedman, "The State in the Dock," *New York Times,* February 18, 1973 (News in Review).
19. *Boston Globe,* February 2, 1973.
20. *Citizens to Preserve Overton Park, Inc.* v. *Volpe,* 401 U.S. 402 (1971).

Act of 1966 barred the Secretary of Transportation from authorizing federal funds for highways through such parks unless (1) there was no "feasible and prudent" alternative to the use of such land and (2) the plan included all possible steps to minimize the harm of such a taking to park and recreation areas. They claimed that both these restrictions had been disregarded in this instance.

The petitioners lost in the district court and again in the court of appeals. Both courts ruled that what was "feasible and prudent" lay within the discretion of the Department of Transportation as long as the department could show that it had not acted in an arbitrary or capricious manner. However, when the protesters reached the Supreme Court, they gained a more sympathetic response.

The Supreme Court reversed the decision of the lower courts and sent the case back to the district court, saying that the record was inadequate for determining whether or not the Secretary of Transportation had exceeded his authority or abused his discretion. This, in itself, did not clearly indicate that the nation's highest tribunal was making a finding of substance. However, comments by the Court in connection with its decision caught the interest of scholars of administrative law.

It seems that in writing up its decision, the Supreme Court refused to accept the argument that building highways through park land could ipso facto be justified simply by showing that to do so was cheaper or more expedient. Although such proof might suffice to establish lack of arbitrariness or capriciousness, said the Court, it would not automatically meet the "feasible and prudent" limitation of the law. The justices noted that putting highways through parks would almost always be cheaper and less disruptive than most other alternatives but that such a fact could not therefore serve as an unconditional rationale for highway builders to do so. On the contrary, said the Court, the preservation of park land is to be given a "paramount" importance in deciding whether or not it is to be used for highways.

The *Duke Law Journal* in analyzing the decision, claimed that "the court chose a more restrictive interpretation of the phrase 'feasible and prudent' than was intended by the Congress." The *Journal* went on to point out that while the decision may be "initially attractive from an environmental perspective," it raised various doubts and dilemmas concerning the Court's role in overseeing administrative agencies. It seemed to mark a departure from the Court's practice of staying out of policy-making. And this, said the journal, could open the door to court intervention in a variety of matters regarding which the courts have no special expertise.

"To ask courts to attempt to make such [policy] decisions on the basis of their limited knowledge vis-a-vis that of an agency in a given

381

area would seem to be a mistake, sacrificing expert and informed judgment for an individual court's notion of desirability in a particular instance," said the *Journal,* "The ultimate result of *Overton Park* then may be a step-up in federal court involvement in many technical and specialized controversies with the consequent delay and loss of efficiency in decision-making."[21]

Whether or not the Overton Park case constitutes a disturbing precedent for the future remains to be seen. By the mid-1970's, however, the thrust of administrative law seems to have followed the lines noted earlier, namely, increasing strictness over procedures accompanied by general reluctance to intervene on matters of policy. Even the Court's rigorous application of administrative due process has had some limits. Thus, while it has stopped the federal government from dismissing homosexuals from any job simply on the ground that they are homosexuals, it has allowed the government's policy of withholding security clearance from homosexuals to stand. The government's rationale that homosexuals are vulnerable to blackmail and therefore constitute a security risk has not been found to go beyond the spirit and scope of due process.[22]

In another matter, a U.S. court of appeals upheld the firing of a 27-year-old unwed air force nurse who became pregnant while on active duty. The nurse claimed that she had been subjected to discrimination since male officers who fathered unwed children were not subject to the same penalty. However, the court ruled that a pregnant nurse serving in a hospital in a combat zone in Vietnam, such as the one where the petitioner was stationed, could suffer a miscarriage during an attack and become "a liability and a burden to the Air Force." On these grounds, then, the court held that the air force was within its rights in dismissing her.[23]

Finally, when the Internal Revenue Service seized some goods and property of the Heck Transfer and Storage Company of San Diego and proceeded to sell them at auction in order to satisfy some back taxes and penalties which the company had resisted paying, the courts upheld the action. Although the company, along with a band of anti-IRS supporters, protested that, among other things, seizure without a court order was a violation of due process, the courts sustained the IRS.[24]

In short, while administrators must tread carefully these days, and while they must respect the rights of employees, clients and the public,

---

21. "Administrative Law Developments—1971," *op. cit.,* pp. 323-324.
22. *New York Times,* April 21, 1971.
23. *New York Times,* November 16, 1971.
24. *Time,* March 19, 1973, p. 45.

they and their agencies still enjoy a fair degree of discretion in carrying out the missions and assignments entrusted to them.

ISSUES IN ADMINISTRATIVE LAW

As the preceding section has indicated, the field of administrative law, after a century of intense litigation and adjudication, remains alive with simmering issues. And with administration being what it is, and the law being what *it* is, it seems unlikely that many of these issues will shrivel up and fade away. Legal complications and complexities appear destined to provide a fertile field of litigation for lawyers and a Pandora's box of perplexities for administrators for many years to come.

One issue which has yet to be fully resolved is the question of hearsay evidence. Hearsay is a report of a statement made by someone who is not present for cross-examination. It is therefore considered second-hand evidence and as such is excluded from American courtrooms. Should it be barred from administrative proceedings as well?

The Administrative Procedures Act of 1946 ruled out any evidence that would be "irrelevant, immaterial or unduly repetitious." However, it did not go so far as to outlaw hearsay evidence as such. In a 1971 case the Supreme Court held that uncorroborated hearsay evidence can constitute "substantial evidence" sufficient to support an administrative ruling.[25] However, this did not mean that all such evidence was to be indiscriminately accepted. It would have to be relevant, reliable and supportive of the point for which it was being used. Material "without a basis in evidence having rationality and probative force" would not meet the Court's standard.

Such a ruling as this one, of course, does not close the door on the issue but only opens it wider. Wrangles can erupt at any time as to whether a particular piece of hearsay evidence meets the criteria for relevance and probative value. Many, meanwhile, still question whether any hearsay evidence at all should be allowed to influence administrative action. Since, as we have seen, the consequences of administrative decision-making can frequently exceed those of a court trial, it is only right and proper, so the argument goes, that those who would have to bear these consequences should benefit from the safeguards enjoyed by those who are subject to a court trial. Others contend, however, that there is nothing inherently evil about hearsay evidence. Such evidence, as a matter of fact, is admissible in even criminal trials in most countries

---

25. *Richardson* v. *Perales,* 402 U.S. 389 (1971).

in the world, including most democratic countries. To bar it from the hearing room, they contend, would only hinder administrative tribunals from making informed and judicious decisions.

A still more lively controversy regarding the administrative process arises over whether an agency should be allowed to play a double role of judge and prosecutor. When an agency discharges or demotes an employee or deprives an individual or a group of some benefit or right the agency first brings the charges and then, during the hearing, sits in judgment on these charges. In effect, it seems to be sitting in judgment on itself. This, to many lawyers, is inherently unfair and is contrary to both the spirit and intent of due process. The affected party should possess the right, they claim, to have the charges decided by a completely external body.

However, while most administrative agencies adjudicate their own charges, in doing so they frequently resort to a special employee called the hearing examiner. The Administrative Procedures Act provided for the creation of such examiners within various federal agencies to hold hearings on matters that would come before these agencies. Thus, when one railroad wants to merge with another or when two or more business groups apply for the same television channel, the case comes before a hearing examiner for determination. The examiner does not make a decision but a finding. He then submits his finding as a recommendation to the agency heads who bear the responsibility for making the final determination.

Federal hearing examiners are generally highly qualified and highly regarded lawyers who possess a good many years of prior legal experience and enjoy a good reputation for sound judgment and sound character. They are well paid and their findings are well regarded. As classified civil servants, they also enjoy a high degree of independence. Consequently, they cannot be easily manipulated or coerced by their agency colleagues and superiors.

Hearing examiners preside over many of the cases which aggrieved parties bring before administrative agencies. Given their independence and integrity, they do provide some degree of separation between the prosecutory and adjudicatory processes even though they are employees of the agency which is involved in the case before them. The record shows that they have often ruled against their own agencies. Hearing examiner David H. Harris of the Food and Drug Administration, in holding hearings in the fall of 1972 on an FDA move to tighten up the regulations on vitamin pills, even refused to allow the FDA's own assistant commissioner in charge of compliance to testify at the stormy proceedings. Harris claimed the record was "entirely barren" of any evidence that the assistant commissioner was qualified as an expert on the subject he wanted to speak on.[26]

The use of hearing examiners has mitigated much of the argument that administrative hearings violate due process in allowing the agency to sit in judgment on itself. However, it has not eliminated it completely. Those who are not satisfied point out that examiners are still not used for many administrative hearings and in any case they are still employees of the agency holding the hearing. Furthermore, their findings are not final and the agency heads still make the ultimate decision.

Suggestions have been made to divorce the examiners completely from any particular agency, setting up, in effect, a new administrative unit in the federal bureaucracy which would assign examiners from one agency to another as cases arose. This would, it is true, give still more independence to the examiners. At the same time, however, it would reduce their expertise in the matters under dispute, for they would no longer be specialized in the work of one agency. Another suggestion calls for examiners to become, in effect, judges, handing down not just recommendations but decisions. The agency head or heads could still overrule an examiner but in doing so they would have to overturn a decision rather than simply disregard a recommendation. Presumably, this would in practice prove more difficult to do.

Underlying these and many other issues which plague the process of administrative law is a basic one: To what extent should the administrative process be subject to all the safeguards found in the judicial process? Spearheading the drive toward ever increasing judicialization of the administrative process has been the American Bar Association. It has sought, with considerable success, to make administrative hearings more and more like court trials. It has fought to give affected parties a greater right to representation by counsel and a greater right to cross-examine witnesses, as well as increased access to judicial review. It has been frequently aided in this drive by civil liberties groups who look with understandable horror at the expanding scope of administrative power.

The idea has obvious attractions for all those who are worried about the nature of governmental power in a democratic society. Certainly, if administrative agencies are, in effect, to legislate and even adjudicate and punish, then those who are to bear the effects of their actions must be supplied with ample weapons to protect themselves. The United States has evolved an elaborate set of procedures to protect the individual who runs afoul of the criminal justice system. Should not

---

26. Mark Bricklin, "Chemicals, Yes; Vitamins, No!" *Prevention,* June 1973.

an equal set of safeguards protect the person who runs afoul of the increasingly powerful bureaucracy?

The problem is that such protection imposes a heavy price. To the extent that administrative activities have already become highly judicialized, they have become costly and complicated to all concerned. Further judicialization, its opponents argue, would only hinder and hamper them all the more. If the demotion of an errant employee or the widening of a street is always going to involve the detailed and difficult process of a full-fledged court proceeding, then agencies simply will not be able to do what they are supposed to do. They will refuse to undertake many of the things which they should undertake simply because of the time and expense involved. Furthermore, many of the activities they do undertake will fail to yield commensurate benefits since they will too often be subjected to months and even years of delay while the full judicial process is gone through. Innovation, flexibility and responsiveness will all suffer.

In this connection, it is interesting to note that civil libertarians are not the only ones who have shown an interest in curbing administrative discretion. Many major corporations and their representatives have shown an even greater zeal for expanding and extending judicial safeguards in the administrative process. Shortly after the enactment of the Administrative Procedures Act, the *New York Times* reported that "utility, rail and numerous other industries" were "celebrating" the law's enactment.[27] Since that time, these interests and their lawyers have eagerly taken advantage of the numerous opportunities the act provides for striking down or at least delaying administrative actions. According to Winton B. Rankin, former deputy commissioner of the Food and Drug Administration, "There is endless repetition of testimony, witnesses saying the same thing over and over. When several industry lawyers are involved, they won't get together and let one of them do the cross-examining. Everyone has to speak. They'll ask for a recess of weeks to study documents that are put into evidence, even though the documents were available in advance. . . . And appeals to the courts at every stage; you set a hearing date, they ask for a postponement, you deny it, they go to court. They seldom win but everything stops while it is argued."[28]

These tactics not only pay off handsomely for many of Washington's 15,000 lawyers but also for the corporations they represent. Joseph C. Goulden has chronicled what happened when the FDA wanted to establish a rule that any product marketed as peanut butter had to con-

---

27. Quoted in Goulden, *The Superlawyers,* p. 186.
28. Quoted in Goulden, *op. cit.,* p. 194.

tain 95 percent peanuts. The commission first proposed the rule on July 2, 1959. However, it was not until March 3, 1971, some twelve years later, that it was finally able to promulgate it, and even then it had been forced to lower the required percentage of peanuts to 90 percent. In the interim, lawyers for the Peanut Butter Manufacturers Association had argued and fought the case all the way to the Supreme Court.[29] In another instance, the FDA wanted to halt the production of a drug called Panalba which, though effective, sometimes produced undesirable and even dangerous side effects. In this instance, the lawyers for the affected party were only able to delay the commission for seventeen months, but that was still time enough to enable the manufacturer to realize an additional $25 million in gross sales of the drug while exposing numerous people to its hazards. The federal government, meanwhile, was subjected to expensive legal proceedings which again reached all the way to the Supreme Court.[30]

Judicialization also converts administrative hearings into adversary proceedings, and this raises additional problems. Lawyers for the affected party or parties treat those testifying for the government as "hostile witnesses" and seek relentlessly to discredit their testimony, their qualifications and even, if possible, their integrity. This tends to make many witnesses, particularly those who fall into the category of professional experts, reluctant to testify. Many scientists turn down FDA work for this reason. Also open to question is whether attacking expert witnesses in this way constitutes the best procedure for ferreting out the facts necessary for making sound administrative decisions.

Judicialization of the administrative process is thus no magic cure-all for making the bureaucracy behave in a responsible and responsive manner. Frequently, it can have the reverse effect. Even when it comes to protecting the rights of the affected party, it can sometimes cut both ways, as the following case study will show.

CASE STUDY

The "Trial" of J. Robert Oppenheimer[31]

On the Monday afternoon of December 21, 1953, J. Robert Oppenheimer showed up by invitation at the office of the chairman of the Atomic Energy Commission, Lewis Strauss. There was certainly nothing unusual in Strauss

---

29. *Ibid.,* pp. 191–194.
30. *Ibid.,* pp. 209–214.
31. The material, including quotations, for this case study was taken almost exclusively from *The Oppenheimer Case; Security on Trial,* by Philip M. Stern with the collaboration of Harold P. Green (New York: Harper & Row, 1969).

having invited the distinguished scientist to pay him a call. Although now heading an institute at Princeton University, Oppenheimer still held a consultant's contract with the AEC. It allowed the Atomic Energy Commission to call upon him for advice and assistance from time to time and presumably this was one of those times.

It was, however, nothing of the sort. While the meeting got underway casually enough with some joint lament over the recent death of a mutual friend, it changed abruptly when Strauss handed Oppenheimer a 3,400-word letter. The letter informed Oppenheimer that the AEC was stripping him of his security clearance and detailed its reasons for doing so.

The action came as a surprise and a shock, not only to Oppenheimer but to most of the world. The renowned physicist had eight years earlier built the atomic bomb, and in so doing had carried around with him more secrets than almost any person in the United States outside of the president. Indeed, just a year previous to his meeting with Strauss, Oppenheimer had received from outgoing President Truman a warm letter praising him for his "lasting and immensely valuable contribution to the national security and to atomic energy progress in the nation." Now, the scientist had been found unfit and untrustworthy for even the most meager of all clearances, one that had been extended to thousands of typists and clerks as well as scientists and officials in numerous government agencies.

What was the basis for the AEC's startling action? The essence of their charges against Oppenheimer, as spelled out in its letter was that he had shown himself indiscreet, at the least, in associating with communists and communist causes and had also on occasion shown himself deceptive in answering questions about such incidents in his past. More specifically, he was accused of having had numerous contacts with communists, with having given money to what were called communist-front causes and with having at one time subscribed to a communist newspaper, *The People's World.* He had also lied about one incident involving his association with a suspected communist agent.

What was unique about these charges was, in effect, that they were not unique at all. All of them dated back to the 1930's and early 1940's and all of them had been presented to Oppenheimer before he was asked to assume the leadership of Los Alamos. At that time, Oppenheimer had satisfied the government's security officers by pointing out his political naivete in associating with communists and communist-linked organizations, and by claiming that in the incident in which he had lied, or at least not quite told the truth, he was prompted by a desire to shield a friend. The government had accepted his explanations at that time and he had gone on to prove himself most worthy of the nation's trust. Why, then, resurrect all these ancient charges at this late date in a move to deny him security clearance?

Philip Stern's detailed and thorough account of the case entitled *In The Matter of J. Robert Oppenheimer* offers three reasons for the sudden about-face in the government's attitude toward the physicist. For one thing, Oppenheimer, the builder of the atomic bomb, had become somewhat remorseful over the weapon he had done so much to give the world, and for this and other reasons he had opposed the development of its successor, the hydrogen bomb. Given his reputation and influence, Oppenheimer's opposition had hampered the government in generating support for the project, particularly in the scientific community. This had scarcely endeared him to the atomic establishment in Washington and had caused many to question once again his degree of devotion to the country's best interests.

Another reason was much more picayune, but, as any student of politics and administration soon learns, often the most innocuous of incidents can lead to dire developments. Although Oppenheimer had maintained a cordial relationship with Strauss, he had, somewhat inadvertently, made a joke at Strauss's expense while testifying before a congressional committee. A proud man, Strauss was not one to take such matters lightly.

The third and perhaps most important reason for the AEC's move was the climate of the times. Senator Joseph McCarthy was then at the height of his powers and his virulent anti-communism was causing government agencies and officials, not excluding the president of the United States, to cringe. All of official Washington was on the defensive concerning potential charges of harboring communists or communist sympathizers. By purging itself of its connection with Oppenheimer, the government was removing a potential source of trouble and exhibiting a get-tough policy toward possible traitors, a policy that could curry public favor.

One rather ironical aspect of the affair should be noted at this time, and that is that the AEC's action, whether justified or not, was completely unnecessary. If the Atomic Energy Commission really felt that Oppenheimer was a security risk, it did not have to deprive him of his clearance since his relationship with the commission left the decision in their hands on when and where to make use of him. They could simply have not availed themselves of his services for the next six months, whereupon his contract would have elapsed and any connection at all between Oppenheimer and the AEC would have ended. Instead, however, the commission determined to go through the formal and publicized procedure of declaring their consultant a risk to the nation's security.

For his part, Oppenheimer could have easily accepted the AEC's decision. He had no financial need of the occasional consulting work it entailed and, in any case, even if he were able to prevent their action, it would be highly unlikely that he would ever again be engaged by them or any other government agency for such duties. His position at Princeton was quite secure and he also possessed substantial inherited wealth. However, after conferring with his lawyers following his meeting with Strauss, he decided that he had no alternative but to fight the AEC's move. To accept termination of his contract, as he expressed it in a letter to Strauss, "would mean that I accept and concur in the view that I am not fit to serve the government that I have served for 12 years. This I cannot do."

The stage was thus set for a hearing. Since this proceeding has become the subject of a lengthy book and even the basis of a Broadway play, it may duly be deemed the most famous administrative hearing in American history. One writer has called it "the century's most famous treason trial." As such, it illuminates a rather inglorious chapter of our national past and points to some weaknesses in our political culture. At the same time, it also illustrates some interesting and important issues in administrative law.

The AEC felt Oppenheimer's stature made it mandatory that it set up a special hearing board of eminent men whose position was roughly comparable to that of the defendant. Only such a board, reasoned the commission, could secure public acceptance of its verdict. To head the panel, the AEC picked Gordon Grey, a former assistant secretary of the army who had gone on to become president of the University of North Carolina. Grey was a Democrat, but a conservative one who came from a southern aristocratic background. He was also a lawyer.

Selected to serve with Grey were Thomas A. Morgan, a self-made businessman who had risen from the job of salesman to president of Sperry Rand, Incorporated, and Ward V. Evans, the chairman of the Chemistry Department at Northwestern University. Known as a "character" because of his idiosyncrasies of dress and manner, Evans was nevertheless an arch-conservative who prided himself on a near perfect Republican voting record.

As its "prosecutor" to present the commission's charges to the board, the AEC chose Roger Robb, a former assistant U.S. attorney who had won esteem for having obtained a high percentage of convictions in the numerous murder cases he had prosecuted during his government service. Robb was also considered a man of strong right-wing convictions.

To defend him, Oppenheimer and his friends settled on Lloyd K. Garrison, a former president of the National Urban League and a leading civil libertarian. Garrison was a bright and even brilliant lawyer and was certainly devoted to Oppenheimer and his cause. However, as Stern describes him, he was "mild-mannered, almost saintly, at home in the world of intellect and compassion" with little experience in, or apparent taste for, the rough-and-tumble world of an adversary, courtroom-type proceeding.

The hearing got underway at 10 o'clock on the morning of April 12, 1954 and ran for three weeks. Oppenheimer was the first witness and spent a grueling twenty hours on the stand. He was followed by a parade of witnesses who testified in his behalf. Among them were two former chairmen of the AEC and three former commissioners. Then the commission presented its own and much shorter list of witnesses. The most distinguished of them was Edward Teller, the noted physicist who later went on to develop the reputation of having been the "father of the H Bomb."

Summations were delivered by the attorneys of both sides with Oppenheimer's Lloyd Garrison making the passionate plea that "America must not devour her own children . . . we must not devour the best and most gifted of our citizens." The hearing panel then voted two-to-one to uphold the commission's charges. The dissenting vote was cast by Professor Evans who summarized his opinion in a little over a page. Grey and Morgan used 15,000 words in stating the majority view. They affirmed Oppenheimer's essential loyalty to the United States but through a convoluted process of legalistic reasoning found him a security risk.

The case then went to the Atomic Energy Commission itself for final action and the commission predictably voted 4 to 1 to accept the majority report and to strip Oppenheimer of his security clearance. The lone physicist on the commission cast the single dissenting vote. Despite this adverse action or perhaps because of it, Oppenheimer went back to Princeton more like a returning hero than a man in disgrace. His colleagues and the scientific community generally rallied to his support and the elderly Albert Einstein personally came to call on him.

Teller, however, remained stricken with remorse over his part in the proceeding and in 1963 he personally nominated Oppenheimer for the Enrico Fermi award, a citation given annually by the AEC. With Joseph McCarthy and the era which he created now dead, and with a new and liberal administration in power, the commission voted unanimously to confer its highest distinction on a man it had previously decreed unworthy of the most rudimentary trust. (Of course, the membership of the commission had also changed in the interim.) President John F. Kennedy said he would personally bestow the award at a White House ceremony, and when an assassin's bullet kept him from doing so, President Lyndon Johnson gladly took on the task.

Three years later, J. Robert Oppenheimer lay dead of cancer at the age of 64. In the eulogy delivered at his funeral, George Kennan said, "The truth is that the United States Government never had a servant more devoted at heart than this one, in the sense of wanting to make a constructive contribution." No discernible public voice arose to dispute his finding.

While the Oppenheimer affair has obvious ramifications which transcend the boundaries of administrative law, it nevertheless sheds a good deal of light on some of the issues we have been examining. To assess some of these implications let us return to the hearing which found Oppenheimer "guilty."

At the outset of the hearing, Chairman Grey pointed out that the proceeding would not be subject to the strict rules and procedures that govern courtroom trials. He implied that such relative informality would prove helpful to the "defendant" in allowing him more flexibility. "Yet," writes Stern, "Oppenheimer, like other security-risk 'defendants' would come to wish that his 'hearing' were governed by certain of the rules and procedures of a trial."

It is easy to see what Stern means. For example, the problem of the administrative agency playing the double role of prosecutor and judge colored the train of events from beginning to end. This first occurred when AEC lawyer Harold P. Green was drafting the statement of charges against Oppenheimer. The commission's general manager, Kenneth D. Nichols, called Green frequently with various ideas and bits of data to help strengthen his case. Comments Stern, "It was as if during a prosecuting attorney's preparation of a criminal case, the prospective trial judge had sought to whet the lawyer's appetite for the impending prosecution." While Stern's characterization is not completely accurate since Nichols did not formally serve on the panel that would adjudicate the case and Green was not really serving as the prosecutor, nevertheless it does have a certain validity. A more obvious instance was the AEC's hiring of Roger Robb to present the charges at the hearing. Since it was the AEC which was to be the final arbiter—the hearing board was only to make a recommendation—the commission would eventually be deciding the validity of a case developed by its own appointee. A further instance of overlapping roles occurred in the appearance of Edward Teller as a prosecution witness. Teller, it was later learned, did not want to testify and only did so under pressure from Nichols. Thus, Nichols, who was associated with the body that was to sit in judgment, worked to strengthen the prosecution's case.

Other aspects of the hearing which failed to conform to courtroom procedure also hampered Oppenheimer and his counsel. Prior to the hearing, he had to hand over all AEC documents in his possession. This helped the government's prosecutor but hindered his own attorneys in preparing his defense.

The right to examine many of the pertinent documents in the case required security clearance. It took the AEC only eight days to give Robb an emergency clearance. It took eight weeks to do the same for Garrison, and since Garrison was late in applying for the clearance to begin with, he did not receive it until the hearing was almost over. As a result, not only was he unable to examine much of the evidence against his client, but he and his associate attorneys had to leave the hearing room on four occasions, leaving his client undefended, when the questioning centered on matters affecting national security.

One persistent and powerful aspect of the hearing which hurt Oppenheimer was the absence of the "blank pad rule," which did not at that time govern security-risk hearings. This meant that Oppenheimer's fate was being decided by "judges" who had already read the investigative file, virtually all of which was negative. Indeed, the members of the tribunal spent a full week going over the file with the prosecuting attorney before the hearing began. Such a practice would have been unthinkable in a court of law. When the hearing got underway, each "judge" had a thick black notebook in front of him full of information about the case, information which Oppenheimer and his attorneys had not seen. No wonder that by the second day of the hearing, before Oppenheimer had begun to testify, Grey was already giving hints that he suspected Oppenheimer of deviousness.

Hearsay played a major role in the case. Statements made by persons who were not only absent but who were not even named were introduced into evidence. One such anonymous informant was later found to be mentally deranged.

In the light of the foregoing, a case can easily be made that the lack of full-scale courtroom procedures proved damaging to Oppenheimer and his case.

However, viewed from another perspective, a case could be made that Oppenheimer suffered because the proceeding was too much like a trial.

First, there were the courtroom tactics which Robb skillfully employed. He badgered and bullied Oppenheimer and Oppenheimer's witnesses almost mercilessly, seeking to score a trial lawyer's points. He would persistently try to catch the defendant and those appearing in his behalf in errors. None of the witnesses, with one exception, had any experience in being exposed to such tactics and most of them proved vulnerable to their use. Oppenheimer in particular showed up badly, at one time even blurting out "I was an idiot." A procedure that smacked less of the adversary proceeding of a courtroom might have served him better.

An adversary courtroom-type proceeding, so the rationale goes, is the best means for discovering the truth. Too often, however, it becomes instead a method for discovering which side has the best lawyer. Certainly, it places a heavy emphasis on the respective legal skills employed by the two contending parties and in this case, the defense was at a distinct disadvantage. Garrison was simply no match for a man who had prosecuted twenty-seven accused murderers. And so thanks to the trial-like nature of the proceeding, Oppenheimer lost again.

A full-blown, trial-like, administrative hearing also tends to run up the same costs as a full-scale courtroom trial. The hearing cost Oppenheimer approximately $25,000 in direct, out-of-pocket expenses. At today's prices, it would cost much more. But even adjusting for inflation would grossly understate the real expense, for Garrison and his associates did not charge him for the six months of work that they put into the case. He only had to pay their travel expenses between New York and Washington. Furthermore, all of Oppenheimer's witnesses paid their own expenses and none of them took a witness fee. If these fortuitous circumstances had not prevailed, then Oppenheimer's defense, adjusted for today's price level, could have cost him close to a quarter of a million dollars.

Thus, the Oppenheimer case provides ammunition for both sides of the argument when it comes to deciding the extent to which the administrative process should be judicialized. While Stern notes that Oppenheimer would have fared better in certain respects if the hearing had been more like a courtroom trial, he nevertheless notes that an ordinary hearing would have been "less formal and combative" and this might have helped rather than hurt the scientist. He quotes Green, the AEC lawyer who drafted the original charges, as saying that some matters injurious to Oppenheimer would not have been raised "if the case had been handled normally before a regular experienced AEC hearing board; as an inquiry, not a trial; and without a full-fledged prosecution." Under such a less judicialized procedure, the panel would call most of the witnesses and do most of the questioning with the government and defense attorneys playing only supplementary roles.

The Oppenheimer case, then, shows the perils of both too much and too little judicialization. It thus can furnish support for each side as the controversy over judicialization of the administrative process continues to rage.

ADMINISTRATIVE CONTROL

In the fifty-first of their famous Federalist Papers, James Madison and Alexander Hamilton pointed out,

> If men were angels no government would be necessary. If angels were to govern men, neither external nor internal controls on government would be necessary. In framing a government which is to be administered by men over men, the great difficulty lies in this: you must first enable the government to control the governed; and in the next place oblige it to control itself. A dependence on the people is, no doubt, the primary control of the government; but experience has taught mankind the necessity of auxiliary precautions.[32]

The judicial safeguards which we have so far examined in this chapter constitute an important part of the "auxiliary precautions" which Hamilton and Madison referred to. However, they by no means embrace them all. As administration has grown in size and scope, as it has become increasingly comprehensive and complex, a welter of "auxiliary precautions" has evolved in a continuing effort to keep it within controllable bounds.

As the writers of *The Federalist* perceptively noted, there are really two aspects to the subject of administrative control. One is the control which agencies must exercise over their own constituent elements, be they subunits or individuals; the other is the control which must be imposed on the agency itself. These two forms of control overlap and even duplicate in many areas. In other areas and respects, however, they diverge and even conflict. An agency may show itself quite zealous in *exercising* internal control but equally zealous in *contesting* external control. Thus the question of administrative control has two quite distinct aspects which, though they often make use of the same techniques and devices, warrant separate consideration.

Internal Control

In chapter three we noted that staff units and their personnel frequently perform a controlling function even when they have no authority or mandate to do so. This is what frequently makes them disliked or at least disfavored by people of the line. The school social worker has no right to tell the teacher what to do. However, the fact that she may be dealing with one or more of the teacher's pupils brings her into contact with the teacher and usually leads, at a minimum, to some joint consul-

---

32. Hamilton, Jay and Madison, *The Federalist*, p. 337.

tation. And while the social worker has no authority to order the teacher to do or refrain from doing anything if her requests are not met, she will most likely appeal to the teacher's department head or principal if her suggestions are rejected. Furthermore, in talking with her pupils, the social worker is, to some extent, checking up and may disclose what she finds to the teacher's colleagues if not her superior. Thus, though teachers do not commonly regard social workers as enemies and instead often welcome their assistance, an element of control is nearly always present in their relationships.

What holds true for the teacher's relationship with the social worker also characterizes the teacher's relationship with the guidance counsellor, the school secretary, the custodian and other non-line personnel. As they carry out their duties they are likely to come into contact with the teacher and are thus likely to become aware of what she may or may not be doing. If the teacher is not doing anything untoward, then she may not feel any pressure at all from these contacts. But if she were to "step out of line" to any degree, she undoubtedly would. At the minimum, "word would get around," causing reverberations which she would subsequently experience as disquieting. All of these staff personnel may also make demands upon her and though she has the option, in most instances, of refusing them, each refusal is likely to cost her something even if it only takes the form of an attenuation of relations which makes her organizational environment a little less pleasant.

In this manner, then, staff services tend to provide internal control even when they are not expressly designed to do so. However, many staff services are expressly designed with a control function at least partly in mind.

One of these is the personnel department. If it enjoys a fair degree of authority, as many such departments do, it can wield a considerable influence in determining how line departments and line officials deal with their personnel problems. But even when a personnel unit has no such authority, i.e., even when it has no power other than to recommend, it still does not lack influence. There is always a price to be paid, no matter how small it may be, for saying no. Thus, personnel departments are inevitably units which perform a controlling function.

When it comes to staff services involving financial matters, the control function becomes still more apparent. The budget bureau or budgeting office of any agency or any government obviously exercises a high degree of control, for it plays a crucial role in deciding who gets what amount of money for what purpose. Since this function has already been the subject of an entire previous chapter, it requires no further elaboration here.

Another staff department which plays a very direct role in exercising financial control is the purchasing office. Generally, line departments as well as staff bureaus must apply to the purchasing agent when they want to buy anything other than small, petty-cash-type items. The purchasing agent, in turn, must usually adhere to certain prescribed rules in filling their requests. One of the most important of these rules requires him to put contracts to purchase the requested item or service out to bid and to accept the lowest qualified bidder. This stipulation is often waived in whole or in part when the contract is quite small or when it calls for an exceptional type of equipment or service which can only be supplied by one firm. However, even in this latter instance he will normally exercise some care to see to it that the exceptions are justified.

Perhaps the most important financial control unit is the auditing branch. Certainly, it is the one which is expressly charged with control and with little else. For obvious reasons, auditing is best performed by a unit that is as separate as possible from the activities that it is auditing. As such, it more often falls into the category of external control. Yet, some organizations, particularly large ones, have their own auditing units and an organization of the size of the Defense Department actually has specialized auditing offices. For example, in 1964 the department set up its Defense Contract Audit Agency to centralize, and hopefully improve, the auditing of defense contracts.

There have been some important changes in the auditing function in recent years. First, there has been a shift of emphasis from pre-audit to post-audit activities. Auditing offices have begun exercising less and less control over expenditures before they are made and instead have begun centering their efforts on checking up afterward. To some, this seems like locking the barn door after the horse is stolen. Others, however, point out that this is really just as effective since awareness that the books will be examined will generally provide the proper deterrent to financial abuses. At the same time, it makes for less work by the auditors and gives less work and aggravation to those they are auditing since they now do not have to clear every expenditure ahead of time.

Another change which follows along these same lines has been to replace complete audits of all expenditures with selected audits of only some expenditures. The selection is usually done through a carefully worked-out sampling procedure. Congress in 1964 gave all federal agencies permission to use such procedures in checking vouchers amounting to $100 or less. This again saves the auditing forces a lot of time and effort, and if the sampling technique is statistically well prepared, it results in no significant loss in financial control. The use of sampling techniques, it should be pointed out, is not confined to simple financial disbursements. Some welfare systems, for example, use such a procedure to check as to whether their clients are eligible, and the Internal Revenue Service uses a complex and highly secret statistical sampling technique for determining which tax returns it will review.

While the internal audit office, when it exists, is usually the only *financial* staff function which has control as its primary purpose, other staff units may also exist expressly to perform such a function in other control areas. Some sizeable organizations maintain special units which do nothing but keep watch on the activities of the rest of the organization. Big city police departments, for example, usually have an internal inspection division or "shoefly squad" as it is often called to maintain surveillance over possibly erring organization members. The Department of Agriculture set up its own Office of Inspector General following some scandals in 1962. Like most such units, it reports directly to the head of the organization, in this case the Secretary of Agriculture. This 850-member unit actually combined both an auditing and investigating function until it was split into two different units, an Office of Investigation and an Office of Audit, in late 1973.[33]

Most organizations of any size also utilize a form of control called the field inspection. Sometimes these inspections are done by internal investigation units, but more often they are performed by simple field inspectors and sometimes by regular line officials. In any case, it has become customary to try to eliminate some of the aura of "snooping" from these field check-ups. Instead, the emphasis is being placed upon the positive aspects of such inspections. The inspectors profess, and often try to fulfill, a goal of only seeking to aid and assist the branch or field office they are inspecting. While their protestations of good intent are often greeted with cynicism, sometimes well merited, by those being inspected, still a change in emphasis is taking place.

The goal of trying to make field inspections into a positive rather than a negative phenomenon is best achieved when field inspections are made on an announced and scheduled basis. Unannounced inspections, it is true, do permit the inspectors to catch the unit unawares, and thus unable to put on a deceptive camouflage or protective coloration for the inspection visit. However, its costs may outweigh its benefits. First, the local officials may be away or tremendously busy on the day the inspectors have chosen to pounce on them and thus may not be able to supply records, answer questions, etc. Then the unit itself may be undergoing an unusually critical or unusually slack period. Consequently, just because the inspectors have arrived unannounced does not mean that they have caught the unit on a typical day and are thus warranted in judging its overall performance on the basis of what they see on any particular occasion.

The fact that the possibilities of deception are supposedly in-

---

33. *New York Times*, November 30, 1973.

creased when inspections are announced beforehand should present no great problem. Experienced and alert inspectors, equipped with the proper tools and techniques and oriented toward inspecting for substantive rather than superficial problems, should have no great difficulty in seeing through any deceptive strategy which they may encounter.

Most important of all, however, is the fact that the announced inspection does not create fear, distrust and hostility. It does not indicate to the people of the subunit that the organization does not trust them. Consequently, it tends to encourage the positive and cooperative attitude which an organization needs to perform in an optimally effective manner.

The Forest Service offers an example of the possibilities inherent in announced inspections. The Service places a great emphasis on its field inspections and tries to use them to strengthen the ranger's affinity to the organization and to develop his skills. "There are no surprise visits," writes Kaufman in *The Forest Ranger*, "for the objectives of inspection are not so much to catch personnel in the wrong as to find out what is happening in the woods and to train forest offices in the organizationally approved methods of resource management. Besides, unless advance notice is given to the units to be visited, there is a chance that the entire staff will be out working when the inspectors arrive, and the inspectors will lose valuable time (and be thrown off their own schedules) while they wait for the return of those they came to see."[34]

After detailing some of the matters that are likely to be covered in such an inspection, Kaufman goes on to point out that "the atmosphere of inspection is not one of a trial or even a competitive examination. In the evenings, when the work is done and the notes written up, the inspectors and the inspected gather socially to discuss personal and organizational affairs. . . . Men in the field, rather than fearing inspections, tend to welcome the opportunities it affords them to keep abreast of developments in the organization, to learn the latest rumors and gossip, and to give their own ideas to their superiors at first hand."[35]

External Control

Along with the courts, whose role in providing external control we have already examined, numerous other agents and agencies exist to curb and check administrative power. Since many of these forces constitute, at the same time, sources of support for administrators, a more detailed analysis of their relationship with administration must await the next chapter. At this juncture, we will limit ourselves to a brief review of their function as agents of restraint and regulation.

---

34. Kaufman, *The Forest Ranger*, p. 142–143.
35. *Ibid.*, p. 145.

The instrumentality that is most expressly and directly charged with controlling administration is the legislative branch of government. Legislatures exercise this function in many different ways. The first is through their customary control over expenditures. Even the least powerful of city councils can usually, at a minimum, cut a mayor's or city manager's budget, while many city councils, to say nothing of state legislatures and the Congress can add, cut and shift around appropriations pretty much as they see fit (subject, of course, in most cases to a chief executive's veto). Joseph Harris, in his authoritative work *Congressional Control of Administration,* says that Congress' power over expenditures is "perhaps the most important single control over the departments."[36]

This power is largely, though not exclusively, exercised during budget hearings. And it is a power which can strike terror into the hearts of administrators. Richard F. Fenno, Jr. in his book *The Power of the Purse* quotes a Washington bureaucrat as saying "There is not a bureau head here whose blood pressure doesn't go up before the appropriations hearing. It's an ordeal. You don't know what questions they might ask or what case they might bring up."[37] Budget hearings, which are annual affairs in most legislative bodies, provide legislative committees excellent opportunities not only to make or to pass on key decisions regarding future agency operations but also to review the agency's activities. Such hearings thus can become probing and quite painful proceedings whose outcomes can prove decisive for an agency's continued well-being or even survival.

Another way in which legislative bodies can exercise control over administration is through confirmation of appointments. The United States Senate must advise and consent on most presidential appointments to agencies situated outside what is called the Executive Office of the President. Since only a small portion of the federal bureaucracy is situated within the Executive Office—they include the Office of Management and Budget, the National Security Council, the Office of Science and Technology and some others—this gives the nation's upper house a fair degree of at least residual power over the administrative branch. In practice the Senate usually goes along with the president's nominee. At the same time, however, presidents not infrequently make at least some appointments at the behest of certain key senators. Furthermore, at times the Senate has succeeded in exacting policy commitments from presidential appointees before confirming them, and, on occasion, it has turned down appointees that it does not like. Many state legislatures and not a few city councils also possess the power to

36. Joseph P. Harris, *Congressional Control of Administration* (Garden City, N.Y.: Doubleday, Anchor Books, 1965), p. 8.
37. Richard F. Fenno, Jr., *The Power of the Purse* (Boston: Little, Brown, 1966), p. 283.

pass on certain gubernatorial or mayoral appointments and they often exhibit a greater interest in influencing such appointments than does the U.S. Senate.

The most well-known power which legislative bodies exercise over administrative ones is the power to investigate and expose. Congress, state legislatures, and city councils can generally summon administrative officials to appear before them to answer questions. Legislatures and their staffs may also examine administrative records and documents. Most investigations are conducted by the legislative committee concerned, though at the municipal level, it is not unusual for the entire town or city council to become engaged in the probe. Congress, all state legislatures and some city councils also possess the subpoena power which, when conferred on one of their committees, enables the committee to command the appearances of witnesses and the production of documents outside the government proper.

One limitation on this power at the federal level involves what is called executive privilege. Presidents have often claimed that their personal staffs are not subject to congressional demands to testify and that many of the in-house documents they generate are similarly off-bounds to congressional scrutinizers. This power has never been adequately demarcated or defined. In the Watergate investigation, President Nixon allowed his aides to testify at the Senate committee's public hearings but refused to surrender the tapes of his White House conferences and telephone calls until forced to do so.

How effective is the legislative investigation as a tool for controlling administration? Dean Acheson answered the question in the negative. "The most publicized weapon of Congress—and one which as often as not proves frustrating to those who employ it—is the investigation," he once noted.[38] He then went on to quote with approval Woodrow Wilson's opinion on this subject: "Congress stands almost helplessly outside the departments. Even the special, irksome, ungracious investigations which it from time to time institutes . . . do not afford it more than a glimpse of the inside of a small province of federal administration. . . ."[39]

There is no question that legislative investigations have their limitations. They lack continuity, often becoming one-shot affairs which, though they may result in some sensational public hearings, do not provide for following through on recommendations. Then, they have often been launched and executed with publicity factors in mind and this, needless to say, limits their depth and, in some cases, their desir-

---

38. Acheson, *Present at the Creation*, p. 146.
39. W. Woodrow Wilson, *Congressional Government* (Boston: Houghton Mifflin, 1885), p. 271. Quoted in Acheson, p. 146.

ability. Finally, they tend to focus on negative aspects alone and this curbs their ability to provide a rounded picture of what is taking place and limits their capacity for offering ideas as to what should be taking place.

Yet, despite these drawbacks, there are reasons for viewing such investigations in a more favorable light. There is, first of all, what might be called the "lighthouse theory." No one ever knows how many ships a lighthouse may save, and in somewhat similar fashion no one knows just how many abuses the investigatory weapon may prevent. It is generally agreed that administrators seldom welcome such probes, and the fear of prompting one may well deter much error and wrong doing in government agencies. The threat of an investigation probably accomplishes more in terms of controlling administration than the actual use of the device.

Then, other factors are improving the possibilities for continuity and follow-up. Legislative committees have begun showing more day-in and day-out responsibility in overseeing the work of the departments entrusted to their care. The Legislative Reorganization Act of 1946 formally mandated to the standing committees of Congress "continuous watchfulness of the execution by the administrative agencies concerned of any new law the subject matter of which falls within the jurisdiction of such committee."[40] Committee staffing, at the state as well as at the congressional level has markedly improved in recent years, thus providing the basis for more diligent and more ongoing oversight over what administrative agencies are doing.

Finally, civil liberties lawyer Charles Rembar has noted a rather sharp change in the focus of congressional investigative committees during the past two decades. They are, he says, becoming more responsible and more useful. "The Senate tries to pry information out of an unwilling Executive and present it to the public. Instead of stifling free expression, the committees, by and large, promote it. And the target of investigations at the present time is fact rather than opinion."[41]

Another means through which Congress and some state and local legislative bodies exercise surveillance over their respective bureaucracies is auditing. Many state legislatures and city councils appoint an auditor to examine the books of the executive department. Congress maintains for this purpose a department of its own, the General Accounting Office. Staffed by 5,600 men and women with headquarters in Washington but with field offices in the various regions, and even at federal installations overseas, the GAO acts as the watchdog of the leg-

---

40. Quoted in Mainzer, *op. cit.,* p. 76.
41. Charles Rembar, "The First Amendment on Trial: The Government, the Press and the Public," *The Atlantic,* April 1973.

islative branch. At its head is the comptroller-general who, though appointed by the president, holds his post for fifteen years, is not eligible for reappointment, and can be fired only by Congress and not by the president. Consequently, there is little dispute over where his loyalty lies and whose interests he and his department serve.

The GAO has seldom been accused of lack of vigor when it comes to monitoring the activities of the executive branch. Indeed, criticism when it has come has often taken the opposite tack, i.e., it is accused of being too meddlesome. The auditing office has, however, somewhat shifted its emphasis in recent years. In line with the current trends in auditing, it has taken to concentrating on post-auditing rather than requiring agencies to clear expenditures in advance. It has also begun to use sampling techniques rather than make complete examinations of expenditure accounts. At the same time, under a congressional mandate to expand its scope beyond the strictly financial sphere, it has begun using the services of economists, engineers, management consultants and other specialists. With such added resources, it now is able to undertake what are called "management audits." As Comptroller-General Elmer Staats has put it, the GAO has begun shifting its focus away from examinations of "individual mismanagement and waste to some of the broader implications of Government operations."[42]

Congress has begun relying more and more heavily on the GAO. If a senator or congressman finds evidence of something going amiss in the federal bureaucracy, he is likely to ask the comptroller-general and his staff to investigate and give him a report. In 1972, Congress established a new Office of Federal Elections within the auditing office. The GAO, however, still lacks the subpoena power and this curtails some of its activities. It cannot, for example, examine income tax records unless the Internal Revenue Service chooses to let it do so.

One last means through which legislatures oversee administration is through "case work." Congressmen, state legislators and city councilors frequently receive complaints against administrative agencies and checking them out provides them with opportunities to find out what these agencies are doing and how they are doing it. The performance of case work frequently blends with, or leads to, many of the other forms of legislative oversight. Thus, if a legislator, in looking into a matter brought to his attention by a disgruntled constituent, finds an indication of some greater wrong, then he may call for an investigation, or ask the auditors to look into the agency, or subject the agency's officials to some tough questioning at the next round of budget hearings.

---

42. Quoted by Philip Shabecoff, "Watching the Money," *New York Times,* February 25, 1972 (Business section).

In some countries and in certain jurisdictions in the United States, the processing of complaints is done by an official expressly charged with this task. Such an official is called the *ombudsman*. The term is a Swedish word meaning representative and in the Scandinavian countries where the office originated, the ombudsman functions as the people's representative against the bureaucracy. He is always a highly esteemed individual, often a distinguished former judge, who has been appointed for a long term. Equipped with a sizable staff and a sizable scope of power, he can conduct searching investigations and even prosecute mis-, mal- or non-feasant administrators. Although in most cases he acts in response to a complaint, he can strike out on his own when he has reason to believe that an administrative agency is not performing its job properly.

The office of ombudsman has a long and successful record in Scandinavia, and during the 1960's other countries began adopting it. Great Britain and many of the Commonwealth nations such as New Zealand, Australia and Canada have set up ombudsmen as have at least ten American states and several American cities. The American governmental units which have adopted the ombudsman concept usually give the office a different title and rarely confer on its holder the sweeping and formal powers which his Scandinavian counterparts enjoy. Nevertheless, the concept has made headway and does seem to be bearing fruit. Dayton, Ohio, for example, established its Joint Office of Citizen Complaints in March of 1971 and named the former chief editorial writer of a local newspaper as its head. With a staff of twenty, including eight volunteers, the office handles two to three thousand complaints a year.

Citizens are not the only ones who lodge complaints against public agencies. Sometimes the agency's own employees find grounds for rebellion and resistance and this too results in a form of administrative control. Thus, the development of public employee unionism can be viewed as a manifestation of control as can the emergence of "underground newspapers" which are published and circulated through some agencies by dissident employees. Such publications flourished at HEW's Washington headquarters during the 1960's. However, a more striking, though not necessarily more important, form of employee control has been the rise of the "whistle blower."

The term *whistle blower* was originated by Ralph Nader to categorize those public employees who, in effect, blow the whistle on acts by their own agencies when they deem such acts to be improper.[43] Some of the more famous whistle blowers during the early 1970's were

---

43. Ralph Nader, Peter Petkas and Kate Blackwell, eds., *Whistle Blowing* (New York: Bantam Books, 1972).

Gordon Rule, the navy's director of procurement who challenged extravagant cost overruns and claims for extra compensation by navy suppliers; A. Earnest Fitzgerald, the Pentagon cost analyst who called attention to some similar cost overruns in conjunction with the air force's C-5A transport jet; and Frank Serpico, the New York City patrolman whose reports on corruption in his department touched off a wide-ranging investigation which culminated in numerous indictments as well as shake-ups in the city's constabulary.

Many factors account for the growing prominence of whistle blowers as agents of administrative control. One of them is the development of administrative law and the safeguards which it extends to public employees. When the Nixon administration attempted to discharge Fitzgerald, for example, by supposedly eliminating his job, he fought back through the courts and won.[44] A midwestern high school teacher who was fired after he sent a letter to a local newspaper criticizing his school board won similar reinstatement. In general, the courts have become increasingly protective of whistle-blowing employees.

Another factor which has encouraged whistle blowing has been the development of the news media. In this connection it is important to note that the press, in and by itself, has long played an active and aggressive role in controlling administrative actions. "I fear three newspapers more than I fear 3,000 bayonets," Napoleon once remarked, while an English philosopher who was his contemporary, Jeremy Bentham, observed that "Without publicity, all checks are inefficient; in comparison to publicity, all checks are of small account."[45]

The development of broadcast journalism, particularly television news, and the growth of public awareness of and interest in government generally, has made the news media today a form of control that rivals if it does not exceed that of legislative bodies. This is particularly true in the United States which does not have a government-owned television and radio network and which has a long "muckraking" tradition. However, the media is not only important for what it does on its own but for the help it provides other forms of control. It has encouraged and strengthened whistle blowing by providing considerable publicity to the whistle blowers. It also has stimulated legislative control by providing headlines and coverage for legislative exposés. Furthermore, many newspapers and radio and TV stations even act as ombudsmen, soliciting citizen complaints against the bureaucracy and then checking them out.

Another instrumentality of control over an administrative agency is its clientele. For reasons which will be more fully discussed in the next chapter, administrators, particularly American ones, usually need

---

44. *Ibid.,* pp. 39–55.
45. Quoted in Berkley, *The Democratic Policeman* (1969), pp. 159–160.

considerable cooperation from their clientele, and the clientele may and often do seize upon this to exercise some countervailing influence over administrators. Sometimes this takes dramatic and violent forms such as the client takeovers of welfare offices and the student rebellions of the 1960's and the prison riots of the early 1970's. More often, however, clients exercise control by simply refusing to cooperate and comply with policies which they do not like.

One final form of control which often receives little attention but which plays an important role in constraining many administrative agencies is the control exercised by competing agencies. As we saw in chapter four, agencies are frequently locked in combat in fights over jurisdiction, funding, etc. In their continual jousting for power and position, agencies tend to control each other. James Madison actually saw this as one of the more effective forms of control. In a well-known passage in *The Federalist,* he noted "Ambition must be made to counteract ambition . . . the constant aim is to divide and arrange the several offices in such a manner that each may be a check on the other—that the private interest of every individual may be a sentinel over the public rights."[46]

In summary, then, it should appear obvious that the substantial grants of powers which have been increasingly conferred on administrative agencies have been accompanied with increasing means and methods of control. This leads us to the question which forms the concluding section of this chapter.

LAW AND CONTROL: HOW MUCH IS ENOUGH?

Democratic government rests on such principles as accountability and responsibility, and the realization of such principles requires a comprehensive system of administrative control. Thus, the public has a right to demand and administrators have a need to accept a widespread network of restraints and restrictions on administrative activity. Democratic government is controlled government.

Of course, administrators often find such controls irksome and irritating. They are by nature active men and women who wish to "get on with the job." It would be strange if they did not frequently chafe at the checks and curbs that are placed upon their actions. However, in the long run, they, too, benefit from a suitable system of control. Such a system will point out their errors before they go too far and will, at the same time, reassure their public that they are not behaving capriciously or coercively. Many administrators in countries which have ombuds-

---

46. *Hamiton, Jay and Madison, op. cit.,* p. 337.

men, for example, have found that the ombudsman helps them more than hurts them. Through giving them timely warnings when they need them, through constructively pointing out errors and through investigating complaints and finding most, though not all, of such complaints invalid, the ombudsman may assist the administrator in carrying out his mission.

However, the idea of bureaucracy as a dominant and power-hungry force in modern life is not the only negative image which administrators have to struggle against. They must also contend with an equally pervasive picture of bureaucracy as an institution mired in sloth and sluggishness. If bureaucratic agencies are frequently accused of becoming too meddlesome and interfering, they are also constantly being flayed for laziness and laxity.

While administrative controls can help allay the first type of criticism, they can aggravate the second. Controls, while they impede administrative abuse, may also inhibit administrative innovation and enterprise. Administrative agencies are continually being scored for the "red tape" which seems to engulf so many of their activities. Yet, this "red tape" is in many instances the direct result of a desire to monitor and control their decisions, of subjecting them to standards of accountability and responsibility. "Too often in American public administration we assure legality and propriety in hiring, purchasing, building and the like, but prevent not only corruption but action prompt and vigorous enough to be effective," writes Lewis Mainzer. And he goes on to add, "Harmless government is not good enough."[47]

Another writer on administration, Peter Woll, expresses the same concern. "Guaranteeing that agencies will follow certain procedures in no way assures that they will take any action at all," he writes. The issue is an important one, he claims, because, due to the limitations of the courts and the chief executive in directing and implementing policy, "the bureaucracy inevitably becomes the primary instrument of positive government to maintain the public interest." As a result, "The central problem today is not how to curb its [the bureaucracy's] power, but how to guarantee that it will take the necessary action to deal with critical public needs."[48]

Looked at in this light, control, or at least extensive control, can be counterproductive. In its way, it can prove as disturbing and as dangerous to the preservation and maintenance of democratic government as its opposite. Carried too far, it can render government ineffectual and even inert, leaving the way clear for less savory and less responsible

47. Mainzer, *op. cit.,* p. 89.
48. Peter Woll, "Administrative Law in the Seventies," *Public Administration Review,* September/October 1972.

forces to operate. As we saw in our examination of administrative law, the judicialization of the administrative process has proven a bonanza to various business interests who use the safeguards imposed on administrative agents to perpetuate or at least prolong questionable activities.

Too much control also breeds a climate of conflict and distrust which can result in a great deal of dysfunctional behavior. An agency straightjacketed with a strict system of controls will, if it refuses to resign itself to relative immobility, expend a good deal of effort squirming to get free. It may dissipate so much of its energies in trying to overcome the obstacles to action that it may have relatively little energy left to serve the public. Furthermore, it may respond to the distrust which extensive control indicates by meriting such distrust. The American statesman Henry L. Stimson, who served in many high government positions before and during World War II, once observed that one way to make a man trustworthy is to trust him.[49] The reverse may also be true. Certainly, the distrust which pervasive control fosters does little to encourage candor and cooperativeness.

It is interesting to note in this connection that while control plays an essential role in the workings of democratic government, it may play an even greater role in the operation of totalitarian regimes. One reason why Russian factories have such a low level of per capita output is that they have a much higher proportion of administrative employees to production workers. The main reason for this disparity is to fulfill the Soviet system of extensive control.

The Nazi regime offers an even better example of this phenomenon. Albert Speer claims that his success in dramatically increasing war production despite the allied bombing raids and the absence of so many workers at the front during World War II resulted from his successful attempt to dismantle, at least in part, the elaborate control apparatus which the Nazi state had established. Speer says he was able to encourage initiative and speed as well as free 600 to 800 thousand workers for the war effort "merely by substituting trust for mistrust within the administrative system."[50]

As the Soviet and Nazi cases suggest, the costs of control are not only felt in the effect it has on the agencies being controlled but also in the costs of maintaining the controllers. Sometimes such costs can reach ludicrous proportions. In 1887 Lord Randolph Churchill, in conducting a campaign against waste in the British armed services, pointed out that one branch of the armed services was spending 5,000 pounds a year to supervise another branch whose expenses amounted to only 250

---

49. McGeorge Bundy, *The Strength of Government* (Cambridge: Harvard University Press, 1968), p. 56.
50. Speer, *Inside The Third Reich*, p. 635.

pounds a year.[51] To take a more recent and closer-to-home example, the United States, according to Robert Presthus, spent $350 million in 1955 to protect the federal government against supposedly subversive elements within it. This program resulted in the firing of between one-twentieth and one-thirtieth percent of all the employees subject to the program's control.[52] Furthermore, given the nature of those rather hysterical times, it is questionable as to how many of those who were actually caught in the elaborate net of the government's security program were really culpable.

One final fact concerning the cost of control should be taken into account. As Peter Drucker has pointed out, control of the last 10 percent of a program or project is nearly always more expensive than control of the preceding 90 percent. Consequently, the cost of control increases significantly as control itself increases. "If control tries to account for everything, it becomes prohibitively expensive," says Drucker.[53]

In conclusion, then, control, whether exercised through legalistic or other means, has its limits if the ends of democratic society are to be served. Fortunately, some of the changes now buffeting administration may help alleviate some of the problems it poses. Programmed budgeting, productivity measures, management by objectives and some of the other new techniques which are coming to the fore may increase responsibility and accountability while replacing or reducing the role of negative controls, that is, control for its own sake. In addition, the growing professionalism which is also starting to characterize public administration may make extensive and elaborate control systems somewhat less necessary. Nevertheless, some systems of control will continue to be needed and the problems they present will doubtlessly persist.

---

51. Parkinson, *The Law and the Profits* (1971), p. 140.
52. Presthus, *The Organizational Society*, p. 304.
53. Drucker, *The Effective Executive* (1967), p. 84.

12

The Search for Support

Perhaps nothing distinguishes the American administrator so much from his European counterpart as the American's frequently unending quest to generate support for his agency and its programs. The reasons for this relate very directly to the distinguishing features of the country's political culture which were denoted and discussed in chapter two. The fragmentation and personalism of our political system in particular tend to make the typical administrative agency something of an isolated entity which must continually develop and maintain its own sources of support.

In his highly regarded and oft-cited essay "The Federal System," the late Morton Grodzins maintained that "the administrator must play politics for the same reason that the politician is able to play in administration: the parties are without program and without discipline. In response to the unprotected position in which the party situation places him, the administrator is forced to seek support where he can find it."[1] Francis Rourke has sounded a similar note. "The political neutralization of bureaucracy is impossible in a country in which the political parties are incapable of performing the functions expected of them in the governmental structure of which they are a part. When the parties do not provide for program development and the mobilization of political support, executive agencies must perform these tasks for themselves."[2]

While these two writers stress the role played by the fragmented nature of our political parties in producing the American administrator's difficult and slippery situation, other factors also enter in. The variability

1. Morton Grodzins, "The Federal System," in *Goals for Americans: The Report of the President's Commission on National Goals* (Englewood Cliffs, N.J.: Prentice-Hall, 1965).
2. Francis E. Rourke, *Bureaucracy, Politics, and Public Policy* (Boston: Little, Brown, 1969), p. 12.

and vigor of the various levels of government, the separation of powers in the various governments found at so many of these levels, the hostility or at least ambiguous feelings with which the American people tend to regard activist government all play a part. The upshot is that the American administrator must indeed cultivate and exercise the skills of the politician if he is to achieve success. He must develop and maintain support.

Where is he to look for such support? As we noted in the previous chapter, those elements and entities which control administration also support it. The courts, for example, in clamping procedural restrictions on administrative behavior also give it sanction, for once the administrator has abided by the prescriptions of procedural due process, he can then look to the courts for legal vindication of his actions. Similarly, the ombudsman, when he investigates a complaint and finds it invalid, tends to bolster the position of the agency in question. Indeed, many administrators in those countries which have ombudsmen have found such investigatory officials to be helpful in deflecting public irritation and encouraging public approval of their actions.

For the most part, however, administrators must assume a more activist role in developing support. This leads them into taking affirmative steps aimed at strengthening and promoting their relationship with other components in their control networks. For example, when the navy set up its Special Projects Office to handle the service's ballistic missile program, the new office wisely saw that it would need the cooperation or at least passive compliance of other navy units in order to succeed. So the Special Projects Office farmed out parts of the program to other navy units in order to gain, if not their active support, then at least their acceptance of the new program.[3]

However, although developing support from other administrative agencies is often useful and even necessary, most public managers tend to concentrate their efforts in support development in three basic areas: clientele, the public and political leaders, particularly legislators. While all three sectors obviously overlap and interrelate, developing and improving relationships with each bring into play somewhat different strategies along with somewhat different skills.

CLIENTELE RELATIONS

American administrators often work hard at developing what Rourke calls "fervent and substantial constituencies." In many cases, such con-

---

3. Sapolsky, *The Polaris System Development* . . . , Chapter 2.

stituencies are as important to the bureaucrat as they are to the elected politician. They not only help the agency to successfully formulate and implement its programs but, more importantly perhaps, may help generate the support necessary to gain the political approval and funding for these programs. A fervent and substantial constituency can produce an outcry that will make any elected political leader think twice before cutting back an agency's scope or reducing its funding. The fact that the Department of Defense has had large and influential clientele groups while the State Department has lacked them explains, at least in part, the ascendancy of the former over the latter during the 1950's and 1960's.

What makes a clientele effective? One rather obvious factor is *size.* Other things being equal, an agency with a larger clientele will benefit from more support than an agency with a smaller one. Another factor is *dispersion.* An agency with a large clientele that is concentrated in only a few states will seldom gain as much influence and power as another agency with an equal number of clients that are more widely dispersed.

A third and quite vital element in assessing clientele support is the clientele's *degree of organization.* The so-called gun lobby which generally supports the Department of Defense is quite well organized. Welfare clients, on the other hand, lack the strong organization which could make them an effective source of support for the Department of Health, Education and Welfare as well as of state and local welfare departments. The fact that programs benefiting the poor suffer from this lack of organized clientele support has often prompted administrators to organize and build up clientele groups on their own initiative. Sometimes this has worked successfully and sometimes not. In the poverty programs of the 1960's, for example, a number of the organizations purporting to speak for the poor, which arose as a result of such initiatives, struck many politicians and members of the public as being too demanding and too controlled by a self-seeking minority of the poor. As a result, such clientele support in many instances proved detrimental to building the programs' overall support base.

A fourth factor which must be taken into account is the *degree of ardor* which the clientele may manifest in rendering their support. The State Department, for instance, does have what might be called clientele groups of a sort. These are World Affairs Councils and similar organizations which, though not organized expressly to support the State Department, do speak for policies and programs that often accrue to the department's benefit. However, the members of such organizations, while sincere and intelligent, lack the intensity of commitment which may characterize some of the support groups of the Defense Depart-

411

ment. Among the latter might be found the defense industries and their unions whose very existence to a great extent depend on the department's well-being.

Usually, the degree of devotion which a clientele group manifests in supporting an agency roughly correlates with its degree of dependence on the agency. However, this may not always be the case. For example, many liberal and humanitarian organizations support programs for the poor even though the membership of most of these organizations is primarily middle or upper class. The fact that these people do not necessarily have an economic interest in the programs they espouse does not ipso facto dampen their degree of dedication. In general, such organizations have rendered more effective support for poverty programs than have the presumed beneficiaries of these programs.

How do administrators go about taking advantage of the potential support which a clientele has to offer? It must, of course, first strive to secure the clientele's cooperation. To this end, it may appoint members of the clientele group to positions, sometimes the highest ones, in the agency. When Franklin D. Roosevelt named financier Joseph P. Kennedy to head the newly created Securities and Exchange Commission, he was motivated in part by the desire to win over the securities industry to cooperate with the new regulatory commission. For the same reason, presidents today usually appoint a businessman to head the Department of Commerce, a labor leader or someone with close ties to the labor movement to serve as Secretary of Labor, and in recent years an American of Indian extraction to preside over the Bureau of Indian Affairs. Similar tendencies are also becoming more widespread at state and local levels. Thus, the greater concern of minority groups with housing problems has led to frequent appointments of blacks to head municipal housing commissions.

Such efforts at clientele involvement are by no means confined to the upper level of administration. At lower echelons, the use of what are sometimes called "para-professionals" has become increasingly popular in many areas of American public administration. School departments are using parents as "teacher's aides," police departments are setting up auxiliaries, correction departments have even begun using rehabilitated offenders to rehabilitate other offenders. Chester Barnard maintained that the customers of an organization should be considered as part of the organization. Modern administration has shown an increasing tendency to carry out this dictum and in so doing has often increased clientele support.

Another and related method of securing clientele support is through the awarding of contracts. This, of course, has played a key role in the powerful support which the Defense Department has managed to build up through the years. Other departments, however, have also not shown themselves lax in this regard. HEW and, to a lesser extent, HUD have also parceled out some of their work to individuals and institutions outside of the government. This does not mean that the sole or even primary purpose of such contracts is to build clientele support. Often, such arrangements are not only useful but necessary for an agency. The alternative for the Defense Department in contracting with war suppliers would be to set up its own armaments industry, a move that would require a major and controversial reversal of a deeply rooted American attitude regarding the relationship of government to the economy. Yet, such contracts and grants do, among other things, foster clientele support.

Important as such activities have become, few agencies can hope to "buy" all the support they need in this manner. They must also learn to gain the backing of their clientele through other means. While space does not permit a full-scale analysis of all the means and methods which administrators have utilized to achieve this end, we can briefly examine three of them before going on to appraise some of the dangers which the task of developing clientele support presents to the administrator and to the society he is supposed to serve.

Strategies of Support: Advisory Committees

If administrators are to elicit the favor and not the fury of their clients, then they must set up effective ways of listening to what their clients have to say. One tool for doing this is the advisory committee.

Ideally, the advisory committee can assist an agency in a variety of ways. It can act as a weather vane, pointing out to the agency what ideological and emotional currents are blowing among its various clientele groups. It can also serve as a sifter for new ideas which the agency may wish to implement. It can further help by serving as a lightning rod, deflecting many of the criticisms and complaints which may be flung at the agency. Finally, it can provide a resource to help the agency carry out its programs.

In order for it to be able to perform all these roles, the advisory committee must be as fully representative as possible of all the segments of the agency's clientele. If it is an advisory committee for a police precinct station in a mixed neighborhood, then it should include residents and business people, blacks and whites, poor and non-poor, young and old. Oftentimes it will be necessary to include not only diverse but divergent interests among its membership. An advisory committee for a housing agency should, for example, include both tenants

413

and landlords. Such a breadth of membership may make committee meetings more tumultuous but also, in the final analysis, more productive.

The Federal Water Pollution Control Act of 1972 charged the Environmental Protection Administration with the duty of making maximum use of public participation. In order to develop guidelines for such participation, the agency set up a committee which included representatives of conservation groups as well as of mining and industrial interests who would have to bear much of the brunt of anti-pollution enforcement. The first meeting, in the words of one EPA official, "blew up" as the conservation members expressed outrage at the presence of the business interests on the committee. They claimed it was equivalent to letting the fox watch the chicken coop. EPA Administrator William Ruckelshaus replied that since in this case the fox had no teeth, the chickens need have no anxieties. Subsequent meetings proved more harmonious and on February 23, 1973, the EPA was able to publish a proposed set of rules for securing the public participation which the act demanded.[4]

Another administrator who made wide and wise use of the advisory committee technique was Chester Bowles. As head of the Office of Price Administration during World War II, Bowles set up an advisory committee for each industry and directed that no significant change could be made in any price, rent or rationing regulation until the appropriate committee had been consulted. The more than one thousand committees established under this mandate contributed much to OPA's generally esteemed efficiency in keeping a lid on inflation during the war years.[5]

Both these examples illustrate the validity of Rourke's observation that at best "the public dialogue as well as the bureaucratic dialogue may be greatly improved by having outsiders participate in the internal deliberations of executive agencies. The bureaucratic dialogue may immediately become more spirited, and the public dialogue may eventually become more informed."[6]

Advisory committees can do more, however, than simply provide useful inputs for policy formulation. They can, like unions, serve as a two-way transmission system for communication, bringing to the agency the concerns of the clients and bringing to the clients the problems of the agency. They can explain the agency's problems and help

---

4. Lackland F. Blair in a short talk at the annual convention, American Society for Public Administration, Los Angeles, 1973.
5. Bowles, *Promises to Keep*, Chapter 5.
6. Rourke, *op. cit.,* p. 103.

win acceptance for its proposed solutions. In some cases, they can even help implement the solutions.

Using advisory committees in this expanded role requires giving them expanded powers. While many agencies and their administrators have been reluctant to take such a step, others have not. One area where clientele advisory committees are assuming more and more authority and responsibility is in public housing. The State Housing Board of Massachusetts promulgated a regulation in 1973 giving representative tenant groups in all the state's housing projects the right to approve all employee hiring. In some cities, tenants have actually won the right to operate the entire project. Meanwhile, the Bureau of Indian Affairs, faced with rising ferment on the nation's reservations, has been moving to shift more of its responsibilities into the hands of the Indians themselves.[7]

Such attempts at clientele involvement are by no means uniformly successful. Frequently, they only produce added stresses and strains. The poverty programs offer an example, in some instances at least, of the wrong kind of clientele involvement, since the "grass roots" leadership that developed did not always represent the interests of the clientele. However, although the trend toward clientele participation in policy-making presents problems and will require caution and care, it seems likely to be a trend that will continue and grow.

Strategies of Support: Complaint Handling

Although involving clients or their representatives in agency operations should do much to allay the fears and appease the demands of the agency's clientele, it can hardly hope to insure complete and continuous contentment. Any agency, no matter how well run it is or thinks it is, will always stir up some dissatisfaction on the part of some of those whom its activities affect. Furthermore, this dissatisfaction will often have a basis in fact for even the best of agencies create occasional injustices. Therefore, any agency of significant size would usually do well to establish a formal and expeditious way of receiving and processing complaints.

A good complaint-handling system can benefit an agency in many ways. The most obvious way is its ability to provide discontented clients with a means of registering their grievances and, if found justified, of having them redressed. Even when the grievance has not been found sufficiently valid for corrective action, the client will often expe-

---

7. *New York Times,* December 3, 1970.

rience some satisfaction in knowing that at least his complaint was heard and examined.

Another and sometimes more important contribution which good complaint handling can make to agency operations is in providing the agency with valuable information. If complaints appear to cluster around one particular segment of the agency's operations or seem to be directed against one or more particular individuals, the agency may want to take a closer look at the operation or the individuals in question. Complaints can aid in the process of internal control and can also assist the agency in evaluating present operations, while helping it in planning future ones.

To make the maximum use of complaint handling for purposes of building clientele support, exercising internal control and evaluating current and planning future operations, administrators may find the following guidelines useful:

1. Adopt an attitude of welcoming complaints and see to it that your agency's clients understand this. Set up a regular procedure and, if possible, a regular branch for receiving and processing complaints and even publicize its operation. If possible have forms printed up to help complainants record their grievances. Above all, try to avoid giving the complainant the impression that he is being given the runaround.

2. Make sure that your complaint-handling procedure provides for following through on the complaint. Too often complaints are accepted but then disappear. Every complainant should be informed of the disposition of his complaint, along with the reasons why no action is to be taken if that, as it turns out, is to be the case.

3. To make sure that the complaint-handling function is taken seriously by all members of the agency, invest those in charge of it with some prestige and power. They will need the cooperation of the rest of the agency in checking out the complaint and they may experience difficulty in obtaining it unless they can speak with some authority. Furthermore, complainants themselves are more apt to feel that they are being given adequate treatment when their dissatisfactions are being heard by someone who holds a position of some authority. U.S. customs officers, for example, usually refer complainants to their supervisors. At one time, the Customs Service ran short of supervisor badges and so aggrieved parties had to be directed to officials who, while supervisors, were wearing ordinary badges. This only compounded the annoyances of the complainants and made many of them outspokenly irate. When the new supervisor badges finally arrived and the supervisors began wearing them, things quieted down considerably.

4. Make sure that you explain the value and need for a complaint-handling procedure to all the agency employees and stress to

them the fact that it should not threaten them in any way. Good employees will actually benefit through receiving a low number of valid complaints. Should such employees receive a high number of complaints, then the problem most likely will come from outside their jurisdiction and investigative action will usually uncover and correct it with benefits to them as well as to the complainants.

5. Make sure you have a system for cataloguing and classifying complaints. Often an agency may want to multi-index them. Thus, a police department may wish to file its complaints according to the area of the city from which they come, according to the type of police work they involve, such as criminal investigation or handling of family disputes, and according to the individuals involved. Only through maintaining a good filing system can an agency make full use of the information which complaint processing can provide.

In recent years, many administrative agencies have begun to institute what they call ombudsmen to handle clientele complaints. These are not ombudsmen in the strict sense since they are employees of the same agency against whom the complaint is being lodged. However, they often enjoy a measure of independence and discretion in seeing to it that the grievances brought to their attention are heard and, if valid, acted upon. The U.S. Immigration Service has set up an ombudsman in its New York City office to process both complaints and appeals for help. "One of my primary functions," says Cono Trubiano, who holds the position, "is to cut through red tape and to zoom in on officials who could attend to a case swiftly."[8] The U.S. Department of Commerce has also set up an "Ombudsman for Business" who, working directly under the department's secretary, gives aid and advice to businessmen in their dealings with the department. Several large business corporations have attempted to do the same, often giving their complaint-handling official vice-presidential status.[9]

Probably no organization in the country, public or private, creates as much clientele disfavor as the Internal Revenue Service. The very nature of its work brings it into an adversary relationship with vast numbers of the country's population every year. However, it gives serious attention to complaints and maintains suggestion boxes in its field offices where such complaints can be submitted. In handling complaints, it also maintains a useful sense of humor. Thus, when an irate taxpayer sent in a turnip with his tax return saying the government was welcome to all the blood they could get out of it, an IRS official cut a slice out of

---

8. *New York Times,* March 4, 1972.
9. Leonard Sloane, "Corporate Ombudsmen Respond to Consumers," *New York Times,* March 21, 1971, (Business section).

the turnip and mailed it back to the taxpayer with a letter saying "enclosed please find refund. Affectionately, U.S. Treasury."[10]

Strategies of Support: Public Hearings

In recounting his adventures as head of OPA during World War II, Chester Bowles relates how a Louisiana senator once frantically called him and asked if he would see "an army of muskrat hunters" who were besieging the senator's office in angry protest over the price ceiling on muskrat hides. Bowles agreed and shortly thereafter a group of angry men clad in hunting shirts and heavy boots trooped into his office. Bowles began by saying that he had trapped muskrats in New England as a boy and was curious as to how it was done in Louisiana. This prompted a discussion which lasted about forty minutes whereupon one of Bowles' aides appeared by pre-arrangement and informed him in urgent tones, "The president wants to see you at the White House immediately." Bowles excused himself and fled to a "sanctuary" elsewhere in the building. "I never heard from the muskrat hunters again."[11]

The story illustrates not only the imagination and enterprise which administrators are frequently called upon to muster, often at little notice, but also of the efficacy of letting people talk. In more recent years, this stratagem has crystallized in the form of the public hearing.

As we saw in the previous chapter, the public hearing has in many instances become part of administrative due process. Administrative agencies are generally required to hold them before they can change their rules, discharge a tenured employee, etc. However, even when they are not required by law to hold such hearings, agencies have increasingly done so, for such hearings may offer opportunities to win support or at least defuse antagonism. New York City's Board of Education, for example, holds a hearing one evening every month, allowing any citizen to speak for four minutes on any topic of his choosing, provided it is related to the city schools.

As a method of improving clientele relations, the hearing is most useful in "clearing the air" rather than in mobilizing support. It brings hostilities, complaints and rumors out into the open and thereby enables administrators to deal with them on a more informed basis. Frequently, it provides new information which can be used to modify and occasionally reverse a course of action which an agency has embarked on. At a minimum, it offers an outlet for resentment which, if kept bottled up, could eventually explode and cause serious damage to the agency and its goals.

---

10. "Diogenes," *The April Game*, pp. 6–7.
11. Bowles, *op. cit.*, pp. 122–123.

Hearings should be adequately advertised and publicized in advance and should be held at convenient times and places. Some sort of record should be kept which should be available for inspection afterward. The agency holding the hearing should also take care to see that both sides are represented and that no one faction dominates the proceedings. To this end, the agency may allocate alternating time periods to proponents and opponents and limit the time of each speaker. Those parties who stand to be the most deeply affected by the issue involved may be given first priority in having their views heard. Thus, an urban renewal agency holding a hearing on a proposed project may allow residents and businessmen in the project area to speak first.

But though sometimes useful, hearings do have their liabilities and limitations. They delay action, consume time, particularly in preparation, and add to expense. The rules which the Environmental Protection Administration eventually promulgated under the Federal Water Pollution Control Act of 1972 required hearings on almost every action the agency would undertake.[12] Frequently, the EPA's field offices found themselves expending a great deal of time and money in locating hearing rooms in areas where the agency was planning to undertake some enforcement action only to find one or two people showing up to be heard.

More important, perhaps, is the fact that despite all the safeguards which an agency may take to see that both sides are adequately heard, the negative side often tends to predominate. Those who are opposed to an action are usually the most vocal and vociferous and so an agency contemplating a proposed move will often find itself confronted with a preponderance of outspoken antagonists when it holds hearings, even though majority sentiment may be in its favor. News reports based on the hearing may thus give the impression that the opposition is much more widespread than it really is. Furthermore, while hearings can clear the air, they can sometimes do the reverse, embittering already rocky relationships and strengthening entrenched positions.

The perils and pitfalls which public hearings sometimes present have prompted many administrators to become somewhat wary about using them to secure citizen input into administrative activity. While required in many instances to meet the standards of administrative due process, and while still useful in some instances in improving clientele relations, they nevertheless may sometimes prove more harmful than helpful. As a result, many administrators and their organizations have begun to look to other devices.

---

12. *Federal Register*, February 23, 1973, Vol. 38, no. 36, Part II.

One interesting and possibly significant development occurred in Seattle in 1972. The Puget Sound Governmental Conference had on two previous occasions, in 1968 and 1970, presented plans for a badly needed mass transit system to the voters. On both occasions, the voters said no. After the second defeat of its referendum proposals, the conference abandoned public hearings as a technique for soliciting citizen views and instead set up work groups consisting of representative citizens and technicians. These work groups gradually fashioned a new set of proposals with citizens participating in nearly all elements of the design process, including selection of routes, schedules and shelters. In the 1972 election, Seattle voters again found a proposed mass transit plan on their ballots. And although this plan was more expensive than the previous ones and would require a 3 percent additional sales tax, the voters this time said yes.[13]

Clientele Support: How Much Is Too Much?

One of the first major federal agencies to undertake a major program of clientele involvement was the Tennessee Valley Authority. It is not difficult to understand why. Censured and condemned from the beginning as a "socialist" and thereby "un-American" enterprise, this New Deal venture faced a compelling need to win local support. To this end, the TVA appointed representatives of influential local institutions to its policy-making body and deferred generally to local customs and sentiments. By assiduously cultivating clientele support, the public power facility was able to prosper and grow.

However, the Authority paid a heavy price for such grass-roots support. It ended up discriminating against blacks, retrenching on conservation measures in order to protect local real estate interests and hindering the programs of other New Deal agencies such as the Soil Conservation Service which it sought to exclude from operating in the valley area. What started out as a highly progressive undertaking became, in large part, a conservative institution as a result of its responsiveness to its presumed clientele.[14]

The TVA case is by no means unique. As Rourke points out, the relationship between a public agency and its clientele is nearly always a two-way street. An agency may achieve great success in marshalling clientele support only to find that it has surrendered its independence and, in so doing, impaired its commitment to the public as a whole. The clientele may manipulate the agency to serve their own limited interests with consequential detriment to general public policy.

---

13. *National Civic Review,* February 1973, p. 100.
14. Philip Selznick, *TVA and the Grass Roots* (Berkeley: University of California Press, 1949).

Examples of clientele capture abound in the federal bureaucracy. The regulatory commissions, for example, have often been accused of actually being regulated by those they are supposed to regulate. The Veterans Administration has become heavily dependent on, and influenced by, veterans' organizations which hold a near veto on much of its policy-making. Even cabinet departments are not immune. Agriculture, Commerce and Labor are often regarded as particularly susceptible to clientele dictation, and many presidents have wanted to merge the latter two departments partly to release them from this bondage.

Agencies that serve only one highly demarcated group are particularly vulnerable to this problem. And when the agency lacks broad public support and when its operations tend to attract insufficient public interest, the problem deepens.

Two current trends in public administration may only serve to increase the amount and degree of clientele capture in American public administration. One of these is the trend toward the clientele basis of organization which was noted in chapter three. Structuring and orienting public agencies on the basis of clientele, while it often offers many advantages in terms of effectiveness and humaneness, will, at the same time, open up more possibilities for clientele influence to get out of hand.

A second trend which could create increasing difficulties is the drive toward decentralization. "Where considerable authority is devolved upon field officials," David Truman once wrote, "there is always the danger . . . that policy will be unduly influenced by those private individuals and groups who are in closer and more intimate contact with the field than are the superior officers." Such a situation, says Truman, "if carried to any great lengths, is likely to beget such differences of policy between field officers that national policy will be a fiction."[15] We saw some of the ramifications of this when we examined the problems of centralization in chapter nine.

Fortunately, some corrective forces are also at work to counter these trends, and, possibly, redress the whole situation. One is the move toward integration of activities. The interdependence between agencies and programs which characterizes today's bureaucratic milieu may make clientele capture of any particular agency increasingly difficult. It is simply becoming necessary for too many agencies to work closely with other agencies. Programs intermesh and sometimes clientele do as well. The sight of a highly differentiated clientele clustered around a highly independent agency may become increasingly rare.

15. David Truman, *Administrative Decentralization; A Study of the United States Department of Agriculture* (Chicago: University of Chicago Press, 1940).

421

In addition, many of the new developments in public administration such as programmed budgeting and management by objectives should make it difficult for a clientele group to induce or coerce an agency to depart from publicly sanctioned policies. Finally, the increased visibility which is being accorded public agencies and their activities, while it will hopefully increase their responsiveness to those they serve, will also increase their responsibility to policies espoused by the entire community. For example, federal regulatory commissions became much less dominated by their clientele groups during the past decade, thanks in part to the increased attention they received from the news media and the public. Such countervailing developments as these may well succeed in offsetting the dangers which increased decentralization and increased clientele orientation may present.

PUBLIC RELATIONS

James Forrestal, who became the country's first Secretary of Defense when the combined department was created after World War II, wrote in his diaries that "the difficulty of government work is that not only has it to be done well, but the public has to be convinced that it is being done well. In other words, there is a necessity both for competence and exposition, and I hold it extremely difficult to combine the two in the same person."[16]

Forrestal, a brooding sort of man who eventually committed suicide, may have overstated the problem but his words do have a ring of truth. Public administrators, or at least good public administrators, would rather do things than talk about doing things, and they often experience the need to explain and expound on what they are doing as a hindrance to getting things done. They frequently begrudge the time and effort that public relations activities take, and even when they do not, they still often find such work distracting and even distasteful.

Compounding the problem is the fact that those who oversee public administration often tend to take a still more critical attitude toward such public relations activity. One might say that the task of image-building has itself acquired a bad image. Congress, for that matter, passed legislation as far back as 1913 barring the use of public funds to pay "any publicity expert unless explicitly appropriated for that purpose."[17] Although no poll has ever been taken on this question, such legislation probably reflects widespread sentiment within the public itself, not only then but also today. To many it does not seem quite

---

16. Quoted in John J. Corson, "Distinguishing Characteristics of Public Administration," *Public Administration Review,* spring 1952.
17. 38 Stat. L. 212.

proper for a public agency to spend public funds to promote itself in the public eye.

Yet, public relations is an integral part of successful public administration. An agency which eschews the public spotlight, which prefers to transact its business in obscurity, may not only fail to generate support for, or at least acceptance of, its programs but may, on the contrary, encourage public distrust and suspicion. Furthermore, in shielding itself from the public view, it is only creating a climate which makes such distrust and suspicion justifiable. The late Supreme Court Justice Felix Frankfurter once defined democratic government as "the government which accepts in the fullest sense the responsibility to explain itself." A public agency that refuses to do so is seldom worthy of the public trust.

On a less lofty level, good public relations may enable an agency to do more and to do it more effectively and expeditiously. It may even enable it to save money. When Chester Bowles asked for $5 million to launch a public relations program for the Office of Price Administration, he claimed that without such a program, he would need $15 million for inspectors to investigate and prosecute minor offenders. Only by intensively disseminating the OPA's rules and regulations as widely as possible, he said, could the new agency keep broad sectors of the public from unwittingly committing illegal acts. His argument persuaded Congress not to slash the OPA's budget request for this purpose.[18]

As a matter of fact, Congress has generally come to accept the idea that public administration requires public relations efforts. Although the 1913 legislation remains on the statute books, federal agencies have easily learned how to circumvent it. For example, they may hire public relations personnel but simply call them public information or even public education employees. It is interesting to note that no one has been prosecuted under the act since it was passed. The same general state of affairs holds true for many state and municipal governments as well. Both public managers and those who oversee their activities have increasingly come to realize the need and even desirability for public relations activities as a way of making public administration more effective.

Working with the News Media

Normally, the most important means through which administrators reach the broad public, i.e., the public which exists beyond their own clientele, is through the news media. Where once such media consisted largely of newspapers, it now encompasses television, radio and a growing number of periodicals. Traditionally and typically, newsmen have

---

18. Bowles, *op. cit.*, p. 93.

tended to slight administrative activity, preferring to concentrate their attention on elective officials. But thanks to the rapid expansion of administrative activity in recent years, their interest is starting slowly to shift. It may be expected that the news media will subject administrative agencies to increasing study and scrutiny as the realization of their growing influence becomes still more widespread.

How does a public administrator work with the news media to create support for his projects and programs? First of all, he should be as frank and open with them and their representatives as he possibly can. Attempts to deceive the news media nearly always eventually backfire. Presidents Johnson and Nixon both experienced a great deal of difficulty through their failure to deal candidly with the White House press corps. Of course, at times the administrator cannot divulge all that the press may want to know. In such cases, it is better to state so frankly than to resort to stratagems in an attempt to cover up and conceal pertinent information. At times, the administrator may be able to ease the tensions which failure to make full disclosure can produce by offering to go "off the record" or by setting a time when further facts will be disclosed. In any case, the press-conscious public manager will try to supply all the information he can as soon as he can, for he knows that refusal to reveal information may not only make newsmen suspicious but may induce them to seek it elsewhere, often from sources which will provide it in a less complete and less objective form.

The administrator who wishes to maintain a "good press" will not, however, simply wait for the press to come to him; he will see to it that he and his agency provide a good bit of news on their own initiative. In selecting and shaping such news, he will be wise to keep certain things in mind.

For one thing, he should focus on those aspects which *directly* rather than indirectly affect the public. For example, an internal reorganization of an agency is not in itself very newsworthy. However, if it brings about a change in the delivery of a service to the public, then this can be singled out and publicized. Or if the reorganization is going to save some money, then this also can be highlighted, assuming that the sum, at least in percentages, represents an appreciable saving. In any case, good public relations at all times requires the ability to see and judge things from the *public's* point of view and this point of view is often quite different from that of someone working for or administering the agency concerned.

In disseminating news about his agency, the administrator should also remember that the specific often scores a greater impact than the general. Thus, a story about one person helped by an agency may ignite more public interest than a general story about all the people who were helped by the agency. This does not mean that the latter should be neglected; it simply means that the former should also be kept in mind. Those concerned with agency public relations should be on the alert for good "human interest" stories that can be distributed to the news media.

Another means for creating legitimate news is to scan agency records and reports for interesting patterns or new trends. Year to year or even month to month changes in requests and demands for services may make newsworthy material and their publication may help to inform the public as to what the agency is doing.

Timing often plays an important role in working with the news media. The administrator should remember that newsmen usually work on tight deadlines and also that they pride themselves on getting a story as soon as possible. Consequently, he should be prepared to cooperate in getting the news to them in an expeditious manner. This does not, however, mean that he must distribute all his news as soon as it is ready. If he has prepared a news story on his own initiative, he may wish to send it out for release at a designated time. This will not only enable the newspeople to study it more carefully before printing or broadcasting it but will also enable the administrator to choose the time he wants it to appear. Some administrators and their public relations assistants, for example, like to "embargo" news stories for Sunday night and Monday morning release. This is because the news is usually light on the weekend and thus their story may not have to compete with too many other newsworthy activities for space and attention. On the other hand, if they have some news to release which they do *not* want highly publicized, such as the closing out of a facility or the phasing out of a popular program, they may release it on late Friday afternoon, knowing that people read fewer newspapers and hear fewer newscasts on Saturday mornings.

The problem of proper timing may involve more than simply choosing appropriate days of the week for releasing material. An organization devoted to traffic safety will find that a news story with a safety message may be more effective if released before a holiday weekend than afterward. A news story that points up the dangers and costs of forest fire will probably fail to score its greatest impact if released in mid-winter. The Internal Revenue Service often seems to time its most newsworthy indictments and prosecutions for tax evasion to coincide with the period when taxpayers are filling out their returns. On April 10, 1973, the IRS brought charges of tax evasion against President Nixon's personal physician. The next day, the IRS secured a similar indictment against a financier whom they accused of owing $1.4 million in back taxes. Both stories created headlines a few short days before the deadline for filing income tax returns.

What about news that places the agency in an unfavorable light?

425

Here, again, a policy of candor and openness usually pays off. When Harry Hopkins took over the newly created Works Progress Administration during the New Deal, he realized that the hastily launched and sprawling organization would encounter numerous problems with corruption. He decided to deal with the situation by aggressively finding out about such corruption before the newspapers did and by announcing it himself.[19] Hopkins exposed more corruption in his own organization than all the newspapers combined, and although it provided some unpleasant headlines for the WPA, most would agree that the agency benefitted from his approach. The air force adopted a similar policy in Vietnam, taking the initiative to announce some of its more grievous errors such as the bombing of friendly villages by mistake. While the announcements hurt the air force, they undoubtedly did less damage than would have occurred had the war correspondents found out about these mistakes themselves. (Unfortunately for the army, it adopted no such policy in regard to the My Lai and Song My massacres with the result that these grim episodes, once they leaked out, created a tremendous furor.)

Another problem which frequently plagues administrators is determining who is to give out the news. Ideally it should be the public manager himself or his public relations office. However, the press often wants to talk to those directly involved, who may be several echelons down or far removed from headquarters. Obviously, the administrator and the public relations officer should know what information other members of the organization are giving out to the press, but they should be wary of trying to establish too firm a control over such interchanges. Carl Friedrich tells the story of how "at one time a federal department head ruled that no official in his organization was to give any more interviews, because one of them had annoyed him. Thereupon," says Friedrich, "six reporters proceeded to that department and got six different stories, all of which were printed and sent to the administrative head to show him that his rule had been foolish and could not really be enforced."[20]

Two incidents during the first term of the Nixon administration point up the dangers of trying to clamp too strong a control over employee contacts with the news media. Doctor Jacqueline Verrett, a research scientist employed by the Food and Drug Administration found that cyclamates could cause severe deformities in chicken embryos. Another scientist learned of her work and mentioned it on a local television show. This, in turn, attracted the interest of a Washington columnist and of a network news show, both of whom asked Dr. Verrett for

19. Robert Sherwood, *Roosevelt and Hopkins* (New York: Harper and Brothers, 1948), Chapter 3.
20. Carl Friedrich, "Public Policy and the Nature of Administrative Responsibility," in *The Politics of the Federal Bureaucracy* (New York: Dodd, Mead & Co. 1968).

interviews. Cyclamates, it should be recalled, were then being heavily used as artificial sweeteners in low-calorie sodas and other beverages.

Dr. Verrett informed her superior and two FDA press officers of the interview requests, and, failing to hear from them, she granted them. Her interviews, along with some pictures of the malformed chicks, caused considerable sensation and when subsequent research by outside investigators showed other potentially harmful effects of cyclamates, the FDA finally banned them from use. However, HEW Secretary Robert Finch, in announcing the ban, expressed displeasure at the way Dr. Verrett had supposedly gone directly to the press without consulting him or her immediate superior. Finch's statement did more injury to him than to Dr. Verrett. It made him the target for considerable criticism, not just from the press but from Congress.[21]

In another incident, the Bureau of Labor Statistics released figures in March of 1971 showing a slight drop in unemployment. The Secretary of Labor issued a statement from the White House calling the figures "heartening" and of "great significance." However, at a subsequent briefing held monthly for the press, the bureau's professional expert Harold Goldstein said the decline was only "marginally significant." When asked if he was contradicting the Secretary of Labor, Goldstein replied, "I am not here to support or not support the secretary's statement. I am here to help you to interpret the figures."[22]

The Labor Department then decided to cancel the monthly press briefing and subsequently assigned Goldstein to analyzing long-term trends rather than monthly figures. But again, such action showed a tendency to boomerang. This time, a Senate subcommittee held a well-publicized hearing to investigate the department's actions.

While cracking down on employees who talk to the press on their own is often a hazardous undertaking, trying to crack down on the press itself is usually even riskier. Politicians generally subscribe to the rule that "you can't win a battle with a newspaper," and administrators would do well to heed the same axiom. Newspeople tend to be critical and somewhat suspicious—when they are not, they are probably not very good newspeople—and they also usually work under great pressure which sometimes makes them slipshod on details. Thus, every administrator will sooner or later find reason to become exasperated over what he feels are misstatements and misquotes or, more seriously, over what he feels is a failure to understand his problems and his point of view. But trying to correct newspeople usually makes the problem worse and trying to fight them can often prove fatal.

When it comes to misstating facts or misquoting statements, the

---

21. Morton Mintz, "Rebuke at HEW," in Peters and Adams, *Inside the System.*
22. Proxmire, *Uncle Sam ...*, pp. 46–48.

administrator can avoid much trouble by issuing as much of his material as possible in written form, usually as a press release, and allowing the media sufficient time to peruse it before a news deadline. When misquotes and misstatements still appear, the administrator would be wise to adopt the attitude that *he* was at fault in not making himself clear and resolve to try harder next time. This approach will usually yield better public relations than calling up the offending journalists and bewailing their mistakes.

When it comes to critical or even hostile reporting on himself, his agency or its programs, the administrator should still try to restrain his rancor. Franklin Roosevelt's Postmaster General and patronage chief James Farley had a unique and useful way of dealing with this problem. Every time a Washington reporter or columnist wrote unfavorably about him he would call the writer and in a good-natured, jocular tone congratulate him on his good work. At no time would he indicate in the slightest that he thought the journalist had written anything which he regarded as wrong.

Every public administrator should accept the fact that no matter how high principled he may feel himself to be, and no matter how well he may think he is handling his job, he will, if he has any continuing contact with the press, sooner or later find himself reading or hearing reports on himself or his agency that he does not like. He should be prepared to shrug them off with good grace. He may experience less pain if he keeps in mind the fact that few people will read or hear the unfavorable story and most of those who do will soon forget it.

On occasion, critical and even caustic comment in the press can help an administrator and his agency. Such comment may uncover weaknesses that he had not been aware of, or it may give him a bargaining point in fending off political demands—look what the press is already doing to me, he can say—or it may, on the other hand, give him a bargaining point for making some demands of his own. For instance, he may cite the unfavorable reports as buttressing his case for increased funding or for increased authority to make changes in the agency's operations. Furthermore, attacks on the agency from any source may help rally the agency's defenders and strengthen the cohesion of its employees. Kaufman found that attacks on the Forest Service often gave its rangers a heightened sense of identification with the Service.[23]

Just as critical press comment may not be all bad, so favorable comment may not be all good. Although every administrator will usually find it to his advantage to maintain generally good press relations, too much favorable publicity can, in the long run, prove injurious to his cause. This is particularly true when it comes to winning political sup-

---

23. Kaufman, *The Forest Ranger.*

port. While elected politicians will often be kinder to an agency that is well regarded by the media, they may become hostile to one which is enjoying too much beneficial attention. "Legislators are capable of being very sensitive to what they regard as improper administrative propagandizing," writes J. Leiper Freeman, "especially when it encroaches on their domain. It does not help administrative leaders and the agencies they represent to become branded as propagandist."[24]

Not only may too much favorable press comment backfire in terms of the agency's relationships with legislators but it may do the same in its relationships with the press itself. The more favorable the media treatment of an agency or its leaders, the more disillusioned they are likely to become when they find that things are not quite so roseate as they have described them. They are then likely to become quite bitter and acrimonious. The administrator who, in their eyes, previously could do no wrong now becomes transformed into one who can do no right. And the fact that the administrator and/or his agency have risen so high in public esteem will only make their fall from grace all the more newsworthy and, therefore, all the more worthy of being publicized.

In brief, while good relationships with the news media are worth any administrator's time and attention, he should be careful not to exaggerate this aspect of his job. In the final analysis, he may do himself and his agency as much harm from doing too much as from doing too little.

Other Public Relations Activities

While cultivating and utilizing good relationships with the news media forms an important part of an administrator's public relations work, it does not or should not comprise it all. There are many other avenues for reaching the public that managers can use, often with quite good results. Furthermore, public relations considerations may properly be integrated into other aspects of agency policy and programs.

One of the more basic ways in which such concerns may make themselves felt is in the choice of a name for a new subunit or for the organization itself. The Internal Revenue Service was once known as the Internal Revenue Bureau; it changed the last word of its title in an attempt to foster a more positive image of its activities. Suggestions have often been made that police departments should refer to themselves as a police service rather than a police force in order to promote a more positive tone. Researchers as well as policemen themselves have often pointed out that over three-quarters of a department's calls are service calls, and consequently such a change in appellation would be more descriptive of what police departments actually do. Correction depart-

---

24. J. Leiper Freeman, "The Bureaucracy in Pressure Politics," *Annals of the American Academy of Political and Social Science*, 319 (September 1958).

ments were once called penal departments; they began changing their titles as the idea of rehabilitation gained favor. And the Social Security Administration's unit for handling requests from congressmen changed its name from Political Inquiries Group to Political Inquiries Branch. The cause of change here was the undesirability of the acronym which the first name gave rise to.

Such concern for titles and names will strike many as quite trivial and no doubt in many instances such a reaction is well justified. Yet, in some cases, titles and names can be important. One of the reasons why so many members of Congress resisted John Kennedy's initial attempt to make the Housing and Home Finance Agency into a cabinet department was the title Kennedy chose for the new department: the Department of Urban Affairs. Many congressmen feared that the department would be unduly oriented toward the larger cities and would thereby neglect smaller municipalities.

Public relations factors should not just influence such seemingly superficial matters as name and title but also some of the most basic features of the organization's structure and style. An organization which is able to infuse its employees with zeal for what it is doing and which is able to demonstrate to its clients that it is achieving its goals can count on having two groups within the community who will speak out on its behalf. Satisfied clients and devoted employees make some of the best public relations people that an organization can hope to have.

At the same time, there are many more specific activities which an organization may undertake to generate public support. It may encourage its employees to participate in community affairs and join various community organizations, and it may, as an organization, take part itself in such community endeavors as United Fund campaigns and blood bank drives. It may also encourage employee sports groups such as bowling and softball teams which play teams from other groups in the community.

A public agency can also maintain a speaker's bureau, sending out employees to describe its programs and policies to fraternal groups, schools, universities, etc. It may operate an intern program which allows high school and/or college students to work for the agency part-time or during the summer. It may hold a periodic open house or give regular tours through its more interesting facilities. It may send out displays and exhibits.

Of course, these forms of public relations can also be overdone. One organization which has often been accused of doing so is the Department of Defense. In 1971, the Columbia Broadcasting System telecast a one-hour documentary detailing what it claimed were the department's excesses in this area. Entitled "The Selling of the Pentagon," the documentary sparked much anti-Defense Department press comment and stirred up considerable furor in Congress. This, in turn, prompted the General Accounting Office to take a closer look at the department's extensive public relations activities, and the following year the GAO reported that the Department of Defense had spent $46 million more than it had reported spending for such efforts.[25] Among the activities which accounted for the overspending, according to GAO, were four special aerial teams which performed at local fairs and other civic events, five military bands which staged over 5,000 performances in 1972 alone, civilian tours of military bases which included 120 costly air tours and the operation of a special school to train military personnel in public relations.[26] The GAO report led to increased surveillance over the Defense Department's public relations activities.

High powered public relations efforts pose still greater dangers to an organization than the possibility of creating, in themselves, adverse reactions from those they are designed to influence. They may also undermine the agency's fundamental role and goals. An agency may become so worried about its image that it actually starts to do less rather than more. It begins to fear new programs and other innovations since they may take it into uncharted and dangerous waters in which it might lose face. It seeks to cover up rather than correct its mistakes and consequently only adds to its problems. In other words, it sacrifices substance for superficiality with results which, in the long term, can prove even more disastrous for itself than for the public it serves. In the following case study we will see examples of both the good and the evil that can come from the active pursuit of public relations.

CASE STUDY

Two Police Forces in Search of an Image[27]

When a young government lawyer named J. Edgar Hoover took over the leadership of the Justice Department's Bureau of Investigation in 1926, he displayed little initiative or interest in public relations. On the contrary, he seemed to prefer keeping the bureau out of the limelight as much as possible. Consequently, during his first years as its head, little was written or said about the FBI's activities. Most Americans did not even know of the bureau's existence.

During the early 1930's the bureau's relative obscurity changed as it sought

---

25. United Press International dispatch in the *Boston Record-American*, August 5, 1973.
26. *Ibid.*
27. Material on the FBI in the following case study is taken principally from *Investigating the FBI*, Pat Walters and Stephen Gillers, eds. (Garden City, N.Y.: Doubleday, 1973). Other sources included Sanford J. Ungar, "The Undoing of the Justice Department," *The Atlantic*, December 1973; "The Heresy of John F. Shaw," *The Nation*, February 8, 1971; "The FBI in Politics," *Time*, March 26, 1973. Material on the German police is from Berkley, *The Democratic Policeman* (1969).

to catch what it regarded as notoriously dangerous criminals in raids that produced considerable gunfire and bloodshed. The first effects of this new and, essentially, unwanted publicity were adverse. The public showed a tendency to identify more with the pursued than the pursuers, and the FBI, in making its captures, seemed to be ganging up in cowardly fashion on brave and desperate men.

This turn of events aggravated and alarmed the still young Mr. Hoover. It prompted him to revise his previous policy of avoiding all unnecessary contacts with the press and, instead, to undertake what a later critic was to call "the most successful job of salesmanship in the history of Western Bureaucracy."

He started by launching a volley of verbal puffery that was to continue up to his death nearly forty years later. Soon books, articles, news stories, letters began to appear, extolling the FBI, its men and its exploits. One magazine published sixteen articles on the agency in less than two years while four books on the FBI, each with an introduction by its director, showed up in bookstores in an even shorter span of time.

Hoover not only encouraged others to write about his agency but did considerable writing himself, (or at least had considerable writing published under his name). By his death in 1972, he had published several books and more than one hundred articles in major magazines alone, along with probably an equal number of articles in magazines not indexed by *Reader's Guide.* His letterwriting campaign was even more remarkable. An editor of an obscure small-town weekly newspaper who might see fit to publish an editorial praising the FBI would soon find a letter on his desk from the agency's director, thanking and commending him for his noble efforts in behalf of the forces of justice. Sometimes letters under Hoover's name were written with the purpose of getting them before the public. When a former Kentucky governor publicly punched a "hippie" in the nose, Hoover sent him a letter of congratulations. The letter itself soon appeared in print and became news.

Hoover's intense utilization of the written word did not lead him to neglect the spoken one. The bureau chief made numerous speeches and encouraged his agents to do the same. Such speeches were designed to glorify the agency and its work before civic groups, school audiences and others. The FBI also stood ready to "assist" others, including congressmen, in preparing speeches that would praise the bureau and its leader.

Radio, meanwhile, was coming into its own as a powerful weapon for influencing public opinion and Hoover eagerly cultivated its potential. "The FBI in Peace and War" became a popular weekly program and recruited its younger listeners into a club which the FBI sponsored called the Junior G-Men. When motion picture producers indicated an interest in the agency, Hoover gladly obliged by opening FBI files for story ideas and by supplying "consultants" for the filming. On occasion, FBI agents served as actors in certain scenes.

Hoover also moved resolutely, though carefully, to take advantage of television. After eight years of deliberation and negotiation, a program on the FBI made its debut in 1957. Soon some 45 million Americans were watching the show every week. Although the program's producers claimed that the scripts were "inspired" by real FBI cases, the plots were usually dreamed up by scriptwriters out of thin air.

In his all-out drive to curry public favor, Hoover also transformed the FBI's Washington headquarters into a major tourist attraction. Visitors frequently were given guided tours through the agency, tours which included exhibitions and other demonstrations of the organization's proficiency. So successful were these tours that a visit to the FBI became almost as much a part of the typical Washington tourist's itinerary as a visit to the Washington Monument or the Lincoln Memorial.

For a while, these efforts paid off handsomely for the FBI. The agency became synonymous with everything good in the minds of a majority of its public and its director became, in the words of a British journalist, "the most powerful police chief in the World." Even Congress often acted as if the FBI could do no wrong. Both branches gave Hoover nearly everything he asked for and seldom disconcerted him during budget hearings by posing an unfriendly or critical question.[28] But Hoover's single-minded pursuit of a glorified image for himself and his bureau led to some dire consequences for the country and eventually for the FBI itself, including its director.

Although Hoover liked to celebrate the FBI as an agency engaged in all sorts of difficult and dangerous missions, in actuality, he centered much of the bureau's efforts on minor matters. One of these was the recovery of stolen cars. Agents would spend long hours going through airport parking lots in the hope of finding a stolen out-of-state vehicle. The reason for this was that if they found one, the FBI could, in effect, give itself a double credit, one for the recovered vehicle, the other for its recovery value which was put into a separate category. Furthermore, prosecution of such crimes was usually quite easy and therefore increased the bureau's conviction rate.

The FBI also focused a good deal of effort on picking up fugitives from justice and eagerly publicized its accomplishments in this area. For example, it claimed to have arrested 30,318 such fugitives in fiscal year 1970. However, more than half of these fugitives were military deserters, not seasoned criminals. Furthermore, most of these fugitives were actually caught by local lawmen. When it came to pursuing and catching those criminals who appeared on its highly touted "public enemy" list, the FBI also managed to score what would seem to be impressive records. However, Washington reporters began to discover that oftentimes a criminal's name would appear on the list shortly before he was captured and speculation grew that a good lead on a miscreant's whereabouts may have been an important factor in securing him a place on the list.

---

28. There were other reasons besides his public acclaim which made members of Congress so hesitant to exercise any genuine oversight over Hoover. Some of these will be touched on in the next section.

Of course, the FBI did not confine itself solely to picking up stolen cars or fugitives from justice, or even its much touted "public enemies." It also entered into other and much more important investigations. However, even here the bureau and its leader liked to pick cases that were not only congenial to their own personal ideologies but also were likely to win headlines and elicit public approval. Thus, the bureau participated vigorously in the wave of anti-communism which swept the country after World War II, catching alleged Russian spies and often prosecuting them with questionable evidence. At the same time, the FBI showed little zeal for cracking down on domestic fascists or enforcing civil rights.

One area where the FBI's lack of interest became increasingly conspicuous was organized crime. For years, indeed, decades, Hoover sought to maintain that there was no real syndicated crime in the United States and his agents did little to prove him wrong. Although records now indicate that Mafia leaders were holding nationwide meetings at least as far back as 1928, the FBI chose to ignore the fact. It was not until the Mafia began engaging in drug traffic during the 1950's and thereby stirred the Treasury Department's T-Men into investigating its activities that the true ramifications of the underworld began to become known. Robert Kennedy as Attorney General in the early 1960's tried to push the FBI into fighting organized crime but with only partial success. The bureau was even reluctant to open its files to the Treasury Department's narcotics agents who by then had plunged into the fight.

Hoover's strange reluctance even to acknowledge the existence of organized crime has given rise to much speculation. Some claim that he did not want to alienate those members of Congress, few in number, perhaps, but sometimes powerful in position, who were in any way beholden to Mafia elements. Others have wondered if he was personally friendly with some of the underworld. The FBI chief was an enthusiastic fan of horse racing and at least one ex-agent mentions taking Hoover to the track and seeing him exchange warm salutations with a local underworld figure. However, most observers believe that Hoover's abstemiousness where organized crime was concerned resulted from a fear of what combatting it could do to his bureau's image. His agents might become corrupted or, worse still, might show themselves ineffective in wrestling with such a serious and powerful enemy.

In general, Hoover was obsessed with avoiding any involvement which could tarnish the bureau's image. This obsession was noted by agent John Shaw who, as we saw in the preceding chapter, wrote a letter which brought about his separation from the agency. In his letter, Shaw claimed that the FBI was so concerned with public approval that "punishment is usually meted out in direct proportion to the amount of bad publicity generated by the particular mistake or incident."[29] Shaw then went on to assess some of the effects of this excessive concern with publicity.

One effect of the Bureau's promoting its image so vociferously through publicity is the acquired characteristic of "over-caution." I believe it is

---

29. "The Heresy of John F. Shaw," *op. cit.*

possible for an organization to become so conscious of its public image—
its unsullied reputation—that it is actually reduced in its effectiveness. At a
time when the entire governmental "establishment" is under assault, the
Bureau of course is even more sensitive to criticism from any quarter. I
suggest that if avoidance of criticism becomes the *chief* consideration of
an agency, there is little likelihood that its members will be distinguishable
for their imagination, initiative and aggressive action. There is a haunting
phrase that echoes throughout the Bureau. "Do not embarrass the Director." This has been so widely interpreted and liberally applied that there is
some question today what action or conduct cannot be considered "em-
barrassing," "indiscreet," "imprudent" or "ill-timed."[30]

Shaw's observations are readily confirmed by many other ex-agents. One of
them, Bernard F. Connors, wrote a novel about the FBI which he entitled
Don't Embarrass the Bureau.

The problem with image building is that it can only be carried so far and
for so long. When it rests upon weak foundations, the facade eventually
buckles. This proved to be the case with the Federal Bureau of Investigation.
As its mania for good publicity caused increasing dysfunction in its operations, its public relations efforts began to backfire. The news media and increasing numbers of the informed public began to question why it was failing
to meet the challenges of the time. As disgruntled former agents began to
speak out, this sentiment grew. Nothing collapses so completely as an over-
swollen balloon and the FBI's bloated image began to suffer the same effects.
Magazines and newspapers that had once lavished fulsome praise on the
agency began to voice increasingly critical and caustic comments.

The tide particularly started to turn with regard to Hoover himself. Having
built himself up as a symbol of his agency, he now began to find himself a
frequent subject of attack. Even members of Congress started to turn hostile.
The very stature which he had acquired seemed only to make him a better
target. Although he clung to a residue of support, his image was crumbling
badly when death finally removed him from the scene and ended a whole era
in federal law enforcement.

Another Police Force, Another Approach
Like the FBI in the early thirties, the West German police in the late forties
found themselves confronting an unfriendly public. Only in their case, the
problem was much more severe. During the latter stages of World War II, the
German police had begun showing in their dealings with ordinary citizens
some of the same brutality and corruption that they had heretofore reserved
for Jews, foreigners and other selected state enemies. As a result, the postwar
German government had to deal with a populace that was distinctly hostile to
any sort of constabulary. In addition, West Germans had now become attracted to the idea of democracy and had an exaggerated idea as to what it

---

30. *Ibid.*

meant. Often, when a policeman would seek to stop a citizen for, say, a traffic offense, the citizen would reply, in effect, "Why are you bothering me? Don't you know that we now have a democracy in Germany?"

To counteract this sentiment, the new postwar police forces launched a sweeping and thorough public relations drive that was unprecedented in the history of law enforcement.

To begin with, the police organizations throughout the country adopted the slogan "The Police: Your Friend and Helper" and set out in determined fashion to put it into effect. They centered much of their attention on children, realizing that this was the best way to start fostering good relations with the public over the long term. For the youngest children, police departments organized three-man squads of theatrically inclined policemen to give puppet shows at kindergartens and play centers. These puppet shows were designed to teach traffic safety and to warn the youngsters about accepting rides from unknown adults. (Child molestation was and still is a severe problem in Germany.) After each such presentation, the policemen-puppeteers would come out and talk with the children. They would always be in uniform because, as one put it, "It is important for the children to know that policemen are staging these things. We want them to develop a positive feeling toward the police so that they would not hesitate to come to a policeman on the street if they were lost or were being bothered by a child molester."

When the children became a little older they would receive invitations to come to their local police station on designated occasions and play in the "traffic kindergarten." These were large rooms equipped with model vehicles which the youngsters could peddle along designated street patterns painted on the floor. A policeman would be present to give traffic signals and instruct the children on how to respond to them. For still older children, the police would hold training classes in how to ride a bicycle. These classes were also held in the local police stations. Once a youngster had satisfactorily completed such a course, he would receive a police certificate saying he had done so. Such a certificate was not required to ride a bicycle, but parents soon began to require their children to obtain one before buying them a bicycle.

Adults were by no means neglected by the police in their all-out attempt to overcome negative attitudes and mobilize public support. Police departments would give bus tours to elderly citizens pointing out pedestrian traffic hazards, sponsor crime clinics for businessmen as well as ordinary citizens to instruct them on ways to prevent crime, maintain lists of doctors available to the public for weekend emergencies and perform a host of other "positive" functions.

Traffic, meanwhile, became a very bothersome problem as car ownership started to rise; it also proved particularly damaging to police-citizen relations since it frequently brought the police into adversary contact with otherwise honest and upright citizens. To meet this challenge, police departments sent out brochures, made TV and radio broadcasts and undertook other efforts to instruct the populace in the safety laws and the need for obeying them. One police force even printed apologetic messages on its parking tickets in an attempt to allay motorist hostility. Another police force began giving annual parties for all younger motorists who had been served traffic summonses during the year. The parties would get underway with a film on traffic safety but would then be followed by a dance with a police band providing the music and policemen and policewomen providing dancing partners for the former offenders.

Each police station began holding an "open house" one day a year, inviting all members of its district to see its facilities and talk with its personnel, and nearly every police force held an annual police show at which men, women and children could, for only a slight charge, see policemen demonstrating various aspects of their jobs and performing somewhat spectacular stunts. The latter might include twelve policemen delicately balanced on three moving motorcycles or dogs jumping through hoops of fire. When people could not come to them, the police would frequently find ways of going to them. Thus, police bands would give concerts at old people's homes while exhibits and speakers would be sent to schools, businesses, clubs.

The new German police forces also adopted a healthy attitude toward complaints and frequently encouraged irate citizens to file them. Oftentimes, a police force would set up a booth at a non-police function or event not only to publicize their work but also to solicit complaints against themselves. Some police training schools began using certain illustrative complaints that had been found valid as part of their instructional material for recruits. At the same time, many police forces did not neglect to take more positive steps to foster better behavior by their members. For example, several would periodically hold a "friendliest policeman of the month contest" in which citizens would submit the name or badge number of a policeman who had proven particularly helpful to them.

The West German police also took several steps to improve their relationship with the news media. Policemen were instructed to cooperate with newsmen as much as possible. News clippings about the police, whether favorable or unfavorable, were frequently posted on the bulletin boards of police stations and, particularly, recruit training schools. Recruits were actually given some instruction in press relations and were cautioned about becoming too irate when the press criticized the police. One basic text used in police training schools reminds recruits that if the press often criticizes the police, it also frequently praises them, and, in any event, a newspaper is only printed for one day so that there is no need to become unduly alarmed.

Nearly all West German policemen soon became union members and these union organizations also sought to improve police-community relations. To children, for example, the unions would distribute calendars showing school holidays as well as balloons emblazoned with the message "The Trade Union of Police: Good Friends." The unions also printed articles in their own publications emphasizing the importance of good public relations programs and detailing ways to carry them out. Every so often, the major police union would hold what it called a "floating press conference." It would invite a representative group of union officials and members along with a group of newsmen for a three-day cruise on the Rhine during which the passengers would engage in lively and productive interchanges regarding police-press relations.

All this zealous activity scored an impact on police work and in almost every respect it was a favorable one. Traffic deaths of children, for example, immediately started to drop when the puppet programs and traffic kindergartens were introduced. Citizen cooperation with the police went up and seldom did a police department have to pay informers to gain needed information. Police behavior on the beat changed and soon the German patrolman, in his non-militaristic uniform with his club and gun carefully kept out of sight, became one of the friendliest and most helpful policemen in Europe.

The West German police, in their way, took public relations as seriously as did the FBI. But though they used at least some of the same basic techniques, they did so with a different emphasis and a different attitude. They adopted a positive image and then changed or modified their basic operations to bolster this image. Thus, they made the image into a goal which they then strove to meet. In so doing, they provide an example of what good public relations is all about.

RELATIONS WITH POLITICIANS

Public administration obviously functions within a political setting and it is probably no exaggeration to say that the relationship of politics to administration is that of sex to life; one engenders the other. Without politics there would be no government and without government there would, of course, be no public administration.

Yet despite this close relationship, administrators rarely look upon politicians as colleagues or cohorts. All too often the reverse is true. A study of federal bureaucrats in the 1950's showed that the majority of them were fairly hostile to congressmen, feeling that the members of our country's highest legislative body tended to be selfish or stupid or both. One Agriculture Department official who had formerly worked in the State Department was quoted as saying, "I've attended lots of these meetings within the department where budget questions and the like were decided, and I've never heard a respectful word spoken about Congress at one of them."[31]

Robert Spadaro of Temple University found that the same atti-

---

31. James Burnham, "Some Administrators Unkindly View Congress," in *Public Administration*, Robert T. Golembiewski, Frank Gibson and Geoffrey Y. Cornog, eds. (Chicago: Rand McNally, 1966).

tudes prevail in state bureaucracies as well. He studied the perceptions that politicians and public administrators had of each other in three states, and in every state he discovered that each group had a low opinion of the other. Over 90 percent of the administrators, he reports, felt that they represented the public interest best. They were willing to concede politicians jurisdiction only on the broadest matters of policy. (The percentage of the politicians who had a low opinion of the administrators also topped 90 percent.)[32]

It is no troublesome task to dig out and designate the sources of this tension. Administrators are subject to the control of politicians and no one likes to be controlled. This situation is particularly true of American administrators for reasons indicated in our discussion of the American political system in chapter two. As we saw then, the fragmentation and personalism in our political system tends to make American administration more politicized than is usually the case in other industrial nations. The American administrator must consequently exert extra efforts to win the favor and backing of political leaders.

This constant and compelling need to placate and persuade politicians is probably a major reason why businessmen often fare poorly when they attempt to put their skills to work in the public sector. Frederick V. Malek who served as a special assistant to President Nixon with the job of getting businessmen involved in government work took note of this particular difficulty. "Most corporate executives are accustomed to giving orders and having them carried out without question," he wrote. "The unaccustomed necessity of cajoling and persuading a large number of strong-willed and diverse men can prove to be a time-consuming, frustrating and humbling exercise."[33]

True, administrators have acquired more and more power in recent decades as we have already noted. However, this power has been granted to them by politicians who are still prone to assert themselves in ways which administrators often find disturbing and even humiliating. For example, Representative Daniel Flood of Pennsylvania chairs the House appropriations subcommittee which oversees HEW's budget. Elizabeth Drew quotes an HEW official as saying, "The budget always reflects political realities. We say, 'That's Dan Flood's favorite program. It's lousy. Let's keep it.' "[34]

The critical and often contemptuous attitude which administrators frequently though secretly manifest toward their political overseers

---

32. Robert Spadaro, "Role Perception of Politicians vis-a-vis Public Administrators," Paper presented at the annual convention, American Society of Public Administration, Los Angeles, 1973.
33. "When Businessmen Turn Their Talents to Government," *U.S. News and World Report*, October 2, 1972.
34. *The Atlantic*, April 1973, p. 12.

is easily understood, for the politicians often seem to emphasize matters which the administrators find picayune or nonsensical. Early in 1964 the motion picture actor Richard Burton applied for and was granted a visa to enter the United States to appear in a Broadway production of *Hamlet*. Burton at that time had separated from his wife and had become the paramour of Elizabeth Taylor, the American film star whom he subsequently married. At this point, however, Miss Taylor was still legally married to someone else.

The fact that Burton had obtained a visa to come to the United States where he presumably would also see Miss Taylor again rankled certain members of House of Representatives, Subcommittee Number 1 of the Committee of the Judiciary which deals with immigration matters. The subcommittee convened a closed hearing to investigate the matter. Abba Schwartz, who at the time was Assistant Secretary of State in charge of immigration, refugee and travel control policies, was summoned as the main witness. In his book *The Open Society*, Schwartz reports the following interchange with Representative Arch Moore of West Virginia.

> Congressman More: . . . I want to know, is Richard Burton guilty of adultery?
>
> Mr. Schwartz: I have no knowledge.
>
> Congressman Moore: I assume, having seen the affectionate embraces spread across the newspapers of America, it is reasonable to conclude that at some time or other, this indiscretion has occurred, but I am talking about legally and technically. Richard Burton is a divorced man?
>
> Mr. Schwartz: I raised the question. I have no answer to it.
>
> Congressman Moore: I would like an answer to it. In our statute it is the United States citizen who has another mate legally.
>
> Mr. Schwartz: . . . I do not have an answer whether or not the divorced person is guilty of adultery. There is no question that the married person is.
>
> Congressman Moore: . . . There is not any question of the fact that his coming to the United States is to deal in an immoral act; whether the term "adultery" or "immoral act" is interchangeable . . . I do not know, but certainly he is going to come in here to fornicate, at least, which is the very, very minimum. But I question whether or not if you are going to exclude him on the fact that he is coming here to commit adultery, legally he is guilty of adultery?
>
> Mr. Schwartz: . . . He is coming in here principally . . . as far as I know . . . to appear in the play *Hamlet* in New York.[35]

Needless to add, this same divergence of viewpoints as to what is important and what is not, and as to what should be done and what

---

35. Abba P. Schwartz, *The Open Society* (New York: Simon and Shuster, 1969), p. 59.

should not, often characterizes politico-administrative relations on the local level as well. The city manager may spend long hours drawing up a comprehensive traffic plan only to find the city council deeply involved and irritated over a crackdown on illegal parking on one or two particular streets. And the school superintendent may eagerly come to the school committee meeting with a new plan to rejuggle the school system only to find the committee members in an uproar over an inadvertent remark dropped by a teacher in a sex education class.

It is not difficult to see, then, why administrators so often view politicians with annoyance and even alarm. Furthermore, this uneasy relationship between the two groups, while perhaps more aggravated in the United States, nevertheless has parallels abroad. Anthony Sampson in his book *The New Anatomy of Britain* mentions how civil servants talk about "politics as a yachtsman might talk of the wind—a wild irrational force, always liable to upset the navigators' calculations, yet having to be calculated for by systems of tacking, reefing or battening down."[36] The French political leader François Mitterand uses a somewhat different metaphor to state the problem. "Administration looks upon politics," he says, "as a wild woman who runs around the streets while she, administration, wise virgin that she is, guards the house."[37]

Administrators and Politicians: Another Approach

In a study done during the mid-1960's, Robert S. Friedman and his associates found that the personnel of government agencies could fall into three basic categories, "politicos," "professionals" and "administrators." The researchers found that it was the politicos who were most likely to be sensitive to outside pressures and interests and who would be most apt to take the broadest view of the constituencies involved in administrative decision-making. Administrators were seen as taking the *narrowest* view of the various interests affected by the agency's activities.[38]

This study substantiates and supports what many politicians and perceptive public managers have learned from experience. Some even feel that American administration, or at least some parts of it, could benefit from more political influence than it now has to contend with. Former North Carolina Governor Terry Sanford, for example, claims that one reason why the health departments of most states are inadequate is that they are over-professionalized and, in a sense, under-politicized. Sanford also feels that many state departments of welfare and education

---

36. Anthony Sampson, *The New Anatomy of Britain* (New York: Stein and Day, 1971), p. 242.
37. Quoted in Charles Debbasch, *L'Administration au pouvoir* (Paris: Calmann-Lévy, 1969), p. 31.
38. Robert S. Friedman et al., "Administrative Agencies and the Publics They Serve," *Public Administration Review*, September 1966.

suffer the same problem.[39] Paul Appleby, who served as assistant to the Secretary of Agriculture during much of the New Deal, felt there was too little rather than too much politics in the federal bureaucracy. He claimed the Washington bureaucrats operated too far from the party in power and resisted it too much. Another college professor who went to Washington learned a similar lesson. Said George Schultz after four years as Secretary of the Treasury in the first Nixon administration, "I have more respect for politicians after four years in Washington. They have an instinct for what's troubling people and why."[40]

What all these people are suggesting is that there is no line of demarcation separating administration and politics. The two are and perhaps should be inextricably intertwined. They are also saying that such a forced marriage is desirable and necessary. "I remember trying to convince a mayor, who was smarter than I, that I would make the administrative decisions and he and the council would make the political decisions," writes William V. Donaldson, the city manager of Tacoma, Washington. "This was a classy way, I thought, of telling him not to bug around with administration but confine himself to the dirty area of politics. I never tried this argument again, when he said, 'Oh! You mean you will handle the easy problems and the council and I will solve the hard ones.' "[41]

Working with Politicians: I

As the foregoing has hopefully made clear, administrators must learn to work with politicians. They must do so not just to insure political support for their programs but to make sure that they have the right programs. So often what has seemed like an expertly worked out project has ended in disaster, not just because it failed to elicit the backing of politicians but because it failed to take into account all the problems and pressures which such a project might encounter from various quarters. Administrators may fume and rage at politicians but all too often the objections which political leaders raise and the concerns they cite are those which administrators need to have called to their attention. Politicians are usually much more knowledgeable about what is going on in society generally than are administrators, and hence they can contribute many valuable insights to, and make many useful inputs into, the administrative process. In any case, their support is ultimately indispensable.

---

39. Terry Sanford, *Storm Over the States* (New York: McGraw-Hill, 1967), p. 199.
40. *Time,* February 26, 1973, p. 80.
41. William V. Donaldson, "Continuing Education for City Managers," *Public Administration Review, November/December 1973.*

The first step toward achieving a good working relationship with politicians is to understand their problems. Any administrator who has ever held elective office or even run for elective office will usually acquire an understanding and tolerance for political leaders that will help him work effectively with them. Of course, the opportunity to acquire such experience is not open to most administrators, but they can obtain some good knowledge about politicians and their problems by assisting in a political campaign. City Manager Donaldson heartily urges all administrators to get involved in such activity providing it lies outside their own area of responsibility. (The Hatch Act, it should be recalled, does not prohibit political activity in non-partisan contests.) "Politics," he writes, "is like lovemaking in that you have to do it to improve. No amount of study of the *Kama Sutra* will be of much value to your love life unless you have someone to practice with. . . ." Donaldson recommends that administrators not just help a person get elected but try to understand the problems he faces once he is elected. "The problems of dealing with the bureacracy and constituents will seem quite different when you see them from this point of view, and that insight will improve your ability to respond intelligently to the demands of your elected masters," he says.[42]

Meanwhile, the demands of one's own "elected masters" continue to pour in and administrators must make sure to maintain good lines of communication with them in order to develop and deepen mutual understanding and trust. Often, administrative agencies maintain special employees and even special subunits to establish and strengthen their rapport with politicians, particularly legislators. While federal legislation was enacted in 1919 to expressly prohibit federal agencies from expending any funds to "influence in any manner a member of Congress, to favor or oppose, by vote or otherwise, any legislation or appropriation by Congress,"[43] nevertheless, the law has, in many respects, been honored more in the breach than in the observance. Data compiled in 1963 showed that federal agencies were spending nearly $5.5 million a year and employing some 500 people for liaison activities with Congress.[44] Indeed, the Hoover Commission itself recommended that the State Department create the post of assistant secretary for congressional relations, a recommendation that was subsequently put into effect.

Occasionally, congressmen have complained about such prac-

---

42. *Ibid.*
43. 41 Stat. L. 68.
44. G. Russell Pipe, "Congressional Liaison: The Executive Branch Consolidates Its Relations with Congress," *Public Administration Review*, spring 1966.

tices, particularly when they seem to have gone too far. But generally, Congress has responded affirmatively to such measures. "Legislators at all levels of government, despite their defensiveness toward bureaucracy, like to hear from the bureaucrats most intimately concerned when making up their minds about proposed legislation, and the bureaucrats oblige them energetically," writes J. Leiper Freeman.[45] He quotes Representative Frank Buchanan, who chaired a House of Representatives committee that investigated bureaucratic lobbying during the 1950's, as saying, "It is equally necessary for the executive branch of government to be able to make its views known to Congress on all matters in which it has responsibilities, duties and opinions. The executive agencies have a definite requirement to express views to Congress, to make suggestions, to request needed legislation, to draft proposed bills or amendments."[46]

However, administrators must often be prepared to do more than this in their quest for good relationships with legislators and other political figures. They must be prepared, within limits, to help them with their more crassly political problems as well. Politicians have to get elected, and once elected they have to appease their constituents. Given the nature of our political system, they must usually succeed on their own with little help from their parties. Administrators should accept this fact and try to work with it. They must therefore often be prepared to give politicians the credit for the good that happens in government while they themselves shoulder the blame.

This takes many forms in actual practice. One typical device is to allow the politician to announce any good news such as a new park, school or other facility for his district. When it is a question of closing down a popular facility or refusing to go ahead with a desired program, then the administrator will offer to make the announcement himself.

James Hagerty, President Eisenhower's dexterous press secretary, began a policy of having all good news concerning major developments in the federal bureaucracy announced by the White House; the departments and agencies, however, were left to announce the bad news. This policy has more or less continued to the present day. At one time during the Vietnam war, President Johnson announced the suspension of the bombing of North Vietnam, a gesture designed ostensibly to encourage peace talks. The bombing suspension had lasted a few days when reporters queried him whether it was leading to anything and whether it would be continued. Johnson replied by saying that Secretary of State Rusk would hold a news conference on this the next day. Experienced

---

45. Freeman, *op. cit.*
46. *Ibid.*

Washington observers were able to guess right away that the administration was going to end the suspension and resume bombing. Otherwise, they reasoned, Johnson would have made the announcement himself. Predictably, Rusk, in his news conference, called the short-lived bombing halt a failure and disclosed that the bombing of the North would resume.

Many a would-be administrator rebels at pursuing a policy that requires him to be the bearer of ill tidings while the politician is allowed to reveal the news that people want to hear. It does seem unfair and even unethical. But a case can be made for its fairness as well as for its practicality in securing political support. A New York City councilman, Matthew J. Troy, Jr., once publicly called upon all city agencies to announce local projects through the councilmen from the districts concerned. He explained his demand by pointing out that a councilman would often fight hard to get a traffic light or a sewer project in the budget only to have it announced a year later by a mayoral appointee. His constituents would then say, "Well, what do we need a councilman for?"[47]

Politicians not only pressure administrators with demands for favorable publicity but also like to pass on to them constituent complaints with a request for action. The wise administrator will do well to respond expeditiously and thoroughly. The Social Security Administration set up its Political Inquiries Branch specifically to handle such complaints. The PIB seeks to acknowledge such complaints within 48 hours and to answer them within a week. This does not mean that it always finds the complaints justified or that it renders the complainant special service simply because his grievance was routed to them by a congressman. However, it does try to check out each such complaint as quickly as possible and inform the congressman concerned of its status.

Politicians do, of course, like to see the administrator "find for the constituent" as it were and act positively to correct whatever the constituent has complained about. But most politicians do not expect administrators to do so unless the complaint is really justified. "Most legislators support constituent cases irrespective of their merit," writes Lewis Mainzer, "but will not press for more than an explanation or prompt action. Speeding up a decision is probably the most frequent consequence."[48] The politician is usually satisfied if he can just show the constituent that he is able and willing to get the constituent's case heard, and most administrators are usually willing to support the politician to this extent. Former Internal Revenue Commissioner Mortimer

---

47. *New York Times,* February 19, 1973.
48. Mainzer, *Political Bureaucracy,* p. 82.

Caplin says, "I never turned down a request for a congressman to see someone, but sometimes I'd reply, 'Sure, I'll see him but why?' What they do a lot of times is pass on a constituent just to get them out of their hair. They know I can't—or wouldn't—do anything for them, but the constituent is satisfied he had a hearing. Part of the job of being commissioner, I suppose."[49]

In disposing of complaints, the administrator may follow the same policy that he follows when it comes to publicizing positive and negative developments. That is, when he finds a complaint justified and sets about correcting it, he may let the politician disclose this fact to his constituent. When he finds the complaint to have no basis, he may offer to inform the constituent of this fact himself. The complainant will then feel that the politician at least took some action and did what he could, and if he remains disgruntled then he will more likely focus his dissatisfaction on the administrator and not the politician.

Politicians, however, may importune administrators for more than just favorable publicity or for an expeditious and fair disposal of complaints. All too often they make demands for actual patronage. To what extent is an administrator justified in meeting such demands?

Paul Appleby relates how in staffing the Department of Agriculture's Civilian Conservation Corps program during the New Deal he called in the head of the Forest Service and asked him to find 100 jobs which could be filled by political appointments. Appleby said that he told the chief forester that he, the chief forester, could determine just what jobs were to be earmarked for the "politicos." He could also set the requirements for those jobs, and could even do all the actual selecting of the people to fill them. If he could not find enough qualified people on the list of politically sponsored nominees to fill the jobs, he could then ask for more names until he was able to do so. But he would have to choose from a list consisting of names submitted by politicians.

The chief forester, according to Appleby, was at first horrified at the prospect of allowing patronage to intrude into one of his agency's programs, but eventually he agreed to go along. The proposal, Appleby later claimed, worked well. It satisfied the demands of numerous members of Congress and other political figures while it did no injury to the new CCC.[50]

The same technique has been adopted by other administrators in dealing with patronage demands. One such administrator was Joseph Lohman, a criminologist who, during one of the reform waves which

49. Quoted in Gouldner, *Patterns of Industrial Democracy*, p. 220.
50. Appleby, *Big Democracy*, Chapter 15.

intermittently sweep Chicago, won election as sheriff of Cook County. Lohman knew he had to achieve some measure of cooperation with the Windy City's numerous and powerful precinct captains, and so he proposed to them the following plan: The precinct captains could send him their nominees for appointment and if these nominees were suitable he would appoint them. If they were not, he would ask for new nominees. "In some instances," said Lohman, "a precinct captain would send me applicant after applicant and I would continually reject them. But always I asked him to send a new applicant and eventually I would get what I was looking for."[51]

Charles Goodwin Sauers made full use of this technique as superintendent of parks in Philadelphia during the 1950's. Sauers felt that the majority of jobs in a park department were non-technical and could be filled by political appointees. He therefore let the proper political leaders know that he would be willing to try almost anybody in these positions provided the probationary period was short and the dismissal fast and firm if the applicant did not work out. He describes some of the responses which he ended up giving to their sponsors when these appointees did turn out to be unsatisfactory.

The fellow you sent me only shows up three days a week—please replace him.

He reports late, skips out early and wants an hour and a half for lunch. Send me another.

He is a good workman but shows up drunk and useless. We will pay him only for the days he is able to work well.

He is not physically well but is willing—we will try him another month and see if his health improves.[52]

Handling patronage demands in the way in which Appleby, Lohman and Sauers dealt with them can produce many benefits for the administrator. First of all, it can actually improve the operations of his agency. As was noted earlier, political appointees can open up an agency and bring in broader and fresher points of view. Even those political appointees who qualify only for the more menial jobs usually have something to offer in this regard. The fact that they have a political connection usually means that they or their families have engaged in

---

51. In an interview with the author at Berkeley, California, April 1967.
52. Charles Goodwin Sauers, Sr., "Parks and Politics," *Parks and Recreation*, April 1959.

some political activity and have acquired some knowledge of what is going on in the community.

In terms of building political support, this system can also work well. It actually allows the politician to submit many names without incurring the blame for those who fail to make the grade. The administrator is still able to pretty much pick and choose the types of people he wants to work in his agency.

Finally, while patronage to many does seem like an unmitigated evil which, while it must sometimes be endured, should never be condoned, it does have benefits for the entire system. Appleby claimed that patronage helps to bring the legislative and executive branches together. It thus may provide a thread of unity to our fragmented political and administrative system.

Working with Politicians: II

Although there are ways in which administrators can work congenially and cooperatively with politicians, they cannot always expect to do so. Sometimes politicians will make demands which an administrator cannot ethically or even practically fulfill. Sometimes politicians will find an administrator's operational practices and policies objectionable. And sometimes politicians will find fault with an administrator on personal grounds, such as disliking his race, religion or the place he comes from. It is not all that unusual for a politician who has a grudge against a member of an administrator's family to take some of his acrimony out on the administrator himself. For these and other reasons, administrators cannot usually hope to achieve uniformly smooth relations with politicians, and on occasion they must prepare themselves to oppose them.

Fighting with politicians is always dangerous. Even when the administrator wins the battle, he sometimes loses the war, for the defeated politician only becomes more hostile toward the administrator and seeks with added zeal another opportunity to denigrate or destroy him. Yet, administrators must at times be prepared to fight back.

In opposing a politician, the administrator can make use of some of the techniques pointed out in chapter six such as choosing his battles and fighting only one front at a time. There are, however, some additional ways in which the administrator can cope with the animosity and opposition of political leaders.

One of these is to try to get someone else to fight his battles for him. Oftentimes, this can take the form of a friendly politician who can be asked or encouraged to stand up to the opponent. "There is, in fact, no better lobbyist for any administrative agency than a legislator," writes Francis Rourke,[53] and the same principle holds true when it comes to defending the agency against onslaughts from its political foes. The administrator can also seek to take advantage of whatever support he can muster among his clientele groups or from the media to put pressure on antagonistic politicians. This must be done carefully, however, for sometimes it will only strengthen the politician's resolution and make him more openly antagonistic than ever.

President Woodrow Wilson and his Secretary of State Robert Lansing adroitly used the press to put pressure on Congress in the case of the famous "Zimmerman Telegram." This was a telegram which revealed Germany's hostile intentions toward the United States at a period during World War I when we were ostensibly neutral. The telegram had been intercepted by the British, decoded, translated and made available to the United States. Wilson and Lansing were alarmed over its contents and wanted desperately to bring it to the attention of Congress. However, many congressmen were belligerently anti-British and also anti-Wilson and would react negatively to anything that smacked of direct presidential pressure.

It was decided that Lansing would call a reporter from the Associated Press to his home, and, without disclosing the actual phrasing of the telegram, would give the newsman a paraphrase of its text and a briefing on its background, at the same time pledging him to the strictest secrecy as to how he had obtained it. The story broke the next morning and, in the words of historian Barbara Tuchman, "The House erupted in patriotic oratory" and hurriedly passed the Wilson administration's armed neutrality bill, giving the United States increased military might to deal with the coming holocaust.[54]

While working indirectly in this fashion is usually more effective, there are times when more direct methods may be called for. Chester Bowles tells of how a senator threatened to hold up the Office of Price Administration's budget appropriation unless the OPA dropped some charges which it had lodged against one of the senator's relatives. Bowles decided to fight back. He was scheduled to give a radio address and prepared for it by writing two speeches. One of them was a general account of how price control was working; the other was a detailed step-by-step account of his problems with the senator and his relative. He showed both speeches to the senator and asked him which one he should give. "The appropriation sailed through without a hitch," says Bowles.[55]

---

53. Rourke, *Bureaucracy, Politics, and Public Policy,* p. 28.
54. Tuchman, *The Zimmerman Telegram,* p. 171.
55. Bowles, *Promises To Keep,* p. 144.

While Bowles' strategy seems to have worked successfully, the incident should be taken as illustrating the exception rather than the rule. Any administrator who attempts to play the role of a noble knight, ready and eager to slay the dragons of petty politics, will usually only succeed in destroying his own effectiveness. Not only will his political opponents scrutinize his every move, waiting for the inevitable misstep in order to pounce upon him, but his political supporters, to say nothing of his superiors, will soon grow tired of defending him. He may soon find himself being given less and less administrative responsibility.

But if administrators must be wary of proceeding too antagonistically toward politicians, they should also be mindful of going too far in the opposite direction. Conciliation does and should not mean capitulation. An administrator who falls at the feet of his political overseers, who stands ready to carry out their every whim and wish, may purchase support at far too high a price. Administrators and agencies which have pursued such a course may have often achieved great growth but they have paid for it not only in terms of ethical responsibility but also in terms of true effectiveness. Furthermore, such a fawning attitude sooner or later breeds suspicion and hostility in other quarters which may eventually bring discredit and disavowal.

Examples of such excessive deference are all too prevalent in the federal bureaucracy, to say nothing of numerous state and local government bureaucracies. The Department of Agriculture, for example, in its efforts to placate its "permanent undersecretary" Representative James Whitten (see chapter two), once expressed a willingness to help underwrite a $265,000 loan for a golf course in Whitten's home district.[56] The Army Corps of Engineers has managed to achieve its remarkable degree of independence from the Pentagon only by becoming a near errand boy for influential congressmen. Both agencies have incurred much bad publicity and public hostility through their over-compliance with congressional directives.

Perhaps the agency which has become the most famous, or infamous, for its currying of congressional favor is the Department of Defense. In their 1968 book *The Case Against Congress*, Drew Pearson and Jack Anderson detailed some of the many ways in which the defense establishment seeks to obtain and maintain congressional support. These include placing military facilities and awarding contracts in the districts of influential congressmen, handing out reserve commissions and medals and providing a host of other favors. "For a worthy Congressional group, the Air Force will provide a plane from Special Air Mis-

---

56. Tolchin, *To the Victor ...*, pp. 191–192.

sion—complete with escort officers, pretty stewardesses, baggage handlers and sometimes even a doctor with a first-aid kit of bicarbonate of soda. The military escorts, boon companions all, pick up the tab for everything."[57]

When it comes to reserve commissions, Pearson and Anderson reported how one congressman who entered the House holding a second lieutenant's commission in the army reserves found himself a major in four years and a major general in seventeen years. Another congressman who had had no previous military service managed to finish his first two-year term as a colonel in the air force reserves. Senator Henry "Scoop" Jackson, who never rose above the rank of an enlisted man during World War II, became a major in the army reserves during his very first year in the Senate. As for medals, the navy once awarded a Silver Star for gallantry to a young congressman who took a short flight as an observer on a navy plane in the South Pacific during World War II. The heroic congressman was Lyndon B. Johnson.

The problems entailed in soliciting political support, as well as those involved in generating clientele and public support, often raise grave issues of administrative responsibility. It is to this sensitive area of public administration that we will now turn.

RESPONSIBILITY

The question of administrative responsibility encompasses the question of accountability but, at the same time, goes far beyond it. Proper and desirable administrative behavior requires something more than accountability, for no set of standards, no matter how clearly set down and no matter how vigorously enforced, can cover the full range of administrative actions. Those who toil at even the lowest levels of the organization will still retain a remarkable degree of discretion. How does one make sure that they, as well as their superiors, exercise this discretion responsibly?

To gain some idea of the complexity which the issue involves, let us take the case of what may be the lowest ranking employee in an administrative office, the receptionist. Let us further assume that she has been instructed to treat all those who come in with fairness and courtesy. Ostensibly, she may do so. However, there will undoubtedly be some clients she will respond to more positively than others and certain subtleties in her demeanor may reflect her preferences and prejudices.

---

57. Drew Pearson and Jack Anderson, *The Case Against Congress* (New York: Simon and Shuster, 1968), pp. 336–339.

She may say the same things and do the same things in her relationships with all those who enter her office, but her manner will convey more warmth in some situations than in others. Some clients may find themselves put off and discouraged by how she treats them, and yet they may find that they have no basis for a valid complaint. Nor will investigation by the office manager produce any evidence that she has failed to conform to the standards set down for her. As Carl Friedrich has observed, "Responsible conduct of administrative functions is not so much enforced as elicited."[58]

Unfortunately, this is only part of the problem of responsibility and quite possibly not the most important part. Let us assume that the receptionist has definitely decided to suppress any personal feelings she may have toward any clients that come into the office and has firmly resolved to carry out the office policy of fairness and courtesy to the utmost. She may then find difficult decisions waiting for her at every turn. She may decide, for example, that living up to such a code means that she should be as helpful as she can to every client that comes in. However, the more helpful she becomes to client A, the more she keeps clients B, C, etc. waiting. And rendering the same amount of service to clients B and C only makes clients D and E wait still longer.

Of course, she may set a maximum of service beyond which she will not go. However, some clients do require more attention than others. They may have special problems or they may be less able to cope with even routine problems than others. For example, a client who is blind or who comes from another part of the country may simply not be able to obtain his or her rightful share of the office's services without some special attention. Thus, treating them in exactly the same manner as everyone else would seem to fall short of achieving the maximum in administrative responsibility.

This means that the responsible receptionist must make what are often difficult decisions. She must decide which clients she will render extra service and, what is perhaps still more troublesome to determine, how much extra service to provide them. Every bit of additional service, we must remember, lengthens the time that other clients must wait for their turn. Often this means keeping them from their jobs or families.

Let us take another example. Suppose a public utility is seeking to increase its rates. The examiner hearing its case looks at the record and finds that the company's profits are at an all-time high. Furthermore, the company's stock is largely in the hands of people who are quite well off. The responsible course of conduct for the hearing examiner therefore seems quite obvious: recommend rejection of the rate rise.

---

58. Friedrich, *op. cit.*

However, some other factors may complicate the situation. The company's profits may be at an all-time high in terms of current dollars but not constant dollars. After adjusting for inflation, its profits may actually have declined or at least stood still. Then, the company may want the rate increase to generate additional funds for expansion. The area it serves may have a good deal of unemployment, and increased electrical power might help it attract more industry. Finally, while much of the company's stock may be owned by wealthy people, some of it is the hands of widows, orphans and others who need its dividends badly. Since the company has not increased its dividends in line with inflation, the real incomes of these particular stockholders are going down. Such considerations do not mean that the responsible decision for the examiner is simply to approve the requested rate increase. They do indicate, however, that with all the best will in the world, the responsible decision is not always easy to determine.

While the above examples are hypothetical, they are by no means unrepresentative of the types of dilemmas which administrators must constantly wrestle with as they seek to plot out responsible courses of action. Shall the personnel officer favor a local resident or a minority group member for a job when he could secure the services of an out-of-state resident or a non-minority group member who may be somewhat more qualified? Shall the environmental inspector shut down the factory which does not quite meet the air pollution standards but whose closing will throw many people out of work and perhaps even bankrupt some small businesses in the bargain? Shall the office manager allow a faithful employee to continue working when the employee has suffered a debilitating illness and can no longer perform an adequate job? Many might seek to answer these questions by saying that it depends on the degree of debilitation, or pollution or difference in skill. But how is the administrator involved to determine the point at which he will take one action and not another?

One problem which many bureaucrats confront on occasion is the need to back a superior's policy before a legislative committee when they really disagree with it. For example, an administrator may be in charge of the federal government's urban renewal program at a time when the administration in power has decided to cut back on urban renewal. The administrator appears before the committee to argue for his budget. A liberal Democrat on the committee notes that the sum of money being requested is less than that of the previous year. He asks questions, seeking to put the administrator on record as personally favoring a much larger appropriation. The administrator knows that the congressman will use any testimony he may give to such effect as a weapon with which to attack the current administration, including his own cabinet secretary. How shall he respond to the congressman's questions?

This brings us to perhaps the most significant decision that any administrator may make regarding his responsibility, and that is under what circumstances should he resign? Philosophy Professor Charles Frankel feels that an administrator should not take such a step lightly. "Assuming that the government for which he works is a constitutional one, a permanent official's conscience must not bleed when he is asked to carry out a policy that doesn't fit his own ideas. Indeed, he requires a conscience which tells him, except in extreme circumstances, to pipe down after he has had his say, and to get to work even in support of what he thinks is wrong. For the electorate hasn't bet on his political opinions or conscience. The only bet it has made, and for which it has paid its taxes, is on his professional integrity and competence."[59]

Seymour Berlin and his associates seem to take a slightly more positive but essentially similar attitude toward the resignation issue, at least as far as the politically appointed administrator is concerned. "Perhaps the most fundamental advice to the political appointee who wants to serve his country well is this: never want the job too much. If you can be clear about your own values, and distinguish between your closely held convictions and your vanity, you will know when you are free to compromise and when you must take a stand. Always be willing to use the power you can acquire when you are ready to resign, but use it only if the cause is vital."[60]

The question of when to resign proved particularly vexing to at least some top-level administrators in the Department of Defense during the latter days of the Johnson administration. They had become increasingly disenchanted with the president's policy in conducting the Vietnam war and thus had begun to give serious thought to the possibility of quitting in protest. They did not have to fear for their livelihood since they could easily have made more money working in the private sector than they were earning in government. But most of them refrained from taking such a step. Their primary rationale for not resigning was that they could work more effectively to change the country's policy if they were inside the government than out of it. However, other considerations may have also stayed their hand.

Townsend Hoopes, who as former undersecretary of the air force was one of those who struggled with this problem, recounts how a blend of such considerations may have kept his chief, Defense Secretary

---

59. Frankel, *High on Foggy Bottom*, p. 109.
60. Berlin et al., "A Guide for Political Appointees...."

Robert MacNamara, from stepping down. According to Hoopes, "Mac-Namara gave evidence that he had ruled out resignation because he believed the situation would grow worse if he left the field to Rusk, Rostow and the joint chiefs, but also because the idea ran strongly against the grain of his temperament and his considered philosophy of organizational effectiveness."[61] Thus, if Hoopes is correct, MacNamara's perseverance in office, until he was transferred by Johnson to the World Bank, was dictated by considerations of responsibility but only as they were filtered through the prism of his own personality and ideology. This offers further support for the contention that even when an administrator has determined to behave as responsibly as he can, he cannot always be sure that he is doing so.

Responsibility: The Search for Solutions

In casting about for answers to the question of responsibility, we are at the outset likely to come across the phrase "the public interest." Many see the entire solution to the question neatly encapsulated in this phrase. An administrator need only resolve himself to serve the public interest and his problems concerning responsibility will vanish.

However, this solution, like so many other easy solutions to difficult problems, only raises more questions than it answers. The most basic one is this: Just what is the public interest? Walter Lippman once claimed that "The public interest may be what men would choose if they saw clearly, thought rationally, and acted disinterestedly and benevolently."[62] But, this leaves us with the task of defining clear vision and rational thought, concepts which, in practice, seem quite susceptible to varying interpretations. Even deciding what course of action is truly benevolent and disinterested may produce more controversy than it settles.

Political scientist Glendon Shubert sought to grapple with the concept of the public interest in a book bearing that title. After exhaustively examining the subject, he says, "It may be somewhat difficult for some readers to accept the conclusion that there is no public interest theory worthy of the name."[63]

Another solution which often presents itself is the maxim of "following one's conscience." Yet, this, too, fails to furnish a usable guideline. The enforcers of the Inquisition who burned hundreds of thousands of heretics at the stake felt they were following the most lofty

---

61. Hoopes, *The Limits of Intervention*, p. 53.
62. Walter Lippman, *The Public Philosophy* (Boston: Little, Brown, 1955), p. 42.
63. Glendon A. Shubert, Jr., *The Public Interest* (New York: The Free Press of Glencoe, 1952), p. 223.

appeals to conscience. The same can be said for so many of the other appalling actions which men have so often taken against their fellows. As Carl Friedrich has noted, "Autocratic and arbitrary abuse of power has characterized the officialdom of a government bound only by the dictates of conscience."[64]

But while Friedrich rules out the use of conscience as a means of insuring responsibility, he does have some positive ideas to offer in its place. "We have a right to call such a policy irresponsible if it can be shown that it was adopted without proper regard to the existing sum of human knowledge concerning the technical issues involved; we have also a right to call it irresponsible if it can be shown that it was adopted without proper regard for existing preference in the community and more particularly its prevailing majority."[65]

In keeping with this admonition, Friedrich sees the solution to the question of administrative responsibility as lying in two areas: professionalism and participation. Professionals generally have been conditioned to uphold certain standards. Furthermore, they usually subscribe to a code of ethics which governs the practice of their profession. As Friedrich sees it, professionalism constitutes something of an "inner check" on administrative irresponsibility. Participation, meanwhile, means that administrators must consult more and more interests and listen to more and more points of view. Allowing diverse and often divergent parties to share in decision-making should make that process less arbitrary and subjective and more responsive and responsible.

To Friedrich's twin safeguards of professionalism and participation can be added a third protective device, publicity. Directing the public spotlight onto administrative decision-making should make such decision-making more responsible. Secrecy and stealth, or even mere obscurity, have rarely led to improved administrative decisions or better administrative behavior.

Professionalism, participation and publicity do not, however, offer ironclad guarantees that administrative behavior will be responsible. Professionals can act irresponsibly and shared decision-making can produce irresponsible decisions. As for publicity, not only can it lead to improper decisions, but many administrative decisions may not receive sufficient publicity for such a safeguard to exert any significant influence. Thus, we need to go still further in order to arrive at a fuller understanding of this problem. Let us return once again to the notion of the public interest.

In his study of the public interest, Shubert, while finding most

---

64. Friedrich, *op. cit.*
65. *Ibid.*

existing definitions unsatisfactory, attempted to develop one of his own. Assuming, he says, that "the peaceful adjustment of conflicting interests" is what we are after, then "a model of administrative due process would be empirically verified if, in practice, the decisions actually made resulted in the maximal accommodation of the affected interests, in comparison with the relative capacities of alternative structures for making the same decisions, and measured by a reciprocally minimal recourse to other centers for public policy change."[66]

A somewhat different and what is to many a more realistic approach to the issue has been taken by Charles E. Lindblom. In "The Science of Muddling Through," an essay that has become quite famous in the annals of American administration, Lindblom seeks to come to terms with some of the difficulties involved in this subject.[67] His essay, to be sure, does not confine itself to the question of administrative responsibility in a narrow sense but rather seeks to encompass the issue of how administrators should and actually do approach their task of policy-making.

In Lindblom's view, it is usually impossible to find the precise policy which will maximize all values. Any administrator, he contends, will simply possess too little information, too little time, too little intellectual capacity and too many political constraints to do so. Even if he could surmount all these impediments, he would still have to contend with additional complications. Values, he emphasizes, are often contradictory. One may have to decide between inflation or employment, freedom or security, speed or accuracy, low taxes or better schools. Furthermore, a social objective may have one value in one situation and another value in another situation. Citizens, politicians, the public generally, superiors and subordinates may all disagree about values, and even the administrator's own set of values contradict each other.

What, then, is the administrator to do?

Lindblom proposed the replacement of what he calls the "rational comprehensive" approach with what he terms the "successive limited comparisons" approach. This approach, he says, is based on the view that values and goals are intertwined with empirical analysis. Means and ends are similarly mixed. Thus, the test of a "good" policy becomes the measure of agreement among various analysts, recognizing that all analysis is itself necessarily limited.

Successive limited comparison means that policies are established in relation to other alternatives that are possible. Decisions are

---

66. Glendon A. Shubert, Jr., "The 'Public Interest' in Administrative Decision-Making," *The American Political Science Review*, June 1957.
67. Charles E. Lindblom, "The Science of Muddling Through," *Public Administration Review*, spring 1959.

made incrementally so that they will be closely related to known and operating policies. Each party of interest must anticipate the moves of other parties and make adjustments to them. "Policy is not made once and for all; it is made and remade endlessly,"[68] says Lindblom. It is always a "very rough process" but the succession of incremental changes helps avoid serious and lasting mistakes.

Lindblom claims that this is what administrators in a democracy not only do but what they should do. On both counts he probably goes too far. Administrators, at least occasionally, approach problems with more basic and long-range considerations in mind than his theory implies. Furthermore, abandoning all attempts at a rational comprehensive approach for the successive limited comparisons approach might lead to foreswearing, or at least avoiding, programmed budgeting, planning and many other new and needed techniques for handling administrative problems. Carried to extremes, his theory of decision-making could encourage treating symptoms of problems rather than the problems themselves.

Nevertheless, Lindblom's theory does point out some of the constraints and compulsions which a public administrator must deal with as he wrestles with his problems of responsibility. In so doing, it introduces a note of humility into the decision-making process. And a measure of humility, combined with the aforementioned safeguards of professionalism, participation and publicity, can carry us a good distance along the road to responsible administrative behavior.

---

68. *Ibid.*

458

13

The Administrative Future

Early in 1972 workers at General Motors' Lordstown plant staged a 22-day strike. While such job actions are certainly no rarity in the auto industry, this one was different. For in staging their walkout, the strikers scarcely mentioned such things as wages, fringe benefits, working hours, safety conditions or any of the other issues which strikers customarily give as the reason for their job action. Instead, their grievances centered almost exclusively on the dull and dehumanizing aspects of their jobs. The Lordstown walkout was probably the first strike in human history to claim boredom as a primary cause.

The eruption in Lordstown was only one of a growing number of signs and signals indicating that in less than a generation the country had undergone a rather profound change. It offered further confirmation to the belief voiced by many social scientists that the age of industrialism is fading from the scene and a new era is taking its place. Social commentators have christened this new age with a variety of names: the post-industrial society, the super-industrial society, the technitronic society or, most commonly, the technological society. They also differ in how they characterize this latest phase in society's development. To some, it is an age of darkness that depersonalizes human relations, enmeshes the individual in a social straitjacket and establishes elite control. To others, it is a messianic age that fosters humanistic values, adds new dimensions to human freedom and makes elite rule increasingly difficult if not impossible. But nearly all agree that the technological, to use the most familiar of the names given it, society differs not only in degree but in kind with the industrial society it is so rapidly replacing.

Without necessarily weighing in on one side or the other regarding its attractiveness and appeal, it is possible to single out certain key

459

and commonly accepted features of the technological society, many of which have been briefly mentioned earlier in this book.

Foremost among these features, the one that appears at or near the top of nearly every futurologist's list, is the high rate of change. The technological society not only represents a fairly dramatic change from the industrial society which preceded it, but makes change itself a stable component of its *modus operandi*. Innovation seems to follow innovation at a mounting pace, frequently leaving the citizen bedazzled, befuddled and breathless. Writes Alvin Toffler in *Future Shock*, the most popular though not the most profound book on this emerging era, "Change sweeps through the highly industrialized country with waves of ever accelerating speed and unprecedented impact. It spawns in its wake all sorts of curious social flora—from psychedelic churches and 'free universities' to science cities in the Arctic and wife-swap clubs in California."[1]

It is fairly easy to discern the ways in which this "accelerating rate of change" is making itself felt in the work organization. At one time, a company engaged in making a product could expect to go on producing it for a number of decades and sometimes even centuries. Buggy whips enjoyed a fairly continuous demand for several centuries during which time their style and features changed very little. The automobile, on the other hand, has undergone numerous transformations during its relatively brief span of existence, and it is by no means certain that it will survive the century in a likeness anywhere near that of the early Model T Fords. Indeed, it may not even survive the century at all.

What is true for the automobile is true for most of the other elements of our everyday life. The National Commission of Technology, Automation and Economic Progress points out that before World War I, it generally took thirty years to make a technical discovery commercially applicable. Between the wars, this time lag decreased to sixteen years, while after World War II it declined to nine years. Undoubtedly it has continued to shrink since then. As one executive of a technologically oriented company remarked, "Half the products we will be making in five years don't even exist today."[2]

Spurring on this rapid rate of innovation has been the mushrooming growth of science in all its manifestations. Science itself is predicated on change. Its basic attitude is that of skepticism; its basic thrust is that of exploration. And science has surged forward in recent years. The number of scientists and engineers in the United States increased five times faster than the population from 1950 to 1965. In an article written in 1962, J. Robert Oppenheimer noted that if the *Physical*

---

1. Alvin Toffler, *Future Shock* (New York: Random House, 1970), p. 9.
2. For a fuller examination of some of the points covered in this paragraph as well as in this entire chapter, see Berkley, *The Administrative Revolution* (1971).

Review, the leading journal for physicists, were to continue growing at the rate it had been growing since World War II, then sometime in the following century the magazine would reach a weight exceeding that of the earth itself![3]

Innovation usually (though not always) correlates with education, and accompanying the increase of the former has been a corresponding growth in the latter. Americans still in their early middle age can remember a time when having a high school diploma signified significant educational achievement while a B.A. degree sufficed to put its holder in the ranks of the educational elite. In those years, most college professors at most universities had only acquired master's degrees. Today, about half of the appropriate age group is in college while even the least notable colleges and universities require a Ph.D. for most of their new faculty.

The same trends are making themselves felt in government service. Only 8 percent of President Truman's appointees had doctorates. The figure inched up to 9 percent under Eisenhower. With John F. Kennedy, the number doubled, reaching 18 percent. But what is perhaps more significant is that the percentage did not go down when Kennedy's less intellectually oriented successor, Lyndon B. Johnson, took over. As a matter of fact, under Johnson the figure crept up another percentage point. No figures are available regarding Richard Nixon's administration in this respect, but the two cabinet members on whom he leaned most heavily during much of his time in office were Drs. Henry Kissinger and George Schultz.

The same push toward increased education is observable at lower levels of government as well. They show up in the burgeoning public administration programs that more and more colleges and universities have instituted in recent years. Often such programs are geared to part-time students who are already employed in government service. Educational requirements for many jobs have become increasingly stiff. Whereas most police forces did not even require a high school diploma in 1960, some were requiring a bachelor's degree by the early 1970's, while others were encouraging their members to pursue such degrees by offering them extra pay, points toward promotion and other inducements. Even the once lowly garbage man has felt the pressure for increased education. The city of Ogden, Utah in 1973 developed a plan to give its street sanitation workers two hours of instruction a day, teaching them how to use heavy and complex equipment as well as developing other skills and knowledge. The plan called for the men to receive some college credits for this educational experience.

The increasing emphasis on education converges with another

---

3.   J. Robert Oppenheimer, "On Science and Culture," *Encounter,* October 1962.

characteristic of the technological society, the rise of professionalism. The percentage of professionals in the work force almost doubled from 1945 to 1965, going from 6.7 percent to 12.3 percent. Professionals now make up a majority of the work force in many of the nation's fastest growing companies. For example, Honeywell has over 60 percent of its employees engaged in professional level activities with only 25 percent of its workers directly involved in production. As for government, an analysis by the Civil Service Commission showed that at sometime during the early 1960's, the percentage of professional-type positions in the federal bureaucracy crossed the halfway mark. In the four-year period from 1961 to 1965, the percentage of professional, technical and administrative jobs went from 46.7 to 52.4 percent while the proportion of clerical and aide jobs of one kind or another dipped from 53.2 percent to 47.3 percent. Undoubtedly, the trend has continued since then.

Accompanying this growth in professionalism has been an equally rapid growth in specialization. As science brings new advances and knowledge it becomes increasingly more difficult for an individual to master the various aspects of any one profession. Thus, while most Americans during the 1930's went to the family doctor for most of their ailments, by the 1960's father was going to an internist, mother was seeing a gynecologist, and the children were being treated by a pediatrician. If any of them developed a serious ailment, then they would consult still another specialist. By the 1970's even fields of medical specialization were hatching new specialties of their own, such as child psychiatry, pediatric neurology, and so forth. The same process was going on at an equally frenetic pace in most other professions as well.

As a result of the growing complexity of knowledge and of society itself, the technological society also gives birth to another phenomenon: interdependence. A faulty light switch can plunge a large section of the country into darkness as it did in the Northeast on one fall evening in 1965. If one state fails to treat its poor humanely or to educate its children properly, the impact will be felt by other states including those that may be far away. Similarly, if any part of an organization fails to work in tandem with another part of the organization, the effect on the whole organization can be disastrous. Almost every person in an organization and in society finds himself increasingly dependent on a host of others to perform his job or simply to survive.

Stepped up mobility is another characteristic component of the technological society. Its citizens are continually on the move, going from job to job, from organization to organization, from place to place, as education expands their horizons and as innovations open up new job possibilities. Mobility, of course, has always played a great part in American life, but with the coming of the technological society, it picks up in both velocity and significance. It also may take many different manifestations. For example, it was not so long ago that large numbers, perhaps even a majority, of young men and women followed in the vocational footsteps of their fathers and mothers. These days, a professor who asks his class of undergraduates how many plan to do what their parents did in life may find that his question fails to produce a single raised hand.

If the technological society makes great demands on its citizens, it also offers them some rewards. One of these is an increase in affluence and leisure. Technological societies are pragmatic and production-oriented, and grow increasingly reluctant to make sacrifices to religious credos and even patriotic ideals. War is often viewed as disturbing and dysfunctional, and most of the violent conflicts that have afflicted the world during the past decade have occurred between or within underdeveloped nations. The Vietnam war was one of those exceptions which proved the rule. The conflict, though not unlike some of America's adventures in the past, became increasingly unpopular with the American people and finally drove President Lyndon Johnson into retirement.

The technological society also gives rise to a new type of person. As we have seen, it rests on and requires increased education and professionalism. These factors, combined with affluence and leisure, produce a more thinking and reflective type of individual. As a British industrial relations expert has expressed it, "The growth of affluence, the growth of education has led to a shortage of morons."[4] People become less and less disposed to take things on faith and more and more inclined to analyze and question. The modern-day advertising man may still be able to sell shoddy goods but he has a harder time doing so than did the patent medicine salesman of bygone days. In politics, we see the same phenomenon in the upsurge in ticket splitting. People are much less inclined these days to vote the straight party ticket than their forebears were.

In similar fashion, organizations, including public ones, are finding it increasingly difficult to sell themselves to their own members through the use of rituals, uniforms, slogans or even lofty ideologies. The claims they can make on an individual in terms of loyalty and conformity grow steadily weaker. Here is how Katz and Kahn put it:

> A technological oriented organization has its rationalized purposes geared to the world of empirical fact rather than transcendental value. Absolutist beliefs, unquestioning loyalty, and the excommunication of heretics just do not fit in to a value system of pragmatic operationalism. Even such a

---

4.   Quoted by Robert Sherrill in the *New York Times Book Review,* July 8, 1973, p. 7.

sacred cow as the prerogatives of management is difficult to assimilate to concepts of consultative management and cooperative effort. The techno-logical system creates experts who are heavily task oriented, who fly no flags, and who are completely bored by ideological considerations. As experts in technology, they move into positions of leadership and pin on the walls their credo, 'Data Win.'[5]

His increased education and professionalism also tend to make technological man more tolerant, broad-minded and committed to a more humanitarian approach. During the crest of the McCarthy era in the 1950's, Samuel A. Stoufer polled a sample of 5,000 Americans as to how they felt regarding civil liberties. Dividing the responses into three categories, less tolerant, in-between, and more tolerant, he found that only 20 percent of all farmers and 30 percent of all blue collar workers fell into the more tolerant category. However, over one-half of all man-agers, proprietors and government officials and a full two-thirds of all professionals and semi-professionals could be so categorized.[6] Similar studies done both here and abroad tend to support his findings. Re-viewing all this research, sociologist Seymour Martin Lipset concludes that "the most important single element differentiating those giving democratic responses from others has been education."[7]

In keeping with this attitudinal aspect, technological man tends to become much more resistant to all kinds of arbitrary authority. His education and his professionalism, together with the very atmosphere which continued change and innovation tends to produce, make him more demanding of his rights and usually more willing to undertake responsibilities. The French general strike of 1968 and the wave of strikes which swept Italy in 1969 both occurred primarily in the more technologically advanced areas of society. In this country, it is interest-ing to note that the upsurge in public employee strikes coincided with the increasing professionalism of the public work force.

College students exemplify this trend of the times. During the 1950's, they were still a relatively docile bunch who generally went along with whatever their institutions demanded of them. During the 1960's, this state of affairs underwent a turbulent transformation, and although things have quieted down considerably since then, the change has left what seems likely to be an indelible imprint on college prac-tices. Student ratings of professors and student participation in tenure, promotion and even presidential selection processes have become stan-

5. Katz and Kahn, *The Social Psychology of Organizations*, p. 471.
6. Samuel A. Stouffer, *Communism, Conformity and Civil Liberties* (Garden City, N.Y.: Doubleday, 1955).
7. Seymour Martin Lipset, *Political Man* (Garden City, N.Y.: Doubleday, 1960), p. 40.

dard procedures on most of the nation's campuses, although such practices would have been deemed unthinkable fifteen years before. Furthermore, a poll taken in 1968 showed only 56 percent of all college students saying that they would not "mind being bossed around on the job." And when the poll was taken again in 1971 the number who said they would not object to being bossed had dropped to 36 percent.[8]

Such data as these support the contention of industrial psychologist Harry Levinson that "we are in the midst of a world-wide social revolution, the central thrust of which is the demand of all people to have a voice in their own fate."[9] Such a revolution seems destined to require a rigorous realignment and reorganization of public administration if the public sector is to cope with, let alone conquer, the manifold challenges of the technological society.

THE PASSING OF THE PYRAMID

Organizations have generally been structured along hierarchical lines. Such concepts and frames of reference as unity of command, chain of command, span of control are based on this fact. Yet, a hierarchical system of organization is good for some things but not for others. Will it be the best way of organizing a technological society?

According to Katz and Kahn, the hierarchical system performs best when it confronts four basic conditions. One is that the tasks its members must execute demand little in the way of creativity; mere compliance often suffices. Second, external or environmental demands on the organization are clear and their implications are obvious. The organization does not require a profusion of contacts with its surroundings. Related to this is a third feature, and that is the ability of the organization to function like a closed and essentially static system, subject to only minimum demands for change from its environment. Finally, the organization is under constant pressure to make decisions speedily.[10]

Rosemary Stewart takes a somewhat similar approach when she itemized the advantages of what she calls "formalization." Such formalization, she contends, promotes a clarity of policy, security or certainty, speed and "efficiency," improved control and, in a certain sense, equity, for it reduces the pressures from special pleaders. She then goes on to list some of the disadvantages which accrue to formalization. It discour-

---

8. Cited in David Jenkins, "Democracy in the Factory," *The Atlantic,* April 1973.
9. Harry Levinson, "Asinine Attitudes Toward Motivation," *Harvard Business Review,* January-February 1973.
10. Katz and Kahn, *op. cit.,* p. 214.

ages initiative, rigidifies routine and hinders adaptation to change. It also promotes deception and insensitivity.[11] We can see all these disadvantages at work when we study or read about the most heavily hierarchical organizations of our society, military ones. Novels such as *Catch 22, The Naked and the Dead, From Here to Eternity* and, best of all from the standpoint of public administration, *Guard of Honor* vividly illustrate some of the problems military organizations suffer from their emphasis on formalization.[12]

Writing along these same lines, Jerald Hage and Michael Aiken in their 1970 book *Social Change in Complex Organizations* postulate that stratification and formalization, along with centralization, and emphasis on "efficiency" and on volume of production (versus quality of production) will generally correlate with a *low* rate of program change. Such things as job complexity and job satisfaction, on the other hand, will usually correlate with a high rate of program change.

Essentially what all these writers seem to be saying is that while formalized and hierarchical systems have their uses, they are becoming less useful all the time. Organizations in a technological society confront pressures for innovation, initiative, flexibility, complexity and job satisfaction, attributes which traditional organizational structures and systems tend to inhibit rather than encourage. True, they may at times function more speedily and this would seem to be a most attractive attribute for an age such as ours. However, even this advantage needs to be qualified, for formalization and hierarchy can slow down as well as speed up the decision-making process. Hierarchical organizations must often sacrifice their formalized procedures and structural design when the pressure for quick action is upon them. As a fire captain in the Los Angeles County Fire Department once remarked, "We're designed in a militaristic fashion, but when we're doing what we are chiefly designed to do, that is fight fires, we function less militaristically than at any other time."[13]

It should be evident, then, that the organizational forms and formulas of an industrial society may prove to be increasingly less satisfactory in a developing technological one. Some of the changes which this new society demands have been touched on in the preceding chapters. It is now time to try to weave them together in an attempt to discern the pattern of the future.

---

11. Stewart, *The Reality of Organizations*, pp. 154–161.
12. While the other novels are better known, *Guard of Honor* is perhaps the most useful novel ever written from the standpoint of public administration. Authored by James Gould Cozzens and published in 1948, it depicts three days of events in a U.S. army air force base during World War II. It won the Pulitzer Prize for 1948.
13. In a conversation with the author in April, 1973, anonymity requested.

The New Organization

In late 1971, the National Academy of Public Administration launched a study to determine just what kind of professional education would be needed to meet the vocational demands of public administration in the future. In conducting the study, the academy contacted nearly 100 "experienced and well-informed leaders in public affairs" and polled them first on what they thought administration itself would be like in the future. The consensus, as reported by the academy, was that there would be a trend toward "flatter organizations with shorter chains of authority but a broader network for providing information and advice. . . . Greater use will be made of temporary ad hoc organizations like task forces and project groups which pull together a small team of people to do a job, and who then disband and return to respective parent organizations or become members of new temporary groups."[14]

In other words, the hierarchical structure will increasingly give way to what has sometimes been called "the all-connected network" or the "matrix organization." There will be less tendency to pass problems up the chain of command and more of a tendency to resolve them laterally in consultation with others. The work teams that result will consist for the most part of individual specialists and, more often than not, will include both line and staff personnel as the distinction between these two categories increasingly blurs. In general, organizational operations will assume an improvisational hue. As an employee of the California State Compensation Fund remarked when that agency was undergoing its remarkable reorganization, "What we need is an organization put together like an airline schedule, subject to change without notice."

The new fluidity in structure and operation will also characterize the public organization's external as well as internal relationships. As it finds itself required to reach beyond its borders for specialized skills and services, and as it finds itself increasingly affected by what happens elsewhere in its environment, it will become less and less of a closed system. Other forces will also tend to further its opening-up process. Clients will become more demanding and newsmen will become more prying. New methods of evaluation will point up both its successes and its shortcomings.

In seeking to motivate its members, the public organization will have to rely more and more on "self-actualization" techniques. This means it will have to focus more and more on meeting the desires of its members for a sense of achievement and self-fulfillment. This will in

---

14. Chapman and Cleaveland, *Meeting the Needs of Tomorrow's Public.*

part spring from the moods and mentalities of these employees who will increasingly insist on their right to satisfaction in the actual performance of their jobs, and who will resist arrangements that detract from their dignity and sense of self-worth. Professionals in particular will demand opportunities to develop and practice the skills which they have labored so long to acquire.

At the same time, another set of conditions will blend and converge with these pressures. Organizations will increasingly see that the arrangements which promote self-actualization also promote effectiveness on other grounds. Work organizations have often striven to break down jobs to their simplest components and then thread them together in linear fashion—employee A doing one single process, employee B doing another, etc.—because such arrangements seemed to them to maximize efficiency. However, the simplification and fractionalization of jobs only increases other costs for it requires more supervision, more communication and more time spent generally in "inter-acting." Katz and Kahn have noted that the greater the number of communication links in a group, the lower the group's efficiency is likely to be in task performance. The specialization, interdependence and general complexity of a technological society greatly increases the number of communication links and that poses grave threats in terms of increased costs and reduced productivity.

Fortunately, the means and methods customarily employed to enhance self-actualization usually run at cross purposes with job simplification and fractionalization. Instead, such self-actualization techniques tend to expand what is sometimes called the work module or slice of work and provide the employee with a greater degree of closure or sense of task completion. In so doing, they reduce the number of communication links and lower the amount of required coordination.

To take a simple example, when employees are allowed to order their own supplies without going through foremen and/or other tiers of middle management, their job satisfaction usually goes up, at least to some degree. At the same time, allowing employees to do this cuts down the number of communication links with all the conferring, paper work and delays that they entail. Thus, in a technological society, job enrichment can yield twofold benefits. It responds to the employee's need for an increased sense of scope and achievement while it mitigates the constantly mounting pressures for more inter-actions.

Other advantages also accrue to the organization which seeks to expand the employee's work module. Reducing the number of interactions and substituting closure for a linear division of work often means that operations will suffer less when any particular employee is absent, feeling poorly or inclined to undercut the work of his fellow employees or that of the organization as a whole. Assume, for instance, that three employees are engaged in producing a product in a linear fashion. Employee A completes the first phase, employee B the second, and employee C the third. If employee B is out sick or is in a non-cooperative mood, the work of employees A and C is likely to be deeply disrupted and the entire operation is likely to sustain a much more than one-third decline in output. However, if each employee handles all three phases of the operation himself, then the other two can continue working in their normal way. Their work will be relatively unaffected.

Another advantage of substituting increased efforts at closure for fragmented work operation is that such efforts enable the employee to gain an increased understanding of the entire operation. He may then perform each part of the operation better because he now has greater insight into how each fits into everything else. Finally it should be noted that increasing closure usually makes it easier for both the employee and the organization to evaluate his performance.

Examples abound which bear out the potentiality of this approach. One is a famous study done by the Tavistock Institute in Great Britain of a coal mining operation. The mining operation involved essentially three phases—widening the coal face, cutting the coal and loading it onto the conveyer. The researchers compared two groups that had been arranged to process these operations in different ways. In the first, the miners were divided into three basic work groups each of which dealt with one phase of the operation exclusively. In the second group, the miners were divided into six-man teams, with each team handling all three phases of the operation. The output of the first group per man-shift was 3.5 tons of coal. The output of the second group was 5.3 tons. Furthermore, the second group required little in the way of supervision or coordination.[15]

A similar experiment in a textile plant in India indicates the nearly universal applicability of such an approach. Management had introduced new and rather expensive looms in this plant only to find out that the new machinery did not improve productivity. Studies showed that the new equipment had fractionated the work process and, in a sense, the workers themselves. Researchers then formed the workers into seven-man groups with each group handling nearly all phases of production. Output quickly rose from 80 to 95 percent of potential while the amount of damaged cloth fell from 32 percent to 15 percent.[16]

These two studies suggest a further advantage of seeking to reduce the fragmentation of the work process and to institute expanded

15. Katz and Kahn, *op. cit.,* pp. 435–442.
16. *Ibid.,* pp. 443–446.

work modules and a greater sense of closure. Thanks to the growing specialization of work, such efforts usually require the establishment of work teams and these work teams not only help meet the employee's self-actualization needs but also his social and emotional needs. Moreover, to the extent that these teams become self-contained units responsible for a complete or nearly complete operation, their members are more likely to achieve a broader view of the organization's entire task. This makes these work teams less likely to substitute interests of their own for those of the organization as a whole. As a result, the informal organization achieves a somewhat better blend with the formal organization and the small group becomes a still more positive force in the organization's functioning.

Personnel

In responding to the rigors and requirements of a technological society, personnel administration like administration generally will perforce become more open and flexible. Recruitment will become expanded and intensified with increased efforts made to tap all sectors of society in order to enroll the best possible talent. While the number of professionals will rise, so will the number of para-professionals. The use of para-professionals not only assuages the demands of minority groups for representation, but gives the professionals better linkages with the clients they are serving. Properly trained and utilized, para-professionals can also reduce costs by freeing those more expensively trained to do the more demanding tasks.

More use will also be made of part-time employees. This will occur partially as a response to demands from mothers of young children and from growing numbers of healthy retired people who will be seeking to maintain some connection with the world of work. Responding to these demands will also tend to improve organizational operations for experiments indicate that part-time employees can make highly effective contributions. In 1969 the Massachusetts Department of Welfare conducted an experiment in which 500 women with young children were hired on a half-time basis. Studies done six months and then a year later found that the average half-timer was handling 89 percent of the number of cases being handled by the average full-time employee. Moreover, the absenteeism of these part-time employees was much less and their turnover rate was only one-third that of the full-time workers.[17]

Personnel classifications will grow increasingly broader and in

---

17. "Ideas in Action," *Harvard Business Review,* September-October 1973. For an interesting article on this subject see Marjorie M. Silverberg, "Part-time Careers in the Federal Government," *The Bureaucrat,* 1, no. 3 (fall 1972).

some cases may become nearly meaningless. Many factors point to such a trend. For one thing, such classifications imply a hierarchical ordering of work. But work, as we have seen, is becoming increasingly professionalized. This means it is becoming knowledge work and, as has been noted previously, there are no higher or lower knowledges. It is difficult and often impossible to say that an employee in one specialty should be a grade above or below an employee in another specialty. Attempting to do so may annoy and antagonize, with considerable justification, the specialist who has been put into the lower classification.

More importantly, such classifications only serve to impede and impair flexibility, and to the extent that they do so, they collide with the most powerful thrust of the technological society, the stepped-up pace of change. The more broadly and loosely personnel classifications are defined and arranged, the easier it becomes for the organization or the individual within it to innovate. As Rosemary Stewart has noted, "The more scope there is for initiative in a job—that is, the less the requirements of the job are precisely defined—the more the man can make the job."[18]

Another factor that will be both a cause and an effect of broadening personnel classifications will be the growing stature of professionalism generally. Moving up the classification ladder usually means moving into supervisory positions. However, many institutions founded on professionalism have already begun to discard this notion. Thus, the outstanding doctor or professor does not always gain his reward by becoming the hospital administrator or dean. More often than not, he does not want recognition in such a form, preferring instead to receive his rewards through increased opportunities to fulfill his ego and self-actualization needs while continuing to exercise his professional skills. Thus, the doctor may be given new facilities and more challenging cases while the professor may receive more chances to teach specialized classes or engage in more extensive research. There is less and less need for putting them into different personnel classifications so that they may have authority over others.

It will be necessary for more and more public organizations to adopt the same approach. The outstanding teacher or patrolman, for example, will need to be rewarded in ways other than by being made principal or desk sergeant. As the task of teaching, policing and other fields of endeavor become more professionalized, those who have invested much time and talent in mastering the skills they require will grow reluctant to abandon opportunities to exercise and develop such skills. Another factor which should further this trend is that administra-

---

18. Stewart, *op. cit.,* p. 35.

tion itself is becoming more professionalized, demanding skills and training that are often quite different from those required for success in the organization's other roles.

The desire for employees to develop their competency and seek new challenges, along with the growing interdependence of organizational life generally, will also increase pressures for mobility. Employees will not only rotate through an organization but will increasingly move outside it. They may not only switch organizations but also levels of government and sectors of society. An employee in the federal bureaucracy, for example, may take a work assignment with a state or local government or with a private organization. Sometimes he may return to his original agency but sometimes he may not. Studies by the Committee for Economic Development and by the Brookings Institute during the mid-1960's both recommended much greater mobility within the civil service, particularly at the higher levels. The CED report called for periodic assignments to universities, tours of duty abroad and, when feasible, temporary assignments in private industry as ways of giving administrators a broader background and perspective. The Brookings study also urged such steps and recommended, among other things, inter-agency career planning.[19]

The federal government has already started to move in this direction. President Johnson issued an executive order in 1966 establishing the Executive Assignment System with a goal of opening up the top grades of the federal service, stepping up internal mobility and bringing in more executives from the outside. Outstanding employees would be circulated throughout the federal service with the aim of sharpening their skills and increasing their identification with the overall purposes of the federal government rather than with those of a particular department or agency. It was also hoped that such a system would make the right man or woman available for the right job at the right time. Some states have begun to adopt similar plans. California actually goes further than the federal government in rotating its top level employees so that they may more fully develop and utilize their abilities.

In 1971 Congress passed the Intergovernmental Personnel Act which is designed to strengthen the human resources of state and local government. One of the means stipulated for doing so is to allow employees in these sub-national governments to work for a while in the federal bureaucracy and to allow federal bureaucrats to spend more time with state and local agencies. There were over 400 such "mobility assignees" in the first year of the act's operation.[20]

---

19. Corson and Paul, *Men Near The Top*. Franklin P. Kilpatrick, Milton C. Cummings and M. Kent Jennings, *The Image of the Federal Service* (Washington, D.C.: The Brookings Institution, 1964).
20. Joseph M. Robertson, "Personnel Administration and the New Federalism," *Civil Service Journal*, 13, no. 3 (January–March 1973).

What is going to happen to civil service under the impact of all these and other changes which the technological society will impose? It should be noted at the outset that the civil service system has been subjected to severe questioning and searching criticism almost since its inception. As long ago as the early 1900's that prescient American theorist Herbert Croly pointed out that the civil service system had only created a conflict between the political appointees at the heads of agencies and their subordinates, and that this conflict operated as a sort of stalemate which made effective administration almost impossible. In his book *The Promise of American Life* Croly noted, "The American Civil Service will never be really reformed by the sort of Civil Service laws which have hitherto been passed—no matter how faithfully those laws may be executed. The only way in which administrative efficiency can be secured is by means of an organization which makes a departmental chief absolutely responsible for energetic work and economical administration in his office; and no such responsibility can exist as long as his subordinates are independent of him."[21]

In recent years, criticism of the civil service system along these as well as other lines has considerably increased. Dr. Emmanuel Sovas, a management consultant with considerable experience in working with government agencies, points out that "when first formulated in the 1850's, Civil Service laws were designed to keep out incompetents. Now they serve to keep them in."[22] Meanwhile, Washington journalist Stewart Alsop has said that "almost everybody—including most intelligent members of the Civil Service—agree that the Civil Service system is a disaster."[23]

Alsop's judgment is undoubtedly too harsh, particularly in the light of more recent developments such as those discussed earlier which have brought increased innovation and flexibility to the federal bureaucracy. However, most knowledgeable observers would agree that the federal civil service system could stand some substantial improvement. They would also judge state and local merit systems, with a few possible exceptions, as warranting even more drastic reform.

To some, the solution seems to lie simply in abolishing the civil service system completely. There is some rational basis for advocating what may seem like an extreme measure. When civil service was inaugurated, jobs in general were at a premium and government jobs with the security they offered were particularly sought after. Therefore, it was necessary to protect government service from the pressures of patronage. However, since World War II, the nation has generally maintained high levels of employment. People may not always be able to find the

---

21. Herbert Croly, *The Promise of American Life* (New York: Capricorn Books, 1964), pp. 335-336.
22. Quoted in Armstrong, "The Re-education of John Lindsay."
23. Alsop, *The Center*, p. 16.

job they want or have been trained to perform but at least some job is nearly always available. Furthermore, unemployment compensation and welfare programs manage to keep most people from actually going under, even though they fail to provide the standard of living that most Americans deem desirable. As a result of such developments, government jobs are no longer quite as prized as they once were, and consequently it can be argued that there is no need to keep such a tight hand on the gates of entry. Frequently, government agencies have trouble finding all the people they need, at least for some of their positions.

Hand in hand with this development has been the rise in professionalism and specialization. This naturally tends somewhat to limit the potentiality of patronage abuses. Already many professionals such as doctors, nurses and teachers frequently become employed by government agencies without going through customary civil service procedures, for it becomes unnecessary to bother with merit system criteria when professional certification programs exist. Furthermore, the growing use of program budgeting and productivity measures may supply a much better means for determining whether an employee should be hired, retained or promoted.

Finally, it can be argued that unions can furnish the employee all the protection he needs against arbitrary treatment by his superiors. If this is so, then why operate a cumbersome personnel system to ensure the same thing? In short, why not let public managers proceed with the same flexibility as private managers in handling their personnel problems, subject to certain basic rules and, of course, union pressures?

Although a reasonable case can be made for outright abolition of civil service, most administrative observers are not quite ready to go so far. But they do concur in the need for change. The National Civil Service League has been wrestling with the civil service problem and has proposed a seven-point plan of reform. Its model public personnel law would abolish the Civil Service Commission, replacing it with a personnel director of cabinet status who, while having to possess certain qualifications, would serve at the pleasure of the chief executive. The league's law would establish a seven-member citizens' advisory board whose members would be appointed by the chief executive but who would be confirmed by the legislature and could not be removed without cause. This board would monitor the personnel system's operation. It would have the right to examine witnesses and papers and issue reports, but it would have no executive or judicial authority. An ombudsman would also be created who, holding life tenure, would hear cases and forward recommendations.

The league's model law further endorses collective bargaining in the public sector, preferential hiring for disadvantaged groups, including handicapped persons and returning veterans, and a broadening of the political rights of public employees. Under its terms, the political activities of a public employee would be subject to only two basic restrictions: (1) he could not be an officer of a political party or hold partisan political office and (2) he could not solicit money or services for any political party from another classified employee. Finally, the act would authorize a "transfusion of talent" between various government agencies and levels of government and it would allow the use of a pass-fail designation for those taking tests for public positions. This presumably means that rank ordering of those who take civil service tests would be abolished, and anyone could be hired who had passed with the minimum grade.[24]

The league's proposed law has not escaped criticism. Opponents claim it would make the chief executive—be he president, governor or mayor—a virtual tzar with nearly unbridled authority. Its detractors also fear that it downgrades the merit principle, opening the door to all kinds of political manipulation. They further claim it could lead to "reverse discrimination" and, in any case, forces government to bear nearly the full burden for society's lapses when it comes to the problems of the disadvantaged.[25]

But while disputes and disagreements may cloud the issue, and while any group's or individual's proposed solution may be another group's or individual's nightmare, an underlying consensus is building up that public personnel administration, like public administration generally, may have to undergo some substantial changes if the needs of a technological society are to be served.

Budgeting, Planning and Centralization

As we noted at the end of chapter one, public administration is currently under considerable pressure to prove and improve its productivity. There is every likelihood that these pressures will only increase in the future. As the role of administration expands, and as politicians, the press and the public become more aware of its presence and its problems, demands for more effectiveness and/or efficiency seem slated to intensify.

This will tend to nudge administration further away from traditional budgeting practices and farther along the road to some form of program budgeting. PPBS in its pure and pristine state may remain a rarity in government circles, but some of its aspects or outgrowths such as productivity measures may well become fixtures in a wide range of

---

24. "League Revises Model Civil Service Law," *National Civil Service League,* November 1970.
25. Harold E. Forbes, "The Model Public Personnel Administration Law: Two Views—Con," *Public Personnel Review,* October 1971.

government activities. Such a development will receive additional impetus from a stepped-up interest in, and practice of, planning, for programmed budgeting and planning are deeply related. The accelerating rate of change will make both short-term and long-term planning ever more necessary. Only by seeking to make change a part of its routine activity will the organization of the future manage to prosper or even survive.

What about centralization? Will it grow or diminish in the administrative future? The report referred to earlier of the National Academy of Public Administration found pressures operating in both directions. Among the pressures making for increased centralization were the need for national solutions to complex public problems now handled at lower levels, the need to utilize complex technology and sophisticated skills, the need to surmount "intractable local conflicts" and the need for displaying greater equality and uniformity in dealing with people. Other centralizing pressures were seen in the expansion of legislative oversight, the further judicialization of the administrative process and the spread of public employee unionism.

At the same time, however, the academy found countervailing pressures at work. These included rising demands for citizen involvement in decision-making, improved methods of service delivery, revenue-sharing, increased concern over and experimentation with attempts at regional organization, increased efforts to upgrade state and local government and increased development of program effective measurements which permit and even require less centralized supervision.

The academy's report did not see these divergent pressures as necessarily irreconcilable. The mounting emphasis on local control, it said, "is not socially incompatible with the trend toward centralization. The efforts to decentralize converge particularly upon the delivery of services and the collecting and analysis of information (including citizen advice and opinion). Thus, both forces may be accommodated by redefining the role of the higher level of government to focus attention upon determining broad policy, defining uniform national standards, program guidelines and the evaluation of information generated at the level of program execution and service delivery. By contrast, local government would manage the delivery of services in a unique local area with all the principles of decentralization met by regular feedback from those receiving the services, opportunity to develop appropriate neighborhood delivery units and emphasis on fitting quality of service to recipient needs—recognizing the value of diversity in program, policy and even objectives."[26]

What the academy seems to be saying is that more *political* cen-

---

26. Chapman and Cleaveland, *op. cit.,* pp. 9–10.

tralization seems likely but that this does not necessarily mean more *administrative* centralization must follow. On the contrary, just the opposite could occur. Thus, a state government could take over its local school system, for example, but operate the system in such a manner that the district school principals would enjoy greater discretion than they previously obtained when their function was part of local government. In many instances this may well occur, for state educational agencies could show less zealousness in closely supervising district principals than did municipal superintendents. The decentralizing forces which the academy noted should only increase the likelihood of this occurring.

Bases and Boundaries

The boundaries of the future organization will stretch much further than the present one. They will tend to be loose and low, easy to bend and easy to break. People and programs will cross through and intersect the organization's borders with less and less difficulty. The public organization will not only have increased contact with other public organizations but with private ones as well. It may frequently contract out for services and sometimes may turn over whole functions to private enterprise. Furthermore, in striving to achieve more flexibility of operation, public organizations may increasingly start to resemble private ones. Programmed budgeting, management by objectives, decentralized service delivery, more flexible personnel policies and other such features will further this end.

Private organizations, meanwhile, will take on more of the features of public ones, for they will find it increasingly more difficult to escape the pressures for social responsibility. "Some of the social forces impacting so effectively on universities and quasi-public institutions will most certainly get stronger and have a powerful effect on business in the future," says Dr. Howard McMahon, president of Arthur D. Little, one of the nation's largest consulting firms.[27] And he points out that many large business firms, confronted with the rising tide of consumerism and conservation, are already starting to assess the social impact of their activities. Such social audits, he has warned, will soon become routine for all corporations. Thus we may find the private and public sectors of society becoming less and less distinguishable from each other.

Finally, the confusion over boundaries may induce more and more public agencies to place more emphasis on the clientele and/or place basis of organization. The client and/or place is a fairly discrete element and there may be less ambiguity and confusion over who is to

---

27. *New York Times*, February 14, 1971.

do what when one or both of them becomes the basis for the organization's structure and activity. However, though the use of such approaches may reduce the costs and frustrations of coordination, they also may limit the use of specialized skills and equipment, prevent certain economies of scale and add to other coordination costs. Here as in most other areas of administration, the future is as replete with problems as it is with promises.

CASE STUDY

The New Administration at Work

In a fast moving, technological society the future becomes the present at a rapidly rising rate. Thus, the trend lines of administration's future path are already beginning to show themselves. While their full development remains for posterity to enjoy, or suffer as the case may be, their impact is already beginning to be felt. European car makers such as Volvo, Volkswagon and Fiat have started to abandon the assembly line and group their workers into teams responsible for producing, if not a whole car, then at least a substantial portion of one.[28] Motorola has experimented with allowing some of its assembly-line workers to make a whole piece of apparatus, Texas Instruments is allowing its janitors to oversee their own supply inventories and to work out their own schedules for keeping buildings clean, and a host of other organizations have taken still greater strides down the paths that point toward the future.

In many respects, the new administration is gaining ground at a greater pace in Europe than in America, and in nearly all countries it is forging ahead faster in the private sector than in the public one. The public sector, particularly in the United States, too often remains stymied by civil service laws, legal and financial controls, political pressures of one kind or another and, perhaps, the lack of generally acceptable productivity measures. Yet, even here, examples and instances of the changes have emerged. The world is moving forward and the world of public administration cannot stand still. Hesitantly and often reluctantly, government bureaucracies are joining other organizations in climbing aboard the bandwagon of change.

Since Europe seems somewhat ahead of the United States, and since the private sector seems a good deal in advance of the public one, let us examine some cases of the new administration at work in Europe and in American industry before going on to study some of the less abundant but still significant instances of major change in American public administration.

Developments Abroad

With 25,000 employees and an $800,000,000-a-year gross income, Gränges AB not only stands as one of Sweden's largest companies, but takes a place

---

28. Clyde Farnsworth, "Companies Raise Role of Workers," *New York Times,* January 28, 1973.

among the world's more significant multi-national conglomerate corporations. Gränges, however, has also shown itself sensitive to the temper of the times, and when its employees began showing signs of disenchantment and disaffection, the firm decided it was time to do things differently.

The first step Gränges took was to institute a "no-firing" policy. This was based on the rationale that if an employee was not performing well the blame should fall on the company for not having recruited well. Then, the Swedish concern began restructuring its work force into small groups, giving these groups authority to plan and assign the work among themselves. Supervision was substantially reduced. In its place arose a bewildering network of management-labor committees. Some labor representatives were also added to the company's board of directors.

The results were generally favorable, sometimes remarkably so. At the company's die-casting foundary production rose 45 percent, employee turnover dropped from 46 to 18 percent and spoilage declined by more than one-third, all within eighteen months of the new scheme's inauguration. As one veteran employee told American journalist David Jenkins, "Everything has changed since I've been here. Now we control the whole job. There is a foreman, sure, but he's busy taking care of materials and administration. He doesn't have to come around every five minutes and tell you what to do."[29] At last report, the company was starting to allow employees to pick their own foremen and was also preparing to let them have a say in replacing a high level executive who was getting ready to retire.

In West Germany, meanwhile, employees at the Hauni Werke of Hamburg have for some years had the right to elect their immediate supervisors by secret ballot. They also elect seven of the seventeen members of the council which selects the higher executives. And since a three-quarters majority is required for such appointments, the workers hold veto power over all executive selection. Under such a plan, the company has prospered, becoming the world's leading firm in its rather specialized field. (It produces machines for making cigarette filters.)[30]

Underlying and underscoring such developments have been governmental efforts in both countries to promote what is sometimes called industrial democracy. Both Sweden and West Germany, along with Norway and Holland, have enacted laws giving workers the right to elect representatives to the boards of directors of their companies. West Germany at the start of 1974 was preparing new legislation to enlarge this right. It would allow employees of the company's 650 largest firms to elect half of the directors of these companies.[31]

In some situations workers have acquired near total control over the firms that employ them. Most of Yugoslavia's industry, for example, is under the

29. David Jenkins, "Industrial Democracy in Sweden," *New York Times,* October 14, 1973 (Business section).
30. Berkley (1971), *op. cit.,* pp. 61–62.
31. David Jenkins, "Industrial Democracy: It Catches on Faster in Europe Than U.S.," *New York Times,* May 13, 1974 (Business section).

479

supervision of employee-elected work councils which, among other things, hire and fire the company's chief executive. In Italy, a metal factory owner in Ovada, bruised, weary, and risking a second heart attack from too many battles with his firm's trade union, turned his plant over to the workers and retired. The workers then hired him back to operate the company but only under their supervision. Absenteeism, which reaches over 20 percent in some Italian firms, has all but vanished and profits, which are divided equally, are rising.[32]

As for the public sector, worker participation in many areas of policy formulation and decision-making has also gone forward. In Great Britain, West Germany and Scandinavia, rank-and-file representatives sit on a variety of policy boards and commissions throughout their respective bureaucracies. Even France, a country not known for having highly developed democratic institutions, has what are called round table commissions in most government departments. Consisting half of employee representatives, these commissions make decisions on promotions and dismissals within their own administrative units.

Developments at Home: The Private Sector

Although the concept of worker control does not enjoy as much government sanction in the United States as it does in the more advanced European countries, and while no American firm has yet made it established policy to put employee representatives on its board of directors, nevertheless the new administration is still starting to take hold. And a few American firms have gone beyond even the more progressive European companies in instituting some of its aspects.

In the late 1960's, General Foods began to experience increasing trouble at its Pet Food plant in Topeka, Kansas. Poor quality production, vandalism and graffiti on the walls was signaling the need for new ways of dealing with its increasingly younger work force. The company's management saw itself compelled to act and it did. It grouped its employees into eight-man processing teams and sixteen-man packaging-warehouse teams and allowed them a rather free hand in arranging and scheduling tasks among themselves. What evolved was a system which calls for employees to rotate throughout the plant, learning and doing nearly all the tasks involved. Each employee learns at his own pace and the more jobs he learns to do, the more he is paid. His progress is judged by his fellow workers.

Journalist Jenkins reports being told by one 34-year-old operator, "They just said this is your baby, you do it. We had to learn everything from the ground up. When you learn one job, you teach it to the next guy, and every guy finds a new and better way of doing things . . . We do our own maintenance work and lubrication. Everything that goes on here, we do it."[33]

---

32. *New York Times,* February 8, 1974.
33. David Jenkins, "Democracy in the Factory," *The Atlantic,* April 1973.

The employee then went on to say how he had acquired additional responsibilities and self-fulfillment by serving as chairman of the plant's safety committee. "Before, I've never been anywhere in the U.S. But now I've been to all the safety meetings in New York, Michigan—they don't send management, they send me. When a salesman comes around to sell safety equipment, Ed Dulworth (the plant manager) sends him to see me." According to Jenkins, the employee claims that "95 percent of the employees are sold on the system. We're the foundation of what's going to be in the future—the Topeka system."[34]

American Telephone and Telegraph Company, long considered one of the stodgiest giants of American business, has also begun to explore fresh ways of doing things. Plagued with high absenteeism and turnover rates, along with a costly high ratio of supervisors, AT&T launched some nineteen experiments in job enrichment. According to the company's personnel director, Robert N. Ford, eighteen of these projects succeeded, nine of them outstandingly so.[35]

One of the projects involved a district business office in suburban St. Louis. Previously, ten separate steps and sometimes as many pairs of hands would be required in this business office as in others to process a service request. Through expanding the work modules of the employees, this figure was reduced to three basic steps involving only three employees. Then, each service representative was given a geographical area of his own to take care of rather than just being assigned the next customer who called in. Finally, the office did some interesting experimentation in changing its physical arrangements. Whereas the desks of the service order representatives had previously been ranged in rows behind the desks of their respective supervisors, now each row of desks was grouped into a circle with the supervisor's desk forming only one not very distinguishable link in a circular chain. When the service order typists began showing signs of feeling left out, they were broken up into groups each stationed in the center of one of the circles. The office called their arrangement "nesting." Within two years these changes had raised the office's productivity from near the bottom to near the top of all telephone districts in the St. Louis area.[36]

Experimentation with new administrative techniques has not been confined to larger firms. In 1932, George Rent set up a fuel oil delivery company in the Boston suburb of Randolph. The firm prospered and was employing fifteen full-time, twenty part-time and summer employees by the mid-1960's. But the owner found himself increasingly dissatisfied. His men, it seemed, would do nothing if not prodded and pushed. Rent had to settle even run-of-the-mill problems and make routine decisions. He was getting along in years, yet he found himself having to work more rather than less every year. Surely, reasoned Rent, there must be a better way to run a fuel oil delivery company.

The first thing he did was to reduce the work week of his employees from

34. *Ibid.*
35. Robert N. Ford, "Job Enrichment Lessons from A.T.&T.," *Harvard Business Review*, February 1973.
36. *Ibid.*

48 to 40 hours while maintaining their existing salaries. Then, he decided to give his workers greatly increased discretion over their own jobs. The truck drivers, for example, could set their own routes, establish the criteria they would use in making automatic deliveries and even pick the days and the times they wanted to work. They would also participate in setting prices and policies as well as in purchasing new equipment. The equipment salesman would have to convince the driver as well as Rent himself before he could sell the firm a new truck. When a customer applied for credit or when a customer had overextended his line of credit, the route driver would discuss the situation with the bookkeeper and they would decide what action to take.

Comparable chunks of discretion were also given service men, office workers and others. As a result, the employees began to work not only more enthusiastically but also more creatively. New ideas suddenly emerged which raised productivity. Drivers who previously drove in from the field to get a decision made, a practice which produced considerable expense in driver time and truck travel costs, would now make such decisions on their own at the scene. The proprietor found his profits rising at a faster rate while his own work schedule dwindled sharply. So far he has only one complaint to make with his system. Many of his drivers have become too well informed in fuel oil company operations and have left him to start competing firms of their own![37]

Developments at Home: The Public Sector

While many might consider the Social Security Administration to be a somewhat dull and drab bureaucracy, it is actually one of the federal government's more enterprising agencies. It was, for example, one of the first government organizations to institute productivity measures. In the 1970's it has become something of a pacesetter in inaugurating the new administration.

When its Bureau of Supplementary Security Income was launched in October 1972, it was organized into four basic divisions—administration, operations, policy and program review. However, the 75 to 100 employees that were to man these divisions were put into a pool. That is, the employees were not assigned on a permanent basis to any particular division but instead found themselves employed on various task forces that were established somewhat on an ad hoc basis. Each employee thus worked for the entire organization and not just for one of its divisions. Moreover, his work unit was not a formalized subunit of the bureau but a temporary work group.

In setting up these flexible task forces, the bureau paid little regard to hierarchy and status. An employee with, say, a G-14 classification might find himself working in a group that was being led by a G-11. In general, people would come and go not only between the work groups but also between the bureau itself and other divisions of the Social Security Administration. Noth-

---

37. Ronald Lawson, "Observations From an Application of Theory Y to a Fuel Oil Dealer," Unpublished paper, Department of Political Science, Northeastern University.

ing quite like it had ever been attempted in any old-line government department. The bureau's leaders and well-wishers were only hoping that the Civil Service Commission would not object to its disregard of the sanctity of grade classifications.

Social Security's Bureau of Retirement and Survivors' Insurance has also been doing some trailblazing along the frontiers of administration. In 1973, following extensive studies and conferences, the bureau launched an experiment at its Philadelphia office. All the office's 280 employees were grouped into six modules with each module covering a nearly complete range of office operations. Every employee is exposed to the whole process and can follow a case from beginning to end. Clerical employees rotate from one job to another every two months, and before taking on a new assignment, they are shown how it relates to the office's entire operation. Everything takes place on one floor and no time is lost in writing memos or engaging in other forms of formal communication. Each employee performs as much of the processing task as he can, and every job done becomes documented in the employee's folder to be noted when promotion time comes around. Each employee is encouraged to make suggestions.

The bureau claims that not only has processing time gone down but that a number of employees have refused promotions that would have forced them to move out of the center. It has gone on to launch similar experiments in its southeastern payments center and its San Francisco and Long Island offices.[38]

Turning to state government, the California State Insurance Compensation Fund, which has been referred to earlier in this book, offers an interesting and encouraging example of the new administration at work. Confronted with sagging fortunes, this quasi-independent government agency undertook a wide-ranging reorganization in 1968. It dismantled much of its hierarchical structure, eliminating such levels and posts as that of divisional manager and regional manager. Instead, the twenty-four district offices were put directly under the fund's president, R. A. Young.

The phrase "directly under" is perhaps not the best one to describe the new arrangement for the fund has striven to make the relationship more collegial than hierarchical. The district managers meet with the president every month to go over problems and discuss new ideas. Otherwise the district managers and their officers are pretty much on their own. Each office receives its budget in a lump sum every year and is free to spend it pretty much as it sees fit. It can, for example, contract out for certain staff services instead of using those provided by the fund's main office, if it finds such private contracting to be cheaper. (If it uses the fund's staff services, the costs will be charged against the district office's budget.) Supervision as such is exercised almost wholly by objectives. Headquarters is primarily interested in the district office's performance as reflected in its annual balance sheet.

Each district office also tries to follow such a collegial pattern and em-

---

38. Evelyn Grgurich, "They Do It Differently," *Oasis,* May 1973. Also see "Making Work More Enjoyable," *Oasis,* October 1973.

ployee committees of various kinds abound. The offices have been restructured on a clientele basis. Each office's operations were formerly divided on the basis of its four main functions which were safety, sales, auditing and claims/rehabilitation. Now the typical district office is divided into work teams, each of which handles all four functions for a group of clients. As a result, a client need make only one phone call to obtain assistance in all four areas of the fund's activity. This not only makes it easier for the client to secure services but also helps prevent him from receiving conflicting advice.[39]

Local government has also witnessed some interesting forays into the administrative future, many of them at the managerial level. When the 1970 census figures indicated that Dayton, Ohio, like so many other American cities, was deteriorating both socially and physically, City Manager James A. Alloway called together over sixty of his top administrators for a two-day seminar to see what could be done. Out of this seminar emerged what was called the Task Force Management System. The system is comprised of eight interdisciplinary teams each of which is concerned with a major problem area that cuts across traditional department lines. Thus, there is one team for youth, another for crime, another for housing, still another for downtown, etc. Each task force consists of nine or ten members, most of whom are city officials, although in some cases outsiders have been brought in. Illustrative of the interdisciplinary approach was the fact that the city's fire chief was made head of the task force on crime while the chief engineer was given leadership of the one on racism. (He has since become quite aggressive, even militant, in locating and attacking racism problems.)

Each task force meets twice a week for two hours or more but since no task force has a budget or staff of its own, many officials soon found that their task force duties were occupying up to half their time. This forced them to delegate more and more of their responsibilities to their subordinates, and many were shocked to see that this rarely produced any major problems. In many instances, their departments actually functioned better without their full-time supervision.

The task forces are charged not just with making recommendations but with implementing solutions. A task force decision normally supersedes that of a department head unless the city manager decides otherwise. The chairman of each task force meets monthly with the city manager to review his team's progress. The concept was launched in 1972 and by the spring of the following year, plans were being worked out for giving the task forces budgetary authority. (Dayton had already instituted program budgeting which, as we saw earlier, lends itself to such an interdepartmental approach.) Proposals for involving more public members in the task forces were also being discussed. Meanwhile, the city has done a good deal of polling in trying to determine the fears and desires of its citizenry.

In the smaller city of Brea, California (population 26,000), a more extensive

---

39. Berkley (1971), *op. cit.*, pp. 28–31.

team management approach is being tried out. In 1972, City Manager William Weeden began moving his department heads into offices near his own. By early 1973 all the city's top-ranking administrative leaders were located in a suite of offices on one floor with no doors and only glass partitions separating one department head's office from another's. In the midst of this arrangement lay the city manager's office which, like that of the other officials, was also doorless. As in Dayton, the task force approach is heavily used, with city officials often heading task forces that were well beyond their own demarcated areas of official responsibility. The police chief, for example, heads the task force on employee development.

The change initially produced some negative effects as the department heads felt isolated from their regular domains and threatened by the new task forces. There are also signs of some unnecessary meddling by one official into another official's business, and frequent eruptions of work were also a problem to some. But generally the system is believed to have worked well. Relationships have for the most part become cordial, and while conflict does arise, it is generally open and reasonably positive. As one city official noted, "Very little goes on here behind closed doors, for after all, there are no doors."

The arrangement has fostered a more city-wide approach to problem solving, thus enabling the city government to function more responsively and more rapidly. Assistant City Manager Michael M. Davis points out that the city negotiated with a nationwide developer of shopping centers to build such a center in Brea. In the course of working out the arrangements, the developer noted that he had never worked with a city that gave him such speedy responses to the matters he would raise.

Perhaps the most dramatic example of the new administration at work in the public sector has occurred in a particular agency of city government not noted for its flexibility, openness, or general humanistic concerns—the police. During the 1960's, American police forces came under increasing pressure to change their ways of doing things. In response to such pressures a new method of local law enforcement arose called team policing.[40]

The idea originated in Syracuse, New York in 1960 when the city decided to set up an eight-man crime control team to cover an inner city district that had been plagued with crime problems. The team was, to a great extent, removed from the department's hierarchical organization and exempted from many of its rules and regulations. The crime control team was to work out for itself when, where and how it wanted to work. Team members would decide singularly or cooperatively, depending on the situation, whether or not they would wear uniforms, look for criminals, patrol on foot or in cars, attend community group meetings or simply talk to citizens, sometimes going into bars and taverns to do so. On a rainy night they might decide to go home

---

40. *Team Policing* (Washington: The Police Foundation, 1973). Also George E. Berkley, "Theory Y Comes to the Police," Paper presented to the annual convention, American Society for Public Administration, 1973.

early, on a busy night they might decide to work late. When any of them came across a crime, he could investigate it on his own without having to turn it over to a detective until such time as he might think he needed extra help. The biggest source of control over the team was the goal that had been set for it: reduce crime.

The results after one year, as described by local newspapers and leading citizens as well as by the police department itself, were little short of phenomenal. The reported crime rate had dropped nearly 60 percent. Much more indicative was the response of the district's residents. They were, for one thing, starting to walk the streets again at night and merchants who had feared to stay open after dark were now doing so.

The team policing concept has gradually spread to other cities such as Holyoke, Massachusetts and Dayton, Ohio. In both cities what began as an experiment in one sensitive area of the city has since been expanded to cover police operations city-wide. The teams operate generally out of store fronts and often have a few paid residents in the neighborhoods they serve to assist them. The response by the residents has been almost uniformly favorable.

These are only a few cases that seem to foreshadow the administrative future. However, some care should be taken in assessing their import and impact. For one thing, there have been undoubtedly many instances where such experiments have fizzled and failed. These, unfortunately, are far less frequently reported. Then, much of the reporting that has been done on the successful experiments has come from those who had a hand in initiating them. While they often make an earnest attempt to use objective evaluative devices, some shading and emphasis, if not distortion, is, at least on occasion, bound to occur. Finally, most of the experiments were accompanied by a good many problems and a good deal of pain before they attained success. And in all cases they represent as yet only partial implementation of the new approach to administration.

But despite such important qualifications, the record of these as well as other developments too numerous to mention here remains impressive. They indicate that administration is changing, and that it is changing in ways which should give it increasing effectiveness in delivering public services to the American people.

"DEMOCRACY IS INEVITABLE"

The heading for this section was the title of an article which appeared in the March–April 1964 issue of the *Harvard Business Review.* The article's authors, administrative theorist and practitioner Warren G. Bennis and sociologist Philip Slater, flatly state at the outset that "democracy (whether capitalistic or socialistic is not at issue here) is the only system that can successfully cope with the changing demands of contemporary civilization. . . . Given a desire to survive in this civilization, democracy is the most effective means to achieve this end."

Bennis and Slater go on to define democracy as a system of values that incorporates such things as full and free communication irrespective of rank and power, reliance on consensus rather than on coercion or even compromise as a way of managing conflict, the substitution of technical competence and knowledge for the "vagaries of personal whims or prerogatives" as a source of power and influence, the creation of an atmosphere conducive to "emotional expression as well as task-oriented tasks" and a "basically human bias."

Having defined democracy, the two writers then proceed to argue for its inevitability on two basic grounds. The first is the need to respond to the continuous and increasing pressures of change. They claim that research shows unmistakably that "the more democratically operated organizations exhibit a much greater adaptability to changing conditions, for rapid acceptance of new ideas, for flexibility in dealing with new and novel problems and for generating high morale and loyalty." Democracy, they also note, creates an attitude of doubt, skepticism and modesty. This also fosters change, for "one cannot believe that change is in itself a good thing and still believe implicitly in the rightness of the present."

Their second reason for believing that the advent of democracy in the organizational world is unavoidable is the growing role of science. "In order for the spirit of inquiry, the foundation of science, to grow and flourish, a democratic environment is a necessity. Science encourages a point of view that is equalitarian, pluralistic, liberal. It accentuates freedom of opinion and dissent." Claiming that the growth of science has always been accompanied by demands for freedom, justice and respect, they reiterate their theme: Democracy is inevitable.[41]

At the time their article appeared, even though its points had been amply foreshadowed by the work of the humanistic theorists such as Argyris, McGregor and Likert, it created something of a stir in the field of administration. Today it seems somewhat less startling. Although administration is far from "democratic," we have already seen some instances of how it may be moving in this direction. And if many writers still deny the validity of democracy's inevitability, a growing number are accepting at least some aspects of this thesis. The 1973 report of the National Academy of Public Administration, while avoiding the use of the term *democratic,* depicted an administrative future consistent in most of its essentials with the one envisioned by Bennis and Slater.[42] Later the same year, the Forty-third American Assembly, sponsored by Columbia University and consisting of eighty people from government,

---

41. Warren G. Bennis and Philip E. Slater, "Democracy Is Inevitable," *Harvard Business Review,* March-April 1964.
42. Chapman and Cleaveland, *op. cit.*

business, labor and the professions, issued a concluding statement on its 1973 topic "The Changing World of Work" which stated:

> Something, clearly, is stirring. In part, we are witnessing changes in personal values that are seen and felt not only in the United States but around the world. In part, we are experiencing the latest chapter in the continuing story of the quest for fulfilling American goals and aspirations; a fair and equitable society; an opportunity for each citizen to participate in the forces that affect his life; a confirmation that the democratic process does, indeed, work for all. Now that challenge is emerging at the most basic level of work itself.[43]

But if there are indications that administration is moving toward increased democratization, do not other indications exist which point in the other direction? What about the trend toward larger organizations? Can this be consistent with democracy? What about the increasing use of automation? Will this not tend to depersonalize administration and introduce a more anti-human bias? And will not the use of work teams stifle individual creativity and lead to a herd mentality?

As for the first of these questions, it is true that the trend line seems to point toward the move of many areas of administrative activity to higher levels of government. States may assume many operations, such as education, now carried on by local governments, and the federal government may take over many activities, such as welfare, now performed by states and/or local governments. Furthermore, there may be a trend to merge more organizations in order to achieve a broader approach to problems. But these developments do not in themselves introduce an anti-democratic element in administration. Large organizations are not necessarily inconsistent with democratic values. They may actually even reinforce such values.

"Many persons believe that size and hierarchy have a tendency to force persons into uniformity," writes John Rehfuss. But, he adds, "there is little empirical data to justify this belief . . . . Intuitively, it seems just as appealing to argue that large bureaucracies have enough organizational slack to tolerate the 'oddball' and to put up with minor and sometimes major variations from 'normal' behavior, while small organizations cannot easily tolerate these aberrations."[44] Rehfuss goes on to cite research supporting such a contention. One study of 1,700 executives in large, medium and small business firms, for example, showed that the large company managers placed a higher value on imagination and

---

43. *The Changing World of Work,* Final Report of the Forty-third American Assembly, November 1–4, 1973 (Harriman, N.Y.: Arden House), p. 10.
44. John Rehfuss, *Public Administration as Political Process* (New York: Charles Scribner's Sons, 1973), p. 91.

forcefulness while the small company managers stressed tact and caution.[45] These and other findings lead Rehfuss to conclude that large organizations often demand more "inner-directed" qualities such as creativity and initiative, while small organizations tend to emphasize group uniformity.

Harlan Cleveland expresses the same basic belief. He maintains that large organizations offer more opportunities for individuals to develop their talents, express their will and whims or simply to escape from conformist pressures. "The result of bigness," he writes, "is actually a diffusion of the decision-making and decision-influencing process. . . . "[46] Bernard Rosen, executive director of the U.S. Civil Service Commission, finds bigness a stimulus of rather than a deterrent to employee participation. "The more complex the system, the larger is the proportion (not just the absolute number) of its members who make professional contributions and participate in policy formulation and decision making. Participative management, in this relative sense, is coming less from behavioral science theory than from the intrinsic requirements of business and complexity," he writes.[47]

Recent trends toward bigness in the book publishing industry offers one illustration of what these writers may have in mind. In describing the takeover of smaller publishing houses by large conglomerates, such as RCA's purchase of the Alfred A. Knopf Company, Victor Navasky writes, "In big companies there's no Alfred Knopf saying I want all (book) jackets to be yellow. At Knopf, nobody but Mr. Knopf could do anything for forty years. In the relative anonymity of a large corporation, there's a lot more latitude and flexibility. They have more latitude at Knopf under RCA than they had under the old man."[48]

The relationship between large organizations and small ones is not unlike the relationship between large cities and small towns. While small towns can offer a feeling of closeness and community, they can also exercise a good deal of control over their residents and can create a good deal of discomfort and distress for those who do not wish to conform to their rules and rituals. People with creativity and initiative have more often found small towns places to flee from rather than places to flee to.

As for the effect of automation, this trend too may spur on the democratizing process. Computers, for example, do not take over decision-making as such but rather expand its role through the organization.

45. Lyman Porter, "Where Is Organization Man?" *Harvard Business Review,* November–December 1963.
46. Harlan Cleveland, "Dinosaurs and Personal Freedom," *The Saturday Review,* February 28, 1959.
47. Bernard Rosen, "The Developing Role of Career Managers," *Civil Service Journal,* January–March 1973.
48. Victor S. Navasky, "In Cold Print: Selling Out and Buying In," *New York Times Book Review,* May 20, 1973, p. 2.

They multiply man's capacity and, in the words of Peter Drucker, force "executives to make, as true decisions, what are today mostly made as on-the-spot adaptations." Drucker claims that "with a computer taking over computation, people all the way down the line in the organization will have to learn to be executives and to make effective decisions."[49]

Similar sentiments are expressed by others who have studied the impact of computers. Writes Gilbert Burck, "Managers at the top levels, freed of the need for analyzing details, will more than ever require the faculties of innovation, creativeness, and vision. . . ," while "at the average worker's level the computer, because it continually reports back on the job, is already improving his sense of personal participation."[50] Herbert Simon voices similar views and determinedly denies the charge that automation in general means dehumanizing work. "On the contrary, in most actual instances of recent automation, jobs were made, on the whole, more pleasant and interesting, as judged by the employees themselves, than they had been before."[51] This claim is further supported by Katz and Kahn who point to research showing that "where automation is feasible, it can actually increase motivation among the employees. . . ."[52]

This brings us to the question of the increasing role of the work group rather than that of the individual in the administrative future. Group decision-making frequently has been denounced as destructive of human individuality. The individual is said to surrender his identity and to become a timorous and pliant tool in the hands of the herd. Furthermore, such "group think," it is contended, has been responsible for some of history's worst and most catastrophic decisions, such as the abortive effort to sponsor an invasion of Cuba by anti-Castro Cubans in the early months of John F. Kennedy's presidency. If group decision-making is going to dominate the future of administration, then, say its opponents, both democracy and efficiency will suffer.[53]

Many administrative theorists, however, disagree with these notions. McGregor ardently argued that group decision-making could and would have the contrary effect. It supports and even catalyzes creativity, he contended. One man's contribution stimulates that of another while the fear of failure, so often an inhibiter to creative problem solving, is reduced by the spread of responsibility.[54] Victor A. Thompson has sum-

---

49. Drucker, *The Effective Executive* (1967), p. 159.
50. Gilbert Burck, *The Computer Age* (New York: Harper Torchbooks, 1965), p. 18.
51. Herbert A. Simon, *The Shape of Automation* (New York: Harper Torchbooks, 1965), p. 35.
52. Katz and Kahn, *op. cit.,* p. 365.
53. For a notable example of the case against "groupthink" see Irving L. James, *Victims of Groupthink: A Psychological Study of Foreign Policy Decisions and Fiascos* (Boston: Houghton Mifflin, 1972).
54. McGregor, *The Professional Manager* (1967), pp. 25-30.

marized research by others showing that group thinking is superior to individual thinking. According to Thompson, group deliberation leads to more considered opinions and maximizes the number of possible solutions. It requires that ideas be communicated and this only serves to sharpen and clarify these ideas. It further may increase motivation toward task completion and obviously fosters attempts to reach an eventual consensus.[55]

History does show many examples of group decision that failed but also offers numerous examples of the opposite. If Napoleon had listened to his generals, he would never have marched to Moscow, and, once there, would have left before the Russian winter decimated his army. If Tzar Nicholas II had shown more disposition toward group decision-making, he would not have launched the ill-fated Russo-Japanese War of 1905 and would probably have refrained from entering World War I. If Hitler had listened to his generals, he would have been far less eager to start World War II. And if Lyndon Johnson had been more willing to elicit and heed the honest opinions of others, the Vietnam conflict might never have become a war. It is hard to see how one-man decision-making, in contrast to group decision-making, has worked to the overall betterment of human history.

Organization Democracy: Its Limits and Liabilities

While rationales and evidence exist to refute many of the arguments made against the Bennis-Slater thesis, this does not mean that the thesis is to be swallowed whole. Democratization along the lines they propose can only be carried so far. The retention of a certain amount of hierarchical structure and rule making seems almost mandatory, at least for the foreseeable future. The California State Insurance Fund cited earlier represents what is probably one of the most extensive and successful efforts yet made in the public sector to introduce the new concepts of administration. Yet, when the fund's sweeping reorganization was completed, R. A. Young was still president (unity of command), district managers were still responsible for district offices (chain of command), and while the more relaxed supervision had greatly increased the number of offices under Young's authority, the number of these offices could not have been increased to, say, one hundred or more (span of control). The traditional concepts of administration were not so much replaced as modified. Thus, the evidence indicates that the Bennis-Slater thesis of democracy's inevitability probably warrants modification. What is inevitable, perhaps, is not organizational democracy as such, but simply increased moves toward it.

A second and more critical qualification is that such increased

---

55. Victor A. Thompson, *Modern Organizations* (New York: Alfred A. Knopf, 1961), p. 88.

democracy as will occur, while it may solve many problems and alleviate others, will create new tensions of its own. Basically, democracy
provides people with more choices, but more choices do not necessarily produce paradise. In some respects they subject the individual to
more strains since they require him to make more decisions. (Alvin
Toffler in his book *Future Shock* describes at great length how this
works.) Furthermore, the additional choices that do open up are almost
never enough. Expectation outstrips realization and each new expansion of possibilities only tends to fuel the demand for still more possibilities. As Bennis and Slater concede, "One cannot find a democracy
anywhere without also discovering an endless pile of contemptuous
and exasperated denunciations of it. And perhaps this is only appropriate. For when a democracy ceases finding fault with itself, it has probably ceased to be a democracy."[56]

Increased democracy in administration will produce similar
problems along with an array of more specific antagonisms and annoyances. The frequent criss-crossing of organizational boundaries and the
rapid rate of change will subject organizations and their members to
increased feelings of stress. Moreover, some of administration's new
trends will clash with each other. For example, the increased insistence
on people's rights may spur on increased judicialization, but such a
move would collide with increasing demands for flexibility and innovation. Project teams will beget problems in overlapping functions, scheduling of resources including manpower, continuity of operations, integration of effort, job classifications, accountability for funds, legal
restrictions, etc. And noisy clientele groups and nosy newsmen will
scarcely add to organizational tranquility. "Democracy," as Senator
Howard Baker remarked during the Watergate hearings, "is not a comfortable form of government. Democracy is a rather painful experience."

The pressures on the public manager under the new administration will particularly pick up. To many of his subordinates, he may become a figure more to be pitied than envied. The National Academy of
Public Administration has itemized some of the factors he will have to
face and some of the burdens he will have to bear:

an educated and professionalized work force;

a unionized work force composed of members insistent on their rights;

complex technology and inter-related disciplines requiring "an improved capability in meshing specialists in a productive fashion";

---

56. Bennis and Slater, "Democracy Is Inevitable." The article appears as Chapter I in their book, *The Temporary Society* (New York: Harper & Row), 1968.

a much more complex array of organizational devices that will intersect in and through various agencies and levels of government;

new knowledge, skills and ways of doing things which will force him to constantly re-educate himself and his subordinates. "No longer can one complete a degree program in the comfort that it will be sufficient to see one through a decade, much less a full career."

more qualified organizational loyalty. "A better educated work force will not automatically follow agency policy when employees see it as in error, unjust or unresponsive to the needs of the time." Increased mobility will make such loyalty still more difficult to elicit as well as posing other problems for the public manager;

increased pressures from politicians, the press, public interest groups and from clientele groups whose interests may run counter to those of the public interest groups and even to those of other clientele groups.[57]

To handle the harassments and confront the crises which will increasingly be his lot, the public manager of the future, in the academy's words, "will be more of a moral leader, broker and coordinator than he will be a boss or issuer of orders."[58] This is in accord with what the French writer Jean-François Revel maintains is the condition confronting all kinds of leaders in present day society. In a perceptive observation Revel notes that "the qualities necessary to acquire power . . . and to exercise power . . . are not the same as the qualities necessary to resolve the problems of modern society. The result is that, *as authority increases, competence decreases.*"[59] (Emphasis added.)

Being compelled to substitute skill and competence for formal authority may, however, only serve to increase the administrator's own sense of self-actualization. Happiness, as Napoleon once noted, lies in the full development and utilization of one's talents. The future administrator will have only too many opportunities to hone and refine to the fullest his administrative capabilities.

Furthermore, although his formal authority may gradually wither away, his power may actually grow. Rensis Likert in his provocative book *New Patterns of Management* refutes the common assumption that power is in fixed supply and that anyone who gives power to others thereby loses it for himself. Utilizing both logic and evidence, Likert builds an impressive case to show that the manager who shares his power increases rather than diminishes his influence.

---

57. Chapman and Cleaveland, *op. cit.*, Chapter II.
58. *Ibid.*, p. 17.
59. Jean-François Revel, *Without Marx or Jesus* (New York: Dell Publishing Co., 1971), p. 22.

An interesting experiment conducted by W. Harvey Hegerty at the University of North Carolina sheds light on both these possibilities. Hegerty asked some 850 non-academic employees in such departments as purchasing, accounting and the university laundry to rate their supervisors. The ratings were then compiled and given to the 54 superiors. Some three months later, he surveyed the employees again, and three-quarters of them said they had noticed some improvement in their superior's behavior. More interesting for our purposes was the response of the superiors. A full 87 percent of them said that the survey helped them to do a better job and that they would recommend the procedure to others. Thus, placing superiors at the mercy of their subordinates, so to speak, helped to improve their capabilities and to heighten their satisfactions.[60]

It is interesting to note in this connection that many writers, including such novelists as Henry James and Henry Adams, have claimed that power leads to isolation, tending to make those who possess it lonely men. The future administrator will have his problems, but loneliness is not likely be one of them.

Tomorrow's public administrator should also derive considerable gratification from knowing that he is engaged in some of society's most vital work. "Government grows," writes Dwight Waldo, "and it grows because society asks it to grow. It remains by the logic of circumstances society's 'chosen instrument' to deal with problems of large scope and great complexity. It could hardly be otherwise short of societal disintegration, or reconstruction in some very different form. The area of *public* problems, that is, the area in which the actions of one or a few affect many, steadily expands; and government, for all its faults, was created to deal with public problems—and there is no obvious and accepted alternative. Except for those whose alienation has led to a 'drop out' status, there is no other important 'game'."[61]

Thus, in sharpening his skills, in increasing his influence and in dealing with the dilemmas that society finds most critical and crucial, the future administrator may find his work to be a source of some joy and even occasional jubilation. And when battle fatigue starts to set in, and he begins to wonder whether the goal is worth the game, he may obtain some measure of inspiration and incentive from Oliver Wendell Holmes, the famous jurist who once noted that where we are at any particular time is often not so important. It is the direction in which we are moving that counts.

---

60. W. Harvey Hegarty, "Supervisors' Reactions to Subordinates' Appraisals," *Personnel,* November–December 1973.
61. Dwight Waldo, "Developments in Public Administration," *The Annals of the American Academy of Political and Social Science,* Vol. 404, November 1972.

SELECTED BIBLIOGRAPHY

Argyris, Chris. *Personality and Organization.* New York: Harper & Row, 1957.

————. *Integrating the Individual and the Organization.* New York: John Wiley, 1964.

Barnard, Chester I. *The Functions of the Executive.* Cambridge: Harvard University Press, 1938.

————. *Organization and Management.* Cambridge: Harvard University Press, 1948.

Bennis, Warren G., and Slater, Philip E. "Democracy Is Inevitable," *Harvard Business Review,* March–April 1964.

————. *The Temporary Society.* New York: Harper & Row, 1968.

Berkley, George E. *The Democratic Policeman.* Boston: Beacon Press, 1969.

————. *The Administrative Revolution.* Englewood Cliffs, N.J.: Prentice-Hall, 1971.

Berlin, Seymour S., et al. "A Guide for Political Appointees: Entering the System." *Good Government,* winter 1972.

Blau, Peter M. *Bureaucracy in Modern Society.* New York: Random House, 1956.

————. *The Dynamics of Bureaucracy.* Chicago: University of Chicago Press, 1955.

Bowles, Chester. *Promises to Keep.* New York: Harper & Row, 1971.

Chapman, Richard L., and Cleaveland, Frederic N. *Meeting the Needs of Tomorrow's Public Service: Guidelines for Professional Education in Public Administration.* Washington, D.C.: National Academy of Public Administration, 1973.

Cleveland, Harlan. "Dinosaurs and Personal Freedom." *Saturday Review,* February 28, 1959.

————. "A Philosophy for the Public Executive." In *Perspectives on Public Management,* edited by Robert T. Golembiewski. Itasca, Ill.: F. E. Peacock, 1968.

Crozier, Michel. *The Bureaucratic Phenomenon.* Chicago: University of Chicago Press, 1973.

————. *La Societé Bloquée.* Paris. Editions du Seuil, 1970.

David, James W., Jr., ed. *Politics, Programs and Budgets.* Englewood Cliffs, N.J.: Prentice-Hall, 1969.

Debbasch, Charles. *L'Administration au pouvoir.* Paris: Calmann-Lévy, 1969.

Downs, Anthony. *Inside Bureaucracy.* Boston: Little, Brown, 1967.

Drucker, Peter F. *The Practice of Management.* New York: Harper & Row, 1954.

————. *The Effective Executive.* New York: Harper & Row, 1968.

Frankel, Charles. *High on Foggy Bottom.* New York: Harper & Row, 1968.

Freeman, J. Leiper. "The Bureaucracy in Pressure Politics." *The Annals of the American Academy of Political and Social Science,* 319 (September 1958).

Friedrich, Carl J. "Public Policy and the Nature of Administrative Responsibility." In *The Politics of the Federal Bureaucracy,* edited by Alan A. Altshuler. New York: Dodd Mead & Co., 1968.

Gellhorn, Ernest. *Administrative Law and Process in a Nutshell.* St. Paul, Minn.: West Publishing Co., 1972.

Gulick, Luther, and Urwick, L., eds. *Papers on the Science of Administration.* New York: Institute of Public Administration, 1937.

Gerth, H. H., and Mills, C. Wright. *From Max Weber: Essays in Sociology.* New York: Oxford University Press, 1946.

Harris, Joseph P. *Congressional Control of Administration.* Washington, D.C.: The Brookings Institution, 1964.

Herzberg, Frederick; Mausner, Bernard; and Snyderman, Barbara Block. *The Motivation to Work.* New York: John Wiley, 1959.

Katz, Daniel, and Kahn, Robert L. *The Social Psychology of Organizations.* New York: John Wiley, 1966.

Kaufman, Herbert. *The Forest Ranger.* Baltimore: Johns Hopkins Press, 1960.

Lindblom, Charles E. "The Science of Muddling Through." *Public Administration Review,* spring 1954.

Likert, Rensis. *New Patterns of Management.* New York: McGraw-Hill, 1961.

————. *The Human Organization: Its Management and Value.* New York: McGraw-Hill, 1967.

Lilienthal, David E. *Management: A Humanist Art.* New York: Columbia University Press (distributor), 1967.

March, J. G., and Simon, H. A. *Organizations.* New York: John Wiley, 1958.

Marini, Frank, ed. *Toward a New Public Administration.* Scranton, Pa.: Chandler Publishing Company, 1971.

Mayo, Elton. *The Human Problems of an Industrial Civilization.* New York: Macmillan, 1933.

McGregor, Douglas. *The Human Side of Enterprise.* New York: McGraw-Hill, 1960.

————. *Leadership and Motivation.* Cambridge: MIT Press, 1966.

————. *The Professional Manager.* New York: McGraw-Hill, 1967.

Newland, Chester A., ed. "Symposium on Productivity in Government." *Public Administration Review,* November/December 1972.

Parkinson, C. Northcote. *Parkinson's Law.* Boston: Houghton Mifflin, 1957.

————. *The Law and the Profits.* Boston: Houghton Mifflin, 1960.

————. *The Law of Delay.* Boston: Houghton Mifflin, 1970.

Peter, Lawrence J., and Hull, Raymond. *The Peter Principle.* New York: William Morrow, 1969.

Peters, Charles, and Rothchild, John, eds. *Inside the System.* 2nd ed. New York: Praeger Publishers, 1973.

Presthus, Robert. *The Organizational Society.* New York: Alfred A. Knopf, 1962.

Proxmire, William. *Uncle Sam: The Last of the Bigtime Spenders.* New York: Simon and Shuster, 1972.

Roethlisberger, F. J., and Dickenson, W. J. *Management and the Worker.* Cambridge: Harvard University Press, 1949.

Rourke, Francis E. *Bureaucracy, Politics and Public Policy.* Boston: Little, Brown, 1969.

Sapolsky, Harvey M. *The Polaris System Development: Bureaucratic and Programmatic Success in Government.* Cambridge: Harvard University Press, 1972.

Selznick, Philip. *TVA and the Grass Roots.* Berkeley: University of California Press, 1949.

Shonfield, Andrew. *Modern Capitalism: The Changing Balance of Public and Private Power.* New York: Oxford University Press, 1965.

Simon, Herbert A. *Administrative Behavior.* 2nd ed. New York: The Free Press, 1957.

———. *The Shape of Automation.* New York: Harper & Row, 1965.

Simon, Herbert A.; Smithburg, Donald W.; and Thompson, Victor A. *Public Administration.* New York: Alfred A. Knopf, 1950.

Smith, Martin R. *I Hate to See a Manager Cry.* Reading, Mass.: Addison-Wesley, 1973.

Snow, C. P. *Science and Government.* Cambridge: Harvard University Press, 1960.

Speer, Albert. *Inside the Third Reich.* New York: Macmillan, 1970.

Stahl, O. Glenn. *Public Personnel Administration.* 6th ed. New York: Harper & Row, 1971.

Stewart, Rosemary. *The Reality of Organizations.* Garden City, N.Y.: Doubleday, 1972.

Taylor, Frederick W. *Scientific Management.* New York: Harper & Row, 1947.

Thompson, Victor A. *Modern Organizations: A General Theory.* New York: Alfred A. Knopf, 1961.

Waldo, Dwight. *The Administrative State.* New York: The Ronald Press, 1948.

———. "Developments in Public Administration." *The Annals of the American Academy of Political and Social Science,* 404 (November 1972).

Waldo, Dwight, ed. Symposium on "Planning-Programming-Budgeting System," *Public Administration Review,* December 1966. Also March-April 1969.

Whyte, William F. *Human Relations in the Restaurant Industry.* New York: McGraw-Hill, 1948.

Wolman, Harold. *Politics of Federal Housing.* New York: Dodd, Mead & Co., 1971.

Index

Index